Fuzzy Number, Fuzzy Difference, Fuzzy Differential: Theory and Applications

Fuzzy Number, Fuzzy Difference, Fuzzy Differential: Theory and Applications

Topic Editors

Changyou Wang
Dong Qiu
Yonghong Shen

MDPI

Basel • Beijing • Wuhan • Barcelona • Belgrade • Novi Sad • Cluj • Manchester

Topic Editors
Changyou Wang
College of Applied Mathematics
Chengdu University of Information Technology
Chengdu
China

Dong Qiu
School of Mathematics and Information Science
Guangxi University
Nanning
China

Yonghong Shen
School of Mathematics and Computer Science
Northwest Minzu University
Lanzhou
China

Editorial Office
MDPI AG
Grosspeteranlage 5
4052 Basel, Switzerland

This is a reprint of the Topic, published open access by the journals *Axioms* (ISSN 2075-1680), *Information* (ISSN 2078-2489), *Mathematics* (ISSN 2227-7390) and *Symmetry* (ISSN 2073-8994), freely accessible at: https://www.mdpi.com/topics/9TRI51D86Q.

For citation purposes, cite each article independently as indicated on the article page online and as indicated below:

Lastname, A.A.; Lastname, B.B. Article Title. *Journal Name* **Year**, *Volume Number*, Page Range.

ISBN 978-3-7258-3819-6 (Hbk)
ISBN 978-3-7258-3820-2 (PDF)
https://doi.org/10.3390/books978-3-7258-3820-2

Contents

Preface . . . . **vii**

Changyou Wang, Dong Qiu and Yonghong Shen
Fuzzy Number, Fuzzy Difference, Fuzzy Differential: Theory and Applications
Reprinted from: *Axioms* **2025**, *14*, 254, https://doi.org/10.3390/axioms14040254 . . . . **1**

Juan J. Font and Sergio Macario
Best Approximation Results for Fuzzy-Number-Valued Continuous Functions
Reprinted from: *Axioms* **2023**, *12*, 192, https://doi.org/10.3390/axioms12020192 . . . . **9**

Hsien-Chung Wu
New Arithmetic Operations of Non-Normal Fuzzy Sets Using Compatibility
Reprinted from: *Axioms* **2023**, *12*, 277, https://doi.org/10.3390/axioms12030277 . . . . **18**

Sadi Bayramov, Çiğdem Gündüz Aras and Ljubiša D. R. Kočinac
Interval-Valued Topology on Soft Sets
Reprinted from: *Axioms* **2023**, *12*, 692, https://doi.org/10.3390/axioms12070692 . . . . **35**

Abdullah Assiry, Sabeur Mansour and Amir Baklouti
S-Embedding of Lie Superalgebras and Its Implications for Fuzzy Lie Algebras
Reprinted from: *Axioms* **2024**, *13*, 2, https://doi.org/10.3390/axioms13010002 . . . . **55**

Xueting Zhao, Kai Duo, Aiping Gan and Yichuan Yang
The Enumeration of $(\odot, \vee)$-Multiderivations on a Finite MV-Chain
Reprinted from: *Axioms* **2024**, *13*, 250, https://doi.org/10.3390/axioms13040250 . . . . **73**

Jingqian Wang and Xiaohong Zhang
Intuitionistic Fuzzy Granular Matrix: Novel Calculation Approaches for Intuitionistic Fuzzy Covering-Based Rough Sets
Reprinted from: *Axioms* **2024**, *13*, 411, https://doi.org/10.3390/axioms13060411 . . . . **97**

Amir Baklouti
Multiple-Attribute Decision Making Based on the Probabilistic Dominance Relationship with Fuzzy Algebras
Reprinted from: *Symmetry* **2023**, *15*, 1188, https://doi.org/10.3390/sym15061188 . . . . **117**

Ali Mert
Defuzzification of Non-Linear Pentagonal Intuitionistic Fuzzy Numbers and Application in the Minimum Spanning Tree Problem
Reprinted from: *Symmetry* **2023**, *15*, 1853, https://doi.org/10.3390/sym15101853 . . . . **133**

Mengran Sun, Yushui Geng and Jing Zhao
Multi-Attribute Group Decision-Making Methods Based on Entropy Weights with q-Rung Picture Uncertain Linguistic Fuzzy Information
Reprinted from: *Symmetry* **2023**, *15*, 2027, https://doi.org/10.3390/sym15112027 . . . . **162**

Na Qin and Zengtai Gong
Special Discrete Fuzzy Numbers on Countable Sets and Their Applications
Reprinted from: *Symmetry* **2024**, *16*, 264, https://doi.org/10.3390/sym16030264 . . . . **179**

Maria N. Rapti, Avrilia Konguetsof and Basil K. Papadopoulos
Two Extensions of the Sugeno Class and a Novel Constructed Method of Strong Fuzzy Negation for the Generation of Non-Symmetric Fuzzy Implications
Reprinted from: *Symmetry* **2024**, *16*, 317, https://doi.org/10.3390/sym16030317 . . . . **200**

Preface

This reprint compiles 16 academic papers spanning fuzzy reasoning, optimization, decision-making, and control. In fuzzy reasoning, a method grounded in symmetric quintuple-implication principles is introduced to manage mixed information, demonstrating strengths in logical foundation and reductivity. This method has been successfully applied to pattern recognition. In fuzzy analysis, trapezoidal-type inequalities within fuzzy frameworks are examined, with an equality derived using the integration by parts formula from fuzzy mathematical analysis. This proven equality, alongside Hölder's inequality, is utilized to establish the trapezoidal-type inequality for functions taking values in the fuzzy number-valued space. In the realm of fuzzy optimization and decision-making, fixed-point theorems are formulated for ψ α- and Fη-contractive mappings in fuzzy bipolar b-metric spaces, furnishing novel tools for tackling complex equations. A novel concept, the intuitionistic fuzzy granular matrix, is introduced within the context of intuitionistic fuzzy covering-based rough sets, offering efficient computational methods for managing noise data in intuitionistic fuzzy (IF) environments. Additionally, fuzzy time series analysis, when integrated with neural networks, is explored to enhance integer time series model estimations, particularly improving the precision of spectral function estimates for the NSINAR(1) model. Within fuzzy set theory, the enumeration of $(\odot,\vee)$-multiderivations on a finite MV-chain is discussed, contributing to a deeper understanding of MV-algebra structures. Extensions of the Sugeno class of fuzzy negations are presented, giving rise to new classes of fuzzy negations, and their properties are investigated for constructing non-symmetric fuzzy implications. In terms of fuzzy number applications, special discrete fuzzy numbers on countable sets are studied, exploring their representation theorems, metrics, and triangular norm operations for image fusion and subjective evaluation aggregation. Non-linear pentagonal intuitionistic fuzzy numbers are defined, and a defuzzification method employing the intuitionistic fuzzy weighted averaging based on levels (IF-WABL) is proposed for application in the minimum spanning tree problem. In communication systems and decision support, an enhanced fuzzy c-means (FCM) algorithm, incorporating particle swarm optimization (PSO) and subtractive clustering, is developed for more accurate modulation identification in low signal-to-noise-ratio (SNR) environments. A multi-attribute group decision-making method, based on entropy weights with q-rung picture uncertain linguistic fuzzy information, is introduced, providing a reliable framework for decision-making when weight information is unknown. Furthermore, new arithmetic operations for non-normal fuzzy sets are explored using compatibility concepts. Lastly, in approximation theory, best approximation results for fuzzy-number-valued continuous functions are investigated. A method to measure the distance between fuzzy-number-valued and real-valued continuous functions is introduced, and the existence of the best approximation is proven using the Michael selection theorem. Collectively, these studies propel forward the theory of fuzzy mathematics and broaden its applications across diverse domains.

Changyou Wang, Dong Qiu, and Yonghong Shen
Topic Editors

axioms

MDPI

Editorial

Fuzzy Number, Fuzzy Difference, Fuzzy Differential: Theory and Applications

Changyou Wang [1,*], Dong Qiu [2] and Yonghong Shen [3]

1 College of Applied Mathematics, Chengdu University of Information Technology, Chengdu 610225, China
2 School of Mathematics and Information Science, Guangxi University, Nanning 530004, China; dongqiumath@163.com or qiudong@gxu.edu.cn
3 School of Mathematics and Computer Science, Northwest Minzu University, Lanzhou 730030, China; shenyonghong2008@hotmail.com or shyh_2004@163.com
* Correspondence: wangchangyou417@163.com or wangcy@cuit.edu.cn

1. Introduction to the Topic Issue

This Topic Issue comprises sixteen pioneering academic papers that delve deeply into the realm of fuzzy reasoning, optimization, decision making, and control. It serves as a testament to the evolving landscape of fuzzy mathematics, increasingly pivotal to addressing complex, real-world problems across diverse domains. At the heart of this reprint lies the exploration of fuzzy numbers, fuzzy differences, and fuzzy differentials foundational concepts which possess both theoretical significance and practical importance.

Fuzzy numbers, which generalize the concept of classical numbers to accommodate imprecision and uncertainty, have revolutionized the way we represent and manipulate data in various fields. Their introduction allows for a more nuanced understanding of inherently ambiguous or ill-defined phenomena. By assigning degrees of membership to elements within a set, fuzzy numbers provide a flexible framework for capturing and analyzing information that lies between the crisp boundaries of classical set theory. This, in turn, has facilitated advancements in fields such as engineering, economics, and medical diagnosis, where the ability to handle imprecise and uncertain data is crucial. The theoretical underpinnings of fuzzy differences and differentials build upon the foundation laid by fuzzy numbers. Fuzzy differences explore how changes in fuzzy values can be represented and analyzed, enabling a more robust understanding of dynamic systems. Similarly, fuzzy differentials extend the concept of classical derivatives to fuzzy-valued functions, providing insights into the behavior of these functions under small perturbations. These developments have been instrumental in refining models and simulations in areas like control systems, where the ability to predict and manage changes is essential for achieving optimal performance. In fuzzy reasoning, a method grounded in symmetric quintuple-implication principles is introduced to manage mixed information, demonstrating strengths in logical foundation and reductivity. This method not only enhances the precision of fuzzy inference but also broadens its applicability to complex, real-world scenarios. By leveraging the principles of symmetry and implication, this approach facilitates a more coherent and consistent reasoning process, making it well suited for tasks such as pattern recognition and decision making under uncertainty. The exploration of trapezoidal-type inequalities within fuzzy frameworks represents another significant contribution to fuzzy analysis. By deriving an equality using the integration-by-parts formula from fuzzy mathematical analysis, researchers have established a robust foundation for analyzing trapezoidal-type inequalities in fuzzy-valued spaces, with important implications for signal processing and image analysis, where the ability to accurately estimate and bind errors is crucial for

Received: 17 March 2025
Accepted: 26 March 2025
Published: 28 March 2025

Citation: Wang, C.; Qiu, D.; Shen, Y. Fuzzy Number, Fuzzy Difference, Fuzzy Differential: Theory and Applications. *Axioms* **2025**, *14*, 254. https://doi.org/10.3390/axioms14040254

achieving high-quality results. In the realm of fuzzy optimization and decision making, the formulation of fixed-point theorems for contractive mappings in fuzzy bipolar b-metric spaces provides novel tools for tackling complex equations. These theorems extend the reach of fixed-point theory into the realm of fuzzy mathematics, enabling more efficient and effective solutions to optimization problems. Additionally, the introduction of the intuitionistic fuzzy granular matrix within the context of intuitionistic fuzzy covering-based rough sets offers efficient computational methods for managing noise data in intuitionistic fuzzy environments. This work has important implications for data mining and machine learning, where the ability to handle noisy and uncertain data is essential for building robust and reliable models. The integration of fuzzy time series analysis with neural networks represents a significant step forward in enhancing integer time series model estimations. By leveraging the strengths of both fuzzy logic and neural networks, researchers have been able to improve the precision of spectral function estimates for models such as NSINAR (1), with important applications in finance, forecasting, and other fields where accurate predictions are crucial for making informed decisions. Within fuzzy set theory, the enumeration of $(\odot,\vee)$-multiderivations on a finite MV-chain contributes to a deeper understanding of MV-algebra structures. This work has important implications for the development of logical systems and formal languages that can handle uncertainty and ambiguity more effectively. Additionally, extensions of the Sugeno class of fuzzy negations give rise to new sets, which have the potential to expand the expressive power of fuzzy logic and enable more nuanced reasoning processes. In terms of fuzzy number applications, special discrete fuzzy numbers on countable sets are being studied, exploring their representation theorems, metrics, and triangular norm operations for image fusion and subjective evaluation aggregation. This work has important implications for fields such as computer vision and data fusion, where the ability to combine and analyze multiple sources of information is crucial for achieving accurate and reliable results. Furthermore, the definition of non-linear pentagonal intuitionistic fuzzy numbers and the proposal of a defuzzification method employing intuitionistic fuzzy weighted averaging based on levels (IF-WABL) have potential applications in the minimum spanning tree problem and other optimization tasks. In communication systems and decision support, the development of an enhanced fuzzy c-means (FCM) algorithm incorporating particle swarm optimization (PSO) and subtractive clustering represents a significant advancement in modulation identification in low signal-to-noise-ratio (SNR) environments. This work has important implications for wireless communication systems, where the ability to accurately identify and decode signals is crucial for maintaining reliable connections. Additionally, the introduction of a multi-attribute group decision-making method based on entropy weights with q-rung picture uncertain linguistic fuzzy information provides a reliable framework for decision making when weight information is unknown. This work has potential applications in fields such as supply chain management and project planning, where the ability to make informed decisions under uncertainty is essential for achieving successful outcomes. Lastly, in approximation theory, the investigation of best approximation results for fuzzy-valued continuous functions introduces a method to measure the distance between fuzzy- and real-valued continuous functions. The proof of the existence of the best approximation using the Michael selection theorem represents a significant theoretical contribution to fuzzy mathematics. This work has important implications for fields such as numerical analysis and computer-aided design, where the ability to approximate complex functions and systems is crucial for achieving accurate and reliable results.

2. Presentation of the Research Papers

Signal modulation recognition commonly relies on clustering algorithms. The fuzzy c-means (FCM) algorithm, which is widely used for such purposes, frequently converges to local optima, posing a challenge particularly in environments with low signal-to-noise ratios (SNRs). An enhanced FCM algorithm, incorporating particle swarm optimization (PSO), has been proposed to improve the accuracy of recognizing M-ary quadrature amplitude modulation (MQAM) signal orders in Contribution 1. This approach involves a two-phase clustering process. In the first phase, a subtractive clustering algorithm, tailored to SNR, utilizes the received signal's constellation diagram to determine the initial number of clustering centers, which are then refined by the PSO-FCM algorithm for greater precision. Accurate signal classification and identification are achieved by evaluating the relative sizes of the radii around the cluster centers within the MQAM constellation diagram and determining the modulation order. Evaluation results indicate that the SNR-based subtractive clustering-assisted PSO-FCM algorithm outperforms traditional FCM in terms of clustering effectiveness, notably enhancing modulation recognition rates in low-SNR conditions when tested against a variety of QAM signals, ranging from 4QAM to 64QAM.

In Contribution 2, a comprehensive study attempts to approximate a fixed fuzzy-valued continuous function to a specific subset of fuzzy-valued continuous functions, primarily focusing on identifying the optimal approximation within this particular context. Additionally, the authors introduce an innovative method specifically designed to quantify the distance between a fuzzy- and real-valued continuous function, providing a precise means to measure the discrepancy between the two types. Furthermore, the paper rigorously proves the existence of the best approximation of a fuzzy-valued continuous function within all real-valued continuous functions, utilizing the well-established Michael selection theorem, renowned in mathematical analysis, to establish a solid theoretical foundation for the approximation process.

In Contribution 3, the authors investigate new arithmetic operations for non-normal fuzzy sets, utilizing the extension principle and taking into account a general aggregation function. Typically, the aggregation functions used in such contexts are the minimum function or t-norms. However, this paper adopts a more general aggregation function to establish arithmetic operations for non-normal fuzzy sets. In practical applications, the arithmetic operations of fuzzy sets are often translated into corresponding operations on their α-level sets. When the aggregation function is specifically the minimum function, this translation becomes straightforward. Given the use of a general aggregation function in this paper, the concept of compatibility with α-level sets is introduced and defined, encompassing the traditional case where minimum functions are employed as a special instance.

In Contribution 4, the authors undertake a study of the concept of interval-valued fuzzy sets within the framework of the family SS (X,E), which comprises all soft sets defined over a set X with a parameter set E. They delve into examining the fundamental properties of these interval-valued fuzzy sets. Subsequently, the researchers introduce the notion of an interval-valued fuzzy topology (or cotopology) τ on SS (X,E). Through their analysis, they derive an important finding: each interval-valued fuzzy topology constitutes a descending family of soft topologies. Furthermore, the paper explores various topological structures related to this concept. Specifically, it examines the interval-valued fuzzy neighborhood system of a soft point, as well as the base and sub-base of τ. The authors meticulously investigate the relationships that exist among these structures. Additionally, the paper presents several key concepts, including direct sum and open and continuous mapping, considering the interconnections between them. To illustrate and support the theoretical results presented, several examples are provided throughout the paper.

Contribution 5 covers an investigation into the s-embedding of the Lie superalgebra $\overrightarrow{(S^{1|1})}$, representing smooth vector fields on a (1,1)-dimensional super-circle. Its primary goal is to precisely define s-embedding, dissecting the Lie superalgebra into the superalgebra of super-pseudodifferential operators ($S\psi D\odot$) on the super-circle $S^{1|1}$. Additionally, it introduces and rigorously defines the central charge within the framework of $\overrightarrow{(S^{1|1})}$, utilizing the canonical central extension of $S\psi D\odot$. The study further explores fuzzy Lie algebras, aiming to elucidate connections between these seemingly distinct mathematical constructs. It covers various aspects such as non-commutative structures, representation theory, central extensions, and central charges, bridging the gap between Lie superalgebras and fuzzy Lie algebras. In summary, this pioneering work makes two key contributions: firstly, it provides a meticulous definition of the s-embedding of the Lie superalgebra $\overrightarrow{(S^{1|1})}$, enhancing fundamental understanding of the topic. Secondly, it examines fuzzy Lie algebras, exploring their associations with conventional Lie superalgebras, and offers a novel deformed representation of the central charge based on these findings.

In Contribution 6, the concept of ($\odot$,V)-multiderivations on an MV-algebra A is introduced, exploring the relations between the former and ($\odot$,V)-derivations. The set MD (A), comprising all ($\odot$,V)-multiderivations on A, can be endowed with a preorder. Furthermore, under a certain equivalence relation ~, the quotient set (MD (A)/~, $\leq$) can be structured as a partially ordered set. Notably, for any finite MV-chain Ln, the quotient set (MD (Ln)/~, $\leq$) evolves into a complete lattice. Lastly, a counting principle is established to enumerate the elements of MD (Ln).

The intuitionistic fuzzy (IF) β-minimal description operators within the framework of IF covering-based rough set theory are adept at managing noisy data, effectively identifying pertinent data within IF environments. In scenarios characterized by IF β-covering approximation spaces with high cardinality, employing IF set representations for calculations becomes cumbersome and intricate. Consequently, there is a pressing need for an efficient method to derive these descriptions. Contribution 7 introduces the concept of IF β-maximal description, building upon the foundation of IF β-minimal description, alongside the IF granular matrix and the notion of IF reduction. The authors further propose matrix-based computational methods for various aspects of IF covering-based rough sets, encompassing IF β-minimal and -maximal descriptions and IF reductions. Firstly, the IF granular matrix, a tool for computing IF β-minimal descriptions, is described, followed by IF β-maximal description and related matrix representations. Subsequently, two types of reductions for IF β-covering approximation spaces are presented, leveraging IF and fuzzy β-minimal descriptions, along with their corresponding matrix representations. Finally, experiments comparing the newly proposed matrix-based calculation methods with their set-based counterparts are conducted.

In multiple-attribute decision-making (MADM) problems, ranking alternatives is crucial for achieving optimal decision outcomes. Intuitionistic fuzzy numbers (IFNs) are highly effective in representing uncertainty and vagueness within these problems. However, current ranking methods for IFNs overlook the probabilistic dominance relationship between alternatives, potentially resulting in inconsistent and unreliable rankings. To address this issue, Contribution 8 introduces a novel ranking method for IFNs that integrates the probabilistic dominance relationship with fuzzy algebras, designed to handle incomplete and uncertain information effectively, ensuring consistent and accurate rankings. By incorporating these elements, the approach offers a significant advancement in the ranking of alternatives in MADM problems.

In recent years, the proliferation of digital objects as information sources has fueled rapid advancements in artificial intelligence (AI) and machine learning (ML). Effective utilization of AI and ML techniques necessitates the conversion of ambient information into reliable data within the framework of information processing theory. It is imperative to model and transform information into data without discarding its inherent uncertainty. To this end, mathematical frameworks such as fuzzy theory and intuitionistic fuzzy theory are employed. The latter uses membership and non-membership functions to describe intuitionistic fuzzy sets and intuitionistic fuzzy numbers (IFNs), mathematically representing the characteristics of IFNs. Given the diverse uncertainties introduced by various information sources, there is a constant need for a more general and inclusive definition of IFNs in AI technologies. In Contribution 9, the authors propose a general and inclusive mathematical definition for IFNs, termed the non-linear pentagonal intuitionistic fuzzy number (NLPIFN), which accommodates a variety of uncertainties. As AI implementations are computer-based, IFNs must be transformed into crisp numbers for their practical application. The techniques used for this transformation are known as defuzzification methods. A shortcut formula for the defuzzification of NLPIFNs using the intuitionistic fuzzy weighted averaging based on levels (IF-WABL) method is introduced. Furthermore, the authors demonstrate the application of their findings in the minimum spanning tree problem by assigning weights as NLPIFNs to more precisely determine uncertainty in the process. This approach underscores the practical significance and versatility of their proposed NLPIFN definition and defuzzification method.

Contribution 10 introduces a novel concept termed q-rung picture uncertain linguistic fuzzy sets (q-RPULSs), offering a robust and comprehensive framework for depicting intricate and uncertain decision-making information. These sets facilitate the integration of quantitative and qualitative assessment inputs from decision makers. Addressing the challenge of multi-attribute group decision making under q-RPULs with unknown attribute weights, the authors propose an entropy-based fuzzy set approach tailored for q-rung picture uncertainty language, taking into account the interdependencies among attributes. Furthermore, the paper delves into the q-RPULMSM operator, which plays a pivotal role in aggregating q-RPULSs and achieving consensus in decision-making contexts, and its associated properties. To validate the efficacy, rationality, and superiority of the proposed methodology, a real-world case study on commodity selection is presented, underscoring the practical benefits and applicability of q-RPULSs in decision-making processes.

Certain drawbacks in the arithmetic and logic operations of general discrete fuzzy numbers hinder their widespread application. Specifically, the sum of general discrete fuzzy numbers, as defined by Zadeh's extension principle, may not itself qualify as a discrete fuzzy number. To address these limitations, Contribution 11 focuses on special discrete fuzzy numbers defined on countable sets. Given that the representation theorem of fuzzy numbers serves as a fundamental tool in fuzzy analysis, the Contribution first examines two types of representation theorems for special discrete fuzzy numbers on countable sets. Subsequently, metrics for these special discrete fuzzy numbers are defined, and their relationship to the uniform Hausdorff metric (also known as the supremum metric) of general fuzzy numbers is discussed. Furthermore, triangular norm and conorm operations (abbreviated as t-norm and t-conorm, respectively) are introduced for special discrete fuzzy numbers on countable sets, proving the properties of these operations. It is demonstrated that these operations satisfy the essential conditions for closure, and illustrative examples are provided. Finally, the Contribution proposes applications of special discrete fuzzy numbers on countable sets in the image fusion and aggregation of subjective evaluations.

In Contribution 12, two novel classes of fuzzy negations are introduced, extending the well-established Sugeno class and serving as the foundation for the first two construction methods discussed. The first method generates rational fuzzy negations through the utilization of a second-degree polynomial with two parameters. This approach necessitates an investigation into the specific conditions these parameters must meet to qualify as a fuzzy negation. The second method replaces the parameter δ of the Sugeno class with an increasing function, thereby producing fuzzy negations which are not limited to rational forms. Instead, by employing an arbitrary increasing function which meets certain criteria, a wider range of fuzzy negations can be generated. Furthermore, a comparison is made between the equilibrium points of the fuzzy negations produced by the first method and those of the Sugeno class. Leveraging the concept of equilibrium points, a novel method for generating strong fuzzy negations is presented. This method employs two decreasing functions that satisfy specific conditions. Additionally, the convexity of the newly introduced fuzzy negations is explored, and conditions are provided for the coefficients of the fuzzy negations generated by the first method to ensure convexity. Examples of the new fuzzy negations are presented, which are then utilized to generate new non-symmetric fuzzy implications using established production methods. Convex fuzzy negations are employed as decreasing functions to construct an Archimedean copula. Finally, the quadratic form of the copula is investigated, and the conditions that the coefficients of the first method and the increasing function of the second method must meet to generate new copulas of this form are discussed.

Contribution 13 delves into the application of fuzzy time series (FTSs) based on neural network models for estimating various spectral functions within integer time series models, with a particular emphasis on the skew integer autoregressive model of order one (NSINAR (1)). To facilitate this estimation, a dataset comprising 1000 realizations of the NSINAR (1) model is created. These input values are subsequently fuzzified using fuzzy logic techniques. The study leverages the powerful capability of artificial neural networks in identifying fuzzy relationships to enhance prediction accuracy by generating output values. A meticulous analysis is conducted to assess the improvement in the smoothing of spectral function estimators for the NSINAR (1) model when both input and output values are utilized. The effectiveness of the output value estimates is rigorously evaluated by comparing them to the input value estimates using a mean-squared error (MSE) analysis, providing insights into the superior performance of the former.

In Contribution 14, novel concepts are introduced within the framework of fuzzy bipolar b-metric spaces, particularly focusing on key mappings such as ψ_α-contractive and F_η-contractive mappings, which play a crucial role in quantifying distances between dissimilar elements. This research establishes fixed-point theorems for these mappings, demonstrating the existence of invariant points under specific conditions. To further strengthen the credibility and applicability of the findings, illustrative examples are provided that support these theorems and contribute to expanding existing knowledge in this field. Moreover, the authors explore practical applications of these theoretical advancements, particularly in solving integral and fractional differential equations, demonstrating the robustness and utility of the proposed concepts. Symmetry, both in its traditional sense and within the fuzzy context, is a fundamental aspect of the study of fuzzy bipolar b-metric spaces. The introduced contractive mappings and fixed-point theorems not only expand the theoretical framework but also offer powerful tools for addressing practical problems in which symmetry is significant. These contributions enhance the understanding and applicability of fuzzy bipolar b-metric spaces in various domains.

Rule-based reasoning, which incorporates various forms of uncertain information, has been recognized in numerous real-world applications. Any reasoning method must be capable of coherently deriving inference results by combining "given if–then" rules with assertions based on input information. The symmetric quintuple-implication principle is formulated by incorporating symmetry into all five implication operators involved. Specifically, the first, third, and fifth implication operators exhibit symmetric properties, meaning they are treated as the same operator type, while the second and fourth operators also satisfy symmetry, implying that they share the same type. Consequently, reasoning methods based on this principle offer significant advantages in terms of logical foundation and reductivity. In Contribution 15, reasoning methods for combining fuzzy and intuitionistic fuzzy information are derived and studied using the symmetric quintuple-implication principle, relying on the notion that the input and "given if–then" rule can only be combined for calculation when their information representations are consistent. An "if–then" rule with inconsistent representations in two different forms should be regarded as the combination of two distinct consistent "if–then" rules, each with its unique representation. The authors further elaborate on these methods by employing possibility and necessity operators along with the quintuple-implication principle, considering whether the representations of the rule antecedent and rule consequent are consistent or not. The reductivity of all proposed reasoning methods is also analyzed in detail. The main contribution is the development of a novel mixed-information reasoning framework incorporating the quintuple-implication principle. The proposed methods have been applied to pattern recognition, with experimental results demonstrating their superiority over corresponding methods based on the triple I principle.

Contribution 16 covers a thorough investigation into trapezoidal-type inequalities within the context of fuzzy settings. The theory of fuzzy analysis is examined in depth, with a particular focus on the integration-by-parts formula from fuzzy mathematics to establish a key equality. By combining this proven equality with the properties of a metric defined on the set of fuzzy-valued space, along with Hölder's inequality, a trapezoidal-type inequality for functions with values in the fuzzy-valued space is proven. The results offer generalizations of previous findings in the field of mathematical inequalities. To validate the theoretical results, an example is designed, involving a function with values in the fuzzy-valued space. Numerical validation is carried out using the latest version (14.1) of Mathematica. Additionally, the p-levels of the defined fuzzy-valued mapping are graphically illustrated for various values of p within the interval $[0, 1]$. This Contribution mainly focuses on its advancement of the theory of fuzzy analysis and mathematical inequalities, as well as a practical demonstration of the results through numerical and graphical validation.

3. Conclusions

In summary, the Topic Issue titled "Fuzzy Numbers, Fuzzy Differences, Fuzzy Differentials: Theory and Applications" propels the theory of fuzzy mathematics forward and broadens its applications across a diverse array of domains. By delving into the theoretical foundations and practical implications of fuzzy numbers, fuzzy differences, and fuzzy differentials, researchers have paved new paths for innovation and discovery in various fields, spanning engineering, economics, medicine, and social sciences. This reprint stands as a testament to the profound power and versatility of fuzzy mathematics. It is our earnest hope that it will ignite the curiosity and passion of future generations of researchers, encouraging them to continue exploring and pushing the boundaries of this exhilarating and dynamic field.

Conflicts of Interest: The authors declare no conflicts of interest.

List of Contributions

1. Quan, Z.; Zhang, H., Luo, J.; Sun, H. Simulation-Enhanced MQAM Modulation Identification in Communication Systems: A Subtractive Clustering-Based PSO-FCM Algorithm Study. *Information* **2024**, *15*, 42. https://doi.org/10.3390/info15010042.
2. Font, J.J.; Macario, S. Best Approximation Results for Fuzzy-Number-Valued Continuous Functions. *Axioms* **2023**, *12*, 192. https://doi.org/10.3390/axioms12020192.

3. Wu, H.C. New Arithmetic Operations of Non-Normal Fuzzy Sets Using Compatibility. *Axioms* **2023**, *12*, 277. https://doi.org/10.3390/axioms12030277.
4. Bayramov, S; Aras, C.G.; Kočinac, L.D.R. Interval-Valued Topology on Soft Sets. *Axioms* **2023**, *12*, 692. https://doi.org/10.3390/axioms12070692.
5. Assiry, A.; Mansour, S.; Baklouti, A. S-Embedding of Lie Superalgebras and Its Implications for Fuzzy Lie Algebras. *Axioms* **2024**, *13*, 2. https://doi.org/10.3390/axioms13010002.
6. Zhao, X; Duo, K.; Gan, A.; Yang, Y. The Enumeration of $(\odot,\vee)$-Multiderivations on a Finite MV-Chain. *Axioms* **2024**, *13*, 250. https://doi.org/10.3390/axioms13040250.
7. Wang, J.; Zhang, X. Intuitionistic Fuzzy Granular Matrix: Novel Calculation Approaches for Intuitionistic Fuzzy Covering-Based Rough Sets. *Axioms* **2024**, *13*, 411. https://doi.org/10.3390/axioms13060411.
8. Baklouti, A. Multiple-Attribute Decision Making Based on the Probabilistic Dominance Relationship with Fuzzy Algebras. *Symmetry* **2023**, *15*, 1188. https://doi.org/10.3390/sym15061188.
9. Mert, A. Defuzzification of Non-Linear Pentagonal Intuitionistic Fuzzy Numbers and Application in the Minimum Spanning Tree Problem. *Symmetry* **2023**, *15*, 1853. https://doi.org/10.3390/sym15101853.
10. Sun, M.; Geng Y.; Zhao, J. Multi-Attribute Group Decision-Making Methods Based on Entropy Weights with q-Rung Picture Uncertain Linguistic Fuzzy Information. *Symmetry* **2023**, *15*, 2027. https://doi.org/10.3390/sym15112027.
11. Qin, N.; Gong, Z. Special Discrete Fuzzy Numbers on Countable Sets and Their Applications. *Symmetry* **2024**, *16*, 264. https://doi.org/10.3390/sym16030264.
12. Rapti, M.N.; Konguetsof, A.; Papadopoulos, B.K. Two Extensions of the Sugeno Class and a Novel Constructed Method of Strong Fuzzy Negation for the Generation of Non-Symmetric Fuzzy Implications. *Symmetry* **2024**, *16*, 317. https://doi.org/10.3390/sym16030317.
13. El-Menshawy, M.H.; Eliwa, M.S.; Al-Essa, L.A.; El-Morshedy, M.; EL-Sagheer, R.M. Enhancing Integer Time Series Model Estimations through Neural Network- Based Fuzzy Time Series Analysis. *Symmetry* **2024**, *16*, 660. https://doi.org/10.3390/sym16060660.
14. Alnabulsi, S.; Salameh, W.M.M.; Rashid, M.H.M. Introducing Fixed-Point Theorems and Applications in Fuzzy Bipolar b-Metric Spaces with ψ_α- and F_η-Contractive Maps. *Symmetry* **2024**, *16*, 777. https://doi.org/10.3390/sym16060777.
15. Yao, N.; Chen, H.; Zhao, R.; Luo, M. Fuzzy Reasoning Symmetric Quintuple- Implication Method for Mixed Information and Its Application. *Symmetry* **2025**, *17*, 369. https://doi.org/10.3390/sym17030369.
16. Latif, M.A. General Trapezoidal-Type Inequalities in Fuzzy Settings. *Mathematics* **2024**, *12*, 3112. https://doi.org/10.3390/math12193112.

Article

Best Approximation Results for Fuzzy-Number-Valued Continuous Functions

Juan J. Font * and Sergio Macario

Institut Universitari de Matemàtiques i Aplicacions de Castelló (IMAC), Universitat Jaume I, Avda. Sos Baynat s/n, 12071 Castelló, Spain
* Correspondence: font@uji.es

Abstract: In this paper, we study the best approximation of a fixed fuzzy-number-valued continuous function to a subset of fuzzy-number-valued continuous functions. We also introduce a method to measure the distance between a fuzzy-number-valued continuous function and a real-valued one. Then, we prove the existence of the best approximation of a fuzzy-number-valued continuous function to the space of real-valued continuous functions by using the well-known Michael selection theorem.

Keywords: best approximation; fuzzy-valued continuous function; Michael selection theorem

MSC: 41A50; 65G40

Citation: Font, J.J.; Macario, S. Best Approximation Results for Fuzzy-Number-Valued Continuous Functions. *Axioms* **2023**, *12*, 192. https://doi.org/10.3390/axioms12020192

Academic Editors: Changyou Wang, Dong Qiu and Yonghong Shen

Received: 27 December 2022
Revised: 3 February 2023
Accepted: 10 February 2023
Published: 11 February 2023

Copyright: © 2023 by the authors. Licensee MDPI, Basel, Switzerland. This article is an open access article distributed under the terms and conditions of the Creative Commons Attribution (CC BY) license (https://creativecommons.org/licenses/by/4.0/).

1. Introduction

Approximation theory originated from the necessity of approximating real-valued continuous functions by a simpler class of functions, such as trigonometric or algebraic polynomials and has attracted the interest of many mathematicians for over a century. Among the most recognized results in this branch of functional analysis, we can mention the Stone–Weierstrass theorem, Korovkin type results and the approximation of functions using neural networks.

More recently, all the above results have also been addressed in the context of fuzzy functions (see, e.g., [1–6]).

Another fundamental problem in approximation theory is the study of the best approximation in spaces of continuous functions, which has a long story with famous results by Chebyshev, Haar, Young, Remez, de la Vallée-Poussin who established the existence of best approximations, as well as characterized and estimated them. In this context, the problem of the uniform approximation of a scalar-valued function continuous on a compact set by a family of continuous functions on such a compact set (see, e.g., [7,8] or [9]) should be mentioned.

The search for the best approximation of a continuous set-valued function by vector-valued ones is another important topic in approximation theory and has been studied by several authors (see, e.g., [10–13] or [14]).

In this paper, we address these two problems of the best approximation type in the context of fuzzy-number-valued continuous functions.

First, we study the best approximation of a fixed fuzzy-number-valued continuous function to a subset of fuzzy-number-valued continuous functions.

Second, we introduce a novel method to measure the distance between a fuzzy-number-valued function and a real-valued one based on the concept of nearest interval approximation of fuzzy numbers [15]. Then, we prove the existence of the best approximation of a fuzzy-number-valued continuous function to the space of real-valued continuous functions by using the well-known Michael selection theorem.

2. Preliminaries

Let $F(\mathbb{R})$ denote the family of all fuzzy subsets on the real numbers $\mathbb{R}$ (see [16]). For $\lambda \in [0,1]$ and a fuzzy set u, its λ-level set is defined as

$$[u]^\lambda := \{\, x \in \mathbb{R} : u(x) \geq \lambda \,\}, \quad \lambda \in]0,1],$$

and $[u]^0$ stands for the closure of $\{\, x \in \mathbb{R} : u(x) > 0 \,\}$.

The family of elements $u \in F(\mathbb{R})$ which satisfies the following properties:

1. There exists an $x_0 \in \mathbb{R}$ with $u(x_0) = 1$, that is, u is normal;
2. $u(\lambda x + (1-\lambda)y) \geq \min\{u(x), u(y)\}$ for all $x, y \in \mathbb{R}, \lambda \in [0,1]$, which is to say that u is convex;
3. $[u]^0$ is a compact set in $\mathbb{R}$;
4. u is upper-semicontinuous,

is called the fuzzy number space $\mathbb{E}^1$ (see, e.g., [17]) and contains the reals. If $u \in \mathbb{E}^1$, then it is known that the λ-level set $[u]^\lambda$ of u is a compact interval for each $\lambda \in [0,1]$. We write $[u]^\lambda = [u^-(\lambda), u^+(\lambda)]$.

The following characterization of fuzzy numbers, which was proved by Goetschel and Voxman [17], is essential in the sequel:

Theorem 1. *Let $u \in \mathbb{E}^1$ and $[u]^\lambda = [u^-(\lambda), u^+(\lambda)]$, $\lambda \in [0,1]$. Then, the functions $u^-(\lambda)$ and $u^+(\lambda)$ satisfy:*

1. *$u^+(\lambda)$ is a nonincreasing bounded left continuous function on $(0,1]$;*
2. *$u^-(\lambda)$ is a nondecreasing bounded left continuous function on $(0,1]$;*
3. *$u^-(1) \leq u^+(1)$;*
4. *$u^-(\lambda)$ and $u^+(\lambda)$ are right continuous at $\lambda = 0$.*

Conversely, if two functions $\gamma(\lambda)$ and $\nu(\lambda)$ fulfill the conditions (i)–(iv), then there is a unique $u \in \mathbb{E}^1$ such that $[u]^\lambda = [\gamma(\lambda), \nu(\lambda)]$ for each $\lambda \in [0,1]$.

As usual, (see, e.g., [17]) given $u, v \in \mathbb{E}^1$ and $k \in \mathbb{R}$, we define the sum $u + v := [u^-(\lambda), u^+(\lambda)] + [v^-(\lambda), v^+(\lambda)]$ and the product $ku := k[u^-(\lambda), u^+(\lambda)]$. With these two operations, $\mathbb{E}^1$ is not a vector space, and $(\mathbb{E}^1, +)$ is not even a group.

The fuzzy number space $\mathbb{E}^1$ can be endowed with several metrics (see, e.g., [16]) but perhaps the most used is the following:

Definition 1 ([16,17]). *For $u, v \in \mathbb{E}^1$,*

$$d_\infty(u,v) := \sup_{\lambda \in [0,1]} \max\{|u^-(\lambda) - v^-(\lambda)|, |u^+(\lambda) - v^+(\lambda)|\}.$$

This metric on $\mathbb{E}^1$ is called the supremum metric. Indeed, $\mathbb{E}^1$ is a complete metric space with this metric. Furthermore, if we consider the Euclidean topology on $\mathbb{R}$, it can be topologically identified with the closed subspace $\tilde{R} = \{\, \tilde{x} : x \in \mathbb{R} \,\}$ of $(\mathbb{E}^1, d_\infty)$ where $\tilde{x}^+(\lambda) = \tilde{x}^-(\lambda) = x$ for all $\lambda \in [0,1]$. We always assume that $\mathbb{E}^1$ is equipped with the supremum metric.

Proposition 1 ([3] Proposition 2.3). *The following properties are satisfied by the metric space $(\mathbb{E}^1, d_\infty)$:*

1. *$d_\infty(\sum_{i=1}^m u_i, \sum_{i=1}^m v_i) \leq \sum_{i=1}^m d_\infty(u_i, v_i)$, where $u_i, v_i \in \mathbb{E}^1$ for $i = 1, \ldots, m$.*
2. *$d_\infty(ku, kv) = k d_\infty(u,v)$, where $u, v \in \mathbb{E}^1$ and $k > 0$.*
3. *$d_\infty(ku, \mu u) = \mid k - \mu \mid d_\infty(u, 0)$, where $u \in \mathbb{E}^1$, $k \geq 0$ and $\mu \geq 0$.*
4. *$d_\infty(ku, \mu v) \leq \mid k - \mu \mid d_\infty(u, 0) + \mu d_\infty(u,v)$, where $u, v \in \mathbb{E}^1$, $k \geq 0$ and $\mu \geq 0$.*

In $C(K, \mathbb{E}^1)$, the space of continuous functions defined on the compact Hausdorff space K which take values in $(\mathbb{E}^1, d_\infty)$, we use the following metric:

$$D(f,g) = \sup_{t \in K} d_\infty(f(t), g(t)),$$

which yields the uniform convergence topology on $C(K, \mathbb{E}^1)$.

Let us next introduce a useful tool for this section.

Definition 2. *Let M be a nonempty subset of $C(K, \mathbb{E}^1)$. We define*

$$Conv(M) := \{\varphi \in C(K,[0,1]) : \varphi f + (1-\varphi)g \in M \ \ for \ \ all \ \ f,g \in M\}.$$

Proposition 2 ([3] Proposition 3.2)**.** *Let M be a nonempty subset of $C(K, \mathbb{E}^1)$. Then, we infer:*

1. *$\phi \in Conv(M)$ implies that $1 - \phi \in Conv(M)$.*
2. *If $\phi, \varphi \in Conv(M)$, then $\phi \cdot \varphi \in Conv(M)$.*

Definition 3. *It is said that $M \subset C(K,[0,1])$ separates the points of K (or it is point-separating) if given $x, y \in K$, there exists $\psi \in M$ such that $\psi(x) \neq \psi(y)$.*

Lemma 1 ([3] Lemma 3.6)**.** *Let $M \subseteq C(K, \mathbb{E}^1)$. If $Conv(M)$ is point-separating, then, given $x_0 \in K$ and an open neighborhood $\mathcal{N}$ of x_0, there is a neighborhood $\mathcal{U}$ of x_0 contained in $\mathcal{N}$ such that for all $0 < \delta < \frac{1}{2}$, there is $\varphi \in Conv(M)$ such that*

1. *$\varphi(t) > 1 - \delta$, for all $t \in \mathcal{U}$;*
2. *$\varphi(t) < \delta$, for all $t \notin \mathcal{N}$.*

3. Best Approximation for Subspaces of $C(K, \mathbb{E}^1)$

Given a metric space (X, d) and a nonempty (closed) subset A of X and given an element $x \in X$, we can define

$$d(x, A) = \inf_{y \in A} d(x, y)$$

and the problem of the best approximation consists in finding an element $y_x \in A$ such that $d(x, A) = d(x, y_x)$. Although we focus on the problem of the best approximation in the space of fuzzy-valued continuous functions endowed with the crisp distance $D(f,g)$ defined above, it is worth noting that this problem has been studied for fuzzy metric spaces as well (see, e.g., [18–20]).

In this section, we get a sharper result, by obtaining that the distance is achieved at a single point.

Definition 4. *Let A be a subspace of $C(K, \mathbb{E}^1)$ and let $f \in C(K, \mathbb{E}^1)$. We define*

$$d(f, A) := \inf_{g \in A} \{\sup_{x \in K} d_\infty(f(x), g(x))\} = \inf_{g \in A} \{D(f,g)\}$$

$$d_x(f, A) := \inf_{g \in A} \{d_\infty(f(x), g(x))\}$$

Theorem 2. *Let W be a subspace of $C(K, \mathbb{E}^1)$ and assume that $Conv(W)$ separates points. For each $f \in C(K, \mathbb{E}^1)$, we have*

$$d(f, W) = d_x(f, W)$$

for some $x \in K$.

Proof. We first show that $d(f, W) = \sup_{x \in K} d_x(f, W)$. It is apparent that $d(f, W) \geq \sup_{x \in K} d_x(f, W)$ since $d(f, W) \geq d_x(f, W)$ for each $x \in K$. Let us prove that $d(f, W) \leq \sup_{x \in K} d_x(f, W)$.

To this end, fix $\varepsilon > 0$. Given $x' \in K$, we can find $f_{x'} \in W$ such that $d_\infty(f(x'), f_{x'}(x')) < \sup_{x \in K} d_x(f, W) + \varepsilon$. We next fix the following open neighborhood of x':

$$N(x') := \{t \in K : d_\infty(f(t), f_{x'}(t)) < \sup_{x \in K} d_x(f, W) + \varepsilon\}.$$

Take an open neighborhood $U(x')$ x' which satisfies the properties in Lemma 1.

Since K is compact, we can find finitely many $\{x_1, \ldots, x_m\}$ in K such that $K \subset U(x_1) \cup \ldots \cup U(x_m)$. Choose $\delta > 0$ such that $\delta < min(1, \frac{\varepsilon}{km})$, where

$$k := \max\{D(f, 0), D(f, f_{x_1}), \ldots D(f, f_{x_m})\}.$$

By Lemma 1, we know that there exist $\phi_1, \cdots, \phi_m \in Conv(W)$ such that for all $i = 1, \ldots, m$,

(i) $\phi_i(t) > 1 - \delta$, for all $t \in U(x_i)$;
(ii) $0 \leq \phi_i(t) < \delta, \quad if \;\; t \notin N(x_i)$.

Let us define the functions

$\psi_1 := \phi_1,$
$\psi_2 := (1 - \phi_1)\phi_2,$
$\vdots$
$\psi_m := (1 - \phi_1)(1 - \phi_2) \cdots (1 - \phi_{m-1})\phi_m.$

By Proposition 2, we know that $\psi_i \in Conv(W)$ for all $i = 1, \ldots, m$. Next, we claim that

$$\psi_1 + \ldots + \psi_j = 1 - (1 - \phi_1)(1 - \phi_2) \cdots (1 - \phi_j),$$

$j = 1, \ldots, m$. Indeed, it is clear that

$$\psi_1 + \psi_2 = \phi_1 + (1 - \phi_1)\phi_2 = 1 - (1 - \phi_1) \cdot (1 - \phi_2).$$

By induction, let us assume that it is true for a certain $j \in \{4, \ldots, m - 1\}$. We claim

$$\psi_1 + \ldots + \psi_j + \psi_{j+1} = 1 - (1 - \phi_1)(1 - \phi_2) \cdots (1 - \phi_j)(1 - \phi_{j+1}).$$

Namely,

$$\begin{gathered} \psi_1 + \ldots + \psi_j + \psi_{j+1} = \\ = 1 - (1 - \phi_1)(1 - \phi_2) \cdots (1 - \phi_j) + (1 - \phi_1)(1 - \phi_2) \cdots (1 - \phi_j)\phi_{j+1} = \\ = 1 - (1 - \phi_1)(1 - \phi_2) \cdots (1 - \phi_j)(1 - \phi_{j+1}), \end{gathered}$$

as was to be checked.

Fix $x_0 \in K$. Then, there is some $i_0 \in \{1, \ldots, m\}$ such that $x_0 \in U(x_{i_0})$. Hence, $\phi_{i_0}(x_0) > 1 - \delta$ and consequently,

$$1 \geq \sum_{i=1}^{m} \psi_i(x_0) = 1 - (1 - \phi_{i_0}(x_0)) \prod_{i \neq i_0} (1 - \phi_i(x_0)) > 1 - \delta.$$

Furthermore, we clearly infer

$$\psi_i(t) < \delta \quad \text{for all } t \notin N(x_{i_0}),\ i = 1, \ldots, m. \tag{1}$$

Let

$$h := \psi_1 f_{x_1} + \psi_2 f_{x_2} + \ldots + \psi_m f_{x_m}. \tag{2}$$

It seems apparent that

$$h = \phi_1 f_{x_1} + (1 - \phi_1)[\phi_2 f_{x_2} + (1 - \phi_2)[\phi_3 f_{x_3} + \cdots + (1 - \phi_{m-1})[\phi_m f_{x_m} \cdots]].$$

Therefore, $h \in W$ since $\phi_i \in Conv(W)$ for $i = 1, ..., m$ (see Definition 2).

From Proposition 1, we know that, given $x \in K$,

$$d_\infty(f(x), h(x)) \leq d_\infty\left(f(x), \sum_{i=1}^{m} \psi_i(x) f(x)\right) + d_\infty\left(\sum_{i=1}^{m} \psi_i(x) f(x), h(x)\right) \leq$$

$$\leq \left|1 - \sum_{i=1}^{m} \psi_i(x)\right| d_\infty(f(x), 0)) + \sum_{i=1}^{m} \psi_i(x) d_\infty(f(x), f_{x_i}(x)).$$

On the one hand, $|1 - \sum_{i=1}^{m} \psi_i(x)| d_\infty(f(x), 0)) \leq \delta D(f, 0) \leq \epsilon$.

On the other hand, let

$$I_x = \{1 \leq i \leq m : x \in N(x_i)\}$$

and

$$J_x = \{1 \leq i \leq m : x \notin N(x_i)\}.$$

Then, for all $i \in I_x$, we have

$$\psi_i(x) d_\infty(f(x), f_{x_i}(x)) \leq \psi_i(x)(\sup_{x \in K} d_x(f, W) + \varepsilon) \leq \sup_{x \in K} d_x(f, W) + \varepsilon$$

and, for all $i \in J$, inequality (1) yields

$$\psi_i(x) d_\infty(f(x), f_{x_i}(x)) \leq \delta d_\infty(f(x), f_{x_i}(x)) \leq \delta D(f, f_{x_i}) \leq \delta k.$$

From the above two paragraphs, we can infer

$$d_\infty(f(x), h(x)) \leq \epsilon + \sup_{x \in K} d_x(f, W) + \varepsilon + \delta k m \leq \sup_{x \in K} d_x(f, W) + 3\varepsilon$$

and, since $x \in K$ is arbitrary,

$$D(f, h) \leq \sup_{x \in K} d_x(f, W) + 3\varepsilon.$$

As a consequence, we deduce that

$$d(f, W) = \inf_{g \in W} \{D(f, g)\} \leq \sup_{x \in K} d(f_x, W_x).$$

Finally, we can define a continuous function $\gamma : K \longrightarrow \mathbb{R}$ as

$$\gamma(x) := \inf_{g \in W} \{d_\infty(f(x), g(x))\}.$$

Since K is compact, we know that γ attains its supremum at some $x' \in K$. Hence, we can write $d(f, W) = d_{x'}(f, W)$. □

4. Best Approximation with Respect to Real-Valued Continuous Functions

In approximation theory, a natural question is when we can approximate a set-valued function by continuous real-valued functions. In the classical setting, Cellina's Theorem [21] is the fundamental result (see also [22–24]). In this section, we introduce a method to measure the distance between a fuzzy-number-valued function and a real-valued one. Then, we prove the existence of the best approximation of a fuzzy-number-valued continuous functions to the space of real-valued continuous functions.

The first problem is to find a suitable definition for the distance between a fuzzy-number-valued function and a real-valued one. Following the ideas in [12], we can define a distance for each level $\lambda \in [0, 1]$.

Definition 5. *Let $f \in C(K, \mathbb{E}^1)$ and let $F \in C(K)$. The distance at level λ between f and F can be defined as*

$$D_\lambda(f, F) := \sup_{x \in K}\{\sup\{|F(x) - t| : t \in I_\lambda := [f(x)^-(\lambda), f(x)^+(\lambda)]\}\}.$$

Now, we need to provide how to choose the best level to measure the distance.

Bearing in mind that the intervals I_λ form a nonincreasing family, it implies that the distances form a nondecreasing family as well, that is,

$$D_\lambda(f, F) \geq D_\eta(f, F) \quad \text{if } 0 \leq \lambda \leq \eta \leq 1.$$

Thus, if we choose

$$D(f, F) := \inf_{\lambda \in [0,1]} D_\lambda(f, F) = D_1(f, F)$$

we measure the distance at the interval with the minimum length (the core), possibly single-valued.

If, on the contrary, we choose

$$D(f, F) := \sup_{\lambda \in [0,1]} D_\lambda(f, F) = D_0(f, F)$$

we get the measurement at the support. As noted in [15], these intervals are not the best to represent the fuzzy number $f(x)$.

Another choice, more accurate, is to find a level λ which represents an average of the length of the level intervals (see, e.g., [25–27]).

The function $g(\lambda) = f(x)^+(\lambda) - f(x)^-(\lambda)$ is a nonincreasing function for each $x \in K$. Theorem 2.4 in [28] can be applied to get $t \in [0, 1]$ and $\lambda \in (0, 1)$ such that

$$\int_0^1 (f(x)^+(\lambda) - f(x)^-(\lambda))d\lambda = t \cdot g(\lambda + 0) + (1 - t) \cdot g(\lambda - 0)$$

where $g(\lambda + 0)$ and $g(\lambda - 0)$ stand for the one-sided limits of g. We choose λ_x as the minimum λ satisfying such a condition and taking $I_{\lambda_x} := [f(x)^-(\lambda_x), f(x)^+(\lambda_x)]$, we can define

$$D(f, F) := D_{\lambda_x}(f, F) = \sup_{x \in K}\left\{\sup_{t \in I_{\lambda_x}}\{|F(x) - t|\}\right\} \tag{3}$$

Definition 6. *Let $f \in C(K, \mathbb{E}^1)$. We can define the distance between f and $C(K)$ as*

$$D(f, C(K)) := \inf_{F \in C(K)} D(f, F).$$

where $D(f, F)$ is given by (3).

Definition 7. *Let $f \in C(K, \mathbb{E}^1)$ and $x \in K$. We can define*

$$rad(x, f) := \inf_{\alpha \in \mathbb{R}}\{\sup\{|\alpha - \beta| \; : \; \beta \in I_{\lambda_x}\}\}$$

It is clear that $rad(x, f)$ turns out to be the radius of the interval $[f(x)^-(\lambda_x), f(x)^+(\lambda_x)]$.

Definition 8. *Let $f \in C(K, \mathbb{E}^1)$. We define the* radius *of f as*

$$rad(f) := \sup_{x \in K} rad(x, f)$$

Remark 1. *From these definitions we infer easily that*

$$D(f,F) \geq rad(f)$$

for all $F \in C(K)$. *Hence,*

$$D(f,C(K)) \geq rad(f).$$

Theorem 3. *Let* $f \in C(K,\mathbb{E}^1)$. *Then, there exists a function* $F_0 \in C(K)$ *such that*

$$D(f,C(K)) = D(f,F_0).$$

Proof. Let us define a map $G : K \longrightarrow 2^{\mathbb{R}}$ such that, for each $x \in K$,

$$G(x) := \{\alpha \in \mathbb{R} : I_{\lambda_x} \subseteq [\alpha - rad(f), \alpha + rad(f)]\}$$

Let us first check that $G(x) \neq \emptyset$ for each $x \in K$. We know that

$$rad(x,f) := \inf_{\alpha\in\mathbb{R}} \sup_{\beta\in I_{\lambda_x}} |\alpha - \beta| \leq rad(f).$$

Since $rad(x,f)$ turns out to be the radius of the interval I_{λ_x}, it is clear that the center of this interval belongs to $G(x)$.

It is apparent that $G(x)$ is closed for each $x \in K$ since the intervals which appear in its definition are closed.

Now we take α_1, α_2 in $G(x)$ and $k_1, k_2 \geq 0$ with $k_1 + k_2 = 1$. Then, given $\alpha \in I_{\lambda_x}$,

$$\begin{aligned} |\alpha - (k_1\alpha_1 + k_2\alpha_2)| &= |\alpha(k_1 + k_2) - (k_1\alpha_1 + k_2\alpha_2)| \\ &\leq k_1|\alpha - \alpha_1| + k_2|\alpha - \alpha_2| \leq rad(f), \end{aligned}$$

which shows that $G(x)$ is convex for each $x \in K$.

Next, we shall prove that the map G is lower semicontinuous, that is, we have to check that the set

$$\mathcal{O} := \{x \in K : G(x) \cap O \neq \emptyset\}$$

is open in K for every open set $O \subset \mathbb{R}$. To this end, fix $x_0 \in \mathcal{O}$ and take $\alpha_0 \in G(x_0) \cap O$ for a certain open set O. Let $\delta_0 > 0$ such that $(\alpha_0 - \delta_0, \alpha_0 + \delta_0) \subset O$. From the continuity of f and from the fact that

$$I_{\lambda_{x_0}} \subset [\alpha_0 - rad(f), \alpha_0 + rad(f)],$$

we infer that, given $\epsilon > 0$, as we have

$$[\alpha_0 - rad(f), \alpha_0 + rad(f)] \subset (\alpha_0 - rad(f) - \epsilon, \alpha_0 + rad(f) + \epsilon),$$

there exists an open neighborhood $Q(\epsilon)$ of x_0 such that

$$I_{\lambda_x} \subset (\alpha_0 - (rad(f) + \epsilon), \alpha_0 + rad(f) + \epsilon)$$

for all $x \in Q(\epsilon)$. Our goal is to prove that $Q(\epsilon) \subseteq \mathcal{O}$ for some $\epsilon > 0$ to get the openness of $\mathcal{O}$.

Fix $x_1 \in Q(\epsilon)$. Since $G(x_1) \neq \emptyset$, there exists $\alpha_1 \in G(x_1)$. That is,

$$I_{\lambda_{x_1}} \subset [\alpha_1 - rad(f), \alpha_1 + rad(f)].$$

Moreover, we know that

$$I_{\lambda_{x_1}} \subset (\alpha_0 - (rad(f) + \epsilon), \alpha_0 + rad(f) + \epsilon).$$

Taking $\epsilon > 0$ as small as necessary, we can find $\delta' < \delta_0$ such that

$$[\alpha_0 - (rad(f) + \epsilon), \alpha_0 + rad(f) + \epsilon] \cap [\alpha_1 - rad(f), \alpha_1 + rad(f)]$$
$$\subset [(\alpha_0 + \delta') - rad(f), (\alpha_0 + \delta') + rad(f)]$$

and consequently

$$I_{\lambda_{x_1}} \subset [(\alpha_0 + \delta') - rad(f), (\alpha_0 + \delta') + rad(f)],$$

which implies that $\alpha_0 + \delta' \in G(x_1) \cap O$. Hence, $x_1 \in \mathcal{O}$, as desired.

Gathering the information we have obtained so far, we know that G is a lower semi-continuous mapping defined between K and the closed convex subsets of $\mathbb{R}$. Hence, by the Michael selection theorem [29], we infer that there exists $F_0 \in C(K)$ such that $F_0(x) \in G(x)$ for all $x \in K$.

As a consequence of the above paragraph, we can deduce that

$$D(f, F_0) \leq rad(f),$$

which, combined with the comments before this theorem, yields $D(f, F_0) = rad(f) = D(f, C(K))$. $\square$

5. Conclusions

In this paper, we addressed two problems of the best approximation type in the context of fuzzy-number-valued continuous functions: (1) the problem of the uniform approximation of a fuzzy-number-valued function continuous on a compact set by a family of continuous functions, continuous on this compact set; and (2) the existence of the best approximation of a fuzzy-number-valued continuous function to the space of real-valued continuous functions. We obtained positive results in both cases.

Author Contributions: All authors contributed equally in writing this article. All authors read and approved the final manuscript.

Funding: This research received no external funding.

Data Availability Statement: Not applicable.

Conflicts of Interest: The authors declare no conflict of interest.

References

1. Anastassiou, G.A. Fuzzy mathematics: Approximation theory. In *Studies in Fuzziness and Soft Computing*; Springer: Berlin, Germany, 2010; p. 251.
2. Bede, B.; Gal, S.G. Best approximation and Jackson-type estimates by generalized fuzzy polynomials. *J. Concr. Appl. Math.* **2004**, *2*, 213–232.
3. Font, J.J.; Sanchis, D.; Sanchis, M. A version of the Stone-Weierstrass theorem in fuzzy analysis. *J. Nonlinear Sci. Appl.* **2017**, *10*, 4275–4283. [CrossRef]
4. Gal, S.G. Approximation theory in fuzzy setting. In *Handbook of Analytic-Computational Methods in Applied Mathematics*; Anastassiou, G., Ed.; Chapman & CRC: New York, NY, USA, 2019.
5. Huang, H.; Wu, C. Approximation of fuzzy-valued functions by regular fuzzy neural networks and the accuracy analysis. *Soft Comput.* **2014**, *18*, 2525–2540. [CrossRef]
6. Liu, P. Analysis of approximation of continuous fuzzy functions by multivariate fuzzy polynomials. *Fuzzy Sets Syst.* **2002**, *127*, 299–313. [CrossRef]
7. Prolla, J.B. On the Weierstrass-Stone Theorem. *J. Approx. Theory* **1994**, *78*, 299–313. [CrossRef]
8. Prolla, J.B. A generalized Bernstein approximation theorem. *Math. Proc. Camb. Phil. Soc.* **1988**, *104*, 317–330. [CrossRef]
9. Chen, D. A note on Machado-Bishop theorem in weighted spaces with applications. *J. Approx. Theory* **2019**, *247*, 1–19. [CrossRef]
10. Cuenya, H.H.; Levis, F.E. Nonlinear Chebyshev approximation to set-valued functions. *Optimization* **2016**, *65*, 1519–1529. [CrossRef]
11. Lau, K.S. Approximation by continuous vector-valued functions. *Stud. Math.* **1980**, *68*, 291–298. [CrossRef]
12. Olech, C. Approximation of set-valued functions by continuous functions. *Colloq. Math.* **1968**, *19*, 285–293. [CrossRef]

13. Prolla, J.B.; Machado, S. Weierstrass-Stone Theorems for set-valued mappings. *J. Approx. Theory* **1982**, *36*, 1–15. [CrossRef]
14. Kashimoto, M.S. A note on a Stone-Weierstrass type theorem for set-valued mappings. *J. Approx. Theory* **2014**, *182*, 59–67. [CrossRef]
15. Grzegorzewski, P. Nearest interval approximation of a fuzzy number. *Fuzzy Sets Syst.* **2002**, *130*, 321–330. [CrossRef]
16. Diamond, P.; Kloeden, P. *Metric Spaces of Fuzzy Sets: Theory and Applications*; World Scientific: Singapore, 1994.
17. Goetschel, R.; Voxman, W. Elementary fuzzy calculus. *Fuzzy Sets Syst.* **1986**, *18*, 31–42. [CrossRef]
18. Abbasi, N.; Golshan, H.M. On best approximation in fuzzy metric spaces. *Kybernetika* **2015**, *51*, 374–386. [CrossRef]
19. Mazaheri, H.; Bizhanzadeh, Z.; Moosavi, S.M.; Dehghan, M.A. Fuzzy farhest points and fuzzy best approximation points in fuzzy normed spaces. *Theory Approx. Appl.* **2019**, *13*, 11–25.
20. Vaezpour, S.M.; Karimi, F. t-best approximation in fuzzy normed spaces. *Iran. J. Fuzzy Syst.* **2008**, *5*, 93–99.
21. Cellina, A. A further result on the approximation of set valued mappings. *Rendi. Acc. Naz. Lincei* **1970**, *48*, 412–416.
22. Beer, G. On a theorem of Cellina for set valued functions. *Rocky Mt. J. Math.* **1988**, *18*, 37–47. [CrossRef]
23. De Blasi, F.S.; Myjak, J. On continuous approximations for multifunction. *Pac. J. Math.* **1986**, *123*, 9–31. [CrossRef]
24. Holá, L'.; McCoy, R.A.; Pelant, J. Approximations of relations by continuous functions. *Topol. Its Appl.* **2007**, *154*, 2241–2247. [CrossRef]
25. Abbasbandy, S.; Amirfakhrian, M. The nearest approximation of a fuzzy quantity in parametric form. *Appl. Math. Comp.* **2006**, *172*, 624–632. [CrossRef]
26. Ban, A.I.; Coroianu, L. Nearest interval, triangular and trapezoidal approximation of a fuzzy number preserving ambiguity. *Int. J. Approx. Reason.* **2012**, *53*, 805–836. [CrossRef]
27. Chanas, S. On the interval approximation of a fuzzy number. *Fuzzy Sets Syst.* **2001**, *122*, 353–356. [CrossRef]
28. Marinescu, D.Ş.; Monea, M.; Mortici, C. About Karamata Mean Value Theorem, Some Consequences and Some Stability Results. *Results Math.* **2017**, *72*, 329–342. [CrossRef]
29. Michael, E. Continuous Selections I. *Ann. Math.* **1956**, *63*, 361–381. [CrossRef]

Article

New Arithmetic Operations of Non-Normal Fuzzy Sets Using Compatibility

Hsien-Chung Wu

Department of Mathematics, National Kaohsiung Normal University, Kaohsiung 802, Taiwan; hsien.chung.wu@gmail.com

Abstract: The new arithmetic operations of non-normal fuzzy sets are studied in this paper by using the extension principle and considering the general aggregation function. Usually, the aggregation functions are taken to be the minimum function or t-norms. In this paper, we considered a general aggregation function to set up the arithmetic operations of non-normal fuzzy sets. In applications, the arithmetic operations of fuzzy sets are always transferred to the arithmetic operations of their corresponding α-level sets. When the aggregation function is taken to be the minimum function, this transformation is clearly realized. Since the general aggregation function was adopted in this paper, the concept of compatibility with α-level sets is needed and is proposed, which can cover the conventional case using minimum functions as the special case.

Keywords: compatibility; extension principle; non-normal fuzzy sets

MSC: 03E72

Citation: Wu, H.-C. New Arithmetic Operations of Non-Normal Fuzzy Sets Using Compatibility. *Axioms* **2023**, *12*, 277. https://doi.org/10.3390/axioms12030277

Academic Editor: Amit K. Shukla

Received: 24 December 2022
Revised: 17 February 2023
Accepted: 2 March 2023
Published: 7 March 2023

Copyright: © 2023 by the authors. Licensee MDPI, Basel, Switzerland. This article is an open access article distributed under the terms and conditions of the Creative Commons Attribution (CC BY) license (https://creativecommons.org/licenses/by/4.0/).

1. Introduction

In order to simplify the notations, the membership function $\xi_{\tilde{F}}$ of a fuzzy set $\tilde{F}$ is identified with $\tilde{F}$ by simply writing $\xi_{\tilde{F}}(x) = \tilde{F}(x)$. Let $\tilde{F}$ and $\tilde{G}$ be two fuzzy sets in $\mathbb{R}$, and let $\odot$ denote any one of the arithmetic operations $\oplus, \ominus, \otimes, \oslash$ between $\tilde{F}$ and $\tilde{G}$. According to the extension principle, the membership function of $\tilde{F} \odot \tilde{G}$ is defined by

$$\tilde{F} \odot \tilde{G}(u) = \sup_{\{(x,y):u=x \circ y\}} \min\{\tilde{F}(x), \tilde{G}(y)\} \qquad (1)$$

for all $u \in \mathbb{R}$, where the arithmetic operations $\odot \in \{\oplus, \ominus, \otimes, \oslash\}$ correspond to the arithmetic operations $\circ \in \{+, -, *, \div\}$. The case of $\circ = \div$ should avoid the division of x/y for $y = 0$.

In general, we can consider the t-norm instead of the minimum function by referring to Dubois and Prade [1] and Weber [2]. For more detailed properties, we can refer to the monographs by Dubois and Prade [3] and Klir and Yuan [4]. In this paper, we used the general function to propose the arithmetic operations of fuzzy sets, and we present the compatibility with the conventional definition using the minimum functions. We can also refer to Gebhardt [5], Fullér and Keresztfalvi [6], Mesiar [7], Ralescu [8], and Yager [9] and Wu [10] for the arithmetic operations of fuzzy sets based on the extension principle.

The generalization of Zadeh's extension principle in (1) can also be used to set up the arithmetic operations without using the minimum function. Coroianua and Fuller [11,12] used the so-called joint probability distribution to generalize the extension principle (1), which is given by

$$\tilde{F} \odot_{\mathfrak{C}} \tilde{G}(u) = \sup_{\{(x,y):u=x \circ y\}} \mathfrak{C}(x,y) \qquad (2)$$

for all $u \in \mathbb{R}$, where $\mathfrak{C} : \mathbb{R}^2 \to [0,1]$ is a joint probability distribution satisfying

$$\sup_{x\in\mathbb{R}} \mathfrak{C}(x,y) = \tilde{G}(y) \text{ and } \sup_{y\in\mathbb{R}} = \mathfrak{C}(x,y) = \tilde{F}(x). \tag{3}$$

Wu [10] considered a general function $\mathfrak{D} : [0,1] \times [0,1] \to [0,1]$ by defining the arithmetic as

$$\tilde{F} \odot_{\mathfrak{D}} \tilde{G}(u) = \sup_{\{(x,y):u=x\circ y\}} \mathfrak{D}\big(\tilde{F}(x), \tilde{G}(y)\big), \tag{4}$$

where $\mathfrak{D}$ does not need to satisfy some extra conditions. The main difference between (2) and (4) is that the domains of the joint probabilitydistribution $\mathfrak{C} : \mathbb{R}^2 \to [0,1]$ and function $\mathfrak{D} : [0,1]^2 \to [0,1]$ are different. We can also refer to Coroianua and Fuller [11] for the comparison between (2) and (4). Although $\mathfrak{D}$ in (4) is a general function, some sufficient conditions regarding $\mathfrak{D}$ are still needed to obtain some desired properties. Therefore, the second motivation of this paper was to propose the concept of compatibility. We shall say that the function $\mathfrak{D}$ is compatible with the arithmetic operations of α-level sets when the following equality:

$$\left(\tilde{F} \odot_{\mathfrak{D}} \tilde{G}\right)_\alpha = \tilde{F}_\alpha \circ \tilde{G}_\alpha$$

is satisfied for each $\alpha \in (0,1]$. The sufficient conditions imposed upon the function $\mathfrak{D}$ will be studied to guarantee the compatibility. Under the general function $\mathfrak{D}$, the associativity of the arithmetic operations is also an important issue. Therefore, many rules regarding the associativity were also studied.

There is some other interesting arithmetic of fuzzy numbers, which will be shown below. Holčapek, Škorupová, and Štěpnička [13,14] proposed the arithmetic of extensional fuzzy numbers based on a similarity relation $S : \mathbb{R}^2 \to [0,1]$ such that S satisfies some required conditions. On the other hand, based on the concept of the extensional hull, given a fixed real number $x \in \mathbb{R}$, the so-called extensional fuzzy number generated by x and a similarity relation S is a fuzzy set $\tilde{x}_S$ in $\mathbb{R}$ with membership degree

$$\tilde{x}_S(y) = S(x,y) \text{ for all } y \in \mathbb{R}.$$

Given any two extensional fuzzy numbers $\tilde{x}_S$ and $\tilde{y}_S$, the addition $\oplus_S$ and multiplication $\otimes_S$ are defined by

$$\tilde{x}_S \oplus_S \tilde{y}_S = (x+y)_S \text{ and } \tilde{x}_S \otimes_S \tilde{y}_S = (xy)_S,$$

where S is assumed to be the so-called separated similarity relation for the purpose of well-defined arithmetic. In general, based on a system $\mathcal{S}$ of so-called nested similarity relations, the addition $\oplus_{\mathcal{S}}$ and multiplication $\otimes_{\mathcal{S}}$ are defined by

$$\tilde{x}_S \oplus_{\mathcal{S}} \tilde{y}_T = (x+y)_{\max(S,T)} \text{ and } \tilde{x}_S \otimes_{\mathcal{S}} \tilde{y}_T = (xy)_{\max(S,T)} \text{ for } S,T \in \mathcal{S}.$$

Esmi et al. [15] and Pedro et al. [16] used the extension principle in (3) to study the fuzzy differential equations. They considered the interactivity between fuzzy numbers. Let $\tilde{P}$ be a fuzzy set in $\mathbb{R}$. Given any fuzzy numbers $\tilde{F}$ and $\tilde{G}$, we say that $\tilde{P}$ is a joint probability distribution of $\tilde{F}$ and $\tilde{G}$ when

$$\sup_{x\in\mathbb{R}} \tilde{P}(x,y) = \tilde{G}(y) \text{ and } \sup_{y\in\mathbb{R}} = \tilde{P}(x,y) = \tilde{F}(x).$$

We say that $\tilde{F}$ and $\tilde{G}$ are non-interactive when

$$\tilde{P}(x,y) = \min\{\tilde{F}(x), \tilde{G}(x)\}.$$

Otherwise, they are called interactive. The disadvantage is that the non-interactivity depends on their joint probability distributions. We cannot just say that $\tilde{F}$ and $\tilde{G}$ are non-interactive without considering the role of the joint probability distribution. Let $\odot$ denote any one of the arithmetic operations $\oplus_{\tilde{P}}, \ominus_{\tilde{P}}, \otimes_{\tilde{P}}, \oslash_{\tilde{P}}$ between fuzzy numbers $\tilde{F}$ and $\tilde{G}$ along with a joint probability distribution $\tilde{P}$. The membership function of $\tilde{F} \odot_{\tilde{P}} \tilde{G}$ is defined by

$$\tilde{F} \odot_{\tilde{P}} \tilde{G}(u) = \sup_{\{(x,y):u=x\circ y\}} \tilde{P}(x,y)$$

for all $u \in \mathbb{R}$, where the case of $\circ_{\tilde{P}} = \div$ should avoid the division of x/y for $y = 0$.

The arithmetic of fuzzy intervals is an important issue. Wu [17] considered the form of expression in the decomposition theorem to study the arithmetic of fuzzy intervals. Wu [18] also used the form of expression in the decomposition theorem to study the different types of binary operations of fuzzy sets, which were also applied to study the difference of fuzzy intervals and covered the so-called generalized differences proposed by Bede and Stefanini [19] and Gomes and Barros [20] as the special cases. The fuzzy axiom of choice, the fuzzy Zorn's lemma, and the fuzzy Hausdorff maximal principle studied by Zulqarnian et al. [21] were also based on normal fuzzy sets. It is also possible to extend those results based on the non-normal fuzzy sets.

The fuzzy sets considered in Wu [17,18] were implicitly assumed to be normal. Without using the form of expression in the decomposition theorem, in this paper, we shall use the extension principle based on a general function rather than the t-norm to study the arithmetic of non-normal fuzzy intervals. In this case, the concept of compatibility with α-level sets can be proposed and the equivalence with conventional arithmetic operations using the minimum function can also be established.

In Section 2, the concept and basic properties of non-normal fuzzy sets will be presented, and the arithmetic operations of non-normal fuzzy sets will be studied using the extension principle based on the general functions. In Section 3, we shall propose the concept of compatibility with the α-level sets, which can cover the conventional case using the minimum functions as the special case.

2. Arithmetic Operations of Fuzzy Sets

Let $\tilde{F}$ be a fuzzy set in $\mathbb{R}$. Recall that a fuzzy set $\tilde{F}$ in a universal set U is called normal when there exists $x \in U$ satisfying $\tilde{F}(x) = 1$. For $\alpha \in (0,1]$, the α-level set of $\tilde{F}$ is denoted and defined by

$$\tilde{F}_\alpha = \{x \in \mathbb{R} : \tilde{F}(x) \geq \alpha\}. \tag{5}$$

The support of a fuzzy set $\tilde{F}$ is the crisp set defined by

$$\tilde{F}_{0+} = \{x \in \mathbb{R} : \tilde{F}(x) > 0\}.$$

The 0-level set $\tilde{F}_0$ is defined to be the topological closure of the support of $\tilde{F}$, i.e., $\tilde{F}_0 = \text{cl}(\tilde{F}_{0+})$. We write $\mathcal{R}_{\tilde{F}}$ to denote the range of the membership function of $\tilde{F}$. In general, we have $\mathcal{R}_{\tilde{F}} \neq [0,1]$. The following result is very useful.

Proposition 1. *Let $\tilde{F}$ be a fuzzy set in $\mathbb{R}$ with membership function $\tilde{F}$. Define $\alpha^* = \sup \mathcal{R}_{\tilde{F}}$ and*

$$I_{\tilde{F}} = \begin{cases} [0,\alpha^*), & \text{if the supremum } \sup \mathcal{R}_{\tilde{F}} \text{ is not obtained} \\ [0,\alpha^*], & \text{if the supremum } \sup \mathcal{R}_{\tilde{F}} \text{ is obtained.} \end{cases} \tag{6}$$

Then, $\tilde{F}_\alpha \neq \emptyset$ for all $\alpha \in I_{\tilde{F}}$ and $\tilde{F}_\alpha = \emptyset$ for all $\alpha \notin I_{\tilde{F}}$. Moreover, we have $\mathcal{R}_{\tilde{F}} \subseteq I_{\tilde{F}}$ and

$$\tilde{F}_{0+} = \bigcup_{\{\alpha \in I_{\tilde{F}}:\alpha>0\}} \tilde{F}_\alpha = \bigcup_{\{\alpha \in \mathcal{R}_{\tilde{F}}:\alpha>0\}} \tilde{F}_\alpha.$$

The interval $I_{\tilde{F}}$ is called an interval range of $\tilde{F}$.

We considered three arithmetic operations $\boxplus, \boxminus$ and $\boxtimes$ between any two fuzzy sets $\tilde{F}$ and $\tilde{G}$ in $\mathbb{R}$. The extension principle says that the membership functions are given by

$$\tilde{F} \boxplus \tilde{G}(u) = \sup_{\{(x,y):u=x+y\}} \min\{\tilde{F}(x), \tilde{G}(y)\} \tag{7}$$

$$\tilde{F} \boxminus \tilde{G}(u) = \sup_{\{(x,y):u=x-y\}} \min\{\tilde{F}(x), \tilde{G}(y)\} \tag{8}$$

$$\tilde{F} \boxtimes \tilde{G}(u) = \sup_{\{(x,y):u=xy\}} \min\{\tilde{F}(x), \tilde{G}(y)\} \tag{9}$$

for all $u \in \mathbb{R}$, where the arithmetic operations $\boxdot \in \{\boxplus, \boxminus, \boxtimes\}$ correspond to the arithmetic operations $\circ \in \{+, -, *\}$. The case of division was not considered in this paper, since it can be similarly obtained.

Instead of the minimum function, we can consider a general function $\mathfrak{D} : [0,1]^2 \to [0,1]$ defined on $[0,1]^2$. In this case, the membership functions are defined by

$$\tilde{F} \oplus_{EP} \tilde{G}(u) = \sup_{\{(x,y):u=x+y\}} \mathfrak{D}(\tilde{F}(x), \tilde{G}(y));$$

$$\tilde{F} \ominus_{EP} \tilde{G}(u) = \sup_{\{(x,y):u=x-y\}} \mathfrak{D}(\tilde{F}(x), \tilde{G}(y));$$

$$\tilde{F} \otimes_{EP} \tilde{G}(u) = \sup_{\{(x,y):u=x\cdot y\}} \mathfrak{D}(\tilde{F}(x), \tilde{G}(y)).$$

In general, the arithmetic operations are defined below.

Definition 1. *Given any fuzzy sets $\tilde{F}^{(1)}, \cdots, \tilde{F}^{(n)}$ in $\mathbb{R}$ and a function $\mathfrak{D}_n : [0,1]^n \to [0,1]$ defined on the product set $[0,1]^n$, regarding the operations $\odot_i \in \{\oplus, \ominus, \otimes\}$ for $i = 1, \cdots, n-1$, the membership function of $\tilde{F} = \tilde{F}^{(1)} \odot_1 \cdots \odot_{n-1} \tilde{F}^{(n)}$ is defined by*

$$\tilde{F}(u) = \tilde{F}^{(1)} \odot_1 \cdots \odot_{n-1} \tilde{F}^{(n)}(u) = \sup_{\{(a_1,\cdots,a_n):u=a_1\circ_1\cdots\circ_{n-1}a_n\}} \mathfrak{D}_n\left(\tilde{F}^{(1)}(a_1), \cdots, \tilde{F}^{(n)}(a_n)\right), \tag{10}$$

where the operations $\odot_i \in \{\oplus, \ominus, \otimes\}$ for $i = 1, \cdots, n-1$ correspond to the operations $\circ_i \in \{+, -, *\}$ for $i = 1, \cdots, n-1$.

When the function $\mathfrak{D}_n$ is taken to be the minimum function given by

$$\mathfrak{D}_n(\alpha_1, \cdots, \alpha_n) = \min\{\alpha_1, \cdots, \alpha_n\},$$

the membership function of $\tilde{F}^{(1)} \boxdot_1 \cdots \boxdot_{n-1} \tilde{F}^{(n)}$ is given by

$$\tilde{F}^{(1)} \boxdot_1 \cdots \boxdot_{n-1} \tilde{F}^{(n)}(u) = \sup_{\{(x_1,\cdots,x_n):u=x_1\circ_1\cdots\circ_{n-1}x_n\}} \min\left\{\tilde{F}^{(1)}(x_1), \cdots, \tilde{F}^{(n)}(x_n)\right\}, \tag{11}$$

where $\boxdot_i \in \{\boxplus, \boxminus, \boxtimes\}$ for $i = 1, \cdots, n-1$ can refer to (7), (8), and (9).

We can also insert the parentheses into the expression $\tilde{F}^{(1)} \odot_1 \cdots \odot_{n-1} \tilde{F}^{(n)}$. The following example shows the way of inserting parentheses.

Example 1. *Given fuzzy sets $\tilde{F}^{(1)}, \cdots, \tilde{F}^{(7)}$ in $\mathbb{R}$, we can consider the membership functions of*

$$\tilde{G} \equiv \tilde{F}^{(1)} \otimes \left(\tilde{F}^{(2)} \oplus \tilde{F}^{(3)}\right) \ominus \left(\tilde{F}^{(4)} \otimes \left(\tilde{F}^{(5)} \oplus \tilde{F}^{(6)} \ominus \tilde{F}^{(7)}\right)\right)$$

and

$$\tilde{H} \equiv \tilde{F}^{(1)} \otimes \tilde{F}^{(2)} \oplus \tilde{F}^{(3)} \ominus \tilde{F}^{(4)} \otimes \tilde{F}^{(5)} \oplus \tilde{F}^{(6)} \ominus \tilde{F}^{(7)}$$

given by

$$\tilde{G}(u) = \sup_{\{(x_1,\cdots,x_7):u=x_1*(x_2+x_3)-(x_4*(x_5+x_6-x_7))\}} \mathfrak{D}_7\left(\tilde{F}^{(1)}(x_1),\cdots,\tilde{F}^{(7)}(x_7)\right)$$

and

$$\tilde{H}(u) = \sup_{\{(x_1,\cdots,x_7):u=x_1*x_2+x_3-x_4*x_5+x_6-x_7\}} \mathfrak{D}_7\left(\tilde{F}^{(1)}(x_1),\cdots,\tilde{F}^{(7)}(x_7)\right),$$

respectively. It is clear that $\tilde{G} \neq \tilde{H}$. *Since*

$$x_1 * x_2 + x_3 - x_4 * x_5 + x_6 - x_7 = (x_1 * x_2) + x_3 - (x_4 * x_5) + x_6 - x_7,$$

the fuzzy set $\tilde{H}$ *means the following form:*

$$\tilde{H} = \left(\tilde{F}^{(1)} \otimes \tilde{F}^{(2)}\right) \oplus \tilde{F}^{(3)} \ominus \left(\tilde{F}^{(4)} \otimes \tilde{F}^{(5)}\right) \oplus \tilde{F}^{(6)} \ominus \tilde{F}^{(7)}.$$

Example 2. *We present an example from mathematical finance. The well-known Black–Scholes formula (see Black and Scholes [22]) for the European call option on a stock is described as follows. Let the function* f *be given by the formula:*

$$f(s,t,K,r,\sigma) = s \cdot N(d_1) - K \cdot e^{-rt} \cdot N(d_2),$$

where s *denotes the stock price,* t *denotes the time,* K *denotes the strike price,* r *denotes the interest rate,* σ *denotes the volatility, and* N *stands for the cumulative distribution function of a standard normal random variable* $N(0,1)$. *The quantities* d_1 *and* d_2 *are given by*

$$d_1 = \frac{\ln(s/K) + (r + \frac{\sigma^2}{2})t}{\sigma \cdot \sqrt{t}} \text{ and } d_2 = d_1 - \sigma \cdot \sqrt{t}.$$

Let T *be the expiry date, and let* C_t *denote the price of a European call option at time* $t \in [0,T]$. *Then, we have*

$$C_t = f(S_t, T-t, K, r, \sigma) \text{ for all } t \in [0,T], \tag{12}$$

where S_t *denotes the stock price at time* t. *On the other hand, the price* P_t *of a European put option at time* t *with the same expiry date* T *and strike price* K *can be obtained by the following put–call parity relationship (see Musiela and Rutkowski [23]):*

$$C_t - P_t = S_t - K \cdot e^{-r(T-t)} \text{ for all } t \in [0,T]. \tag{13}$$

Under the considerations of the fuzzy interest rate $\tilde{r}$, *fuzzy volatility* $\tilde{\sigma}$, *and fuzzy stock price* $\tilde{S}$, *we can obtain the fuzzy price* $\tilde{H}_t$ *of a European call option at time* t *according to (12) and the extension principle. Therefore, the membership function of* $\tilde{H}_t$ *is given by*

$$\tilde{H}_t(c) = \sup_{\{(s,r,\sigma):c=f(s,T-t,K,r,\sigma)\}} \mathfrak{D}_3\left(\tilde{S}_t(s),\tilde{r}(r),\tilde{\sigma}(\sigma)\right).$$

According to the put–call parity relationship in (13), we can also study the fuzzy price $\tilde{P}_t$ *of a European put option at time* t. *Let*

$$g(s,t,K,r,\sigma) = f(s,t,K,r,\sigma) - s + K \cdot e^{-rt}.$$

Then, we can obtain the fuzzy price $\tilde{P}_t$ *of a European put option at time* t *in which the membership function of* $\tilde{P}_t$ *is given by*

$$\tilde{P}_t(p) = \sup_{\{(s,r,\sigma):p=g(s,T-t,K,r,\sigma)\}} \mathfrak{D}_3\left(\tilde{S}_t(s),\tilde{r}(r),\tilde{\sigma}(\sigma)\right)).$$

Let $\tilde{F}^{(1)}, \cdots, \tilde{F}^{(n)}$ be fuzzy sets in $\mathbb{R}$, and let $\alpha_i^* = \sup \mathcal{R}_{\tilde{F}^{(i)}}$. From Proposition 1, we see that $\tilde{F}_\alpha^{(i)} \neq \emptyset$ for all $\alpha \in I_{\tilde{F}^{(i)}}$ and $\tilde{F}_\alpha^{(i)} = \emptyset$ for all $\alpha \notin I_{\tilde{F}^{(i)}}$, where the interval range $I_{\tilde{F}^{(i)}}$ is given by

$$I_{\tilde{F}^{(i)}} = \begin{cases} [0, \alpha_i^*), & \text{if the supremum } \sup \mathcal{R}_{\tilde{F}^{(i)}} \text{ is not obtained} \\ [0, \alpha_i^*], & \text{if the supremum } \sup \mathcal{R}_{\tilde{F}^{(i)}} \text{ is obtained.} \end{cases} \tag{14}$$

Let $I^* = I_{\tilde{F}^{(1)}} \cap \cdots \cap I_{\tilde{F}^{(n)}}$. Then, I^* is also an interval of the form $[0, \alpha]$ or $[0, \alpha)$ for some $\alpha \in (0, 1]$. For $\alpha \in I^*$, we see that $\tilde{F}_\alpha^{(i)} \neq \emptyset$ for all $i = 1, \cdots, n$.

Let $\tilde{F} = \tilde{F}^{(1)} \odot_1 \cdots \odot_{n-1} \tilde{F}^{(n)}$, and let $I_{\tilde{F}}$ be the interval range of $\tilde{F}$. We also write $\mathcal{R}_i \equiv \mathcal{R}_{\tilde{F}^{(i)}}$ to denote the range of the membership function of $\tilde{F}^{(i)}$ for $i = 1, \cdots, n$. The supremum of the range $\mathcal{R}_{\tilde{F}}$ of the membership function of $\tilde{F}$ is given by

$$\begin{aligned} \sup \mathcal{R}_{\tilde{F}} &= \sup_{u \in \mathbb{R}} \tilde{F}(u) = \sup_{u \in \mathbb{R}} \sup_{\{(x_1, \cdots, x_n): u = x_1 \circ_1 \cdots \circ_{n-1} x_n\}} \mathfrak{D}_n\left(\tilde{F}^{(1)}(x_1), \cdots, \tilde{F}^{(n)}(x_n)\right) \\ &= \sup_{(\alpha_1, \cdots, \alpha_n) \in \mathcal{R}_1 \times \cdots \times \mathcal{R}_n} \mathfrak{D}_n(\alpha_1, \cdots, \alpha_n) \equiv \alpha^*. \end{aligned} \tag{15}$$

Therefore, the definition of interval range says

$$I_{\tilde{F}} = \begin{cases} [0, \alpha^*] & \text{if the supremum } \mathcal{R}_{\tilde{F}} \text{ is obtained} \\ [0, \alpha^*) & \text{if the supremum } \mathcal{R}_{\tilde{F}} \text{ is not obtained} \end{cases} \tag{16}$$

Proposition 2. *Let $\tilde{F}^{(1)}, \cdots, \tilde{F}^{(n)}$ be fuzzy sets in $\mathbb{R}$, and let $\tilde{F} = \tilde{F}^{(1)} \odot_1 \cdots \odot_{n-1} \tilde{F}^{(n)}$ with interval range $I_{\tilde{F}}$. Suppose that the function $\mathfrak{D}_n : [0, 1]^n \to [0, 1]$ satisfies the following condition:*

$$\alpha_i \leq \beta_i \text{ for } i = 1, \cdots, n \text{ imply } \mathfrak{D}_n(\alpha_1, \cdots, \alpha_n) \leq \mathfrak{D}_n(\beta_1, \cdots, \beta_n). \tag{17}$$

We also assumed that the supremum $\alpha_i^* = \sup \mathcal{R}_{\tilde{F}^{(i)}}$ is obtained for $i = 1, \cdots, n$. Then, the following supremum:

$$\sup \mathcal{R}_{\tilde{F}} = \alpha^* = \mathfrak{D}_n(\alpha_1^*, \cdots, \alpha_n^*)$$

is obtained. Moreover, we have

$$I_{\tilde{F}} = [0, \alpha^*] \text{ and } I^* = [0, \alpha^\bullet],$$

where

$$\alpha^\bullet = \min\{\alpha_1^*, \cdots, \alpha_n^*\}.$$

In particular, suppose that

$$\mathfrak{D}_n(\alpha_1^*, \cdots, \alpha_n^*) = \min\{\alpha_1^*, \cdots, \alpha_n^*\}. \tag{18}$$

Then, we have

$$I_{\tilde{F}} = I_{\tilde{F}^{(1)}} \cap \cdots \cap I_{\tilde{F}^{(n)}} = I^* = [0, \alpha^*].$$

Proof. Since the supremum $\sup \mathcal{R}_{\tilde{F}^{(i)}}$ is obtained for $i = 1, \cdots, n$, we have

$$I_{\tilde{F}^{(i)}} = [0, \alpha_i^*] \text{ and } \alpha_i^* = \tilde{F}^{(i)}(x_i^*) \in \mathcal{R}_{\tilde{F}^{(i)}} \equiv \mathcal{R}_i \tag{19}$$

for some $x_i^* \in \mathbb{R}$ and for all $i = 1, \cdots, n$. It is also clear that

$$I^* = I_{\tilde{F}^{(1)}} \cap \cdots \cap I_{\tilde{F}^{(n)}} = [0, \alpha^\bullet].$$

From (15), we have

$$\alpha^* = \sup_{(\alpha_1,\cdots,\alpha_n)\in\mathcal{R}_1\times\cdots\times\mathcal{R}_n} \mathfrak{D}_n(\alpha_1,\cdots,\alpha_n) \geq \mathfrak{D}_n(\alpha_1^*,\cdots,\alpha_n^*).$$

On the other hand, since $\tilde{F}^{(i)}(x_i) \leq \alpha_i^*$ for all $i = 1,\cdots,n$, from (15), again, we also have

$$\begin{aligned}
\alpha^* &= \sup_{u\in\mathbb{R}} \sup_{\{(x_1,\cdots,x_n):u=x_1\circ_1\cdots\circ_{n-1}x_n\}} \mathfrak{D}_n\left(\tilde{F}^{(1)}(x_1),\cdots,\tilde{F}^{(n)}(x_n)\right) \\
&\leq \sup_{u\in\mathbb{R}} \sup_{\{(x_1,\cdots,x_n):u=x_1\circ_1\cdots\circ_{n-1}x_n\}} \mathfrak{D}_n(\alpha_1^*,\cdots,\alpha_n^*) \text{ (using (17))} \\
&= \mathfrak{D}_n(\alpha_1^*,\cdots,\alpha_n^*),
\end{aligned}$$

which proves

$$\alpha^* = \mathfrak{D}_n(\alpha_1^*,\cdots,\alpha_n^*).$$

We take $u^* = x_1^* \circ_1 \cdots \circ_{n-1} x_n^*$. Then, we have

$$\begin{aligned}
\tilde{F}(u^*) &= \sup_{\{(x_1,\cdots,x_n):u^*=x_1\circ_1\cdots\circ_{n-1}x_n\}} \mathfrak{D}_n\left(\tilde{F}^{(1)}(x_1),\cdots,\tilde{F}^{(n)}(x_n)\right) \\
&\geq \mathfrak{D}_n\left(\tilde{F}^{(1)}(x_1^*),\cdots,\tilde{F}^{(n)}(x_n^*)\right) \text{ (since } u^* = x_1^* \circ_1 \cdots \circ_{n-1} x_n^*) \\
&= \mathfrak{D}_n(\alpha_1^*,\cdots,\alpha_n^*) = \alpha^*
\end{aligned}$$

and

$$\begin{aligned}
\tilde{F}(u^*) &= \sup_{\{(x_1,\cdots,x_n):u^*=x_1\circ_1\cdots\circ_{n-1}x_n\}} \mathfrak{D}_n\left(\tilde{F}^{(1)}(x_1),\cdots,\tilde{F}^{(n)}(x_n)\right) \\
&\leq \sup_{\{(x_1,\cdots,x_n):u^*=x_1\circ_1\cdots\circ_{n-1}x_n\}} \mathfrak{D}_n\left(\tilde{F}^{(1)}(x_1^*),\cdots,\tilde{F}^{(n)}(x_n^*)\right) \text{ (using (17))} \\
&= \mathfrak{D}_n(\alpha_1^*,\cdots,\alpha_n^*) = \alpha^*
\end{aligned}$$

Therefore, we obtain $\tilde{F}(u^*) = \alpha^*$. From (15), we conclude that the supremum $\sup \mathcal{R}_{\tilde{F}}$ is obtained at u^*. From (16), it follows that $I_{\tilde{F}} = [0, \alpha^*]$. This completes the proof. □

3. Compatibility

Let $S_1,\cdots,S_n$ be subsets of $\mathbb{R}$. We write

$$S_1 \circ_1 \cdots \circ_{n-1} S_n = \{x_1 \circ_1 \cdots \circ_{n-1} x_n : x_i \in S_i \text{ for } i = 1,\cdots,n\},$$

where the arithmetic operations $\circ_i \in \{+,-,*\}$ for $i = 1,\cdots,n-1$.

Given any fuzzy sets $\tilde{F}^{(1)},\cdots,\tilde{F}^{(n)}$ in $\mathbb{R}$, let $\tilde{F} = \tilde{F}^{(1)} \odot_1 \cdots \odot_{n-1} \tilde{F}^{(n)}$ be defined in Definition 1. For any

$$\alpha \in I^* \cap I_{\tilde{F}} = I_{\tilde{F}^{(1)}} \cap \cdots \cap I_{\tilde{F}^{(n)}} \cap I_{\tilde{F}},$$

it is clear that the α-level sets $\tilde{F}_\alpha$ and $\tilde{F}_\alpha^{(i)}$ are nonempty for $i = 1,\cdots,n$. Therefore, we propose the following definition.

Definition 2. *Given any fuzzy sets $\tilde{F}^{(1)},\cdots,\tilde{F}^{(n)}$ in $\mathbb{R}$, we considered the arithmetic operations $\odot_i \in \{\oplus,\ominus,\otimes\}$, which correspond to the arithmetic operations $\circ_i \in \{+,-,*\}$ for $i = 1,\cdots,n-1$:*

- *The function $\mathfrak{D}_n : [0,1]^n \to [0,1]$ is said to be compatible with the arithmetic operations of α-level sets when the following equality is satisfied:*

$$\left(\tilde{F}^{(1)} \odot_1 \cdots \odot_{n-1} \tilde{F}^{(n)}\right)_\alpha = \tilde{F}_\alpha^{(1)} \circ_1 \cdots \circ_{n-1} \tilde{F}_\alpha^{(n)} \text{ for all } \alpha \in I^* \cap I_{\tilde{F}} \text{ with } \alpha > 0.$$

- *The function* $\mathfrak{D}_n : [0,1]^n \to [0,1]$ *is said to be strongly compatible with the arithmetic operations of* α*-level sets when the following equality is satisfied:*

$$\left(\tilde{F}^{(1)} \odot_1 \cdots \odot_{n-1} \tilde{F}^{(n)}\right)_\alpha = \tilde{F}^{(1)}_\alpha \circ_1 \cdots \circ_{n-1} \tilde{F}^{(n)}_\alpha \text{ for all } \alpha \in I^* \cap I_{\tilde{F}}.$$

The purpose of this paper was to present some sufficient conditions such that the compatibility with the arithmetic operations of α-level sets can be satisfied.

Recall that the real-valued function $f : \mathbb{R} \to \mathbb{R}$ is upper semi-continuous on $\mathbb{R}$ if and only if the set $\{x \in \mathbb{R} : f(x) \geq \alpha\}$ is a closed set in $\mathbb{R}$ for each $\alpha \in \mathbb{R}$. Especially, if $\tilde{F}$ is a fuzzy set in $\mathbb{R}$ such that its membership function $\tilde{F}$ is upper semi-continuous on $\mathbb{R}$, then each α-level set $\tilde{F}_\alpha$ is a closed subset of $\mathbb{R}$ for $\alpha \in I_{\tilde{F}}$.

Lemma 1 (Royden ([24] p. 161)). *Let K be a closed and bounded subset of* $\mathbb{R}$*, and let f be a real-valued function defined on* $\mathbb{R}$*. Suppose that f is upper semi-continuous on* $\mathbb{R}$*. Then, f assumes its maximum on K; that is, the supremum is obtained in the following sense:*

$$\sup_{x \in K} f(x) = \max_{x \in K} f(x).$$

Theorem 1. *Given any fuzzy sets* $\tilde{F}^{(1)}, \cdots, \tilde{F}^{(n)}$ *in* $\mathbb{R}$*, we considered the arithmetic operations* $\odot_i \in \{\oplus, \ominus, \otimes\}$*, which correspond to the arithmetic operations* $\circ_i \in \{+, -, *\}$ *for* $i = 1, \cdots, n - 1$*. Then, we have the following properties:*

(i) *For any* $\alpha \in I^* \cap I_{\tilde{F}}$ *with* $\alpha > 0$*, we assumed that the function* $\mathfrak{D}_n$ *satisfies the following condition:*

$$\alpha_i \geq \alpha \text{ for all } i = 1, \cdots, n \text{ imply } \mathfrak{D}_n(\alpha_1, \cdots, \alpha_n) \geq \alpha. \tag{20}$$

Then, the following inclusion:

$$\tilde{F}^{(1)}_\alpha \circ_1 \cdots \circ_{n-1} \tilde{F}^{(n)}_\alpha \subseteq \left(\tilde{F}^{(1)} \odot_1 \cdots \odot_{n-1} \tilde{F}^{(n)}\right)_\alpha$$

holds true for all $\alpha \in I^* \cap I_{\tilde{F}}$.

(ii) *Suppose that the membership functions of* $\tilde{F}^{(i)}$ *are upper semi-continuous for all* $i = 1, \cdots, n$*. We also assumed that the function* $\mathfrak{D}_n$ *satisfies the following conditions:*

- *given any* $\alpha \in I^* \cap I_{\tilde{F}}$ *with* $\alpha > 0$,

$$\mathfrak{D}_n(\alpha_1, \cdots, \alpha_n) \geq \alpha \text{ if and only if } \alpha_i \geq \alpha \text{ for all } i = 1, \cdots, n. \tag{21}$$

- *Given any* $\alpha \notin I^*$ *with* $\alpha \in (0,1]$,

$$\alpha_i < \alpha \text{ for some } i \in \{1, \cdots, n\} \text{ imply } \mathfrak{D}_n(\alpha_1, \cdots, \alpha_n) < \alpha \tag{22}$$

for any $\alpha_j \in [0,1]$ *with* $j \neq i$.

Then, the following equality:

$$\left(\tilde{F}^{(1)} \odot_1 \cdots \odot_{n-1} \tilde{F}^{(n)}\right)_\alpha = \tilde{F}^{(1)}_\alpha \circ_1 \cdots \circ_{n-1} \tilde{F}^{(n)}_\alpha \tag{23}$$

holds true for all $\alpha \in I^* \cap I_{\tilde{F}}$ *with* $\alpha > 0$*. We further assumed that the supports* $\tilde{F}^{(i)}_{0+}$ *are bounded for all* $i = 1, \cdots, n$*. Then, the following equality:*

$$\left(\tilde{F}^{(1)} \odot_1 \cdots \odot_{n-1} \tilde{F}^{(n)}\right)_0 = \tilde{F}^{(1)}_0 \circ_1 \cdots \circ_{n-1} \tilde{F}^{(n)}_0. \tag{24}$$

regarding the 0-level sets holds true.

Proof. To prove Part (i), given any $\alpha \in I^* \cap I_{\tilde{F}}$ with $\alpha > 0$, we have $\tilde{F}_\alpha \neq \emptyset$ and $\tilde{F}_\alpha^{(i)} \neq \emptyset$ for all $i = 1, \cdots, n$. Given any

$$u_\alpha \in \tilde{F}_\alpha^{(1)} \circ_1 \cdots \circ_{n-1} \tilde{F}_\alpha^{(n)}.$$

there exist $x_\alpha^{(i)} \in \tilde{F}_\alpha^{(i)}$ for all $i = 1, \cdots, n$ satisfying

$$u_\alpha = x_\alpha^{(1)} \circ_1 \cdots \circ_{n-1} x_\alpha^{(n)}.$$

We see that

$$\tilde{F}^{(i)}(x_\alpha^{(i)}) \geq \alpha \text{ for all } i = 1, \cdots, n.$$

Using the assumption (20) of $\mathfrak{D}_n$, we also have

$$\mathfrak{D}_n\left(\tilde{F}^{(1)}(x_\alpha^{(1)}), \cdots, \tilde{F}^{(n)}(x_\alpha^{(n)})\right) \geq \alpha \tag{25}$$

Therefore, we have

$$\begin{aligned} \tilde{F}^{(1)} \odot_1 \cdots \odot_{n-1} \tilde{F}^{(n)}(u_\alpha) &= \sup_{\{(x_1, \cdots, x_n) : u_\alpha = x_1 \circ_1 \cdots \circ_{n-1} x_n\}} \mathfrak{D}_n\left(\tilde{F}^{(1)}(x_1), \cdots, \tilde{F}^{(n)}(x_n)\right) \\ &\geq \mathfrak{D}_n\left(\tilde{F}^{(1)}(x_\alpha^{(1)}), \cdots, \tilde{F}^{(n)}(x_\alpha^{(n)})\right) \geq \alpha \text{ (using (25))}. \end{aligned}$$

This shows

$$u_\alpha \in (\tilde{F}^{(1)} \odot_1 \cdots \odot_{n-1} \tilde{F}^{(n)})_\alpha.$$

Therefore, we obtain the following inclusion:

$$\tilde{F}_\alpha^{(1)} \circ_1 \cdots \circ_{n-1} \tilde{F}_\alpha^{(n)} \subseteq \left(\tilde{F}^{(1)} \odot_1 \cdots \odot_{n-1} \tilde{F}^{(n)}\right)_\alpha$$

for all $\alpha \in I^* \cap I_{\tilde{F}}$ with $\alpha > 0$.

Next, we considered the 0-level sets. For $\alpha = 0$, given any

$$u_0 \in \tilde{F}_0^{(1)} \circ_1 \cdots \circ_{n-1} \tilde{F}_0^{(n)},$$

there exist $x_0^{(i)} \in \tilde{F}_0^{(i)}$ for all $i = 1, \cdots, n$ satisfying

$$u_0 = x_0^{(1)} \circ_1 \cdots \circ_{n-1} x_0^{(n)}.$$

For each fixed i, since

$$x_0^{(i)} \in \tilde{F}_0^{(i)} = \text{cl}\left(\{x \in \mathbb{R} : \tilde{F}^{(i)}(x) > 0\}\right),$$

the concept of closure says that there exists a sequence

$$\{x_m^{(i)}\}_{m=1}^\infty \subseteq \{x \in \mathbb{R} : \tilde{F}^{(i)}(x) > 0\} \tag{26}$$

satisfying

$$\lim_{m \to \infty} x_m^{(i)} = x_0^{(i)}.$$

We considered a function $\eta : \mathbb{R}^n \to \mathbb{R}$ defined by

$$\eta(x_1, \cdots, x_n) = x_1 \circ_1 \cdots \circ_{n-1} x_n,$$

where the binary operations $\circ_i \in \{+,-,*\}$ for $i = 1,\cdots,n$. Then, it is clear that η is continuous. We define

$$u_m = x_m^{(1)} \circ_1 \cdots \circ_{n-1} x_m^{(n)} = \eta\left(x_m^{(1)},\cdots,x_m^{(n)}\right).$$

Using (26) and the continuity of η, we obtain

$$\lim_{m\to\infty} u_m = \lim_{m\to\infty} \eta\left(x_m^{(1)},\cdots,x_m^{(n)}\right) = \eta\left(x_0^{(1)},\cdots,x_0^{(n)}\right) = x_0^{(1)} \circ_1 \cdots \circ_{n-1} x_0^{(n)} = u_0. \quad (27)$$

Given any $\alpha_i \in I_{\tilde{F}^{(i)}}$ with $\alpha_i > 0$ for $i = 1,\cdots,n$ and any $\bar{\alpha} \in I_{\tilde{F}}$ with $\bar{\alpha} > 0$, let

$$\alpha = \min\{\bar{\alpha},\alpha_1,\cdots,\alpha_n\}.$$

Then, we have $0 < \alpha \le \bar{\alpha}$ and $0 < \alpha \le \alpha_i$ for $i = 1,\cdots,n$. From (14), we also see $\alpha \in I_{\tilde{F}}$ and $\alpha \in I_{\tilde{F}^{(i)}}$ for all $i = 1,\cdots,n$, i.e., $\alpha \in I^* \cap I_{\tilde{F}}$. The assumption (20) of $\mathfrak{D}_n$ says

$$\mathfrak{D}_n(\alpha_1,\cdots,\alpha_n) \ge \alpha > 0.$$

Therefore, the following statement holds true:

$$0 < \alpha_i \in I_{\tilde{F}^{(i)}} \text{ for all } i = 1,\cdots,n \text{ imply } \mathfrak{D}_n(\alpha_1,\cdots,\alpha_n) > 0. \quad (28)$$

Now, we have

$$\begin{aligned}\tilde{F}^{(1)} \odot_1 \cdots \odot_{n-1} \tilde{F}^{(n)}(u_m) &= \sup_{\{(x_1,\cdots,x_n):u_m = x_1\circ_1\cdots\circ_{n-1}x_n\}} \mathfrak{D}_n\left(\tilde{F}^{(1)}(x_1),\cdots,\tilde{F}^{(n)}(x_n)\right)\\ &\ge \mathfrak{D}_n\left(\tilde{F}^{(1)}(x_m^{(1)}),\cdots,\tilde{F}^{(n)}(x_m^{(n)})\right) > 0 \text{ (using (28))},\end{aligned}$$

which also says

$$u_m \in \{u \in \mathbb{R} : \tilde{F}^{(1)} \odot_1 \cdots \odot_{n-1} \tilde{F}^{(n)}(u) > 0\} \text{ for all } m.$$

From (27), we obtain

$$u_0 \in \text{cl}\left(\{u \in \mathbb{R} : \tilde{F}^{(1)} \odot_1 \cdots \odot_{n-1} \tilde{F}^{(n)}(u) > 0\}\right) = \left(\tilde{F}^{(1)} \odot_1 \cdots \odot_{n-1} \tilde{F}^{(n)}\right)_0,$$

which shows the following inclusion:

$$\tilde{F}_0^{(1)} \circ_1 \cdots \circ_{n-1} \tilde{F}_0^{(n)} \subseteq \left(\tilde{F}^{(1)} \odot_1 \cdots \odot_{n-1} \tilde{F}^{(n)}\right)_0.$$

Therefore, we obtain the desired inclusion.

Proving Part (ii) means proving another direction of inclusion. Now, we further assumed that the membership functions of $\tilde{F}^{(i)}$ are upper semi-continuous for all $i = 1,\cdots,n$. In other words, the nonempty α-level sets $\tilde{F}_\alpha^{(i)}$ are closed sets in $\mathbb{R}$ for all $\alpha \in I^*$ and $i = 1,\cdots,n$. Given any $\alpha \in I^* \cap I_{\tilde{F}}$ with $\alpha > 0$ and any

$$u_\alpha \in (\tilde{F}^{(1)} \odot_1 \cdots \odot_{n-1} \tilde{F}^{(n)})_\alpha,$$

we have

$$\sup_{\{(x_1,\cdots,x_n):u_\alpha = x_1\circ_1\cdots\circ_{n-1}x_n\}} \mathfrak{D}_n\left(\tilde{F}^{(1)}(x_1),\cdots,\tilde{F}^{(n)}(x_n)\right) = \tilde{F}^{(1)} \odot_1 \cdots \odot_{n-1} \tilde{F}^{(n)}(u_\alpha) \ge \alpha. \quad (29)$$

Since u_α is a finite number, we see that

$$F \equiv \{(x_1,\cdots,x_n) : u_\alpha = x_1 \circ_1 \cdots \circ_{n-1} x_n\}$$

is a bounded set in $\mathbb{R}^n$. We also see that the function

$$\eta(x_1, \cdots, x_n) = x_1 \circ_1 \cdots \circ_{n-1} x_n$$

is continuous on $\mathbb{R}^n$. Since the singleton set $\{u_\alpha\}$ is a closed set in $\mathbb{R}$, the continuity of η says that the inverse image $F = \eta^{-1}(\{u_\alpha\})$ of $\{u_\alpha\}$ is also a closed set in $\mathbb{R}^n$. This says that F is a bounded and closed set in $\mathbb{R}^n$. Next, we want to claim that the function

$$f(x_1, \cdots, x_n) = \mathfrak{D}_n\left(\tilde{F}^{(1)}(x_1), \cdots, \tilde{F}^{(n)}(x_n)\right)$$

is upper semi-continuous. In other words, we want to show that

$$\{(x_1, \cdots, x_n) : f(x_1, \cdots, x_n) \geq \alpha\}$$

is a closed set in $\mathbb{R}^n$ for any $\alpha \in \mathbb{R}$. We considered the different cases as follows:

- Suppose that $\alpha \leq 0$. Then, we have

$$\{(x_1, \cdots, x_n) : f(x_1, \cdots, x_n) \geq \alpha\} = \mathbb{R}^n,$$

which is a closed set in $\mathbb{R}^n$.

- Suppose that $\alpha > 1$. Then, we have

$$\{(x_1, \cdots, x_n) : f(x_1, \cdots, x_n) \geq \alpha\} = \emptyset,$$

which is also a closed set in $\mathbb{R}^n$.

- Suppose that $\alpha \in I^* \cap I_{\tilde{F}}$ with $\alpha > 0$, i.e., $\tilde{F}_\alpha^{(i)} \neq \emptyset$ for all $i = 1, \cdots, n$. Then, we have

$$\begin{aligned}
\{(x_1, \cdots, x_n) : f(x_1, \cdots, x_n) \geq \alpha\} &= \left\{(x_1, \cdots, x_n) : \mathfrak{D}_n\left(\tilde{F}^{(1)}(x_1), \cdots, \tilde{F}^{(n)}(x_n)\right) \geq \alpha\right\} \\
&= \left\{(x_1, \cdots, x_n) : \tilde{F}^{(i)}(x_i) \geq \alpha \text{ for all } i = 1, \cdots, n\right\} \text{ (using (21))} \\
&= \left\{(x_1, \cdots, x_n) : x_i \in \tilde{F}_\alpha^{(i)} \text{ for all } i = 1, \cdots, n\right\} = \tilde{F}_\alpha^{(1)} \times \cdots \times \tilde{F}_\alpha^{(n)},
\end{aligned}$$

which is a closed set in $\mathbb{R}^n$, since $\tilde{F}_\alpha^{(i)}$ are closed sets in $\mathbb{R}$ for all $i = 1, \cdots, n$.

- Suppose that $\alpha \notin I^*$ with $\alpha \in (0, 1]$. Then, we have $\tilde{F}_\alpha^{(i)} = \emptyset$ for some i, i.e., $\alpha \notin I_{\tilde{F}^{(i)}}$. By referring to (14), it follows that $\tilde{F}^{(i)}(x) < \alpha$ for all $x \in \mathbb{R}$. Therefore, using the assumption (22), we obtain

$$f(x_1, \cdots, x_n) = \mathfrak{D}_n\left(\tilde{F}^{(1)}(x_1), \cdots, \tilde{F}^{(n)}(x_n)\right) < \alpha \text{ for all } (x_1, \cdots, x_n) \in \mathbb{R}^n.$$

This shows

$$\{(x_1, \cdots, x_n) : f(x_1, \cdots, x_n) \geq \alpha\} = \emptyset,$$

which is also a closed set in $\mathbb{R}^n$.

- Suppose that $\alpha \notin I_{\tilde{F}}$ with $\alpha \in (0, 1]$. Then, we have

$$\begin{aligned}
\emptyset &= \left\{(x_1, \cdots, x_n) : \mathfrak{D}_n\left(\tilde{F}^{(1)}(x_1), \cdots, \tilde{F}^{(n)}(x_n)\right) \geq \alpha\right\} \\
&= \{(x_1, \cdots, x_n) : f(x_1, \cdots, x_n) \geq \alpha\},
\end{aligned}$$

which is a closed set in $\mathbb{R}^n$.

The above cases conclude that the function $f(x_1, \cdots, x_n)$ is indeed upper semi-continuous. Lemma 1 says that the function f assumes the maximum on the set F. Therefore, using (29), we have

$$\max_{(x_1,\cdots,x_n)\in F} f(x_1,\cdots,x_n) = \max_{\{(x_1,\cdots,x_n):u_\alpha = x_1 \circ_1 \cdots \circ_{n-1} x_n\}} f(x_1,\cdots,x_n)$$
$$= \sup_{\{(x_1,\cdots,x_n):u_\alpha = x_1 \circ_1 \cdots \circ_{n-1} x_n\}} f(x_1,\cdots,x_n) \geq \alpha. \quad (30)$$

Therefore, there exists $(x_1^*, \cdots, x_n^*) \in F$ satisfying

$$u_\alpha = x_1^* \circ_1 \cdots \circ_{n-1} x_n^*$$

and

$$\mathfrak{D}_n\left(\tilde{F}^{(1)}(x_1^*), \cdots, \tilde{F}^{(n)}(x_n^*)\right) = f(x_1^*, \cdots, x_n^*) = \max_{(x_1,\cdots,x_n)\in F} f(x_1,\cdots,x_n) \geq \alpha.$$

Using the assumption (21), we obtain $\tilde{F}^{(i)}(x_i^*) \geq \alpha$, which says $x_i^* \in \tilde{F}_\alpha^{(i)}$ for all $i = 1, \cdots, n$. Therefore, we obtain

$$u_\alpha \in \tilde{F}_\alpha^{(1)} \circ_1 \cdots \circ_{n-1} \tilde{F}_\alpha^{(n)},$$

which shows the following inclusion:

$$\left(\tilde{F}^{(1)} \odot_1 \cdots \odot_{n-1} \tilde{F}^{(n)}\right)_\alpha \subseteq \tilde{F}_\alpha^{(1)} \circ_1 \cdots \circ_{n-1} \tilde{F}_\alpha^{(n)}$$

for all $\alpha \in I^* \cap I_{\tilde{F}}$ with $\alpha > 0$. Using Part (i), we obtain the desired equality (23).

Considering the 0-level sets, for $\alpha = 0$, we further assumed that the supports $\tilde{F}_{0+}^{(i)}$ are bounded for all $i = 1, \cdots, n$. Suppose that $\mathfrak{D}_n(\alpha_1 \cdots, \alpha_n) > 0$ for $\alpha_i \in I_{\tilde{F}^{(i)}}$ and $i = 1, \cdots, n$. Since $I^* \cap I_{\tilde{F}}$ is an interval beginning from 0, using the denseness of $\mathbb{R}$, there exists $\alpha \in I^* \cap I_{\tilde{F}}$ with $\alpha > 0$ satisfying

$$\mathfrak{D}_n(\alpha_1 \cdots, \alpha_n) \geq \alpha > 0.$$

Using the assumption (21), we have $\alpha_i \geq \alpha > 0$ for all $i = 1, \cdots, n$, which says that the following statement holds true:

$$\mathfrak{D}_n(\alpha_1 \cdots, \alpha_n) > 0 \text{ for } \alpha_i \in I_{\tilde{F}^{(i)}} \text{ and } i = 1, \cdots, n \text{ imply } \alpha_i > 0 \text{ for all } i = 1, \cdots, n. \quad (31)$$

Now, considering the 0-level set, we have

$$u_0 \in \left(\tilde{F}^{(1)} \odot_1 \cdots \odot_{n-1} \tilde{F}^{(n)}\right)_0 = \text{cl}\left(\left(\tilde{F}^{(1)} \odot_1 \cdots \odot_{n-1} \tilde{F}^{(n)}\right)_{0+}\right)$$
$$= \text{cl}\left(\left\{u \in \mathbb{R} : \tilde{F}^{(1)} \odot_1 \cdots \odot_{n-1} \tilde{F}^{(n)}(u) > 0\right\}\right).$$

Therefore, there exists a sequence $\{u_m\}_{m=1}^\infty$ in the following set:

$$\left\{u \in \mathbb{R} : \tilde{F}^{(1)} \odot_1 \cdots \odot_{n-1} \tilde{F}^{(n)}(u) > 0\right\}$$

satisfying

$$\lim_{m\to\infty} u_m = u_0.$$

Using the above arguments by referring to (30), we can obtain

$$0 < \tilde{F}^{(1)} \odot_1 \cdots \odot_{n-1} \tilde{F}^{(n)}(u_m) = \sup_{\{(x_1,\cdots,x_n):u_m=x_1\circ_1\cdots\circ_{n-1}x_n\}} \mathfrak{D}_n\left(\tilde{F}^{(1)}(x_1),\cdots,\tilde{F}^{(n)}(x_n)\right)$$
$$= \max_{\{(x_1,\cdots,x_n):u_m=x_1\circ_1\cdots\circ_{n-1}x_n\}} \mathfrak{D}_n\left(\tilde{F}^{(1)}(x_1),\cdots,\tilde{F}^{(n)}(x_n)\right).$$

Therefore, there exist $x_{1m},\cdots,x_{nm}$ satisfying

$$u_m = x_{1m} \circ_1 \cdots \circ_{n-1} x_{nm}$$

and

$$\mathfrak{D}_n\left(\tilde{F}^{(1)}(x_{1m}),\cdots,\tilde{F}^{(n)}(x_{nm})\right) = \max_{\{(x_1,\cdots,x_n):u_m=x_1\circ_1\cdots\circ_{n-1}x_n\}} \mathfrak{D}_n\left(\tilde{F}^{(1)}(x_1),\cdots,\tilde{F}^{(n)}(x_n)\right) > 0,$$

Using (31), we have $\tilde{F}^{(i)}(x_{im}) > 0$ for all $i = 1,\cdots,n$, which shows that the sequence $\{x_{im}\}_{m=1}^{\infty}$ is in the support $\tilde{F}^{(i)}_{0+}$ for all $i = 1,\cdots,n$. Since each $\tilde{F}^{(i)}_{0+}$ is bounded for $i = 1,\cdots,n$, it follows that $\{x_{im}\}_{m=1}^{\infty}$ is also a bounded sequence. Therefore, there exists a convergent subsequence $\{x_{im_k}\}_{k=1}^{\infty}$ of $\{x_{im}\}_{m=1}^{\infty}$. In other words, we have

$$\lim_{k\to\infty} x_{im_k} = x_{i0} \text{ for all } i = 1,\cdots,n,$$

which also says $x_{i0} \in \mathrm{cl}(\tilde{F}^{(i)}_{0+}) = \tilde{F}^{(i)}_0$ for all $i = 1,\cdots,n$. Let

$$u_{m_k} = x_{1m_k} \circ_1 \cdots \circ_{n-1} x_{nm_k}.$$

Then, we see that $\{u_{m_k}\}_{k=1}^{\infty}$ is a subsequence of $\{u_m\}_{n=1}^{\infty}$, i.e.,

$$\lim_{k\to\infty} u_{m_k} = u_0.$$

Since

$$u_0 = \lim_{k\to\infty} u_{m_k} = \lim_{k\to\infty} \left(x_{1m_k} \circ_1 \cdots \circ_{n-1} x_{nm_k}\right)$$
$$= \left(\lim_{k\to\infty} x_{1m_k}\right) \circ_1 \cdots \circ_{n-1} \left(\lim_{k\to\infty} x_{nm_k}\right) = x_{10} \circ_1 \cdots \circ_{n-1} x_{n0},$$

which shows

$$u_0 \in \tilde{F}^{(1)}_0 \circ_1 \cdots \circ_{n-1} \tilde{F}^{(n)}_0.$$

Therefore, we obtain the following inclusion:

$$\left(\tilde{F}^{(1)} \odot_1 \cdots \odot_{n-1} \tilde{F}^{(n)}\right)_0 \subseteq \tilde{F}^{(1)}_0 \circ_1 \cdots \circ_{n-1} \tilde{F}^{(n)}_0.$$

Using Part (i), we obtain the desired equality (24), and the proof is complete. □

Theorem 2. *Given any fuzzy sets $\tilde{F}^{(1)},\cdots,\tilde{F}^{(n)}$ in $\mathbb{R}$, we considered the arithmetic operations $\odot_i \in \{\oplus,\ominus,\otimes\}$, which correspond to the arithmetic operations $\circ_i \in \{+,-,*\}$ for $i = 1,\cdots,n-1$. Suppose that the function $\mathfrak{D}_n$ satisfies the following conditions:*

- *Given any $\alpha \in I^* \cap I_{\tilde{F}}$ with $\alpha > 0$,*

$$\mathfrak{D}_n(\alpha_1,\cdots,\alpha_n) \geq \alpha \text{ if and only if } \alpha_i \geq \alpha \text{ for all } i = 1,\cdots,n.$$

- *Given any $\alpha \notin I^*$ with $\alpha \in (0,1]$,*

$$\alpha_i < \alpha \text{ for some } i \in \{1,\cdots,n\} \text{ imply } \mathfrak{D}_n(\alpha_1,\cdots,\alpha_n) < \alpha$$

for any $\alpha_j \in [0,1]$ *with* $j \neq i$.

Then, we have the following properties:

(i) *Suppose that the membership functions of* $\tilde{F}^{(i)}$ *are upper semi-continuous for all* $i = 1, \cdots, n$. *Then, the function* $\mathfrak{D}_n$ *is compatible with arithmetic operations of* α*-level sets. In other words, given any* $\alpha \in I^* \cap I_{\tilde{F}}$ *with* $\alpha > 0$, *we have*

$$\left(\tilde{F}^{(1)} \odot_1 \cdots \odot_{n-1} \tilde{F}^{(n)}\right)_\alpha = \tilde{F}^{(1)}_\alpha \circ_1 \cdots \circ_{n-1} \tilde{F}^{(n)}_\alpha. \tag{32}$$

In particular, if $\tilde{F}^{(1)}, \cdots, \tilde{F}^{(n)}$ *are normal, the equality (32) holds true for all* $\alpha \in (0,1]$.

(ii) *Suppose that the membership functions of* $\tilde{F}^{(i)}$ *are upper semi-continuous and that the supports* $\tilde{F}^{(i)}_{0+}$ *are bounded for all* $i = 1, \cdots, n$. *Then, the function* $\mathfrak{D}_n$ *is strongly compatible with the arithmetic operations of* α*-level sets. In other words, the equality (32) holds true for all* $\alpha \in I^* \cap I_{\tilde{F}}$. *In particular, if* $\tilde{F}^{(1)}, \cdots, \tilde{F}^{(n)}$ *are normal, the equality (32) holds true for all* $\alpha \in [0,1]$.

Proof. To prove Part (i), the equality (32) follows immediately from Part (ii) of Theorem 1. In particular, if each $\tilde{F}^{(i)}$ is assumed to be normal for $i = 1, \cdots, n$, then we have $I_{\tilde{F}^{(i)}} = [0,1]$ for all $i = 1, \cdots, n$, which also says $I^* = [0,1]$. Part (ii) can be easily realized from Part (ii) of Theorem 1 and Part (i) of this theorem. This completes the proof. □

Corollary 1. *Given any fuzzy sets* $\tilde{F}^{(1)}, \cdots, \tilde{F}^{(n)}$ *in* $\mathbb{R}$, *we considered the arithmetic operations* $\boxdot_i \in \{\boxplus, \boxminus, \boxtimes\}$, *which correspond to the arithmetic operations* $\circ_i \in \{+, -, *\}$ *for* $i = 1, \cdots, n-1$. *Then, we have the following properties:*

(i) *Suppose that the membership functions of* $\tilde{F}^{(i)}$ *are upper semi-continuous for all* $i = 1, \cdots, n$. *Then, given any* $\alpha \in I^* \cap I_{\tilde{F}}$ *with* $\alpha > 0$, *we have*

$$\left(\tilde{F}^{(1)} \boxdot_1 \cdots \boxdot_{n-1} \tilde{F}^{(n)}\right)_\alpha = \tilde{F}^{(1)}_\alpha \circ_1 \cdots \circ_{n-1} \tilde{F}^{(n)}_\alpha. \tag{33}$$

In particular, if $\tilde{F}^{(1)}, \cdots, \tilde{F}^{(n)}$ *are normal, the equality (33) holds true for all* $\alpha \in (0,1]$.

(ii) *Suppose that the membership functions of* $\tilde{F}^{(i)}$ *are upper semi-continuous and that the supports* $\tilde{F}^{(i)}_{0+}$ *are bounded for all* $i = 1, \cdots, n$. *Then, the equality (33) holds true for all* $\alpha \in I^* \cap I_{\tilde{F}}$. *In particular, if* $\tilde{F}^{(1)}, \cdots, \tilde{F}^{(n)}$ *are normal, the equality (33) holds true for all* $\alpha \in [0,1]$.

Proof. Since we considered the arithmetic operations $\boxdot_i \in \{\boxplus, \boxminus, \boxtimes\}$, this means that we take

$$\mathfrak{D}_n(\alpha_1, \cdots, \alpha_n) = \min\{\alpha_1, \cdots, \alpha_n\},$$

which clearly satisfies all the assumptions of Theorem 2. Therefore, the desired results follow immediately from Theorem 2. □

Definition 3. *We denote by* $\mathcal{F}_{cc}(\mathbb{R})$ *the family of all fuzzy sets in* $\mathbb{R}$ *such that each* $\tilde{a} \in \mathcal{F}_{cc}(\mathbb{R})$ *satisfies the following conditions:*

- *The supremum* $\sup \mathcal{R}_{\tilde{a}}$ *is obtained, i.e.,* $\sup \mathcal{R}_{\tilde{a}} = \max \mathcal{R}_{\tilde{a}}$.
- *The membership function of* $\tilde{a}$ *is upper semi-continuous and quasi-concave on* $\mathbb{R}$.
- *The* 0*-level set* $\tilde{a}_0$ *is a closed and bounded subset of* $\mathbb{R}$.

Each $\tilde{a} \in \mathcal{F}_{cc}(\mathbb{R})$ *is also called a* fuzzy interval. *If the fuzzy interval* $\tilde{a}$ *is normal and the one-level set* $\tilde{a}_1$ *is a singleton set* $\{a\}$, *where* $a \in \mathbb{R}$, *then* $\tilde{a}$ *is also called a* fuzzy number *with* core value *a*.

If $\tilde{a}$ is a fuzzy interval, then its 0-level set $\tilde{a}_0$ is a closed and bounded subset of $\mathbb{R}$. The conditions in Definition 3 says that each α-level set $\tilde{a}_\alpha$ is a bounded closed interval for $\alpha \in [0,1]$. It is also clear that

$$\tilde{a}_\alpha = \begin{cases} \emptyset & \text{if } \alpha \notin I_{\tilde{a}} \\ [\tilde{a}^L_\alpha, \tilde{a}^U_\alpha] & \text{if } \alpha \in I_{\tilde{a}}, \end{cases}$$

where $I_{\tilde{a}}$ denotes the interval range of $\tilde{a}$ and $[\tilde{a}^L_\alpha, \tilde{a}^U_\alpha]$ is a bounded closed interval with endpoints $\tilde{a}^L_\alpha$ and $\tilde{a}^U_\alpha$. The α-level set $\tilde{a}_\alpha$ can be interpreted as a bounded closed interval $[\tilde{a}^L_\alpha, \tilde{a}^U_\alpha]$ with degree α, which explains the terminology of the fuzzy interval.

Proposition 3. *Given any fuzzy intervals $\tilde{a}$ and $\tilde{b}$ with interval ranges $I_{\tilde{a}}$ and $I_{\tilde{b}}$, respectively, let $I_{\tilde{a}\boxdot\tilde{b}}$ denote the interval range of $\tilde{a} \boxdot \tilde{b}$ for $\boxdot \in \{\boxplus, \boxminus, \boxtimes\}$. Then, $\tilde{a} \boxdot \tilde{b}$ is also a fuzzy interval, and its α-level set is given by*

$$(\tilde{a} \boxdot \tilde{b})_\alpha = \tilde{a}_\alpha \circ \tilde{b}_\alpha \text{ for all } \alpha \in I_{\tilde{a}} \cap I_{\tilde{b}} \cap I_{\tilde{a}\boxdot\tilde{b}}.$$

More precisely, we have

$$\begin{aligned}
(\tilde{a} \boxplus \tilde{b})_\alpha &= \left[\tilde{a}^L_\alpha + \tilde{b}^L_\alpha, \tilde{a}^U_\alpha + \tilde{b}^U_\alpha\right] \\
(\tilde{a} \boxminus \tilde{b})_\alpha &= \left[\tilde{a}^L_\alpha - \tilde{b}^U_\alpha, \tilde{a}^U_\alpha - \tilde{b}^L_\alpha\right], \\
(\tilde{a} \boxtimes \tilde{b})_\alpha &= \left[\min\left\{\tilde{a}^L_\alpha\tilde{b}^L_\alpha, \tilde{a}^L_\alpha\tilde{b}^U_\alpha, \tilde{a}^U_\alpha\tilde{b}^L_\alpha, \tilde{a}^U_\alpha\tilde{b}^U_\alpha\right\}, \max\left\{\tilde{a}^L_\alpha\tilde{b}^L_\alpha, \tilde{a}^L_\alpha\tilde{b}^U_\alpha, \tilde{a}^U_\alpha\tilde{b}^L_\alpha, \tilde{a}^U_\alpha\tilde{b}^U_\alpha\right\}\right],
\end{aligned}$$

for any $\alpha \in I_{\tilde{a}} \cap I_{\tilde{b}} \cap I_{\tilde{a}\boxdot\tilde{b}}$. We further assumed that the suprema:

$$\alpha^* = \sup \mathcal{R}_{\tilde{a}} \text{ and } \beta^* = \sup \mathcal{R}(\tilde{b})$$

are obtained. Then,

$$I_{\tilde{a}} \cap I_{\tilde{b}} = I_{\tilde{a}\boxdot\tilde{b}} = [0, \min\{\alpha^*, \beta^*\}]$$

is a closed interval.

Proof. Given any $\alpha \in I_{\tilde{a}} \cap I_{\tilde{b}} \cap I_{\tilde{a}\boxdot\tilde{b}}$, it is clear that the α-level sets $(\tilde{a} \boxdot \tilde{b})_\alpha$, $\tilde{a}_\alpha$, and $\tilde{b}_\alpha$ are nonempty. Therefore, the desired results follow immediately from Corollary 1 and Proposition 2. This completes the proof. □

4. Conclusions

The arithmetic operations of non-normal fuzzy sets using the extension principle based on general functions were investigated in this paper. The membership function of arithmetic operation $\tilde{F}^{(1)} \odot_1 \cdots \odot_{n-1} \tilde{F}^{(n)}$ is defined by

$$\tilde{F}^{(1)} \odot_1 \cdots \odot_{n-1} \tilde{F}^{(n)}(u) = \sup_{\{(a_1,\cdots,a_n):u=a_1\circ_1\cdots\circ_{n-1}a_n\}} \mathfrak{D}_n\left(\tilde{F}^{(1)}(a_1), \cdots, \tilde{F}^{(n)}(a_n)\right),$$

where the way of calculation $\tilde{F}^{(1)} \odot_1 \cdots \odot_{n-1} \tilde{F}^{(n)}$ for $\odot_i \in \{\oplus, \ominus, \otimes\}$ and $i = 1, \cdots, n-1$ corresponds to the way of calculation for $a_1 \circ_1 \cdots \circ_{n-1} a_n$ for $\circ_i \in \{+, -, *\}$ and $i = 1, \cdots, n-1$. This kind of arithmetic operation generalizes the conventional one given by

$$\tilde{F}^{(1)} \boxdot_1 \cdots \boxdot_{n-1} \tilde{F}^{(n)}(u) = \sup_{\{(x_1,\cdots,x_n):u=x_1\circ_1\cdots\circ_{n-1}x_n\}} \min\left\{\tilde{F}^{(1)}(x_1), \cdots, \tilde{F}^{(n)}(x_n)\right\},$$

where $\boxdot_i \in \{\boxplus, \boxminus, \boxtimes\}$ for $i = 1, \cdots, n-1$.

The main issue of arithmetic operations is studying their α-level sets. Therefore, the concept of compatibility with α-level sets is proposed by saying that the function

$\mathfrak{D}_n : [0,1]^n \to [0,1]$ is (strongly) compatible with the arithmetic operations of α-level sets when

$$\left(\tilde{F}^{(1)} \odot_1 \cdots \odot_{n-1} \tilde{F}^{(n)}\right)_\alpha = \tilde{F}^{(1)}_\alpha \circ_1 \cdots \circ_{n-1} \tilde{F}^{(n)}_\alpha \text{ for all } \alpha \in I^* \cap I_{\tilde{F}} \text{ with } \alpha > 0.$$

It is clear that the minimum function:

$$\mathfrak{D}(\alpha_1, \cdots, \alpha_n) = \min\{\alpha_1, \cdots, \alpha_n\}$$

considered in the conventional case is compatible with arithmetic operations of α-level sets.

Theorems 1 and 2 present the sufficient conditions to guarantee the compatibility with the arithmetic operations of α-level sets. This means that Theorems 1 and 2 are the general situation. Therefore, Corollary 1 and Proposition 3, which are the conventional cases, are the special cases of Theorems 1 and 2. This was the main purpose of this paper: to generalize the conventional cases. In other words, from some other functions $\mathfrak{D}_n$ that can satisfy the sufficient conditions, the desired results can be obtained as the conventional cases. The main focus was on the functions $\mathfrak{D}_n$ and the non-normal fuzzy sets, rather than the t-norm and the normal fuzzy sets. As we can see in Part (i) of Theorem 2, the equality (32) holds true for non-normal fuzzy sets. The case of normal fuzzy sets is just the special case of (32). Therefore, Theorems 1 and 2 indeed generalize the conventional cases. The limitation of Theorems 1 and 2 is checking the assumptions of general function $\mathfrak{D}_n$. Since those assumptions are satisfied for the conventional cases, as shown in Corollary 1 and Proposition 3, this also means that those assumptions are not too strong to be used in real applications.

The interval ranges of non-normal fuzzy sets comprise an important tool to handle the arithmetic of non-normal fuzzy sets. The future research will focus on the applications by using non-normal fuzzy sets and will solve the difficulty caused by the different forms of the interval ranges of non-normal fuzzy sets.

Funding: The APC was funded by NSTC Taiwan.

Conflicts of Interest: The author declares no conflict of interest.

References

1. Dubois, D.; Prade, H. A Review of Fuzzy Set Aggregation Connectives. *Inf. Sci.* **1985**, *36*, 85–121. [CrossRef]
2. Weber, S. A General Concept of Fuzzy Connectives, Negations and Implications Based on t-Norms and t-Conorms. *Fuzzy Sets Syst.* **1983**, *11*, 115–134. [CrossRef]
3. Dubois, D.; Prade, H. *Possibility Theory*; Springer: New Yourk, NY, USA, 1988.
4. Klir, G.J.; Yuan, B. *Fuzzy Sets and Fuzzy Logic: Theory and Applications*; Prentice-Hall: New York, NY, USA, 1995.
5. Gebhardt, A. On Types of Fuzzy Numbers and Extension Principles. *Fuzzy Sets Syst.* **1995**, *75*, 311–318. [CrossRef]
6. Fullér, R.; Keresztfalvi, T. On Generalization of Nguyen's Theorem. *Fuzzy Sets Syst.* **1990**, *41*, 371–374. [CrossRef]
7. Mesiar, R. Triangular-Norm-Based Addition of Fuzzy Intervals. *Fuzzy Sets Syst.* **1997**, *91*, 231–237. [CrossRef]
8. Ralescu, D.A. A generalization of the representation theorem. *Fuzzy Sets Syst.* **1992**, *51*, 309–311. [CrossRef]
9. Yager, R.R. A Characterization of the Extension Principle. *Fuzzy Sets Syst.* **1986**, *18*, 205–217. [CrossRef]
10. Wu, H.-C. Generalized Extension Principle for Non-Normal Fuzzy Sets. *Fuzzy Optim. Decis. Mak.* **2019**, *18*, 399–432. [CrossRef]
11. Coroianua, L.; Fuller, R. Nguyen Type Theorem For Extension Principle Based on a Joint Possibility Distribution. *Int. J. Approx. Reason.* **2018**, *95*, 22–35. [CrossRef]
12. Coroianua, L.; Fuller, R. Necessary and Sufficient Conditions for The Equality of Interactive and Non-Interactive Extensions of Continuous Functions. *Fuzzy Sets Syst.* **2018**, *331*, 116–130. [CrossRef]
13. Holčapek, M.; Štěpnixcxka, M. MI-Algebras: A New Framework for Arithmetics of (Extensional) Fuzzy Numbers. *Fuzzy Sets Syst.* **2014**, *257*, 102–131. [CrossRef]
14. Holčapek, M.; Škorupová, N.; xSxtěpnixcxka, M. Fuzzy Interpolation with Extensional Fuzzy Numbers. *Symmetry* **2021**, *13*, 170. [CrossRef]
15. Esmi, E.; Sánchez, D.E.; Wasques, V.F.; de Barros, L.C. Solutions of Higher Order Linear Fuzzy Differential Equations with Interactive Fuzzy Values. *Fuzzy Sets Syst.* **2021**, *419*, 122–140. [CrossRef]
16. Pedro, F.S.; de Barros, L.C.; Esmi, E. Population Growth Model via Interactive Fuzzy Differential Equation. *Inf. Sci.* **2019**, *481*, 160–173. [CrossRef]

17. Wu, H.-C. Decomposition and Construction of Fuzzy Sets and Their Applications to the Arithmetic Operations on Fuzzy Quantities. *Fuzzy Sets Syst.* **2013**, *233*, 1–25. [CrossRef]
18. Wu, H.-C. Compatibility between Fuzzy Set Operations and Level Set Operations: Applications to Fuzzy Difference. *Fuzzy Sets Syst.* **2018**, *353*, 1–43. [CrossRef]
19. Bede, B.; Stefanini, L. Generalized Differentiability of Fuzzy-Valued Functions. *Fuzzy Sets Syst.* **2013**, *230*, 119–141. [CrossRef]
20. Gomes, L.T.; Barros, L.C. A Note on the Generalized Difference and the Generalized Differentiability. *Fuzzy Sets Syst.* **2015**, *280*, 142–145. [CrossRef]
21. Zulqarnian, R.M.; Xin, X.L.; Jun, Y.B. Fuzzy axiom of choice, fuzzy Zorn's lemma and fuzzy Hausdorff maximal principle. *Soft Comput.* **2021**, *25*, 11421–11428. [CrossRef]
22. Black, F.; Scholes, M. The Pricing of Options and Corporate Liabilities. *J. Political Econ.* **1973**, *81*, 637–659. [CrossRef]
23. Musiela, M.; Rutkowski, M. *Martingale Methods in Financial Modelling*; Springer: New York, NY, USA, 1997.
24. Royden, H.L. *Real Analysis*, 2nd ed.; Macmillan: London, UK, 1968.

axioms

MDPI

Article

Interval-Valued Topology on Soft Sets

Sadi Bayramov [1,†], Çiğdem Gündüz Aras [2,†] and Ljubiša D. R. Kočinac [3,*]

1 Department of Algebra and Geometry, Baku State University, Baku AZ 1148, Azerbaijan; baysadi@gmail.com
2 Department of Mathematics, Kocaeli University, Kocaeli 41380, Turkey; carasgunduz@gmail.com
3 Faculty of Sciences and Mathematics, University of Niš, 18000 Niš, Serbia
* Correspondence: lkocinac@gmail.com
† These authors contributed equally to this work.

Abstract: In this paper, we study the concept of interval-valued fuzzy set on the family $\mathsf{SS}(X,E)$ of all soft sets over X with the set of parameters E and examine its basic properties. Later, we define the concept of interval-valued fuzzy topology (cotopology) τ on $\mathsf{SS}(X,E)$. We obtain that each interval-valued fuzzy topology is a descending family of soft topologies. In addition, we study some topological structures such as interval-valued fuzzy neighborhood system of a soft point, base and subbase of τ and investigate some relationships among them. Finally, we give some concepts such as direct sum, open mapping and continuous mapping and consider connections between them. A few examples support the presented results.

Keywords: interval-valued fuzzy topology (cotopology); interval-valued fuzzy neighborhood; base; subbase; continuous mapping; direct sum

MSC: 54A40; 54A05; 03E72; 06D72

Citation: Bayramov, S.; Aras, Ç.G.; Kočinac, L.D.R. Interval-Valued Topology on Soft Sets. *Axioms* **2023**, *12*, 692. https://doi.org/10.3390/axioms12070692

Academic Editors: Changyou Wang, Dong Qiu and Yonghong Shen

Received: 12 June 2023
Revised: 12 July 2023
Accepted: 13 July 2023
Published: 16 July 2023

1. Introduction

The concept of interval-valued fuzzy set was given by Zadeh [1]. This set is an extension of fuzzy sets in the sense that the values of the membership degrees are intervals of numbers instead of the numbers. Chang [2] introduced the concept of fuzzy topology in 1968. But, since the concept of openness of a fuzzy set was not given, Samanta et al. [3,4] introduced the concept of gradation of openness (closedness) of a fuzzy set in 1992. Furthermore, the concept of intuitionistic gradation of openness of fuzzy sets in Sostak's sense [5] was defined by some researchers [6–8]. In [9], D. L. Shi et al. introduced the concept of ordinary interval-valued fuzzifying topology and investigated some of its important properties. It is known that to describe and deal with uncertainties, a lot of mathematical approaches put forward a proposal such as probability theory, fuzzy set theory, rough set theory, interval set theory etc. But all these theories have inherent difficulties. In [10], Molodtsov presented soft set theory in order to overcome difficulties affecting the existing methods. Later, many papers were written on soft set theory. Since soft set theory has many application areas, it has progressed very quickly until today. Maji et al. [11] defined some operations on soft sets. In recent years, topological structures of soft sets have been studied by some authors. M. Shabir and M. Naz [12] have initiated the concept of soft topological space. A large number of papers was devoted to the study of soft topological spaces from various aspects [13–22]. Moreover, C.G. Aras et al. [23] gave the definition of gradation of openness τ which is a mapping from $\mathsf{SS}(X,E)$ to $[0,1]$ which satisfies some conditions and showed that a fuzzy topological space gives a parameterized family of soft topologies on X. Also, S. Bayramov et al. [24] gave the concepts of continuous mapping, open mapping and closed mapping by using soft points in intuitionistic fuzzy topological spaces.

The importance and applications of interval-valued analysis is given in the book [25]. Our aim in this paper is to demonstrate applications of interval-valued mathematics in the context of fuzzy and soft topologies. We study the concept of interval-valued fuzzy set on the family $SS(X,E)$ of all soft sets over X and examine its basic properties. We also define the concept of interval-valued fuzzy topology τ (called also cotopology) on $SS(X,E)$. We prove that each interval-valued fuzzy topology is actually a descending family of soft topologies. Further, we study some topological structures such as interval-valued fuzzy neighborhood system of a soft point, base and subbase of τ and investigate some relationships among them. Finally, we give some concepts such as direct sum, open mappings and continuous mappings and consider connections between them.

2. Preliminaries

In this section we give basic notions about soft sets and soft topology which will be used in the sequel.

Definition 1 ([10]). *Let X be a set, called an initial universal set, and E a nonempty set, called the set of parameters. A pair (F,E) is called a soft set over X, where $F: E \to P(X)$ is a mapping from E into a power set of X.*

The family of all soft sets over X with the set of parameters E is denoted by $SS(X,E)$.

Definition 2 ([11]). *If for all $e \in E$, $F(e) = \emptyset$, (F,E) is said to be the null soft set denoted by Φ. If for all $e \in E$, $F(e) = X$, then (F,E) is said to be the* absolute soft set *denoted by $\widetilde{X}$.*

Definition 3 ([14,16]). *Let (F,E) be a soft set over X. The soft set (F,E) is called a soft point if for some element $e \in E$, $F(e) = \{x\}$ and $F(e') = \emptyset$ for all $e' \in E \setminus \{e\}$ (briefly denoted by x_e).*

Note that since each soft set can be expressed as a union of soft points, to give the family of all soft sets on X it is sufficient to give only soft points on X.

Notice that in the literature there are other definitions of soft points, but we think that our approach gives an easier applications of these points.

Definition 4 ([14]). *The soft point x_e is said to belong to the soft set (F,E), denoted by $x_e \widetilde{\in} (F,E)$, if $x_e(e) \in F(e)$, i.e., $\{x\} \subseteq F(e)$.*

Definition 5 ([12]). *A soft topology on a non-empty set X is a collection τ of soft sets over X with a set of parameters E satisfying the following axioms:*
(ST1) $\widetilde{X}$ and Φ belong to τ;
(ST2) The soft intersection of finitely many members in τ belongs to τ;
(ST3) The soft union of any family of members in τ belongs to τ.

The triple (X,τ,E) is called a soft topological space. Members of τ are called soft open sets.

Notice that if (X,τ,E) is a soft topological space, then $\tau_e = \{F(e) : (F,E) \in \tau\}$ defines a topology on X, for each $e \in E$. This topology is called *e-parametric topology* [12].

Throughout this paper, I denotes the closed unit interval $[0,1]$, and $[I]$ represents the set of all closed subintervals of I. The members of $[I]$ are called *interval numbers* and are denoted by $\widetilde{a}, \widetilde{b}, \widetilde{c}, \ldots$ Here $\widetilde{a} \in [I]$, $\widetilde{a} = [a^-, a^+]$ and $0 \le a^- \le a^+ \le 1$. Especially, if $a^- = a^+$, then we take $\widetilde{a} = a$. Also, it is defined an order relation $\le$, on $[I]$ as follows:

(1) $\left(\forall \widetilde{a}, \widetilde{b} \in [I]\right)\ \widetilde{a} \le \widetilde{b} \Longleftrightarrow a^- \le b^-, a^+ \le b^+$,

(2) $\left(\forall \widetilde{a}, \widetilde{b} \in [I]\right)\ \widetilde{a} = \widetilde{b} \Longleftrightarrow \widetilde{a} \le \widetilde{b}$ and $\widetilde{b} \le \widetilde{a}$, (i.e., $a^- = b^-, a^+ = b^+$),

(3) For any $\widetilde{a}, \widetilde{b} \in [I]$, maximum and minimum of $\widetilde{a}, \widetilde{b}$, respectively

$$\begin{aligned} \widetilde{a} \vee \widetilde{b} &= \left[a^- \vee b^-, a^+ \vee b^+\right], \\ \widetilde{a} \wedge \widetilde{b} &= \left[a^- \wedge b^-, a^+ \wedge b^+\right]. \end{aligned}$$

Let $\{\widetilde{a}_i\}_{i\in J} \subset [I]$. Then inf and sup of $\{\widetilde{a}_i\}_{i\in J}$ are defined as follows:

$$\bigwedge_{i\in J}\widetilde{a}_i = \left[\bigwedge_{i\in J} a_j^-, \bigwedge_{i\in J} a_j^+\right],$$
$$\bigvee_{i\in J}\widetilde{a}_i = \left[\bigvee_{i\in J} a_j^-, \bigvee_{i\in J} a_j^+\right].$$

Also, for each $\widetilde{a} \in [I]$, the complement of $\widetilde{a}$, denoted by $\widetilde{a}^c$, is defined as:

$$\widetilde{a}^c = \left[1 - a^+, 1 - a^-\right].$$

3. Introduction to Interval-Valued Topology on Soft Sets

We introduce now the main notion in this paper, the notion of interval-valued fuzzy topology on the set $\mathsf{SS}(X, E)$.

Definition 6. *A mapping $A : \mathsf{SS}(X, E) \to [I]$ is called an interval-valued fuzzy set in $\mathsf{SS}(X, E)$ and is denoted briefly as $IVFS$.*

Let $[I]^{\mathsf{SS}(X,E)}$ represent the set of all $IVFSs$ in $\mathsf{SS}(X, E)$. For each $A \in [I]^{\mathsf{SS}(X,E)}$ and $(F, E) \in \mathsf{SS}(X, E)$. $A(F, E) = [A^-(F, E), A^+(F, E)]$ is a closed interval. Thus $A^-, A^+ : \mathsf{SS}(X, E) \to I$ are two fuzzy sets. For each $A \in [I]^{\mathsf{SS}(X,E)}$, we write $A = [A^-, A^+]$. In particular, $\widetilde{0}, \widetilde{1}$ denote the interval-valued fuzzy empty set and the interval-valued fuzzy whole set in $\mathsf{SS}(X, E)$, respectively.

Now we give the relations $\subset$ and $=$ on $[I]^{\mathsf{SS}(X,E)}$ as follows:

$$\left(\forall A, B \in [I]^{\mathsf{SS}(X,E)}\right) [A \subset B \Longleftrightarrow (\forall (F, E) \in \mathsf{SS}(X, E))\ A(F, E) \leq B(F, E)],$$
$$\left(\forall A, B \in [I]^{\mathsf{SS}(X,E)}\right) [A = B \Longleftrightarrow (\forall (F, E) \in \mathsf{SS}(X, E))\ A(F, E) = B(F, E)].$$

Definition 7. *Let $A \in [I]^{\mathsf{SS}(X,E)}$ and $\{A_i\}_{i\in J}$ be arbitrary subfamily of $[I]^{\mathsf{SS}(X,E)}$. The complement, union and intersection of A are denoted by A^c, $\bigcup_{i\in J} A_i$ and $\bigcap_{i\in J} A_i$, respectively, are defined for each $(F, E) \in \mathsf{SS}(X, E)$ as follows respectively,*

$$A^c(F, E) = [1 - A^+(F, E), 1 - A^-(F, E)],$$
$$\left(\bigcup_{i\in J} A_i\right)(F, E) = \bigvee_{i\in J} A_i(F, E),$$
$$\left(\bigcap_{i\in J} A_i\right)(F, E) = \bigwedge_{i\in J} A_i(F, E).$$

Proposition 1. *Let $A, B, C \in [I]^{\mathsf{SS}(X,E)}$ and $\{A_i\}_{i\in J} \subset [I]^{\mathsf{SS}(X,E)}$. Then the following statements hold:*

(1) $\widetilde{0} \subset A \subset \widetilde{1}$,
(2) $A \cup B = B \cup A$, $A \cap B = B \cap A$,
(3) $A \cup (B \cup C) = (A \cup B) \cup C$, $A \cap (B \cap C) = (A \cap B) \cap C$,
(4) $A, B \subset A \cup B$, $A \cap B \subset A, B$,
(5) $A \cap \left(\bigcup_{i\in J} A_i\right) = \bigcup_{i\in J}(A \cap A_i)$, $A \cup \left(\bigcap_{i\in J} A_i\right) = \bigcap_{i\in J}(A \cup A_i)$,
(6) $\left(\widetilde{0}\right)^c = \widetilde{1}$, $\left(\widetilde{1}\right)^c = \widetilde{0}$,
(7) $(A^c)^c = A$,

(8) $\left(\bigcup_{i\in J} A_i\right)^c = \bigcap_{i\in J} A_i^c, \left(\bigcap_{i\in J} A_i\right)^c = \bigcup_{i\in J} A_i^c.$

Proof. It is immediately obtained. □

Definition 8. *A mapping* $\tau = [\tau^-, \tau^+] : \mathrm{SS}(X,E) \to [I]$ *is called an interval-valued fuzzy topology over* $\mathrm{SS}(X,E)$ *if it satisfies the following conditions:*

(1) $\tau(\Phi) = \tau\left(\widetilde{X}\right) = 1,$

(2) $\tau((F,E) \cap (G,E)) \geq \tau(F,E) \wedge \tau(G,E), \forall (F,E),(G,E) \in \mathrm{SS}(X,E),$

(3) $\tau\left(\bigcup_{i\in J}(F_i,E)\right) \geq \bigwedge_{i\in J} \tau(F_i,E), \forall \{(F_i,E)\}_{i\in J} \subset \mathrm{SS}(X,E).$

The interval-valued fuzzy topology is denoted briefly $IVFT$ and the triple (X,τ,E) is called an *interval-valued fuzzy topological space over* $\mathrm{SS}(X,E)$ (in short $IVFTS$)

It is clear that $\tau \in IVFT$ consists of two fuzzy topologies over $\mathrm{SS}(X,E)$, τ^- and τ^+. Also, for each $(F,E) \in \mathrm{SS}(X,E)$, $\tau^-(F,E) \leq \tau^+(F,E)$.

Example 1. *Let* $X = \{x,y,z\}$ *and* $E = \{e\}$. *The set of all soft points on X is* $\{x_e, y_e, z_e\}$. *Then the soft sets are:*

$$F_1(e) = \{x\}, F_2(e) = \{y\}, F_3(e) = \{z\}, F_4(e) = \{x,y\},$$
$$F_5(e) = \{x,z\}, F_6(e)\{y,z\}, F_7(e) = \varnothing, F_8(e) = X.$$

Define the mapping $\tau : \mathrm{SS}(X,E) \to [I]$ *as follows:*

$$\begin{aligned}
\tau(\Phi) &= \tau\left(\widetilde{X}\right) = 1,\\
\tau(F_1) &= [0.2, 0.5],\\
\tau(F_2) &= [0.3, 0.4],\\
\tau(F_3) &= [0.4, 0.5],\\
\tau(F_4) &= [0.2, 0.4],\\
\tau(F_5) &= [0.3, 0.5],\\
\tau(F_6) &= [0.3, 0.5].
\end{aligned}$$

Then it is clear that τ *is an* $IVFT$.

Example 2. *Let* $X = \{x\}$ *and* $E = \{a,b,c\}$. *The set of all soft points on X is* $\{x_a, x_b, x_c\}$. *Then the soft sets are*

$$\begin{aligned}
F_1(a) &= \{x\}, F_1(b) = \varnothing, F_1(c) = \varnothing,\\
F_2(a) &= \varnothing, F_2(b) = \{x\}, F_2(c) = \varnothing,\\
F_3(a) &= \varnothing, F_3(b) = \varnothing, F_3(c) = \{x\},\\
F_4(a) &= \{x\}, F_4(b) = \{x\}, F_4(c) = \varnothing,\\
F_5(a) &= \{x\}, F_5(b) = \varnothing, F_5(c) = \{x\},\\
F_6(a) &= \varnothing, F_6(b) = \{x\}, F_6(c) = \{x\},\\
F_7 &= \Phi,\ F_8 = \widetilde{X}.
\end{aligned}$$

We define the mapping $\tau : \mathrm{SS}(X,E) \to [I]$ *as follows:*

$$\begin{aligned}\tau(\Phi) &= \tau\left(\widetilde{X}\right) = 1,\\ \tau(F_1) &= [0.3, 0.5],\\ \tau(F_2) &= [0.2, 0.4],\\ \tau(F_3) &= [0.3, 0.6],\\ \tau(F_4) &= [0.2, 0.5],\\ \tau(F_5) &= [0.4, 0.5],\\ \tau(F_6) &= [0.2, 0.4].\end{aligned}$$

Then it is clear that τ is an $IVFT$.

Definition 9. *A mapping $C = (\mu_C, \upsilon_C) : \mathsf{SS}(X, E) \to [I]$ is called an interval-valued fuzzy cotopology (in short $IVFCT$) over $\mathsf{SS}(X, E)$ if it satisfies the following conditions:*

(1) $C(\Phi) = C\left(\widetilde{X}\right) = 1$,

(2) $C((F, E) \cup (G, E)) \geq C(F, E) \wedge C(G, E), \forall (F, E), (G, E) \in \mathsf{SS}(X, E)$,

(3) $C\left(\bigcap_{i \in J} (F_i, E)\right) \geq \bigwedge_{i \in J} C(F_i, E), \forall \{(F_i, E)\}_{i \in J} \subset \mathsf{SS}(X, E)$.

The triple (X, C, E) is called an *interval-valued fuzzy cotopological space over* $\mathsf{SS}(X, E)$ and denoted by IVFCTS.

Proposition 2. (1) *If $\tau : \mathsf{SS}(X, E) \to [I]$ is an $IVFT$, then $C(F, E) = \tau((F, E)^c)$ is a $IVFCT$, $\forall (F, E) \in \mathsf{SS}(X, E)$.*

(2) *If $C : \mathsf{SS}(X, E) \to [I]$ is an $IVFCT$, then $\tau(F, E) = C((F, E)^c)$ is an $IVFT$, $\forall (F, E) \in \mathsf{SS}(X, E)$.*

Proof. (1) It is clear that

$$C(\Phi) = \tau(\Phi^c) = \tau\left(\widetilde{X}\right) = 1,$$

$$C\left(\widetilde{X}\right) = \tau\left(\widetilde{X}^c\right) = \tau(\Phi) = 1.$$

$$\begin{aligned}C((F, E) \cup (G, E)) &= \tau(((F, E) \cup (G, E))^c) = \tau((F, E)^c \cap (G, E)^c)\\ &\geq \tau((F, E)^c) \wedge \tau((G, E)^c) = C(F, E) \wedge C(G, E).\end{aligned}$$

$$\begin{aligned}C\left(\bigcap_{i \in J} (F_i, E)\right) &= \tau\left(\left(\bigcap_{i \in J} (F_i, E)\right)^c\right) = \tau\left(\bigcup_{i \in J} (F_i, E)^c\right)\\ &\geq \bigwedge_{i \in J} \tau(F_i, E)^c = \bigwedge_{i \in J} C(F_i, E).\end{aligned}$$

(2) The proof is done similarly to (1). □

Definition 10. *Let (X, τ, E) be an $IVFTS$ and $\widetilde{a} \in [I]$. We define two families $\tau_{\widetilde{a}}$ and $\tau^*_{\widetilde{a}}$ as follows, respectively:*

(1) $\tau_{\widetilde{a}} = \{(F, E) \in \mathsf{SS}(X, E) : \tau(F, E) \geq \widetilde{a}\}$,

(2) $\tau^*_{\widetilde{a}} = \{(F, E) \in \mathsf{SS}(X, E) : \tau(F, E) > \widetilde{a}\}$.

Proposition 3. *Let (X, τ, E) be an $IVFTS$ and $\widetilde{a}, \widetilde{b} \in [I]$. Then:*

(1) *$\tau_{\widetilde{a}}$ is a soft topology.*

(2) *If $\widetilde{a} \leq \widetilde{b}$, then $\tau_{\widetilde{b}} \subset \tau_{\widetilde{a}}$.*

(3) *$\tau_{\widetilde{a}} = \bigcap_{\widetilde{b} < \widetilde{a}} \tau_{\widetilde{b}}$, where $\widetilde{a} \neq 0$.*

(4) *$\tau^*_{\widetilde{a}}$ is a soft topology.*

(5) *If* $\widetilde{a} \leq \widetilde{b}$, *then* $\tau^*_{\widetilde{b}} \subset \tau^*_{\widetilde{a}}$.
(6) $\tau^*_{\widetilde{a}}. = \bigcup_{\widetilde{a}<\widetilde{b}} \tau^*_{\widetilde{b}}$, *where* $\widetilde{a} \neq 1$.
Thus each interval-valued fuzzy topology is a descending family of soft topologies.

Proof. The proofs of (1), (2), (4) and (5) are clear.

(3) From (2), $\{\tau_{\widetilde{a}}\}_{\widetilde{a}\neq 0}$ is a descending family of soft topologies. Then for each $\widetilde{a} \neq 0$, $\mathrm{SS}(X, E)$

$$\tau_{\widetilde{a}} \subset \bigcap_{\widetilde{b}<\widetilde{a}} \tau_{\widetilde{b}}. \qquad \text{(i)}$$

Suppose that $(F, E) \notin \tau_{\widetilde{a}}$. Then $\tau(F, E) < \widetilde{a}$. Hence there exists $\widetilde{b} \neq 0$ such that $\tau(F, E) < \widetilde{b} < \widetilde{a}$. So $(F, E) \notin \tau_{\widetilde{b}}$ for $\widetilde{b} < \widetilde{a}$. Thus $(F, E) \notin \bigcap_{\widetilde{b}<\widetilde{a}} \tau_{\widetilde{b}}$ is obtained, i.e.,

$$\bigcap_{\widetilde{b}<\widetilde{a}} \tau_{\widetilde{b}} \subset \tau_{\widetilde{a}}. \qquad \text{(ii)}$$

Hence from (i) and (ii), $\tau_{\widetilde{a}} = \bigcap_{\widetilde{b}<\widetilde{a}} \tau_{\widetilde{b}}$, where $\widetilde{a} \neq 0$.

(6) The proof is obtained similarly to the proof of (3). □

Remark 1. *It is clear that for each* $\tau \in IVFT$, $\{\tau_{\widetilde{a}}\}_{\widetilde{a}\in[I]}$ *is a descending family of soft topologies.*

Proposition 4. *Let* $\{\tau_{\widetilde{a}}\}_{\widetilde{a}\in[I]}$ *be a descending family of soft topologies on X. We define the mapping* $\tau : \mathrm{SS}(X, E) \to [I]$ *as follows: for each* $(F, E) \in \mathrm{SSS}(X, E)$,

$$\tau(F, E) = \bigvee_{(F,E)\in\tau_{\widetilde{a}}} \widetilde{a}.$$

Then $\tau \in IVFT$.

Proof. Obviously $\tau(\Phi) = \tau\left(\widetilde{X}\right) = 1$ is met.

Suppose $(F, E), (G, E) \in \mathrm{SS}(X, E)$ such that $\tau(F, E) = \widetilde{a}$ and $\tau(G, E) = \widetilde{b}$. If $\widetilde{a} = 0$ or $\widetilde{b} = 0$, then

$$\begin{aligned} \tau^-((F, E) \cap (G, E)) &\geq \tau^-(F, E) \wedge \tau^-(G, E), \\ \tau^+((F, E) \cap (G, E)) &\geq \tau^+(F, E) \wedge \tau^+(G, E). \end{aligned}$$

Thus $\tau((F, E) \cap (G, E)) \geq \tau(F, E) \wedge \tau(G, E)$. Since

$$\tau(F, E) = \bigvee_{(F,E)\in\tau_{\widetilde{a}}} \widetilde{a} = \bigvee_{(F,E)\in\tau_{\widetilde{a}}} [a^-, a^+],$$

we can find $\varepsilon > 0$, $\widetilde{c_1}$ and $\widetilde{c_2}$ such that

$$\begin{aligned} a^- - \varepsilon &< c_1^- \leq a^-,\ a^+ - \varepsilon < c_1^+ \leq a^+, \\ b^- - \varepsilon &< c_2^- \leq b^-,\ b^+ - \varepsilon < c_2^+ \leq b^+ \end{aligned}$$

and $(F, E) \in \tau_{\tau_{c_1^-}}, (G, E) \in \tau_{\tau_{c_2^-}}$. Let

$$\begin{aligned} c^- &= c_1^- \wedge c_2^-,\ c^+ = c_1^+ \wedge c_2^+, \\ d^- &= a^- \wedge b^-,\ d^+ = a^+ \wedge b^+. \end{aligned}$$

Then $\widetilde{c} \leq \widetilde{a}, \widetilde{c} \leq \widetilde{b}$. Since $\{\tau_{\widetilde{a}}\}_{\widetilde{a} \in [I]}$ is a descending family, then $\tau_{\widetilde{a}}, \tau_{\widetilde{b}} \subset \tau_{\widetilde{c}}$. Since $(F, E) \in \tau_{\widetilde{a}}$, $(G, E) \in \tau_{\widetilde{b}}$, then $(F, E) \cap (G, E) \in \tau_{\widetilde{c}}$. So we have

$$\begin{aligned} \tau^-((F,E) \cap (G,E)) &\geq c^- > d^- - \varepsilon, \\ \tau^+((F,E) \cap (G,E)) &\geq d^+ > d^+ - \varepsilon. \end{aligned}$$

Since $\varepsilon > 0$ was arbitrary,

$$\begin{aligned} \tau^-((F,E) \cap (G,E)) &\geq c^- \geq d^- = a^- \wedge b^-, \\ \tau^+((F,E) \cap (G,E)) &\geq d^+ = a^+ \wedge b^+. \end{aligned}$$

Hence $\tau((F,E) \cap (G,E)) \geq \tau(F,E) \wedge \tau(G,E)$ is obtained.

Finally, let $\{(F_i, E)\}_{i \in J} \subset \mathsf{SS}(X, E)$ and $\tau(F_i, E) = \widetilde{a}_i, \widetilde{a} = \bigwedge_{i \in J} \widetilde{a}_i$. If $\widetilde{a} = 0$, then obviously

$$\tau\left(\bigcup_{i \in J} (F_i, E)\right) \geq 0 = \bigwedge_{i \in J} \tau(F_i, E).$$

If $\widetilde{a} > 0$, choose $\varepsilon > 0$ such that $\widetilde{a} > \varepsilon$. Then for $i \in J$, $0 < a^- - \varepsilon < a_i^-$ and $0 < a^+ - \varepsilon < a_i^+$. Thus $(F_i, E) \in \tau_{[a^- - \varepsilon, a^+ - \varepsilon]}$. So $\bigcup_{i \in J} (F_i, E) \in \tau_{[a^- - \varepsilon, a^+ - \varepsilon]}$ and $\tau^-\left(\bigcup_{i \in J} (F_i, E)\right) \geq a^- - \varepsilon$, $\tau^+\left(\bigcup_{i \in J} (F_i, E)\right) \geq a^+ - \varepsilon$. Since $\varepsilon > 0$ was arbitrary,

$$\begin{aligned} \tau^-\left(\bigcup_{i \in J} (F_i, E)\right) &\geq a^- = \bigwedge_{i \in J} \tau^-(F_i, E), \\ \tau^+\left(\bigcup_{i \in J} (F_i, E)\right) &\geq a^+ = \bigwedge_{i \in J} \tau^+(F_i, E). \end{aligned}$$

Hence $\tau\left(\bigcup_{i \in J} (F_i, E)\right) \geq \bigwedge_{i \in J} \tau(F_i, E)$ is met. □

Theorem 1. *Let (X, τ, E) be an IVFTS and let $Y \subset X$. We define the mapping $\tau_Y : \mathsf{SS}(Y, E) \to [I]$ as follows: for each $(F, E) \in \mathsf{SS}(Y, E)$,*

$$\tau_Y(F, E) = \bigwedge_{\substack{(G,E) \in \mathsf{SS}(X,E) \\ (F,E) = (G,E) \cap \widetilde{Y}}} \tau(G, E).$$

Then $(X, \tau, E) \in IVFT$ and $\tau_Y(F, E) \geq \tau(F, E)$ for each $(F, E) \in \mathsf{SS}(Y, E)$. Then (Y, τ_Y, E) is said to be an interval-valued fuzzy subspace of (X, τ, E), and τ_Y is said to be induced interval-valued fuzzy topology on Y by τ.

Proof. It is obvious that $\tau_Y(\Phi) = \tau_Y\left(\widetilde{Y}\right) = 1$. Let $(F, E), (G, E) \in \mathsf{SS}(Y, E)$. Then

$$\tau_Y(F,E) \wedge \tau_Y(G,E) = \left(\bigwedge_{\substack{(C_1,E)\in SS(X,E)\\ (F,E)=(C_1,E)\cap\widetilde{Y}}} \tau(C_1,E) \right)$$

$$\wedge \left(\bigwedge_{\substack{(C_2,E)\in SS(X,E)\\ (G,E)=(C_2,E)\cap\widetilde{Y}}} \tau(C_2,E) \right)$$

$$= \bigwedge_{\substack{(C_1,E),(C_2,E)\in SS(X,E)\\ (F,E)\cap(G,E)=((C_1,E)\cap(C_2,E))\cap\widetilde{Y}}} [\tau(C_1,E)\wedge\tau(C_2,E)]$$

$$\leq \bigwedge_{\substack{(C_1,E),(C_2,E)\in SS(X,E)\\ (F,E)\cap(G,E)=((C_1,E)\cap(C_2,E))\cap\widetilde{Y}}} [\tau((C_1,E)\cap(C_2,E))]$$

$$= \tau_Y((F,E)\cap(G,E)).$$

Now, let $\{(F_i,E)\}_{i\in J} \subset SS(Y,E)$. Then

$$\tau_Y\left(\bigcup_{i\in J}(F_i,E)\right) = \bigwedge_{\substack{(B_i,E)\in SS(X,E)\\ \bigcup_{i\in J}(F_i,E)=\bigcup_{i\in J}(B_i,E)\cap\widetilde{Y}}} \tau\left(\bigcup_{i\in J}(B_i,E)\right)$$

$$\geq \bigwedge_{\substack{(B_i,E)\in SS(X,E)\\ \bigcup_{i\in J}(F_i,E)=\bigcup_{i\in J}(B_i,E)\cap\widetilde{Y}}} \left(\bigwedge_{i\in J}\tau(B_i,E)\right)$$

$$= \bigwedge_{i\in J}\left[\bigwedge_{\substack{(B_i,E)\in SS(X,E)\\ \bigcup_{i\in J}(F_i,E)=\bigcup_{i\in J}(B_i,E)\cap\widetilde{Y}}} \tau(B_i,E)\right]$$

$$= \bigwedge_{i\in J}\tau_Y(F_i,E).$$

Also, for each $(F,E)\in SS(Y,E)$, $\tau_Y(F,E)\geq\tau(F,E)$ is satisfied. □

4. Interval-Valued Neighborhood Structures

In this section we define and study the concept of interval-valued fuzzy neighborhood system of a soft point.

Definition 11. *Let (X,τ,E) be an IVFTS and let x_e be a soft point. Then a mapping N_{x_e} : $SS(X,E)\to[I]$ is called the interval-valued fuzzy neighborhood system of x_e if for each $(F,E)\in SS(X,E)$,*

$$N_{x_e} = \bigvee_{x_e\in(G,E)\subset(F,E)} \tau(G,E).$$

Proposition 5. *Let (X, τ, E) be an IVFTS and let $(F, E) \in \mathrm{SS}(X, E)$. Then*

$$\bigwedge_{x_e \in (F,E)} \bigvee_{x_e \in (G,E) \subset (F,E)} \tau(G, E) = \tau(F, E).$$

Proof. Since $(F, E) = \bigcup_{x_e \in (F,E)} \{x_e\}$, it is clear that

$$\bigwedge_{x_e \in (F,E)} \left(\bigvee_{x_e \in (G,E) \subset (F,E)} \tau(G, E) \right) \geq \tau(F, E).$$

Let $G_{x_e} = \{(G, E) \in \mathrm{SS}(X, E) : x_e \in (G, E) \subset (F, E)\}$. If $f \in \prod_{x_e \in (F,E)} G_{x_e}$, then obviously $\bigcup_{x_e \in (F,E)} f(x_e) = (F, E)$. Then

$$\bigwedge_{x_e \in (F,E)} \tau(f(x_e)) \leq \tau\left(\bigcup_{x_e \in (F,E)} f(x_e) \right) = \tau(F, E).$$

So

$$\bigwedge_{x_e \in (F,E)} \left(\bigvee_{x_e \in (G,E) \subset (F,E)} \tau(G, E) \right) = \bigvee_{f \in \prod_{x_e \in (F,E)} G_{x_e}} \left(\bigwedge_{x_e \in (F,E)} \tau(f(x_e)) \right) \leq \tau(F, E).$$

Hence

$$\bigwedge_{x_e \in (F,E)} \left(\bigvee_{x_e \in (G,E) \subset (F,E)} \tau(G, E) \right) = \tau(F, E).$$

□

Definition 12. *Let (X, τ, E) be an IVFTS.*

(1) $\beta : \mathrm{SS}(X, E) \to [I]$ is called a base of τ if β satisfies the following condition: $(F, E) \in \mathrm{SS}(X, E)$

$$\tau(F, E) = \bigvee_{\bigcup_{i \in J} (G_i, E) = (F,E)} \bigwedge_{i \in J} \beta(G_i, E).$$

(2) $\varphi : \mathrm{SS}(X, E) \to [I]$ is called a subbase of τ if $\widetilde{\varphi} : \mathrm{SS}(X, E) \to [I]$ is a base of τ, where

$$\widetilde{\varphi}(F, E) = \bigvee_{\bigcap_{i \in J} (G_i, E) = (F,E)} \bigwedge_{i \in J} \varphi(G_i, E)$$

and J is a finite set.

We now give an example of a base for a topology.

Example 3. *Let $X = \{x\}$, $E = \{e_1, e_2, e_3\}$. The set of soft points in X is $\{x_{e_1}, x_{e_2}, x_{e_3}\}$. Let $\widetilde{a} \in [I]$ be fixed. We define the mapping $\tau : \mathrm{SS}(X, E) \to [I]$ as follows: for $(F, E) \in \mathrm{SS}(X, E)$ we set*

$$\tau(F, E) = \begin{cases} 1, & \text{if } (F, E) \in \{\Phi, \widetilde{X}, \{x_{e_2}\}, \{x_{e_1}, x_{e_2}\}, \{x_{e_2}, x_{e_3}\}\}, \\ \widetilde{a}, & \text{otherwise.} \end{cases}$$

The mapping $\beta : \mathrm{SS}(X, E) \to [I]$ defined by

$$\beta(F, E) = 1, \text{ if } (F, E) \in \{\{x_{e_2}\}, \{x_{e_1}, x_{e_2}\}, \{x_{e_2}, x_{e_3}\}\}$$

is a base for τ.

Theorem 2. *Let* (X, τ, E) *be an IVFTS and let* $\beta : SS(X, E) \to [I]$ *be a mapping such that* $\beta \subset \tau$. *Then* β *is an interval-valued fuzzy base for* τ *if and only if for each soft point* x_e *and each* $(F, E) \in SS(X, E)$,

$$N_{x_e}(F, E) \leq \bigvee_{x_e \in (G,E) \subset (F,E)} \beta(G, E).$$

Proof. Let β be an interval-valued fuzzy base for τ, x_e be a soft point and $(F, E) \in SS(X, E), x_e \in (F, E)$. Thus from the definition of interval-valued fuzzy neighborhood system of x_e,

$$\begin{aligned} N_{x_e}(F, E) &= \bigvee_{x_e \in (G,E) \subset (F,E)} \tau(G, E) \\ &= \bigvee_{x_e \in (G,E) \subset (F,E)} \bigvee_{\bigcup_{i \in J}(G_i,E)=(G,E)} \bigwedge_{i \in J} \beta(G_i, E). \end{aligned}$$

If $x_e \in (G, E) = \bigcup_{i \in J} (G_i, E)$, then there is $i_0 \in J$ such that $x_e \in \left(G_{i_0}, E\right)$. Hence

$$\bigwedge_{i \in J} \beta(G_i, E) \leq \beta\left(G_{i_0}, E\right) \leq \bigvee_{x_e \in (G,E) \subset (F,E)} \beta(G, E).$$

So

$$N_{x_e}(F, E) \leq \bigvee_{x_e \in (G,E) \subset (F,E)} \beta(G, E)$$

is obtained.

Conversely, suppose the condition of necessary holds and for $(F, E) \in SS(X, E)$,

$$(F, E) = \bigcup_{i \in J} (G_i, E).$$

Then

$$\tau(F, E) \geq \bigwedge_{i \in J} \tau(G_i, E) \geq \bigwedge_{i \in J} \beta(G_i, E).$$

Hence

$$\tau(F, E) \geq \bigvee_{\bigcup_{i \in J}(G_i,E)=(F,E)} \bigwedge_{i \in J} \beta(G_i, E) \quad \text{(i)}$$

On the other hand, from Proposition 5,

$$\begin{aligned} \tau(F, E) &= \bigwedge_{x_e \in (F,E)} \bigvee_{x_e \in (G,E) \subset (F,E)} \tau(G, E) \\ &= \bigwedge_{x_e \in (F,E)} N_{x_e}(F, E) \\ &\leq \bigwedge_{x_e \in (F,E)} \bigvee_{x_e \in (G,E) \subset (F,E)} \beta(G, E) \\ &= \bigvee_{f \in \prod_{x_e \in (F,E)} G_{x_e}} \left(\bigwedge_{x_e \in (F,E)} \beta(f(x_e)) \right). \end{aligned}$$

So, for each $f \in \prod_{x_e \in (F,E)} G_{x_e}$, since $(F,E) = \bigcup_{x_e \in (F,E)} f(x_e)$,

$$\bigvee_{f \in \prod_{x_e \in (F,E)} G_{x_e}} \left(\bigwedge_{x_e \in (F,E)} \beta(f(x_e)) \right) = \bigvee_{\bigcup_{i \in J} (G_i,E)=(F,E)} \bigwedge_{i \in J} \beta(G_i, E).$$

Therefore

$$\tau(F,E) \leq \bigvee_{\bigcup_{i \in J} (G_i,E)=(F,E)} \bigwedge_{i \in J} \beta(G_i, E). \quad \text{(ii)}$$

Hence from (i) and (ii),

$$\tau(F,E) = \bigvee_{\bigcup_{i \in J} (G_i,E)=(F,E)} \bigwedge_{i \in J} \beta(G_i, E),$$

i.e., β is an interval-valued fuzzy base for τ. □

Theorem 3. *If $\beta : \mathrm{SS}(X,E) \to [I]$ satisfies the following conditions:*
(1) $\beta(\Phi) = \beta\left(\widetilde{X}\right) = 1$,
(2) $\beta((F,E) \cap (G,E)) \geq \beta(F,E) \wedge \beta(G,E), \forall (F,E),(G,E) \in \mathrm{SS}(X,E)$, then

$$\tau_\beta(F,E) = \bigvee_{\bigcup_{i \in J} (G_i,E)=(F,E)} \bigwedge_{i \in J} \beta(G_i, E)$$

is an interval-valued fuzzy topology and β is a base of τ_β.

Proof. From the condition (1), $\tau_\beta(\Phi) = \tau_\beta\left(\widetilde{X}\right) = 1$ hold. For $\forall (F,E),(G,E) \in \mathrm{SS}(X,E)$,

$$\begin{aligned}
\tau_\beta(F,E) \quad \wedge \quad \tau_\beta(G,E) &= \left(\bigvee_{\bigcup_{i \in J_1} (F_i,E)=(F,E)} \bigwedge_{i \in J} \beta(F_i, E) \right) \\
&\wedge \left(\bigvee_{\bigcup_{j \in J_2} (G_j,E)=(G,E)} \bigwedge_{j \in J} \beta(G_j, E) \right) \\
&= \bigvee_{\bigcup_{i \in J_1} (F_i,E)=(F,E)} \bigvee_{\bigcup_{j \in J_2} (G_j,E)=(G,E)} \left(\left(\bigwedge_{i \in J_1} \beta(F_i, E) \right) \wedge \left(\bigwedge_{j \in J_2} \beta(G_j, E) \right) \right) \\
&\leq \bigvee_{\bigcup_{i \in J_1, j \in J_2} ((F_i,E) \cap (G_j,E))=(F,E) \cap (G,E)} \left(\bigwedge_{i \in J_1, j \in J_2} \beta((F_i,E) \cap (G_j,E)) \right) \\
&\leq \bigvee_{\bigcup_{k \in J_3} (H_k,E)(H_k,E)=(F,E) \cap (G,E)} \left(\bigwedge_{k \in J_3} \beta(H_k, E) \right) \\
&= \tau_\beta((F,E) \cap (G,E)).
\end{aligned}$$

is obtained. Let let $\{(F_i, E)\}_{i\in J} \subset \mathrm{SS}(X,E)$. We consider a family

$$B_i = \left\{ \{(G_{l_i}, E)\} : l_i \in J_i : \bigcup_{l_i \in J_i} (G_{l_i}, E) = (F_i, E) \right\}.$$

Then

$$(F,E) = \bigcup_{i\in J}(F_i, E) = \bigcup_{i\in J}\bigcup_{l_i\in K_i} (G_{l_i}, E).$$

For an arbitrary $f \in \prod B_i$, since $\bigcup\limits_{i\in J} \bigcup\limits_{i\in J\left(G_{l_i},E\right)\in f(i)} (G_{l_i}, E) = \bigcup\limits_{i\in J}(F_i, E)$,

$$\begin{aligned}
\tau_\beta(F,E) &= \bigvee_{\bigcup\limits_{l\in J}(G_l,E)=(F,E)} \bigwedge_{l\in J} \beta(G_l, E) \\
&\geq \bigvee_{f\in\prod\limits_{i\in J} B_i} \bigwedge_{i\in J} \bigwedge_{\left(G_{l_i},E\right)\in f(i)} \beta(G_{l_i}, E) \\
&= \bigwedge_{i\in J} \bigwedge_{\left\{\left(G_{l_i},E\right):l_i\in J_i\right\}} \bigwedge_{l_i\in J_i} \beta(G_{l_i}, E) \\
&= \bigwedge_{i\in J} \tau_\beta(F_i, E)
\end{aligned}$$

is obtained. Thus τ_β is an interval-valued fuzzy topology. It is clear that β is a base of τ_β. □

5. Mappings

In this section we define and study continuous and open mappings between interval-valued fuzzy topological spaces.

Definition 13. *Let (X, τ, E) and (Y, ζ, E^*) be two IVFTSs and $(f, \varphi) : (X, \tau, E) \to (Y, \zeta, E^*)$ be a mapping. Then (f, φ) is called a continuous mapping at the soft point $x_e \in (X, E)$ if for each arbitrary soft set $(f, \varphi)(x_e) = (f(x))_{\varphi(e)} \in (G, E^*) \in \mathrm{SS}(Y, E^*)$, there exists $(F, E) \in \mathrm{SS}(X, E)$ such that*

$$\tau(F,E) \geq \zeta(G, E^*) \text{ and } (f,\varphi)(F,E) \subset (G, E^*).$$

(f, φ) is called a continuous mapping *if (f, φ) is a continuous mapping for each soft point.*

The following example illustrates the definition of continuity.

Example 4. *Let $X = \{x, y\}$, $E = \{e\}$. The set of all soft points in X is $\{x_e, y_e\}$, and the soft sets are*

$$F_1(e) = \{x\},\ F_2(e) = \{y\},\ F_3(e) = \Phi,\ F_4(e) = \tilde{X}.$$

Let $Y = \{u\}$, $E' = \{e_1', e_2'\}$. The soft sets in Y are:

$$\begin{gathered}
G_1(e_1') = u,\ G_1(e_2') = \Phi, \\
G_2(e_1') = \Phi,\ G_2(e_2') = u, \\
G_3(e_1') = G_3(e_2') = \tilde{Y}, \\
G_4(e_1') = G_4(e_2') = \Phi.
\end{gathered}$$

Define $\tau : \mathrm{SS}(X,E) \to [I]$ and $\tau' : \mathrm{SS}(Y,E') \to [I]$ by

$$\begin{gathered}
\tau(F_1, E) = [0.1, 0.6],\ \tau(F_2, E) = [0.3, 0.5],\ \tau(F_3, E) = \tau(F_4, E) = 1; \\
\tau'(G_1, E') = [0.2, 0.7],\ \tau'(G_2, E') = [0.4, 0.6],\ \tau'(G_3, E') = \tau'(G_4, E') = 1.
\end{gathered}$$

Consider mappings $f : X \to Y$ and $\varphi : E \to E'$ defined by

$$f(x) = f(y) = u,$$
$$\varphi(e) = e_1'.$$

Then $(f,\varphi) : (X,\tau,E) \to (Y,\tau',E')$ *is a continuous mapping. Indeed, we have*

$$(f,\varphi)^{-1}(G_1,E')(e) = f^{-1}(G_1(\varphi(e))) = f^{-1}(u) = \{x,y\},$$
$$\tau((f,\varphi)^{-1}(G_1,E')) = 1 \geq \tau'(G_1,E');$$
$$(f,\varphi)^{-1}(G_2,E')(e) = f^{-1}(G_2(\varphi(e))) = f^{-1}(\Phi) = \Phi,$$
$$\tau((f,\varphi)^{-1}(G_2,E')) = 1 \geq \tau'(G_2,E').$$

Theorem 4. *Let* (X,τ,E) *and* (Y,ζ,E^*) *be two IVFTSs and* $(f,\varphi) : (X,\tau,E) \to (Y,\zeta,E^*)$ *be a mapping. Then* (f,φ) *is a continuous mapping if and only if*

$$\tau\Big((f,\varphi)^{-1}(G,E^*)\Big) \geq \zeta(G,E^*)$$

is satisfied for each $(G,E^*) \in SS(Y,E^*)$.

Proof. Let (f,φ) be a continuous mapping and $\forall(G,E^*) \in SS(Y,E^*)$. Suppose $x_e \in (f,\varphi)^{-1}(G,E^*)$ be an arbitrary soft point. Since (f,φ) is a continuous mapping, there exists $x_e \in (F,E) \in SS(X,E)$ such that

$$\tau(F,E) \geq \zeta(G,E^*) \text{ and } (f,\varphi)(F,E) \subset (G,E^*).$$

Then

$$(f,\varphi)^{-1}(G,E^*) = \bigcup_{x_e \in (f,\varphi)^{-1}(G,E^*)} x_e \subset \bigcup_{x_e \in (f,\varphi)^{-1}(G,E^*)} (F,E) \subset (f,\varphi)^{-1}(G,E^*).$$

We have

$$\tau\Big((f,\varphi)^{-1}(G,E^*)\Big) = \tau\left(\bigcup_{x_e \in (f,\varphi)^{-1}(G,E^*)} (F,E)\right) \geq \wedge\tau(F,E) \geq \zeta(G,E^*).$$

Conversely, let $x_e \in SS(X,E)$ be an arbitrary soft point and $(f,\varphi)(x_e) \in (G,E^*)$. From the condition of the theorem, $x_e \in (f,\varphi)^{-1}(G,E^*)$,

$$\tau\Big((f,\varphi)^{-1}(G,E^*)\Big) \geq \zeta(G,E^*),$$

and $(f,\varphi)\Big((f,\varphi)^{-1}(G,E^*)\Big) \subset (G,E^*)$ hold. So (f,φ) is a continuous mapping. □

Theorem 5. *Let* (X,τ,E) *and* (Y,ζ,E^*) *be two IVFTSs and* $(f,\varphi) : (X,\tau,E) \to (Y,\zeta,E^*)$ *be a mapping. Then* (f,φ) *is a continuous mapping if and only if for* $\forall\widetilde{a} = [a^-,a^+] \in [I]$,

$$(f_{a^-},\varphi_{a^-}) \; : \; (X,\tau_{a^-},E) \to (Y,\zeta_{a^-},E^*),$$
$$(f_{a^+},\varphi_{a^+}) \; : \; (X,\tau_{a^+},E) \to (Y,\zeta_{a^+},E^*)$$

are soft continuous mappings.

Proof. Let (f,φ) be a continuous mapping and $(G,E^*) \in \zeta_{\widetilde{a}}$. Then $\zeta(G,E^*) \geq \widetilde{a}$. For each $(G,E^*) \in SS(Y,E^*)$, $\zeta^-(G,E^*) \geq a^-$, $\zeta^+(G,E^*) \geq a^+$. Since

$$\tau\Big((f,\varphi)^{-1}(G,E^*)\Big) \geq \zeta(G,E^*) \geq \widetilde{a},$$

then

$$\tau^-\Big((f,\varphi)^{-1}(G,E^*)\Big) \geq a^-, \tau^+\Big((f,\varphi)^{-1}(G,E^*)\Big) \geq a^+,$$
$$(f,\varphi)^{-1}(G,E^*) \in \tau_{a^-}, (f,\varphi)^{-1}(G,E^*) \in \tau_{a^+}.$$

Conversely, suppose that for $\forall\widetilde{a} = [a^-, a^+] \in [I]$,

$$\begin{aligned}(f_{a^-}, \varphi_{a^-}) &: (X, \tau_{a^-}, E) \to (Y, \zeta_{a^-}, E^*),\\ (f_{a^+}, \varphi_{a^+}) &: (X, \tau_{a^+}, E) \to (Y, \zeta_{a^+}, E^*)\end{aligned}$$

are soft continuous mappings. If for each $(G, E^*) \in SS(Y, E^*)$, $\zeta(G, E^*) = \widetilde{a}$, then $(G, E^*) \in \zeta_{\widetilde{a}}$, so $(G, E^*) \in \zeta_{a^-}$ and $(G, E^*) \in \zeta_{a^+}$. Since (f_{a^-}, φ_{a^-}), (f_{a^+}, φ_{a^+}) are continuous mappings, $(f_{a^-}, \varphi_{a^-})^{-1}(G, E^*) \in \tau_{a^-}$, $(f_{a^+}, \varphi_{a^+})^{-1}(G, E^*) \in \tau_{a^+}$. Then

$$\tau\Big((f, \varphi)^{-1}(G, E^*)\Big) \geq \widetilde{a} = \zeta(G, E^*),$$

i.e., (f, φ) is a continuous mapping. □

Theorem 6. *Let (X, τ, E) and (Y, ζ, E^*) be two IVFTSs and β^* be an interval-valued fuzzy base for ζ. Then $(f, \varphi) : (X, \tau, E) \to (Y, \zeta, E^*)$ is a continuous mapping if and only if $\beta^*(G, E^*) \leq \tau\Big((f, \varphi)^{-1}(G, E^*)\Big)$ for each $(G, E^*) \in SS(Y, E^*)$.*

Proof. Let $(f, \varphi) : (X, \tau, E) \to (Y, \zeta, E^*)$ be a continuous mapping and $(G, E^*) \in SS(Y, E^*)$. Then $\zeta(G, E^*) \geq \beta^*(G, E^*)$. So,

$$\tau\Big((f, \varphi)^{-1}(G, E^*)\Big) \geq \zeta(G, E^*) \geq \beta^*(G, E^*)$$

is obtained.

Conversely, let $\beta^*(G, E^*) \leq \tau\Big((f, \varphi)^{-1}(G, E^*)\Big)$ for each $(G, E^*) \in SS(Y, E^*)$. Let $(G, E^*) = \bigcup\limits_{i\in J}(G_j, E^*)$. Hence

$$\begin{aligned}\tau\Big((f, \varphi)^{-1}(G, E^*)\Big) &= \tau\left((f, \varphi)^{-1}\left(\bigcup_{i\in J}(G_j, E^*)\right)\right)\\ &= \tau\left(\bigcup_{i\in J}(f, \varphi)^{-1}(G_j, E^*)\right)\\ &\geq \bigwedge_{i\in J}\tau\Big((f, \varphi)^{-1}(G_j, E^*)\Big)\\ &\geq \bigwedge_{i\in J}\beta^*(G_j, E^*).\end{aligned}$$

So we have $\tau\Big((f, \varphi)^{-1}(G, E^*)\Big) \geq \bigvee\limits_{(G,E^*)=\bigcup\limits_{i\in J}(G_j,E^*)} \bigwedge\limits_{i\in J}\beta^*(G_j, E^*) = \zeta(G, E^*)$. □

Theorem 7. *Let (X, τ, E) and $(Y, \zeta\zeta, E^*)$ be two IVFTSs and δ^* be a subbase for ζ. Then $(f, \varphi) : (X, \tau, E) \to (Y, \zeta, E^*)$ is a continuous mapping if $\delta^*(G, E^*) \leq \tau\Big((f, \varphi)^{-1}(G, E^*)\Big)$ is satisfied, for each $(G, E^*) \in SS(Y, E^*)$.*

Proof. For each $(G,E^*) \in SS(Y,E^*)$,

$$\begin{aligned}
\delta^*(G,E^*) &= \bigvee_{\bigcup_{i\in J}(G_i,E^*)=(G,E^*)} \bigwedge_{i\in J} \bigvee_{\bigcap_{\mu\in A}(F_i,E^*)=(G_i,E^*)} \bigwedge_{\mu\in A} \zeta(F_\mu,E^*) \\
&\leq \bigvee_{\bigcup_{i\in J}(G_i,E^*)=(G,E^*)} \bigwedge_{i\in J} \bigvee_{\bigcap_{\mu\in A}(F_i,E^*)=(G_i,E^*)} \bigwedge_{\mu\in A} \tau\Big((f,\varphi)^{-1}(F_\mu,E^*)\Big) \\
&\leq \bigvee_{\bigcup_{i\in J}(G_i,E^*)=(G,E^*)} \bigwedge_{i\in J} \tau\Big((f,\varphi)^{-1}(G_i,E^*)\Big) \\
&\leq \bigvee_{\bigcup_{i\in J}(G_i,E^*)=(G,E^*)} \tau\left((f,\varphi)^{-1}\left(\bigcup_{i\in J}(G_i,E^*)\right)\right) \\
&= \tau\Big((f,\varphi)^{-1}(G,E^*)\Big)
\end{aligned}$$

is obtained. □

Definition 14. *Let (X,τ,E) and (Y,ζ,E^*) be two IVFTSs and $(f,\varphi):(X,\tau,E)\to(Y,\zeta,E^*)$ be a mapping. Then (f,φ) is called an open mapping if it the following condition*

$$\tau(F,E) \leq \zeta((f,\varphi)(F,E))$$

is satisfied for each $(F,E) \in SS(X,E)$.

Now we give an example of an open mapping.

Example 5. *Let $X=\{x\}$, $E=\{e_1,e_2\}$; $Y=\{u,v\}$, $E'=\{e'\}$.*
The soft sets in X are

$$\begin{gathered}
F_1(e_1)=\{x\},\ F_1(e_2)=\Phi, \\
F_2(e_1)=\Phi,\ F_2(e_2)=\{x\}, \\
F_3(e_1)=F_3(e_2)=\{x\}, \\
F_4(e_1)=F_4(e_2)=\Phi,
\end{gathered}$$

and the soft sets in Y are

$$G_1(e')=\{u\},\ G_2(e')=\{v\},\ G_3(e')=\widetilde{Y},\ G_4(e')=\Phi.$$

Define topologies τ on X and τ' on Y by

$$\begin{gathered}
\tau(F_1,E)=[0.2,0.5],\ \tau(F_2,E)=[0.1,0.7],\ \tau(F_3,E)=\tau(F_4,E)=1; \\
\tau'(G_1,E')=1,\ \tau'(G_2,E')=[0.4,0.8], \tau'(G_3,E')=\tau'(G_4,E')=1.
\end{gathered}$$

Consider mappings $f:X\to Y$ and $\varphi:E\to E'$ given by

$$\begin{gathered}
f(x)=u, \\
\varphi(e_1)=\varphi(e_2)=e'.
\end{gathered}$$

Then

$$\begin{gathered}
(f,\varphi)(F_1,E)(e')=f(F_1(e_1))\cup f(F_1(e_2))=f(x)=u=G_1(e'), \\
\tau(F_1,E)=[0.2,0.5]\leq\tau'(G_1,e')=[1,1]; \\
(f,\varphi)(F_2,E)(e')=f(F_2(e_1))\cup f(F_2(e_2))=f(x)=u=G_1(e'), \\
\tau(F_2,E)=[0.1,0.7]\leq\tau'(G_1,e')=[1,1].
\end{gathered}$$

It follows that (f,φ) is an open mapping.

Theorem 8. *Let* (X, τ, E) *and* (Y, ζ, E^*) *be two IVFTSs and* $(f, \varphi) : (X, \tau, E) \to (Y, \zeta, E^*)$ *be a mapping and* β *be a base of* τ. *If*

$$\beta(F, E) \leq \zeta((f, \varphi)(F, E))$$

is satisfied for each $(F, E) \in \mathrm{SS}(X, E)$, *then* (f, φ) *is an open mapping.*

Proof. For each $(F, E) \in \mathrm{SS}(X, E)$,

$$\begin{aligned}
\tau(F, E) &= \tau(F, E) = \bigvee_{\bigcup_{i \in J} (F_i, E) = (F, E)} \bigwedge_{i \in J} \beta(F_i, E) \\
&\leq \bigvee_{\bigcup_{i \in J} (F_i, E) = (F, E)} \bigwedge_{i \in J} \zeta((f, \varphi)(F_i, E)) \\
&\leq \bigvee_{\bigcup_{i \in J} (F_i, E) = (F, E)} \zeta\left((f, \varphi)\left(\bigcup_{i \in J} (F_i, E)\right)\right) \\
&= \zeta((f, \varphi)(F, E))
\end{aligned}$$

is satisfied. □

Theorem 9. *Let* (Y, ζ, E^*) *be an IVFTS and* $(f, \varphi) : \mathrm{SS}(X, E) \to (Y, \zeta, E^*)$ *be a mapping of soft sets. Then define* $\tau : \mathrm{SS}(X, E) \to [I]$ *as follows:*

$$\tau(F, E) = \bigvee_{(f, \varphi)^{-1}(G, E^*) = (F, E)} \zeta(G, E^*).$$

Then τ *is an interval-valued fuzzy topology over* $\mathrm{SS}(X, E)$ *and* (f, φ) *is a continuous mapping.*

Proof. It is obvious that $\tau(\Phi) = \tau\left(\widetilde{X}\right) = 1$.

$$\begin{aligned}
&\tau((F_1, E) \cap (F_2, E)) = \bigvee\left\{\zeta(G, E^*) : (f, \varphi)^{-1}(G, E^*) = (F_1, E) \cap (F_2, E)\right\} \\
&\geq \bigvee\left\{\zeta((G_1, E^*) \cap (G_2, E^*)) : (f, \varphi)^{-1}((G_1, E^*) \cap (G_2, E^*)) = (F_1, E) \cap (F_2, E)\right\} \\
&\geq \left(\bigvee\left\{\zeta(G_1, E^*) : (f, \varphi)^{-1}(G_1, E^*) = (F_1, E)\right\}\right) \\
&\wedge \bigvee\left\{\zeta(G_2, E^*) : (f, \varphi)^{-1}(G_2, E^*) = (F_2, E)\right\} \\
&= \tau(F_1, E) \wedge \tau(F_2, E)
\end{aligned}$$

is obtained. Also,

$$\begin{aligned}
&\tau\left(\bigcup_{i \in J} (F_i, E)\right) = \bigvee\left\{\zeta(G, E^*) : (f, \varphi)^{-1}(G, E^*) = \bigcup_{i \in J} (F_i, E)\right\} \\
&\geq \bigvee\left\{\zeta\left(\bigcup_{i \in J} (G_i, E^*)\right) : (f, \varphi)^{-1}\left(\bigcup_{i \in J} (G_i, E^*)\right) = \bigcup_{i \in J} (F_i, E)\right\} \\
&\geq \bigvee\left\{\left(\bigwedge_{i \in J} \zeta(G_i, E^*)\right) : (f, \varphi)^{-1}(G_i, E^*) = (F_i, E)\right\} \\
&= \bigwedge_{i \in J}\left(\bigvee\left\{\zeta(G_i, E^*) : (f, \varphi)^{-1}(G_i, E^*) = (F_i, E)\right\}\right) = \bigwedge_{i \in J} \tau(F_i, E).
\end{aligned}$$

So τ is an interval-valued fuzzy topology over $\mathrm{SS}(X, E)$ and (f, φ) is a continuous mapping. □

Theorem 10. *Let (X, τ, E) be an IVFTS and $(f, \varphi) : (X, \tau, E) \to \mathrm{SS}(Y, E^*)$ be a mapping of soft sets. Then define $\zeta : \mathrm{SS}(Y, E^*) \to [I]$ as follows:*

$$\zeta(G, E^*) = \tau\left((f, \varphi)^{-1}(G_i, E^*)\right).$$

Then ζ is an interval-valued fuzzy topology over $\mathrm{SS}(Y, E^*)$ and (f, φ) is a continuous mapping.

Proof. It is clear that $\zeta(\Phi) = \zeta\left(\widetilde{Y}\right) = 1$.

$$\zeta((G_1, E^*) \cap (G_2, E^*)) = \tau\left((f, \varphi)^{-1}((G_1, E^*) \cap (G_2, E^*))\right)$$
$$= \tau\left(\left((f, \varphi)^{-1}(G_1, E^*)\right) \cap \left((f, \varphi)^{-1}(G_2, E^*)\right)\right)$$
$$\geq \tau\left((f, \varphi)^{-1}(G_1, E^*)\right) \wedge \tau\left((f, \varphi)^{-1}(G_2, E^*)\right) = \zeta(G_1, E^*) \wedge \zeta(G_2, E^*)$$

is obtained. Furthermore,

$$\zeta\left(\bigcup_{i\in J}(G_i, E^*)\right) = \tau\left((f, \varphi)^{-1}\left(\bigcup_{i\in J}(G_i, E^*)\right)\right) = \tau\left(\bigcup_{i\in J}(f, \varphi)^{-1}(G_i, E^*)\right)$$
$$\geq \bigwedge_{i\in J}\tau\left((f, \varphi)^{-1}(G_i, E^*)\right) = \bigwedge_{i\in J}\zeta(G_i, E^*).$$

So ζ is an interval-valued fuzzy topology over $\mathrm{SS}(Y, E^*)$ and (f, φ) is a continuous mapping. □

6. Direct Sum

Now let $\{(X_\lambda, \tau_\lambda, E_\lambda)\}_{\lambda\in\Lambda}$ be a family of fuzzy topological spaces, $X_\lambda \cap X_v = \varnothing$ and $E_\lambda \cap E_v = \varnothing$ for $\lambda \neq v$. Let $\widetilde{X}$ be union of all soft points which belong to this space and $E = \bigcup_{\lambda\in\Lambda} E_\lambda$. Then $\left(\widetilde{X}, E\right)$ is the family of soft sets on $X = \bigcup_{\lambda\in\Lambda} X_\lambda$ with parameters E. For soft point $x_e \in \left(\widetilde{X}, E\right)$ if $x \in X_\lambda$, then $e \in E_\lambda$. If $e \in E_\lambda$, then $x \in X_\lambda$ is satisfied. For an arbitrary $(F, E) \in \left(\widetilde{X}, E\right)$, $(F, E)_\lambda = \{F(e) \cap X_\lambda\}_{\lambda\in\Lambda}$ [23].

Theorem 11. *Let $\{(X_\lambda, \tau_\lambda, E_\lambda)\}_{\lambda\in\Lambda}$ be a family of interval-valued fuzzy topological spaces, X_λ's be pairwise disjoint. Then τ defined by*

$$\tau(F, E) = \bigwedge_{\lambda\in\Lambda} \tau_\lambda((F, E)_\lambda),$$

for each $(F, E) \in \left(\widetilde{X}, E\right)$ is an interval-valued fuzzy topology on $\left(\widetilde{X}, E\right)$.

Proof. Let $(F_1, E), (F_2, E) \in \left(\widetilde{X}, E\right)$. Then

$$\tau((F_1, E) \cap (F_2, E)) = \bigwedge_{\lambda\in\Lambda} \tau_\lambda(((F_1, E) \cap (F_2, E))_\lambda)$$
$$= \bigwedge_{\lambda\in\Lambda} \tau_\lambda((F_1, E)_\lambda \cap (F_2, E)_\lambda)$$
$$\geq \bigwedge_{\lambda\in\Lambda} (\tau_\lambda((F_1, E)_\lambda) \wedge \tau_\lambda((F_2, E)_\lambda))$$
$$= \left(\bigwedge_{\lambda\in\Lambda} \tau_\lambda((F_1, E)_\lambda)\right) \wedge \left(\bigwedge_{\lambda\in\Lambda} \tau_\lambda((F_2, E)_\lambda)\right) = \tau(F_1, E) \wedge \tau(F_2, E)$$

holds.

Now, let $\{(F_i, E_i)\}_{i\in J}$ be a family of soft sets. Then

$$\tau\left(\bigcup_{i\in J}(F_i, E_i)\right) = \bigwedge_{\lambda\in\Lambda} \tau_\lambda\left(\left(\bigcup_{i\in J}(F_i, E_i)\right)_\lambda\right) = \bigwedge_{\lambda\in\Lambda} \tau_\lambda\left(\bigcup_{i\in J}(F_i, E_i)_\lambda\right)$$
$$\geq \bigwedge_{\lambda\in\Lambda} \bigwedge_{i\in J}\tau_\lambda((F_i, E_i)_\lambda) = \bigwedge_{i\in J}\left(\bigwedge_{\lambda\in\Lambda} \tau_\lambda((F_i, E_i))_\lambda\right) = \bigwedge_{i\in J}\tau(F_i, E_i)$$

is satisfied. Hence, (X, τ, E) is an $IVFTS$. □

Definition 15. *The interval-valued fuzzy topological space* (X, τ, E) *in the previous theorem is called the direct sum of* $\{(X_\lambda, \tau_\lambda, E_\lambda)\}_{\lambda\in\Lambda}$, *denoted by* $(X, \tau, E) = \bigoplus_{\lambda\in\Lambda} (X_\lambda, \tau_\lambda, E_\lambda)$.

It is obvious that $i_\lambda : X_\lambda \to X = \bigcup_{\lambda\in\Lambda} X_\lambda$ and $j_\lambda : E_\lambda \to E = \bigcup_{\lambda\in\Lambda} E_\lambda$ are embedding mappings for all $\lambda \in \Lambda$. Then

$$(i_\lambda, j_\lambda) : (X_\lambda, \tau_\lambda, E_\lambda) \to (X, \tau, E)$$

is a continuous mapping.

Theorem 12. *Let* $\{(X_\lambda, \tau_\lambda, E_\lambda)\}_{\lambda\in\Lambda}$ *be a family of interval-valued fuzzy topological spaces,* $X = \prod_{\lambda\in\Lambda} X_\lambda$ *be a set,* $E = \prod_{\lambda\in\Lambda} E_\lambda$ *be a parameter set and* $p_\lambda : X \to X_\lambda$, $q_\lambda : E \to E_\lambda$ *be two projections mappings for* $\forall\lambda \in \Lambda$. *Define* $\beta : \mathsf{SS}(Y, E) \to [I]$ *as follows:*

$$\beta(G, E^*) = \bigvee \left\{ \bigwedge_{j=1}^{n} \tau_{\alpha_i}(F_{\alpha_i}, E_{\alpha_i}) : (F, E) = \bigcap_{j=1}^{n} (p_{\alpha_i}, q_{\alpha_i})^{-1}(F_{\alpha_i}, E_{\alpha_i}) \right\}.$$

Then β *is a base of the topology* $\tau_\beta R$ *on* (X, E), *and* $(p_\lambda, q_\lambda) : (X, \tau_\beta, E) \to (X_\lambda, \tau_\lambda, E_\lambda)$ *are continuous mapping for* $\forall\lambda \in \Lambda$.

Proof. We show that β is a base. Indeed,

$$\begin{aligned} \beta\left(\widetilde{X}\right) &= \bigvee \left\{ \bigwedge_{j=1}^{n} \tau_{\alpha_i}(F_{\alpha_i}, E_{\alpha_i}) : \widetilde{X} = \bigcap_{j=1}^{n} (p_{\alpha_i}, q_{\alpha_i})^{-1}(F_{\alpha_i}, E_{\alpha_i}) \right\} \\ &= \bigvee \left\{ \bigwedge_{j=1}^{n} \tau_{\alpha_i}(X_{\alpha_i}, E_{\alpha_i}) \right\} = 1 \end{aligned}$$

is satisfied. Similarly, $\beta(\Phi)$ is obtained.

$$\beta(F, E) \wedge \beta(G, E) = \left(\bigvee_{(F,E) = \bigcap_{j=1}^{n} (p_{\alpha_i}, q_{\alpha_i})^{-1}(F_{\alpha_i}, E_{\alpha_i})} \bigwedge_{j=1}^{n} \tau_{\alpha_i}(F_{\alpha_i}, E_{\alpha_i}) \right)$$

$$\wedge \left(\bigvee_{(G,E) = \bigcap_{j=1}^{k} (p_{\delta_i}, q_{\delta_i})^{-1}(G_{\delta_i}, E_{\delta_i})} \bigwedge_{j=1}^{k} \tau_{\delta_i}(G_{\delta_i}, E_{\delta_i}) \right)$$

$$= \bigvee_{(F,E) = \bigcap_{j=1}^{n} (p_{\alpha_i}, q_{\alpha_i})^{-1}(F_{\alpha_i}, E_{\alpha_i})} \bigvee_{(G,E) = \bigcap_{j=1}^{k} (p_{\delta_i}, q_{\delta_i})^{-1}(G_{\delta_i}, E_{\delta_i})} \left(\left(\bigwedge_{j=1}^{n} \tau_{\alpha_i}(F_{\alpha_i}, E_{\alpha_i}) \right) \wedge \left(\bigwedge_{j=1}^{k} \tau_{\delta_i}(G_{\delta_i}, E_{\delta_i}) \right) \right)$$

$$= \bigvee_{\left(\bigcap_{j=1}^{n} (p_{\alpha_i}, q_{\alpha_i})^{-1}(F_{\alpha_i}, E_{\alpha_i})\right) \cap \left(\bigcap_{j=1}^{k} (p_{\delta_i}, q_{\delta_i})^{-1}(G_{\delta_i}, E_{\delta_i})\right) = (F,E) \cap (G,E)} \left(\left(\bigwedge_{j=1}^{n} \tau_{\alpha_i}(F_{\alpha_i}, E_{\alpha_i}) \right) \wedge \left(\bigwedge_{j=1}^{k} \tau_{\delta_i}(G_{\delta_i}, E_{\delta_i}) \right) \right)$$

$$\leq \bigvee_{\bigcap_{\lambda\in\Lambda} (p_{\varpi_\lambda}, q_{\varpi_\lambda})^{-1}(H_{\varpi_\lambda}, E_{\varpi_\lambda}) = (F,E) \cap (G,E)} \tau_{\varpi_\lambda}(H_{\varpi_\lambda}, E_{\varpi_\lambda}) = \beta((F, E) \cap (G, E)).$$

Hence β is a base.

Now we check that the projection mapping $(p_\lambda, q_\lambda) : (X, \tau_\beta, E) \to (X_\lambda, \tau_\lambda, E_\lambda)$ are continuous mapping for $\forall \lambda \in \Lambda$. Indeed, for each $(F_\lambda, E_\lambda) \in SS(X_\lambda, E_\lambda)$,

$$\tau\Big((p_\lambda, q_\lambda)^{-1}(F_\lambda, E_\lambda)\Big) \geq \beta\Big((p_\lambda, q_\lambda)^{-1}(F_\lambda, E_\lambda)\Big)$$

$$= \left\{ \bigwedge_{j=1}^{n} \tau_{\alpha_i}(F_{\alpha_i}, E_{\alpha_i}) : (p_{\alpha_i}, q_{\alpha_i})^{-1}(F_{\alpha_i}, E_{\alpha_i}) = (p_\lambda, q_\lambda)^{-1}(F_\lambda, E_\lambda) \right\}$$

$$\geq \tau_\lambda(F_\lambda, E_\lambda)$$

is satisfied. □

Remark 2. *In general, we cannot obtain an interval-valued fuzzy topology by utilizing τ^- and τ^+, with τ^- and τ^+ being fuzzy topologies. If τ^-, τ^+ are two fuzzy topologies and $(F, E) \in SS(X, E)$, $\tau^-(F, E) \leq \tau^+(F, E)$, then $\tau = [\tau^-, \tau^+]$ is an interval-valued fuzzy topology.*

7. Conclusions

We introduce the interval-valued fuzzy set on the family of all soft sets over X. Later we give interval-valued fuzzy topology (cotopology) on $SS(X, E)$. We obtain that each interval-valued fuzzy topology is a descending family of soft topologies. In addition to, we study some topological structures such as interval-valued fuzzy neighborhood system of a soft point, base and subbase of τ and investigate some relationship between them. Finally, we give some concepts such as direct sum, open mapping and continuous mapping,consider relationships between them and illustrate it by examples.

The relations between soft topologies and crisp topologies explained in the paper [19,21] may be used for the future research in this field. Also, the relations between fuzzy soft and soft topologies might suggest a new lines of investigation related to our article.

Author Contributions: The authors contributed equally to this work. All authors have read and agreed to the published version of the manuscript.

Funding: This research received no external funding.

Data Availability Statement: Not applicable.

Conflicts of Interest: The authors declare no conflict of interest.

References

1. Zadeh, L.A. The concept of a lingusistic variable and its application to approximate reasoning. *Inf. Sci.* **1975**, *9*, 199–249. [CrossRef]
2. Chang, C.L. Fuzzy topological spaces. *J. Math. Anal. Appl.* **1968**, *24*, 182–190. [CrossRef]
3. Chattopadhyay, K.C.; Hazra, R.N.; Samanta, S.K. Gradation of openness: Fuzzy topology. *Fuzzy Sets Syst.* **1992**, *49*, 237–242. [CrossRef]
4. Hazra, R.N.; Samanta, S.K.; Chattopadhyay, K.C. Fuzzy topology redefined. *Fuzzy Sets Syst.* **1992**, *45*, 79–82. [CrossRef]
5. Šostak, A. On a fuzzy topological structure. *Rend. Circ. Mat. Palermo Suppl. Ser. II* **1985**, *11*, 89–103.
6. Coker, D.; Demirci, M. An introduction to intuitionistic fuzzy topological spaces in Sostak's sense. *Busefal* **1996**, *67*, 67–76.
7. Samanta, S.K.; Mondal, T.K. Intuitionistic gradation of openness: Intuitionistic fuzzy topology. *Busefal* **1997**, *73*, 8–17.
8. Samanta, S.K.; Mondal, T.K. On intuitionistic gradation of openness. *Fuzzy Sets Syst.* **2002**, *131*, 323–336.
9. Shi, D.L.; Baek, J.I.; Cheong, M.; Han, S.H.; Hur, K. Ordinary interval-valued fuzzifying topological spaces. *Ann. Fuzzy Math. Inform.* **2023**, *25*, 175–203.
10. Molodtsov, D. Soft set theory-first results. *Comput. Math. Appl.* **1999**, *37*, 19–31. [CrossRef]
11. Maji, P.K.; Biswas, R.; Roy, A.R. Soft set theory. *Comput. Math. Appl.* **2013**, *45*, 555–562. [CrossRef]
12. Shabir, M.; Naz, M. On soft topological spaces. *Comput. Math. Appl.* **2011**, *61*, 1786–1799. [CrossRef]
13. Aras, C.G.; Bayramov, S. On the Tietze extension theorem in soft topological spaces. *Proc. Inst. Math. Mech. Nat. Acad. Sci. Azer.* **2017**, *43*, 105–115.
14. Bayramov, S.; Gunduz, C. Soft locally compact spaces and soft paracompact spaces. *J. Math. System Sci.* **2013**, *3*, 122–130.
15. Cagman, N.; Enginoglu, S. Soft topology. *Comput. Math. Appl.* **2011**, *62*, 351–358.
16. Das, S.; Samanta, S.K. Soft metric. *Ann. Fuzzy Math. Inform.* **2013**, *6*, 77–94.
17. Hussain, S.; Ahmad, B. Some properties of soft topological spaces. *Comput. Math. Appl.* **2011**, *62*, 4058–4067. [CrossRef]

18. Kočinac, L.D.R.; Al-Shami, T.M.; Çetkin, V. Selection principles in the context of soft sets: Menger spaces. *Soft Comput.* **2021**, *25*, 12693–12702. [CrossRef]
19. Matejdes, M. Methodological remarks on soft topology. *Soft Comput.* **2021**, *25*, 4149–4156. [CrossRef]
20. Min, W.K. A note on soft topological spaces. *Comput. Math. Appl.* **2011**, *62*, 3524–3528. [CrossRef]
21. Alcantud, J.C.R. An operational characterization of soft topologies by crisp topologies. *Mathematics* **2021**, *9*, 1656. [CrossRef]
22. Al-shami, T.M.; Kočinac, L.D.R. The equivalence between the enriched and extended soft topologies. *Appl. Comput. Math.* **2019**, *18*, 149–162.
23. Aras, C.G.; Bayramov, S.; Veliyeva, K. Introduction to fuzzy topology on soft sets. *Trans. Nat. Acad. Sci. Azerb. Ser. Phys. Tech. Math. Sci. Math.* **2021**, *41*, 1–13.
24. Bayramov, S.; Gunduz, C. Mappings on intuitionistic fuzzy topology of soft sets. *Filomat* **2021**, *35*, 4341–4351. [CrossRef]
25. Moore, R.E.; Kearfott, R.B.; Cloud, M.J. *Introduction to Interval Analysis*; SIAM: Philadelphia, PA, USA, 2009.

axioms

MDPI

Article

S-Embedding of Lie Superalgebras and Its Implications for Fuzzy Lie Algebras

Abdullah Assiry, Sabeur Mansour and Amir Baklouti *

Department of Mathematics, College of Sciences, Umm Al-Qura University, Mecca 21955, Saudi Arabia; aaassiry@uqu.edu.sa (A.A.); samansour@uqu.edu.sa (S.M.)
* Correspondence: ambaklouti@uqu.edu.sa; Tel.: +966-567612436

Abstract: This paper performed an investigation into the s-embedding of the Lie superalgebra $\vec{(}S^{1|1})$, a representation of smooth vector fields on a (1,1)-dimensional super-circle. Our primary objective was to establish a precise definition of the s-embedding, effectively dissecting the Lie superalgebra into the superalgebra of super-pseudodifferential operators ($S\psi D\odot$) residing on the super-circle $S^{1|1}$. We also introduce and rigorously define the central charge within the framework of $\vec{(}S^{1|1})$, leveraging the canonical central extension of $S\psi D\odot$. Moreover, we expanded the scope of our inquiry to encompass the domain of fuzzy Lie algebras, seeking to elucidate potential connections and parallels between these ostensibly distinct mathematical constructs. Our exploration spanned various facets, including non-commutative structures, representation theory, central extensions, and central charges, as we aimed to bridge the gap between Lie superalgebras and fuzzy Lie algebras. To summarize, this paper is a pioneering work with two pivotal contributions. Initially, a meticulous definition of the s-embedding of the Lie superalgebra $\vec{(}S^{1|1})$ is provided, emphasizing the representationof smooth vector fields on the (1,1)-dimensional super-circle, thereby enriching a fundamental comprehension of the topic. Moreover, an investigation of the realm of fuzzy Lie algebras was undertaken, probing associations with conventional Lie superalgebras. Capitalizing on these discoveries, we expound upon the nexus between central extensions and provide a novel deformed representation of the central charge.

Keywords: Lie superalgebra; s-embedding; central charge; fuzzy Lie algebras; canonical central extension

MSC: 17B66; 17B68; 16S32; 81R10; 46L87; 81T60

Citation: Assiry, A.; Mansour, S.; Baklouti, A. S-Embedding of Lie Superalgebras and Its Implications for Fuzzy Lie Algebras. *Axioms* **2024**, *13*, 2. https://doi.org/10.3390/axioms13010002

Academic Editors: Changyou Wang, Dong Qiu and Yonghong Shen

Received: 23 October 2023
Revised: 12 November 2023
Accepted: 14 November 2023
Published: 19 December 2023

1. Introduction

The study of multi-parameter deformations (MLDs) within the framework of the standard embedding (s-embedding) of the Lie algebra (LA) $\vec{(}S^{1})$ has long been a subject of profound mathematical interest. This embedding represents the vector fields on the circle S^1 and finds applications in various mathematical and physical contexts. The exploration of the MLD involves examining how this standard embedding evolves when subjected to multi-parameter deformations, thus unveiling intricate structures and revealing hidden symmetries.

In recent decades, the intersection of Lie algebras and multi-parameter deformations has been the subject of considerable exploration and debate. The work of Pogudin et al. [1] laid the groundwork, introducing the foundational concepts of the standard embedding of Lie algebras. Their focus on the vector fields on the circle was later expanded upon by Bahturin [2], who found wide-ranging applications in both mathematical and physical realms. However, it was the breakthrough research by Kanel-Belov et al. [3] that began delving into the intricacies of pseudodifferential operators, emphasizing their invaluable role in mathematical physics. However, amid this flourishing area of study, the critical review in [4–6] cautioned the academic community to ensure rigorous proofs and validations.

As the field continues to grow, the convergence of these diverse perspectives promises richer understandings and breakthroughs. In the realm of pseudodifferential operators, particularly within the algebra of pseudodifferential operators denoted as $\psi\mathcal{D}\odot$ on S^1, the s-embedding has been a topic of extensive research. The pseudodifferential operator algebra is an invaluable tool in mathematical physics and provides insights into a wide array of phenomena. References [7,8] have laid a solid foundation for understanding the s-embedding within this context.

One of the central objectives of this study was to delve into the cohomology space $H^1(\vec{(}S^{1|1}), \mathcal{S}\psi\mathcal{D}\odot)$. This cohomology space plays a pivotal role in understanding the deformations of the s-embedding. Remarkably, our analysis revealed that this cohomology space is four-dimensional. Furthermore, we provide explicit formulations for four generating one-cocycles. These cocycles serve as key elements in the classification and characterization of tiny deformations (def) of the standard embedding (SE) of the Lie superalgebra $\vec{(}S^{1|1})$. This Lie superalgebra represents vector fields on the super-circle $S^{1|1}$ and resides within the larger Lie superalgebra $\mathcal{S}\psi\mathcal{D}\odot$, which comprises super-pseudodifferential operators defined on $S^{1|1}$.

Some works appear to operate within the framework of Lie superalgebras, central extensions, vertex superalgebras, and superalgebras (cf. [9–11]). These are common mathematical structures in both cases. But, in our work, we had distinct research objectives and a mathematical focus. We emphasize the s-embedding of $\vec{(}S^{1|1})$ and its connections to various mathematical domains, while the cited work concentrated on minimal generating sets, root systems, and commutant vertex algebras within the context of a different Lie superalgebra.

In the course of our investigation into these deformations and cohomology spaces, we uncovered intriguing connections with fuzzy Lie algebras. Fuzzy Lie algebras are a unique and emerging area of research that introduces non-commutative structures into the realm of Lie algebras. For more detail about these structures, see [12–14]. By examining the deformations and cohomology spaces in parallel with the concepts from fuzzy Lie algebras, we aimed to establish a deeper connection between these two mathematical domains. This interdisciplinary exploration sought to bridge the gap between traditional Lie theory and non-commutative algebra, offering new insights and perspectives on both.

The second phase of our study focused on the integrability relations of the defined quantity. This analysis revealed the existence of four distinct families of non-trivial definitions, each parameterized by an even parameter. Our objective was to derive explicit formulas that meticulously describe these families. It was through a careful contraction procedure applied to these definitions that we obtained four one-parameter definitions of the superembedding of $\vec{(}S^{1|1})$ into the Poisson–Lie superalgebra $\mathcal{S}\varrho$ of super-pseudodifferential operators defined on $S^{1|1}$. Each parameter within these definitions corresponds to a fascinating algebraic curve within the parameter space, creating a rich interplay between deformation theory and the fuzzy Lie algebra framework.

The well-established non-trivial central extension of $\mathcal{S}\psi\mathcal{D}\odot$ significantly influences the central extension of the superalgebra $\vec{(}S^{1|1})$, as detailed in [15]. In particular, the two-cocycle that generates this extension plays a critical role in defining the central extension of $\vec{(}S^{1|1})$. Leveraging our findings, we not only elucidated this intricate relationship, but also derived a "deformed" representation of the central charge. This central charge arises from the deformations of the superembedding we constructed, further emphasizing the connections between central extensions and fuzzy Lie algebra structures.

In summary, the novelty in this paper is represented by two key contributions. Firstly, we provide a precise definition for the s-embedding of the Lie superalgebra $\vec{(}S^{1|1})$, focusing on its representation of smooth vector fields on a $(1,1)$-dimensional super-circle, enhancing the foundational understanding. Secondly, we explored the domain of fuzzy Lie algebras, seeking connections with traditional Lie superalgebras. Leveraging these findings, we elucidated the relationship between central extensions and derived a novel "deformed" representation of the central charge.

MLD = multi-parameter deformation.
LA = Lie algebra.
LSA = Lie superalgebra.
$\vec{(}S^1)$ = Lie algebra of vector fields on the circle (S^1).
$\vec{(}S^{1|1})$ = Lie superalgebra of vector fields on the super-circle $(S^{1|1})$.
$\psi\mathcal{D}\odot$ = algebra of pseudodifferential operators on S^1.
$\mathcal{S}\psi\mathcal{D}\odot$ = superalgebra of pseudodifferential operators on $S^{1|1}$.
(SE) = standard embedding.

2. Background

2.1. The Lie Superalgebra of (Contact) Vector Fields on $S^{1|1}$

The super-circle $S^{1|1}$ is defined by $\mathbb{C}^\infty(S^{1|1})$. Let us explicate the elements of $\mathbb{C}^\infty(S^{1|1})$. An element $\mathbb{C}^\infty(S^{1|1})$ must be written as

$$\mathsf{T}(a,\vartheta) = f_0(a) + \vartheta f_1(a),$$

where $f_0(a)$ and $f_1(a)$ are in $\mathbb{C}^\infty(S^1)$ and a and ϑ are even and odd variables, respectively. Let us remark that we have $\vartheta^2 = 0$. In fact, the even elements in $\mathbb{C}^\infty(S^{1|1})$ are the functions $\mathsf{T}(a,0) = f_0(a)$, and the functions $\mathsf{T}(a,\vartheta) - \mathsf{T}(a,0) = \vartheta f_1(a)$ are odd elements. The parity of a homogeneous function T is denoted by $p(\mathsf{T})$.

Assume that $\vec{(}S^{1|1})$ is the super-space of vector fields on $S^{1|1}$:

$$\vec{(}S^{1|1}) = \{\mathsf{T}(a,\vartheta)\partial_a + \tilde{\mathsf{T}}(a,\vartheta)\partial_\vartheta\},$$

where ∂_ϑ and ∂_a stand, respectively, for $\frac{\partial}{\partial\vartheta}$ and $\frac{\partial}{\partial a}$. The even vector fields are linear combination of the fields $f(a)\partial_a$ and $\vartheta f(a)\partial_\vartheta$, while the odd ones are a combination of the fields $\vartheta f(a)\partial_a$ and $f(a)\partial_\vartheta$. The bilinear operation of the superbracket between two vector fields is defined for two homogeneous vector fields as follows:

$$[\chi,\, \aleph] = \chi \circ \aleph - (-1)^{p(\chi)p(\aleph)}\aleph \circ \chi,$$

where $p(\chi)$ and $p(\aleph)$ are the parities of χ and $\aleph$, respectively.

The structure of the contact on $S^{1|1}$ can be given by the one-form:

$$\alpha = da + \vartheta d\vartheta.$$

Denoting $\mathcal{K}(1)$ as the Lie-sub-superalgebra of $\vec{(}S^{1|1})$, where the Lie action on α corresponds to a function multiplication, it can be observed that any element in $\mathcal{K}(1)$ follows the form described in [15].

$$v_\mathsf{T} = \mathsf{T}\partial_a + \frac{(-1)^{p(\mathsf{T})+1}}{2}\gamma(\mathsf{T})\gamma,$$

where $\mathsf{T} \in \mathbb{C}^\infty(S^{1|1})$, $p(\mathsf{T})$ is the parity of T and $\gamma = \partial_\vartheta - \vartheta\partial_a$. The bracket is given by

$$[v_\mathsf{T},\, v_H] = v_{\{\mathsf{T},H\}},$$

where

$$\{\mathsf{T},H\} = \mathsf{T}H' - \mathsf{T}'H + \frac{(-1)^{p(\mathsf{T})+1}}{2}\gamma(\mathsf{T})\gamma(H);\ H' := \partial_a(H). \quad (1)$$

Equation (1) is taken directly from [16].

The LSA $\mathcal{K}(1)$ is called the LSA of contact vector fields. The vector field $\gamma = \partial_\theta - \vartheta\partial_a$ on $S^{1|1}$ maps $\mathsf{T} = f(a) + \vartheta g(a)$ to $\gamma(\mathsf{T}) = g(a) - f'(a)\vartheta$, so that $\gamma^2 = \frac{1}{2}[\gamma,\gamma] = -\partial_a$. The usual rule of Leibniz: $\frac{\partial}{\partial a} \circ g = g'(a) + g(a)\frac{\partial}{\partial a}$ on $\mathbb{C}^\infty(S^1)$, is replaced on $\mathbb{C}^\infty(S^{1|1})$ by:

$$\gamma \circ \mathsf{T} = \gamma(\mathsf{T}) + (-1)^{p(\mathsf{T})}\, \mathsf{T}\,\gamma.$$

2.2. Detailed Overview of the Super-Space $\mathcal{S}\psi\mathcal{DO}$

This subsection elaborates on the intricate concepts and mathematical formulations derived from the seminal work referenced as ABO. Central to this discussion is the series defined as follows:

$$\mathcal{SP} = \Big\{ X = \sum_{k=-M}^{\infty} \sum_{\epsilon} x_{k,\epsilon}(a,\vartheta) y^{-k} \bar{\vartheta}^{\epsilon} \,\Big|\, x_{k,\epsilon} \in \mathbb{C}^\infty(S^{1|1}), \epsilon \in \{0,1\}, M \in \mathbb{N} \Big\}, \qquad (2)$$

where the series X represents an aggregation of terms indexed by k and ϵ, with $x_{k,\epsilon}$ as complex-valued smooth functions on the super-circle $S^{1|1}$. In this formulation, y is analogous to the derivative with respect to the coordinate a, and $\bar{\vartheta}$ corresponds to the derivative with respect to the Grassmannian variable ϑ, bearing a parity of one.

This framework gives rise to the super-space, which forms the foundational structure for the super-commutative algebra of super-pseudodifferential symbols on $S^{1|1}$. This algebra is characterized by conventional multiplication operations. The space $\mathcal{SP}$ is endowed with a Poisson LSA (Lie superalgebra) structure, which is articulated by the brackets defined as:

$$\{X,Y\} = \frac{\partial X}{\partial y}\frac{\partial Y}{\partial a} - \frac{\partial X}{\partial a}\frac{\partial Y}{\partial y} - (-1)^{p(X)}\left(\frac{\partial X}{\partial \vartheta}\frac{\partial Y}{\partial \bar{\vartheta}} + \frac{\partial X}{\partial \bar{\vartheta}}\frac{\partial Y}{\partial \vartheta}\right). \qquad (3)$$

Here, the Poisson brackets incorporate both the even and odd derivatives, reflecting the supergeometry underlying the algebra.

Furthermore, the associative superalgebra of super-pseudodifferential operators, $\mathcal{S}\psi\mathcal{DO}$, is constructed on the same super-circle $S^{1|1}$. Although it shares a similar vector space structure with $\mathcal{SP}$, the multiplication in $\mathcal{S}\psi\mathcal{DO}$ adheres to a distinct rule, expanding the algebraic interactions:

$$X \circ Y = \sum_{\alpha \geq 0, \nu = 0,1} \frac{(-1)^{p(X)+1}}{\alpha!} (\partial_y^\alpha \partial_{\bar{\vartheta}}^\nu X)(\partial_a^\alpha \partial_\vartheta^\nu Y). \qquad (4)$$

This rule of composition is pivotal as it induces a super-commutator, a fundamental element in the study of superalgebras, defined by:

$$[X,Y] = X \circ Y - (-1)^{p(X)p(Y)} Y \circ X.$$

The super-commutator, thus, encapsulates the non-commutative nature of the algebra, offering a nuanced view of the interactions between different elements in this superalgebraic structure.

The format of the LSA can be constructed as $\mathcal{S}\psi\mathcal{D}\odot$ to the Poisson algebra $\mathcal{S}\varrho$. Consider the super-commutative SA Λ generated by $(\vartheta;\bar{\vartheta})$. Then, $\mathcal{S}\varrho = \varrho \otimes \Lambda$, where ϱ is the space of symbols of ordinary pseudodifferential operators $\psi\mathcal{D}\odot(S^1)$. Let us define the linear isomorphisms:

$$\Phi_h : \varrho \longrightarrow \varrho \qquad (5)$$

as

$$\Phi_h(x(a)y^l) = a(x)h^l y^l, \text{where } 0 < h \leq 1.$$

Now, the multiplication on ϱ is given by

$$X \circ_h Y = \Phi_h^{-1}(\Phi_h(X) \circ \Phi_h(Y)).$$

The rule of Leibniz in the odd variables can take a form by letting:

$$\bar{\vartheta} \circ_h \vartheta = h - \vartheta\bar{\vartheta}.$$

Now, the composition on $\mathcal{S}\varrho$ affected by h is:

$$(X \otimes \alpha) \circ_h (Y \otimes \beta) = (X \circ_h Y)\alpha \cdot \beta,$$

where $X,\ Y \in \varrho$ and $\alpha, \beta \in \Lambda$. We will denote by $\mathcal{S}\psi\mathcal{D}\odot_h$ the associative algebra $\mathcal{S}\varrho$ endowed with the farmer composition $\circ_h$. This compositioninduces the usual LSA structure on $\mathcal{S}\psi\mathcal{D}\odot_h$ given by the super-commutator $[X,Y]_h = X \circ_h Y - (-1)^{p(X)p(Y)} Y \circ_h X$. One has

$$[X,Y]_h = \{X,Y\} + O(h)$$

and therefore, $\lim_{h\to 0}[X,Y]_h = \{X,Y\}$. This is mean that the LSA $\mathcal{S}\psi\mathcal{D}\odot$ belongs to the Poisson superalgebra $\mathcal{S}\varrho$.

Moreover, $\mathcal{S}\psi\mathcal{D}\odot$ injects the similarity of the Adler trace expressed on the LA $\psi\mathcal{D}\odot$ of pseudodifferential operators on S^1 (cf. [15,17]). The right super-residue of the super-pseudodifferential operator $X = \sum_{k=-M}^{\infty} \sum_{\epsilon=0,1} a_{k,\epsilon}(a,\vartheta) y^{-k}\bar{\vartheta}^{\epsilon}$ (see (2)) is given by

$$\mathrm{Sres}(X) = a_{-1,\,1}(a,\vartheta)$$

and the functional $\mathrm{Str}(X)$ known from the Gelfand–Adler trace will be defined on $\mathcal{S}\psi\mathcal{D}\odot$ by

$$\mathrm{Str}(X) = \int_{S^{1|1}} \mathrm{Sres}(X) Ber(a,\vartheta).$$

while the Berezin integral is of the form

$$\int_{S^{1|1}} (g_0(a) + \vartheta g_1(a)) Ber(a,\vartheta) = \int_{S^1} g_1 da$$

2.3. Fuzzy Lie Algebras

Given the detailed mathematical context of the super-space $\mathcal{S}\psi\mathcal{D}\mathcal{O}$ and its underlying principles, we now explore the concept of fuzzy subsets within the realm of vector spaces. This exploration extends the notion of traditional vector spaces into the domain of fuzzy logic, providing a unique perspective on how subsets can be characterized in a less binary and more-gradual manner.

In the world of linear algebra, vector spaces over a field F are fundamental constructs. These spaces are typically defined with crisp, clear boundaries. However, when we introduce the concept of fuzzy subsets, these boundaries become more nuanced. A fuzzy subset μ of a vector space V can be thought of as a "soft" or "blurred" version of a traditional subset. Unlike conventional subsets, where an element either belongs or does not belong to a set, a fuzzy subset assigns a degree of membership to each element, ranging from 0 (completely outside the set) to 1 (completely inside the set).

Let V be a vector space over a field F. A fuzzy subset μ of V is considered a fuzzy subspace of V if it satisfies the following conditions:

$$\mu(x+y) \geq \min\{\mu(x), \mu(y)\} \text{ for all } x, y \in V,$$
$$\mu(\alpha x) \geq \mu(x) \text{ for all } x \in V, \alpha \in F.$$

Note: Condition (2) implies that $\mu(-x) \geq \mu(x)$ and $\mu(0) \geq \mu(x)$ for all x in V.

If μ is a fuzzy subspace of a vector space V, then the following properties hold:

$$\mu(x) = \mu(-x),$$
$$\mu(x-y) = \mu(0) \text{ implies } \mu(x) = \mu(y),$$
$$\mu(x) < \mu(y) \text{ implies } \mu(x-y) = \mu(x) = \mu(y-x),$$

for all $x, y \in V$.

For a fuzzy subset μ of a vector space V, the following statements are equivalent:

1. μ is a fuzzy subspace of V;
2. Each nonempty $U(\mu, t) = \{x \in L | \mu(x) \geq t\}$ is a subspace of V.

Note: This theorem establishes the equivalence between fuzzy subspaces and conventional subspaces within the context of fuzzy sets.

A fuzzy set μ, defined as a map $\mu : L \to [0, 1]$, is termed a fuzzy Lie subalgebra of L over a field F if it is a fuzzy subspace of L and satisfies the additional condition:

$$\mu([x, y]) \geq \min\{\mu(x), \mu(y)\},$$

for all $x, y \in L$ and $\alpha \in F$.

Example 1. *Consider the real vector space $\mathbb{R}^3$ with the Lie bracket operation $[x, y] = x \times y$, where $x, y \in \mathbb{R}^3$. Define a fuzzy set μ on $\mathbb{R}^3$ such that:*

$$\mu(x) = \begin{cases} 0.9, & \text{if } x = (0,0,0), \\ 0.6, & \text{if } x = (c,0,0), c = 0, \\ 0.2, & \text{otherwise.} \end{cases}$$

By direct calculations, it is observed that μ satisfies the conditions of a fuzzy Lie subalgebra, making it a fuzzy Lie algebra (cf. [18–20]).

A fuzzy set $\mu : L \to [0, 1]$ is considered a fuzzy Lie ideal of a Lie algebra L if it satisfies the following conditions:

$$\mu(x+y) \geq \min\{\mu(x), \mu(y)\},$$
$$\mu(\alpha x) \geq \mu(x) \text{ for all } x \in L \text{ and } \alpha \in F,$$
$$\mu([x, y]) \geq \mu(x) \text{ for all } x, y \in L \text{ and } \alpha \in F.$$

A fuzzy set $\mu : L \to [0, 1]$ is considered a fuzzy Lie ideal of a Lie algebra L if it satisfies the following conditions:

$$\mu(x+y) \geq \min\{\mu(x), \mu(y)\} \text{ for all } x, y \in L,$$
$$\mu(\alpha x) \geq \mu(x) \text{ for all } x \in L \text{ and } \alpha \in F,$$
$$\mu([x, y]) \geq \min\{\mu(x), \mu(y)\} \text{ for all } x, y \in L.$$

The definition of a fuzzy Lie ideal is equivalent to the condition that, for each nonempty set, $U(\mu, t) = \{x \in L | \mu(x) \geq t\}$, $U(\mu, t)$ is a Lie ideal of L.

2.4. The Structure of $\mathcal{S}_\varrho$ as a $\vec{(}S^{1|1})$-Module

In this section, we will follow the same method used in [8,16]. We define the usual embedding of $\vec{(}S^{1|1})$ into $\mathcal{S}_\varrho$ as follows:

$$\pi(\mathsf{T}\partial_a + H\partial_\vartheta) = \mathsf{T}y + H\bar{\vartheta}, \tag{6}$$

which induces a $\vec{(}S^{1|1})$-module structure on $\mathcal{S}_\varrho$.

We assign the following $\mathbb{Z}$-grading to the PSA $\mathcal{S}\varrho$:

$$\mathcal{S}\varrho = \widetilde{\bigoplus}_{n\in\mathbb{Z}} \mathcal{S}\varrho_n, \tag{7}$$

where $\widetilde{\bigoplus}_{n\in\mathbb{Z}} = (\bigoplus_{n<0}) \bigoplus \prod_{n\geq 0}$, and

$$\mathcal{S}\varrho_n = \left\{ \left(\mathsf{T} y^{-n} + H y^{-n-1}\bar{\vartheta} \right) \,\middle|\, \mathsf{T},\, H \in \mathbb{C}^\infty(S^{1|1}) \right\}$$

is the homogeneous degree $-n$ subspace.

Each element A of $\mathcal{S}\psi\mathcal{D}\odot$ can be defined as

$$A = \sum_{k\in\mathbb{Z}} (\mathsf{T}_k + H_k y^{-1}\bar{\vartheta}) y^{-n}, \quad \mathsf{T}_k,\, H_k \in \mathbb{C}^\infty(S^{1|})$$

The *order* of A is defined as

$$\mathrm{o}(A) = \sup\{k \mid \mathsf{T}_k \neq 0 \text{ or } H_k \neq 0\}.$$

This defines a non-decreasing filtration on $\mathcal{S}\psi\mathcal{D}\odot$ as follows:

$$\mathsf{T}_n = \{A \in \mathcal{S}\psi\mathcal{D}\odot,\, \mathrm{o}(A) \leq -n\},$$

where n is an integer. Consequently, we have the filtration:

$$\ldots \subset \mathsf{T}_{n+1} \subset \mathsf{T}_n \subset \ldots \tag{8}$$

This filtration is compatible with the multiplication and the Poisson bracket. Specifically, for $X \in \mathsf{T}_n$ and $Y \in \mathsf{T}_m$, we have $X \circ Y \in \mathsf{T}_{n+m}$ and $\{X, Y\} \in \mathsf{T}_{n+m-1}$. This filtration endows $\mathcal{S}\psi\mathcal{D}\odot$ with an associative filtered superalgebra structure.

Let $Hr(\mathcal{S}\psi\mathcal{D}\odot) = \widetilde{\bigoplus}_{n\in\mathbb{Z}} \mathsf{T}_n/\mathsf{T}_{n+1}$ denote the associated graded space. The filtration (8) is also compatible with the usual action of $\vec{(}S^{1|1})$ on $\mathcal{S}\psi\mathcal{D}\odot$. In fact, if $v \in \vec{(}S^{1|1})$ and $X \in \mathsf{T}_n$, then

$$v.X = [\pi(v), X] \in \mathsf{T}_n.$$

The induced $\vec{(}S^{1|1})$-module structure on the quotient $\mathsf{T}_n/\mathsf{T}_{n+1}$ is isomorphic to the $\vec{(}S^{1|1})$-module $\mathcal{S}\varrho_n$. Therefore, the $\vec{(}S^{1|1})$-module $Hr(\mathcal{S}\psi\mathcal{D}\odot)$ is isomorphic to the graded $\vec{(}S^{1|1})$-module $\mathcal{S}\varrho$, i.e.,

$$\mathcal{S}\varrho \simeq \widetilde{\bigoplus}_{n\in\mathbb{Z}} \mathsf{T}_n/\mathsf{T}_{n+1}.$$

3. Computations of the Space $H^1(\vec{(}S^{1|1}), \mathcal{S}\psi\mathcal{D}\odot))$

In the current section, we will adopt the same policy as in [8,16,21] to establish the first CHS of $\vec{(}S^{1|1})$ with coefficients in $\mathcal{S}\psi\mathcal{D}\odot$.

Let an LSA $\mathfrak{h} = \mathfrak{h}_0 \oplus \mathfrak{h}_1$ be acting on a super-space $\mathrm{Y} = \mathrm{Y}_0 \oplus \mathrm{Y}_1$. For $p \geq 1$, let the space $\mathbb{C}^p(\mathfrak{h}, \mathrm{Y})$ of p-cochains be the $\mathbb{Z}_2$ graded space of skew symmetric P-linear functions on $\mathfrak{h}$ with the range in V, and let $\mathbb{C}^0(\mathfrak{h}, \mathrm{Y}) = V$. The Chevalley–Eilenberg operator δ (see [22]) transforms $\mathbb{C}^p(\mathfrak{h}, \mathrm{Y})$ into $\mathbb{C}^{p+1}(\mathfrak{h}, V)$. In particular, δ converts a linear function $c : \mathfrak{h} \to \mathrm{Y}$ ($\in \mathbb{C}^1(\mathfrak{h}, V)$) into a bilinear function $\delta c : \mathfrak{h} \times \mathfrak{h} \to \mathrm{Y}$ defined by

$$\delta c(a, b) = c([a, b]) - (-1)^{p(a)p(c)} a.c(b) + (-1)^{p(b)(p(a)+p(c))} b.c(a), \; \forall\, b, a \in \mathfrak{h} \tag{9}$$

where $p(a) \in \mathbb{Z}_2$ represents the parity of a.

Set

$$\begin{aligned} Z^1(\mathfrak{h}, \mathrm{Y}) &= \{c \in \mathrm{Hom}(\mathfrak{h},\, V) | \delta c = 0\} \\ B^1(\mathfrak{h}, \mathrm{Y}) &= \{c \in \mathrm{Hom}(\mathfrak{h},\, V) | \exists v \in \mathrm{Y} \text{ and } c(a) = a \cdot v, \forall a \in \mathfrak{h}\} \\ H^1(\mathfrak{h}, \mathrm{Y}) &= Z^1(\mathfrak{h}, \mathrm{Y}) / B^1(\mathfrak{h}, \mathrm{Y}). \end{aligned} \tag{10}$$

The spaces $Z^1(\mathfrak{h}, Y)$, $B^1(\mathfrak{h}, Y)$ and $H^1(\mathfrak{h}, Y)$ are the space of one-cocycles, the space of one coboundaries, and the first CHS.

The space Hom($\mathfrak{h}$, Y) is $\mathbb{Z}_2$-graded via

$$\mathrm{Hom}(\mathfrak{h}, Y)_b = \oplus_{a\in\mathbb{Z}_2}\mathrm{Hom}(\mathfrak{h}_x, Y_{x+y});\ y \in \mathbb{Z}_2. \tag{11}$$

According to the $\mathbb{Z}_2$-grading (11), each c in $\mathbb{Z}^1(\mathfrak{h}, Y)$ is converted into $(c', c'') \in \mathrm{Hom}(\mathfrak{h}_0, Y)\oplus \mathrm{Hom}(\mathfrak{h}_1, Y)$ with respect to the equations below:

$$\begin{array}{llcll} (\mathfrak{E}_1) & c'([h_1,h_2]) + h_2 \times c'(h_1) - h_1 \times c'(h_2) & = & 0 \text{ for-each} & h_1, h_2 \in \mathfrak{h}_0, \\ (\mathfrak{E}_2) & c''([h,g]) + g \times c'(g) - h \times c''(g) & = & 0 \text{ for-any} & h \in \mathfrak{h}_0, h \in \mathfrak{h}_1, \\ (\mathfrak{E}_3) & c'([g_1,g_2]) - g_1 c''(g_2) - g_2 c''(h_1) & = & 0 \text{ for-each} & h_1, h_2 \in \mathfrak{h}_1. \end{array} \tag{12}$$

A differential operator on $S^{1|1}$ is an operator on $C^\infty(S^{1|1})$ of the following form:

An element c in $\mathrm{Hom}(\vec{(}S^{1|1}), \mathcal{S}\varrho_n)$ is called differential if it is written in the following form: $c(\mathrm{T}(a,\vartheta)\partial_a + \tilde{\mathrm{T}}(a,\vartheta)\partial_\vartheta) = \Big(A_1(\mathrm{T}(a,\vartheta)) + A_2(\tilde{\mathrm{T}}(a,\vartheta))\Big)y^{-n} + \Big(A_3(\mathrm{T}(a,\vartheta)) + A_4(\tilde{\mathrm{T}}(a,\vartheta))\Big)y^{-n-1}\bar{\vartheta}$ where $A_i; i = 1,2,3,4$, are differential operators on $S^{1|1}$.

We define:

(1) The space:

$$Hom^1_{diff}(\vec{(}S^{1|1}), \mathcal{S}\varrho_n) = \{c \in \mathrm{Hom}(\vec{(}S^{1|1}), \mathcal{S}\varrho_n) |\ c \text{ is differential.}\}$$

(2) The space of one-differential cocycles:

$$Z^1_{diff}(\vec{(}S^{1|1}), \mathcal{S}\varrho_n) = \{c \in \mathrm{Hom}_{diff}(\vec{(}S^{1|1}), \mathcal{S}\varrho_n) | \delta c = 0\}$$

(13)

(3) The space of one-coboundaries:

$$B^1(\vec{(}S^{1|1}), \mathcal{S}\varrho_n) = \{c \in \mathrm{Hom}(\vec{(}S^{1|1}), \mathcal{S}\varrho_n) | \exists T \in \mathcal{S}\varrho_n \text{ and } c(v) = \{\pi(v), T\}, \forall v \in \vec{(}S^{1|1})\}$$

(4) The first differential cohomology space:

$$H^1_{diff}(\vec{(}S^{1|1}), \mathcal{S}\varrho_n) = Z^1_{diff}(\vec{(}S^{1|1}), \mathcal{S}\varrho_n)/B^1(\vec{(}S^{1|1}), \mathcal{S}\varrho_n).$$

Lemma 1. *Let an even differential one-cocycle $\mathbb{C}_0$ from $\vec{(}S^{1|1})$ to $\mathcal{S}\varrho_n$. Then, if the restriction of $\mathbb{C}_0$ to $\mathcal{K}(1)$ is a coboundary, then $\mathbb{C}_0$ is a coboundary over $\vec{(}\mathcal{S}^{1|1})$.*

Proof. Let $\mathbb{C}_0$ be an even differential one-cocycle. If the restriction of $\mathbb{C}_0$ to $\mathcal{K}(1)$ is a coboundary, then there exists $x(a)y^{-n} + b(a)y^{-n-1}\vartheta\bar{\vartheta} \in \mathcal{S}\varrho_n^0$ such that

$$\mathbb{C}_0(\mathrm{T}\partial_a + H\partial_\vartheta) = \{\pi(\mathrm{T}\partial_a + H\partial_\vartheta), x(a)y^{-n} + b(a)y^{-n-1}\vartheta\bar{\vartheta}\}$$

for all $\mathrm{T}\partial_a + H\partial_\vartheta \in \mathcal{K}(1)$.

If we apply the equation (E_1), (E_2) and (E_3) from (12), we will obtain that

$$\mathbb{C}_0(v) = \{\pi(v), x(a)y^{-n} + b(a)y^{-n-1}\vartheta\bar{\vartheta}\}$$

for all $v\ in\ \vec{(}S^{1|1})$. Then, $\mathbb{C}_0$ is a coboundary over $\vec{(}S^{1|1})$. □

The following lemma is an immediate deduction of the previous lemma and Theorem 5.5 from [16].

Lemma 2. *We have:*

$$\dim(H^1_{diff}(\vec{(}S^{1|1}),\ \mathcal{S}\varrho)_0) \leq \dim(H^1_{diff}(\mathcal{K}(1),\ \mathcal{S}\varrho)_0) = 4$$

and

$$\dim(H^1_{diff}(\vec{(}S^{1|1}),\ \mathcal{S}\varrho)_1) \leq \dim(H^1_{diff}(\mathcal{K}(1),\ \mathcal{S}\varrho)_1) = 0$$

Lemma 3. *The $H^1_{diff}(\vec{(}S^{1|1}),\ \mathcal{S}\varrho)$ space is totally even if it has the following structure:*

$$H^1_{diff}(\vec{(}S^{1|1}),\ \mathcal{S}\varrho_n)_0 = \begin{cases} R^3 & \textit{with } n = 0 \\ R & \textit{if } n = 1 \\ 0 & \textit{elsewhere.} \end{cases}$$

When n is zero, the non-trivial one-cocycles are:

$$\begin{aligned} \Xi_0(\mathsf{T}\partial_a + H\partial_\vartheta) &= \mathsf{T}, \\ \Xi_1(\mathsf{T}\partial_a + H\partial_\vartheta) &= \mathsf{T}' - \partial_\vartheta(H), \\ \Xi_2(\mathsf{T}\partial_a + H\partial_\vartheta) &= -\partial_\vartheta(\mathsf{T}')\vartheta + H'y^{-1}\bar{\vartheta}, \end{aligned} \tag{14}$$

If n is one, then the non-trivial one-cocycle is:

$$\Xi_3(\mathsf{T}\partial_a + H\partial_\vartheta) = \mathsf{T}''y^{-1} - H''y^{-2}\bar{\vartheta} - 2\partial_\vartheta(H')y^{-1}, \tag{15}$$

Proof. The first thing we should know is that the CHS inherits the Z-grading of $\mathcal{S}\varrho$. It is important to calculate it in each homogeneous component $\mathcal{S}\varrho_n$. Furthermore, the Z_2-grading of $\mathcal{S}\varrho_n$ is inherited by the CHS, and it is important to calculate the even cohomology and the odd one independently. But, this calculation is directly followed by the above two results. □

Theorem 1. *The space $H^1(\vec{(}S^{1|1}), \mathcal{S}\psi\mathcal{D}\odot)$ is totally even. It is generated by the families of the following insignificant one-cocycles:*

$$\begin{aligned} \Gamma_0(\mathsf{T}\partial_a + H\partial_\vartheta) =&\ \mathsf{T}, \\ \Gamma_1(\mathsf{T}\partial_a + H\partial_\vartheta) =&\ \mathsf{T}' - \partial_\vartheta(H), \\ \Gamma_2(\mathsf{T}\partial_a + H\partial_\vartheta) =&\ \sum_{\ell=1}^{\infty} \frac{(-1)^{\ell-1}}{\ell}\mathsf{T}^{(\ell)}\, y^{-\ell+1} + \sum_{\ell=1}^{\infty} \frac{(-1)^{\ell-1}}{\ell} H^{(\ell)} y^{-\ell}\bar{\vartheta} \\ \Gamma_3(\mathsf{T}\partial_a + H\partial_\vartheta) =&\ \sum_{\ell=1}^{\infty}(-1)^{(\ell+1)}\frac{2}{\ell+1}\mathsf{T}^{(\ell+1)}\, y^{-\ell} + \sum_{\ell=1}^{\infty}(-1)^{(\ell+1)}\frac{2\ell}{\ell+1}H^{(\ell+1)}y^{-\ell-1}\bar{\vartheta} \\ &+ \sum_{\ell=1}^{\infty} 2(-1)^n\partial_\vartheta(H^{(\ell)})y^{-\ell}. \end{aligned}$$

Proof. First of all, we refer the readers to [23], for comprehensive studies of the homological algebra used to structure the spectral sequences. We only mention the filtered module $\mathfrak{M}$ alone with nonincreasing filtration $\{\mathfrak{M}_n\}_{n\in Z}$ over an LSA $\mathfrak{h}$ so that $\mathfrak{M}_{n+1} \subset \mathfrak{M}_n$, $\cup_{n\in Z}$ $\mathfrak{M}_n = \mathfrak{M}$ and $\mathfrak{h}\mathfrak{M}_n \subset \mathfrak{M}_n$.

Now, denote the induced usual filtration on the space of co-chains by providing the following context:

$$\mathsf{T}^n(\mathbb{C}^*(\mathfrak{h}, \mathfrak{M})) = \mathbb{C}^*(\mathfrak{h}, \mathfrak{M}_n),$$

lead us to

$$d\,\mathsf{T}^n\,(\mathbb{C}^*(\mathfrak{h},\mathfrak{M}))\subset\mathsf{T}^n(\mathbb{C}^*(\mathfrak{h},\mathfrak{M}))\ \text{(that is, d preserves the filtration)};$$
$$\mathsf{T}^{n+1}(\mathbb{C}^*(\mathfrak{h},\mathfrak{M}))\subset\mathsf{T}^n(\mathbb{C}^*(\mathfrak{h},\mathfrak{M}))\ \text{(that is, the filtrationis nonincreasing)}.$$

Then there is a spectral sequence $(\mathfrak{E}_r^{*,*},d_r)$ for $r\in\mathbb{N}$ with d_r of degree $(r,1-r)$ and

$$\mathfrak{E}_0^{\rho,\sigma}=\mathsf{T}^p(\mathbb{C}^{\rho+\sigma}(\mathfrak{h},\mathfrak{M}))\,\mathsf{T}^{\rho+1}\,(\mathbb{C}^{\rho+\sigma}(\mathfrak{h},\mathfrak{M}))\quad\text{and}\quad\mathfrak{E}_1^{\rho,\sigma}=H^{\rho+\sigma}(\mathfrak{h},\,Gr^\rho(\mathfrak{M})).$$

To simplify the notations, we have to replace $\mathsf{T}^n(\mathbb{C}^*(\mathfrak{h},\mathfrak{M}))$ with $\mathsf{T}^n\mathbb{C}^*$. We define

$$\begin{aligned}\mathcal{Z}_r^{\rho,\sigma}&=\mathsf{T}^\rho\mathbb{C}^{\rho+\sigma}\bigcap d^{-1}(\mathsf{T}^{\rho+r}\mathbb{C}^{\rho+\sigma+1}),\\ Y_r^{\rho,\sigma}&=\mathsf{T}^\rho C^{\rho+\sigma}\bigcap d(\mathsf{T}^{\rho-r}C^{\rho+\sigma-1}),\\ \mathfrak{E}_r^{\rho,\sigma}&=\mathcal{Z}_r^{\rho,\sigma}(\mathcal{Z}_{r-1}^{\rho+1,\sigma-1}+Y_{r-1}^{\rho,\sigma}).\end{aligned}$$

The differential d maps $\mathcal{Z}_r^{\rho,\sigma}$ into $\mathcal{Z}_r^{\rho+r,\sigma-r+1}$ and hence, includes a homomorphism:

$$d_r:\mathfrak{E}_r^{\rho,\sigma}\longrightarrow\mathfrak{E}_r^{\rho+r,\sigma-r+1}$$

The spectral sequence converges to $H^*(\mathbb{C},d)$, that is

$$\mathfrak{E}_\infty^{\rho,\sigma}\simeq\mathsf{T}^\rho H^{\rho+\sigma}(\mathbb{C},d)/\,\mathsf{T}^{\rho+1}\,H^{\rho+\sigma}(\mathbb{C},d),$$

where $\mathsf{T}^\rho H^*(\mathbb{C},d)$ is the image of the map $H^*(\mathsf{T}^\rho\mathbb{C},d)\to H^*(\mathbb{C},d)$ induced by the inclusion $\mathsf{T}^\rho\mathbb{C}\to\mathbb{C}$.

Now, let us come back to our general case, in which we are able to test the behavior of the cocycles $\Xi_0,\ldots,\Xi_3$ with the help of consecutive differentials of the spectral sequence. The one-cocycles Ξ_0,Ξ_1, and Ξ_2 are in $\mathfrak{E}_1^{0,1}$ and Ξ_3 belong to $\mathfrak{E}_1^{1,0}$. Imagine a one-cocycle $\in\mathcal{S}\varrho$, but let us find its differentialas if its values belong to $\mathcal{S}\psi\mathcal{D}\odot$ and keep the rest of the symbolic piece of the theorem. This implies that there is a new cocycle of a degree similar to the degree of the previous one plus one, and its image under d_1 is shown by its class. The differentials d_r of highers order are calculated by an iterative process of this procedure. Now, the space $\mathfrak{E}_r^{\rho+r,\sigma-r+1}$ contains the subspace coming from $G^{\rho+\sigma+1}((\vec{S}^{1|1});\ Hr^{\rho+1}(\mathcal{S}\psi\mathcal{D}\odot))$.

It is not a difficult task to see that the cocycles Ξ_0 and Ξ_1 survive in a similar form. Finding supplementary higher-order terms for the cocycles Ξ_2 and Ξ_3 leads us to the following result: □

Using the isomorphism $\Phi_\mathfrak{h}$ (5), we obtain the following corollary:

Corollary 1. *The space $H^1((\vec{S}^{1|1}),\mathcal{S}\psi\mathcal{D}\odot_\mathfrak{h})$ is totally even. It is generated by the family of the following insignificant one-cocycles:*

$$\begin{aligned}\Gamma_0(\mathsf{T}\partial_a+H\partial_\vartheta)=&\quad\mathsf{T},\\ \Gamma_1(\mathsf{T}\partial_a+H\partial_\vartheta)=&\quad\mathsf{T}'-\partial_\vartheta(H),\\ \Gamma_{2_\mathfrak{h}}(\mathsf{T}\partial_a+H\partial_\vartheta)=&\quad\sum_{\ell=1}^{\infty}\frac{(-\mathfrak{h})^{\ell-1}}{\ell}\,\mathsf{T}^{(\ell)}\,y^{-\ell+1}+\sum_{\ell=1}^{\infty}\frac{(-\mathfrak{h})^{\ell-1}}{\ell}H^{(\ell)}y^{-\ell}\bar{\vartheta}\\ \Gamma_{3_\mathfrak{h}}(\mathsf{T}\partial_a+H\partial_\vartheta)=&\quad\sum_{\ell=1}^{\infty}(-1)^{(\ell+1)}\frac{2\mathfrak{h}^{\ell-1}}{\ell+1}\,\mathsf{T}^{(\ell+1)}\,y^{-\ell}+\sum_{\ell=1}^{\infty}(-1)^{(\ell+1)}\frac{2\ell\mathfrak{h}^{\ell-1}}{\ell+1}H^{(\ell+1)}y^{-\ell}\bar{\vartheta}\\ &+\sum_{\ell=1}^{\infty}2(-1)^\ell\mathfrak{h}^{\ell-1}\partial_\vartheta(H^{(\ell)})y^{-\ell}\end{aligned}$$

where $\mathfrak{h}\in[0,1]$.

Remark 1. *If $\mathfrak{h}\to 0$, we obtain the first CHS $H^1((\vec{S}^{1|1}),\mathcal{S}\varrho)$.*

4. Deformations, Cohomology, and Integrability of Infinitesimal Deformations

4.1. Deformations

Let $\eta : \vec{(}S^{1|1}) \to \mathcal{S}\psi\mathcal{D}\odot(S^{1|1})$ be an embedding of Lie superalgebras:

$$\widetilde{\eta}_\tau = \eta + \sum_{k=1}^{\infty} \tau^k \eta_k \ : Vect(S^{1|1}) \to \mathcal{S}\psi\mathcal{D}\odot(S^{1|1}), \quad \text{satisfying } \widetilde{\eta}_\tau([A,B]) = [\widetilde{\eta}_\tau(A), \widetilde{\eta}_\tau(B)], \tag{16}$$

Here, $\eta_k : Vect(S^{1|1}) \to \mathcal{S}\psi\mathcal{D}\odot$ are linear even functions, a *formal deformation* of η.

The right-hand bracket in (16) is a obvious extension of the LB in $\mathcal{S}\psi\mathcal{D}\odot$ to $\mathcal{S}\psi\mathcal{D}\odot[[\tau]]$. Two formal deformations $\widetilde{\eta}_\tau$ and $\widetilde{\eta}'_\tau$ are *equivalent* if there is an inner automorphism $\jmath_\tau$: $\mathcal{S}\psi\mathcal{D}\odot[[\tau]] \to \mathcal{S}\psi\mathcal{D}\odot[[\tau]]$

$$\jmath_\tau = \exp(\tau \text{ ad } \mathrm{T}_1 + \tau^2 \text{ ad } \mathrm{T}_2 + \cdots), \tag{17}$$

where $\mathrm{T}_i \in \mathcal{S}\psi\mathcal{D}\odot$ such that $p(\mathrm{T}_i) = p(\tau^i)$, satisfying

$$\widetilde{\eta}'_\tau = \jmath_\tau \circ \widetilde{\eta}_\tau. \tag{18}$$

Now, we explore a polynomial deformation (poly deformation) that is not a special case of the formal definition. Specifically, we define the $\widetilde{\Pi}$ deformation of a homomorphism $\Pi : \vec{(}S^1) \to \psi\mathcal{D}\odot$ as **polynomial** if it takes the form:

$$\widetilde{\Pi}(z) = \Pi + \sum_{k\in\mathbb{Z}} \widetilde{\Pi}_k(z)\, y^k, \quad \text{where } z \in R^n$$

For sufficiently large k and $\widetilde{\Pi}_k(0) = 0$, each linear function $\widetilde{\Pi}_k(z) : \vec{(}S^1) \to \mathbb{C}^\infty(S^1)$ is a polynomial in z and satisfies the conditions $\widetilde{\Pi}_k \equiv 0$.

Additionally, we considered an LSA homomorphism $\widetilde{\eta}(z) : \vec{(}S^{1|1}) \to \mathcal{S}\psi\mathcal{D}\odot$ in the following form:

$$\widetilde{\eta}(c) = \eta + \sum_{k\in\mathbb{Z}} \widetilde{\eta}_k(c), \tag{19}$$

where $\widetilde{\eta}_k(c) : \vec{(}S^{1|1}) \to \mathcal{S}\varrho_k$ are even linear mappings that are polynomial in the deformation parameters $z \in \mathbb{R}^n$. When k is sufficiently large and $\widetilde{\eta}_k(0) = 0$, these maps satisfy the conditions $\widetilde{\eta}_k \equiv 0$.

To denote equivalence in terms of poly deformations, we replaced the formal automorphism $\jmath_t$ in (17) with an automorphism:

$$\jmath(z) : \mathcal{S}\psi\mathcal{D}\odot \longrightarrow \mathcal{S}\psi\mathcal{D}\odot, \tag{20}$$

which depends on $z \in \mathbb{R}^\ell$. The automorphism $\jmath(z)$ is defined as follows:

$$\jmath(z) = \exp\left(\sum_{i=1}^{\ell} z_i \text{ ad } \mathrm{T}_i + \sum_{i,j=1}^{\ell} z_i z_j \text{ ad } \mathrm{T}_{i,j} + \cdots \right), \tag{21}$$

where $\mathrm{T}_i, \mathrm{T}_{i,j}, \cdots, \mathrm{T}_{i_1\cdots i_k}$ are the even elements of $\mathcal{S}\psi\mathcal{D}\odot$.

Remark 2. *The theory of poly deformations looks to be important as compared to formal ones. In the poly deformations, the equivalence problem has more attractive aspects related to the parameter transformations.*

Next, we explore the relationship between the polynomial and formal deformations of LSA homologyand cohomology, cf. Nijenhuis and Richardson [24]. If $\eta : \mathfrak{h} \to \mathfrak{y}$ is an LSA homology, then $\mathfrak{y}$ is usually a $\mathfrak{h}$-module. A function

$$\eta + t\eta_1 : \mathfrak{h} \to \mathfrak{y}, \tag{22}$$

where $\eta_1 \in Z^1(\mathfrak{h}, \mathfrak{y})$ is an LSA homologyup to second-order terms in τ; and it is known as **infinitesimal deformation (inf deformation)**.

Now, it is a matter of finding higher-order prolongations of these inf deformations. Fix $\zeta_\tau = \widetilde{\eta}_\tau - \eta$, then (16) can be rewritten in the following way:

$$[\zeta_\tau(A), \eta(B)] + [\eta(A), \zeta_\tau(B)] - \zeta_\tau([A, B]) + \sum_{i,j>0} [\eta_i(A), \eta_j(B)]\tau^{i+j} = 0\,. \tag{23}$$

The initial few terms are $(\delta\zeta_\tau)(A, B)$, where δ is known as the coboundary. For linear function $\zeta, \zeta' : \mathfrak{h} \longrightarrow \mathfrak{y}$, define:

$$\begin{aligned} &[[\zeta, \zeta']] : \mathfrak{h} \otimes \mathfrak{h} \longrightarrow \mathfrak{y} \\ &[[\zeta, \zeta']](A, B) = [\zeta(A), \zeta'(B)] + [\zeta'(A), \zeta(B)]. \end{aligned} \tag{24}$$

The relation (23) becomes now equivalent to:

$$\delta\zeta_\tau + \frac{1}{2}[[\zeta_\tau, \zeta_\tau]] = 0. \tag{25}$$

Exploring (25) in series in τ, we obtain the equation for η_k:

$$\delta\eta_k + \frac{1}{2}\sum_{i+j=k}[[\eta_i, \eta_j]] = 0. \tag{26}$$

The initial insignificant relation is $\delta\eta_2 + \frac{1}{2}[[\eta_1, \eta_1]] = 0$, which gives us the initial obstruction to the integration of an inf deformation. Indeed, it is not difficult to test that, for any couple of 1-cocycles Υ_1 and $\Upsilon_2 \in Z^1(\mathfrak{h}, \mathfrak{y})$, the bi-linear function $[[\Upsilon_1, \Upsilon_2]]$ is a 2-cocycle. This is the first non-trivial relationship (26), which is clearly the condition for this cocycle to be a coboundary. Furthermore, if one of the cocycles Υ_1 or Υ_2 is a coboundary, then $[[\Upsilon_1, \Upsilon_2]]$ is a two-coboundary. This means that the operation (24) defines a bi-linear function:

$$H^1(\mathfrak{h}, \mathfrak{y}) \otimes H^1(\mathfrak{h}, \mathfrak{y}) \longrightarrow H^2(\mathfrak{h}, \mathfrak{y}), \tag{27}$$

known to be a *cup product*.

All the obstructions can be found in $H^2(\mathfrak{h}, \mathfrak{y})$, and under the cup product, they can be in the image of $H^1(\mathfrak{h}, \mathfrak{y})$.

4.2. Integrability of Infinitesimal Deformation

The first objective of this section is to learn the deformation of canonical embedding $\eta : \vec{(}S^{1|1}) \to \mathcal{S}\psi\mathcal{D}\odot$ defined by

$$\eta(\mathrm{T}\partial_a + H\partial_\theta) = \mathrm{T}y + H\bar{\vartheta}, \tag{28}$$

to a one-parameter family of LSA homomorphisms.

The space $H^1(\vec{(}S^{1|1}), \mathcal{S}\psi\mathcal{D}\odot)$ categorizes the infinitesimal deformation of the s-embedding $\vec{(}S^{1|1}) \longrightarrow \mathcal{S}\psi\mathcal{D}\odot$ expressed in (28). Here, we will attempt to determine the integrability conditions of the inf deformation into polynomial ones. Any non-trivial infinitesimal deformation can be expressed as follows:

$$\eta_1 = \eta + \sum_{0\le i\le 3} \tau_i \Gamma_i\,, \text{ where } \tau_0, \tau_1, \tau_2, \tau_3 \in \mathbb{R}. \tag{29}$$

The integrability condition (below) implies that either $\tau_0 = 0$ or $\tau_2 = \tau_3 = 0$.

As operators with zero ordercommute in $\mathcal{S}\psi\mathcal{D}\odot$, this is clear evidence that the cup products $[[\Gamma_0, \Gamma_0]]$, $[[\Gamma_0, \Gamma_1]]$, and $[[\Gamma_1, \Gamma_1]]$ terminate identically, and that is why the map:

$$\eta_{\nu,\lambda} : \vec{(}S^{1|1}) \to \mathcal{S}\psi\mathcal{D}\odot, \; v \mapsto \eta_{\nu,\lambda}(v) = \eta(v) + \nu\,\Gamma_0(v) + \lambda\,\Gamma_1(v) \tag{30}$$

is infected, a non-trivial definitionof the s-embedding; since it is of order one, it is a poly deformation.

Lemma 4. *Any non-trivial deformation of the embedding (28) resulting from Γ_0 and Γ_1 is equivalent to a deformation of order one, which is expressed in (22).*

Proof. Using Γ_0 and Γ_1 to generate the embedding (28), the embedding is deformed as follows:

$$\widetilde{\eta}_\tau = \eta + \tau_0\,\Gamma_0 + \tau_1\,\Gamma_1 + \sum_{m\geq 2}\sum_{i+j=m} \tau_0^i\,\tau_1^j\,\eta_{ij}^{(m)}, \tag{31}$$

where $\eta_{ij}^{(m)}$ represents the even linear functions with the largest order terms. It is known from previous works [25,26] that different choices of solutions for $\eta_{ij}^{(2)}$, which arise from (26), lead to equivalent deformations. Therefore, it is possible to neglect $\eta_{ij}^{(2)}$. Moreover, by recurrence, it can be shown that the largest-order terms satisfy $\delta\eta_{ij}^{(m)} = 0$, and they can also be neglected. □

Before giving the main theorem of this section, let us recall the following result of [16,27].

The space $H^1(\mathcal{K}(1), \mathcal{S}\psi\mathcal{D}\odot)$ is truly even. It is generated by the family of the following non-trivial one-cocycles:

$$\begin{aligned}
\Phi_0(\mathfrak{v}_{\mathsf{T}}) &= -\mathsf{T} + \frac{1}{2}\vartheta'(\mathsf{T}),\\
\Phi_1(\mathfrak{v}_{\mathsf{T}}) &= \mathsf{T}',\\
\Phi_2(\mathfrak{v}_{\mathsf{T}}) &= \sum_{\ell=1}^{\infty}(-1)^{\ell}\left(\frac{\ell-2}{\ell}(-1)^{p(\mathsf{T})}(\varphi(\mathsf{T}^{(\ell)})y^{-\ell}\varphi - \frac{\ell-3}{\ell+1}\,\mathsf{T}^{\ell+1}\,y^{-\ell}\right),\\
\Phi_3(\mathfrak{v}_{\mathsf{T}}) &= \sum_{\ell=2}^{\infty}(-1)^{\ell}\left(\frac{\ell-1}{\ell}(-1)^{p(\mathsf{T})}(\varphi(\mathsf{T}^{(\ell)}))y^{-\ell}\varphi - \frac{\ell-1}{\ell+1}\,\mathsf{T}^{\ell+1}\,y^{-\ell}\right),
\end{aligned} \tag{32}$$

Now, suppose the following inf deformation of the s-embedding of $\eta' : \mathcal{K}(1) \hookrightarrow \mathcal{S}\psi\mathcal{D}\odot$ defined by the cocycle Φ_1, Φ_2, Φ_3 and depending on the real parameters τ_1, τ_2, τ_3 :

$$\widetilde{\eta}'(\tau)(\mathfrak{v}_{\mathsf{T}}) = \eta'(\mathfrak{v}_{\mathsf{T}}) + \tau_1\Phi_1(\mathfrak{v}_{\mathsf{T}}) + \tau_2\Phi_2(\mathfrak{v}_{\mathsf{T}}) + \tau_3\Phi_3(\mathfrak{v}_{\mathsf{T}}). \tag{33}$$

The infinitesimal deformation (33) with respect to a polynomial deformation existsif and only if the following conditions hold:

$$\begin{cases} 3\tau_1\tau_3 - 2\tau_1^3 - 2\tau_1^2\tau_3 + \tau_1^2 + 2\tau_3^2 = 0 \\ \tau_1 = \tau_2 \end{cases} \tag{34}$$

or

$$\begin{cases} \tau_3\tau_1 - 2\tau_3\tau_1^2 - 2\tau_3^2 = 0 \\ \tau_2 = 0 \end{cases} \tag{35}$$

Now, Let us suppose an infinitesimal deformation of the s-embedding of $\vec{(}S^{1|1})$ into $\mathcal{S}\psi\mathcal{D}\odot$ defined with the help of cocycles $\Gamma_1, \Gamma_2, \Gamma_3$ and depending on the real parameters τ_1, τ_2, τ_3:

$$\widetilde{\eta}(\tau)(v) = \eta(v) + \tau_1\Gamma_1(v) + \tau_2\Gamma_2(v) + \tau_3\Gamma_3(v). \tag{36}$$

where $\tau = (\tau_1, \tau_2, \tau_3)$.

Theorem 2. *The infinitesimal deformation (36) corresponds to a polynomial deformation if and only if the following relations are satisfied:*

$$\begin{cases} 4\tau_3^2 + 2\tau_1^2\tau_3 + 2\tau_1\tau_3 + \tau_1^3 = 0 \\ \tau_1 = -\tau_2 \end{cases} \tag{37}$$

or

$$\begin{cases} 2\tau_3^2 + \tau_1\tau_3 - \tau_1^2\tau_3 = 0 \\ \tau_2 = 0 \end{cases} \tag{38}$$

We can modify the relations to obtain a deformation in $\mathcal{S}\psi\mathcal{D}\odot_h$ by considering the weight of the scalar h with separate powers in the respective terms of Formulas (37) and (38). This leads us to the following conditions:

$$\begin{cases} 4\tau_3^2 + 2\tau_1^2\tau_3 + h(2\tau_1\tau_3 + \tau_1^3) = 0 \\ \tau_1 = -\tau_2 \end{cases} \quad \text{or} \quad \begin{cases} 2\tau_3^2 + h\tau_1\tau_3 - \tau_1^2\tau_3 = 0 \\ \tau_2 = 0 \end{cases} \tag{39}$$

These conditions are crucial for the integrability of the inf deformation (36) in $\mathcal{S}\psi\mathcal{D}\odot_h$.

The following lemma gives a rational parameterization of the curves (39):

Lemma 5. *(i) $\forall\omega \in R$, the constants:*

$$\begin{cases} \tau_1 &= 2\omega \\ \tau_2 &= -2\omega \\ \tau_3 &= -h\omega \end{cases} \quad or \quad \begin{cases} \tau_1 &= 2\omega \\ \tau_2 &= -2\omega \\ \tau_3 &= -2\omega^2 \end{cases} \tag{40}$$

satisfy the first of the relations (39).

(ii) For all $\omega \in R$, the constants:

$$\begin{cases} \tau_1 &= -2\omega \\ \tau_2 &= \tau_3 = 0 \end{cases} \quad or \quad \begin{cases} \tau_1 &= -2\omega \\ \tau_2 &= 0 \\ \tau_3 &= 2\omega^2 + h\omega \end{cases} \tag{41}$$

satisfy the second of the relations (39).

(iii) Any triple $\tau_1, \tau_2, \tau_3 \in \mathbb{R}$ satisfying (39) is of the form (40) or (41) for the same ω.

Remark 3. *Geometrically, the curves (40) and (41) are simply lines and parabolas, respectively.*

Now, we are ready to give the main theorem of this section.

Proof. Since the contact LSA $\mathcal{K}(1)$ is a subalgebra of $\vec{(}S^{1|1}$, then the obstructions to the integrability of the embedding of $\vec{(}S^{1|1}$ in $\mathcal{S}\psi\mathcal{D}\odot$ will be a part of the obstructions to the integrability of the embedding of $\mathcal{K}(1)$ in $\mathcal{S}\psi\mathcal{D}\odot$. To prove the necessary condition of Theorem 2, we need the two following theorems from [16,27].

Now, the restriction can be mentioned as follows: $\mathcal{K}(1)$ of the deformation $\widetilde{\eta}(\tau)$ given by (36) is not separate from the deformation $\widetilde{\eta}'(\tau)$ below in Equations (34) and (35) found by N. Ben Fraj and S. Omri in [27]. The restriction of the tiny deformation (36) to $\mathcal{K}(1)$ is found by

$$\widetilde{\eta}(\tau)(\mathfrak{v}_\mathsf{T}) = \eta(\mathfrak{v}_\mathsf{T}) + \tau_1\Phi_1(\mathfrak{v}_\mathsf{T}) + \tau_2\Phi_2(\mathfrak{v}_\mathsf{T}) + \tau_3\Phi_3(\mathfrak{v}_\mathsf{T})$$

where $\tau_1 := \frac{1}{2}\tau_1 + \tau_2$, $\tau_2 := \frac{1}{2}\tau_2$, and $\tau_3 := -\frac{1}{2}\tau_3 - \frac{1}{4}\tau_2$. If we interchange these values of τ_1, τ_2, τ_3 in Equations (34) and (35), we will obtain the required conditions (37) and (38) of Theorem 2.

To prove the converse of Theorem 2, we constructed a poly deformation that satisfies the necessary relations (39) with respect to the infinitesimal deformation (33). These relations play a crucial role in ensuring the integrability of the infinitesimal deformation (33).

Within the space $H^1_0(\mathcal{S}\psi\mathcal{D}\odot, \mathcal{S}\psi\mathcal{D}\odot)$, which consists of even outer superderivations of the LSA $\mathcal{S}\psi\mathcal{D}\odot$, there exists a linear operator denoted as $\operatorname{ad}\log\xi$ on $\mathcal{S}\psi\mathcal{D}\odot$ (refer to [15]). This outer superderivation can be integrated into a one-parameter family of outer automorphisms, represented by Ψ_ν, and defined as follows:

$$\Psi_\nu(\mathrm{T}) = y^\nu \circ \mathrm{T} \circ y^{-\nu}, \tag{42}$$

where $\eta = \partial_\vartheta - \vartheta\partial_x$ should be considered as a Laurent series.

By applying the automorphism (42) to the elementary deformation $\eta_{0,2\omega}$ (22), we obtain:

$$\begin{aligned}\widetilde{\eta}_1^{\omega}(\mathrm{T}\partial_x + H\partial_\vartheta) &= \Psi_{\frac{-2\omega}{h}}(\eta(\mathrm{T}\partial_x + H\partial_\vartheta) + 2\omega\Omega_1(\mathrm{T}\partial_x + H\partial_\vartheta)) \\ &= \eta(\mathrm{T}\partial_x + H\partial_\vartheta) - 2\omega(H'\bar{\vartheta}y^{-1} + \partial_\vartheta(H)) \\ &-2\omega^2(\mathrm{T}''y^{-1} - H''y^{-2}\bar{\vartheta} - 2\partial_\vartheta(H')y^{-1}) + \cdots \end{aligned} \tag{43}$$

Since $\Psi_{\frac{-2\omega}{h}}$ is an automorphism, it is, in fact, a poly deformation of the embedding (6) for any $\omega \in R$, corresponding to any inf deformation (33) satisfying the second condition in (40).

The function defined by

$$\widetilde{\eta}_2^{\lambda} : \mathrm{T}\partial_a + G\partial_\vartheta \to \eta(\mathrm{T}\partial_a + H\partial_\vartheta) + \omega;\widetilde{\Gamma}_h(\mathrm{T}\partial_a + G\partial_\theta), \tag{44}$$

represents a polynomial and formal deformation of the embedding (6). This holds true for any value of $\omega \in R$ corresponding to an infinitesimal deformation (33) that satisfies the first condition stated in (40). Here, $\widetilde{\Gamma}_h = -h\Gamma_{3_h} - 2\Gamma_{2_h} + 2\Gamma_1$.

In fact, Since $\widetilde{\Gamma}_h$ is an even one-cocycle, the function $\widetilde{\eta}_2^{\lambda}$ is a poly deformation if the supercommutator $[\widetilde{\Gamma}_h, \widetilde{\Gamma}_h]$ vanishes. Notice that the one-cocycle $\widetilde{\Gamma}_h(\mathrm{T}\partial_a) = 0$. Furthermore, we have:

$$\widetilde{\Gamma}_h(\mathrm{T}\partial_a + H\partial_\vartheta) = \widetilde{\Theta}_h(v_H)$$

where $\widetilde{\Theta}_h : \mathcal{K}(1) \to \mathcal{S}\psi\mathcal{D}\odot$ is the one-cocycle defined in [27], Section 6, Proposition 4.

Since the supercommutator $[\widetilde{\Theta}_h, \widetilde{\Theta}_h]$ terminates, as proven by N. Ben Fraj and S. Omri in [27], Section 6, it follows that $[\widetilde{\Gamma}_h, \widetilde{\Gamma}_h]$ vanishes. □

Finally, we structured a polynomial deformation with respect to any inf deformation (33) satisfying the condition (41). The automorphismcan be applied (42) to the polynomial deformation (44):

$$\begin{aligned}\widetilde{\eta}_3^{\omega}(\mathrm{T}\partial_x + G\partial_\vartheta) &= \Psi_{\frac{-2\omega}{h}} \circ \widetilde{\eta}_2^{\omega}(\mathrm{T}\partial_a + H\partial_\vartheta) \\ &= \eta(\mathrm{T}\partial_a + H\partial_\vartheta) - 2\omega(\mathrm{T}' - \partial_\vartheta(H)) \\ &+ (2\omega^2 + h\omega)(\mathrm{T}''y^{-1} - H''y^{-2}\bar{\vartheta} - 2\partial_\vartheta(H')y^{-1}) + \cdots, \end{aligned} \tag{45}$$

so we arrive at a polynomial deformation satisfying the second of the conditions (41) with respect to any inf deformation (33).

4.2.1. Exploring Integrable Infinitesimal Deformations in Fuzzy Lie Algebras

Consider the defining relations for a fuzzy torus and a deformed (squashed) sphere. These defining relations can be rewritten as a new algebra that incorporates q-deformed commutators. Let $\mathcal{A}$ be this algebra, and let q be the quantum parameter with $|q| = 1$. Furthermore, assume that $\mathcal{A}$ contains the parameter μ as a constant.

Lemma 6. *For generic values of q such that $qN \neq 1$ for any positive integer N, $\mathcal{A}$ admits a representation that corresponds to the "string solution" of the algebra.*

Proof. Consider the defining relations for $\mathcal{A}$ with generic values of q, where $qN \neq 1$ for any positive integer N. These defining relations lead to the "string solution" of the algebra, which has a well-defined representation. The representation in this case is finite-dimensional and corresponds to a fuzzy torus or a similar structure. □

Theorem 3. *If q is a root of unity, i.e., $qN = 1$ for some positive integer N, then $\mathcal{A}$ admits a representation corresponding to the "loop solution" of the algebra. This representation contains undetermined parameters. Moreover, in the case of the squashed sphere, where $q = 1$ and $\mu < 0$, the algebra $\mathcal{A}$ can be regarded as a new kind of quantum S^2. The value of the invariant of the algebra, which defines the constraint for the surfaces, is not restricted to be one. This lack of restriction allows the parameter q to be treated as independent of N (the dimension of the representation) and μ.*

Proof. When q is a root of unity, the defining relations of $\mathcal{A}$ lead to the "loop solution" of the algebra. In this case, the representation contains undetermined parameters because the algebraic relations are not uniquely fixed. This undeterminedness is a consequence of the special properties of q as a root of unity, allowing multiple representations. Moreover, when $q = 1$ and $\mu < 0$, the defining relations of $\mathcal{A}$ take on a unique form that distinguishes it from a fuzzy torus or other cases. This specific form corresponds to a different algebraic structure, and its properties are reminiscent of those of a quantum S^2, making it a new kind of quantum S^2. On the other hand, The invariant value in the algebra $\mathcal{A}$ is not fixed at one, but can take various values depending on the specific algebraic relations and structure. This flexibility in the invariant value allows the parameter q to be treated independently of N and μ when considering different representations or scenarios. □

Corollary 2. *It is shown that, for generic values of q (where $qN \neq 1$), the allowed range of the value $q + q^{-1}$ must be restricted for each fixed positive integer N to ensure consistency in the representation of $\mathcal{A}$.*

Proof. The restrictions on $q + q^{-1}$ arises from the need to maintain consistency in the representation of $\mathcal{A}$. For generic values of q where $qN \neq 1$, certain values of $q + q^{-1}$ may lead to inconsistencies in the algebraic structure or representations. Therefore, to ensure a consistent representation of $\mathcal{A}$ for each fixed positive integer N, the allowed range of $q + q^{-1}$ must be carefully restricted. □

4.2.2. A Variation of the Central Charge

The non-trivial two-cocycle with scalar values, denoted as $\widetilde{C}_1(X, Y)$, is defined by the outer superderivation $\operatorname{ad}\log y$ in $H^1_0(\mathcal{S}\psi\mathcal{D}\odot, \mathcal{S}\psi\mathcal{D}\odot)$. This is given by the formula [15]:

$$\widetilde{C}_1(X, Y) = Str([\log y, X] \circ Y). \tag{46}$$

It is known that $\dim H^2(\vec{(}S^{1|1}), C) = 1$ [28,29], and $H^2(\vec{(}S^{1|1}), C)$ is generated by the two-cocycle:

$$C(v_1, v_2) = \int_{S^{1|1}} (2\,\mathrm{T}_1''\, G_2 + 2(-1)^{p(\mathrm{T}_2)}\, \mathrm{T}_2''\, G_1 + \mathrm{T}_2'\partial_\vartheta(G_2))\ \mathrm{vol}(x, \vartheta), \tag{47}$$

where $v_1 = \mathrm{T}_1\partial_a + \mathrm{T}_2\partial_\vartheta$ and $v_1 = G_1\partial_a + G_2\partial_\vartheta$, with $\mathrm{T}_1, \mathrm{T}_2, G_1, G_2 \in C^\infty(S^{1|1})$.

Remark 4. *The restriction to the Lie superalgebra $\vec{(}S^{1|1})$ of the 2-cocycle (46) is identical to the 2-cocycle (47).*

Corollary 3. *The restriction to $\vec{(}S^{1|1}) \hookrightarrow \mathcal{S}\psi\mathcal{D}\odot_h$ of the cocycle $\widetilde{C}_1$ with respect to the embedding (43), (44), or (45) is given by:*

$$\widetilde{\eta^{\omega}}^*(\widetilde{C}_1) = (-h - 4\omega)C. \tag{48}$$

Proof. This is arrived at by straightforward calculations from the previous theorem. □

5. Conclusions

In summary, our study focused on a mathematical relationship that intricately intertwines several fundamental elements within the domain of Lie superalgebras ($\mathfrak{g}$). We explored the multifaceted interplay of multi-parameter deformations, cohomology spaces, integrability relations, and central extensions.

We delved into an examination of the s-embedding within the Lie superalgebra $\vec{(}S^{1|1})$, representing smooth vector fields on the ((1,1))-dimensional super-circle. Our principal endeavor was to ascertain a precise delineation of the s-embedding, which entailed deconstructing the Lie superalgebra to unveil the superalgebra of super-pseudodifferential operators $(S\psi D\odot)$ situated on the super-circle $(S^{1|1})$. Additionally, we delineated and rigorously defined the central charge within the framework of $\vec{(}S^{1|1})$, capitalizing on the canonical central extension of $(S\psi D\odot)$. Our inquiry was further broadened to traverse the realm of fuzzy Lie algebras, with the aim to unearth potential associations and analogies between these seemingly disparate mathematical frameworks. Spanning a gamut of aspects including non-commutative structures, representation theory, central extensions, and central charges, our investigation fosters a foundational bridge between Lie superalgebras and fuzzy Lie algebras, enriching the understanding of the interconnections within these mathematical domains.

Author Contributions: Conceptualization, A.A. and A.B.; methodology, A.B. and S.M.; software, A.A. and A.B.; validation, S.M. and A.B.; formal analysis, A.A.; investigation, S.M.; resources, A.B.; data curation, S.M.; writing—original draft preparation, A.A., A.B. and S.M.; writing—review and editing, A.B.; supervision, A.A.; project administration, A.A. All authors have read and agreed to the published version of the manuscript.

Funding: This research received no external funding.

Data Availability Statement: There is no dataset related to this manuscript.

Conflicts of Interest: The authors declare no conflict of interest.

References

1. Pogudin, G.; Razmyslov, Y.P. Prime Lie algebras satisfying the standard Lie identity of degree 5. *J. Algebra* **2016**, *468*, 182–192. [CrossRef]
2. Bahturin, Y. *Identical Relations in Lie Algebras*; Walter de Gruyter GmbH & Co KG: Berlin, Germany, 2021; Volume 68.
3. Kanel-Belov, A.; Rowen, L.H. *Computational Aspects of Polynomial Identities*; AK Peters/CRC Press: Boca Raton, FL, USA, 2005.
4. Davies, J.M. Elliptic cohomology is unique up to homotopy. *J. Aust. Math. Soc.* **2023**, *115*, 99–118. [CrossRef]
5. Baklouti, A. Quadratic Hom-Lie triple systems. *J. Geom. Phys.* **2017**, *121*, 166–175. [CrossRef]
6. Baklouti, A.; Benayadi, S. Symplectic Jacobi-Jordan algebras. *Linear Multilinear Algebra* **2021**, *69*, 1557–1578. [CrossRef]
7. Roger, C.; Ovsienko, V. Deforming the Lie algebra of vector fields on S^1 inside the Lie algebra of pseudodifferential symbols on S^1. *arXiv* **1998**, arXiv:math/9812074.
8. Ovsienko, V.; Roger, C. Deforming the Lie algebra of vector fields on S1 inside the Lie algebra of pseudodifferential symbols on S1, Differential topology, infinite-dimensional Lie algebras, and applications. *Am. Math. Soc. Transl.* **1999**, *194*, 211–226.
9. Creutzig, T.; Linshaw, A. The super $W_{(1\infty)}$ algebra with integral central charge. *Trans. Am. Math. Soc.* **2015**, *367*, 5521–5551. [CrossRef]
10. Cheng, S.J.; Wang, W. Lie subalgebras of differential operators on the super circle. *Publ. Res. Inst. Math. Sci.* **2003**, *39*, 545–600. [CrossRef]
11. García, J.I.; Liberati, J.I. Quasifinite Representations of Classical Subalgebras of the Lie Superalgebra of Quantum Pseudodifferential Operators. *Int. Sch. Res. Not.* **2013**, *2013*, 672872.
12. Yehia, S.E.B. The adjoint representation of fuzzy Lie algebras. *Fuzzy Sets Syst.* **2001**, *119*, 409–417. [CrossRef]
13. Assiry, A.; Baklouti, A. Exploring Roughness in Left Almost Semigroups and Its Connections to Fuzzy Lie Algebras. *Symmetry* **2023**, *15*, 1717. [CrossRef]
14. Baklouti, A. Multiple-Attribute Decision Making Based on the Probabilistic Dominance Relationship with Fuzzy Algebras. *Symmetry* **2023**, *15*, 1188. [CrossRef]
15. Radul, A.O. Non-trivial central extensions of Lie algebras of differential operators in two and higher dimensions. *Phys. Lett. B* **1991**, *265*, 86–91. [CrossRef]

16. Agrebaoui, B.; Ben Fraj, N. On the cohomology of the Lie superalgebra of contact vector fields on S1 | 1. *Belletin Soc. R. Sci. Liege* **2004**, *72*, 365–375. [CrossRef]
17. Manin, Y.I.; Radul, A.O. A supersymmetric extension of the Kadomtsev-Petviashvili hierarchy. *Commun. Math. Phys.* **1985**, *98*, 65–77. [CrossRef]
18. Ali, A.; Alali, A.S.; Zishan, A. Applications of Fuzzy Semiprimary Ideals under Group Action. *Axioms* **2023**, *12*, 606. [CrossRef]
19. Altassan, A.; Mateen, M.H.; Pamucar, D. On Fundamental Theorems of Fuzzy Isomorphism of Fuzzy Subrings over a Certain Algebraic Product. *Symmetry* **2021**, *13*, 998. [CrossRef]
20. Shaqaqha, S. Fuzzy Hom–Lie Ideals of Hom–Lie Algebras. *Axioms* **2023**, *12*, 630. [CrossRef]
21. Agrebaoui, B.; Ben Fraj, N.; Omri, S. On the cohomology of the Lie superalgebra of contact vector fields on S1 | 2. *J. Nonlinear Math. Phys.* **2006**, *13*, 523–534. [CrossRef]
22. Fuks, D.B. *Cohomology of Infinite-Dimensional Lie Algebras*; Springer Science & Business Media: New York, NY, USA, 2012.
23. Poletaeva, E. The analogs of Riemann and Penrose tensors on supermanifolds. *arXiv* **2005**, arXiv:math/0510165.
24. Nijenhuis, A.; Richardson, R.W., Jr. Deformations of homomorphisms of Lie groups and Lie algebras. *Bull. Am. Math. Soc.* **1967**, *73*, 175–179. [CrossRef]
25. Agrebaoui, B.; Ammar, F.; Lecomte, P.; Ovsienko, V. Multi-parameter deformations of the module of symbols of differential operators. *Int. Math. Res. Not.* **2002**, *2002*, 847–869. [CrossRef]
26. Fialowski, A.; Fuchs, D. Construction of miniversal deformations of Lie algebras. *J. Funct. Anal.* **1999**, *161*, 76–110. [CrossRef]
27. Fraj, N.B.; Omri, S. Deforming the Lie superalgebra of contact vector fields on S1 | 1 inside the Lie superalgebra of superpseudodifferential operators on S1 | 1. *J. Nonlinear Math. Phys.* **2006**, *13*, 19–33. [CrossRef]
28. Grozman, P.; Leites, D.; Shchepochkina, I. Lie superalgebras of string theories. *arXiv* **1997**, arXiv:hep-th/9702120.
29. Radul, A.O. Superstring schwartz derivative and the bott cocycle. In *Integrable and Superintegrable Systems*; World Scientific: Singapore, 1990.

axioms

MDPI

Article

The Enumeration of $(\odot,\vee)$-Multiderivations on a Finite MV-Chain

Xueting Zhao [1], Kai Duo [1], Aiping Gan [2] and Yichuan Yang [1,*]

1 School of Mathematical Sciences, Shahe Campus, Beihang University, Beijing 102206, China; xtzhao@buaa.edu.cn (X.Z.); duokai@buaa.edu.cn (K.D.)
2 School of Mathematics and Statistics, Jiangxi Normal University, Nanchang 330022, China; 003191@jxnu.edu.cn
* Correspondence: ycyang@buaa.edu.cn

Abstract: In this paper, $(\odot,\vee)$-multiderivations on an MV-algebra A are introduced, the relations between $(\odot,\vee)$-multiderivations and $(\odot,\vee)$-derivations are discussed. The set $\mathrm{MD}(A)$ of $(\odot,\vee)$-multiderivations on A can be equipped with a preorder, and $(\mathrm{MD}(A)/\sim,\preccurlyeq)$ can be made into a partially ordered set with respect to some equivalence relation $\sim$. In particular, for any finite MV-chain L_n, $(\mathrm{MD}(L_n)/\sim,\preccurlyeq)$ becomes a complete lattice. Finally, a counting principle is built to obtain the enumeration of $\mathrm{MD}(L_n)$.

Keywords: MV-algebra; $(\odot,\vee)$-multiderivation; complete lattice; enumeration; cardinality

MSC: 3G20; 06D35; 06B10; 08B26

1. Introduction

The concept of derivation originating from analysis has been delineated for a variety of algebraic structures which come in analogy with the Leibniz rule

$$\frac{d}{dx}(fg)=\frac{d}{dx}(f)g+f\frac{d}{dx}(g).$$

Posner [1] introduced the derivation on prime rings $(R,+,\cdot)$ as a mapping d from R to R such that for all $x,y\in R$:

$$(1)\ d(x\cdot y)=d(x)\cdot y+x\cdot d(y),\quad (2)\ d(x+y)=d(x)+d(y).$$

It implies that

$$(3)\ \ d(1)=0,\quad (4)\ \ d(0)=0,$$

which are the 0-ary version of (1) and (2), respectively.

The derivations on lattices $(L,\vee,\wedge)$ were defined in [2] by Szász and were developed in [3] by Ferrari as a map d from L to L such that for all elements x,y in L:

$$(i)\ d(x\wedge y)=(d(x)\wedge y)\vee(x\wedge d(y)),\quad (ii)\ d(x\vee y)=d(x)\vee d(y).$$

Xin et al. [4,5] investigated the derivations on a lattice satisfying only condition (i). In fact, a derivation d on L with both the Leibniz rule (i) and the linearity (ii) implies that $d(x)=x\wedge u$ for some $u\in L$ [6] (Proposition 2.5). If u is the maximum of a lattice, then such a derivation is actually the identity. It seems that this is an important reason for the derivations on, for instance, BCI-algebra [7], residuated lattices [8], basic algebra [9], L-algebra [10], and differential lattices [6], which are defined with the unique requirement of the Leibniz rule (i) (for the discussion in detail, cf. Section 2).

The derivation on an MV-algebra $(A,\oplus,^*,0)$ was firstly introduced by Alshehri [11] as a mapping d from A to A satisfying an $(\odot,\ \oplus)$-condition: $\forall x,y\in A$,

Citation: Zhao, X.; Duo, K.; Gan, A.; Yang, Y. The Enumeration of $(\odot,\vee)$-Multiderivations on a Finite MV-Chain. *Axioms* **2024**, *13*, 250. https://doi.org/10.3390/axioms13040250

Academic Editors: Changyou Wang, Dong Qiu, Yonghong Shen and Cristina Flaut

Received: 21 February 2024
Revised: 27 March 2024
Accepted: 29 March 2024
Published: 10 April 2024

$$d(x \odot y) = (d(x) \odot y) \oplus (x \odot d(y)),$$

where $x \odot y$ is defined to be $(x^* \oplus y^*)^*$. Then, several derivations on MV-algebras have been considered in [12–15]. However, the interplay of the ring operations $\cdot$ and $+$ is more similar to the interplay between the MV-operations $\odot$ and $\vee$ rather than that between the MV-operations $\odot$ and $\oplus$. In fact, the main interplay between $\cdot$ and $+$ in rings is the distributivity of $\cdot$ over $+$. In MV-algebras, $\odot$ distributes over $\vee$, as in rings, while it is not true that $\odot$ distributes over $\oplus$. It is also true that $\odot$ distributes over $\wedge$, but $\vee$ is preferable because the identity element of $\vee$ is absorbing for $\odot$, that is, $0 \odot x = 0$ for any element x in an MV-algebra A, as in rings, while the same is not true for $\wedge$. Therefore, the $(\odot, \vee)$-derivation on MV-algebras [16] is a nature improvement of Alshehri's celebrated work [11] of the $(\odot, \oplus)$-derivation (cf. Section 2 for more discussion).

Let E and F be nonempty sets. A multifunction f: $E \to \Delta(F)$ is a map (or function) from E into $\Delta(F)$, the collection of nonempty subsets of F. The multifunction [17] is also known as set-valued function [18]. Significantly, multifunctions have many diverse and interesting applications in control problems [19,20] and mathematical economics [21,22]. Motivated by the role played by derivations on MV-algebras and the work of multiderivations on lattices [23], it is imperative to undertake a systematic study of the corresponding algebraic structure for derivations on MV-algebras.

This article is a continuation of work on $(\odot, \vee)$-multiderivations based on the nature $(\odot, \vee)$-derivation on MV-algebras [16], that is, a set-valued generalization of point-valued $(\odot, \vee)$-derivations. Section 2 starts with a review of the $(\odot, \vee)$-derivations on an MV-algebra A. In Section 3, we first define a natural preorder on $\Delta(A)$ that $M \preceq N$ iff for every $m \in M$ there exists $n \in N$ such that $m \leq n$. Then, we introduce $(\odot, \vee)$-multiderivations on MV-algebras. The relations between $(\odot, \vee)$-derivations and $(\odot, \vee)$-multiderivations on an MV-algebra are given (Propositions 5–7). In Section 4, we investigate the set of $(\odot, \vee)$-multiderivations $\mathrm{MD}(A)$ on an MV-algebra A. Let $\sigma, \sigma' \in \mathrm{MD}(A)$. Define $\sigma \preccurlyeq \sigma'$ if $\sigma(x) \preceq \sigma'(x)$ for any $x \in A$, and an equivalence relation $\sim$ on $\mathrm{MD}(A)$ by $\sigma \sim \sigma'$ iff $\sigma \preccurlyeq \sigma'$ and $\sigma' \preccurlyeq \sigma$. Then, $(\mathrm{MD}(A)/\sim, \preccurlyeq)$ is a poset. For an n-element MV-chain L_n, we show that $(\mathrm{MD}(L_n)/\sim, \preccurlyeq)$ is isomorphic to the complete lattice $\mathrm{Der}(L_n)$, the underlying set of $(\odot, \vee)$-derivations on L_n (Theorem 1), so we deduce that $|\,\mathrm{MD}(L_n)/\sim| = |\,\mathrm{Der}(L_n)|$, then [16] (Theorem 3.11) can be applied. Moreover, we define an equivalence relation $\sim$ on $\Delta(A)$, and present the fact that the poset $\Delta(L_n \times L_2)/\sim$ is isomorphic to the complete lattice $\mathrm{Der}(L_{n+1})$ (Proposition 11). However, the cardinalities of different equivalence classes with respect to the equivalence relation $\sim$ are different in general (Example 5). In Section 5, by building a counting principle (Theorem 3) for $(\odot, \vee)$-multiderivations on an n-element MV-chain L_n, we finally obtain the enumeration of $\mathrm{MD}(L_n)$: $(7 \cdot 3^{n-1} - 2^{n+2} + 1)/2$.

Notation. Throughout this paper, A denotes an MV-algebra; $|X|$ denotes the cardinality of a set X; $\Delta(X)$ denotes the set of nonempty subsets of a set X; $\sqcup$ means disjoint union; $\mathbb{N}$ denotes the set of natural numbers; "iff" is the abbreviation for "if and only if".

2. Preliminaries

Definition 1 ([24]). *An algebra $(A, \oplus, ^*, 0)$ is an* MV-algebra *if the following axioms are satisfied:*

(MV1) (associativity) $x \oplus (y \oplus z) = (x \oplus y) \oplus z$.
(MV2) (commutativity) $x \oplus y = y \oplus x$.
(MV3) (existence of the unit 0) $x \oplus 0 = x$.
(MV4) (involution) $x^{**} = x$.
(MV5) (maximal element 0^*) $x \oplus 0^* = 0^*$.
(MV6) (Łukasiewicz axiom) $(x^* \oplus y)^* \oplus y = (y^* \oplus x)^* \oplus x$.

Define $1 = 0^*$ and **the natural order** on A as follows: $y \geq x$ iff $x \odot y^* = 0$. Then, the interval $[a, b] = \{r \in A \mid a \leq r \leq b\}$ for any $a, b \in A$ and $a \leq b$. Note that A is a bounded distributive lattice with respect to the natural order [24] (Proposition 1.5.1) with 0, 1, and

$$x \vee y = (x \odot y^*) \oplus y \ , \ x \wedge y = x \odot (x^* \oplus y). \tag{1}$$

An MV-chain is an MV-algebra which is linearly ordered with respect to the natural order.

Example 1 ([24]). *Let $L = [0,1]$ be the real unit interval. Define*

$$x \oplus y = \min\{1, x+y\} \text{ and } x^* = 1 - x \text{ for any } x, y \in L.$$

Then $(L, \oplus, ^*, 0)$ is an MV*-chain. Note that $x \odot y = \max\{0, x+y-1\}$.*

Example 2. *For every $2 \leq n \in \mathbb{N}_+$, let*

$$L_n = \left\{0, \frac{1}{n-1}, \frac{2}{n-1}, \cdots, \frac{n-2}{n-1}, 1\right\}.$$

Then the n-element subset L_n is an MV*-subalgebra of L.*

Lemma 1 ([24,25]). *If A is an* MV*-algebra, then the following statements are true $\forall x, y, z \in A$:*

1. $x \oplus y \geq x \vee y \geq x \geq x \wedge y \geq x \odot y$.
2. $x \oplus y = 0$ *iff* $x = y = 0$. $x \odot y = 1$ *iff* $x = y = 1$.
3. *If* $y \geq x$, *then* $y \vee z \geq x \vee z$, $y \wedge z \geq x \wedge z$.
4. *If* $y \geq x$, *then* $y \oplus z \geq x \oplus z$, $y \odot z \geq x \odot z$.
5. $y \geq x$ *iff* $x^* \geq y^*$.
6. $x \odot (y \wedge z) = (x \odot y) \wedge (x \odot z)$.
7. $x \odot (y \vee z) = (x \odot y) \vee (x \odot z)$.
8. $x \odot y \leq z$ *iff* $x \leq y^* \oplus z$.

Let Ω be an index set. The **direct product** $\prod_{i \in \Omega} A_i$ [24] of a family of MV-algebras $\{A_i\}_{i \in \Omega}$ is the MV-algebra with cartesian product of the family and pointwise MV-operations. We denote $A_1 \times A_2 \times \cdots \times A_n$ when Ω is a positive integer n. We call $a \in A$ **idempotent** if $a \oplus a = a$. Let $\mathbf{B}(A)$ be the set of idempotent elements of A and B_{2^n} be the 2^n-element Boolean algebra. Note that B_4 is actually $L_2 \times L_2$ [24].

Lemma 2 ([24], Proposition 3.5.3). *Let A be a subalgebra of $[0,1]$. Let $A^+ = \{x \in A \mid x > 0\}$ and $a = \inf A^+$ be the infimum of A^+. If $a = 0$, then A is a dense subchain of $[0,1]$. If $a > 0$, then $A = L_n$ for some $n \geq 2$.*

Definition 2 ([16]). *If A is an* MV*-algebra, then a map d from A to A is an $(\odot, \vee)$-**derivation** on A if $\forall x, y \in A$,*

$$d(x \odot y) = (d(x) \odot y) \vee (x \odot d(y)). \tag{2}$$

Let $\mathrm{Der}(A)$ *be the set of $(\odot, \vee)$-derivations on A. For $X = \{x_1, x_2, \cdots, x_n\}$ and a map $d : X \to X$, we shall write d as*

$$\begin{pmatrix} x_1 & x_2 & \cdots & x_n \\ d(x_1) & d(x_2) & \cdots & d(x_n) \end{pmatrix}.$$

The mappings Id_A and $\mathbf{0}_A$, defined by $\mathrm{Id}_A(x) = x$ and $\mathbf{0}_A(x) = 0$ $(\forall x \in A)$, respectively, are $(\odot, \vee)$-derivations on A. For $u \in A$, the operator $\chi^{(u)}(x) := \begin{cases} u, & \text{if } x = 1 \\ x. & \text{otherwise} \end{cases} \in \mathrm{Der}(A)$. More examples are given in [16].

Proposition 1 ([16]). *If A is an* MV*-algebra and $d \in \mathrm{Der}(A)$, then the followings hold for all $x, y \in A$:*

1. $0 = d(0)$.
2. $x \geq d(x)$.
3. *If* $d(x) = x$, *then* $d(y) = y$ *for* $y \leq x$.

Remark 1. *Now let us give some explanations of the naturality of an* $(\odot, \vee)$*-derivation in Definition 2. The interplay of the ring operations* $\cdot$ *and* $+$ *is more similar to the interplay between the MV-operations* $\odot$ *and* $\vee$ *rather than that between the MV-operations* $\odot$ *and* $\oplus$.

Next we discuss why we include only Equation (2). Recall that $d(0) = 0$ *is the 0-ary version of* $d(x+y) = d(x) + d(y)$ *in derivations on a ring. For MV-algebras,* $d(0) = 0$ *is the 0-ary version of (a); see Proposition 1 (1).* $d(1) = 0$ *is the 0-ary version of* $d(x \cdot y) = d(x) \cdot d(y)$ *in derivations on a ring. Hence, it seems that the most faithful and natural derivation notion on A as a translation of the ring-theoretic notion of derivation (cf. Introduction) would include:*

(a) $d(x \odot y) = (d(x) \odot y) \vee (x \odot d(y))$,
(b) $d(1) = 0$,
(c) $d(x \vee y) = d(x) \vee d(y)$,
(d) $d(0) = 0$.

However, (b) and (c) imply that d is trivial (note that (a) is automatically assumed).

Lemma 3. *If A is an* MV*-algebra and* $d : A \to A$ *is a map satisfying* (a), (b) *and* (c) *for any* $x, y \in A$. *Then,* $d = \mathbf{0}_A$.

Proof. Assume $x \leq y$, it follows from (c) that $d(y) = d(x \vee y) = d(x) \vee d(y)$ and thus $d(x) \leq d(y)$. Together with (b) $d(1) = 0$, we have $d(x) = 0$ for any $x \in A$ since $x \leq 1$. Hence, $d = \mathbf{0}_A$. □

Next, we consider what will happen if the condition (b′) $d(1) = 1$ replaces (b) $d(1) = 0$.

Lemma 4. *If* $d : A \to A$ *is a mapping from an* MV*-algebra A to A with* (a) *and* (b′) *for any* $x, y \in A$, *then,* $d = \mathrm{Id}_A$.

Proof. Assume d satisfies (a) and (b′). We obtain that d satisfies Proposition 1 (3) since d satisfies (a). Both with (b′) $d(1) = 1$, we obtain $d(x) = x$ for any $x \in A$. Therefore, $d = \mathrm{Id}_A$. □

Recall that for a given $a \in A$, a **principal** $(\odot, \vee)$-derivation d_a on A [16] is defined by $d_a(x) := a \odot x$ for all $x \in A$. An $(\odot, \vee)$-derivation d is **isotone** [16] if $\forall x, y \in A$, $y \geq x$ implies that $d(y) \geq d(x)$. Note that $\mathbf{0}_A$ and Id_A are both principal and isotone. More generally, we obtain the following.

Proposition 2 ([16] (Proposition 3.19)). *Let A be an MV-algebra and d be a map satisfying* (a) *and* (b″). *Then, the followings are equivalent:*

1. *d is isotone;*
2. $d(1) \odot x = d(x)$ *for all* $x \in A$;
3. $d(x) \vee d(y) = d(x \vee y)$.

If d satisfies (b), then the principal derivations on MV-algebra A will not be included, expect $\mathbf{0}_A$. Even identity derivations Id_A will not be within our scope of consideration. Hence, the scope of the study will be significantly narrowed.

Remark 2. *Note that d is isotone if d satisfies* (c). *In fact, if* $x \leq y$, *then* $d(y) = d(x \vee y) = d(x) \vee d(y)$ *and thus* $d(x) \leq d(y)$. *The isotone case is a special case of d, thus the scope of research will be narrowed. This case has been partially studied in [16], Section 3.3.*

Therefore, we use the derivation meaning from Definition 2 in our series papers since [16] on.

3. $(\odot, \vee)$-Multiderivations on an MV-Algebra

Let X and Y be two nonempty sets. Recall that a **set-valued function** or **multivalued function** (for short, **multifunction**) F between X and Y is a map $F : X \to \Delta(Y)$. The set $F(x)$ is called the image of x under F (cf. [26], Appendix A).

Definition 3. *Let A be an* MV*-algebra and $M, N \in \Delta(A)$. We define four binary operations $\oplus, \odot, \vee, \wedge$ and an unary operation $*$ on $\Delta(A)$ by:*

$$M \star N = \{m \star n \mid m \in M, n \in N\} \text{ and } M^* = \{m^* \mid m \in M\}$$

where $\star \in \{\oplus, \odot, \vee, \wedge\}$.

Remark 3.

1. *Note that $M \vee N$ means the pointwise $m \vee n$ operation from Equation* (1) *of sets, which is different from the supremum of M and N. $M \wedge N$ has a similar meaning.*
2. *We abbreviate $M \star \{x\}$ and $\{x\}^*$ by $M \star x$ and x^*, respectively. But if $\{x\}$ appears by itself such as $M \preceq \{x\}$, we still use $\{x\}$.*

We define a binary relation $M \preceq N$ iff for every $m \in M$ there exists $n \in N$ such that $m \leq n$. Denote $M \prec N$ if $M \preceq N$ and $M \neq N$.

Then, $\preceq$ is a preorder on $\Delta(A)$. In fact, the reflexivity and transitivity of $\preceq$ are clear. However, $\preceq$ does not satisfy antisymmetry in general. In fact, $\preceq$ satisfies antisymmetry iff the MV-algebra A is trivial: If A is trivial, we have $\Delta(A) = \{\{0\}\}$ and $\{0\} \preceq \{0\}$. Hence, $\preceq$ satisfies antisymmetry. Conversely, suppose A is nontrivial, we have $A \neq \{1\}$, but $\{1\} \preceq A$ and $A \preceq \{1\}$, a contradiction.

Lemma 5. *Let A be an* MV*-algebra and $x, a, b, c, e, f \in A$. Then, the followings hold:*

1. *If $x \leq b \odot c$, then there exists $t \in A$ such that $t \leq b$ and $x = t \odot c$.*
2. *If $x \leq b \vee c$, then there exist $t, s \in A$ such that $t \leq b, s \leq c$ and $x = t \vee s$.*
3. *$[a, b] \odot c = [a \odot c, b \odot c]$.*
4. *$[a, b] \vee [e, f] = [a \vee e, b \vee f]$.*

Proof. (1) Assume $x \leq b \odot c$, then

$$x = (b \odot c) \wedge x = (b \odot c) \odot ((b \odot c)^* \oplus x) = b \odot ((b \odot c)^* \oplus x) \odot c.$$

Thus, we may choose $t = b \odot ((b \odot c)^* \oplus x)$.

(2) Assume $x \leq b \vee c$. Recall that A is a distributive lattice. So

$$x = (b \vee c) \wedge x = (b \wedge x) \vee (c \wedge x).$$

Hence, we can obtain $x = t \vee s$ by taking $t = b \wedge x, s = c \wedge x$.

(3) For each $x \in [a, b]$, we obtain $a \odot c \leq x \odot c \leq b \odot c$ by Lemma 1 (4). Thus, $[a, b] \odot c \subseteq [a \odot c, b \odot c]$. It suffices to prove that $[a \odot c, b \odot c] \subseteq [a, b] \odot c$. For any $a \odot c \leq x \leq b \odot c$, by (1) there is $t = b \odot ((b \odot c)^* \oplus x) \leq b$ such that $x = t \odot c$. If we can prove $a \leq t$, then the result follows immediately. Note that

$$t = b \odot ((b \odot c)^* \oplus x) = b \odot (b^* \oplus c^* \oplus x) = b \wedge (c^* \oplus x).$$

Since $a \odot c \leq x$, we have $a \leq c^* \oplus x$ by Lemma 1 (8). Together with $a \leq b$, we obtain $a \leq b \wedge (c^* \oplus x) = t$. Thus, we conclude that $[a, b] \odot c = [a \odot c, b \odot c]$.

(4) For any $t \in [a, b], s \in [e, f]$, we have $a \vee e \leq t \vee s \leq b \vee f$ by Lemma 1 (3). Thus, $[a, b] \vee [e, f] \subseteq [a \vee e, b \vee f]$. It is enough to prove that $[a \vee e, b \vee f] \subseteq [a, b] \vee [e, f]$. For any $a \vee e \leq x \leq b \vee f$, there exist $t, s \in A$ such that

$$t = b \wedge x \leq b, \quad s = f \wedge x \leq f \quad \text{and} \quad x = t \vee s$$

by (2). If we can prove $a \leq t$ and $e \leq s$, then the result follows. Note that since $a \leq b$ and $a \leq a \vee e \leq x$, we have $a \leq b \wedge x = t$. Similarly, $e \leq s$. Therefore, $[a \vee e, b \vee f] = [a, b] \vee [e, f]$. □

The following result holds for any MV-algebra A since it is a distributive lattice under the natural order.

Lemma 6 ([23] (Lemma 2.1)). *Let L be a lattice and $M, N, P, Q \in \Delta(L)$. Then, the following statements hold:*

1. $M \wedge N \preceq M \preceq M \vee N$.
2. *If* $M \preceq N$ *and* $P \preceq Q$, *then* $M \wedge P \preceq N \wedge Q$ *and* $M \vee P \preceq N \vee Q$. *In particular,* $M \preceq N$ *implies* $M \wedge P \preceq N \wedge P$.
3. $M \subseteq M \wedge M, M \subseteq M \vee M$. *If M is a sublattice of L, then* $M = M \vee M$.
4. $M \vee N = N \vee M$.
5. $(M \vee N) \vee P = M \vee (N \vee P)$.
6. *If* $M \vee N \subseteq M$, *then* $N \preceq M$.
7. *If L is distributive, then* $(M \vee N) \wedge P \subseteq (M \wedge P) \vee (N \wedge P)$.

Remark 4.

1. *Note that the converse inclusion of Lemma 6 (3), i.e.,* $M \wedge M \subseteq M$ *and* $M \vee M \subseteq M$, *does not hold in general. For example, consider the Boolean lattice* $B_4 = \{0, a, b, 1\}$ *(see Figure 1),* $M = \{a, b\} \subseteq B_4$, *then* $0 = a \wedge b \in M \wedge M$ *and* $1 = a \vee b \in M \vee M$, *but* $0, 1 \notin M$.
2. *The converse of Lemma 6 (6), i.e.,* $N \preceq M$ *implies* $M \vee N \subseteq M$ *may not hold. For example, in* L_3, *let* $N = \{0, \frac{1}{2}\}, M = \{0, 1\}$. *We have* $N \preceq M$ *but* $M \vee N = \{0, \frac{1}{2}, 1\} \nsubseteq M$.
3. *The converse inclusion of Lemma 6 (7) holds if P is a singleton but need not hold in general. This is slightly different from [23]. For example, let* $B_8 = \{0, a, b, c, u, v, w, 1\}$ *be the 8-element Boolean lattice as Figure 2,* $M = \{u\}, N = \{w\}$ *and* $P = \{a, b, c\}$. *We can check that* $u = a \vee b = (u \wedge a) \vee (w \wedge b) \in (M \wedge P) \vee (N \wedge P)$ *but* $u \notin P = (M \vee N) \wedge P$.

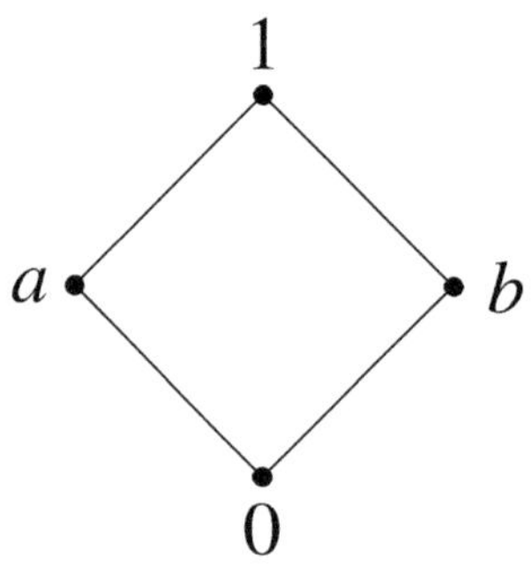

Figure 1. Hasse diagram of B_4.

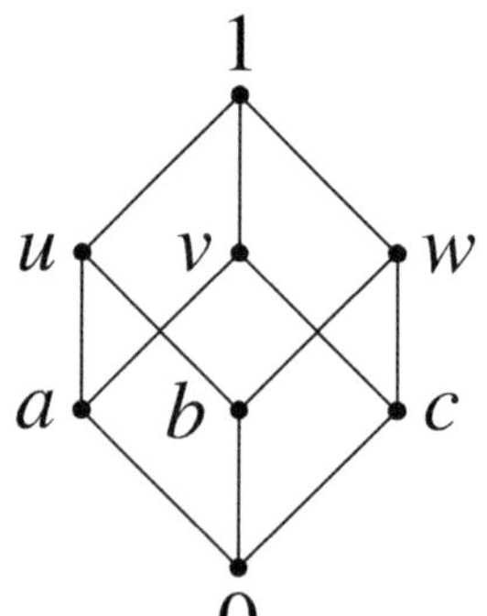

Figure 2. Hasse diagram of B_8.

According to Lemma 1, one obtains

Lemma 7. *Assume that A is an MV-algebra, $M, N, P, Q \in \Delta(A)$, and $m \in M$. Then, the following statements hold:*

1. *If $M \preceq N$ and $P \preceq Q$, then $M \oplus P \preceq N \oplus Q$ and $M \odot P \preceq N \odot Q$. In particular, $M \preceq N$ implies $M \oplus P \preceq N \oplus P$ and $M \odot P \preceq N \odot P$.*
2. $m \odot (P \vee Q) = (m \odot P) \vee (m \odot Q)$.
3. $m \odot (P \cup Q) = (m \odot P) \cup (m \odot Q)$.
4. $M \odot N \preceq M \wedge N \preceq M \preceq M \vee N \preceq M \oplus N$.
5. *If $M \oplus N \subseteq M$, then $N \preceq M$.*

Proof. (1) Suppose $M \preceq N$ and $P \preceq Q$. For any $x = m \oplus p \in M \oplus P$, there are $n \in N$ and $q \in Q$ such that $m \leq n$ and $p \leq q$. It follows from Lemma 1 (4) that $m \oplus p \leq m \oplus q \leq n \oplus q$, where $n \oplus q \in N \oplus Q$. Thus, $M \oplus P \preceq N \oplus Q$. Similarly, we have $M \odot P \preceq N \odot Q$. In particular, we obtain $M \oplus P \preceq N \oplus P$ and $M \odot P \preceq N \odot P$.

(2) For any $p \in P$ and $q \in Q$, we have $m \odot (p \vee q) = (m \odot p) \vee (m \odot q) \in (m \odot P) \vee (m \odot Q)$ by Lemma 1 (7). Thus, $m \odot (P \vee Q) \subseteq (m \odot P) \vee (m \odot Q)$. The reverse inclusion can be verified similarly. Therefore, $m \odot (P \vee Q) = (m \odot P) \vee (m \odot Q)$.

(3) We have $x \in m \odot (P \cup Q)$, iff there is $y \in P \cup Q$ such that $x = m \odot y$, iff there is $y \in P$ or $y \in Q$ such that $x = m \odot y$, iff $x \in m \odot P$ or $x \in m \odot Q$, iff $x \in (m \odot P) \cup (m \odot Q)$. Hence, $m \odot (P \cup Q) = (m \odot P) \cup (m \odot Q)$.

(4) For any $m \in M$ and $n \in N$, we know $m \odot n \leq m \wedge n \leq m \leq m \vee n \leq m \oplus n$ by Lemma 1 (1). The result follows immediately.

(5) Assume $M \oplus N \subseteq M$, then for any $n \in N$, there exists $m \in M$ such that $m \oplus n \in M$. So by Lemma 1 (1) we obtain $n \leq m \oplus n$. Therefore, $N \preceq M$. □

To study whether $(\Delta(A), \oplus, ^*, \{0\})$ is an MV-algebra, we first give

Lemma 8. *If A is an MV-algebra, then, for any $M, N, P \in \Delta(A)$, the followings hold:*

1. $(M \oplus N) \oplus P = M \oplus (N \oplus P)$.
2. $M \oplus N = N \oplus M$.
3. $M \oplus 0 = M$.
4. $M^{**} = M$.
5. $M \oplus 0^* = \{0^*\}$.

Proof. (1)–(5) follow from (MV1)–(MV5), respectively. □

Remark 5. *Since (MV1)–(MV5) are satisfied on $\Delta(A)$, it is natural to consider whether (MV6) $(M^* \oplus N)^* \oplus N = (N^* \oplus M)^* \oplus M$ holds on $\Delta(A)$. The answer is no. For example, let $M = \{\frac{1}{2}\}$ and $N = \{0, 1\}$ on three-element MV-chain L_3. It is easy to see that $(\frac{1}{2}^* \oplus \{0,1\})^* \oplus \{0,1\} = \{0, \frac{1}{2}\} \oplus \{0,1\} = \{0, \frac{1}{2}, 1\} \neq \{\frac{1}{2}, 1\} = (\{0,1\}^* \oplus \frac{1}{2})^* \oplus \frac{1}{2}$. That is, $(M^* \oplus N)^* \oplus N \neq (N^* \oplus M)^* \oplus M$.*

If A is a nontrivial MV-algebra, and $\varphi : A \to \Delta(A)$ is a multifunction on A. φ is called additive and negative, if $\varphi(x \oplus y) = \varphi(x) \oplus \varphi(y)$ and $\varphi(x^*) = (\varphi(x))^*$ for all $x, y \in A$, respectively.

Proposition 3. *Let A be an MV-algebra and $\varphi : A \to \Delta(A)$ be a multifunction on A. If φ is additive and negative, then $(\varphi(A), \oplus, ^*, \varphi(0))$ is an MV-algebra, where $\varphi(A) = \{\varphi(x) \mid x \in A\}$.*

Proof. It is sufficient to prove (MV3), (MV5) and (MV6), since we know that $(\varphi(A), \oplus, ^*, \varphi(0))$ satisfies (MV1), (MV2) and (MV4) by Lemma 8. Since φ is additive and negative, it follows that $\varphi(x) \oplus \varphi(0) = \varphi(x \oplus 0) = \varphi(x)$ and $\varphi(x) \oplus \varphi(0)^* = \varphi(x \oplus 0^*) = \varphi(0^*) = \varphi(0)^*$. Furthermore, $(\varphi(x)^* \oplus \varphi(y))^* \oplus \varphi(y) = \varphi(x^* \oplus y)^* \oplus \varphi(y) = \varphi((x^* \oplus y)^* \oplus y) = \varphi((y^* \oplus x)^* \oplus x) = \varphi(y^* \oplus x)^* \oplus \varphi(x) = (\varphi(y)^* \oplus \varphi(x))^* \oplus \varphi(x)$ for any $x, y \in A$. Thus, $(\varphi(A), \oplus, ^*, \varphi(0))$ is an MV-algebra. □

Now let us define the $(\odot, \vee)$-multiderivation.

Definition 4. If A is an MV-algebra, a multifunction $\sigma : A \to \Delta(A)$ is called an $(\odot, \vee)$-**multiderivation on** A if

$$\sigma(x \odot y) = (\sigma(x) \odot y) \vee (x \odot \sigma(y)) \tag{3}$$

for all $x, y \in A$. Denote the set of $(\odot, \vee)$-multiderivations on A by $\mathrm{MD}(A)$.

Example 3. *(i) Consider the* MV*-chain* L_4*. We define a multifunction* σ *on* L_4 *by* $\sigma(0) = \{0\}$, $\sigma(\frac{1}{3}) = \{0, \frac{1}{3}\}, \sigma(\frac{2}{3}) = \{0, \frac{2}{3}\}, \sigma(1) = \{0, 1\}$*. Then, we can check* σ *is an* $(\odot, \vee)$*-multiderivation on* L_4*. In fact,* $\sigma = \beta_1$ *(see Corollary 1).*

(ii) Consider the standard MV*-algebra* $L = [0, 1]$*. We define a multifunction* $\sigma : L \to \Delta(L)$ *by* $\sigma(x) = [0, x]$ *for all* $x \in L$*. Then, we can verify that* σ *is an* $(\odot, \vee)$*-multiderivation on* L *(see Proposition 6).*

(iii) Let A *be an* MV*-algebra and* $S \subseteq A$ *be a subalgebra of* A*. Define a multifunction* σ_S *on* A *by* $\sigma_S(x) = x \odot S$, $\forall x \in A$*, then* $\sigma_S \in \mathrm{MD}(A)$*, which is called a* ***principal*** $(\odot, \vee)$*-****multiderivation****. In fact, for any* $x, y \in A$*, since the subalgebra* S *must be a sublattice of* A*, it follows that* $S = S \vee S$ *by Lemma 6 (3). According to Lemma 7 (2), we immediately have* $\sigma_S(x \odot y) = x \odot y \odot S = x \odot y \odot (S \vee S) = (x \odot y \odot S) \vee (x \odot y \odot S) = (\sigma_S(x) \odot y) \vee (x \odot \sigma_S(y))$.

Proposition 4. *If* A *is an* MV*-algebra and* $\sigma \in \mathrm{MD}(A)$*. Then, the followings hold for all* $x, y \in A$,

1. $\sigma(0) = \{0\}$.
2. $\sigma(x) \preceq \{x\}$.
3. $\sigma(x) \odot \sigma(y) \preceq \sigma(x \odot y) \preceq \sigma(x) \vee \sigma(y)$.
4. $x \odot \sigma(1) \preceq \sigma(x)$.
5. *If* I *is a lower set of* A*, then* $\sigma(x) \subseteq I$ *holds for any* $x \in I$*.*
6. *Let* $1 \in \sigma(1)$*. Then,* $x \in \sigma(x)$*.*

Proof. (1) Taking $x = y = 0$ in Equation (3), we obtain $\sigma(0) = \sigma(0 \odot 0) = (\sigma(0) \odot 0) \vee (0 \odot \sigma(0)) = \{0\}$.

(2) Since $x \odot x^* = 0$, we know that $\{0\} = \sigma(0) = \sigma(x \odot x^*) = (\sigma(x) \odot x^*) \vee (x \odot \sigma(x^*))$ by (1). So $\sigma(x) \odot x^* = \{0\}$ and we obtain $\sigma(x) \preceq \{x\}$.

(3) By Lemma 6 (3), we have $\sigma(x) \odot \sigma(y) \subseteq (\sigma(x) \odot \sigma(y)) \vee (\sigma(x) \odot \sigma(y))$. Moreover, $\sigma(x) \odot \sigma(y) \preceq \sigma(x) \odot y$ and $\sigma(x) \odot \sigma(y) \preceq x \odot \sigma(y)$ by (2) and Lemma 7 (1). Thus,

$$\sigma(x) \odot \sigma(y) \subseteq (\sigma(x) \odot \sigma(y)) \vee (\sigma(x) \odot \sigma(y)) \preceq (\sigma(x) \odot y) \vee (x \odot \sigma(y)) = \sigma(x \odot y)$$

by Lemma 6 (2). Moreover, by Lemma 7 (1) and Lemma 6 (2) we have

$$\sigma(x \odot y) = (\sigma(x) \odot y) \vee (x \odot \sigma(y)) \preceq \sigma(x) \vee \sigma(y).$$

(4) Since $x = 1 \odot x$, it follows that $\sigma(x) = \sigma(1 \odot x) = \sigma(x) \vee (x \odot \sigma(1))$ by Equation (3). Then, we can obtain $x \odot \sigma(1) \preceq \sigma(x)$ by Lemma 6 (6).

(5) For any $x \in I$, we know $\sigma(x) \preceq \{x\}$ by (2). It induces that $y \leq x$ holds for any $y \in \sigma(x)$. Then, $y \in I$ since I is a lower set. Thus, $\sigma(x) \subseteq I$.

(6) Since $1 \in \sigma(1)$, there must exist $y \in \sigma(x)$ such that $x = x \odot 1 \leq y$ by (4). Moreover, by (2) we know $y \leq x$ always holds for y. Hence, we obtain $x = y$ and $x \in \sigma(x)$. □

Now, let us explore the relations between $(\odot, \vee)$-derivation d and $(\odot, \vee)$-multiderivation σ on A.

On the one hand, given an $(\odot, \vee)$-derivation d on A, how can we construct an $(\odot, \vee)$-multiderivation on A? We get started with a direct construction. Assume $d \in \mathrm{Der}(A)$. Define a multifunction $\alpha : A \to \Delta(A)$ as follows:

$$\alpha(x) = \{d(x)\} \quad \text{for any } x \in A.$$

Then, $\alpha \in \mathrm{MD}(A)$.

Proposition 5. *If A is an* MV*-algebra and $d \in \mathrm{Der}(A)$, define a multifunction $\beta : A \to \Delta(A)$ on A as follows*

$$\beta(x) := \{0, d(x)\}.$$

Then, $\beta \in \mathrm{MD}(A)$ iff $d(x) \odot y = x \odot d(y)$ holds for any $x, y \in A$ with $d(x) \odot y > 0$ and $x \odot d(y) > 0$.

Proof. Assuming $\beta \in \mathrm{MD}(A)$, it follows that

$$\begin{aligned}\{0, d(x \odot y)\} &= \beta(x \odot y) \\ &= (\beta(x) \odot y) \vee (x \odot \beta(y)) \\ &= (\{0, d(x)\} \odot y) \vee (x \odot \{0, d(y)\}) \\ &= \{0, d(x) \odot y\} \vee \{0, x \odot d(y)\} \\ &= \{0, d(x) \odot y, x \odot d(y), d(x \odot y)\}\end{aligned}$$

for any $x, y \in A$. From the chain of equalities, we know that $d(x) \odot y, x \odot d(y) \in \{0, d(x \odot y)\}$. If both $d(x) \odot y > 0$ and $x \odot d(y) > 0$, then $d(x) \odot y = d(x \odot y) = x \odot d(y)$.

Conversely, let $x, y \in A$.

Then,

$$\beta(x \odot y) = \{0, d(x \odot y)\}$$

and

$$(\beta(x) \odot y) \vee (x \odot \beta(y)) = \{0, d(x) \odot y, x \odot d(y), d(x \odot y)\}.$$

There are only two cases:

If $d(x) \odot y = 0$ or $x \odot d(y) = 0$, without loss of generality, assume that $d(x) \odot y = 0$. Then,

$$d(x \odot y) = 0 \vee (x \odot d(y)) = x \odot d(y).$$

Thus, $(\beta(x) \odot y) \vee (x \odot \beta(y)) = \{0, d(x \odot y)\} = \beta(x \odot y)$.

If $d(x) \odot y = x \odot d(y)$, then

$$d(x \odot y) = d(x) \odot y = x \odot d(y).$$

Thus, $(\beta(x) \odot y) \vee (x \odot \beta(y)) = \{0, d(x \odot y)\} = \beta(x \odot y)$.

Consequently, we infer $\beta \in \mathrm{MD}(A)$. □

Corollary 1. *If A is an* MV*-algebra, and $a \in A$, a multifunction $\beta_a : A \to \Delta(A)$ on A is defined as follows*

$$\beta_a(x) := \{0, d_a(x)\}.$$

Then $\beta_a \in \mathrm{MD}(A)$.

Proof. If $d = d_a$ in Proposition 5, then for any $x, y \in A$, we know $d(x) \odot y = a \odot x \odot y = x \odot d(y)$. Hence, we infer that $\beta_a \in \mathrm{MD}(A)$ by Proposition 5. □

Remark 6. *The conclusion is not necessarily true for general $(\odot, \vee)$-derivations. For example, $d = \begin{pmatrix} 0 & \frac{1}{3} & \frac{2}{3} & 1 \\ 0 & \frac{1}{3} & \frac{2}{3} & \frac{2}{3} \end{pmatrix}$ is an $(\odot, \vee)$-derivation on L_4. But $\beta(\frac{2}{3} \odot 1) = \{0, \frac{2}{3}\} \neq \{0, \frac{1}{3}, \frac{2}{3}\} = \{0, \frac{2}{3}\} \vee \{0, \frac{1}{3}\} = (\{0, \frac{2}{3}\} \odot 1) \vee (\frac{2}{3} \odot \{0, \frac{2}{3}\}) = (\beta(\frac{2}{3}) \odot 1) \vee (\frac{2}{3} \odot \beta(1))$.*

Proposition 6. *Let A be an* MV*-algebra and $d \in \mathrm{Der}(A)$. Define a multifunction $\gamma : A \to \Delta(A)$ on A as follows*

$$\gamma(x) := [0, d(x)].$$

Then $\gamma \in \mathrm{MD}(A)$.

Proof. Since $d \in \mathrm{Der}(A)$, we obtain $\gamma(x \odot y) = [0, d(x \odot y)] = [0, (d(x) \odot y) \vee (x \odot d(y))]$. Moreover, we have

$$\begin{aligned}(\gamma(x) \odot y) \vee (x \odot \gamma(y)) &= ([0, d(x)] \odot y) \vee (x \odot [0, d(y)]) && \text{(Definition 3)}\\ &= [0, d(x) \odot y] \vee [0, x \odot d(y)] && \text{(Lemma 5 (3))}\\ &= [0, (d(x) \odot y) \vee (x \odot d(y))]. && \text{(Lemma 5 (4))}\end{aligned}$$

Hence, we conclude that $\gamma \in \mathrm{MD}(A)$. □

On the other hand, if there is a given $(\odot, \vee)$-multiderivation σ on A, then we can construct a corresponding $(\odot, \vee)$-derivation d from σ. We need the following lemma to prepare.

Lemma 9. *If A is an* MV*-algebra, and $M, N \in \Delta(A)$, if both* $\sup(M)$ *and* $\sup(N)$ *exist, then*

1. $\sup(M \odot N)$ *exists and* $\sup(M \odot N) = \sup(M) \odot \sup(N)$.
2. $\sup(M \vee N)$ *exists and* $\sup(M \vee N) = \sup(M) \vee \sup(N)$.

Proof. Denote $m_0 = \sup(M)$ and $n_0 = \sup(N)$.

(1) Firstly, we prove that $m_0 \odot n_0$ is an upper bound of $M \odot N$. For any $m \in M$ and $n \in N$, we immediately have $m \odot n \leq m_0 \odot n_0$ by Lemma 1 (4). Hence, it is enough to show that $m_0 \odot n_0$ is the least upper bound. Assume that $m \odot n \leq x$ for all $m \in M, n \in N$. It tells us that $m \leq n^* \oplus x$ and so $m_0 \leq n^* \oplus x$ by Lemma 1 (8) and the definition of least upper bound. Then, we have $m_0 \odot n \leq x$. Similarly, we obtain $n \leq m_0^* \oplus x$ and $n_0 \leq m_0^* \oplus x$. Thus, we can prove that $m_0 \odot n_0 \leq x$. Finally, $\sup(M \odot N) = \sup(M) \odot \sup(N)$ holds.

(2) For any $m \in M$ and $n \in N$, we have $m \leq m_0$ and $n \leq n_0$. So, $m \vee n \leq m_0 \vee n_0$ and $\sup(M \vee N) \leq \sup(M) \vee \sup(N)$. Conversely, since $M \vee N \succeq M, N$, it implies that $\sup(M \vee N) \geq \sup(M), \sup(N)$ and thus $\sup(M \vee N) \geq \sup(M) \vee \sup(N)$. Therefore, $\sup(M \vee N) = \sup(M) \vee \sup(N)$. □

Proposition 7. *If A is an* MV*-algebra, $\sigma \in \mathrm{MD}(A)$, and $\sup(\sigma(x))$ exists for any $x \in A$, define $\sup\sigma : A \to A$ by $(\sup\sigma)(x) = \sup(\sigma(x))$. Then, $\sup\sigma \in \mathrm{Der}(A)$.*

Proof. For any $x, y \in A$, we have

$$\begin{aligned}(\sup\sigma)(x \odot y) &= \sup(\sigma(x \odot y)) && \text{(Definition of } \sup\sigma)\\ &= \sup((\sigma(x) \odot y) \vee (x \odot \sigma(y))) && \text{(Equation (3))}\\ &= \sup(\sigma(x) \odot y) \vee \sup(x \odot \sigma(y)) && \text{(Lemma 9 (2))}\\ &= (\sup(\sigma(x)) \odot \sup\{y\}) \vee (\sup\{x\} \odot \sup(\sigma(y))) && \text{(Lemma 9 (1))}\\ &= ((\sup\sigma)(x) \odot y) \vee (x \odot (\sup\sigma)(y)). && \text{(Definition of } \sup\sigma)\end{aligned}$$

Hence, $\sup\sigma \in \mathrm{Der}(A)$. □

Remark 7. (1) *If* MV*-algebra A is complete, then $\sup\sigma$ is always an $(\odot, \vee)$-derivation on A for an arbitrary $(\odot, \vee)$-multiderivation σ on A.*

(2) *If $\sigma \in \mathrm{MD}(A)$ and the image $\sigma(x)$ is finite for any $x \in A$, then $\sup\sigma$ is always an $(\odot, \vee)$-derivation on A.*

Next, we construct $(\odot, \vee)$-multiderivations on subalgebras and direct products of MV-algebras from a given $(\odot, \vee)$-multiderivation.

Proposition 8. *Let A be an* MV*-algebra and $\sigma \in \mathrm{MD}(A)$. If S is a subalgebra of A and $\sigma(x) \subseteq S$ for any $x \in S$, then $\sigma|_S \in \mathrm{MD}(S)$.*

Proof. For any $x, y \in S$, we know that $\sigma(x), \sigma(y) \subseteq S$ and so $\sigma(x) \odot y, x \odot \sigma(y) \subseteq S$. Then,

$$\sigma|_S(x \odot y) = (\sigma(x) \odot y) \vee (x \odot \sigma(y)) = (\sigma|_S(x) \odot y) \vee (x \odot \sigma|_S(y)) \subseteq S \vee S = S$$

by Lemma 6 (3). Thus, $\sigma|_S \in \mathrm{MD}(S)$. □

Definition 5. If Ω is a nonempty set, for each $i \in \Omega$, let σ_i be a multifunction on A_i. The **direct product of** $\{\sigma_i\}_{i\in\Omega}$ $\prod_{i\in\Omega}\sigma_i : \prod_{i\in\Omega} A_i \to \Delta(\prod_{i\in\Omega} A_i)$ is defined by

$$\left(\prod_{i\in\Omega}\sigma_i\right)(g) = \prod_{i\in\Omega}\sigma_i(g(i)) = \{(x_i)_{i\in\Omega} \mid x_i \in \sigma_i(g(i))\}$$

for all $g \in \prod_{i\in\Omega} A_i$.

Lemma 10. *Let Ω be a nonempty set, $\{A_i\}_{i\in\Omega}$ be a family of* MV*-algebras, and $M_i, N_i \in \Delta(A_i)$. Then, $\prod_{i\in\Omega}(M_i \vee N_i) = \prod_{i\in\Omega} M_i \vee \prod_{i\in\Omega} N_i$.*

Proof. We first show that $\prod_{i\in\Omega}(M_i \vee N_i) \subseteq \prod_{i\in\Omega} M_i \vee \prod_{i\in\Omega} N_i$. For any $x \in \prod_{i\in\Omega}(M_i \vee N_i)$, there are $m_i \in M_i, n_i \in N_i$ for any $i \in \Omega$ such that $x = (m_i \vee n_i)_{i\in\Omega}$. Denote $m = (m_i)_{i\in\Omega}, n = (n_i)_{i\in\Omega}$, we have $x = (m_i \vee n_i)_{i\in\Omega} = (m_i)_{i\in\Omega} \vee (n_i)_{i\in\Omega} = m \vee n \in \prod_{i\in\Omega} M_i \vee \prod_{i\in\Omega} N_i$. And vice versa. Therefore, $\prod_{i\in\Omega}(M_i \vee N_i) = \prod_{i\in\Omega} M_i \vee \prod_{i\in\Omega} N_i$. □

Proposition 9. *Assume that Ω is a nonempty set and $\{A_i\}_{i\in\Omega}$ is a family of* MV*-algebras. Then, $\sigma_i \in \mathrm{MD}(A_i)$ for any $i \in \Omega$ iff $\prod_{i\in\Omega}\sigma_i \in \mathrm{MD}(\prod_{i\in\Omega} A_i)$.*

Proof. Denote $A = \prod_{i\in\Omega} A_i$ and $\sigma = \prod_{i\in\Omega}\sigma_i$. For all $x = (x_i)_{i\in\Omega}, y = (y_i)_{i\in\Omega} \in A$, we have

$$\sigma(x \odot y) = \sigma((x_i)_{i\in\Omega} \odot (y_i)_{i\in\Omega}) = \prod_{i\in\Omega}\sigma_i(x_i \odot y_i),$$

$$\begin{aligned}
(\sigma(x) \odot y) \vee (x \odot \sigma(y)) &= \left(\prod_{i\in\Omega}\sigma_i(x_i) \odot (y_i)_{i\in\Omega}\right) \vee \left((x_i)_{i\in\Omega} \odot \prod_{i\in\Omega}\sigma_i(y_i)\right) \\
&= \prod_{i\in\Omega}(\sigma_i(x_i) \odot y_i) \vee \prod_{i\in\Omega}(x_i \odot \sigma_i(y_i)) \\
&= \prod_{i\in\Omega}((\sigma_i(x_i) \odot y_i) \vee (x_i \odot \sigma_i(y_i))). && \text{(Lemma 10)}
\end{aligned}$$

We can immediately obtain $\sigma_i \in \mathrm{MD}(A_i)$ for all $i \in \Omega$ iff $\sigma(x \odot y) = (\sigma(x) \odot y) \vee (x \odot \sigma(y))$ by Equation (3). □

Finally, we investigate the condition when an $(\odot, \vee)$-multiderivation σ is isotone.

Definition 6. *If A is an* MV*-algebra, and $\sigma \in \mathrm{MD}(A)$, we say σ is* ***isotone*** *if $\sigma(x) \preceq \sigma(y)$ whenever $x \leq y$.*

Proposition 10. *If A is an* MV*-algebra, and $\sigma \in \mathrm{MD}(A)$, then σ is isotone iff $\sigma(x \wedge y) \preceq \sigma(x) \wedge y$ for all $x, y \in A$.*

Proof. Assume σ is isotone, then,

$$\sigma(x \wedge y) \subseteq \sigma(x \wedge y) \wedge \sigma(x \wedge y) \preceq \sigma(x) \wedge \sigma(y) \preceq \sigma(x) \wedge y$$

by Lemma 6 (3) and (2). Conversely, assume that $\sigma(x \wedge y) \preceq \sigma(y) \wedge x$ for all $x, y \in A$. Let $x, y \in A$ with $x \leq y$. Then, $\sigma(x) = \sigma(y \wedge x) \preceq \sigma(y) \wedge x$. Thus, for every $a \in \sigma(x)$ there is $b \in \sigma(y)$ such that $a \leq b \wedge x$. Hence, $a \leq b$ and so $\sigma(x) \preceq \sigma(y)$. □

Corollary 2. *If A is an* MV*-algebra, and $S \subseteq A$ is a subalgebra of A, then the principal $(\odot, \vee)$-multiderivation σ_S is isotone.*

Proof. Method 1: Let $x, y \in A$ and $x \leq y$. For any $s \in S$, Lemma 1 (4) implies $x \odot s \leq y \odot s$. Thus, $\sigma_S(x) \preceq \sigma_S(y)$.

Method 2: It is enough to verify that $\sigma_S(x \wedge y) \preceq \sigma_S(x) \wedge y$ for all $x, y \in A$ by Proposition 10. For any $s \in S$, Lemma 1 (6) implies

$$(x \wedge y) \odot s = (x \odot s) \wedge (y \odot s) \leq (x \odot s) \wedge y.$$

Thus, $\sigma_S(x \wedge y) = (x \wedge y) \odot S \preceq (x \odot S) \wedge y = \sigma_S(x) \wedge y$. □

4. The Order Structure of $(\odot, \vee)$-Multiderivations on a Finite MV-Chain

Let $\mathrm{MF}(A)$ be the set of multifunctions on an MV-algebra A. Define $\preccurlyeq$ on $\mathrm{MF}(A)$ by:

$$(\forall\, \sigma, \sigma' \in \mathrm{MF}(A)) \quad \sigma \preccurlyeq \sigma' \text{ if } \sigma(x) \preceq \sigma'(x), \forall x \in A.$$

Then, $\preccurlyeq$ is a preorder on $\mathrm{MF}(A)$ and $\mathbf{0}_{\mathrm{MF}(A)} \preccurlyeq \sigma \preccurlyeq \mathbf{1}_{\mathrm{MF}(A)}$ for any $\sigma \in \mathrm{MF}(A)$, where $\mathbf{0}_{\mathrm{MF}(A)}$ and $\mathbf{1}_{\mathrm{MF}(A)}$ are defined by $\mathbf{0}_{\mathrm{MF}(A)}(x) := \{0\}$ and $\mathbf{1}_{\mathrm{MF}(A)}(x) := \{1\}$ for any $x \in A$, respectively. For any $\sigma \in \mathrm{MD}(A)$, we have $\mathbf{0}_{\mathrm{MF}(A)} \preccurlyeq \sigma \preccurlyeq \mathrm{Id}_{\mathrm{MF}(A)}$, where $\mathrm{Id}_{\mathrm{MF}(A)}(x) = \{x\}$, and it is plain that $\{0\} \preceq \sigma(x) \preceq \{x\}, \forall x \in A$.

For $\sigma, \sigma' \in \mathrm{MF}(A)$, set

$$(\sigma \boxtimes \sigma')(x) := \sigma(x) \boxtimes \sigma'(x), \tag{4}$$

for any $x \in A$ and $\boxtimes \in \{\vee, \wedge, \cup, \cap\}$.

Remark 8.

1. *Note that $\sigma(x) \vee \sigma'(x)$ is meant in the sense of Definition 3, rather than the supremum of $\sigma(x)$ and $\sigma'(x)$.*
2. *Note that $\sigma \vee \sigma'$ is an upper bound of σ and σ' by Lemma 6 (1) but is not necessarily a least upper bound. For example, define $\sigma \in \mathrm{MF}(B_4)$ by $\sigma(a) = \sigma(b) = \{a, b\}$, $\sigma(0) = \{0\}, \sigma(1) = \{1\}$. Then,*

$$(\sigma \vee \sigma)(a) = (\sigma \vee \sigma)(b) = \{a, b, 1\}.$$

It is clear that both σ and $\sigma \vee \sigma$ are upper bounds of σ and σ, but $\sigma \prec \sigma \vee \sigma$. In a word, $\sigma \vee \sigma$ is not a least upper bound of σ and σ.

More generally, let A be an MV*-algebra which is not an* MV*-chain with two incomparable elements a, b. Define $\sigma \in \mathrm{MF}(A)$ as $\sigma(a) = \sigma(b) = \{a, b\}, \sigma(x) = \{x\}$ for $x \in A \backslash \{a, b\}$. $\sigma \vee \sigma$ is not a least upper bound of σ and σ.*

In the sense of category theory, a preordered set P is called **complete** [27] (Section 8.5) if for every subset S of P both $\sup S$ and $\inf S$ exist (in P). Note that $\sup S$ and $\inf S$ need not be unique. For example, let $P = \{a, b\}$ and define a preorder $\preceq$ as follows: $a \preceq b, b \preceq a$. Take $S = \{a, b\}$. Then, both a and b are $\sup S$, also $\inf S$. Therefore, we use "a" rather than "the" concerning $\sup S$ and $\inf S$ in the following.

Let $\{\sigma_i\}_{i \in \Omega}$ be a nonempty family of multifunctions on an MV-algebra A. Define a multifunction $\bigcup_{i \in \Omega} \sigma_i$ on A, by

$$\left(\bigcup_{i \in \Omega} \sigma_i\right)(x) := \bigcup_{i \in \Omega} \sigma_i(x),$$

for any $x \in A$.

Analogue to [28] (Theorem I.4.2), we have the following.

Lemma 11. *If A is an* MV*-algebra, then* $(\mathrm{MF}(A), \preccurlyeq, \mathbf{0}_{\mathrm{MF}(A)}, \mathbf{1}_{\mathrm{MF}(A)})$ *is a complete bounded preordered set, where* $\bigcup_{i\in\Omega}\sigma_i$ *is a least upper bound of* $\{\sigma_i\}_{i\in\Omega}$*, and* $\sigma \wedge \sigma'$ *is a greatest lower bound of* σ *and* σ'*, respectively.*

Proof. Note that $\mathbf{0}_{\mathrm{MF}(A)} \preccurlyeq \sigma \preccurlyeq \mathbf{1}_{\mathrm{MF}(A)}$ for any $\sigma \in \mathrm{MF}(A)$.

Let $\{\sigma_i\}_{i\in\Omega}$ be a nonempty family of $\mathrm{MF}(A)$. Then, $\sigma_i \preccurlyeq \bigcup_{i\in\Omega}\sigma_i$. Now we will prove that $\bigcup_{i\in\Omega}\sigma_i$ is a least upper bound of $\{\sigma_i\}_{i\in\Omega}$. Assume that $\sigma_i \preccurlyeq \eta$ for every $i \in \Omega$. For any $y \in (\bigcup_{i\in\Omega}\sigma_i)(x)$ where $x \in A$, there exists $k \in \Omega$ such that $y \in \sigma_k(x)$. Since $\sigma_k(x) \preceq \eta(x)$, there is $z \in \eta(x)$ such that $y \leq z$, which shows $\bigcup_{i\in\Omega}\sigma_i \preccurlyeq \eta$. Therefore, $\bigcup_{i\in\Omega}\sigma_i$ is a least upper bound of $\{\sigma_i\}_{i\in\Omega}$.

Let
$$X^\ell = \{\lambda \in \mathrm{MF}(A) \mid \lambda \preccurlyeq \sigma_i, \forall i \in \Omega\}$$
be the set of lower bounds of $\{\sigma_i\}_{i\in\Omega}$ in $\mathrm{MF}(A)$. Next, we verify that $\bigcup_{\lambda\in X^\ell}\lambda$ is indeed a greatest lower bound of $\{\sigma_i\}_{i\in\Omega}$. For any $i \in \Omega$ and $\lambda \in X^\ell$, we have $\lambda \preccurlyeq \sigma_i$. Thus, $\bigcup_{\lambda\in X^\ell}\lambda \preccurlyeq \sigma_i$ and $\bigcup_{\lambda\in X^\ell}\lambda \in X^\ell$. Hence, $\bigcup_{\lambda\in X^\ell}\lambda$ is a greatest lower bound of $\{\sigma_i\}_{i\in\Omega}$. Therefore, $\mathrm{MF}(A)$ is complete.

For any $\sigma, \sigma' \in \mathrm{MF}(A)$, since $\sigma \wedge \sigma' \preccurlyeq \sigma, \sigma'$, it follows that $\sigma \wedge \sigma'$ is a lower bound of σ and σ'. To verify that $\sigma \wedge \sigma'$ is a greatest lower bound, let $\eta \preccurlyeq \sigma, \sigma'$. Then, for any $y \in \eta(x)$ ($x \in A$), there are $z \in \sigma(x)$ and $w \in \sigma'(x)$ such that $y \leq z$ and $y \leq w$ by $\eta(x) \preceq \sigma(x), \sigma'(x)$. Hence,
$$y \leq z \wedge w \in \sigma(x) \wedge \sigma'(x).$$
Therefore, $\eta(x) \preceq \sigma(x) \wedge \sigma'(x)$. Thus, $\eta \preccurlyeq \sigma \wedge \sigma'$. □

As already mentioned, $\preceq$ is not always a partial order on $\Delta(A)$, where $M \preceq N$ iff for each $m \in M$ there exists $n \in N$ such that $m \leq n$. The binary relation $\sim$ on $\Delta(A)$ defined by $M \sim N$ iff $M \preceq N$ and $N \preceq M$ is an equivalence relation. Given $M \in \Delta(A)$, the equivalence class of M with respect to $\sim$ will be denoted by $\overline{M}$. If $M = \{x\}$ is a singleton, then we abbreviate $\overline{\{x\}}$ by $\overline{x}$. Thus, we can obtain a partial order $\preceq$ on $\Delta(A)/\!\sim$ defined by $\overline{M} \preceq \overline{N}$ iff $M \preceq N$. We claim that $\preceq$ is well defined. In fact, if $M \sim M', N \sim N'$ and $M \preceq N$, then $M' \preceq M \preceq N \preceq N'$.

Recall that for a subset M of A, the **lower set generated by** $\boldsymbol{M}$ [29] is the set
$$\downarrow\! M = \{x \in A \mid \text{there exists } m \in M \text{ such that } x \leq m\}.$$

Lemma 12. *Let $M, N \in \Delta(A)$. Then,* $\overline{M} = \overline{N}$ *iff* $\downarrow\! M = \downarrow\! N$.

Proof. It is sufficient to show that $M \preceq N$ iff $\downarrow\! M \subseteq \downarrow\! N$.

Let $M \preceq N$. For every $x \in \downarrow\! M$, there is $m \in M$ such that $x \leq m$. Then, $M \preceq N$ gives $m \leq n$ for some $n \in N$. Hence, $x \leq n$ and $x \in \downarrow\! N$. Therefore, $\downarrow\! M \subseteq \downarrow\! N$.

Conversely, assume that $\downarrow\! M \subseteq \downarrow\! N$. For any $m \in M$, we have $m \in \downarrow\! M \subseteq \downarrow\! N$. Thus, there exists $n \in N$ such that $m \leq n$. Hence, $M \preceq N$.

Similarly, $N \preceq M$ iff $\downarrow\! N \subseteq \downarrow\! M$. □

Corollary 3. *In general, let A be an* MV*-algebra, $M \in \Delta(A)$, and $a \in A$. Then,* $\overline{M} = \overline{a}$ *iff* $\sup M$ *exists and* $\sup M = a \in M$.

Assume $\overline{M} = \overline{a}$. *Then a is an upper bound of M since $M \preceq \{a\}$. To prove a is a least upper bound of M, let b be an upper bound of M. Since $\{a\} \preceq M$, there exists $m \in M$ such that $a \leq m$. Hence, $a \leq m \leq b$, which shows* $\sup M = a \in M$.

Conversely, let $\sup M = a \in M$. *It suffices to verify that $\downarrow\! M = \downarrow\! a$ by Lemma 12. If $x \in \downarrow\! M$, then there is $m \in M$ such that $x \leq m \leq a$. It follows that $x \in \downarrow\! a$ and $\downarrow\! M \subseteq \downarrow\! a$. If $x \in \downarrow\! a$, then $x \leq a \in M$. Thus, $x \in \downarrow\! M$ and $\downarrow\! a \subseteq \downarrow\! M$. Therefore, $\downarrow\! M = \downarrow\! a$.*

Corollary 4. *Let L_n with $n \geq 2$ and $M \in \Delta(L_n)$. Then,* $\overline{M} = \overline{\sup M}$.

Proof. Observe that $\sup M$ is exactly $\frac{i}{n-1}$ for a certain $0 \leq i \leq n-1$. It suffices to verify that $\downarrow M = \downarrow \sup M$ by Lemma 12. Suppose $x \in \downarrow M$, there is $m \in M$ such that $x \leq m$. Since $m \leq \sup M$, it follows that $x \leq \sup M$. Hence, $x \in \downarrow \sup M$. Conversely, assume $x \in \downarrow \sup M$, which means $x \leq \sup M = \frac{i}{n-1}$. Since $\sup M \in M$, it follows that $x \in \downarrow M$. Therefore, $\downarrow M = \downarrow \sup M$ and $\overline{M} = \overline{\sup M}$. □

Note that the family of all lower sets of a poset A is a complete lattice by [30] (Example O-2.8). We will prove that the family of all nonempty lower sets of A is also a complete lattice, denoted by $(L_0(A), \subseteq)$.

Corollary 5. *Let A be an* MV*-algebra, then $\Delta(A)/\sim$ is isomorphic to the complete lattice $(L_0(A), \subseteq)$.*

Proof. Since A has a least element 0, the intersection of a family of nonempty lower sets of A is still a nonempty lower set. Therefore, $L_0(A)$ is a complete lattice.

Define $\varphi : \Delta(A)/\sim \to L_0(A)$ by $\overline{M} \mapsto \downarrow M$. Lemma 12 shows that φ is well defined and injective, and φ is also surjective since $M = \downarrow M$ if $M \in L_0(A)$. As discussed in the proof of Lemma 12, $\overline{M} \preceq \overline{N}$ iff $\downarrow M \subseteq \downarrow N$ for all $M, N \in \Delta(A)$, which gives both φ and φ^{-1} are order preserving. Hence, φ is an isomorphism. □

Next, we study the order structure on $\Delta(L_n)/\sim$. First, we need

Lemma 13. *Let A be an* MV*-chain, $M, N \in \Delta(A)$, and $\sup M, \sup N$ exist.*

1. *If $\overline{M} \preceq \overline{N}$, then $\sup M \leq \sup N$.*
2. *If $\sup M < \sup N$, then $\overline{M} \preceq \overline{N}$.*
3. *$\overline{M} = \overline{N}$ iff the following conditions hold:*
   - *(a)* $\sup M = \sup N$.
   - *(b)* $\sup M \in M \Leftrightarrow \sup N \in N$.

   In particular, if A is a finite MV*-chain, then $\overline{M} = \overline{N}$ iff (a) holds.*

Proof. (1) Suppose $\overline{M} \preceq \overline{N}$, then $M \preceq N$. For any $m \in M$ there is $n \in N$ such that $m \leq n \leq \sup N$. According to the definition of $\sup M$, we have $\sup M \leq \sup N$.

(2) Let $\sup M < \sup N$. Assume on the contrary $M \not\preceq N$. Then, there is $m \in M$ such that $m > n$ for any $n \in N$. The definition of $\sup N$ implies $m \geq \sup N$. Thus, $\sup N \leq m \leq \sup M$, which contradicts the fact that $\sup M < \sup N$.

(3) Assume that $\overline{M} = \overline{N}$. (a) follows from (1).

To prove that $\sup M \in M \Leftrightarrow \sup N \in N$, we assume $\sup M \in M$. Then, there exists $n_0 \in N$ such that $\sup M \leq n_0$ by $M \preceq N$. Since $N \preceq M$, we have $n_0 \leq \sup M$. Hence, $n_0 = \sup M$. Therefore, $\sup N = \sup M = n_0 \in N$ by (a). Symmetrically, $\sup N \in N \Rightarrow \sup M \in M$.

Conversely, assume that (a) and (b) hold, it suffices to show that $\downarrow M = \downarrow N$ by Lemma 12. Assume that $\downarrow M \neq \downarrow N$; without loss of generality, there is $y \in \downarrow M$ but $y \notin \downarrow N$. That is to say, for arbitrary $n \in N$ we have $n < y$. So, $\sup N \in N$ implies $\sup N < y$. Since $y \in \downarrow M$, there is $m \in M$ such that $y \leq m$. It follows $\sup N < y \leq m < \sup M$ by the definition of $\sup N$, which is contrary to $\sup M = \sup N$. Thus, $\overline{M} = \overline{N}$.

Assume A is a finite MV-chain, and (b) always holds. Hence, $\overline{M} = \overline{N}$ iff (a) holds. □

Remark 9. *Note that $\sup M = \sup N$ may not imply $\overline{M} \preceq \overline{N}$. For example, let $A = [0,1]$ be the standard* MV*-algebra and $\frac{1}{2} \in A$. Define $M = \downarrow \frac{1}{2}$ and $N = \{a \in A \mid 0 \leq a < \frac{1}{2}\}$. Then, $\sup M = \sup N = \frac{1}{2}$, but $\overline{M} \not\preceq \overline{N}$, since $\frac{1}{2} \in M$, there is no $y \in N$ such that $\frac{1}{2} \leq y$.*

Example 4. *Consider the MV-chain L_n with $n \geq 2$. Then, $\Delta(L_n)/\sim$ is order isomorphic to L_n.*

Proof. Define $f : L_n \to \Delta(L_n)/\sim$ by $f(x) = \overline{x}$ for any $x \in L_n$. If $\overline{x} = \overline{y}$, then $x = \sup\{x\} = \sup\{y\} = y$ by Lemma 13 (3). Thus, f is injective. To prove f is surjective, assume $\overline{M} \in \Delta(L_n)/\sim$, then $f(\sup M) = \overline{\sup M} = \overline{M}$ by Corollary 4.

It is enough to verify that f and f^{-1} are order preserving. If $x \leq y$, then $f(x) = \overline{x} \preceq \overline{y} = f(y)$ since $\{x\} \preceq \{y\}$ and Corollary 4. Conversely, suppose $\overline{x} \preceq \overline{y}$, we have $x = \sup\{x\} \leq \sup\{y\} = y$ by Lemma 13 (1). Therefore, f is an isomorphism. □

We next investigate the preorder on the set of $(\odot, \vee)$-multiderivations.

Similar to $\Delta(A)$, we can define an equivalence relation on $\mathrm{MD}(A)$ by $\sigma \sim \sigma'$ iff $\sigma \preccurlyeq \sigma'$ and $\sigma' \preccurlyeq \sigma$, and define $\overline{\sigma} \preccurlyeq \overline{\sigma'}$ in $\mathrm{MD}(A)/\sim$ iff $\sigma \preccurlyeq \sigma'$. Observe that $\preccurlyeq$ in $\mathrm{MD}(A)/\sim$ is a well-defined partial order by the hereditary order of $\preceq$. Clearly, $(\mathrm{MD}(A)/\sim, \preccurlyeq)$ is a poset. By the definition of $\preceq$, we know $\overline{\sigma} = \overline{\sigma'}$ iff $\overline{\sigma(x)} = \overline{\sigma'(x)}$ for any $x \in A$.

For any $\sigma \in \mathrm{MD}(A)$, $\downarrow\sigma\colon A \to \Delta(A)$ is defined as $(\downarrow\sigma)(x) = \downarrow\sigma(x)$. We claim that $\overline{\sigma} = \overline{\downarrow\sigma}$. In fact, $\sigma \preccurlyeq \downarrow\sigma$ is trivial. For any $y \in \downarrow\sigma(x)$, there exists $z \in \sigma(x)$ such that $y \leq z$ by the definition of $\downarrow\sigma(x)$. Therefore, $\downarrow\sigma(x) \preceq \sigma(x)$ for any $x \in A$ and $\downarrow\sigma \preccurlyeq \sigma$.

Lemma 14. *If A is an* MV*-algebra, then:*

1. $\sigma \vee \sigma' \in \mathrm{MD}(A)$ *for all* $\sigma, \sigma' \in \mathrm{MD}(A)$.
2. $\downarrow\sigma \in \mathrm{MD}(A)$ *for any* $\sigma \in \mathrm{MD}(A)$.

Proof. (1) Let $\sigma, \sigma' \in \mathrm{MD}(A)$ and $x, y \in A$. Then, we have

$$
\begin{aligned}
(\sigma \vee \sigma')(x \odot y) &= \sigma(x \odot y) \vee \sigma'(x \odot y) && \text{(Definition of } \sigma \vee \sigma')\\
&= ((\sigma(x) \odot y) \vee (x \odot \sigma(y))) \vee ((\sigma'(x) \odot y) \vee (x \odot \sigma'(y))) && (\sigma, \sigma' \in \mathrm{MD}(A))\\
&= ((\sigma(x) \odot y) \vee (\sigma'(x) \odot y)) \vee ((x \odot \sigma(y)) \vee (x \odot \sigma'(y))) && \text{(Lemma 6 (4) and (5))}\\
&= ((\sigma(x) \vee \sigma'(x)) \odot y) \vee (x \odot (\sigma(y) \vee \sigma'(y))) && \text{(Lemma 7 (2))}\\
&= ((\sigma \vee \sigma')(x) \odot y) \vee (x \odot (\sigma \vee \sigma')(y)) && \text{(Definition of } \sigma \vee \sigma')
\end{aligned}
$$

and so $\sigma \vee \sigma' \in \mathrm{MD}(A)$.

(2) Assume $\sigma \in \mathrm{MD}(A)$. Let $a \in (\downarrow\sigma)(x \odot y) = \downarrow\sigma(x \odot y) = \downarrow((\sigma(x) \odot y) \vee (x \odot \sigma(y)))$. There exist $x_1 \in \sigma(x)$ and $y_1 \in \sigma(y)$ such that $a \leq (x_1 \odot y) \vee (x \odot y_1)$. It follows that

$$
\begin{aligned}
a &= a \wedge ((x_1 \odot y) \vee (x \odot y_1))\\
&= (a \wedge (x_1 \odot y)) \vee (a \wedge (x \odot y_1)) && \text{(Distributivity of } A)\\
&= (b \odot y) \vee (x \odot c), && \text{(Lemma 5 (1))}
\end{aligned}
$$

where $b \leq x_1$ and $c \leq y_1$. Hence, $a \in ((\downarrow\sigma)(x) \odot y) \vee (x \odot (\downarrow\sigma)(y))$.

Conversely, let $a \in ((\downarrow\sigma)(x) \odot y) \vee (x \odot (\downarrow\sigma)(y))$. There exist $x_1 \in \sigma(x)$ and $y_1 \in \sigma(y)$ such that

$$a = (b \odot y) \vee (x \odot c) \leq (x_1 \odot y) \vee (x \odot y_1),$$

where $b \leq x_1$ and $c \leq y_1$. Thus, $a \in (\downarrow\sigma)(x \odot y)$.

Therefore, $\downarrow\sigma \in \mathrm{MD}(A)$. □

Remark 10. *When A is an* MV*-chain, $\sigma \vee \sigma' \in \mathrm{MD}(A)$ is a least upper bound of σ and σ' in $\mathrm{MD}(A)$. We know $\sigma \cup \sigma'$ is a least upper bound of σ and σ' in $\mathrm{MF}(A)$. Note that $\mathrm{MD}(A) \subseteq \mathrm{MF}(A)$ and the preordered on $\mathrm{MF}(A)$. It suffices to verify that $\sigma \vee \sigma' \sim \sigma \cup \sigma'$. For all $x \in A$, $(\sigma \cup \sigma')(x) \preceq (\sigma \vee \sigma')(x)$ is trivial. For any $y \in (\sigma \vee \sigma')(x)$, there exist $z \in \sigma(x)$ and $z' \in \sigma'(x)$ such that $y = z \vee z'$. Since A is an* MV*-chain, $y = z$ or $y = z'$. Hence, $y \in (\sigma \cup \sigma')(x)$, which implies $(\sigma \vee \sigma')(x) \preceq (\sigma \cup \sigma')(x)$. Therefore, $(\sigma \cup \sigma')(x) \sim (\sigma \vee \sigma')(x)$ for all $x \in A$, and hence, $\sigma \vee \sigma' \in \mathrm{MD}(A)$ is a least upper bound of σ and σ' in $\mathrm{MD}(A)$.*

At the end of this section, we characterize the lattice $\mathrm{MD}(L_n)/\sim$ $(n \geq 2)$.

Theorem 1. *If L_n is the n-element* MV*-chain with $n \geq 2$, then the lattices* $\mathrm{MD}(L_n)/\sim$ *and* $\mathrm{Der}(L_n)$ *are isomorphic.*

Proof. Define a map $f : \mathrm{MD}(L_n)/\sim \to \mathrm{Der}(L_n)$ by

$$f(\overline{\sigma}) = \sup \sigma.$$

By Proposition 7 we know $\sup \sigma \in \mathrm{Der}(L_n)$. The order $\leqq$ on $\mathrm{Der}(L_n)$ is defined as $d \leqq d'$ iff $d(x) \leq d'(x), \forall x \in L_n$.

Firstly, we prove that f is well defined. Suppose $\overline{\sigma} = \overline{\sigma'}$, that is, $\overline{\sigma(x)} = \overline{\sigma'(x)}$ for any $x \in L_n$. We get

$$(\sup \sigma)(x) = \sup(\sigma(x)) = \sup(\sigma'(x)) = (\sup \sigma')(x)$$

for any $x \in L_n$ by Lemma 13 (3). Thus, $f(\overline{\sigma}) = \sup(\sigma) = \sup(\sigma') = f(\overline{\sigma'})$.

If $f(\overline{\sigma}) = f(\overline{\sigma'})$, that is, $\sup(\sigma) = \sup(\sigma')$, then $\sup(\sigma(x)) = \sup(\sigma'(x))$ for any $x \in L_n$. Lemma 13 (3) implies $\overline{\sigma(x)} = \overline{\sigma'(x)}$ for any $x \in L_n$ and thus $\overline{\sigma} = \overline{\sigma'}$. Hence, f is injective. For any $d \in \mathrm{Der}(L_n)$, there is $\gamma_d \in \mathrm{MD}(L_n)$ where $\gamma_d(x) := [0, d(x)]$ such that

$$f(\overline{\gamma_d})(x) = (\sup \gamma_d)(x) = \sup(\gamma_d(x)) = \sup[0, d(x)] = d(x)$$

for all $x \in L_n$ by Propositions 6 and 7. Thus, $f(\overline{\gamma_d}) = d$ and f is surjective.

To prove that f is an order-isomorphism, let $\overline{\sigma} \preccurlyeq \overline{\sigma'}$, that is, for any $x \in L_n$, $\overline{\sigma(x)} \preceq \overline{\sigma'(x)}$. Corollary 4 implies that $\overline{\sigma(x)} = \overline{\sup(\sigma(x))}$ for any $x \in L_n$. It follows that

$$\overline{(\sup \sigma)(x)} = \overline{\sup(\sigma(x))} \preceq \overline{\sup(\sigma'(x))} = \overline{(\sup \sigma')(x)}$$

and thus $(\sup \sigma)(x) \leq (\sup \sigma')(x)$ for any $x \in L_n$ since $(\sup \sigma)(x)$ is a singleton. Hence, $f(\overline{\sigma}) = \sup \sigma \leqq \sup \sigma' = f(\overline{\sigma'})$. Conversely, assume $d, d' \in \mathrm{Der}(L_n)$ and $d \leqq d'$, which means $d(x) \leq d'(x)$ for all $x \in L_n$. Now the construction in Proposition 6 gives $\gamma_d = f^{-1} : A \to \Delta(A)$, where $\gamma_d(x) = [0, d(x)]$. Furthermore, we have

$$\gamma_d(x) = [0, d(x)] \preceq [0, d'(x)] = \gamma_{d'}(x)$$

for any $x \in L_n$ by the definition of $\preceq$. Thus, $\gamma_d \preccurlyeq \gamma_{d'}$ and $f^{-1}(d) = \overline{\gamma_d} \preccurlyeq \overline{\gamma_{d'}} = f^{-1}(d')$. □

Proposition 11. *If L_n is the n-element* MV*-chain with $n \geq 2$, then the lattices $\Delta(L_n \times L_2)/\sim$ and $\mathrm{Der}(L_{n+1})$ are isomorphic.*

Proof. Recall that $\mathrm{Der}(L_{n+1})$ is isomorphic to the lattice $(\mathcal{A}(L_{n+1}), \leqq)$ where $\mathcal{A}(L_{n+1}) = \{(x, y) \in L_{n+1} \times L_{n+1} \mid y \leq x\} \backslash \{(0, 0)\}$ [16, Theorem 5.6] and $\leqq$ is defined by: for any $(x_1, y_1), (x_2, y_2) \in L_{n+1} \times L_{n+1}$, $(x_1, y_1) \leqq (x_2, y_2)$ iff $x_1 \leq x_2$ and $y_1 \leq y_2$. Moreover, $\Delta(L_n \times L_2)/\sim$ is isomorphic to the lattice $L_0(L_n \times L_2)$ by Corollary 5.

Define a map $f : \mathcal{A}(L_{n+1}) \to L_0(L_n \times L_2)$ by:

$$f\left(\tfrac{k}{n}, \tfrac{\ell}{n}\right) = \begin{cases} \downarrow(\frac{k-1}{n-1}, 0), & \text{if } \ell = 0; \\ \downarrow(\frac{k-1}{n-1}, 0) \cup \downarrow(\frac{\ell-1}{n-1}, 1), & \text{if } \ell > 0, \end{cases}$$

where $0 \leq k, \ell \leq n-1$. It is easy to see that f is injective. Now we show that f is surjective. For any $M \in L_0(L_n \times L_2)$, we claim M has at most two maximal elements. By way of contradiction, assume M has three different maximal elements denoted by (a_n, b_n), $n = 1, 2, 3$; then, there exist $1 \leq i < j \leq 3$ such that $b_i = b_j$ since $b_n \in L_2$. Thus, (a_i, b_i) and (a_j, b_j) are comparable, which contradicts the fact that (a_i, b_i) and (a_j, b_j) are different maximal elements. If M has only one maximal element denoted by $(\frac{k}{n-1}, a)$, then

$$M = \downarrow(\tfrac{k}{n-1}, a) = \begin{cases} f\left(\frac{k+1}{n}, 0\right), & \text{if } a = 0; \\ f\left(\frac{k+1}{n}, \frac{k+1}{n}\right), & \text{if } a = 1. \end{cases}$$

If M has exactly two maximal elements denoted by $(\frac{k}{n-1}, 0)$ and $(\frac{\ell}{n-1}, 1)$, then

$$M = \downarrow(\tfrac{k}{n-1}, 0) \cup \downarrow(\tfrac{\ell}{n-1}, 1) = f\left(\tfrac{k+1}{n}, \tfrac{\ell+1}{n}\right).$$

Therefore, f is surjective.

Since a bijection with supremum preserving is an order isomorphism, it suffices to verify that f preserves the supremum, that is,

$$f\left((\tfrac{k}{n}, \tfrac{\ell}{n}) \vee (\tfrac{p}{n}, \tfrac{q}{n})\right) = f\left(\tfrac{k}{n}, \tfrac{\ell}{n}\right) \cup f(\tfrac{p}{n}, \tfrac{q}{n})$$

for all $(\frac{k}{n}, \frac{\ell}{n}), (\frac{p}{n}, \frac{q}{n}) \in \mathcal{A}(L_{n+1})$.

Case 1. If $\ell = q = 0$, then

$$\begin{aligned} f\left(\tfrac{k}{n}, 0\right) \cup f(\tfrac{p}{n}, 0) &= \downarrow(\tfrac{k-1}{n-1}, 0) \cup \downarrow(\tfrac{p-1}{n-1}, 0) \\ &= \downarrow(\max\{\tfrac{k-1}{n-1}, \tfrac{p-1}{n-1}\}, 0) \\ &= \downarrow(\tfrac{\max\{k,p\}-1}{n-1}, 0) \\ &= f\left((\tfrac{k}{n}, 0) \vee (\tfrac{p}{n}, 0)\right). \end{aligned}$$

Case 2. If $\ell = 0, q > 0$, then

$$\begin{aligned} f\left(\tfrac{k}{n}, 0\right) \cup f(\tfrac{p}{n}, \tfrac{q}{n}) &= \downarrow(\tfrac{k-1}{n-1}, 0) \cup \left(\downarrow(\tfrac{p-1}{n-1}, 0) \cup \downarrow(\tfrac{q-1}{n-1}, 1)\right) \\ &= \downarrow(\tfrac{\max\{k,p\}-1}{n-1}, 0) \cup \downarrow(\tfrac{q-1}{n-1}, 1) \\ &= f\left((\tfrac{k}{n}, 0) \vee (\tfrac{p}{n}, \tfrac{q}{n})\right). \end{aligned}$$

The case $\ell > 0, q = 0$ is similar.

Case 3. If $\ell > 0, q > 0$, then

$$\begin{aligned} f\left(\tfrac{k}{n}, \tfrac{\ell}{n}\right) \cup f(\tfrac{p}{n}, \tfrac{q}{n}) &= \left(\downarrow(\tfrac{k-1}{n-1}, 0) \cup \downarrow(\tfrac{\ell-1}{n-1}, 1)\right) \cup \left(\downarrow(\tfrac{p-1}{n-1}, 0) \cup \downarrow(\tfrac{q-1}{n-1}, 1)\right) \\ &= \downarrow(\tfrac{\max\{k,p\}-1}{n-1}, 0) \cup \downarrow(\tfrac{\max\{\ell,q\}-1}{n-1}, 1) \\ &= f\left(\tfrac{\max\{k,p\}}{n}, \tfrac{\max\{\ell,q\}}{n}\right) \\ &= f\left((\tfrac{k}{n}, \tfrac{\ell}{n}) \vee (\tfrac{p}{n}, \tfrac{q}{n})\right). \end{aligned}$$

Now we verify that f is an isomorphism of posets and hence an isomorphism of lattices. For all $x, y \in \mathcal{A}(L_{n+1})$,

$$x \leq y \Leftrightarrow x \vee y = y \Leftrightarrow f(x) \cup f(y) = f(x \vee y) = f(y) \Leftrightarrow f(x) \subseteq f(y).$$

Hence, f is an isomorphism of lattices.

Therefore, $\mathcal{A}(L_{n+1}) \cong L_0(L_n \times L_2)$ and then $\Delta(L_n \times L_2)/\sim \cong \mathrm{Der}(L_{n+1})$. □

Corollary 6. *If L_n is the n-element* MV*-chain with $n \geq 2$, then* $\mathrm{MD}(L_{n+1})/\sim$ *is isomorphic to the lattice* $\Delta(L_n \times L_2)/\sim$.

Proof. It follows from Theorem 1 and Proposition 11. □

Note that according to the isomorphism in Theorem 1, $|\,\mathrm{MD}(L_n)/{\sim}\,| = |\,\mathrm{Der}(L_n)\,| = \frac{(n-1)(n+2)}{2}$ by [16] (Theorem 3.11). However, the following Example 5 shows that the cardinalities of different equivalence classes with respect to the equivalence relation $\sim$ are different in general.

Example 5. *Let $n = 2$ and define $\delta \in \mathrm{MF}(L_2)$ by $\delta(0) = \{0\}, \delta(1) = \{0,1\}$. Then, it is easy to check that*

$$\mathrm{MD}(L_2) = \{\mathbf{0}_{\mathrm{MF}(L_2)}, \mathrm{Id}_{\mathrm{MF}(L_2)}, \delta\},$$
$$\mathrm{MD}(L_2)/{\sim} = \{\{\mathbf{0}_{\mathrm{MF}(L_2)}\}, \{\mathrm{Id}_{\mathrm{MF}(L_2)}, \delta\}\}.$$

It is clear that $|\,\overline{\mathbf{0}_{\mathrm{MF}(L_2)}}\,| = 1$ but $|\,\overline{\mathrm{Id}_{\mathrm{MF}(L_2)}}\,| = 2$. Hence, $2 = |\,\mathrm{MD}(L_2)/{\sim}\,| \nmid |\,\mathrm{MD}(L_2)\,| = 3$.

So, the cardinality of $\mathrm{MD}(L_n)$ is not easy to deduce from Theorem 1. In the next section, we will investigate the enumeration of the set of $(\odot, \vee)$-multiderivations on L_n by constructing a counting principle (Theorem 3).

5. The Enumeration of $(\odot, \vee)$-Multiderivations on a Finite MV-Chain

In this section, we determine the cardinality of $\mathrm{MD}(L_n)$. For small values of n, this can be performed with calculations using Python (see the Appendix A Figure A1) in Table 1:

Table 1. The cardinality of $\mathrm{MD}(L_n)$.

n	2	3	4	5	6
$\lvert\mathrm{MD}(L_n)\rvert$	3	16	63	220	723

The result cannot be obtained after $n \geq 6$ due to the limitation of computing resources. But we have shown the following general formula.

Theorem 2. *Let $n \geq 2$ be a positive integer. Then, $|\,\mathrm{MD}(L_n)| = \dfrac{7 \cdot 3^{n-1} - 2^{n+2} + 1}{2}$.*

In order to prove Theorem 2, we need the following Lemmas.

Lemma 15. *Assume that A is an MV-chain and $\sigma \in \mathrm{MD}(A)$; then, the following results hold:*

1. *If $M \subseteq A$, then $M = M \vee M$.*
2. *For any $x \in A, n \in \mathbb{N}_+$, we have $\sigma(x^n) = x^{n-1} \odot \sigma(x)$, where $x^0 = 1$, $x^n = \underbrace{x \odot x \odot \cdots \odot x}_{n}$.*

Proof. (1) It follows immediately from Lemma 6 (3), as M is a sublattice.

(2) We prove $\sigma(x^n) = x^{n-1} \odot \sigma(x)$ by induction on n. Obviously, $\sigma(x^1) = \sigma(x) = 1 \odot \sigma(x) = x^{1-1} \odot \sigma(x)$.

Now, assume that $\sigma(x^n) = x^{n-1} \odot \sigma(x)$. By Equation (3), we have

$$\begin{aligned}
\sigma(x^{n+1}) &= \sigma(x^n \odot x) \\
&= (\sigma(x^n) \odot x) \vee (x^n \odot \sigma(x)) \\
&= (x^{n-1} \odot \sigma(x) \odot x) \vee (x^n \odot \sigma(x)) \\
&= x^n \odot \sigma(x),
\end{aligned}$$

so (2) holds. □

Note that an MV-chain can be completely characterized by (1). That is, if A is an MV-algebra, then A is an MV-chain iff $M = M \vee M$ for every $M \subseteq A$. In fact, by way of contraposition, assume that $x, y \in A$ and x, y are incomparable, denote $z = x \vee y$. Let $M = \{x, y\}$. Then, $z = x \vee y \in M \vee M$ but $z \notin M$. This leads to a contradiction.

Let $n \in \mathbb{N}_+$ and $n \geq 2$. In L_n, we know $\frac{n-m-1}{n-1} = (\frac{n-2}{n-1})^m$ for every $m \in \{1, 2, \cdots, n-1\}$. So, any $x \in L_n \backslash \{1\}$ has a representation as a power of $\frac{n-2}{n-1}$.

Next, we give a counting principle for $(\odot, \vee)$-multiderivations on a finite MV-chain L_n.

Theorem 3. *Let σ be a multifunction on L_n and $v = \frac{n-2}{n-1}$. Then, $\sigma \in \mathrm{MD}(L_n)$ iff σ satisfies the following conditions:*

1. $\sigma(v^m) = v^{m-1} \odot \sigma(v), \forall m \in \{1, 2, \cdots, n-1\}$.
2. $\sigma(v) = \sigma(v) \vee (v \odot \sigma(1))$.
3. $\sigma(v) \preceq \{v\}$.

Proof. Assume $\sigma \in \mathrm{MD}(L_n)$; then, for each $m \in \{1, 2, \cdots, n-1\}$, we have $\sigma(v^m) = v^{m-1} \odot \sigma(v)$ by Lemma 15 (2), and $\sigma(v) = \sigma(v \odot 1) = \sigma(v) \vee (v \odot \sigma(1))$ by Equation (3). Thus, σ satisfies (1) and (2). Furthermore, (3) holds by Proposition 4 (2).

Conversely, suppose that σ satisfies (1), (2) and (3). Let $x, y \in L_n$. There are four cases:

If $x = y = 1$, then it is easy to see that $\sigma(1 \odot 1) = \sigma(1) = \sigma(1) \vee \sigma(1)$ by Lemma 15 (1).

If $x = 1$ or $y = 1$, and $x \neq y$. With out loss of generality, suppose that $x \neq 1$ and $y = 1$, then $x = v^k$ for some $k \in \{1, 2, \cdots, n-1\}$. By (1), we have $\sigma(x \odot 1) = \sigma(x) = \sigma(v^k) = v^{k-1} \odot \sigma(v)$. Also, we have

$$\begin{aligned}
\sigma(x) \vee (x \odot \sigma(1)) &= (v^{k-1} \odot \sigma(v)) \vee (v^k \odot \sigma(1)) \\
&= (v^{k-1} \odot \sigma(v)) \vee (v^{k-1} \odot (v \odot \sigma(1))) \\
&= v^{k-1} \odot (\sigma(v) \vee (v \odot \sigma(1)) && \text{(Lemma 7 (2))} \\
&= v^{k-1} \odot \sigma(v). && \text{((2) of Theorem 3)}
\end{aligned}$$

Hence, $\sigma(x \odot 1) = \sigma(x) = (\sigma(x) \odot 1) \vee (x \odot \sigma(1))$.

If $x \neq 1$ and $y \neq 1$, then assume that $x = v^k$ and $y = v^\ell$ for some $k, \ell \in \{1, 2, \cdots, n-1\}$. We have

$$\sigma(x \odot y) = \sigma(v^k \odot v^\ell) = \sigma(v^{k+\ell})$$

and

$$(\sigma(x) \odot y) \vee (x \odot \sigma(y)) = ((v^{k-1} \odot \sigma(v)) \odot v^\ell) \vee (v^k \odot (v^{\ell-1} \odot \sigma(v))) = v^{k+\ell-1} \odot \sigma(v)$$

by Lemma 15 (1). Then, there are three cases:

For $k + \ell < n-1$, by (1) we obtain $\sigma(v^{k+\ell}) = v^{k+\ell-1} \odot \sigma(v)$.

For $k + \ell = n-1$, by (3) we have $\sigma(v^{k+\ell}) = \sigma(v^{n-1}) = \sigma(0) \preceq \{0\}$ and so $\sigma(0) = \{0\}$. And $v^{k+\ell-1} \odot \sigma(v) = v^{n-2} \odot \sigma(v) = v^* \odot \sigma(v) = \{0\}$. Thus, $\sigma(x \odot y) = (\sigma(x) \odot y) \vee (x \odot \sigma(y))$.

For $n-1 < k+\ell \leq 2n-2$, we have $\sigma(v^{k+\ell}) = \sigma(0) = \{0\} = 0 \odot \sigma(v) = v^{k+\ell-1} \odot \sigma(v)$ by (3) and thus Equation (3) holds.

Therefore, we conclude that $\sigma \in \mathrm{MD}(L_n)$. □

Lemma 16. *Let $P, Q \in \Delta(L_n)$. Then, the following results hold:*

1. $P \subseteq P \vee Q$ *iff* $\min Q \leq \min P$.
2. $P \vee Q \subseteq P$ *iff* $[\min P, 1] \cap Q \subseteq P$.

Proof. Denote $p_0 = \min P$, $q_0 = \min Q$.

(1) Assume $P \subseteq P \vee Q$, then there exist $p \in P, q \in Q$ such that $p_0 = p \vee q \geq q$. Thus, $q_0 \leq q \leq p_0$.

Conversely, suppose $q_0 \leq p_0$, then $p = p \vee q_0$ for any $p \in P$ since $p_0 \leq p$. Hence, $P \subseteq P \vee Q$.

(2) Assume $P \vee Q \subseteq P$; then, for all $q \in [p_0, 1] \cap Q$, we have $q = p_0 \vee q \in P \vee Q \subseteq P$. Thus, $[p_0, 1] \cap Q \subseteq P$.

Conversely, assume $[p_0, 1] \cap Q \subseteq P$ and $p \in P, q \in Q$. If $q \leq p$, then $p \vee q = p \in P$. If $q > p$, then $p \vee q = q \in [p_0, 1] \cap Q \subseteq P$. In either case, $p \vee q \in P$ and so $P \vee Q \subseteq P$. □

Lemma 17. *Let $Q, Q' \in \Delta(L_n)$ and $1 \notin Q$. Denote $v = \frac{n-2}{n-1}$. Then, the following results hold:*

1. *If $0 \notin Q$, then $Q = v \odot Q'$ iff $Q' = Q \oplus v^*$.*
2. *If $0 \in Q$, denote $Q_1 = Q \setminus \{0\}$. Then, $Q = v \odot Q'$ iff $Q' = \{0\} \sqcup (Q_1 \oplus v^*)$, $\{v^*\} \sqcup (Q_1 \oplus v^*)$ or $\{0, v^*\} \sqcup (Q_1 \oplus v^*)$.*

Proof. (1) Let $0 \notin Q$ and $Q = v \odot Q'$. Then, $0 \notin Q'$, otherwise, $0 = v \odot 0 \in v \odot Q' = Q$, a contradiction. Thus, $0 \notin Q'$, which implies $\{v^*\} \preceq Q'$. Hence, we have

$$\begin{aligned} Q' = Q' \vee v^* &= \{q' \vee v^* \mid q' \in Q'\} \\ &= \{(q' \odot v) \oplus v^* \mid q' \in Q'\} \\ &= (Q' \odot v) \oplus v^* \\ &= Q \oplus v^*. \end{aligned}$$

Conversely, assume $Q' = Q \oplus v^*$. Since $1 \notin Q$, we have $Q \preceq \{v\}$. Hence,

$$\begin{aligned} Q = Q \wedge v &= \{q \wedge v \mid n \in Q\} \\ &= \{v \odot (q \oplus v^*) \mid n \in Q\} \\ &= v \odot (Q \oplus v^*) \\ &= v \odot Q'. \end{aligned}$$

(2) Assume $0 \in Q$ and $Q = v \odot Q'$; then, $0 = v \odot q'$ for some $q' \in Q'$. Thus, $0 \in Q'$ or $v^* \in Q'$. Denote $Q'_0 = \{0, v^*\} \cap Q'$ and $Q'_1 = Q' \setminus Q'_0$. By $v \odot Q'_0 = \{0\}$ and $\{v^*\} \preceq v \odot Q'_1$, we have

$$\begin{aligned} Q_1 = Q \setminus \{0\} &= (v \odot Q') \setminus \{0\} \\ &= (v \odot (Q'_0 \cup Q'_1)) \setminus \{0\} \\ &= ((v \odot Q'_0) \cup (v \odot Q'_1)) \setminus \{0\} \quad \text{(Lemma 7 (3))} \\ &= (\{0\} \cup (v \odot Q'_1)) \setminus \{0\} \\ &= v \odot Q'_1. \end{aligned}$$

Since $0 \notin Q_1$, we obtain $Q'_1 = Q_1 \oplus v^*$ by (1). Therefore,

$$Q' = Q'_0 \sqcup Q'_1 = Q'_0 \sqcup (Q_1 \oplus v^*),$$

where $Q'_0 = \{0\}$, $\{v^*\}$ or $\{0, v^*\}$.

Conversely, assume $0 \in Q$ and $Q' = Q'_0 \sqcup (Q_1 \oplus v^*)$, where $Q'_0 = \{0\}$, $\{v^*\}$ or $\{0, v^*\}$. From $1 \notin Q_1$, it follows that $Q_1 \preceq \{v\}$ and

$$\begin{aligned} v \odot Q' &= v \odot (Q'_0 \cup (Q_1 \oplus v^*)) \\ &= (v \odot Q'_0) \cup (v \odot (Q_1 \oplus v^*)) \qquad \text{(Lemma 7 (3))} \\ &= \{0\} \cup (Q_1 \wedge v) = \{0\} \cup Q_1 = Q. \end{aligned}$$

Hence, we complete the proof. □

We are now in a position to prove Theorem 2:

Proof of Theorem 2. Assume that σ is a multifunction on L_n and denote $\frac{n-2}{n-1}$ by v. According to Theorem 3, σ is uniquely determined by $\sigma(v)$ and $\sigma(1)$ if $\sigma \in \mathrm{MD}(L_n)$. Hence, it is enough to consider the values of $\sigma(v)$ and $\sigma(1)$. By Theorem 3, $\sigma \in \mathrm{MD}(L_n)$ iff

$$\sigma(v) \preceq \{v\}, \tag{5}$$

and

$$\sigma(v) = \sigma(v) \vee (v \odot \sigma(1)). \tag{6}$$

For convenience, we denote $P = \sigma(v)$, $Q' = \sigma(1)$, $Q = v \odot \sigma(1)$, $p_0 = \min P$ and $q_0 = \min Q$. Equation (5) implies $1 \notin P$. By Lemma 16, we know Equation (6) implies that $q_0 \le p_0$ and $[p_0, 1] \cap Q \subseteq P$. Assume that $p_0 = \frac{k}{n-1}$ and $|P| = \ell$, where $0 \le k \le n-2$ and $1 \le \ell \le n-k-1$. Then, $P \setminus \{p_0\} \subseteq \left[\frac{k+1}{n-1}, \frac{n-2}{n-1}\right]$. Thus, P has $C_{n-k-2}^{\ell-1}$ choices with respect to k and ℓ. Now, we will determine all choices of Q and Q'.

Case 1. If $q_0 = p_0$, then $Q = [q_0, 1] \cap Q = [p_0, 1] \cap Q \subseteq P$. Hence, $Q \setminus \{q_0\}$ can take any subset of $P \setminus \{p_0\}$ and so Q has $2^{\ell-1}$ choices.

If $q_0 > 0$, then $0 \notin Q$, and by Lemma 17 (1) and $Q = v \odot Q'$ we know $Q' = Q \oplus v^*$. Hence, Q' has $2^{\ell-1}$ choices.

If $q_0 = 0$, then $0 \in Q$, by Lemma 17 (2) and $Q = v \odot Q'$ we have $Q' = \{0\} \sqcup (Q_1 \oplus v^*)$, $\{v^*\} \sqcup (Q_1 \oplus v^*)$ or $\{0, v^*\} \sqcup (Q_1 \oplus v^*)$. Thus, Q' has $3 \cdot 2^{\ell-1}$ choices.

Case 2. If $0 < q_0 < p_0$, denote $Q_1 = (0, p_0) \cap Q$ and $Q_2 = [p_0, 1] \cap Q$. Since $0 \notin Q$, we have $Q = Q_1 \sqcup Q_2$. Notice that $Q_1 \ne \varnothing$, so there are $2^{k-1} - 1$ choices of Q_1. Furthermore, since $Q_2 = [p_0, 1] \cap Q \subseteq P$, Q_2 can take any subset of P and so has 2^ℓ choices. Thus, there are $(2^{k-1} - 1) \cdot 2^\ell$ choices of Q in this case. Since $0 \notin Q$, it follows that Q' has also $(2^{k-1} - 1) \cdot 2^\ell$ choices by Lemma 17 (1).

Case 3. If $0 = q_0 < p_0$, denote $Q_1 = (0, p_0) \cap Q$ and $Q_2 = [p_0, 1] \cap Q$, so we have $Q = \{0\} \sqcup Q_1 \sqcup Q_2$. Since $Q_1 \subset (0, p_0)$, there are 2^{k-1} choices of Q_1. Moreover, Q_2 has 2^ℓ choices as in Case 2. Thus, there are $2^{k+\ell-1}$ choices of Q in this case. Since $0 \in Q$, it follows that Q' has $3 \cdot 2^{k+\ell-1}$ choices by Lemma 17 (2).

According to Theorem 3, we can determine the unique $(\odot, \vee)$-multiderivation for each choices of $\sigma(1)$ and $\sigma(v)$.

Therefore, it follows

$$\begin{aligned}
|\mathrm{MD}(L_n)| &= \sum_{k=1}^{n-2} \sum_{\ell=1}^{n-k-1} \binom{n-k-2}{\ell-1} (2^{\ell-1} + (2^{k-1} - 1) \cdot 2^\ell + 3 \cdot 2^{k-1} \cdot 2^\ell) + \sum_{\ell=1}^{n-1} \binom{n-2}{\ell-1} (3 \cdot 2^{\ell-1}) \\
&= \sum_{k=0}^{n-2} \sum_{\ell=1}^{n-k-1} \binom{n-k-2}{\ell-1} (2^{k+\ell+1} - 2^{\ell-1}) \\
&= \sum_{k=0}^{n-2} \left((2^{k+2} - 1) \sum_{\ell=1}^{n-k-1} \binom{n-k-2}{\ell-1} \cdot 2^{\ell-1} \right) \\
&= \sum_{k=0}^{n-2} (2^{k+2} - 1)(2+1)^{n-k-2} \\
&= 3^n \sum_{k=0}^{n-2} \left(\left(\frac{2}{3}\right)^{k+2} - \left(\frac{1}{3}\right)^{k+2} \right) \\
&= \frac{7 \cdot 3^{n-1} - 2^{n+2} + 1}{2}. \quad \square
\end{aligned}$$

6. Conclusions and Questions

In this paper, the point-to-point $(\odot, \vee)$-derivations on MV-algebras have been extended to point-to-set $(\odot, \vee)$-multiderivations. We show that $(\mathrm{MD}(L_n)/\!\sim, \preccurlyeq)$ is isomorphic to the complete lattice $\mathrm{Der}(L_n)$, the underlying set of $(\odot, \vee)$-derivations on L_n. This unveils a certain relevance between $(\odot, \vee)$-multiderivations and $(\odot, \vee)$-derivations. Moreover, by building a counting principle, we obtain the enumeration of $\mathrm{MD}(L_n)$.

This general study of $(\odot, \vee)$-multiderivations has the advantage of developing into a system theory of sets and has potential wide applications: other logical algebras, control theory, interval analysis, and artificial intelligence.

We list three questions to be considered in the future:

(1) We have found two ways to construct $(\odot, \vee)$-multiderivations from $(\odot, \vee)$-derivations in Propositions 5 and 6. Are there other ways?

(2) We ask whether the equivalent characterization and enumeration of $(\odot, \vee)$- multiderivations on finite MV-chains can be extended to finite MV-algebras.

(3) We ask whether MV-algebras A and A' are isomorphic if $(\mathrm{MD}(A), \preccurlyeq)$ and $(\mathrm{MD}(A'), \preccurlyeq)$ are order isomorphic.

Author Contributions: Conceptualization, X.Z. and Y.Y.; methodology, X.Z., K.D. A.G., and Y. Y.; software, K,D.; validation, X.Z. and K.D.; investigation, X.Z. and Y.Y.; writing—original draft preparation, X.Z.; writing—review and editing, Y.Y.; supervision, Y.Y. All authors have read and agreed to the published version of the manuscript.

Funding: The work is partially supported by CNNSF (Grants: 12171022, 62250001).

Data Availability Statement: Data sharing is not applicable to this article as no new data were created or analyzed in this study.

Conflicts of Interest: The authors declare that they have no conflicts of interest.

Appendix A. Calculation Program by Python in Table 1

```
from itertools import product

#the set of MV-chain Ln
n = 6  # Adjust n as needed
L = list(range(n))

# operators on Ln
def omul(a, b):
    return max(a + b + 1 - n, 0)

def join(a, b):
    return max(a, b)

# operators on Delta(Ln)
def Omul(A, B):
    C = []
    for i in A:
        for j in B:
            k = omul(i, j)
            if k not in C:
                C.append(k)
    return C

def Join(A, B):
    C = []
    for i in A:
        for j in B:
            k = join(i, j)
            if k not in C:
```

Figure A1. *Cont.*

```
                C.append(k)
    return C

# judge whether F is a multiderivation
def IsMulDer(F):
    for i in range(n):
        for j in range(n):
            if set(F[omul(i, j)]) != set(Join(Omul(F[i], [j
                ]), Omul([i], F[j]))):
                return False
    return True

# get the list of all multifunctions on Ln
def powerset(s):
    for i in range(1 << len(s)):
        yield [s[j] for j in range(len(s)) if (i & (1 << j))
            ]

def generate_PLn(n):
    elements = []
    for i in range(1, n+1):
        a = list(powerset(range(i)))
        if [] in a:
            a.remove([])
        elements.append(a)
    return list(product(*elements))

def find_MulDer():
    MulDer = 0
    for F in generate_PLn(n):
        if IsMulDer(F):
            MulDer += 1
            print(F)
    return MulDer

MulDer_count = find_MulDer()
print(MulDer_count)
```

Figure A1. MD(L_n).py.

References

1. Posner, E. Derivations in prime rings. *Proc. Amer. Math Soc.* **1957**, *8*, 1093–1100. [CrossRef]
2. Szász, G. Derivations of lattices. *Acta Sci. Math.* **1975**, *37*, 149–154.
3. Ferrari, L. On derivations of lattices. *Pure Math Appl.* **2001**, *12*, 365–382.
4. Xin, X.L.; Li, T.Y.; Lu, J.H. On derivations of lattices. *Inf. Sci.* **2008**, *178*, 307–316. [CrossRef]
5. Xin, X.L. The fixed set of a derivation in lattices. *Fixed Point Theory Appl.* **2012**, *218*, 218. [CrossRef]
6. Gan, A.P.; Guo, L. On differential lattices. Soft Comput. **2022**, *26*, 7043–7058. [CrossRef]
7. Jun, Y.B.; Xin, X.L. On derivations on BCI-algebras. *Inf. Sci.* **2004**, *159*, 167–176. [CrossRef]
8. He, P.F.; Xin, X.L.; Zhan, J.M. On derivations and their fixed point sets in residuated lattices. *Fuzzy Sets Syst.* **2016**, *303*, 97–113. [CrossRef]
9. Krňávek, J.; Kühr, J. A note on derivations on basic algebras. *Soft Comput.* **2015**, *19*, 1765–1771. [CrossRef]
10. Hua, X.J. State L-algebras and derivations of L-algebras. *Soft Comput.* **2021**, *25*, 4201–4212. [CrossRef]
11. Alshehri, N.O. Derivations of MV-algebras. *Int. J. Math. Math. Sci.* **2010**, *2010*, 312027. [CrossRef]
12. Hamal, A. Additive derivative and multiplicative coderivative operators on MV-algebras. *Turk. J. Math.* **2019**, *43*, 879–893. [CrossRef]
13. Wang, J.T.; He, P.F.; She, Y.H. Some results on derivations of MV-algebras. *Appl. Math. J. Chin. Univ. Ser. B* **2023**, *38*, 126–143. [CrossRef]

14. Yazarli, H. A note on derivations in MV-algebras. *Miskolc Math. Notes* **2013**, *14*, 345–354. [CrossRef]
15. Rachůnek, J.; Šalounová, D. Derivations on algebras of a non-commutative generalization of the Łukasiewicz logic. *Fuzzy Sets Syst.* **2018**, *333*, 11–16. [CrossRef]
16. Zhao, X.T.; Gan, A.P.; Yang, Y.C. $(\odot, \vee)$-derivations on MV-algebras. *Soft Comput.* **2024**, *28*, 1833–1849. [CrossRef]
17. Eilenberg, S.; Montgomery, D. Fixed Point Theorems for Multi-Valued Transformations. *Amer. J. Math.* **1946**, *68*, 214. [CrossRef]
18. Aumann, R.J. Integrals of set-valued functions. *J. Math. Anal. Appl.* **1965**, *12*, 1–12. [CrossRef]
19. Filippov, A.F. Classical solutions of differential equations with multivalued right-hand side. *SIAM J. Control* **1967**, *5*, 609–621. [CrossRef]
20. Hermes, H. Calculus of set valued functions and control. *J. Math. Mech.* **1968**, *18*, 47–60. [CrossRef]
21. Aumann, R.J. Existence of a competitive equilibrium in markets with a continuum of traders. *Econometrica* **1966**, *34*, 1–17. [CrossRef]
22. Neumann, J.V.; Morgenstern, O. *Theory of Games and Economic Behavior*; Princeton: Princeton, NJ, USA, 1944.
23. Rezapour, S.; Sami, S. Some properties of isotone and joinitive multiderivations on lattices. *Filomat* **2016**, *30*, 2743–2748. [CrossRef]
24. Cignoli, R.; D'Ottaviano, I.M.L.; Mundici, D. *Algebraic Foundations of Many-Valued Reasoning*; Kluwer Academic Publishers: Dordrecht, The Netherlands, 2000.
25. Chang, C.C. Algebraic analysis of many-valued logic. *Trans. Am. Math. Soc.* **1958**, *88*, 467–490. [CrossRef]
26. Ansari, Q.H.; Köbis, E.; Yao, J.C. *Vector Variational Inequalities and Vector Optimization*; Springer International Publishing: Cham, Switzerland, 2018.
27. Awodey, S. *Category Theory*; Oxford University Press: New York, NY, USA, 2010.
28. Burris, S.; Sankappanavar, H.P. *A Course in Universal Algebra*; Springer: New York, NY, USA, 2012.
29. Almeida, J.; Cano, A.; Klíma, O.; Pin, J.E. On fixed points of the lower set operator. *Internat. J. Algebra Comput.* **2015**, *25*, 259–292. [CrossRef]
30. Gierz, G.; Hofmann, K.H.; Keimel, K.; Lawson, J.D.; Mislove, M.; Scott, D.S. *Continuous Lattices and Domains*; Cambridge University Press: Cambridge, UK, 2003.

axioms

MDPI

Article

Intuitionistic Fuzzy Granular Matrix: Novel Calculation Approaches for Intuitionistic Fuzzy Covering-Based Rough Sets

Jingqian Wang [1] **and Xiaohong Zhang** [1,2,*]

[1] School of Mathematics and Data Science, Shaanxi University of Science and Technology, Xi'an 710021, China; wangjingqianw@163.com or wangjingqianw@sust.edu.cn
[2] Shaanxi Joint Laboratory of Artificial Intelligence, Shaanxi University of Science and Technology, Xi'an 710021, China
* Correspondence: zhangxiaohong@sust.edu.cn

Abstract: Intuitionistic fuzzy (IF) β-minimal description operators can deal with noise data in the IF covering-based rough set theory. That is to say, they can be used to find data that we need in IF environments. For an IF β-covering approximation space (i.e., an IF environment) with a high cardinality, it would be tedious and complicated to use IF set representations to calculate them. Therefore, it is necessary to find a quick method to obtain them. In this paper, we present the notion of IF β-maximal description based on the definition of IF β-minimal description, along with the concepts of IF granular matrix and IF reduction. Moreover, we propose matrix calculation methods for IF covering-based rough sets, such as IF β-minimal descriptions, IF β-maximal descriptions, and IF reductions. Firstly, the notion of an IF granular matrix is presented, which is used to calculate IF β-minimal description. Secondly, inspired by IF β-minimal description, we give the notion of IF β-maximal description. Furthermore, the matrix representations of IF β-maximal descriptions are presented. Next, two types of reductions for IF β-covering approximation spaces via IF β-minimal and fuzzy β-minimal descriptions are presented, along with their matrix representations. Finally, the new calculation methods are compared with corresponding set representations by carrying out several experiments.

Keywords: IF covering-based rough set; IF β-minimal description; IF β-maximal description; IF granular matrix; IF reduction

MSC: 03E72

Citation: Wang, J.; Zhang, X. Intuitionistic Fuzzy Granular Matrix: Novel Calculation Approaches for Intuitionistic Fuzzy Covering-Based Rough Sets. *Axioms* **2024**, *13*, 411. https://doi.org/10.3390/axioms13060411

Academic Editors: Oscar Castillo and Andreja Tepavčević

Received: 16 April 2024
Revised: 23 May 2024
Accepted: 13 June 2024
Published: 18 June 2024

1. Introduction

Covering-based rough set theory [1] was proposed to deal with the type of covering data, which enriched classical rough set theory [2]. Nearly forty covering rough set models [3–5] have been developed in covering approximation space. These models popularized their application to practical problems such as decision rule synthesis [6–8], knowledge reduction [9–11] and other fields [12–14]. Using set representations to investigate issues in real-life problems would be complicated and tedious in a covering approximation space with a high cardinality. As computer-implemented methods, matrix approaches are the ideal tools for managing this problem; these include matrices for axiomatizing three types of covering approximation operators [15], matrices for studying knowledge reduction in dynamic covering decision information systems [16], matrices for representing 32 pairs of neighborhood-based upper and lower approximation operators [17], and matrices for minimal and maximal descriptions in covering-based rough sets [18].

Fuzzy set theory [19] addresses the issue of how to understand and manipulate imperfect knowledge. It and rough set theory are related, but distinct and complementary [20]. The first type of fuzzy rough set model based on an fuzzy similarity relation was established in [21]. Then, some essential research on fuzzy rough set models was finished by different fuzzy logical connectives [22,23] and fuzzy relations [24,25]. Recently, some fuzzy rough set models were constructed under a fuzzy covering approximation space [26,27]. In particular, Ma [28] presented the concept of a fuzzy β-covering approximation space by replacing "1" with a parameter β, where "1" is a condition for the definition of fuzzy covering. Inspired by Ma's work, many fuzzy covering-based rough set models were established. For example, several newly important notions and other types of fuzzy β-covering rough set models are presented in [29]. Multigranulation fuzzy rough covering models based on fuzzy β-neighborhoods were used to solve the problem of multi-criteria group decision making in [30]. At the same time, the matrix approaches are the most used in these studies. For example, Ma [28] proposed the matrix representations of two pairs of fuzzy β-covering approximation operators. Yang and Hu [31] used matrices to represent three pairs of L-fuzzy covering-based approximation operators, as well as other fuzzy covering approximation operators in [32]. Wang et al. [33] used matrices to calculate fuzzy β-minimal descriptions, β-maximal descriptions and fuzzy β-neighborhoods.

As a generalization of fuzzy set theory, intuitionistic fuzzy (IF) set theory [34] expresses stronger information uncertainty. Therefore, IF β-covering rough set models [35] were first presented in IF β-covering approximation spaces. They were extended to other models [36,37], which were used in decision making and feature selection. Since an IF set explains the degrees of membership and non-membership of an element, it is difficult to use matrices to study these IF β-covering rough sets. To solve this problem, we use matrix approaches in IF β-covering approximation spaces, providing a new viewpoint to investigate IF β-covering rough set models and optimize complex computations expressed by IF sets. The motivations and contents of this paper are listed as follows:

- Huang et al. [35] presented the notion of IF β-minimal description. But the dual notion of IF β-maximal description is not proposed. Therefore, this new notion will be given in this paper, which reflects a different method of information screening.
- In [33], matrix methods are used for calculating minimal and maximal descriptions in covering approximation spaces. In [33,38], fuzzy matrix methods are used for calculating fuzzy β-minimal and fuzzy β-maximal descriptions in fuzzy β-covering approximation spaces. Therefore, we can also present IF matrix methods for calculating IF β-minimal and IF β-maximal descriptions in IF β-covering approximation spaces.
- There are many different notions of reductions in covering and fuzzy β-covering approximation spaces, respectively. It is interesting to define reductions in IF β-covering approximation spaces by IF β-minimal and IF β-maximal descriptions in this paper, respectively. Based on the matrix representations of IF β-minimal and β-maximal descriptions, these new notions of IF reductions can be represented by matrices.

The rest of this article is arranged as follows: Section 2 reviews some basic definitions about coverings, IF sets and IF β-covering approximation space. In Section 3, the notion of an IF granular matrix is presented in an IF β-covering approximation space. Then, IF matrix approaches are used to calculate the IF β-minimal and β-maximal descriptions. In Section 4, two types of reductions in an IF β-covering approximation space are presented through IF β-minimal and β-maximal descriptions, respectively. Moreover, these two types of reductions are represented in the IF granular matrix. Section 5 compares the existing set representation method with the new IF matrix method through a number of experiments. The advantages and efficiency of the new method are explained from different viewpoints. Section 6 provides the conclusion and prospects.

2. Basic Definitions

This section recalls some fundamental definitions related to coverings, IF sets and IF covering-based rough sets. Suppose U is a nonempty and finite set called a "universe" unless stated to the contrary.

Definition 1 ([39,40]). *Let U be a universe and $\mathbf{C}$ be a family of subsets of U. If no element in $\mathbf{C}$ is empty and $\bigcup \mathbf{C} = U$, then $\mathbf{C}$ is called a covering of U. We call $(U, \mathbf{C})$ a covering approximation space.*

We show the notions of minimal and maximal descriptions in the covering approximation space as follows:

Let $\mathbf{C}$ be a covering of U. For any $x \in U$, we call

$$Md_{\mathbf{C}}(x) = \{K \in \mathbf{C} : x \in K \wedge (\forall S \in \mathbf{C})(x \in S \wedge S \subseteq K \Rightarrow K = S)\}$$

the minimal description of x [1,41], and call

$$MD_{\mathbf{C}}(x) = \{K \in \mathbf{C} : x \in K \wedge (\forall S \in \mathbf{C})(x \in S \wedge K \subseteq S \Rightarrow K = S)\}$$

the maximal description of x [42].

In [18], we showed the advantages of matrix approaches for obtaining the minimal description and the maximal description in covering rough sets. Moreover, in [33], we showed the advantages of fuzzy minimal description and fuzzy maximal description in fuzzy covering rough sets. For example, they can be used in granular reductions (see Example 17 in [33]), and can also be used to obtain fuzzy neighborhoods (see Figure 4 in [33]).

In the following, we introduce some basic notions of IF set theory.

Definition 2 ([34]). *Let U be a universe. An intuitionistic fuzzy set (IFS) A in U is defined as follows:*

$$A = \{\langle x, \mu_A(x), \nu_A(x)\rangle : x \in U\},$$

where $\mu_A : U \to [0,1]$ is called the degree of membership of the element $x \in U$ to A, $\nu_A : U \to [0,1]$ is called the degree of non-membership. They satisfy $\mu_A(x) + \nu_A(x) \leq 1$ for all $x \in U$. The family of all intuitionistic fuzzy sets in U is denoted by $IF(U)$.

We call $\langle a, b\rangle$ with $0 < a, b \leq 1$ and $a + b \leq 1$ an IF value. As is well known, for two IF values $\alpha = \langle a, b\rangle$ and $\beta = \langle c, d\rangle$, $\alpha \leq \beta \Leftrightarrow a \leq c$ and $b \geq d$.

For any family $\gamma_i \in [0,1], i \in I, I \subseteq \mathbb{N}^+$ ($\mathbb{N}^+$ is the set of all positive integers), we write $\vee_{i\in I}\gamma_i$ for the supremum of $\{\gamma_i : i \in I\}$, and $\wedge_{i\in I}\gamma_i$ for the infimum of $\{\gamma_i : i \in I\}$. Some basic operations on $IF(U)$ are listed as follows [34]: $A, B \in IF(U)$,

(1) $A \subseteq B$ iff $\mu_A(x) \leq \mu_B(x)$ and $\nu_B(x) \leq \nu_A(x)$ for all $x \in U$;
(2) $A = B$ iff $A \subseteq B$ and $B \subseteq A$;
(3) $A \cup B = \{\langle x, \mu_A(x) \vee \mu_B(x), \nu_A(x) \wedge \nu_B(x)\rangle : x \in U\}$;
(4) $A \cap B = \{\langle x, \mu_A(x) \wedge \mu_B(x), \nu_A(x) \vee \nu_B(x)\rangle : x \in U\}$;
(5) $A' = \{\langle x, \nu_A(x), \mu_A(x)\rangle : x \in U\}$.

Definition 3 ([35]). *Let U be a universe and $\beta = \langle a, b\rangle$ be an IF value. Then, we call $\widehat{\mathbf{C}} = \{C_1, C_2, \ldots, C_m\}$, with $C_i \in IF(U) (i = 1, 2, \ldots, m)$, an IF β-covering of U, if for any $x \in U$ there exists $C_i \in \widehat{\mathbf{C}}$ such that $C_i(x) \geq \beta$. We also call $(U, \widehat{\mathbf{C}})$ an IF β-covering approximation space.*

Finally, we introduce some notions in the IF β-covering approximation space.

Definition 4 ([35]). *Let $(U, \widehat{\mathbf{C}})$ be an IF β-covering approximation space. For each $x \in U$, the IF β-neighborhood $\widetilde{N}^{\beta}_{\widehat{\mathbf{C}}(x)}$ of x induced by $\widehat{\mathbf{C}}$ can be defined as follows:*

$$\widetilde{N}^{\beta}_{\widehat{\mathbf{C}}(x)} = \bigcap\{C \in \widehat{\mathbf{C}} : C(x) \geq \beta\}.$$

Definition 5 ([35]). *Let $(U, \widehat{\mathbf{C}})$ be an IF β-covering approximation space. For any $x \in U$, its IF β-minimal description $\widetilde{Md}^{\beta}_{\widehat{\mathbf{C}}}(x)$ is defined as follows:*

$$\widetilde{Md}^{\beta}_{\widehat{\mathbf{C}}}(x) = \{C \in \widehat{\mathbf{C}} : C(x) \geq \beta \wedge (\forall D \in \widehat{\mathbf{C}})(D(x) \geq \beta \wedge D \subseteq C \Rightarrow C = D)\}.$$

For better reading and understanding, we explain relevant symbols in Table 1.

Table 1. Relevant symbols in this paper.

	Full Name	Relevant Symbol
Original Symbols	Covering approximation space	$(U, \mathbf{C})$
	Minimal description of x	$Md_{\mathbf{C}}(x)$
	Maximal description of x	$MD_{\mathbf{C}}(x)$
	IF β-covering approximation space	$(U, \widehat{\mathbf{C}})$
	IF β-neighborhood	$\widetilde{N}^{\beta}_{\widehat{\mathbf{C}}(x)}$
	IF β-minimal description of x	$\widetilde{Md}^{\beta}(\widehat{\mathbf{C}}, x)$
New Symbols	IF β-maximal description of x	$\widetilde{MD}^{\beta}(\widehat{\mathbf{C}}, x)$
	IF granular matrix representation of $\widehat{\mathbf{C}}$	$M_{\widehat{\mathbf{C}}}$
	IF eigenmatrix of x	$M_{\widehat{\mathbf{C}}}(x)$
	IF β-covering number matrix of $\widehat{\mathbf{C}}$	$\overline{M_{\widehat{\mathbf{C}}}}$

3. Matrix Representations of IF β-Minimal and β-Maximal Descriptions

In this section, IF β-minimal and β-maximal descriptions are computed by matrices. First, some new matrices and corresponding operations are proposed in an IF β-covering approximation space. Then, several properties of these new matrices are presented. Finally, we give the matrix representations of IF β-minimal and β-maximal descriptions based on the results above.

3.1. Matrix Representations of IF β-Minimal Descriptions

In this subsection, we present some new matrices and matrix operations in the IF β-covering approximation space. Moreover, the matrix representations of IF β-minimal and β-maximal descriptions are presented.

Definition 6. *Let $(U, \widehat{\mathbf{C}})$ be an IF β-covering approximation space, where $U = \{x_1, \cdots, x_n\}$ and $\widehat{\mathbf{C}} = \{C_1, C_2, \ldots, C_m\}$. We call $M_{\widehat{\mathbf{C}}} = (C_j(x_i))_{n \times m}$ an IF granular matrix representation of $\widehat{\mathbf{C}}$.*

Example 1. *Let $U = \{x_1, x_2, x_3, x_4, x_5, x_6\}$ and $\widehat{\mathbf{C}} = \{C_1, C_2, C_3, C_4, C_5\}$, where*

$$C_1 = \frac{\langle 0.6,0.3\rangle}{x_1} + \frac{\langle 0.5,0.2\rangle}{x_2} + \frac{\langle 0.7,0.3\rangle}{x_3} + \frac{\langle 0.6,0.4\rangle}{x_4} + \frac{\langle 0.7,0.3\rangle}{x_5} + \frac{\langle 0.6,0.2\rangle}{x_6},$$
$$C_2 = \frac{\langle 0.7,0.3\rangle}{x_1} + \frac{\langle 0.2,0.6\rangle}{x_2} + \frac{\langle 0.1,0.7\rangle}{x_3} + \frac{\langle 0.6,0.2\rangle}{x_4} + \frac{\langle 0.5,0.2\rangle}{x_5} + \frac{\langle 0.5,0.3\rangle}{x_6},$$
$$C_3 = \frac{\langle 0.7,0.2\rangle}{x_1} + \frac{\langle 0.6,0.1\rangle}{x_2} + \frac{\langle 0.8,0.1\rangle}{x_3} + \frac{\langle 0.6,0.3\rangle}{x_4} + \frac{\langle 0.8,0.1\rangle}{x_5} + \frac{\langle 0.6,0.1\rangle}{x_6},$$
$$C_4 = \frac{\langle 0.3,0.5\rangle}{x_1} + \frac{\langle 0.5,0.5\rangle}{x_2} + \frac{\langle 0.5,0.3\rangle}{x_3} + \frac{\langle 0.4,0.5\rangle}{x_4} + \frac{\langle 0.6,0.2\rangle}{x_5} + \frac{\langle 0.5,0.3\rangle}{x_6},$$
$$C_5 = \frac{\langle 0.5,0.1\rangle}{x_1} + \frac{\langle 0.6,0.4\rangle}{x_2} + \frac{\langle 0.7,0.2\rangle}{x_3} + \frac{\langle 0.6,0.3\rangle}{x_4} + \frac{\langle 0.7,0.2\rangle}{x_5} + \frac{\langle 0.6,0.2\rangle}{x_6}.$$

Suppose $\beta = \langle 0.6, 0.3\rangle$. By Definition 3, we know $\widehat{\mathbf{C}}$ is an IF β-covering of U. By Definition 6, we have

$$M_{\widehat{C}} = \begin{array}{c} \\ x_1 \\ x_2 \\ x_3 \\ x_4 \\ x_5 \\ x_6 \end{array} \begin{array}{c} \begin{array}{ccccc} C_1 & C_2 & C_3 & C_4 & C_5 \end{array} \\ \begin{pmatrix} \langle 0.6,0.3\rangle & \langle 0.7,0.3\rangle & \langle 0.7,0.2\rangle & \langle 0.3,0.5\rangle & \langle 0.5,0.1\rangle \\ \langle 0.5,0.2\rangle & \langle 0.2,0.6\rangle & \langle 0.6,0.1\rangle & \langle 0.5,0.5\rangle & \langle 0.6,0.4\rangle \\ \langle 0.7,0.3\rangle & \langle 0.1,0.7\rangle & \langle 0.8,0.1\rangle & \langle 0.5,0.3\rangle & \langle 0.7,0.2\rangle \\ \langle 0.6,0.4\rangle & \langle 0.6,0.2\rangle & \langle 0.6,0.3\rangle & \langle 0.4,0.5\rangle & \langle 0.6,0.3\rangle \\ \langle 0.7,0.3\rangle & \langle 0.5,0.2\rangle & \langle 0.8,0.1\rangle & \langle 0.6,0.2\rangle & \langle 0.7,0.2\rangle \\ \langle 0.6,0.2\rangle & \langle 0.5,0.3\rangle & \langle 0.6,0.1\rangle & \langle 0.5,0.3\rangle & \langle 0.6,0.2\rangle \end{pmatrix} \end{array}.$$

Based on Definition 6, another two matrices about $M_{\widehat{C}}$ are proposed in the following definition.

Definition 7. *Let $(U, \widehat{C})$ be an IF β-covering approximation space and $M_{\widehat{C}} = (C_j(x_i))_{n\times m}$ be a matrix representation of $\widehat{C}$, where $U = \{x_1, \cdots, x_n\}$ and $\widehat{C} = \{C_1, C_2, \ldots, C_m\}$.*

(1) For any $1 \leq j \leq m$, $M_{\widehat{C}}(x_i) = (\alpha_{kj})_{n\times m}$ is called an IF eigenmatrix of x_i, where $1 \leq k \leq n$,

$$\alpha_{kj} = \begin{cases} C_j(x_k), & C_j(x_i) \geq \beta; \\ \langle 0,0\rangle, & \text{otherwise.} \end{cases}$$

(2) $\overline{M_{\widehat{C}}} = (n)_{m\times m}$ is called the IF β-covering number matrix of $\widehat{C}$.

Remark 1. *In Definition 7, for $M_{\widehat{C}}(x_i)$, if $C_j(x_i) \geq \beta$, then the jth column of $M_{\widehat{C}}(x_i)$ is the jth of $M_{\widehat{C}}$; otherwise, all elements in the jth column of $M_{\widehat{C}}(x_i)$ are $\langle 0,0\rangle$.*

Example 2 (Continued from Example 1). *By Definition 7, we have*

$$M_{\widehat{C}}(x_1) = \begin{pmatrix} \langle 0.6,0.3\rangle & \langle 0.7,0.3\rangle & \langle 0.7,0.2\rangle & \langle 0,0\rangle & \langle 0,0\rangle \\ \langle 0.5,0.2\rangle & \langle 0.2,0.6\rangle & \langle 0.6,0.1\rangle & \langle 0,0\rangle & \langle 0,0\rangle \\ \langle 0.7,0.3\rangle & \langle 0.1,0.7\rangle & \langle 0.8,0.1\rangle & \langle 0,0\rangle & \langle 0,0\rangle \\ \langle 0.6,0.4\rangle & \langle 0.6,0.2\rangle & \langle 0.6,0.3\rangle & \langle 0,0\rangle & \langle 0,0\rangle \\ \langle 0.7,0.3\rangle & \langle 0.5,0.2\rangle & \langle 0.8,0.1\rangle & \langle 0,0\rangle & \langle 0,0\rangle \\ \langle 0.6,0.2\rangle & \langle 0.5,0.3\rangle & \langle 0.6,0.1\rangle & \langle 0,0\rangle & \langle 0,0\rangle \end{pmatrix},$$

$$M_{\widehat{C}}(x_2) = \begin{pmatrix} \langle 0,0\rangle & \langle 0,0\rangle & \langle 0.7,0.2\rangle & \langle 0,0\rangle & \langle 0,0\rangle \\ \langle 0,0\rangle & \langle 0,0\rangle & \langle 0.6,0.1\rangle & \langle 0,0\rangle & \langle 0,0\rangle \\ \langle 0,0\rangle & \langle 0,0\rangle & \langle 0.8,0.1\rangle & \langle 0,0\rangle & \langle 0,0\rangle \\ \langle 0,0\rangle & \langle 0,0\rangle & \langle 0.6,0.3\rangle & \langle 0,0\rangle & \langle 0,0\rangle \\ \langle 0,0\rangle & \langle 0,0\rangle & \langle 0.8,0.1\rangle & \langle 0,0\rangle & \langle 0,0\rangle \\ \langle 0,0\rangle & \langle 0,0\rangle & \langle 0.6,0.1\rangle & \langle 0,0\rangle & \langle 0,0\rangle \end{pmatrix},$$

$$M_{\widehat{C}}(x_3) = \begin{pmatrix} \langle 0.6,0.3\rangle & \langle 0,0\rangle & \langle 0.7,0.2\rangle & \langle 0,0\rangle & \langle 0.5,0.1\rangle \\ \langle 0.5,0.2\rangle & \langle 0,0\rangle & \langle 0.6,0.1\rangle & \langle 0,0\rangle & \langle 0.6,0.4\rangle \\ \langle 0.7,0.3\rangle & \langle 0,0\rangle & \langle 0.8,0.1\rangle & \langle 0,0\rangle & \langle 0.7,0.2\rangle \\ \langle 0.6,0.4\rangle & \langle 0,0\rangle & \langle 0.6,0.3\rangle & \langle 0,0\rangle & \langle 0.6,0.3\rangle \\ \langle 0.7,0.3\rangle & \langle 0,0\rangle & \langle 0.8,0.1\rangle & \langle 0,0\rangle & \langle 0.7,0.2\rangle \\ \langle 0.6,0.2\rangle & \langle 0,0\rangle & \langle 0.6,0.1\rangle & \langle 0,0\rangle & \langle 0.6,0.2\rangle \end{pmatrix},$$

$$M_{\widehat{C}}(x_4) = \begin{pmatrix} \langle 0,0\rangle & \langle 0.7,0.3\rangle & \langle 0.7,0.2\rangle & \langle 0,0\rangle & \langle 0.5,0.1\rangle \\ \langle 0,0\rangle & \langle 0.2,0.6\rangle & \langle 0.6,0.1\rangle & \langle 0,0\rangle & \langle 0.6,0.4\rangle \\ \langle 0,0\rangle & \langle 0.1,0.7\rangle & \langle 0.8,0.1\rangle & \langle 0,0\rangle & \langle 0.7,0.2\rangle \\ \langle 0,0\rangle & \langle 0.6,0.2\rangle & \langle 0.6,0.3\rangle & \langle 0,0\rangle & \langle 0.6,0.3\rangle \\ \langle 0,0\rangle & \langle 0.5,0.2\rangle & \langle 0.8,0.1\rangle & \langle 0,0\rangle & \langle 0.7,0.2\rangle \\ \langle 0,0\rangle & \langle 0.5,0.3\rangle & \langle 0.6,0.1\rangle & \langle 0,0\rangle & \langle 0.6,0.2\rangle \end{pmatrix},$$

$$M_{\widehat{C}}(x_5) = \begin{pmatrix} \langle 0.6,0.3\rangle & \langle 0,0\rangle & \langle 0.7,0.2\rangle & \langle 0.3,0.5\rangle & \langle 0.5,0.1\rangle \\ \langle 0.5,0.2\rangle & \langle 0,0\rangle & \langle 0.6,0.1\rangle & \langle 0.5,0.5\rangle & \langle 0.6,0.4\rangle \\ \langle 0.7,0.3\rangle & \langle 0,0\rangle & \langle 0.8,0.1\rangle & \langle 0.5,0.3\rangle & \langle 0.7,0.2\rangle \\ \langle 0.6,0.4\rangle & \langle 0,0\rangle & \langle 0.6,0.3\rangle & \langle 0.4,0.5\rangle & \langle 0.6,0.3\rangle \\ \langle 0.7,0.3\rangle & \langle 0,0\rangle & \langle 0.8,0.1\rangle & \langle 0.6,0.2\rangle & \langle 0.7,0.2\rangle \\ \langle 0.6,0.2\rangle & \langle 0,0\rangle & \langle 0.6,0.1\rangle & \langle 0.5,0.3\rangle & \langle 0.6,0.2\rangle \end{pmatrix},$$

$$M_{\widehat{C}}(x_6) = \begin{pmatrix} \langle 0.6, 0.3 \rangle & \langle 0, 0 \rangle & \langle 0.7, 0.2 \rangle & \langle 0, 0 \rangle & \langle 0.5, 0.1 \rangle \\ \langle 0.5, 0.2 \rangle & \langle 0, 0 \rangle & \langle 0.6, 0.1 \rangle & \langle 0, 0 \rangle & \langle 0.6, 0.4 \rangle \\ \langle 0.7, 0.3 \rangle & \langle 0, 0 \rangle & \langle 0.8, 0.1 \rangle & \langle 0, 0 \rangle & \langle 0.7, 0.2 \rangle \\ \langle 0.6, 0.4 \rangle & \langle 0, 0 \rangle & \langle 0.6, 0.3 \rangle & \langle 0, 0 \rangle & \langle 0.6, 0.3 \rangle \\ \langle 0.7, 0.3 \rangle & \langle 0, 0 \rangle & \langle 0.8, 0.1 \rangle & \langle 0, 0 \rangle & \langle 0.7, 0.2 \rangle \\ \langle 0.6, 0.2 \rangle & \langle 0, 0 \rangle & \langle 0.6, 0.1 \rangle & \langle 0, 0 \rangle & \langle 0.6, 0.2 \rangle \end{pmatrix},$$

$$\overline{M_{\widehat{C}}} = \begin{pmatrix} 6 & 6 & 6 & 6 & 6 \\ 6 & 6 & 6 & 6 & 6 \\ 6 & 6 & 6 & 6 & 6 \\ 6 & 6 & 6 & 6 & 6 \\ 6 & 6 & 6 & 6 & 6 \end{pmatrix}.$$

Then, a new matrix operation is presented in the following definition.

Definition 8. *Let $A = (\alpha_{ik})_{n\times m}$ and $B = (\gamma_{kj})_{m\times s}$ be two matrices, where $\alpha_{ik} = \langle a^+_{ik}, a^-_{ik} \rangle$ and $\gamma_{kj} = \langle b^+_{kj}, b^-_{kj} \rangle$. We define $C = A \trianglerighteq B = (c_{ij})_{n\times s}$, where*

$$c_{ij} = \begin{cases} \sum\limits_{k=1}^{m} (\alpha_{ik} \trianglerighteq \gamma_{kj}), & \text{row } i \text{ of } A \text{ and column } j \text{ of } B \text{ are not } \mathbf{0}; \\ 0, & \text{otherwise}, \end{cases} \quad \text{and}$$

$$\alpha_{ik} \trianglerighteq \gamma_{kj} = \begin{cases} 1, & a^+_{ik} \geq b^+_{kj} \wedge a^-_{ik} \leq b^-_{kj}; \\ 0, & \text{otherwise}. \end{cases}$$

In Definition 8, $\mathbf{0}$ denotes the vector with any element $\langle 0, 0 \rangle$. Then, two characteristics of $M^T_{\widehat{C}}(x) \trianglerighteq M_{\widehat{C}}(x)$ $(\forall x \in U)$ are presented in the following two propositions, respectively.

Proposition 1. *Let $(U, \widehat{\mathbf{C}})$ be an IF β-covering approximation space and $M^T_{\widehat{C}}(x_k) \trianglerighteq M_{\widehat{C}}(x_k) = (a_{ij})_{m\times m}$, where $x_k \in U$ $(k = 1, 2, \cdots, n)$ and $\widehat{\mathbf{C}} = \{C_1, C_2, \ldots, C_m\}$. Then, $a_{ij} = |\{x \in U : (C_i \cap C_j)(x_k) \geq \beta \wedge C_i(x) \geq C_j(x)\}|$.*

Proof.

$$\begin{aligned} a_{ij} &= \begin{cases} \sum\limits_{x\in U} (C_i(x) \trianglerighteq C_j(x)), & C_i(x_k) \geq \beta \text{ and } C_j(x_k) \geq \beta; \\ 0, & \text{otherwise}. \end{cases} \\ &= \begin{cases} |\{x \in U : C_i(x) \geq C_j(x)\}|, & (C_i \cap C_j)(x_k) \geq \beta; \\ 0, & \text{otherwise}. \end{cases} \\ &= |\{x \in U : (C_i \cap C_j)(x_k) \geq \beta \wedge C_i(x) \geq C_j(x)\}|. \end{aligned}$$

□

Proposition 2. *Let $(U, \widehat{\mathbf{C}})$ be an IF β-covering approximation space, $x_k \in U$, $M^T_{\widehat{C}}(x_k) \trianglerighteq M_{\widehat{C}}(x_k) = (a_{ij})_{m\times m}$ and $\overline{M_{\widehat{C}}} = (b_{ij})_{m\times m}$. For any $(t \in \{1, 2, \cdots, m\})$, $a_{tt} = b_{tt}$ if and only if $a_{tt} > 0$.*

Proof. Suppose $U = \{x_1, \cdots, x_n\}$ and $\widehat{\mathbf{C}} = \{C_1, C_2, \ldots, C_m\}$. Then,

$$a_{tt} = |\{x \in U : C_t(x_k) \geq \beta\}| = b_{tt} = n = |\{x : x \in U\}| \Leftrightarrow C_t(x_k) \geq \beta \Leftrightarrow a_{tt} > 0.$$

□

Finally, the matrix representation of the IF β-minimal description is presented in Theorem 1. Let $A = (a_{ij})_{n\times n}$ and $B = (b_{ij})_{n\times n}$ be two matrices. We define $C = A \oplus B = (c_i)_{n\times 1}$, where

$$c_i = \begin{cases} 1, & a_{ij} = b_{ij} \Leftrightarrow i = j; \\ 0, & \text{otherwise}. \end{cases}$$

Let $\widehat{\mathbf{C}} = \{C_1, C_2, \ldots, C_m\}$ be an IF β-covering of U and $\widehat{\mathbf{C}}_1 \subseteq \widehat{\mathbf{C}}$. We call $f(\widehat{\mathbf{C}}_1) = (y_i)_{m\times 1}$ the membership function of $\widehat{\mathbf{C}}_1$ in $\widehat{\mathbf{C}}$, where

$$y_i = \begin{cases} 1, & C_i \in \widehat{\mathbf{C}}_1; \\ 0, & C_i \notin \widehat{\mathbf{C}}_1. \end{cases}$$

Note that "$\trianglerighteq$" is before "$\oplus$" in operations.

Theorem 1. *Let $(U, \widehat{\mathbf{C}})$ be an IF β-covering approximation space, where $U = \{x_1, \cdots, x_n\}$ and $\widehat{\mathbf{C}} = \{C_1, C_2, \ldots, C_m\}$. Then,*

$$f(\widetilde{Md}^{\beta}_{\widehat{\mathbf{C}}}(x_k)) = M^T_{\widehat{\mathbf{C}}}(x_k) \trianglerighteq M_{\widehat{\mathbf{C}}}(x_k) \oplus \overline{M_{\widehat{\mathbf{C}}}},\ k = 1, 2, \cdots, n.$$

Proof. Suppose $M^T_{\widehat{\mathbf{C}}}(x_k) \trianglerighteq M_{\widehat{\mathbf{C}}}(x_k) = (a_{ij})_{m\times m}$, $\overline{M_{\widehat{\mathbf{C}}}} = (b_{ij})_{m\times m}$ and $f(\widetilde{Md}^{\beta}_{\widehat{\mathbf{C}}}(x_k)) = (y_j)_{m\times 1}$. For any $C_t \in \mathbf{C}$,

$$\begin{aligned} C_t \in \widetilde{Md}^{\beta}_{\widehat{\mathbf{C}}}(x_k) \ &\Leftrightarrow (C_t(x_k) \geq \beta) \wedge (\forall C_j \in \widehat{\mathbf{C}} \wedge (C_j(x_k) \geq \beta) \wedge (C_j \subseteq C_t \Rightarrow C_t = C_j)) \\ &\Leftrightarrow (C_t(x_k) \geq \beta) \wedge (\forall j \in \{1, 2, \cdots, m\} \wedge (C_j(x_k) \geq \beta) \wedge (C_j \subseteq C_t \Rightarrow C_t = C_j)) \\ &\Leftrightarrow (C_t(x_k) \geq \beta) \wedge (\forall j \in \{1, 2, \cdots, m\} \wedge (C_j(x_k) \geq \beta) \wedge \\ &\quad (|\{x \in U : C_t(x) \geq C_j(x)\}| = n \Rightarrow C_t = C_j)) \\ &\Leftrightarrow (C_t(x_k) \geq \beta) \wedge (\forall j \in \{1, 2, \cdots, m\} \wedge (a_{tj} = b_{tj} \Rightarrow t = j)) \\ &\Leftrightarrow (a_{tt} > 0) \wedge (a_{tj} = b_{tj} \Rightarrow t = j) \\ &\Leftrightarrow (a_{tt} = b_{tt}) \wedge (a_{tj} = b_{tj} \Rightarrow t = j) \\ &\Leftrightarrow y_t = 1. \end{aligned}$$

Hence, $f(\widetilde{Md}^{\beta}_{\widehat{\mathbf{C}}}(x_k)) = M^T_{\widehat{\mathbf{C}}}(x_k) \trianglerighteq M_{\widehat{\mathbf{C}}}(x_k) \oplus \overline{M_{\widehat{\mathbf{C}}}}$. □

Example 3 (Continued from Example 1). *All $M_{\widehat{\mathbf{C}}}(x_k)$ $(k = 1, 2, \cdots, 6)$ and $\overline{M_{\widehat{\mathbf{C}}}}$ are calculated in Examples 1 and 2. Hence,*

$$\begin{aligned} f(\widetilde{Md}^{\beta}_{\widehat{\mathbf{C}}}(x_1)) &= M^T_{\widehat{\mathbf{C}}}(x_1) \trianglerighteq M_{\widehat{\mathbf{C}}}(x_1) \oplus \overline{M_{\widehat{\mathbf{C}}}} \\ &= \begin{pmatrix} \langle 0.6,0.3\rangle & \langle 0.5,0.2\rangle & \langle 0.7,0.3\rangle & \langle 0.6,0.4\rangle & \langle 0.7,0.3\rangle & \langle 0.6,0.2\rangle \\ \langle 0.7,0.3\rangle & \langle 0.2,0.6\rangle & \langle 0.1,0.7\rangle & \langle 0.6,0.2\rangle & \langle 0.5,0.2\rangle & \langle 0.5,0.3\rangle \\ \langle 0.7,0.2\rangle & \langle 0.6,0.1\rangle & \langle 0.8,0.1\rangle & \langle 0.6,0.3\rangle & \langle 0.8,0.1\rangle & \langle 0.6,0.1\rangle \\ \langle 0,0\rangle & \langle 0,0\rangle & \langle 0,0\rangle & \langle 0,0\rangle & \langle 0,0\rangle & \langle 0,0\rangle \\ \langle 0,0\rangle & \langle 0,0\rangle & \langle 0,0\rangle & \langle 0,0\rangle & \langle 0,0\rangle & \langle 0,0\rangle \end{pmatrix} \trianglerighteq \\ &\begin{pmatrix} \langle 0.6,0.3\rangle & \langle 0.7,0.3\rangle & \langle 0.7,0.2\rangle & \langle 0,0\rangle & \langle 0,0\rangle \\ \langle 0.5,0.2\rangle & \langle 0.2,0.6\rangle & \langle 0.6,0.1\rangle & \langle 0,0\rangle & \langle 0,0\rangle \\ \langle 0.7,0.3\rangle & \langle 0.1,0.7\rangle & \langle 0.8,0.1\rangle & \langle 0,0\rangle & \langle 0,0\rangle \\ \langle 0.6,0.4\rangle & \langle 0.6,0.2\rangle & \langle 0.6,0.3\rangle & \langle 0,0\rangle & \langle 0,0\rangle \\ \langle 0.7,0.3\rangle & \langle 0.5,0.2\rangle & \langle 0.8,0.1\rangle & \langle 0,0\rangle & \langle 0,0\rangle \\ \langle 0.6,0.2\rangle & \langle 0.5,0.3\rangle & \langle 0.6,0.1\rangle & \langle 0,0\rangle & \langle 0,0\rangle \end{pmatrix} \oplus \begin{pmatrix} 6 & 6 & 6 & 6 & 6 \\ 6 & 6 & 6 & 6 & 6 \\ 6 & 6 & 6 & 6 & 6 \\ 6 & 6 & 6 & 6 & 6 \\ 6 & 6 & 6 & 6 & 6 \end{pmatrix} \\ &= \begin{pmatrix} 6 & 3 & 0 & 0 & 0 \\ 2 & 6 & 1 & 0 & 0 \\ 6 & 5 & 6 & 0 & 0 \\ 0 & 0 & 0 & 0 & 0 \\ 0 & 0 & 0 & 0 & 0 \end{pmatrix} \oplus \begin{pmatrix} 6 & 6 & 6 & 6 & 6 \\ 6 & 6 & 6 & 6 & 6 \\ 6 & 6 & 6 & 6 & 6 \\ 6 & 6 & 6 & 6 & 6 \\ 6 & 6 & 6 & 6 & 6 \end{pmatrix} = \begin{pmatrix} 1 \\ 1 \\ 0 \\ 0 \\ 0 \end{pmatrix}, \end{aligned}$$

i.e., $\widetilde{Md}^{\beta}_{\widehat{C}}(x_1) = \{C_1, C_2\}$.

$$\begin{aligned} f(\widetilde{Md}^{\beta}_{\widehat{C}}(x_2)) &= M^T_{\widehat{C}}(x_2) \trianglerighteq M_{\widehat{C}}(x_2) \oplus \overline{M_{\widehat{C}}} \\ &= \begin{pmatrix} 0 & 0 & 0 & 0 & 0 \\ 0 & 0 & 0 & 0 & 0 \\ 0 & 0 & 6 & 0 & 0 \\ 0 & 0 & 0 & 0 & 0 \\ 0 & 0 & 0 & 0 & 0 \end{pmatrix} \oplus \begin{pmatrix} 6 & 6 & 6 & 6 & 6 \\ 6 & 6 & 6 & 6 & 6 \\ 6 & 6 & 6 & 6 & 6 \\ 6 & 6 & 6 & 6 & 6 \\ 6 & 6 & 6 & 6 & 6 \end{pmatrix} = \begin{pmatrix} 0 \\ 0 \\ 1 \\ 0 \\ 0 \end{pmatrix}, \end{aligned}$$

i.e., $\widetilde{Md}^{\beta}_{\widehat{C}}(x_2) = \{C_3\}$.

$$\begin{aligned} f(\widetilde{Md}^{\beta}_{\widehat{C}}(x_3)) &= M^T_{\widehat{C}}(x_3) \trianglerighteq M_{\widehat{C}}(x_3) \oplus \overline{M_{\widehat{C}}} \\ &= \begin{pmatrix} 6 & 0 & 0 & 0 & 1 \\ 0 & 0 & 0 & 0 & 0 \\ 6 & 0 & 6 & 0 & 5 \\ 0 & 0 & 0 & 0 & 0 \\ 4 & 0 & 1 & 0 & 6 \end{pmatrix} \oplus \begin{pmatrix} 6 & 6 & 6 & 6 & 6 \\ 6 & 6 & 6 & 6 & 6 \\ 6 & 6 & 6 & 6 & 6 \\ 6 & 6 & 6 & 6 & 6 \\ 6 & 6 & 6 & 6 & 6 \end{pmatrix} = \begin{pmatrix} 1 \\ 0 \\ 0 \\ 0 \\ 1 \end{pmatrix}, \end{aligned}$$

i.e., $\widetilde{Md}^{\beta}_{\widehat{C}}(x_3) = \{C_1, C_5\}$.

$$\begin{aligned} f(\widetilde{Md}^{\beta}_{\widehat{C}}(x_4)) &= M^T_{\widehat{C}}(x_4) \trianglerighteq M_{\widehat{C}}(x_4) \oplus \overline{M_{\widehat{C}}} \\ &= \begin{pmatrix} 0 & 0 & 0 & 0 & 0 \\ 0 & 6 & 1 & 0 & 1 \\ 0 & 5 & 6 & 0 & 5 \\ 0 & 0 & 0 & 0 & 0 \\ 0 & 4 & 1 & 0 & 6 \end{pmatrix} \oplus \begin{pmatrix} 6 & 6 & 6 & 6 & 6 \\ 6 & 6 & 6 & 6 & 6 \\ 6 & 6 & 6 & 6 & 6 \\ 6 & 6 & 6 & 6 & 6 \\ 6 & 6 & 6 & 6 & 6 \end{pmatrix} = \begin{pmatrix} 0 \\ 1 \\ 1 \\ 0 \\ 1 \end{pmatrix}, \end{aligned}$$

i.e., $\widetilde{Md}^{\beta}_{\widehat{C}}(x_4) = \{C_2, C_3, C_5\}$.

$$\begin{aligned} f(\widetilde{Md}^{\beta}_{\widehat{C}}(x_5)) &= M^T_{\widehat{C}}(x_5) \trianglerighteq M_{\widehat{C}}(x_5) \oplus \overline{M_{\widehat{C}}} \\ &= \begin{pmatrix} 6 & 0 & 0 & 5 & 1 \\ 0 & 0 & 0 & 0 & 0 \\ 6 & 0 & 6 & 6 & 5 \\ 0 & 0 & 0 & 6 & 0 \\ 4 & 0 & 1 & 6 & 6 \end{pmatrix} \oplus \begin{pmatrix} 6 & 6 & 6 & 6 & 6 \\ 6 & 6 & 6 & 6 & 6 \\ 6 & 6 & 6 & 6 & 6 \\ 6 & 6 & 6 & 6 & 6 \\ 6 & 6 & 6 & 6 & 6 \end{pmatrix} = \begin{pmatrix} 1 \\ 0 \\ 0 \\ 1 \\ 0 \end{pmatrix}, \end{aligned}$$

i.e., $\widetilde{Md}^{\beta}_{\widehat{C}}(x_5) = \{C_1, C_4\}$.

$$\begin{aligned} f(\widetilde{Md}^{\beta}_{\widehat{C}}(x_6)) &= M^T_{\widehat{C}}(x_6) \trianglerighteq M_{\widehat{C}}(x_6) \oplus \overline{M_{\widehat{C}}} \\ &= \begin{pmatrix} 6 & 0 & 0 & 0 & 1 \\ 0 & 0 & 0 & 0 & 0 \\ 6 & 0 & 6 & 0 & 5 \\ 0 & 0 & 0 & 0 & 0 \\ 4 & 0 & 1 & 0 & 6 \end{pmatrix} \oplus \begin{pmatrix} 6 & 6 & 6 & 6 & 6 \\ 6 & 6 & 6 & 6 & 6 \\ 6 & 6 & 6 & 6 & 6 \\ 6 & 6 & 6 & 6 & 6 \\ 6 & 6 & 6 & 6 & 6 \end{pmatrix} = \begin{pmatrix} 1 \\ 0 \\ 0 \\ 0 \\ 1 \end{pmatrix}, \end{aligned}$$

i.e., $\widetilde{Md}^{\beta}_{\widehat{C}}(x_6) = \{C_1, C_5\}$.

3.2. Matrix Representations of IF β-Maximal Descriptions

Based on Section 3.1, we present the matrix representation of the IF β-maximal description in this subsection. Firstly, the concept of IF β-maximal description is given in the following definition.

Definition 9. *Let $(U, \widehat{\mathbf{C}})$ be an IF β-covering approximation space. For any $x \in U$, its IF β-maximal description $\widetilde{MD}^{\beta}_{\widehat{\mathbf{C}}}(x)$ is defined as follows:*

$$\widetilde{MD}^{\beta}_{\widehat{\mathbf{C}}}(x) = \{C \in \widehat{\mathbf{C}} : C(x) \geq \beta \wedge (\forall D \in \widehat{\mathbf{C}})(D(x) \geq \beta \wedge C \subseteq D \Rightarrow C = D)\}.$$

To investigate the matrix representation of the IF β-maximal description, another new matrix operation is presented in the following definition.

Definition 10. *Let $A = (\alpha_{ik})_{n\times m}$ and $B = (\gamma_{kj})_{m\times s}$ be two matrices, where $\alpha_{ik} = \langle a^+_{ik}, a^-_{ik}\rangle$ and $\gamma_{kj} = \langle b^+_{kj}, b^-_{kj}\rangle$. We define $C = A \trianglelefteq B = (c_{ij})_{n\times s}$, where*

$$c_{ij} = \begin{cases} \sum\limits_{k=1}^{m} (\alpha_{ik} \trianglelefteq \gamma_{kj}), & \text{row } i \text{ of } A \text{ and column } j \text{ of } B \text{ are not } \mathbf{0}; \\ 0, & \text{otherwise,} \end{cases} \quad \text{and}$$

$$\alpha_{ik} \trianglelefteq \gamma_{kj} = \begin{cases} 1, & a^+_{ik} \leq b^+_{kj} \wedge a^-_{ik} \geq b^-_{kj}; \\ 0, & \text{otherwise.} \end{cases}$$

By Definition 10, two characteristics of $M^T_{\widehat{\mathbf{C}}}(x) \trianglelefteq M_{\widehat{\mathbf{C}}}(x)$ $(\forall x \in U)$ are presented in the following two propositions.

Proposition 3. *Let $\widehat{\mathbf{C}} = \{C_1, C_2, \ldots, C_m\}$ be an IF β-covering of $U = \{x_1, \cdots, x_n\}$, $x_k \in U$ and $M^T_{\widehat{\mathbf{C}}}(x_k) \trianglelefteq M_{\widehat{\mathbf{C}}}(x_k) = (a_{ij})_{m\times m}$. Then, $a_{ij} = |\{x \in U : (C_i \cap C_j)(x_k) \geq \beta \wedge C_i(x) \leq C_j(x)\}|$.*

Proof.

$$\begin{aligned} a_{ij} &= \begin{cases} \sum\limits_{x\in U} (C_i(x) \trianglelefteq C_j(x)), & C_i(x_k) \geq \beta \text{ and } C_j(x_k) \geq \beta; \\ 0, & \text{otherwise.} \end{cases} \\ &= \begin{cases} |\{x \in U : C_i(x) \leq C_j(x)\}|, & (C_i \cap C_j)(x_k) \geq \beta; \\ 0, & \text{otherwise.} \end{cases} \\ &= |\{x \in U : (C_i \cap C_j)(x_k) \geq \beta \wedge C_i(x) \leq C_j(x)\}|. \end{aligned}$$

□

Proposition 4. *Let $\widehat{\mathbf{C}} = \{C_1, C_2, \ldots, C_m\}$ be an IF β-covering of $U = \{x_1, \cdots, x_n\}$, $x_k \in U$, $M^T_{\widehat{\mathbf{C}}}(x_k) \trianglelefteq M_{\widehat{\mathbf{C}}}(x_k) = (a_{ij})_{m\times m}$ and $\overline{M_{\widehat{\mathbf{C}}}} = (b_{ij})_{m\times m}$. $a_{tt} = b_{tt}$ if and only if $a_{tt} > 0$ $(t \in \{1, 2, \cdots, m\})$.*

Proof. $a_{tt} = |\{x \in U : C_t(x_k) \geq \beta\}| = b_{tt} = n = |\{x : x \in U\}| \Leftrightarrow C_t(x_k) \geq \beta \Leftrightarrow a_{tt} > 0$. □

Finally, the matrix representation of the IF β-maximal description is presented in the following theorem. Note that "$\trianglelefteq$" is before "$\oplus$" in operations.

Theorem 2. *Let $\widehat{\mathbf{C}} = \{C_1, C_2, \ldots, C_m\}$ be an IF β-covering of $U = \{x_1, \cdots, x_n\}$. Then,*

$$f(\widetilde{MD}^{\beta}_{\widehat{\mathbf{C}}}(x_k)) = M^T_{\widehat{\mathbf{C}}}(x_k) \trianglelefteq M_{\widehat{\mathbf{C}}}(x_k) \oplus \overline{M_{\widehat{\mathbf{C}}}}, \; k = 1, 2, \cdots, n.$$

Proof. Suppose $M^T_{\widehat{\mathbf{C}}}(x_k) \trianglelefteq M_{\widehat{\mathbf{C}}}(x_k) = (a_{ij})_{m\times m}$, $\overline{M_{\widehat{\mathbf{C}}}} = (b_{ij})_{m\times m}$ and $f(\widetilde{MD}^{\beta}_{\widehat{\mathbf{C}}}(x_k)) = (y_j)_{m\times 1}$. For any $C_t \in \mathbf{C}$,

$$\begin{aligned} C_t \in \widetilde{MD}^{\beta}_{\widehat{\mathbf{C}}}(x_k) &\Leftrightarrow (C_t(x_k) \geq \beta) \wedge (\forall C_j \in \widehat{\mathbf{C}} \wedge (C_j(x_k) \geq \beta) \wedge (C_j \supseteq C_t \Rightarrow C_t = C_j)) \\ &\Leftrightarrow (C_t(x_k) \geq \beta) \wedge (\forall j \in \{1,2,\cdots,m\} \wedge (C_j(x_k) \geq \beta) \wedge (C_j \supseteq C_t \Rightarrow C_t = C_j)) \\ &\Leftrightarrow (C_t(x_k) \geq \beta) \wedge (\forall j \in \{1,2,\cdots,m\} \wedge (C_j(x_k) \geq \beta) \wedge \\ &\quad (|\{x \in U : C_t(x) \leq C_j(x)\}| = n \Rightarrow C_t = C_j)) \\ &\Leftrightarrow (C_t(x_k) \geq \beta) \wedge (\forall j \in \{1,2,\cdots,m\} \wedge (a_{tj} = b_{tj} \Rightarrow t = j)) \\ &\Leftrightarrow (a_{tt} = b_{tt}) \wedge (a_{tj} = b_{tj} \Rightarrow t = j) \\ &\Leftrightarrow y_t = 1. \end{aligned}$$

Hence, $f(\widetilde{MD}^{\beta}_{\widehat{\mathbf{C}}}(x_k)) = M^T_{\widehat{\mathbf{C}}}(x_k) \trianglelefteq M_{\widehat{\mathbf{C}}}(x_k) \oplus \overline{M_{\widehat{\mathbf{C}}}}$. □

Example 4 (Continued from Example 1). *All $M_{\widehat{\mathbf{C}}}(x_k)$ ($k = 1,2,\cdots,6$) and $\overline{M_{\widehat{\mathbf{C}}}}$ are calculated in Example 2. Then,*

$$\begin{aligned} f(\widetilde{MD}^{\beta}_{\widehat{\mathbf{C}}}(x_1)) &= M^T_{\widehat{\mathbf{C}}}(x_1) \trianglelefteq M_{\widehat{\mathbf{C}}}(x_1) \oplus \overline{M_{\widehat{\mathbf{C}}}} \\ &= \begin{pmatrix} 6 & 2 & 6 & 0 & 0 \\ 3 & 6 & 5 & 0 & 0 \\ 0 & 1 & 6 & 0 & 0 \\ 0 & 0 & 0 & 0 & 0 \\ 0 & 0 & 0 & 0 & 0 \end{pmatrix} \oplus \begin{pmatrix} 6 & 6 & 6 & 6 & 6 \\ 6 & 6 & 6 & 6 & 6 \\ 6 & 6 & 6 & 6 & 6 \\ 6 & 6 & 6 & 6 & 6 \\ 6 & 6 & 6 & 6 & 6 \end{pmatrix} = \begin{pmatrix} 0 \\ 1 \\ 1 \\ 0 \\ 0 \end{pmatrix}, \end{aligned}$$

i.e., $\widetilde{MD}^{\beta}_{\widehat{\mathbf{C}}}(x_1) = \{C_2, C_3\}$.

$$\begin{aligned} f(\widetilde{MD}^{\beta}_{\widehat{\mathbf{C}}}(x_2)) &= M^T_{\widehat{\mathbf{C}}}(x_2) \trianglelefteq M_{\widehat{\mathbf{C}}}(x_2) \oplus \overline{M_{\widehat{\mathbf{C}}}} \\ &= \begin{pmatrix} 0 & 0 & 0 & 0 & 0 \\ 0 & 0 & 0 & 0 & 0 \\ 0 & 0 & 6 & 0 & 0 \\ 0 & 0 & 0 & 0 & 0 \\ 0 & 0 & 0 & 0 & 0 \end{pmatrix} \oplus \begin{pmatrix} 6 & 6 & 6 & 6 & 6 \\ 6 & 6 & 6 & 6 & 6 \\ 6 & 6 & 6 & 6 & 6 \\ 6 & 6 & 6 & 6 & 6 \\ 6 & 6 & 6 & 6 & 6 \end{pmatrix} = \begin{pmatrix} 0 \\ 0 \\ 1 \\ 0 \\ 0 \end{pmatrix}, \end{aligned}$$

i.e., $\widetilde{MD}^{\beta}_{\widehat{\mathbf{C}}}(x_2) = \{C_3\}$.

$$\begin{aligned} f(\widetilde{MD}^{\beta}_{\widehat{\mathbf{C}}}(x_3)) &= M^T_{\widehat{\mathbf{C}}}(x_3) \trianglelefteq M_{\widehat{\mathbf{C}}}(x_3) \oplus \overline{M_{\widehat{\mathbf{C}}}} \\ &= \begin{pmatrix} 6 & 0 & 6 & 0 & 4 \\ 0 & 0 & 0 & 0 & 0 \\ 0 & 0 & 6 & 0 & 1 \\ 0 & 0 & 0 & 0 & 0 \\ 1 & 0 & 5 & 0 & 6 \end{pmatrix} \oplus \begin{pmatrix} 6 & 6 & 6 & 6 & 6 \\ 6 & 6 & 6 & 6 & 6 \\ 6 & 6 & 6 & 6 & 6 \\ 6 & 6 & 6 & 6 & 6 \\ 6 & 6 & 6 & 6 & 6 \end{pmatrix} = \begin{pmatrix} 0 \\ 0 \\ 1 \\ 0 \\ 1 \end{pmatrix}, \end{aligned}$$

i.e., $\widetilde{MD}^{\beta}_{\widehat{\mathbf{C}}}(x_3) = \{C_3, C_5\}$.

$$\begin{aligned} f(\widetilde{MD}^{\beta}_{\widehat{\mathbf{C}}}(x_4)) &= M^T_{\widehat{\mathbf{C}}}(x_4) \trianglelefteq M_{\widehat{\mathbf{C}}}(x_4) \oplus \overline{M_{\widehat{\mathbf{C}}}} \\ &= \begin{pmatrix} 0 & 0 & 0 & 0 & 0 \\ 0 & 6 & 5 & 0 & 4 \\ 0 & 1 & 6 & 0 & 1 \\ 0 & 0 & 0 & 0 & 0 \\ 0 & 1 & 5 & 0 & 6 \end{pmatrix} \oplus \begin{pmatrix} 6 & 6 & 6 & 6 & 6 \\ 6 & 6 & 6 & 6 & 6 \\ 6 & 6 & 6 & 6 & 6 \\ 6 & 6 & 6 & 6 & 6 \\ 6 & 6 & 6 & 6 & 6 \end{pmatrix} = \begin{pmatrix} 0 \\ 1 \\ 1 \\ 0 \\ 1 \end{pmatrix}, \end{aligned}$$

i.e., $\widetilde{MD}^{\beta}_{\widehat{\mathbf{C}}}(x_4) = \{C_2, C_3, C_5\}$.

$$
\begin{aligned}
f(\widetilde{MD}^{\beta}_{\widehat{\mathbf{C}}}(x_5)) &= M^{T}_{\widehat{\mathbf{C}}}(x_5) \trianglelefteq M_{\widehat{\mathbf{C}}}(x_5) \oplus \overline{M_{\widehat{\mathbf{C}}}} \\
&= \begin{pmatrix} 6 & 0 & 6 & 0 & 4 \\ 0 & 0 & 0 & 0 & 0 \\ 0 & 0 & 6 & 0 & 1 \\ 5 & 0 & 6 & 6 & 6 \\ 1 & 0 & 5 & 0 & 6 \end{pmatrix} \oplus \begin{pmatrix} 6 & 6 & 6 & 6 & 6 \\ 6 & 6 & 6 & 6 & 6 \\ 6 & 6 & 6 & 6 & 6 \\ 6 & 6 & 6 & 6 & 6 \\ 6 & 6 & 6 & 6 & 6 \end{pmatrix} = \begin{pmatrix} 0 \\ 0 \\ 1 \\ 0 \\ 1 \end{pmatrix},
\end{aligned}
$$

i.e., $\widetilde{MD}^{\beta}_{\widehat{\mathbf{C}}}(x_5) = \{C_3, C_5\}$.

$$
\begin{aligned}
f(\widetilde{MD}^{\beta}_{\widehat{\mathbf{C}}}(x_6)) &= M^{T}_{\widehat{\mathbf{C}}}(x_6) \trianglelefteq M_{\widehat{\mathbf{C}}}(x_6) \oplus \overline{M_{\widehat{\mathbf{C}}}} \\
&= \begin{pmatrix} 6 & 0 & 6 & 0 & 4 \\ 0 & 0 & 0 & 0 & 0 \\ 0 & 0 & 6 & 0 & 1 \\ 0 & 0 & 0 & 0 & 0 \\ 1 & 0 & 5 & 0 & 6 \end{pmatrix} \oplus \begin{pmatrix} 6 & 6 & 6 & 6 & 6 \\ 6 & 6 & 6 & 6 & 6 \\ 6 & 6 & 6 & 6 & 6 \\ 6 & 6 & 6 & 6 & 6 \\ 6 & 6 & 6 & 6 & 6 \end{pmatrix} = \begin{pmatrix} 0 \\ 0 \\ 1 \\ 0 \\ 1 \end{pmatrix},
\end{aligned}
$$

i.e., $\widetilde{MD}^{\beta}_{\widehat{\mathbf{C}}}(x_6) = \{C_3, C_5\}$.

4. Matrix Approaches for Reductions in IF β-Covering Approximation Spaces

In this section, we present two kinds of reductions in IF β-covering approximation spaces based on IF β-minimal and β-maximal descriptions, respectively. Moreover, they are calculated by matrices.

4.1. Reductions of IF β-Covering Approximation Spaces via IF β-Minimal Descriptions

The definitions of IF β-minimal reduction and corresponding matrix approaches are mainly presented in this subsection. Firstly, the notion of the subspace of the original IF β-covering approximation space is presented in the following definition.

Definition 11. *Let $(U, \widehat{\mathbf{C}})$ be an IF β-covering approximation space and $\widehat{\mathbf{D}} \subseteq \widehat{\mathbf{C}}$. We call $(U, \widehat{\mathbf{D}})$ an IF sub-β-covering approximation space of $(U, \widehat{\mathbf{C}})$ if $\widehat{\mathbf{D}}$ is also an IF β-covering of U. The family of all IF sub-β-covering approximation spaces of $(U, \widehat{\mathbf{C}})$ is denoted by $\mathcal{S}(\widehat{\mathbf{C}})$.*

By Definition 11, $\widehat{\mathbf{C}} \in \mathcal{S}(\widehat{\mathbf{C}})$ for any IF β-covering approximation space $(U, \widehat{\mathbf{C}})$. We denote $\widetilde{\mathcal{N}}^{\beta}_{\widehat{\mathbf{C}}}(x) = \{C \in \widehat{\mathbf{C}} : C(x) \geq \beta\}$. Then, Propositions 5 and 6 show two properties of IF β-minimal descriptions in the IF sub-β-covering approximation space.

Proposition 5. *Let $(U, \widehat{\mathbf{C}})$ be an IF β-covering approximation space and $\widehat{\mathbf{D}} \in \mathcal{S}(\widehat{\mathbf{C}})$. For any $x \in U$, if $|\widetilde{\mathcal{N}}^{\beta}_{\widehat{\mathbf{C}}}(x)| = 1$, then $\widetilde{Md}^{\beta}_{\widehat{\mathbf{C}}}(x) = \widetilde{Md}^{\beta}_{\widehat{\mathbf{D}}}(x)$.*

Proof. If $|\widetilde{\mathcal{N}}^{\beta}_{\widehat{\mathbf{C}}}(x)| = 1$, then we suppose $\widetilde{\mathcal{N}}^{\beta}_{\widehat{\mathbf{C}}}(x) = \{C'\}$, where $C' \in \widehat{\mathbf{C}}$ and $C'(x) \geq \beta$. Since $\widehat{\mathbf{D}} \in \mathcal{S}(\widehat{\mathbf{C}})$, $C' \in \widehat{\mathbf{D}}$. Hence, $\widetilde{\mathcal{N}}^{\beta}_{\widehat{\mathbf{D}}}(x) = \{C'\}$. By Definition 5, $\widetilde{Md}^{\beta}_{\widehat{\mathbf{C}}}(x) = \{C \in \widehat{\mathbf{C}} : C(x) \geq \beta \wedge (\forall D \in \widehat{\mathbf{C}})(D(x) \geq \beta \wedge D \subseteq C \Rightarrow C = D)\} = \{C \in \widetilde{\mathcal{N}}^{\beta}_{\widehat{\mathbf{C}}}(x) : \forall D \in \widetilde{\mathcal{N}}^{\beta}_{\widehat{\mathbf{C}}}(x) \wedge D \subseteq C \Rightarrow C = D)\} = \{C'\}$ and $\widetilde{Md}^{\beta}_{\widehat{\mathbf{D}}}(x) = \{C \in \widetilde{\mathcal{N}}^{\beta}_{\widehat{\mathbf{D}}}(x) : \forall D \in \widetilde{\mathcal{N}}^{\beta}_{\widehat{\mathbf{D}}}(x) \wedge D \subseteq C \Rightarrow C = D)\} = \{C'\}$. Therefore, $\widetilde{Md}^{\beta}_{\widehat{\mathbf{C}}}(x) = \widetilde{Md}^{\beta}_{\widehat{\mathbf{D}}}(x)$. □

Proposition 6. *Let $(U, \widehat{\mathbf{C}})$ be an IF β-covering approximation space and $\widehat{\mathbf{D}} \in \mathcal{S}(\widehat{\mathbf{C}})$. For any $x \in U$, if $\widetilde{\mathcal{N}}^{\beta}_{\widehat{\mathbf{C}}}(x) = \widetilde{\mathcal{N}}^{\beta}_{\widehat{\mathbf{D}}}(x)$, then $\widetilde{Md}^{\beta}_{\widehat{\mathbf{C}}}(x) = \widetilde{Md}^{\beta}_{\widehat{\mathbf{D}}}(x)$.*

Proof. Since $\widetilde{\mathcal{N}}^{\beta}_{\widehat{\mathbf{C}}}(x) = \widetilde{\mathcal{N}}^{\beta}_{\widehat{\mathbf{D}}}(x)$, $\widetilde{Md}^{\beta}_{\widehat{\mathbf{C}}}(x) = \{C \in \widehat{\mathbf{C}} : C(x) \geq \beta \wedge (\forall D \in \widehat{\mathbf{C}})(D(x) \geq \beta \wedge D \subseteq C \Rightarrow C = D)\} = \{C \in \widetilde{\mathcal{N}}^{\beta}_{\widehat{\mathbf{C}}}(x) : \forall D \in \widetilde{\mathcal{N}}^{\beta}_{\widehat{\mathbf{C}}}(x) \wedge D \subseteq C \Rightarrow C = D)\} = \{C \in \widetilde{\mathcal{N}}^{\beta}_{\widehat{\mathbf{D}}}(x) : \forall D \in \widetilde{\mathcal{N}}^{\beta}_{\widehat{\mathbf{D}}}(x) \wedge D \subseteq C \Rightarrow C = D)\} = \widetilde{Md}^{\beta}_{\widehat{\mathbf{D}}}(x)$. □

The converse of Proposition 6 is incorrect. That is to say, "for any $x \in U$, if $\widetilde{Md}^{\beta}_{\widehat{\mathbf{C}}}(x) = \widetilde{Md}^{\beta}_{\widehat{\mathbf{D}}}(x)$, then $\widetilde{\mathcal{N}}^{\beta}_{\widehat{\mathbf{C}}}(x) = \widetilde{\mathcal{N}}^{\beta}_{\widehat{\mathbf{D}}}(x)$" is not true. We use the following example to explain this.

Example 5 (Continued from Example 1). *In Example 1, $\widehat{\mathbf{C}} = \{C_1, \cdots, C_5\}$ is an IF β-covering of U. In Example 3, we have $f(\widetilde{Md}^{\beta}_{\widehat{\mathbf{C}}}(x_5)) = (1,0,0,1,0)^T$, i.e., $\widetilde{Md}^{\beta}_{\widehat{\mathbf{C}}}(x_5) = \{C_1, C_4\}$. Suppose $\widehat{\boldsymbol{D}} = \{C_1, \cdots, C_4\}$. Then, $\widehat{\boldsymbol{D}} \in \mathcal{S}(\widehat{\boldsymbol{C}})$.*

$$M_{\widehat{\mathbf{D}}} = \begin{array}{c} \\ x_1 \\ x_2 \\ x_3 \\ x_4 \\ x_5 \\ x_6 \end{array} \begin{array}{c} \begin{array}{cccc} C_1 & C_2 & C_3 & C_4 \end{array} \\ \begin{pmatrix} \langle 0.6,0.3\rangle & \langle 0.7,0.3\rangle & \langle 0.7,0.2\rangle & \langle 0.3,0.5\rangle \\ \langle 0.5,0.2\rangle & \langle 0.2,0.6\rangle & \langle 0.6,0.1\rangle & \langle 0.5,0.5\rangle \\ \langle 0.7,0.3\rangle & \langle 0.1,0.7\rangle & \langle 0.8,0.1\rangle & \langle 0.5,0.3\rangle \\ \langle 0.6,0.4\rangle & \langle 0.6,0.2\rangle & \langle 0.6,0.3\rangle & \langle 0.4,0.5\rangle \\ \langle 0.7,0.3\rangle & \langle 0.5,0.2\rangle & \langle 0.8,0.1\rangle & \langle 0.6,0.2\rangle \\ \langle 0.6,0.2\rangle & \langle 0.5,0.3\rangle & \langle 0.6,0.1\rangle & \langle 0.5,0.3\rangle \end{pmatrix} \end{array} \textit{ and}$$

$$f(\widetilde{Md}^{\beta}_{\widehat{\mathbf{D}}}(x_5)) = M^T_{\widehat{\mathbf{D}}}(x_5) \trianglerighteq M_{\widehat{\mathbf{D}}}(x_5) \oplus \overline{M_{\widehat{\mathbf{D}}}} = \begin{pmatrix} 6 & 0 & 0 & 5 \\ 0 & 0 & 0 & 0 \\ 6 & 0 & 6 & 6 \\ 0 & 0 & 0 & 6 \end{pmatrix} \oplus \begin{pmatrix} 6 & 6 & 6 & 6 \\ 6 & 6 & 6 & 6 \\ 6 & 6 & 6 & 6 \\ 6 & 6 & 6 & 6 \end{pmatrix} = \begin{pmatrix} 1 \\ 0 \\ 0 \\ 1 \end{pmatrix},$$

i.e., $\widetilde{Md}^{\beta}_{\widehat{\mathbf{D}}}(x_5) = \{C_1, C_4\}$. Hence, $\widetilde{Md}^{\beta}_{\widehat{\mathbf{C}}}(x_5) = \widetilde{Md}^{\beta}_{\widehat{\mathbf{D}}}(x_5) = \{C_1, C_4\}$. But $\widetilde{\mathcal{N}}^{\beta}_{\widehat{\mathbf{C}}}(x_5) = \{C_1, C_3, C_4, C_5\}$ and $\widetilde{\mathcal{N}}^{\beta}_{\widehat{\mathbf{D}}}(x_5) = \{C_1, C_3, C_4\}$, i.e., $\widetilde{\mathcal{N}}^{\beta}_{\widehat{\mathbf{C}}}(x_5) \neq \widetilde{\mathcal{N}}^{\beta}_{\widehat{\mathbf{D}}}(x_5)$.

Definition 12. *Let $(U, \widehat{\mathbf{C}})$ be an IF β-covering approximation space and $\widehat{\mathbf{D}} \in \mathcal{S}(\widehat{\mathbf{C}})$. $\widehat{\mathbf{D}}$ is called the IF β-minimal reduction of $\widehat{\mathbf{C}}$ if $\widehat{\mathbf{D}}$ satisfies the following conditions:*

(1) For any $x \in U$, $\widetilde{Md}^{\beta}_{\widehat{\mathbf{C}}}(x) = \widetilde{Md}^{\beta}_{\widehat{\mathbf{D}}}(x)$;

(2) For any $\widehat{\mathbf{E}} \in \mathcal{S}(\widehat{\mathbf{D}}) - \{\widehat{\mathbf{D}}\}$, there exists $x \in U$ such that $\widetilde{Md}^{\beta}_{\widehat{\mathbf{E}}}(x) \neq \widetilde{Md}^{\beta}_{\widehat{\mathbf{D}}}(x)$.

Let $\mathbf{A}$ be a family of subsets of $IF(U)$. We denote $Min(\mathbf{A}) = \{X \in \mathbf{A} : \forall Y \in \mathbf{A}, Y \subseteq X \Rightarrow X = Y\}$.

Proposition 7. *Let $(U, \widehat{\mathbf{C}})$ be an IF β-covering approximation space. $\widehat{\mathbf{D}}$ is the IF β-minimal reduction of $\widehat{\mathbf{C}}$ if and only if $\widehat{\mathbf{D}} \in Min(\{\widehat{\mathbf{E}} \in \mathcal{S}(\widehat{\mathbf{C}}) : \forall x \in U, \widetilde{Md}^{\beta}_{\widehat{\mathbf{C}}}(x) = \widetilde{Md}^{\beta}_{\widehat{\mathbf{E}}}(x)\})$.*

Proof. By Definition 12, it is immediate. □

Theorem 3. *Let $(U, \widehat{\mathbf{C}})$ be an IF β-covering approximation space. The IF β-minimal reduction of $\widehat{\mathbf{C}}$ is unique.*

Proof. By Definition 12, the existence of the IF β-minimal reduction is true. Then, we use proof by contradiction to prove uniqueness. Suppose $\widehat{\mathbf{D}}_1$ is an IF β-minimal reduction of $\widehat{\mathbf{C}}$ and $\widehat{\mathbf{D}}_2$ is the other one. Then, $\widetilde{Md}^{\beta}_{\widehat{\mathbf{C}}}(x) = \widetilde{Md}^{\beta}_{\widehat{\mathbf{D}}_1}(x) = \widetilde{Md}^{\beta}_{\widehat{\mathbf{D}}_2}(x)$ for any $x \in U$. Hence, there exists $K \in \widehat{\mathbf{D}}_2 - \widehat{\mathbf{D}}_1$ such that $K \notin \widetilde{Md}^{\beta}_{\widehat{\mathbf{D}}_1}(x)$ for any $x \in U$. That is to say, $K \notin \widetilde{Md}^{\beta}_{\widehat{\mathbf{D}}_2}(x)$ for any $x \in U$. $\widehat{\mathbf{D}}_2 - \{K\}$ is also an IF β-covering, since for any $x \in U$ there exists $C \in \widetilde{Md}^{\beta}_{\widehat{\mathbf{D}}_2}(x)$ such that $C(x) \geq \beta$. Therefore, $\widetilde{Md}^{\beta}_{\widehat{\mathbf{D}}_2 - \{K\}}(x) = \widetilde{Md}^{\beta}_{\widehat{\mathbf{D}}_2}(x)$ for any $x \in U$. So, $\widehat{\mathbf{D}}_2$ is not an IF

β-minimal reduction of $\widehat{\mathbf{C}}$, which is contradictory with $\widehat{\mathbf{D}}_2$ being an IF β-minimal reduction of $\widehat{\mathbf{C}}$. Thus, the IF β-minimal reduction of $\widehat{\mathbf{C}}$ is unique. □

By Proposition 7 and Theorem 3, the steps of calculating all IF β-minimal reductions in the IF β-covering approximation space $(U, \widehat{\mathbf{C}})$ are presented as follows:

Step 1: Compute the family of all IF sub-β-covering approximation spaces of $(U, \widehat{\mathbf{C}})$ according to Definition 11, i.e., $\mathcal{S}(\widehat{\mathbf{C}})$.

Step 2: For any $x \in U$ and $\widehat{\mathbf{D}} \in \mathcal{S}(\widehat{\mathbf{C}})$, compute $\widetilde{Md}^{\beta}_{\widehat{\mathbf{D}}}(x)$ according to Theorem 1, i.e., $f(\widetilde{Md}^{\beta}_{\widehat{\mathbf{D}}}(x)) = M^{T}_{\widehat{\mathbf{D}}}(x) \unrhd M_{\widehat{\mathbf{D}}}(x) \oplus \overline{M_{\widehat{\mathbf{D}}}}$.

Step 3: Compute $F = Min(\{\widehat{\mathbf{D}} \in \mathcal{S}(\widehat{\mathbf{C}}) : \forall x \in U, \widetilde{Md}^{\beta}_{\widehat{\mathbf{C}}}(x) = \widetilde{Md}^{\beta}_{\widehat{\mathbf{D}}}(x)\})$. The element of F is the IF β-minimal reduction of $\widehat{\mathbf{C}}$ according to Proposition 7 and Theorem 3.

Hence, the IF β-minimal reduction of $\widehat{\mathbf{C}}$ belongs to F.

4.2. Reductions of IF β-Covering Approximation Spaces via IF β-Maximal Descriptions

Based on Section 4.1, we present the definition of IF β-maximal reduction and corresponding matrix approaches in this subsection. Firstly, we present two properties of IF β-minimal descriptions in the IF sub-β-covering approximation space in the following two propositions, respectively.

Proposition 8. *Let $(U, \widehat{\mathbf{C}})$ be an IF β-covering approximation space and $\widehat{\mathbf{D}} \in \mathcal{S}(\widehat{\mathbf{C}})$. For any $x \in U$, if $|\widetilde{\mathcal{N}}^{\beta}_{\widehat{\mathbf{C}}}(x)| = 1$, then $\widetilde{MD}^{\beta}_{\widehat{\mathbf{C}}}(x) = \widetilde{MD}^{\beta}_{\widehat{\mathbf{D}}}(x)$.*

Proof. If $|\widetilde{\mathcal{N}}^{\beta}_{\widehat{\mathbf{C}}}(x)| = 1$, then we suppose $\widetilde{\mathcal{N}}^{\beta}_{\widehat{\mathbf{C}}}(x) = \{C'\}$, where $C' \in \widehat{\mathbf{C}}$ and $C'(x) \geq \beta$. Since $\widehat{\mathbf{D}} \in \mathcal{S}(\widehat{\mathbf{C}})$, $C' \in \widehat{\mathbf{D}}$. Hence, $\widetilde{\mathcal{N}}^{\beta}_{\widehat{\mathbf{D}}}(x) = \{C'\}$. By Definition 9, $\widetilde{MD}^{\beta}_{\widehat{\mathbf{C}}}(x) = \{C \in \widehat{\mathbf{C}} : C(x) \geq \beta \wedge (\forall D \in \widehat{\mathbf{C}})(D(x) \geq \beta \wedge C \subseteq D \Rightarrow C = D)\} = \{C \in \widetilde{\mathcal{N}}^{\beta}_{\widehat{\mathbf{C}}}(x) : \forall D \in \widetilde{\mathcal{N}}^{\beta}_{\widehat{\mathbf{C}}}(x) \wedge C \subseteq D \Rightarrow C = D)\} = \{C'\}$ and $\widetilde{Md}^{\beta}_{\widehat{\mathbf{D}}}(x) = \{C \in \widetilde{\mathcal{N}}^{\beta}_{\widehat{\mathbf{D}}}(x) : \forall D \in \widetilde{\mathcal{N}}^{\beta}_{\widehat{\mathbf{D}}}(x) \wedge C \subseteq D \Rightarrow C = D)\} = \{C'\}$. Therefore, $\widetilde{MD}^{\beta}_{\widehat{\mathbf{C}}}(x) = \widetilde{MD}^{\beta}_{\widehat{\mathbf{D}}}(x)$. □

Proposition 9. *Let $(U, \widehat{\mathbf{C}})$ be an IF β-covering approximation space and $\widehat{\mathbf{D}} \in \mathcal{S}(\widehat{\mathbf{C}})$. For any $x \in U$, if $\widetilde{\mathcal{N}}^{\beta}_{\widehat{\mathbf{C}}}(x) = \widetilde{\mathcal{N}}^{\beta}_{\widehat{\mathbf{D}}}(x)$, then $\widetilde{MD}^{\beta}_{\widehat{\mathbf{C}}}(x) = \widetilde{MD}^{\beta}_{\widehat{\mathbf{D}}}(x)$.*

Proof. Since $\widetilde{\mathcal{N}}^{\beta}_{\widehat{\mathbf{C}}}(x) = \widetilde{\mathcal{N}}^{\beta}_{\widehat{\mathbf{D}}}(x)$, $\widetilde{MD}^{\beta}_{\widehat{\mathbf{C}}}(x) = \{C \in \widehat{\mathbf{C}} : C(x) \geq \beta \wedge (\forall D \in \widehat{\mathbf{C}})(D(x) \geq \beta \wedge C \subseteq D \Rightarrow C = D)\} = \{C \in \widetilde{\mathcal{N}}^{\beta}_{\widehat{\mathbf{C}}}(x) : \forall D \in \widetilde{\mathcal{N}}^{\beta}_{\widehat{\mathbf{C}}}(x) \wedge C \subseteq D \Rightarrow C = D)\} = \{C \in \widetilde{\mathcal{N}}^{\beta}_{\widehat{\mathbf{D}}}(x) : \forall D \in \widetilde{\mathcal{N}}^{\beta}_{\widehat{\mathbf{D}}}(x) \wedge C \subseteq D \Rightarrow C = D)\} = \widetilde{MD}^{\beta}_{\widehat{\mathbf{D}}}(x)$. □

The converse of Proposition 9 is incorrect. That is to say, "for any $x \in U$, if $\widetilde{MD}^{\beta}_{\widehat{\mathbf{C}}}(x) = \widetilde{MD}^{\beta}_{\widehat{\mathbf{D}}}(x)$, then $\widetilde{\mathcal{N}}^{\beta}_{\widehat{\mathbf{C}}}(x) = \widetilde{\mathcal{N}}^{\beta}_{\widehat{\mathbf{D}}}(x)$" is not true. We use the following example to explain this.

Example 6. *(Continued from Example 1.) In Example 1, $\widehat{\mathbf{C}} = \{C_1, \cdots, C_5\}$ is an IF β-covering of U. In Example 4, we have $f(\widetilde{MD}^{\beta}_{\widehat{\mathbf{C}}}(x_1)) = (0,1,1,0,0)^T$, i.e., $\widetilde{MD}^{\beta}_{\widehat{\mathbf{C}}}(x_1) = \{C_2, C_3\}$. Suppose $\widehat{\mathbf{D}} = \{C'_1, C'_2, C'_3\}$, where $C'_1 = C_2, C'_2 = C_3, C'_3 = C_5\}$. Then, $\widehat{\mathbf{D}} \in \mathcal{S}(\widehat{\mathbf{C}})$.*

$$M_{\widehat{\mathbf{D}}} = \begin{array}{c} \\ x_1 \\ x_2 \\ x_3 \\ x_4 \\ x_5 \\ x_6 \end{array} \begin{array}{c} \begin{array}{ccc} C'_1 & C'_2 & C'_3 \end{array} \\ \begin{pmatrix} \langle 0.7,0.3\rangle & \langle 0.7,0.2\rangle & \langle 0.5,0.1\rangle \\ \langle 0.2,0.6\rangle & \langle 0.6,0.1\rangle & \langle 0.6,0.4\rangle \\ \langle 0.1,0.7\rangle & \langle 0.8,0.1\rangle & \langle 0.7,0.2\rangle \\ \langle 0.6,0.2\rangle & \langle 0.6,0.3\rangle & \langle 0.6,0.3\rangle \\ \langle 0.5,0.2\rangle & \langle 0.8,0.1\rangle & \langle 0.7,0.2\rangle \\ \langle 0.5,0.3\rangle & \langle 0.6,0.1\rangle & \langle 0.6,0.2\rangle \end{pmatrix} \end{array} = \begin{array}{c} \\ x_1 \\ x_2 \\ x_3 \\ x_4 \\ x_5 \\ x_6 \end{array} \begin{array}{c} \begin{array}{ccc} C_2 & C_3 & C_5 \end{array} \\ \begin{pmatrix} \langle 0.7,0.3\rangle & \langle 0.7,0.2\rangle & \langle 0.5,0.1\rangle \\ \langle 0.2,0.6\rangle & \langle 0.6,0.1\rangle & \langle 0.6,0.4\rangle \\ \langle 0.1,0.7\rangle & \langle 0.8,0.1\rangle & \langle 0.7,0.2\rangle \\ \langle 0.6,0.2\rangle & \langle 0.6,0.3\rangle & \langle 0.6,0.3\rangle \\ \langle 0.5,0.2\rangle & \langle 0.8,0.1\rangle & \langle 0.7,0.2\rangle \\ \langle 0.5,0.3\rangle & \langle 0.6,0.1\rangle & \langle 0.6,0.2\rangle \end{pmatrix} \end{array} \text{ and}$$

$$f(\widetilde{MD}^{\beta}_{\widehat{\mathbf{D}}}(x_1)) = M^T_{\widehat{\mathbf{D}}}(x_1) \trianglelefteq M_{\widehat{\mathbf{D}}}(x_1) \oplus \overline{M_{\widehat{\mathbf{D}}}} = \begin{pmatrix} 6 & 5 & 0 \\ 1 & 6 & 0 \\ 0 & 0 & 0 \end{pmatrix} \oplus \begin{pmatrix} 6 & 6 & 6 \\ 6 & 6 & 6 \\ 6 & 6 & 6 \end{pmatrix} = \begin{pmatrix} 1 \\ 1 \\ 0 \end{pmatrix},$$

i.e., $\widetilde{MD}^{\beta}_{\widehat{\mathbf{D}}}(x_1) = \{C'_1, C'_2\} = \{C_2, C_3\}$. *Hence,* $\widetilde{MD}^{\beta}_{\widehat{\mathbf{C}}}(x_1) = \widetilde{MD}^{\beta}_{\widehat{\mathbf{D}}}(x_1) = \{C_2, C_3\}$. *But* $\widetilde{\mathcal{N}}^{\beta}_{\widehat{\mathbf{C}}}(x_1) = \{C_1, C_2, C_3\}$ *and* $\widetilde{\mathcal{N}}^{\beta}_{\widehat{\mathbf{D}}}(x_1) = \{C_2, C_3\}$, *i.e.,* $\widetilde{\mathcal{N}}^{\beta}_{\widehat{\mathbf{C}}}(x_1) \neq \widetilde{\mathcal{N}}^{\beta}_{\widehat{\mathbf{D}}}(x_1)$.

Definition 13. *Let* $(U, \widehat{\mathbf{C}})$ *be an IF* β*-covering approximation space and* $\widehat{\mathbf{D}} \in \mathcal{S}(\widehat{\mathbf{C}})$. $\widehat{\mathbf{D}}$ *is called an IF* β*-maximal reduction of* $\widehat{\mathbf{C}}$ *if* $\widehat{\mathbf{D}}$ *satisfies the following conditions:*

(1) For any $x \in U$, $\widetilde{MD}^{\beta}_{\widehat{\mathbf{C}}}(x) = \widetilde{MD}^{\beta}_{\widehat{\mathbf{D}}}(x)$*;*

(2) For any $\widehat{\mathbf{E}} \in \mathcal{S}(\widehat{\mathbf{D}}) - \{\widehat{\mathbf{D}}\}$, *there exists* $x \in U$ *such that* $\widetilde{MD}^{\beta}_{\widehat{\mathbf{E}}}(x) \neq \widetilde{MD}^{\beta}_{\widehat{\mathbf{D}}}(x)$.

Proposition 10. *Let* $(U, \widehat{\mathbf{C}})$ *be an IF* β*-covering approximation space.* $\widehat{\mathbf{D}}$ *is an IF* β*-maximal reduction of* $\widehat{\mathbf{C}}$ *if and only if* $\widehat{\mathbf{D}} \in Min(\{\widehat{\mathbf{E}} \in \mathcal{S}(\widehat{\mathbf{C}}) : \forall x \in U, \widetilde{MD}^{\beta}_{\widehat{\mathbf{C}}}(x) = \widetilde{MD}^{\beta}_{\widehat{\mathbf{E}}}(x)\})$.

Proof. By Definition 13, it is immediate. □

Theorem 4. *Let* $(U, \widehat{\mathbf{C}})$ *be an IF* β*-covering approximation space and* $\widehat{\mathbf{D}} \in \mathcal{S}(\widehat{\mathbf{C}})$. *The IF* β*-maximal reduction of* $\widehat{\mathbf{C}}$ *is unique.*

Proof. By Definition 13, the existence of the IF β-maximal reduction is true. Then, we use proof by contradiction to prove the uniqueness. Suppose $\widehat{\mathbf{D}}_1$ is an IF β-maximal reduction of $\widehat{\mathbf{C}}$ and $\widehat{\mathbf{D}}_2$ is the other one. Then, $\widetilde{MD}^{\beta}_{\widehat{\mathbf{C}}}(x) = \widetilde{MD}^{\beta}_{\widehat{\mathbf{D}}_1}(x) = \widetilde{MD}^{\beta}_{\widehat{\mathbf{D}}_2}(x)$ for any $x \in U$. Hence, there exists $K \in \widehat{\mathbf{D}}_2 - \widehat{\mathbf{D}}_1$ such that $K \notin \widetilde{MD}^{\beta}_{\widehat{\mathbf{D}}_1}(x)$ for any $x \in U$. That is to say, $K \notin \widetilde{MD}^{\beta}_{\widehat{\mathbf{D}}_2}(x)$ for any $x \in U$. $\widehat{\mathbf{D}}_2 - \{K\}$ is also an IF β-covering, since for any $x \in U$, there exists $C \in \widetilde{MD}^{\beta}_{\widehat{\mathbf{D}}_2}(x)$ such that $C(x) \geq \beta$. Therefore, $\widetilde{MD}^{\beta}_{\widehat{\mathbf{D}}_2 - \{K\}}(x) = \widetilde{MD}^{\beta}_{\widehat{\mathbf{D}}_2}(x)$ for any $x \in U$. So, $\widehat{\mathbf{D}}_2$ is not an IF β-maximal reduction of $\widehat{\mathbf{C}}$, which is contradictory with $\widehat{\mathbf{D}}_2$ is an IF β-maximal reduction. Thus, the IF β-maximal reduction of $\widehat{\mathbf{C}}$ is unique. □

By Proposition 10 and Theorem 4, the steps of calculating the IF β-maximal reduction in the IF β-covering approximation space $(U, \widehat{\mathbf{C}})$ are presented as follows:

Step 1: Compute the family of all IF sub-β-covering approximation spaces of $(U, \widehat{\mathbf{C}})$ according to Definition 11, i.e., $\mathcal{S}(\widehat{\mathbf{C}})$.

Step 2: For any $x \in U$ and $\widehat{\mathbf{D}} \in \mathcal{S}(\widehat{\mathbf{C}})$, compute $\widetilde{MD}^{\beta}_{\widehat{\mathbf{D}}}(x)$ according to Theorem 2, i.e., $f(\widetilde{MD}^{\beta}_{\widehat{\mathbf{D}}}(x)) = M^T_{\widehat{\mathbf{D}}}(x) \trianglelefteq M_{\widehat{\mathbf{D}}}(x) \oplus \overline{M_{\widehat{\mathbf{D}}}}$.

Step 3: Compute $F = Min(\{\widehat{\mathbf{D}} \in \mathcal{S}(\widehat{\mathbf{C}}) : \forall x \in U, \widetilde{MD}^{\beta}_{\widehat{\mathbf{C}}}(x) = \widetilde{MD}^{\beta}_{\widehat{\mathbf{D}}}(x)\})$. The element of F is the IF β-maximal reduction of $\widehat{\mathbf{C}}$ according to Proposition 10 and Theorem 4.

Example 7. *A customer wants to choose suitable attributes to evaluate a house. Let* $U = \{x_1, x_2, \cdots, x_6\}$ *be a set of houses and* $\widehat{\mathbf{C}} = \{C_1, C_2, \cdots, C_5\}$ *be five attributes given by merchants, where* $C_1, C_2, \cdots, C_5$ *represent expensive, beautiful, large, convenient traffic and green surroundings, respectively. Suppose* $C_j(x_i) = \langle \mu_{C_j(x_i)}, \nu_{C_j(x_i)} \rangle$, $(i = 1, 2, \cdots, 6; j = 1, 2, \cdots, 5)$, *where* $\mu_{C_j(x_i)}$ *and* $\nu_{C_j(x_i)}$ *are the degrees of membership and non-membership of the alternative* x_i *to the attribute* C_j*, respectively. Let* $\beta = \langle 0.6, 0.3 \rangle$ *be the critical value. Suppose that for each alternative* x_i *there exists the attribute* C_j *such that* $C_j(x_i) \geq \beta$. *It is obvious that* $\widehat{\mathbf{C}}$ *is an IF* β*-covering presented in Example 1.*

Step 1: $\mathcal{S}(\widehat{\mathbf{C}}) = \{\{C_1, C_2, C_3, C_4, C_5\}, \{C_1, C_3, C_4, C_5\}, \{C_1, C_2, C_3, C_5\}, \{C_2, C_3, C_4, C_5\}, \{C_1, C_2, C_3, C_4\}, \{C_3, C_4, C_5\}, \{C_1, C_2, C_3\}, \{C_1, C_3, C_4\}, \{C_1, C_3, C_5\}, \{C_2, C_3, C_5\}, \{C_2, C_3, C_4\}, \{C_3, C_4, C_5\}, \{C_1, C_3\}, \{C_2, C_3\}, \{C_2, C_5\}, \{C_3, C_4\}, \{C_3, C_5\}, \{C_3\}\}$.

***Step 2**: For any $x \in U$ and $\widehat{\mathbf{D}} \in \mathcal{S}(\widehat{\mathbf{C}})$, we compute $\widetilde{MD}^{\beta}_{\widehat{\mathbf{D}}}(x)$ by matrices. All $\widetilde{MD}^{\beta}_{\widehat{\mathbf{C}}}(x)$ for any $x \in U$ were calculated in Example 4. Here, we show the process about $\widehat{\mathbf{D}} = \{C_2, C_3, C_4, C_5\}$ only.*

Suppose $\widehat{\mathbf{D}} = \{C'_1, C'_2, C'_3, C'_4\}$, where $C'_1 = C_2, C'_2 = C_3, C'_3 = C_4, C'_4 = C_5$. Then,

$$M_{\widehat{D}} = \begin{array}{c} \\ x_1 \\ x_2 \\ x_3 \\ x_4 \\ x_5 \\ x_6 \end{array} \begin{array}{c} \begin{array}{cccc} C'_1 & C'_2 & C'_3 & C'_4 \end{array} \\ \begin{pmatrix} \langle 0.7,0.3\rangle & \langle 0.7,0.2\rangle & \langle 0.3,0.5\rangle & \langle 0.5,0.1\rangle \\ \langle 0.2,0.6\rangle & \langle 0.6,0.1\rangle & \langle 0.5,0.5\rangle & \langle 0.6,0.4\rangle \\ \langle 0.1,0.7\rangle & \langle 0.8,0.1\rangle & \langle 0.5,0.3\rangle & \langle 0.7,0.2\rangle \\ \langle 0.6,0.2\rangle & \langle 0.6,0.3\rangle & \langle 0.4,0.5\rangle & \langle 0.6,0.3\rangle \\ \langle 0.5,0.2\rangle & \langle 0.8,0.1\rangle & \langle 0.6,0.2\rangle & \langle 0.7,0.2\rangle \\ \langle 0.5,0.3\rangle & \langle 0.6,0.1\rangle & \langle 0.5,0.3\rangle & \langle 0.6,0.2\rangle \end{pmatrix} \end{array} =$$

$$\begin{array}{c} \\ x_1 \\ x_2 \\ x_3 \\ x_4 \\ x_5 \\ x_6 \end{array} \begin{array}{c} \begin{array}{cccc} C_2 & C_3 & C_4 & C_5 \end{array} \\ \begin{pmatrix} \langle 0.7,0.3\rangle & \langle 0.7,0.2\rangle & \langle 0.3,0.5\rangle & \langle 0.5,0.1\rangle \\ \langle 0.2,0.6\rangle & \langle 0.6,0.1\rangle & \langle 0.5,0.5\rangle & \langle 0.6,0.4\rangle \\ \langle 0.1,0.7\rangle & \langle 0.8,0.1\rangle & \langle 0.5,0.3\rangle & \langle 0.7,0.2\rangle \\ \langle 0.6,0.2\rangle & \langle 0.6,0.3\rangle & \langle 0.4,0.5\rangle & \langle 0.6,0.3\rangle \\ \langle 0.5,0.2\rangle & \langle 0.8,0.1\rangle & \langle 0.6,0.2\rangle & \langle 0.7,0.2\rangle \\ \langle 0.5,0.3\rangle & \langle 0.6,0.1\rangle & \langle 0.5,0.3\rangle & \langle 0.6,0.2\rangle \end{pmatrix} \end{array}.$$

Hence,

$$f(\widetilde{MD}^{\beta}_{\widehat{D}}(x_1)) = M^T_{\widehat{D}}(x_1) \trianglelefteq M_{\widehat{D}}(x_1) \oplus \overline{M_{\widehat{D}}} = \begin{pmatrix} 6 & 5 & 0 & 0 \\ 1 & 6 & 0 & 0 \\ 0 & 0 & 0 & 0 \\ 0 & 0 & 0 & 0 \end{pmatrix} \oplus \begin{pmatrix} 6 & 6 & 6 & 6 \\ 6 & 6 & 6 & 6 \\ 6 & 6 & 6 & 6 \\ 6 & 6 & 6 & 6 \end{pmatrix} = \begin{pmatrix} 1 \\ 1 \\ 0 \\ 0 \end{pmatrix},$$

i.e., $\widetilde{MD}^{\beta}_{\widehat{D}}(x_1) = \{C'_1, C'_2\} = \{C_2, C_3\}$.

$$f(\widetilde{MD}^{\beta}_{\widehat{D}}(x_2)) = M^T_{\widehat{D}}(x_2) \trianglelefteq M_{\widehat{D}}(x_2) \oplus \overline{M_{\widehat{D}}} = \begin{pmatrix} 0 & 0 & 0 & 0 \\ 0 & 6 & 0 & 0 \\ 0 & 0 & 0 & 0 \\ 0 & 0 & 0 & 0 \end{pmatrix} \oplus \begin{pmatrix} 6 & 6 & 6 & 6 \\ 6 & 6 & 6 & 6 \\ 6 & 6 & 6 & 6 \\ 6 & 6 & 6 & 6 \end{pmatrix} = \begin{pmatrix} 0 \\ 1 \\ 0 \\ 0 \end{pmatrix},$$

i.e., $\widetilde{MD}^{\beta}_{\widehat{D}}(x_2) = \{C'_2\} = \{C_3\}$.

$$f(\widetilde{MD}^{\beta}_{\widehat{D}}(x_3)) = M^T_{\widehat{D}}(x_3) \trianglelefteq M_{\widehat{D}}(x_3) \oplus \overline{M_{\widehat{D}}} = \begin{pmatrix} 0 & 0 & 0 & 0 \\ 0 & 6 & 0 & 1 \\ 0 & 0 & 0 & 0 \\ 0 & 5 & 0 & 6 \end{pmatrix} \oplus \begin{pmatrix} 6 & 6 & 6 & 6 \\ 6 & 6 & 6 & 6 \\ 6 & 6 & 6 & 6 \\ 6 & 6 & 6 & 6 \end{pmatrix} = \begin{pmatrix} 0 \\ 1 \\ 0 \\ 1 \end{pmatrix},$$

i.e., $\widetilde{MD}^{\beta}_{\widehat{D}}(x_3) = \{C'_2, C'_4\} = \{C_3, C_5\}$.

$$f(\widetilde{MD}^{\beta}_{\widehat{D}}(x_4)) = M^T_{\widehat{D}}(x_4) \trianglelefteq M_{\widehat{D}}(x_4) \oplus \overline{M_{\widehat{D}}} = \begin{pmatrix} 6 & 5 & 0 & 4 \\ 1 & 6 & 0 & 1 \\ 0 & 0 & 0 & 0 \\ 1 & 5 & 0 & 6 \end{pmatrix} \oplus \begin{pmatrix} 6 & 6 & 6 & 6 \\ 6 & 6 & 6 & 6 \\ 6 & 6 & 6 & 6 \\ 6 & 6 & 6 & 6 \end{pmatrix} = \begin{pmatrix} 1 \\ 1 \\ 0 \\ 1 \end{pmatrix},$$

i.e., $\widetilde{MD}^{\beta}_{\widehat{D}}(x_4) = \{C'_1, C'_2, C'_4\} = \{C_2, C_3, C_5\}$.

$$f(\widetilde{MD}^{\beta}_{\widehat{D}}(x_5)) = M^T_{\widehat{D}}(x_5) \trianglelefteq M_{\widehat{D}}(x_5) \oplus \overline{M_{\widehat{D}}} = \begin{pmatrix} 0 & 0 & 0 & 0 \\ 0 & 6 & 0 & 1 \\ 0 & 6 & 6 & 6 \\ 0 & 5 & 0 & 6 \end{pmatrix} \oplus \begin{pmatrix} 6 & 6 & 6 & 6 \\ 6 & 6 & 6 & 6 \\ 6 & 6 & 6 & 6 \\ 6 & 6 & 6 & 6 \end{pmatrix} = \begin{pmatrix} 0 \\ 1 \\ 0 \\ 1 \end{pmatrix},$$

i.e., $\widetilde{MD}^{\beta}_{\widehat{D}}(x_5) = \{C'_2, C'_4\} = \{C_3, C_5\}$.

$$f(\widetilde{MD}^{\beta}_{\widehat{D}}(x_6)) = M^T_{\widehat{D}}(x_6) \trianglelefteq M_{\widehat{D}}(x_6) \oplus \overline{M_{\widehat{D}}} = \begin{pmatrix} 0 & 0 & 0 & 0 \\ 0 & 6 & 0 & 1 \\ 0 & 0 & 0 & 0 \\ 0 & 5 & 0 & 6 \end{pmatrix} \oplus \begin{pmatrix} 6 & 6 & 6 & 6 \\ 6 & 6 & 6 & 6 \\ 6 & 6 & 6 & 6 \\ 6 & 6 & 6 & 6 \end{pmatrix} = \begin{pmatrix} 0 \\ 1 \\ 0 \\ 1 \end{pmatrix},$$

i.e., $\widetilde{MD}^{\beta}_{\widehat{D}}(x_6) = \{C'_2, C'_4\} = \{C_3, C_5\}$.

Step 3: *$Min(\{\widehat{\mathbf{D}} \in \mathcal{S}(\widehat{\mathbf{C}}) : \forall x \in U, \widetilde{MD}^{\beta}_{\widehat{C}}(x) = \widetilde{MD}^{\beta}_{\widehat{D}}(x)\}) = Min(\{\{C_1, C_2, C_3, C_5\}, \{C_2, C_3, C_4, C_5\}, \{C_2, C_3, C_5\}\}) = \{\{C_2, C_3, C_5\}\}$. Therefore, $\{C_2, C_3, C_5\}$ is the IF β-maximal reduction of $\widehat{\mathbf{C}}$.*

5. Experimental Evaluations

Compared with the set representations, it is necessary to show the advantage of matrix representations of IF β-minimal and β-maximal descriptions. In this section, we call the presented matrix methods of IF β-minimal and β-maximal descriptions as "M-IFMin" and "M-IFMax", respectively. Hence, we compare them with the set-based algorithms of IF β-minimal and β-maximal descriptions (which are named "S-IFMin" and "S-IFMax", respectively) through several experiments.

5.1. The Process of Experiments

We construct some IF β-covering approximation spaces to run M-IFMin, M-IFMax, S-IFMin and S-IFMax on them. In Definition 6, we know that any IF β-covering approximation space can be seen as an IF granular matrix. The procedure of constructing the IF β-matrix is as follows: (1) The elements of the matrix are IF numbers, which are randomly chosen from $\{0, 0.1, 0.2, \cdots, 0.9, 1\}$. (2) For any row of the matrix, if the maximal number of the row is less than β, then we denote β as its maximal number. Hence, the matrix is the IF β-matrix, i.e., an IF β-covering approximation space.

Finally, we compare the computational time of M-IFMin, M-IFMax, S-IFMin and S-IFMax with different values of β, sizes of a universe and sizes of an IF β-covering. All of the experiments were carried out on a personal computer with 64-bit Windows 10, Intel(R) Core(TM) i7-8565U CPU @1.80 GHz 1.99 GHz, and 8 GB memory. The programming language was Matlab r2016a.

5.2. Results and Analysis

To compare the computational time of M-IFMin, M-IFMax, S-IFMin and S-IFMax with different values of β in Figure 1, we set the size of U to 200 and the size of $\widehat{\mathbf{C}}$ to 600. The one value of β ranges from 0.2 to 0.6, gradually increasing by a step of 0.1, and the other value is 0.3. Figure 1a,c show the computational time of M-IFMin and S-IFMin. In Figure 1a, the first value of β ranges from 0.2 to 0.6, gradually increasing by a step of 0.1, and the second value is 0.3. In Figure 1c, the first value is 0.3 and the second value of β ranges from 0.2 to 0.6, gradually increasing by a step of 0.1. Figure 1b,d show the computational time of M-IFMax and S-IFMax. In Figure 1b, the first value of β ranges from 0.2 to 0.6, gradually increasing by a step of 0.1, and the second value is 0.3. In Figure 1d, the first value is 0.3 and the second value of β ranges from 0.2 to 0.6, gradually increasing by a step of 0.1. In Figure 1, we can see that the computational time of M-IFMin, M-IFMax, S-IFMin and S-IFMax decreases with the gradual increase in the value of β. M-IFMin (or M-IFMax) is more efficient than S-IFMin (or S-IFMax) with different values of β, especially with small values of β.

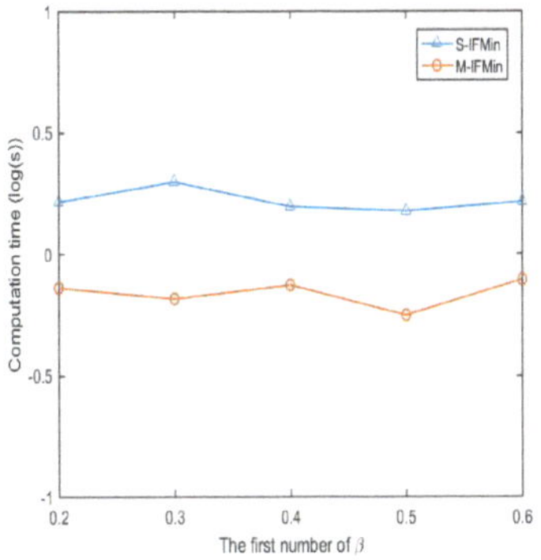

(**a**) Comparison of S-IFMin and M-IFMin with different β (the first value changes, the other is 0.3).

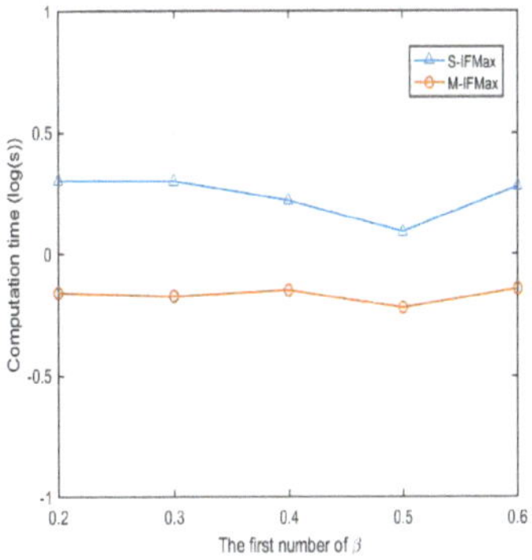

(**b**) Comparison of S-IFMax and M-IFMax with different β (the first value changes, the other is 0.3).

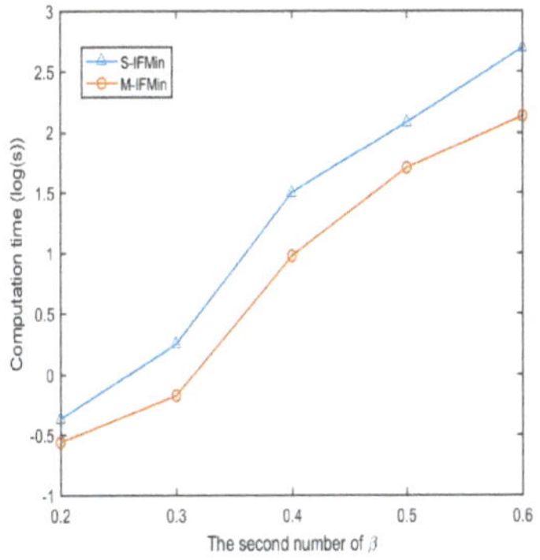

(**c**) Comparison of S-IFMin and M-IFMin with different β (the first value is 0.3, the other changes).

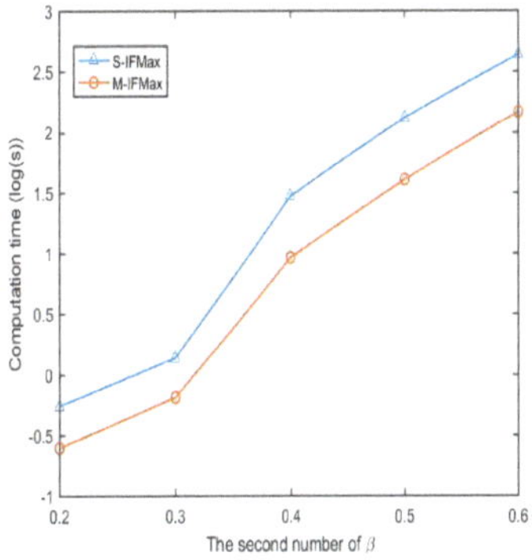

(**d**) Comparison of S-IFMax and M-IFMax with different β (the first value is 0.3, the other changes).

Figure 1. Computational time of M-IFMin, M-IFMax, S-IFMin and S-IFMax with different β ($|U| = 200$, $|\widehat{\mathbf{C}}| = 600$).

To compare the computational time of M-IFMin, M-IFMax, S-IFMin and S-IFMax with different sizes of U in Figure 2, we set the value of β to $\langle 0.6, 0.3 \rangle$ and the size of $\widehat{\mathbf{C}}$ to 200. The size of U ranges from 200 to 600, gradually increasing by a step of 100. In Figure 2, we can see that the computational time of M-IFMin, M-IFMax, S-IFMin and S-IFMax increases with the gradual increase in the size of U. M-IFMin (or M-IFMax) is more efficient than S-IFMin (or S-IFMax) with different sizes of U. Hence, for large universe sizes, M-IFMin (or M-IFMax) is feasible.

To compare the computational time of M-IFMin, M-IFMax, S-IFMin and S-IFMax with different sizes of $\widehat{\mathbf{C}}$ in Figure 3, we set the value of β to $\langle 0.6, 0.3 \rangle$ and the size of U to 200. The size of $\widehat{\mathbf{C}}$ ranges from 100 to 500, gradually increasing by a step of 100. In Figure 3, we can see that the computational time of M-IFMin, M-IFMax, S-IFMin and S-IFMax increases with the gradual increase in the size of U. M-IFMin (or M-IFMax) is more efficient than S-IFMin (or S-IFMax) with different sizes of $\widehat{\mathbf{C}}$, especially with large $\widehat{\mathbf{C}}$.

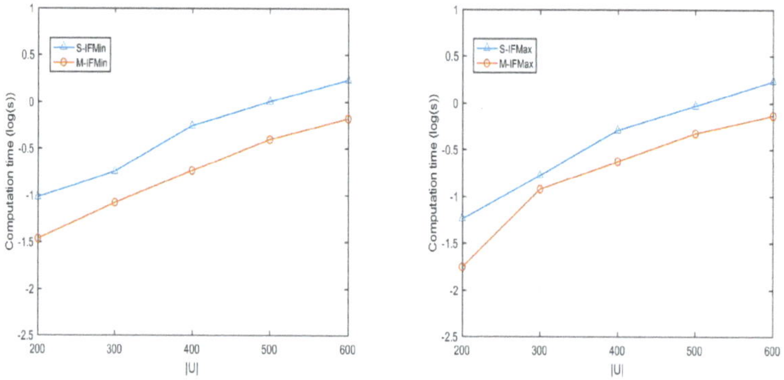

(**a**) Comparison of S-IFMin and M-IFMin with different sizes of U.

(**b**) Comparison of S-IFMax and M-IFMax with different sizes of U.

Figure 2. Computational time of M-IFMin, M-IFMax, S-IFMin and S-IFMax with different sizes of U ($\beta = \langle 0.6, 0.3 \rangle$, $|\widehat{\mathbf{C}}| = 200$).

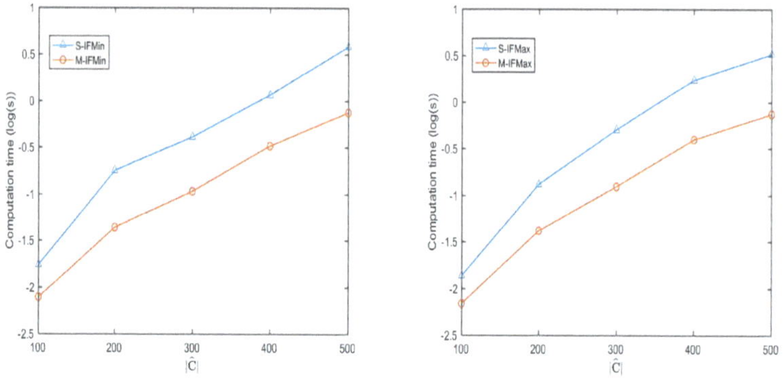

(**a**) Comparison of S-IFMin and M-IFMin with different sizes of $\widehat{\mathbf{C}}$.

(**b**) Comparison of S-IFMin and M-IFMin with different sizes of $\widehat{\mathbf{C}}$.

Figure 3. Computational time of M-IFMin, M-IFMax, S-IFMin and S-IFMax with different sizes of $\widehat{\mathbf{C}}$ ($\beta = \langle 0.6, 0.3 \rangle$, $|U| = 200$).

By Figures 2 and 3, we can see that M-IFMin and M-IFMax are feasible for large U and $\widehat{\mathbf{C}}$, respectively. That is to say, they are scalable on big data sets.

6. Conclusions

In this paper, we mainly use matrix approaches to study IF β-covering rough sets by IF β-minimal and β-maximal descriptions. Moreover, the feasibility of the proposed matrix approaches is studied by several experiments. The main conclusions of this paper are as follows:

1. The matrix representations of IF β-minimal and β-maximal descriptions are proposed. Moreover, the comparative analysis illustrates that the proposed calculus based on matrices is feasible for large IF β-coverings as well as big data sets.
2. Two new types of reductions of IF β-covering approximation spaces are proposed via IF β-minimal and β-maximal descriptions, respectively. They are calculated based on the matrix representations of IF β-minimal and β-maximal descriptions. It is a new viewpoint to study IF β-covering rough sets using IF β-minimal and β-maximal descriptions.

Although the matrix method proposed by us is faster than the existing set method in IF set theory, it is still somewhat time-consuming in the environment of big data, and further faster calculation methods need to be proposed. In the future, the following research topics are deserving of attention. These matrix approaches can be used in fuzzy soft covering-based multi-granulation fuzzy rough sets [43]. Moreover, Choquet-like integrals [44,45] were recently combined with fuzzy rough sets, which can connected with the content of this paper in further research.

Author Contributions: J.W. analyzed the existing work of IF rough sets with matrices, and wrote the paper. X.Z. improved and funded this paper. All authors have read and agreed to the published version of the manuscript.

Funding: This research was funded by the National Natural Science Foundation of China (Grant Nos. 12201373 and 12271319) and the China Postdoctoral Science Foundation (Grant No. 2023T160402).

Data Availability Statement: The data presented in this study are available on request from the corresponding author.

Conflicts of Interest: The authors declare no conflicts of interest.

References

1. Zhu, W.; Wang, F. Reduction and axiomatization of covering generalized rough sets. *Inf. Sci.* **2003**, *152*, 217–230. [CrossRef]
2. Pawlak, Z. Rough sets. *Int. J. Comput. Inf. Sci.* **1982**, *11*, 341–356. [CrossRef]
3. Zhao, Z. Reductions of a covering approximation space from algebraic points of view. *Int. J. Approx. Reason.* **2023**, *153*, 101–114. [CrossRef]
4. Shakiba, A.; Hooshmandasl, M.R. Data volume reduction in covering approximation spaces with respect to twenty-two types of covering based rough sets. *Int. J. Approx. Reason.* **2016**, *75*, 13–38. [CrossRef]
5. Yao, Y.; Yao, B. Covering based rough set approximations. *Inf. Sci.* **2012**, *200*, 91–107. [CrossRef]
6. Du, Y.; Hu, Q.; Zhu, P.; Ma, P. Rule learning for classification based on neighborhood covering reduction. *Inf. Sci.* **2011**, *181*, 5457–5467. [CrossRef]
7. Mohammed, A.; Shokry, N.; Ashraf, N. Covering soft rough sets and its topological properties with application. *Soft Comput.* **2023**, *27*, 4451–4461.
8. Qian, Y.; Liang, J.; Pedrycz, W.; Dang, C. Positive approximation: An accelerator for attribute reduction in rough set theory. *Artif. Intell.* **2010**, *174*, 597–618. [CrossRef]
9. Jing, Y.; Li, T.; Fujita, H.; Yu, Z.; Wang, B. An incremental attribute reduction approach based on knowledge granularity with a multi-granulation view. *Inf. Sci.* **2017**, *411*, 23–38. [CrossRef]
10. Wang, C.; Shi, Y.; Fan, X.; Shao, M. Attribute reduction based on κ-nearest neighborhood rough sets. *Int. J. Approx. Reason.* **2019**, *106*, 18–31. [CrossRef]
11. Long, Z.; Cai, M.; Li, Q.; Li, Y.; Cai, W. Convex granules and convex covering rough sets. *Eng. Appl. Artif. Intell.* **2023**, *124*, 106509. [CrossRef]
12. Dai, J.; Wang, W.; Xu, Q.; Tian, H. Uncertainty measurement for interval-valued decision systems based on extended conditional entropy. *Knowl.-Based Syst.* **2012**, *27*, 443–450. [CrossRef]
13. El-Bably, M.K.; Abo-Tabl, E.A. A topological reduction for predicting of a lung cancer disease based on generalized rough sets. *J. Intell. Fuzzy Syst.* **2021**, *41*, 3045–3060. [CrossRef]
14. Huang, Z.; Li, J. Covering based multi-granulation rough fuzzy sets with applications to feature selection. *Expert Syst. Appl.* **2024**, *238*, 121908. [CrossRef]
15. Wang, S.; Zhu, W.; Zhu, Q.; Min, F. Characteristic matrix of covering and its application to Boolean matrix decomposition. *Inf. Sci.* **2014**, *263*, 186–197. [CrossRef]
16. Lang, G.; Li, Q.; Cai, M.; Yang, T. Characteristic matrixes-based knowledge reduction in dynamic covering decision information systems. *Knowl.-Based Syst.* **2015**, *85*, 1–26. [CrossRef]
17. Ma, L. The investigation of covering rough sets by Boolean matrices. *Int. J. Approx. Reason.* **2018**, *100*, 69–84. [CrossRef]
18. Wang, J.; Zhang, X.; Liu, C. Grained matrix and complementary matrix: Novel methods for computing information descriptions in covering approximation spaces. *Inf. Sci.* **2022**, *591*, 68–87. [CrossRef]
19. Zadeh, L.A. Fuzzy sets. *Inf. Control.* **1965**, *8*, 338–353. [CrossRef]
20. Yao, Y. A comparative study of fuzzy sets and rough sets. *Inf. Sci.* **1998**, *109*, 227–242. [CrossRef]
21. Dubois, D.; Prade, H. Rough fuzzy sets and fuzzy rough sets. *Int. J. Gen. Syst.* **1990**, *17*, 191–208. [CrossRef]
22. Morsi, N.N.; Yakout, M.M. Axiomatics for fuzzy rough sets. *Fuzzy Sets Syst.* **1998**, *100*, 327–342. [CrossRef]
23. Radzikowska, A.M.; Kerre, E.E. A comparative study of fuzzy rough sets. *Fuzzy Sets Syst.* **2002**, *126*, 137–155. [CrossRef]
24. Greco, S.; Matarazzo, B.; Slowinski, R. Rough set processing of vague information using fuzzy similarity relations. In *Finite Versus Infinite*; Calude, C.S., Paun, G., Eds.; Springer: London, UK, 2000; pp. 149–173.
25. Wu, W.; Mi, J.; Zhang, W. Generalized fuzzy rough sets. *Inf. Sci.* **2003**, *151*, 263–282. [CrossRef]

26. D'eer, L.; Cornelis, C.; Godo, L. Fuzzy neighborhood operators based on fuzzy coverings. *Fuzzy Sets Syst.* **2017**, *312*, 17–35. [CrossRef]
27. Feng, T.; Zhang, S.; Mi, J. The reduction and fusion of fuzzy covering systems based on the evidence theory. *Int. J. Approx. Reason.* **2012**, *53*, 87–103. [CrossRef]
28. Ma, L. Two fuzzy covering rough set models and their generalizations over fuzzy lattices. *Fuzzy Sets Syst.* **2016**, *294*, 1–17. [CrossRef]
29. Yang, B.; Hu, B. Fuzzy neighborhood operators and derived fuzzy coverings. *Fuzzy Sets Syst.* **2019**, *370*, 1–33. [CrossRef]
30. Zhan, J.; Zhang, X.; Yao, Y. Covering based multigranulation fuzzy rough sets and corresponding applications. *Artif. Intell. Rev.* **2020**, *53*, 1093–1126. [CrossRef]
31. Yang, B.; Hu, B. Matrix representations and interdependency on L-fuzzy covering-based approximation operators. *Int. J. Approx. Reason.* **2018**, *96*, 57–77. [CrossRef]
32. Yang, B.; Hu, B. A fuzzy covering-based rough set model and its generalization over fuzzy lattice. *Inf. Sci.* **2016**, *367–368*, 463–486. [CrossRef]
33. Wang, J.; Zhang, X.; Yao, Y. Matrix approach for fuzzy description reduction and group decision-making with fuzzy β-covering. *Inf. Sci.* **2022**, *597*, 53–85. [CrossRef]
34. Atanassov, K. Intuitionistic fuzzy sets. *Fuzzy Sets Syst.* **1986**, *20*, 87–96. [CrossRef]
35. Huang, B.; Guo, C.; Li, H.; Feng, G.; Zhou, X. An intuitionistic fuzzy graded covering rough set. *Knowl.-Based Syst.* **2016**, *107*, 155–178. [CrossRef]
36. Ye, J.; Zhan, J.; Ding, W.; Fujita, H. A novel fuzzy rough set model with fuzzy neighborhood operators. *Inf. Sci.* **2021**, *544*, 266–297. [CrossRef]
37. Jain, P.; Som, T. Multigranular rough set model based on robust intuitionistic fuzzy covering with application to feature selection. *Int. J. Approx. Reason.* **2023**, *156*, 16–37. [CrossRef]
38. Liu, C.; Cai, K.; Miao, D.; Qian, J. Novel matrix-based approaches to computing MinD and MaxD in covering-based rough sets. *Inf. Sci.* **2020**, *539*, 312–326. [CrossRef]
39. Bonikowski, Z.; Bryniarski, E.; Wybraniec-Skardowska, U. Extensions and intentions in the rough set theory. *Inf. Sci.* **1998**, *107*, 149–167. [CrossRef]
40. Pomykala, J.A. Approximation operations in approximation space. *Bull. Pol. Acad. Sci.* **1987**, *35*, 653–662.
41. Zhu, W. Relationship among basic concepts in covering-based rough sets. *Inf. Sci.* **2009**, *179*, 2478–2486. [CrossRef]
42. Wang, Z.; Shu, L.; Ding, X. Minimal description and maximal description in covering-based rough sets. *Fundam. Inform.***2013**, *128*, 503–526. [CrossRef]
43. Atef, M.; Ali, M.I.; Al-Shami, T.M. Fuzzy soft covering-based multi-granulation fuzzy rough sets and their applications. *Comput. Appl. Math.* **2021**, *40*, 115. [CrossRef]
44. Wang, J.; Shao, S.; Zhang, X. Choquet-like integrals with multi-neighborhood approximation numbers for novel covering granular reduction methods. *Mathematics* **2023**, *11*, 4650. [CrossRef]
45. Wang, J.; Zhang, X.; Shen, Q. Choquet-like integrals with rough attribute fuzzy measures for data-driven decision-making. *IEEE Trans. Fuzzy Syst.* **2024**, *32*, 2825–2836. [CrossRef]

symmetry

MDPI

Article

Multiple-Attribute Decision Making Based on the Probabilistic Dominance Relationship with Fuzzy Algebras

Amir Baklouti

Departmentof Mathematical Sciences, College of Applied Sciences, Umm Al-Qura University, Mecca 21955, Saudi Arabia; ambaklouti@uqu.edu.sa; Tel.: +96-65-6761-2436

Abstract: In multiple-attribute decision-making (MADM) problems, ranking the alternatives is an important step for making the best decision. Intuitionistic fuzzy numbers (IFNs) are a powerful tool for expressing uncertainty and vagueness in MADM problems. However, existing ranking methods for IFNs do not consider the probabilistic dominance relationship between alternatives, which can lead to inconsistent and inaccurate rankings. In this paper, we propose a new ranking method for IFNs based on the probabilistic dominance relationship and fuzzy algebras. The proposed method is able to handle incomplete and uncertain information and can generate consistent and accurate rankings.

Keywords: fuzzy algebra; intuitionistic fuzzy numbers; multiple-attribute decision making; probabilistic dominance relationship; hesitant intuitionistic fuzzy numbers

Citation: Baklouti, A. Multiple-Attribute Decision Making Based on the Probabilistic Dominance Relationship with Fuzzy Algebras. *Symmetry* **2023**, *15*, 1188. https://doi.org/10.3390/sym15061188

Academic Editors: Sergei D. Odintsov, Changyou Wang, Dong Qiu and Yonghong Shen

Received: 28 April 2023
Revised: 26 May 2023
Accepted: 31 May 2023
Published: 2 June 2023

1. Introduction

In multiple-attribute decision making (MADM), evaluating various alternatives based on multiple criteria and selecting the most suitable one is a complex process that involves dealing with uncertainty and vagueness. Fuzzy set theory is a valuable tool for handling imprecise information, and intuitionistic fuzzy sets (IFSs) are an extension of fuzzy sets that can model uncertainty and vagueness in a more effective way.

Ranking the alternatives is an essential step in MADM, and several ranking methods for IFSs have been developed. However, most of these methods do not consider the probabilistic dominance relationship between alternatives, which can lead to limitations in terms of consistency, accuracy, and applicability. The probabilistic dominance relationship considers the probability of an alternative being better than another alternative in terms of a certain criterion, which can lead to more accurate and consistent rankings.

Recent research has focused on developing ranking methods for IFSs based on fuzzy algebras. Some of these methods include probabilistic dominance-based ranking methods for hesitant fuzzy linguistic term sets proposed by Peng et al. [1], a novel ranking method for intuitionistic fuzzy sets based on probabilistic dominance and cross entropy proposed by Yuan et al. [2], and a method for ranking intuitionistic fuzzy sets based on expected values of the probability distribution functions proposed by Khan and Parvez [3]. These methods are designed to handle the complex structure and uncertain nature of IFSs and can generate accurate and consistent rankings.

Fuzzy algebras are algebraic structures that can represent the operations on fuzzy sets and IFSs. Fuzzy algebra-based ranking methods have shown promising results in terms of consistency, accuracy, and applicability. For instance, Huang et al. [4] proposed a new ranking method for IFSs based on the probabilistic dominance relationship and fuzzy algebras. The proposed method transformed IFSs into fuzzy sets using the degree of membership and non-membership functions and compared the fuzzy sets using the concept of fuzzy algebras.

However, there is still a need to develop more effective ranking methods for IFSs that can handle incomplete and uncertain information. For example, Huang et al. [4] proposed a new method based on hesitant intuitionistic fuzzy sets, which can handle incomplete and uncertain information in MADM.

In multiple-attribute decision-making (MADM) problems, ranking the alternatives is a crucial step in achieving optimal decision making. Intuitionistic fuzzy numbers (IFNs) serve as a powerful tool for expressing uncertainty and vagueness in MADM problems. However, existing ranking methods for IFNs often overlook the probabilistic dominance relationship between alternatives, resulting in inconsistent and inaccurate rankings. To address this issue, this paper proposes a novel ranking method for IFNs based on the probabilistic dominance relationship and fuzzy algebras. The proposed method effectively handles incomplete and uncertain information, leading to consistent and accurate rankings.

In recent years, several researchers have contributed to developing new ranking methods for IFSs. These methods aim to tackle the challenges posed by the uncertainty of information expression and applicability in practical problems, as the uncertainty of fuzzy sets is described by the degree of membership (DM) and degree of non-membership (DN). Scholarly efforts have been dedicated to various aspects of IFS research, including distance measure [5–9], similarity measure [10], model generalization, such as interval-type IFS and Atanassov-type intuitionistic fuzzy [11], and other achievements, such as intuitionistic fuzzy soft sets [12], intuitionistic fuzzy rough sets [13,14], intuitionistic fuzzy set and three-way decision [15–19], and intuitionistic fuzzy set and dominance relationship [20,21]. These advancements in IFS research have found practical applications in fault diagnosis [22], multi-attribute decision-making [23], deep learning [24], imbalance learning [25], and other fields. Baklouti et al. [26,27] give relevant examples of the application of optimization techniques in solar photovoltaic systems and the consideration of energetic types and maintenance costs in the decision-making process of selling or leasing used vehicles, respectively. The reader can find some other interesting references in [4].

Moreover, researchers have also applied fuzzy algebras and the probabilistic dominance relationship in real-world applications. For instance, Wang et al. [28] used fuzzy algebras and the probabilistic dominance relationship to evaluate the sustainability of transportation systems. Additionally, Wu et al. [29] applied the probabilistic dominance relationship and fuzzy algebras to rank the preferences of investors in the stock market.

In this paper, we propose a new ranking method for IFSs based on the probabilistic dominance relationship and fuzzy algebras. The proposed method extends the existing method by considering hesitant IFSs and can generate consistent and accurate rankings in complex decision-making problems.

Regarding the outline of the paper, the rest of the paper is organized as follows: Section 2 is a review of the basic knowledge. Section 3 is devoted to exploring the concepts of the probabilistic dominance relationship and fuzzy algebras in the context of ranking intuitionistic fuzzy sets. Section 4 is a ranking method for IFSs based on hesitant IFSs and the probabilistic dominance relationship. Section 5 is the conclusion.

2. Basic Knowledge

An IFS is defined as a 3-tuple (A, μ_A, ν_A), where A is the universe of discourse, $\mu_A{:}A \to [0,1]$ is the membership function, and $\nu_A{:}A \to [0,1]$ is the non-membership function. The degree of hesitation, denoted by h_A, is defined as $h_A = 1 - \max_{x\in A}(\mu_A(x) + \nu_A(x))$.

Ranking IFSs is an important task in decision-making problems, as it allows us to compare and prioritize multiple alternatives based on their degree of desirability. Various ranking methods for IFSs have been proposed in the literature, each with their own strengths and weaknesses. In this section, we provide a review of some of the most commonly used ranking methods.

Before introducing ranking methods, we define some basic probabilistic indices for IFSs, which will be used in the subsequent discussion. Let us recall some definitions from [30,31].

Definition 1. *Let A be a universe of discourse and* (A, μ_A, ν_A) *be an IFS. The* ***possibility degree*** *of A is defined as* $P(A) = \max_{x \in A} \mu_A(x)$.

Definition 2. *Let A be a universe of discourse and* (A, μ_A, ν_A) *be an IFS. The* ***necessity degree*** *of A is defined as* $N(A) = \min_{x \in A} \nu_A(x)$.

Definition 3. *Let A be a universe of discourse and* (A, μ_A, ν_A) *be an IFS. The* ***probability degree*** *of A is defined as* $Pr(A) = P(A) - h_A$.

Remark 1. *The possibility degree* $P(A)$ *represents the maximum degree of membership of any element in A, while the necessity degree* $N(A)$ *represents the minimum degree of non-membership of any element in A. The probability degree* $Pr(A)$ *is a measure of the overall plausibility of A, taking into account both its membership and non-membership degrees as well as its degree of hesitation.*

A fuzzy algebra is an algebraic structure that extends classical algebra to handle fuzzy sets. A fuzzy algebra is defined over a set X and a set of fuzzy sets $F(X)$ on X. A fuzzy set is defined as a mapping $\mu : X \to [0, 1]$ that assigns a degree of membership between 0 and 1 to each element in X. A fuzzy algebra is defined as a tuple $(X, F(X), \oplus, \odot)$, where $\oplus$ and $\odot$ are binary operations on $F(X)$.

Example 1. *A basic and concrete example of a fuzzy set is the set of people's heights, where the height can be described as "tall", "medium", or "short". We can define a fuzzy set called "tall" as including all the heights greater than 1.80 meters, a fuzzy set called "medium" as including all the heights between 1.60 and 1.80 m, and a fuzzy set called "short" as including all the heights less than 1.60 m. This way, any height can belong to multiple fuzzy sets, with a degree of membership between 0 and 1.*

Remark 2. *Fuzzy algebras provide a framework for dealing with fuzzy sets and operations on them. They have applications in various fields, such as decision making, control theory, and pattern recognition.*

Example 2. *Consider a decision-making problem, where we need to select the best car among a set of alternatives based on criteria such as fuel efficiency, price, and safety. We can use fuzzy logic to represent the preferences of the decision maker, who may not be able to provide precise numerical values for each criterion. For example, the decision maker may say that fuel efficiency is "very important", price is "somewhat important", and safety is "not very important". We can then use fuzzy sets and membership functions to represent these preferences, and apply a fuzzy inference system to rank the alternatives based on their degree of satisfaction of the criteria.*

The above example illustrates the application of fuzzy logic in a multiple criteria decision-making problem. Fuzzy logic has been widely used in such problems, and several methods have been developed to handle the complexity of comparing alternatives based on multiple criteria. Some of these methods are reviewed in [32,33]. In addition, the procedure for ordering fuzzy subsets of the unit interval, which is an important step in fuzzy decision making, is described in [34].

In multiple-attribute decision making, PDR is used to compare two alternatives based on the probability of one alternative being better than the other. PDR is defined as follows:

Definition 4 (Probabilistic Dominance Relationship). *Let A and B be two alternatives, and let D be a set of attributes. PDR between A and B with respect to D is defined as follows:*

- *Let* $D(A)$ *and* $D(B)$ *be the sets of values of attributes in D for alternatives A and B, respectively.*
- *Let n be the number of attributes in D.*
- *For each* $d_i \in D$*, let* A_i *and* B_i *denote the* d_i*-value of alternatives A and B, respectively.*

- *Let m_A be the number of attributes, where A is at least as good as B, i.e., $A_i \geq B_i$ for $i = 1, \ldots, n$. Similarly, let m_B be the number of attributes, where B is at least as good as A, i.e., $B_i \geq A_i$ for $i = 1, \ldots, n$.*
- *The probabilistic dominance degree (PDD) of A over B is defined as*

$$PDD(A, B) = \frac{m_A}{n}.$$

One of the main advantages of PDR is that it can handle incomplete and uncertain information. However, the classical PDR approach assumes that the attribute values are precise and that the preferences are crisp. To overcome these limitations, fuzzy set theory and fuzzy algebra can be used.

Fuzzy set theory is an extension of classical set theory that allows for partial membership, where an element can belong to a set with a degree of membership between 0 and 1. Fuzzy algebra is a branch of algebra that deals with fuzzy sets and their operations. The basic operations in fuzzy algebra are fuzzy complement, fuzzy union, and fuzzy intersection.

In the context of PDR, fuzzy algebra can be used to represent the uncertainty and imprecision in the attribute values and the preferences.

Many researchers have proposed different fuzzy algebraic approaches for PDR. Some of these approaches are based on fuzzy relation equations, fuzzy preference relations, fuzzy numbers, and fuzzy sets.

In particular, the use of intuitionistic fuzzy sets (IFSs) in PDR has received increasing attention in recent years. IFSs were first introduced by Atanassov in 1986 [35] as an extension of fuzzy sets to handle uncertainty and indeterminacy. IFSs consist of three components: the membership function, the non-membership function, and the hesitation function, which represents the degree of uncertainty or indecision about the membership and non-membership of an element in a set.

Several studies have proposed the use of IFSs in PDR. For example, Khalil et al. [36] proposed a PDR approach based on IFSs to handle uncertain and incomplete information. Zhu et al. [37] proposed a PDR approach based on hesitant fuzzy sets, which are a generalization of IFSs that allow for multiple degrees of hesitation. The proposed approach was applied to the evaluation of water resource security in China.

3. Intuitionistic Fuzzy Set Ranking: Integrating Probabilistic Dominance Relationship and Fuzzy Algebras

In this section, we will explore the concepts of the probabilistic dominance relationship and fuzzy algebras in the context of ranking intuitionistic fuzzy sets. Both of these approaches provide valuable tools for comparing and ordering intuitionistic fuzzy sets based on different criteria.

It is worth noting that the choice of ranking method depends on the application domain and the specific problem being addressed. Therefore, it is important to carefully select the appropriate ranking method based on the specific requirements and constraints of the problem. In the following subsections, we provide a detailed review of the most commonly used ranking methods for IFSs.

After discussing the different ranking methods for intuitionistic fuzzy sets (IFSs), we can make some remarks on their properties and applicability.

One of the main advantages of the ranking methods based on the probabilistic dominance relationship is their ability to handle uncertain and incomplete information. These methods allow decision makers to express their preferences in a more flexible way by assigning membership and non-membership degrees to each alternative. Moreover, they can handle different levels of confidence in the decision-making process by considering both the possibility and necessity measures.

Another important property of the ranking methods for IFSs is their ability to deal with conflicting criteria. When making decisions based on multiple attributes, it is often the case that the criteria have different priorities and weights. In this context, the use of IFSs can provide a more comprehensive and accurate representation of the decision problem. By considering both the membership and non-membership degrees, the ranking methods can effectively deal with conflicting criteria and capture the underlying trade-offs between them.

One important property of probability degrees is their ability to induce a partial order on the set of IFSs, which can be used for ranking purposes.

Proposition 1. *Let* (A, μ_A, ν_A) *and* (B, μ_B, ν_B) *be two IFSs. If* $Pr(A) > Pr(B)$*, then* (A, μ_A, ν_A) *is considered more desirable than* (B, μ_B, ν_B)*.*

Proof. Let $Pr(A) > Pr(B)$, which means

$$\int_0^1 \mu_A(x)dx - \int_0^1 \nu_A(x)dx > \int_0^1 \mu_B(x)dx - \int_0^1 \nu_B(x)dx.$$

Then, we can rewrite the inequality as

$$\int_0^1 \mu_A(x)dx + \int_0^1 \nu_B(x)dx > \int_0^1 \mu_B(x)dx + \int_0^1 \nu_A(x)dx.$$

By using the definition of the probabilistic dominance relationship, we have $(A, \mu_A, \nu_A) \geq_P (B, \mu_B, \nu_B)$, which implies that (A, μ_A, ν_A) is more desirable than (B, μ_B, ν_B). Hence, the proposition holds. □

Based on the above propositions, we obtain the following theorem.

Theorem 1. *Let* (X, μ, ν) *be an IFS, where X is a finite set, and* μ *and* ν *are the membership and non-membership degrees, respectively. Suppose that* $f : X \to \mathbb{R}$ *is a real-valued function on X. Then, the ranking of the elements of X based on f and the probabilistic dominance relationship is the same as the ranking based on the probability measure* $Pr(\mu)$*.*

Proof. Let $x, y \in X$ be two elements of X, and let $\mu(x)$, $\mu(y)$, $\nu(x)$, and $\nu(y)$ be their corresponding membership and non-membership degrees. Suppose that $f(x) > f(y)$. Then, we have

$$\begin{aligned} Pr(\mu(x) > \mu(y)) &= Pr(\mu(x) - \mu(y) > 0) \\ &= Pr(\mu(x) - \mu(y) + \nu(x) - \nu(y) > \nu(x) - \nu(y)) \\ &\geq Pr(\mu(x) - \mu(y) + \nu(x) - \nu(y) > 0) \\ &= Pr(\mu(x) + \nu(x) > \mu(y) + \nu(y)) \\ &= Pr(\mu(x) \geq \mu(y)) \end{aligned}$$

where the inequality follows from the fact that $\nu(x) - \nu(y) \geq 0$.

Conversely, if $f(x) < f(y)$, we have

$$\begin{aligned} Pr(\mu(x) < \mu(y)) &= Pr(\mu(y) > \mu(x)) \\ &\geq Pr(\mu(y) + \nu(y) > \mu(x) + \nu(x)) \\ &= Pr(\mu(y) \geq \mu(x)) \end{aligned}$$

Therefore, we show that the ranking of the elements of X based on f and the probabilistic dominance relationship is the same as the ranking based on $Pr(\mu)$. □

Theorem 1 provides an important result for the ranking of IFSs. It states that if we have a real-valued function f on X, then the ranking based on f and the probabilistic dominance relationship is equivalent to the ranking based on the probability measure $Pr(\mu)$. This theorem can be useful in practice, as it allows the following.

Corollary 1. *Given a set X and a collection of n IFSs* $(A_i, \mu_{A_i}, \nu_{A_i})i = 1^n$ *defined on X, let* D_i *be the set of desirable elements in* A_i *as defined in Theorem 1. Then, a possible way to rank the IFSs* $(A_i, \mu A_i, \nu_{A_i})_{i=1}^n$ *is to order them according to the cardinality of their set of desirable elements, in decreasing order, that is,*

$$D_1 \geq D_2 \geq \ldots \geq D_n.$$

This corollary follows directly from Theorem 1, as we can consider the set of desirable elements D_i as the set A_i^{des} defined in the theorem, and compare them using the order relation $\geq$ defined in the theorem. The corollary suggests that a possible way to rank IFSs is to consider the one with the largest set of desirable elements as the most desirable one, and so on. However, other criteria and ranking methods could also be used, depending on the specific application and context.

Remark 3. *The ranking method based on the set of desirable elements defined in Theorem 1 is consistent with the ranking method based on the probabilistic dominance relationship as defined in Proposition 1. That is, if IFS* (A, μ_A, ν_A) *is more desirable than* (B, μ_B, ν_B) *according to the probabilistic dominance relationship, then* A^{des} *is a superset of* B^{des}*, and so* $|A^{des}| \geq |B^{des}|$.

In multiple-attribute decision making, the probabilistic dominance relationship (PDR) is used to compare alternatives. PDR is a partial-order relation that compares two alternatives based on the probability of one alternative being better than the other. Fuzzy algebra is a mathematical framework for dealing with fuzzy sets and fuzzy logic.

Proposition 2. *Let A and B be two alternatives, and let D be a set of attributes. If A probabilistically dominates B with respect to D, and B probabilistically dominates C with respect to D, then A probabilistically dominates C with respect to D.*

Remark 4. *Note that the converse of Proposition 2 may not be true, i.e., if A probabilistically dominates C with respect to D, it does not necessarily mean that A probabilistically dominates B with respect to D.*

Remark 5. *Let* $(L, \oplus, \odot, \neg)$ *be a fuzzy algebra. Then, the following properties hold:*
1. $\forall x, y \in L, (x \oplus y)' = x' \oplus y', (x \odot y)' = x' \odot y'$.
2. $\forall x, y, z \in L, x \oplus (y \oplus z) = (x \oplus y) \oplus z, x \odot (y \odot z) = (x \odot y) \odot z$.
3. $\forall x, y \in L, x \oplus y = y \oplus x, x \odot y = y \odot x$.
4. $\forall x, y, z \in L, x \oplus (y \odot z) = (x \oplus y) \odot (x \oplus z)$.

Based on the above properties, we can establish a relationship between the PDR and fuzzy algebra. The following theorem illustrates this relationship.

Theorem 2. *Let* $(L, \oplus, \odot, \neg)$ *be a fuzzy algebra, and let A and B be two alternatives with respect to a set of attributes D. Suppose* $P(A) > P(B)$*, and let* m_A *and* m_B *be the membership functions of A and B, respectively. Then A is preferred to B with respect to D if and only if*

$$\sum_{i=1}^{n}(m_A(d_i) \odot \neg m_B(d_i)) \neq \sum_{i=1}^{n}(m_B(d_i) \odot \neg m_A(d_i)), \tag{1}$$

where d_i *denotes the i-th attribute in D.*

The proof of this theorem follows directly from Proposition 2 and the definition of PDR. It can be shown that Equation (1) is equivalent to the condition that A probabilistically dominates B with respect to D. Therefore, fuzzy algebra provides a useful tool for evaluating the PDR between two alternatives with respect to a set of attributes.

Corollary 2. *Let A, B, C be alternatives, and let D be a set of attributes. If $A \geq_p B$ and $B \geq_p C$, then $A \geq_p C$.*

4. Proposed Ranking Method for IFSs Based on Hesitant IFSs and the Probabilistic Dominance Relationship

4.1. Intuitionistic Fuzzy Sets

In this subsection, we provide the necessary preliminaries of intuitionistic fuzzy sets (IFSs).

Definition 5 (Intuitionistic Fuzzy Set). *An intuitionistic fuzzy set (IFS) A in a universe of discourse X is defined by a membership function $\mu_A : X \to [0,1]$ and a non-membership function $\nu_A : X \to [0,1]$, which assign each element $x \in X$ a degree of membership $\mu_A(x)$ and a degree of non-membership $\nu_A(x)$, respectively. The value $1 - \mu_A(x) - \nu_A(x)$ is called the degree of hesitancy of x with respect to A. The triplet (X, μ_A, ν_A) is called an intuitionistic fuzzy set.*

Definition 6 (Support and Core of IFS). *The support and core of an IFS $A = (X, \mu_A, \nu_A)$ are defined as follows:*

- *Support of A:* $\text{supp}(A) = x \in X : \mu_A(x) > 0$;
- *Core of A:* $\text{core}(A) = x \in X : \nu_A(x) = 0$.

Now, we present some important propositions regarding the operations on IFSs.

Proposition 3 (Union and Intersection of IFSs). *Let $A = (X, \mu_A, \nu_A)$ and $B = (X, \mu_B, \nu_B)$ be two IFSs. Then, the union and intersection of A and B are defined as follows:*

- $A \cup B = (X, \max(\mu_A, \mu_B), \max(\nu_A, \nu_B))$;
- $A \cap B = (X, \min(\mu_A, \mu_B), \min(\nu_A, \nu_B))$.

Proof. Straightforward. □

Proposition 4 (Complement of IFS). *Let $A = (X, \mu_A, \nu_A)$ be an IFS. Then, the complement of A is defined as follows:*

- $\overline{A} = (X, \nu_A, \mu_A)$.

Proof. To show that $\overline{A} = (X, \nu_A, \mu_A)$ is the complement of A, we need to show that $\mu_{\overline{A}}(x) = 1 - \mu_A(x)$ and $\nu_{\overline{A}}(x) = 1 - \nu_A(x)$ for all $x \in X$.

First, we have

$$\mu_{\overline{A}}(x) = \nu_A(x) \qquad = 1 - \mu_A(x)$$

Therefore, $\mu_{\overline{A}}(x) = 1 - \mu_A(x)$.

Similarly, we have

$$\nu_{\overline{A}}(x) = \mu_A(x) \qquad = 1 - \nu_A(x)$$

Therefore, $\nu_{\overline{A}}(x) = 1 - \nu_A(x)$.

Hence, we showed that $\overline{A} = (X, \nu_A, \mu_A)$ is the complement of A. □

Remark 6. *Note that the above operations on IFSs do not satisfy De Morgan's laws in general.*

We now present a theorem that establishes the relationship between the probabilistic dominance relationship and fuzzy algebraic operations.

Theorem 3. *Let (X, μ_A, ν_A) and (X, μ_B, ν_B) be two IFSs. Then, A dominates B probabilistically if and only if $\overline{A} \cap B = \emptyset$.*

Proof. (⇒) Assume that A dominates B probabilistically. Then, we have $Pr(A) > Pr(B)$. This means that for each attribute i, $D_i(A) \geq D_i(B)$ and $P_i(A) > P_i(B)$. Since $P_i(A) + P_i(\overline{A}) = P_i(B) + P_i(\overline{B}) = 1$ for each attribute i, we have $P_i(\overline{A}) < P_i(\overline{B})$. Therefore, $\mu_A(x) \leq \mu_B(x)$ and $\nu_A(x) \geq \nu_B(x)$ for all $x \in X$.

Assume, for the sake of contradiction, that there exists $x \in X$ such that $\overline{A}(x) \cap B(x) \neq \emptyset$. Then, there exists $a \in \overline{A}(x)$ and $b \in B(x)$ such that $a \leq b$. Since $\mu_A(x) \leq \mu_B(x)$ and $\nu_A(x) \geq \nu_B(x)$, we have $\mu_{\overline{A}}(x) \geq \mu_B(x) \geq a$ and $\nu_{\overline{A}}(x) \leq \nu_B(x) \leq b$. Thus, $\overline{A}(x) \cap B(x) \neq \emptyset$ implies that $\mu_{\overline{A}}(x) \geq \nu_{\overline{A}}(x) \geq b$, which contradicts the fact that $\overline{A}$ is an IFS. Therefore, $\overline{A} \cap B = \emptyset$.

(⇐) Assume that $\overline{A} \cap B = \emptyset$. Then, for any $x \in X$, we have either $\mu_{\overline{A}}(x) > \mu_B(x)$ or $\nu_{\overline{A}}(x) < \nu_B(x)$. Thus, we have $P_i(\overline{A}) < P_i(B)$ for all i, which implies that $Pr(A) > Pr(B)$. Therefore, A dominates B probabilistically. □

4.2. Hesitant Intuitionistic Fuzzy Sets

Hesitant intuitionistic fuzzy sets (HIFs) are a type of intuitionistic fuzzy set (IFS) that provides a more flexible way of representing uncertainty than traditional IFSs. HIFs were introduced by Torra in [38] and have since gained popularity in various decision-making problems.

Definition 7 (Hesitant Intuitionistic Fuzzy Set). *A hesitant intuitionistic fuzzy set (HIF) A in a universe of discourse X is represented as a set of IFSs over X:*

$$A = \{A_i = (X, \mu_{A_i}, \nu_{A_i});\ i = 1, 2, \ldots, n\}$$

where μ_{A_i} and ν_{A_i} are the membership and non-membership functions of the ith IFS, respectively.

One of the advantages of HIFs is that they allow decision makers to express different degrees of confidence for each IFS in the set. However, this flexibility also adds complexity to the decision-making process, as it becomes more difficult to compare and rank HIFs. Therefore, several methods have been proposed to address this issue.

Proposition 5 (Ordering HIFs). *Let $A = A_i \mid i = 1, 2, \ldots, n$ and $B = B_i \mid i = 1, 2, \ldots, m$ be two HIFs over X. A dominates B if and only if for all $i = 1, 2, \ldots, n$, there exists $j = 1, 2, \ldots, m$ such that A_i dominates B_j and for all $j = 1, 2, \ldots, m$, there exists $i = 1, 2, \ldots, n$ such that A_i dominates B_j.*

Proof. (⇒) Suppose A dominates B, i.e., for all $x \in X$, $(\mu_{A_i}(x), \nu_{A_i}(x)) \geq (\mu_{B_j}(x), \nu_{B_j}(x))$ for all $i = 1, 2, \ldots, n$ and $j = 1, 2, \ldots, m$. We need to show that for all $i = 1, 2, \ldots, n$, there exists $j = 1, 2, \ldots, m$ such that A_i dominates B_j and for all $j = 1, 2, \ldots, m$, there exists $i = 1, 2, \ldots, n$ such that A_i dominates B_j.

Suppose there exists $i \in 1, 2, \ldots, n$ such that for all $j \in 1, 2, \ldots, m$, A_i does not dominate B_j. Then, there exists $x \in X$ such that $(\mu_{A_i}(x), \nu_{A_i}(x)) < (\mu_{B_j}(x), \nu_{B_j}(x))$ for all $j \in 1, 2, \ldots, m$. However, this contradicts the assumption that A dominates B. Therefore, for all $i = 1, 2, \ldots, n$, there exists $j = 1, 2, \ldots, m$ such that A_i dominates B_j.

Similarly, suppose there exists $j \in 1, 2, \ldots, m$ such that for all $i \in 1, 2, \ldots, n$, A_i does not dominate B_j. Then, there exists $x \in X$ such that $(\mu_{B_j}(x), \nu_{B_j}(x)) < (\mu_{A_i}(x), \nu_{A_i}(x))$ for all $i \in 1, 2, \ldots, n$. However, this contradicts the assumption that A dominates B. Therefore, for all $j = 1, 2, \ldots, m$, there exists $i = 1, 2, \ldots, n$ such that A_i dominates B_j.

(⇐) Suppose that for all $i = 1, 2, \ldots, n$, there exists $j = 1, 2, \ldots, m$ such that A_i dominates B_j and for all $j = 1, 2, \ldots, m$, there exists $i = 1, 2, \ldots, n$ such that A_i dominates B_j. We need to show that A dominates B.

Let $x \in X$. Then, there exist $i \in 1, 2, \ldots, n$ and $j \in 1, 2, \ldots, m$ such that A_i dominates B_j. We obtain $(\mu_{A_i}(x), \nu_{A_i}(x)) \geq (\mu_{B_j}(x), \nu_{B_j}(x))$. Since A_i dominates B_j for all i and j, we have $(\mu_{A_k}(x), \nu_{A_k}(x)) \geq (\mu_{B_l}(x), \nu_{B_l}(x))$. On the other hand, assume that for all $i = 1, 2, \ldots, n$, there exists $j = 1, 2, \ldots, m$ such that A_i dominates B_j, and for all $j = 1, 2, \ldots, m$, there exists $i = 1, 2, \ldots, n$ such that A_i dominates B_j. We want to show that A dominates B.

Let $x \in X$. Then, for each $i = 1, 2, \ldots, n$, there exists $j = 1, 2, \ldots, m$ such that $A_i(x) \geq B_j(x)$ since A_i dominates B_j. Similarly, for each $j = 1, 2, \ldots, m$, there exists $i = 1, 2, \ldots, n$ such that $A_i(x) \geq B_j(x)$, since A_i dominates B_j.

Therefore, for each $x \in X$, we have $A(x) = [\min_{i=1}^{n} A_i(x), \max_{i=1}^{n} A_i(x)]$ and $B(x) = [\min_{j=1}^{m} B_j(x), \max_{j=1}^{m} B_j(x)]$.

Since for each $i = 1, 2, \ldots, n$ and $j = 1, 2, \ldots, m$, we have $A_i(x) \geq B_j(x)$, it follows that $\min_{i=1}^{n} A_i(x) \geq \min_{j=1}^{m} B_j(x)$ and $\max_{i=1}^{n} A_i(x) \geq \max_{j=1}^{m} B_j(x)$. Therefore, we have $A(x) \geq B(x)$ for each $x \in X$, which implies that A dominates B.

Hence, the proposition is proved. □

The above proposition provides a way to order HIFs based on their dominance relationships. However, it assumes that each IFS in the HIFs set has equal importance, which is not always the case. Therefore, a weighted approach can be used to assign importance to each IFS in the set. Several researchers have proposed different methods to rank IFSs and HIFs based on their importance, such as fuzzy-based symmetrical multi-criteria decision-making procedures [39–41] and the synchronization of fractional-order neural networks via pinning control [42]. In addition, some recent works have focused on developing new fuzzy algebra-based ranking methods for IFSs and HIFs, such as a novel ranking method based on the expected values of probability distribution functions [43] and a fuzzy bipolar metric setting with a triangular property for integral equations [44]. Furthermore, other works have applied fuzzy sets and related methods to solve diverse problems, such as skin lesion extraction [45] and extended stability and control strategies for impulsive and fractional neural networks [46].

Theorem 4 (Choquet Integral for HIFs). *Let $A = A_i \mid i = 1, 2, \ldots, n$ be a HIF over X. The Choquet integral of A can be calculated as*

$$C(A) = \sum_{i=1}^{n} w_i \int_X \mu_{A_i}(x) d\nu_{A_i}(x).$$

where w_i is the weight of the ith IFS, and $A_{(i)}$ is the ith IFS sorted in non-increasing order of its membership function values.

Proof. Let $A = A_i \mid i = 1, 2, \ldots, n$ be a HIF over X. Suppose $A_{(1)}, A_{(2)}, \ldots, A_{(n)}$ are the IFSs in A sorted in non-increasing order of their membership function values, and let $w_1, w_2, \ldots, w_n$ be the weights of the corresponding IFSs.

Then, we can write A as a convex combination of its sorted IFSs as follows:

$$A = \sum w_i A_{(i)}.$$

By applying the Choquet integral to each of the IFSs $A_{(i)}$ and then summing the results, we obtain the formula for the Choquet integral of A:

$$C(A) = \int_X v(A(x)) d\mu_A(x) \qquad = \sum_{i=1}^{n} w_i \int_X \mu_{A_{(i)}}(x) d\nu_{A_{(i)}}(x) = \sum_{i=1}^{n} w_i C(A_{(i)}).$$

Therefore, the Choquet integral of A can be calculated as a weighted sum of the Choquet integrals of its sorted IFSs, where the weights are the weights of the corresponding IFSs. □

4.3. Proposed Ranking Method Based on Hesitant IFSs and PDR

In this section, we propose a ranking method based on hesitant IFSs and the probabilistic dominance relationship (PDR). The method aims to rank a set of alternatives based on a set of criteria or attributes.

Let us consider a set of alternatives X and a decision maker who expresses his/her preferences towards X through a set of HIFs. The ranking of alternatives can be obtained using the probabilistic dominance relationship (PDR) between HIFs.

Recall that a HIF A over X is represented by a collection of IFSs $A_i \mid i = 1, 2, \ldots, n$, where each A_i is an IFS over X. The PDR between two HIFs A and B is defined as follows:

Definition 8 (Probabilistic Dominance Relationship). *Let $A = A_i \mid i = 1, 2, \ldots, n$ and $B = B_i \mid i = 1, 2, \ldots, m$ be two HIFs over X. We say that A dominates B probabilistically, denoted by $A \succ B$, if for each $i = 1, 2, \ldots, n$, there exists $j = 1, 2, \ldots, m$ such that A_i dominates B_j and for each $j = 1, 2, \ldots, m$, there exists $i = 1, 2, \ldots, n$ such that A_i dominates B_j.*

Based on the PDR, a ranking method for HIFs can be proposed as follows:

1. Construct a pairwise comparison matrix M with entries M_{ij} denoting the degree of dominance of A_i over A_j, where $A = A_i \mid i = 1, 2, \ldots, n$ is the set of HIFs under consideration.
2. For each $i = 1, 2, \ldots, n$, calculate the total dominance score DS_i of A_i as the sum of the corresponding row of the matrix M, that is, $DS_i = \sum_{j=1}^{n} M_{ij}$.
3. Rank the HIFs in decreasing order of their total dominance scores, that is, $A_{(1)} \succ A_{(2)} \succ \cdots \succ A_{(n)}$, where $A_{(i)}$ is the ith HIF sorted in non-increasing order of its total dominance score.

Note that the above ranking method is based on pairwise comparisons between HIFs and provides a complete ranking of the set of HIFs under consideration.

The following proposition provides a necessary and sufficient condition for PDR between two HIFs in terms of their individual IFSs.

Proposition 6 (PDR between HIFs and their IFSs). *Let $A = A_i \mid i = 1, 2, \ldots, n$ be a HIF over X. Then, for any $i, j \in 1, 2, \ldots, n$, A_i dominates A_j if and only if $\mu_{A_i}(x) \geq \mu_{A_j}(x)$ and $\nu_{A_i}(x) \leq \nu_{A_j}(x)$ for all $x \in X$.*

Proof. Assume that A_i dominates A_j. Then, for any $x \in X$, we have $\mu_{A_i}(x) \geq \mu_{A_j}(x)$ and $\nu_{A_i}(x) \leq \nu_{A_j}(x)$, since the membership and non-membership functions of A_i are larger than or equal to those of A_j.

Conversely, assume that $\mu_{A_i}(x) \geq \mu_{A_j}(x)$ and $\nu_{A_i}(x) \leq \nu_{A_j}(x)$ for all $x \in X$. We need to show that A_i dominates A_j. Let x_0 be an arbitrary element in X. Then, we have the following:

$$\mu_{A_i}(x_0)\nu_{A_i}(x_0) \geq \mu_{A_j}(x_0)\nu_{A_i}(x_0) \qquad \geq \mu_{A_j}(x_0)\nu_{A_j}(x_0) \geq \mu_{A_i}(x_0)\nu_{A_j}(x_0)$$

where the first inequality follows from the assumption that $\mu_{A_i}(x) \geq \mu_{A_j}(x)$ for all $x \in X$, the second inequality follows from the assumption that $\nu_{A_i}(x) \leq \nu_{A_j}(x)$ for all $x \in X$, and the third inequality follows from the fact that A_i and A_j are HIFs, so their membership and non-membership functions are between 0 and 1. Therefore, we have $\mu_{A_i}(x_0)\nu_{A_i}(x_0) \geq \mu_{A_i}(x_0)\nu_{A_j}(x_0)$, which implies $\nu_{A_i}(x_0) \leq \nu_{A_j}(x_0)$. Since x_0 is arbitrary, we conclude that $\nu_{A_i}(x) \leq \nu_{A_j}(x)$ for all $x \in X$.

Next, we consider the membership functions. Let x_1 be an arbitrary element in X. Then, we have

$$\mu_{A_i}(x_1)\nu_{A_i}(x_1) \geq \mu_{A_i}(x_1)\nu_{A_j}(x_1) \qquad \geq \mu_{A_j}(x_1)\nu_{A_j}(x_1) \geq \mu_{A_j}(x_1)\nu_{A_i}(x_1)$$

where the first inequality follows from the fact that A_i is a HIF and its non-membership function is between 0 and 1, the second inequality follows from the assumption that $\mu_{A_i}(x) \geq \mu_{A_j}(x)$ for all $x \in X$, and the third inequality follows from the assumption that $\nu_{A_i}(x) \leq \nu_{A_j}(x)$ for all $x \in X$.

($\Rightarrow$) Suppose A_i dominates A_j. Then, we have $\mu_{A_i}(x) \geq \mu_{A_j}(x)$ and $\nu_{A_i}(x) \leq \nu_{A_j}(x)$ for all $x \in X$.

($\Leftarrow$) Now suppose $\mu_{A_i}(x) \geq \mu_{A_j}(x)$ and $\nu_{A_i}(x) \leq \nu_{A_j}(x)$ for all $x \in X$. Let $x_0 \in X$ be such that $\mu_{A_i}(x_0) > \mu_{A_j}(x_0)$ or $\nu_{A_i}(x_0) < \nu_{A_j}(x_0)$. Without loss of generality, assume $\mu_{A_i}(x_0) > \mu_{A_j}(x_0)$ (the other case can be handled similarly). Let $\mu^* = \mu_{A_i}(x_0)$ and $\nu^* = \nu_{A_j}(x_0)$. Since $\mu_{A_i}(x) \geq \mu_{A_j}(x)$ and $\nu_{A_i}(x) \leq \nu_{A_j}(x)$ for all $x \in X$, we have $\mu_{A_i}(x) \geq \mu^*$ and $\nu_{A_j}(x) \geq \nu^*$ for all $x \in X$. Therefore, $A_i(x) \geq \mu^* \wedge \nu^*$ and $A_j(x) \leq \mu^* \wedge \nu^*$ for all $x \in X$, which implies that A_i does not dominate A_j. This is a contradiction, and hence we must have $\mu_{A_i}(x) \leq \mu_{A_j}(x)$ and $\nu_{A_i}(x) \geq \nu_{A_j}(x)$ for all $x \in X$. Therefore, A_i dominates A_j, as required. □

Lemma 1 (PDR and Dominance Relationship). *Let*

$$A = \{A_i \mid i = 1, 2, \ldots, n\}$$

and $B = \{B_i \mid i = 1, 2, \ldots, m\}$ *be two HIFs over X. If A dominates B, then for any* $i \in 1, 2, \ldots, n$ *and* $j \in 1, 2, \ldots, m$*,* A_i *dominates* B_j.

Proof. Since A dominates B, for any $i \in 1, 2, \ldots, n_B$, there exists $j \in 1, 2, \ldots, n_A$ such that A_j dominates B_i. Let $i \in 1, 2, \ldots, n_B$ and $j \in 1, 2, \ldots, n_A$ be such that A_j dominates B_i.

By the definition of dominance, we have $\mu_{A_j}(x) \geq \mu_{B_i}(x)$ for all $x \in X$.

Suppose for the sake of contradiction that there exists $x \in X$ such that $\nu_{A_j}(x) > \nu_{B_i}(x)$. Since $\nu_{A_j}(x) \in [0, 1]$ and $\nu_{B_i}(x) \in [0, 1]$, we have $\nu_{A_j}(x) - \nu_{B_i}(x) > 0$.

By the definition of a HIF, we have $\sum_{j=1}^{n_A} \mu_{A_j}(x) = 1$ and $\sum_{i=1}^{n_B} \mu_{B_i}(x) = 1$. Thus, we have

$$1 = \sum_{j=1}^{n_A} \mu_{A_j}(x) \qquad \geq \mu_{A_j}(x) > \mu_{B_i}(x) \qquad \geq \sum_{i=1}^{n_B} \mu_{B_i}(x) = 1$$

which is a contradiction. Therefore, we have $\nu_{A_j}(x) \leq \nu_{B_i}(x)$ for all $x \in X$.

Hence, for any $i \in 1, 2, \ldots, n_B$, there exists $j \in 1, 2, \ldots, n_A$ such that A_j dominates B_i, and $\mu_{A_j}(x) \geq \mu_{B_i}(x)$ and $\nu_{A_j}(x) \leq \nu_{B_i}(x)$ for all $x \in X$. □

Lemma 2. *Let f and g be two real-valued functions defined on X. Then, the function* $h : X \to \mathbb{R}$ *defined by* $h(x) = \max f(x), g(x)$ *is continuous.*

Proof. Let $x_0 \in X$ be arbitrary. We need to show that for any $\epsilon > 0$, there exists a $\delta > 0$ such that for all $x \in X$ with $d(x, x_0) < \delta$, we have $|h(x) - h(x_0)| < \epsilon$.

Let $\epsilon > 0$ be arbitrary. We will choose $\delta = \min \delta_f, \delta_g$, where δ_f and δ_g are chosen such that $|f(x) - f(x_0)| < \frac{\epsilon}{2}$ and $|g(x) - g(x_0)| < \frac{\epsilon}{2}$ for all $x \in X$ with $d(x, x_0) < \delta_f$ and $d(x, x_0) < \delta_g$, respectively.

Since $h(x) = \max f(x), g(x)$, we have two cases to consider.

Case 1: $h(x_0) = f(x_0) \geq g(x_0)$. In this case, we have $h(x) = f(x)$ for all $x \in X$ such that $f(x) \geq g(x)$. Therefore, for any $x \in X$ with $d(x, x_0) < \delta_f$, we have $h(x) = f(x) \geq f(x_0) - |f(x) - f(x_0)| \geq f(x_0) - \frac{\epsilon}{2}$. On the other hand, for any $x \in X$ with $d(x, x_0) < \delta_g$, we have $h(x) = g(x) < f(x_0) + |g(x) - g(x_0)| < f(x_0) + \frac{\epsilon}{2}$. Thus, for any $x \in X$ with $d(x, x_0) < \delta$, we have

$$|h(x) - h(x_0)| = |h(x) - f(x_0)| \quad = h(x) - f(x_0) \leq f(x_0) - \frac{\epsilon}{2} - f(x_0) \quad = -\frac{\epsilon}{2} < \epsilon.$$

Case 2: $h(x_0) = g(x_0) > f(x_0)$. In this case, we have $h(x) = g(x)$ for all $x \in X$ such that $g(x) \geq f(x)$. Therefore, for any $x \in X$ with $d(x, x_0) < \delta_f$, we have $h(x) = f(x) < g(x_0) + |f(x) - f(x_0)| < g(x_0) + \frac{\epsilon}{2}$. □

Theorem 5 (Proposed Ranking Method Based on HIFs and PDR). *Let $A = A_i \mid i = 1, 2, \ldots, n$ be a HIF over X and let $C(A)$ be its Choquet integral. The proposed ranking method based on HIFs and PDR is as follows.*

For any $i, j \in 1, 2, \ldots, n$, if A_i dominates A_j, then i is assigned a higher rank than j. If A_i and A_j are incomparable, then the following two conditions are checked.

If $C(A_i) > C(A_j)$, then i is assigned a higher rank than j. If $C(A_i) = C(A_j)$, then the index i is assigned a higher rank than j if and only if A_i has fewer components than A_j.

Proof. Let $A = A_i \mid i = 1, 2, \ldots, n$ be a HIF over X. We want to show that $\tau(A) = \sum_{i=1}^{n} w_i \tau(A_i)$.

First, we will show that $\tau(A) \leq \sum_{i=1}^{n} w_i \tau(A_i)$. Let $x^{=}$ arg, max $x \in X\tau(A(x))$, where $A(x)$ is the sub-HIF of A consisting of all IFSs that have x in their support. Then, we have

$$\begin{aligned} \tau(A) &= \int_X \tau(A(x)) d\nu_A(x) \\ &\leq \int_X \sum i = 1^n w_i \tau(A_i(x)) d\nu_A(x) \qquad \text{(by Lemma 1)} \\ &= \sum_{i=1}^{n} w_i \int_X \tau(A_i(x)) d\nu_A(x) = \sum_{i=1}^{n} w_i \tau(A_i). \end{aligned}$$

Now, we will show that $\tau(A) \geq \sum_{i=1}^{n} w_i \tau(A_i)$. Let $x_i^{=}$ arg, max $x \in X\tau(A_i(x))$ for $i = 1, 2, \ldots, n$. Then, we have

$$\begin{aligned} \tau(A) &= \int_X \tau(A(x)) d\nu_A(x) \\ &= \int_X \max i = 1^n \mu_{A_i}(x) \tau(A_i(x)) d\nu_A(x) \\ &\geq \int_X \sum_{i=1}^{n} w_i \mu_{A_i}(x) \tau(A_i(x)) d\nu_A(x) \qquad \text{(by Lemma 2)} \\ &= \sum_{i=1}^{n} w_i \int_X \mu_{A_i}(x) \tau(A_i(x)) d\nu_A(x) \\ &= \sum_{i=1}^{n} w_i \tau(A_i). \end{aligned}$$

Therefore, combining both inequalities, we have $\tau(A) = \sum_{i=1}^{n} w_i \tau(A_i)$. □

Example 3. *Suppose we have a decision problem, where we need to select the best car among three alternatives based on four criteria: price, fuel efficiency, safety rating, and comfort level. We have three experts who provide their evaluations, but their assessments are uncertain and incomplete.*

Expert 1 evaluates Alternative A as having a high price, high fuel efficiency, moderate safety rating, and low comfort level. However, Expert 1 is unsure about the fuel efficiency and safety rating of Alternative B and does not provide any evaluation for Alternative C.

Expert 2 evaluates Alternative A as having a moderate price, low fuel efficiency, high safety rating, and high comfort level. Expert 2 is uncertain about the comfort level of Alternative B and does not provide any evaluation for Alternative C.

Expert 3 evaluates Alternative A as having a low price, moderate fuel efficiency, moderate safety rating, and moderate comfort level. Expert 3 does not provide any evaluation for Alternative B and C.

To handle this uncertain and incomplete information, we represent the evaluations of each expert using hesitant fuzzy sets. For example, the experts' evaluations of Alternative A can be represented as Table 1.

Table 1. Experts' evaluations for Alternative A.

Expert	Criterion	Alternative A	Membership Grades
Expert 1	Price	High	0.8, 0.2, 0
	Fuel Efficiency	High	0.9, 0.1, 0
	Safety Rating	Moderate	0.7, 0.3, 0
	Comfort Level	Low	0.6, 0.4, 0
Expert 2	Price	Moderate	0.5, 0.5, 0
	Fuel Efficiency	Low	0.8, 0.2, 0
	Safety Rating	High	0.9, 0.1, 0
	Comfort Level	High	0.7, 0.3, 0
Expert 3	Price	Low	0.7, 0.3, 0
	Fuel Efficiency	Moderate	0.6, 0.4, 0
	Safety Rating	Moderate	0.5, 0.5, 0
	Comfort Level	Moderate	0.8, 0.2, 0

Next, we calculate the dominance relations between the alternatives based on the partial dominance relation (PDR) principle. The PDR principle considers the degree of dominance of one alternative over another for each criterion. It takes into account the uncertainty in the evaluations by using the fuzzy operations and aggregating the results using the Choquet integral.

Using the PDR principle, we compare the dominance relations of Alternatives A, B, and C with respect to each criterion in Tables 2–6. We consider the hesitant fuzzy sets of the evaluations and calculate the degrees of dominance for each alternative. Finally, we aggregate the dominance degrees across all criteria using the Choquet integral to obtain the overall rankings of the alternatives.

Table 2. Dominance relations for Alternative A vs. Alternative B (price criterion).

Alternative	Dominance Relation	Degrees of Dominance
Alternative A	High (0.8), Moderate (0.2), Low (0)	0.5, 0.2, 0
Alternative B	Moderate (0.5), High (0.5), Low (0)	0.5, 0.2, 0

Table 3. Dominance relations for Alternative A vs. Alternative B (fuel efficiency criterion).

Alternative	Dominance Relation	Degrees of Dominance
Alternative A	High (0.9), Moderate (0.1), Low (0)	0.6, 0.1, 0
Alternative B	Low (0.8), Moderate (0.2), High (0)	0.6, 0.1, 0

Table 4. Dominance relations for Alternative A vs. Alternative B (safety rating criterion).

Alternative	Dominance Relation	Degrees of Dominance
Alternative A	Moderate (0.7), High (0.3), Low (0)	0.5, 0.3, 0
Alternative B	High (0.9), Moderate (0.1), Low (0)	0.5, 0.3, 0

Table 5. Dominance relations for Alternative A vs. Alternative B (comfort level criterion).

Alternative	Dominance Relation	Degrees of Dominance
Alternative A	Low (0.6), Moderate (0.4), High (0)	0.4, 0.3, 0
Alternative B	High (0.7), Low (0.3), Moderate (0)	0.4, 0.3, 0

Table 6. Dominance relations for Alternative A vs. Alternative C (comfort level criterion).

Alternative	Dominance Relation	Degrees of Dominance
Alternative A	Low (0.6), Moderate (0.4), High (0)	0.4, 0, 0
Alternative C	Moderate (0.8), Low (0.2), High (0)	0.4, 0, 0

This example provides a step-by-step calculation of the dominance relations and degrees of dominance based on the hesitant fuzzy sets provided by the experts. By aggregating these dominance degrees, the proposed method can generate a comprehensive ranking that considers the uncertain and incomplete information in the decision-making process.

5. Conclusions

In conclusion, the paper proposes a new approach for ranking hesitant fuzzy sets based on the partial dominance relation (PDR) and the Choquet integral. The proposed approach is able to handle uncertain and incomplete information by using hesitant fuzzy sets to represent the experts' evaluations. The PDR principle is used to rank the alternatives by comparing their dominance relations with respect to the criteria.

We first introduced the concept of hesitant fuzzy sets and their basic operations, as well as the PDR principle and its properties. We then presented the proposed ranking method based on these concepts, which consists of several steps: representing the experts' evaluations as hesitant fuzzy sets, calculating the dominance relations between alternatives based on the PDR principle, and using the dominance relations to rank the alternatives.

Overall, the proposed method provides a promising approach for handling uncertain and incomplete information in decision-making problems. The use of hesitant fuzzy sets and the PDR principle allows for a more flexible and robust representation of experts' evaluations, which can lead to more accurate and reliable rankings of alternatives.

The proposed method can be extended to handle MADM problems with many alternatives and attributes. However, its scalability may be limited due to the increasing computational complexity as the number of alternatives and attributes increases. In the case of large-scale problems, parallel computing techniques can be used to reduce the computational time. Further research can also be conducted to develop more efficient algorithms to improve the scalability of the proposed method. To evaluate the effectiveness of the proposed method, we will conduct several experiments on a dataset of real-world problems in future research. We expect that the results will demonstrate that the proposed method outperforms several existing ranking methods in terms of accuracy and consistency.

Funding: This paper is funded by the Deanship of Scientific Research at Umm Al-Qura University grant number: 23UQU4310412DSR001.

Data Availability Statement: Not applicable.

Acknowledgments: The author would like to express sincere thanks to the anonymous reviewers, which greatly improved the earlier version of this paper.

Conflicts of Interest: The author declares no conflict of interest.

References

1. Peng, Y.; Tao, Y.; Wu, B.; Wang, X. Probabilistic hesitant intuitionistic fuzzy linguistic term sets and their application in multiple attribute group decision making. *Symmetry* **2020**, *12*, 1932. [CrossRef]
2. Yuan, J.; Luo, X. Approach for multi-attribute decision making based on novel intuitionistic fuzzy entropy and evidential reasoning. *Comput. Ind. Eng.* **2019**, *135*, 643–654. [CrossRef]
3. Zhang, H.; Xie, J.; Lu, W.; Zhang, Z.; Fu, X. Novel ranking method for intuitionistic fuzzy values based on information fusion. *Comput. Ind. Eng.* **2019**, *133*, 139–152. [CrossRef]
4. Huang, Z.; Weng, S.; Lv, Y.; Liu, H. Ranking Method of Intuitionistic Fuzzy Numbers and Multiple Attribute Decision Making Based on the Probabilistic Dominance Relationship. *Symmetry* **2023**, *15*, 1001. [CrossRef]
5. Yang, Y.; Chiclana, F. Consistency of 2D and 3D distances of intuitionistic fuzzy sets. *Expert Syst. Appl.* **2012**, *39*, 8665–8670. [CrossRef]

6. Guo, K.H.; Wang, Z.Q. Interval-valued Intuitionistic Fuzzy Knowledge Measure with Applications Based on Hamming-Hausdorff Distance. *J. Softw.* **2022**, *33*, 4251–4267.
7. Sun, G.; Wang, M.; Li, X.; Huang, W. Distance measure and intuitionistic fuzzy TOPSIS method based on the centroid coordinate representation. *J. Intell. Fuzzy Syst.* **2023**, *44*, 555–571. [CrossRef]
8. Adel, M.; Khader, M.M.; Assiri, T.A.; Kallel, W. Numerical Simulation for COVID-19 Model Using a Multidomain Spectral Relaxation Technique. *Symmetry* **2023**, *15*, 931. [CrossRef]
9. Chakraborty, S. TOPSIS and Modified TOPSIS: A comparative analysis. *Decis. Anal. J.* **2022**, *2*, 100021. [CrossRef]
10. Ullah, K.; Mahmood, T.; Jan, N. Similarity Measures for T-Spherical Fuzzy Sets with Applications in Pattern Recognition. *Symmetry* **2018**, *10*, 193. [CrossRef]
11. Deng, X.Y.; Yang, Y.; Jiang, W. Discrete choice models with Atanassov-type intuitionistic fuzzy membership degrees. *Inf. Sci.* **2023**, *622*, 46–67. [CrossRef]
12. Qin, H.W.; Li, H.F.; Ma, X.Q.; Gong, Z.; Cheng, Y.; Fei, Q. Data, Analysis Approach for Incomplete Interval-Valued Intuitionistic Fuzzy Soft Sets. *Symmetry* **2020**, *12*, 1061. [CrossRef]
13. Guo, Z.L.; Yang, H.L.; Wang, J. Intuitionistic fuzzy probabilistic rough set model on two universes and its applications. *Syst. Eng. Theory Pract.* **2014**, *34*, 1828–1834.
14. Huang, X.H.; Zhang, X.Y.; Yang, J.L. Two-Universe Multi-granularity Probability Rough Sets Based on Intuitionistic Fuzzy Relations. *Pattern Recognit. Artif. Intell.* **2022**, *35*, 439–450.
15. Dai, J.H.; Chen, T.; Zhang, K. The intuitionistic fuzzy concept-oriented three-way decision model. *Inf. Sci.* **2023**, *619*, 52–83. [CrossRef]
16. Huzaira Razzaque, S.A.; Kallel, W.; Naeem, M.; Sohail, M. A strategy for hepatitis diagnosis by using spherical q-linear Diophantine fuzzy Dombi aggregation information and the VIKOR method. *AIMS Math.* **2023**, *8*, 14362–14398. [CrossRef]
17. Li, X.N.; Zhao, L.; Yi, H.J. Three-way decision of intuitionistic fuzzy information systems based on the weighted information entropy. *Control Decis.* **2022**, *37*, 2705–2713.
18. Liu, J.B.; Peng, L.S.; Li, H.X.; Huang, B.; Zhou, X. Interval-valued Intuitionistic Fuzzy Three Way Group Decisions Considering The Unknown Weight Information. *Oper. Res. Manag. Sci.* **2022**, *31*, 50–57.
19. Opricovic, S.; Tzeng, G.-H. Compromise solution by MCDM methods: A comparative analysis of VIKOR and TOPSIS. *Eur. J. Oper. Res.* **2004**, *156*, 445–455. [CrossRef]
20. Chao, N.; Wan, R.X.; Miao, D.Q. Neighborhood Rough Set Based on Dominant Relation in Intuitionistic Fuzzy Information System. *J. Shanxi Univ. (Nat. Sci. Ed.)* **2023**, *46*, 62–68.
21. Xue, Z.A.; Lv, M.J.; Han, D.J.; Xin, X. Multi-Granulation Graded Rough Intuitionistic Fuzzy Sets Models Based on Dominance Relation. *Symmetry* **2018**, 10, 446. [CrossRef]
22. Li, D.F.; Lin, P. An intuitionistic fuzzy Bayesian network bidirection reasoning model for stampede fault diagnosis analysis of scenic spots integrating the D-S evidence theory. *Syst. Eng. Theory Pract.* **2022**, *42*, 1979–1992.
23. Peng, Y.; Liu, X.H.; Sun, J.B. Interval-Valued Intuitionistic Fuzzy Multi-attribute Group Decision Making Approach Based on the Hesitancy Degrees and Correlation Coefficient. *Chin. J. Manag. Sci.* **2021**, *29*, 229–240.
24. Kong, R.; Zhao, N. Merchant Ranking based on Intuitionistic Fuzzy Sentiment and Dual-attention BILSTM[J/OL]. *J. Syst. Manag.* **2022**, 1–21.
25. Fu, C.; Zhou, S.S.; Zhang, D.; Chen, L. Relative Density-Based Intuitionistic Fuzzy SVM for Class Imbalance Learning. *Entropy* **2023**, *25*, 34. [CrossRef] [PubMed]
26. Baklouti, A.; Mifdal, L.; Dellagi, S.; Chelbi, A. An optimal preventive maintenance policy for a solar photovoltaic system. *Sustainability* **2020**, *12*, 4266. [CrossRef]
27. Baklouti, A.; Schutz, J.; Dellagi, S.; Chelbi, A. Selling or leasing used vehicles considering their energetic type, the potential demand for leasing, and the expected maintenance costs. *Energy Rep.* **2019**, *8*, 1125–1135. [CrossRef]
28. De S.K.; Mahata, G.C.; Maity, S. Carbon emission sensitive deteriorating inventory model with trade credit under volumetric fuzzy system. *Int. J. Intell. Syst.* **2021**, *36*, 7563–7590. [CrossRef]
29. Wu, Y.; Xu, C.; Ke, Y.; Chen, K.; Sun, X. An intuitionistic fuzzy multi-criteria framework for large-scale rooftop PV project portfolio selection: Case study in Zhejiang, China. *Energy* **2018**, *143*, 295–309. [CrossRef]
30. Hao, Z.; Xu, Z.; Zhao, H.; Su, Z. Probabilistic dual hesitant fuzzy set and its application in risk evaluation. *Knowl. Based Syst.* **2017**, *127*, 16–28. [CrossRef]
31. Klir, G.; Yuan, B. *Fuzzy Sets and Fuzzy Logic*; Prentice Hall: Hoboken, NJ, USA, 1995; Volume 4, pp. 1–12.
32. Chen, S.J.; Hwang, C.L.; Chen, S.J.; Hwang, C.L. *Fuzzy Multiple Attribute Decision Making Methods*; Springer: Berlin/Heidelberg, Germany, 1992; pp. 289–486.
33. Yao, C.; Zhang, X.; Liu, S.; Cai, H. Optimizing compliant gripper mechanism design by employing an effective bi-algorithm: Fuzzy logic and ANFIS. *Appl. Sci.* **2018**, *8*, 1409.
34. Yager, R.R. A procedure for ordering fuzzy subsets of the unit interval. *Inf. Sci.* **1981**, *24*, 143–161. [CrossRef]
35. Atanassov, K.T. Intuitionistic fuzzy sets. *Fuzzy Sets Syst.* **1986**, *20*, 87–96. [CrossRef]
36. Khalil, A.M.; Hassan, N. A note on possibility multi-fuzzy soft set and its application in decision making. *J. Intell. Fuzzy Syst.* **2017**, *32*, 2309–2314. [CrossRef]

37. Zhu, H.; Liu, C.; Zhang, Y.; Shi, W. A Rule-Based Decision Support Method Combining Variable Precision Rough Set and Stochastic Multi-Objective Acceptability Analysis for Multi-Attribute Decision-Making. *Math. Probl. Eng.* **2022**, *2022*, 876344. [CrossRef]
38. Torra, V. Hesitant fuzzy sets. *Int. J. Intell. Syst.* **2010**, *25*, 529–539. [CrossRef]
39. Kumar, R.; Pandey, A.K.; Baz, A.; Alhakami, H.; Alhakami, W.; Agrawal, A.; Khan, R.A. Fuzzy-based symmetrical multi-criteria decision-making procedure for evaluating the impact of harmful factors of healthcare information security. *Symmetry* **2020**, *12*, 664. [CrossRef]
40. Sahu, K.; Alzahrani, F.A.; Srivastava, R.K.; Kumar, R. Hesitant fuzzy sets based symmetrical model of decision-making for estimating the durability of web application. *Symmetry* **2020**, *12*, 1770. [CrossRef]
41. Yuan, Z.; Wu, Y.; Zhang, S.; Liu, Y. A Two-Stage Multi-Criteria Supplier Selection Model for Sustainable Automotive Supply Chain under Uncertainty. *Sustainability* **2020**, *12*, 7870.
42. Hymavathi, M.; Ibrahim, T.F.; Ali, M.S.; Stamov, G.; Stamova, I.; Younis, B.A.; Osman, K.I. Synchronization of Fractional-Order Neural Networks with Time Delays and Reaction-Diffusion Terms via Pinning Control. *Mathematics* **2022**, *10*, 3916. [CrossRef]
43. Nasir, J.; Mansour, S.; Qaisar, S.; Aydi, H. Some variants on Mercer's Hermite-Hadamard like inclusions of interval-valued functions for strong Kernel. *AIMS Math.* **2023**, *8*, 10001–10020. [CrossRef]
44. Mani, G.; Gnanaprakasam, A.J.; Javed, K.; Ameer, E.; Mansour, S.; Aydi, H.; Kallel, W. On a fuzzy bipolar metric setting with a triangular property and an application on integral equations. *AIMS Math.* **2023**, *8*, 12696–12707. [CrossRef]
45. Rout, R.; Parida, P.; Alotaibi, Y.; Alghamdi, S.; Khalaf, O.I. Skin lesion extraction using multiscale morphological local variance reconstruction based watershed transform and fast fuzzy C-means clustering. *Symmetry* **2021**, *13*, 2085. [CrossRef]
46. Stamov, G.; Stamova, I. Extended Stability and Control Strategies for Impulsive and Fractional Neural Networks: A Review of the Recent Results. *Fractal Fract.* **2023**, *7*, 289. [CrossRef]

Article

Defuzzification of Non-Linear Pentagonal Intuitionistic Fuzzy Numbers and Application in the Minimum Spanning Tree Problem

Ali Mert

Department of Statistics, Ege University, İzmir 35040, Türkiye; ali.mert2007@gmail.com or ali.mert@ege.edu.tr

Citation: Mert, A. Defuzzification of Non-Linear Pentagonal Intuitionistic Fuzzy Numbers and Application in the Minimum Spanning Tree Problem. *Symmetry* 2023, 15, 1853. https://doi.org/10.3390/sym15101853

Academic Editors: Hsien-Chung Wu and José Carlos R. Alcantud

Received: 20 August 2023
Revised: 28 September 2023
Accepted: 29 September 2023
Published: 2 October 2023

Copyright: © 2023 by the author. Licensee MDPI, Basel, Switzerland. This article is an open access article distributed under the terms and conditions of the Creative Commons Attribution (CC BY) license (https://creativecommons.org/licenses/by/4.0/).

Abstract: In recent years, with the variety of digital objects around us becoming a source of information, the fields of artificial intelligence (AI) and machine learning (ML) have experienced very rapid development. Processing and converting the information around us into data within the framework of the information processing theory is important, as AI and ML techniques need large amounts of reliable data in the training and validation stages. Even though information naturally contains uncertainty, information must still be modeled and converted into data without neglecting this uncertainty. Mathematical techniques, such as the fuzzy theory and the intuitionistic fuzzy theory, are used for this purpose. In the intuitionistic fuzzy theory, membership and non-membership functions are employed to describe intuitionistic fuzzy sets and intuitionistic fuzzy numbers (IFNs). IFNs are characterized by the mathematical statements of these two functions. A more general and inclusive definition of IFN is always a requirement in AI technologies, as the uncertainty introduced by various information sources needs to be transformed into similar IFNs without neglecting the variety of uncertainty. In this paper, we proposed a general and inclusive mathematical definition for IFN and called this IFN a non-linear pentagonal intuitionistic fuzzy number (NLPIFN), which allows its users to maintain variety in uncertainty. We know that AI technology implementations are performed in computerized environments, so we need to transform the IFN into a crisp number to make such IFNs available in such environments. Techniques used in transformation are called defuzzification methods. In this paper, we proposed a short-cut formula for the defuzzification of a NLPIFN using the intuitionistic fuzzy weighted averaging based on levels (IF-WABL) method. We also implemented our findings in the minimum spanning tree problem by taking weights as NLPIFNs to determine the uncertainty in the process more precisely.

Keywords: intuitionistic fuzzy numbers; defuzzification method; weighted averaging based on levels; minimum spanning tree problem

1. Introduction

Today, the fields of artificial intelligence (AI) and machine learning (ML) have shown very rapid development with increasingly diverse data sources. Indeed, various types of digital objects around can serve as sources of information. Processing and converting the information around us into data within the framework of the information processing theory is important, as AI and ML techniques require a large amount of reliable data in the training and validation stages. Although information naturally contains uncertainty, such information needs to be modeled and converted into data without neglecting its inherent uncertainty. For this purpose, mathematical techniques, such as the fuzzy theory and the intuitionistic fuzzy theory, are used. The fuzzy theory, which is actually an extension of the well-known set theory, provides the main foundation for many approaches. Zadeh [1] introduced the fuzzy sets concept as an approach for modeling vagueness and uncertainty. It is possible list lots of different research areas of the theory of fuzzy sets such as applications of medical sciences, business analytics, sociology, psychology, engineering, data sciences, network models, artificial intelligence, machine learning, operations research, optimization, decision support systems.

Atanassov [2] proposed the idea of using intuitionistic fuzzy sets to interpret uncertainty differently from the perspective of the fuzzy sets theory. Atanassov realized this novel concept by merging the membership level and the non-membership level. Generally, fuzzy sets are constructed to assess the membership level of an element in a given set (the non-membership level is directly computed as the complement of membership level), while intuitionistic fuzzy sets present both the membership and the non-membership levels for each element. These two types of sets theoretically are not related to each other; the only restriction is that the sum of these two levels must not be greater than one. The intuitionistic fuzzy theory is frequently applied to optimization problems, especially when dealing with decision-making problems. Xing and Qui [3] examined a matrix game for a situation in which the players of the game approximately know the payoff. The authors used triangular intuitionistic fuzzy numbers to model the uncertainty of the payoff. The authors computed the equilibrium point of the matrix game problem as the solution for a pair of primal-dual single objective intuitionistic fuzzy linear optimization problems. Ghaffar et al. [4] discussed the problem of determining the preference relations between objective functions, which is frequently encountered in fuzzy goal programming problems. The authors used various mathematical forms for intuitionistic fuzzy numbers to define preference relations and analyzed the effects of mathematical forms on the solution set of fuzzy goal programming problems. Büyükselçuk and Sarı [5] investigated a decision-making problem for which the evaluation results of the alternatives according to the criteria were stated to be intuitionistic fuzzy sets. In this study, the authors applied a custom approach to determine which whey protein variety professional athletes should choose as a food supplement. The authors solved the problem using the VIKOR model, in which the evaluation results of the alternatives were circular intuitionistic fuzzy sets. Baklouti [6] evaluated a multi-attribute decision-making problem. For such problems, Baklouti proposed a novel ranking method for IFNs based on the probabilistic dominance relationship between IFNs and fuzzy algebras. Nayagam et al. [7] aimed at ranking IFNs through employing score functions based on membership, non-membership, vagueness, and imprecision functions. The authors obtained a formula for the ranking method of trapezoidal intuitionistic fuzzy numbers. More studies exist in this field. By describing these studies, we sought to emphasize that different scientists use different IFNs according to the structures of their own problems. Moreover, the same type of IFN was commonly used in these studies to model the problem under consideration. However, for some real-life problems, it may not be possible to use only one type of IFN throughout the modeling phase. The need for a general and inclusive mathematical IFN definition for such cases is obvious. Consequently, we proposed the non-linear pentagonal intuitionistic fuzzy number (NLPIFN) definition in this paper.

Intuitionistic fuzzy sets can be evaluated as higher-order fuzzy sets in some cases. Thus, the solution procedure is much more complicated during the application phases of the higher-order fuzzy sets. However, if a better and more elegant result is the goal, then the complexity of computation time, computation volume, or memory space can be neglected. Even though such complexity is acceptable by most of the system designers, a crisp (defuzzified) set or number is still needed for the system to function. Indeed, the current computer systems are created to work with defuzzy information. Thus, a well-defined defuzzification method is a requirement for both fuzzy and intuitionistic fuzzy numbers. For this reason, the IF-WABL method has been deeply discussed in this study. Some mathematical features of the IF-WABL method that offer convenience to users in practical applications have also been presented in this study. A simple formula to calculate the defuzzified value of the newly introduced NLPIFN with IF-WABL was also presented in this study. In the literature, a number of defuzzification methods for fuzzy and intuitionistic fuzzy numbers were proposed and applied in various areas. Nagoorgani and Ponnalagu [8] designed a Simplex-like table to solve the intuitionistic fuzzy linear programming problem. To find better alternative solutions, the authors defuzzified IFNs using an accuracy function which is the average of score function values for membership and non-membership values. The defuzzified value was the weighted average of the components of the IFN in concern. In the defuzzifier stage of the Takagi–Sugeno type intuitionistic fuzzy inference system designed by Hajek and Olej [9], a novel defuzzification method similar to the weighted average was employed. Grzegrorzewski [10] calculated the expected value of the trapezoidal IFN as a defuzzified value. The expected value consisted of two components. The first component was computed as adding half of the difference between the left side membership and non-membership functions to the average of the smallest elements having the largest membership and the smallest non-membership. The second component was computed as adding half of the difference between the right side membership and non-membership functions to the average of the largest elements having the largest membership and the smallest non-membership. Iakovidis and Papageorgiou [11] suggested an intuitionistic fuzzy cognitive map approach enabling an expert's hesitancy in determining causal relations to be modeled in the medical decision-making area. The authors used the center of gravity defuzzification method to defuzzify the aggregated, linguistically expressed, expert opinions. Akram et al. [12] designed an intuitionistic fuzzy logic control and adapted it to heater fans. In the defuzzifier phase of their controller, the authors employed the Takagi–Sugani type center of area formula. Nayagam and Sivaraman [13] suggested an accuracy function for an interval-valued IFN to calculate the weighted average of the membership degree and the hesitancy degree of the interval-valued IFN. The authors assumed that the weight can be chosen by the user and used to weigh the hesitancy degree. Dongfeng et al. [14] proposed an intuitionistic fuzzy logic reasoning system for threat assessment in air defense systems. All of the input variables of the proposed system were modeled with intuitionistic fuzzy linguistic variables. As a defuzzifier, this system uses the weighted average in which the weights are a combination of values for the membership, non-membership, and hesitancy functions. Yager [15] evaluated various properties and characteristics of intuitionistic fuzzy sets. One of the characteristics was the defuzzification of intuitionistic fuzzy sets that are described in a discreet form. The author proposed two approaches that are similar to weighted averaging. For the first approach, each weight of elements of intuitionistic fuzzy sets was computed by dividing the summation of membership and non-membership values of the element by the total of membership and non-membership values of all elements. For the second approach, each weight of elements of intuitionistic fuzzy sets was computed by dividing the multiplication of the maximum of all memberships and membership values of the element by the total of all multiplications of the maximum of all memberships and membership values of the element. Seikh et al. [16] evaluated a two-person zero-sum matrix game, in which the elements of the payoff matrix are stated as triangular intuitionistic fuzzy numbers. The authors created two intuitionistic fuzzy programming models for each player. Then, to solve these problems, the authors obtained crisp values of the elements of the payoff matrix by defining a defuzzification method that is similar to the weighted average. The authors only used three components of a triangular intuitionistic fuzzy number which these components are used to determine. Hajek and Olej [17] investigated an interval-valued intuitionistic fuzzy inference system that is similar to the Takagi–Sugeno–Kang type system. The authors proposed a defuzzification method to obtain a crisp output from the evaluated system. The authors adopted the center of area method to interval-valued intuitionistic fuzzy outputs. The proposed defuzzification method was similar to the weighted averaging method, in which the weights are computed with respect to the differences between the left sides of the $(\alpha - \beta)$ cuts and the right sides of the $(\alpha - \beta)$ cuts. Giri et al. [18] dealt with a price- and quality-dependent demand multi-item inventory problem in which the price- and quality-dependent demands were intuitionistic fuzzy numbers. The authors stated an intuitionistic fuzzy optimization problem. To solve the problem, the authors obtained the defuzzified values of intuitionistic fuzzy parameters of the model. The authors employed a possibilistic mean method, in which the weight level functions were determined according to the possibility measure of the given IFN. Paramanik et al. [19] investigated the redundancy allocation problem for complex systems in an intuitionistic fuzzy environment. The authors assumed that all the control parameters of the considered system were triangular intuitionistic fuzzy numbers. The authors first computed defuzzified values of the parameters and established an optimization problem using these values. Then, the authors solved the optimization problem with the Genetic Algorithm. The authors utilized Yager's ranking method to defuzzify all the control parameters. In the employed defuzzification method, there were weights for sides of the membership and non-membership functions and for the membership and non-membership values. Singh et al. [20] dealt with the c-control charts problem with an intuitionistic fuzzy number scenario. With respect to the definition of the intuitionistic fuzzy number given by the authors, there was no hesitancy measure, so they actually employed a fuzzy number. The authors assumed that the limits of the control chart were calculated based on specific $(\alpha - \beta)$ cuts values. On the other hand, intuitionistic fuzzy observations were defuzzified using the method proposed by the authors. The authors obtained defuzzified values using only the membership function and only employed weights to sides of the membership function. Karthick and Uthayakumar [21] evaluated a closed-loop supply chain model with intuitionistic fuzzy parameters. The model was used to investigate the delivery process of an item from a manufacturer to a retailer. In the model, there were various uncertain inventory cost variables that were modeled using intuitionistic triangular fuzzy numbers. The authors first established the model using defuzzified values of these intuitionistic triangular fuzzy numbers and then solved the model by means of theoretical way and using the Genetic Algorithm. The proposed defuzzification method was stated using the distance between the intuitionistic fuzzy number and the origin. If the defuzzification method was applied to an intuitionistic triangular fuzzy number, the result was just the arithmetic mean of the components of the intuitionistic triangular fuzzy number. Maity et al. [22] investigated a green inventory model, in which the demand rate was related to the selling price, stock, and green concern level, and the holding cost was assumed to be a quadratic function of time. To model the demand rate, which possesses uncertainty due to market flexibility, the authors employed a pentagonal intuitionistic fuzzy number. First, the authors stated an intuitionistic fuzzy model, and then, to solve the model, they presented a defuzzification technique and a solution algorithm. The defuzzification technique was an adoption of the centroid method. The authors used the difference between the membership function and non-membership function as the weights of the defuzzification methods. In the aforementioned studies [8–17,21,22], scientists preferred using weighted-averaging-based defuzzification methods. In actual applications, the authors chose different weights, such as membership values, non-membership values, hesitancy values, accuracy values, the difference between sides of $(\alpha - \beta)$ cuts, and possibility values. All of these methods only use the part of IFN for processing, so the information kept in the shape of the IFN cannot be injected into the defuzzification computations. On the other hand, the IF-WABL method can utilize all information that an IFN contains through its various parameters, $c_L^\mu, c_R^\mu, c_L^\nu, c_R^\nu$, $p(\alpha)$, and $s(\beta)$. The remaining studies published by the authors of [18–20] mentioned this part, in which scientists aimed at using more information kept in the IFN, so they employed various weights to various parts of the IFN. The common disadvantageous part of these methods is that their weights are constant and cannot be adjustable. Thus it is clear that these methods are special cases of the IF-WABL method due to the adjustable manner of the IF-WABL method.

As in the aforementioned studies, there are various precious studies in the literature concerning the implementation of defuzzification methods. However, we have not evaluated one of the important implementation areas of the defuzzification methods which is ordering or ranking. We know that crisp numbers have total ordering; on the other hand, intuitionistic fuzzy numbers have partial ordering. In multi-criteria decision-making problems, ranking or ordering the alternatives has been one of the widely studied topics. Ye [23] investigated intuitionistic trapezoidal fuzzy multi-criteria decision-making problems, in which the preference values of an alternative on the criteria and the weight values of criteria were stated as intuitionistic trapezoidal fuzzy numbers. The author applied Grzegrorzewski's method to multi-criteria decision-making problems for ranking alternatives in the problem. Yue [24] dealt with interval-valued intuitionistic fuzzy group decision-making problems. The author focused on obtaining the decision makers' weights in a group decision-making setting. In this setup, the decision information was provided as interval-valued intuitionistic fuzzy numbers. First, the author computed similarity measures between ideal decisions and all individual decisions. Then, the author used these similarity measures to compute the weights of decision makers. To reach the collective decision, all individual decisions, which were stated as interval-valued intuitionistic fuzzy numbers, were aggregated using the weights. To rank all the alternatives, the scores and accuracy degrees of the aggregated overall assessment of each alternative were computed. Wang et al. [25] proposed a novel score function using the prospect value function. This function includes three components: (i) α power of the difference between the average difference of the membership and non-membership values of all interval-valued intuitionistic fuzzy numbers and the difference of the membership and non-membership values of the interval-valued intuitionistic fuzzy number that are being concerned, (ii) α power of the difference between the average total of the membership and non-membership values of all interval-valued intuitionistic fuzzy numbers and, the total of the membership and non-membership values of the interval-valued intuitionistic fuzzy number that are being concerned, (iii) the hesitancy degree. The authors implemented the score function into interval-valued intuitionistic fuzzy multi-criteria decision -making. Wan et al. [26] extended the classic VIKOR method to solve the multi-attribute group decision-making problem with sub-normal triangular IFNs. The authors used weighted possibility means for both membership and non-membership functions as the defuzzifier of the method. The authors employed the defuzzifier and Shannon entropy to compute the attribute weight. Meng et al. [27] proposed two novel approaches to multi-criteria group decision-making under an interval-valued intuitionistic fuzzy environment. These operators were weighted averaging of interval-valued intuitionistic fuzzy numbers. One of these methods was based on arithmetic averaging, which is called the arithmetical interval-valued intuitionistic fuzzy generalized λ-Shapley Choquet operator, and the other one was based on geometric averaging, which is called the geometric interval-valued intuitionistic fuzzy generalized λ-Shapley Choquet operator. For these operators, weights were determined by first employing the λ fuzzy measure, then Shapley indices, and finally the Choquet integral. These operators were employed to reach the comprehensive interval-valued intuitionistic fuzzy variable of criteria values. Then, using the score and accuracy functions, the authors ranked the alternatives. Wu and Chiclana [28] proposed novel score and accuracy functions for ranking interval-valued intuitionistic fuzzy numbers. The authors used these functions to propose a total order on the set of interval-valued intuitionistic fuzzy numbers and to develop an interval-valued intuitionistic fuzzy multi-attribute decision-making selection process. The expected score function value was the weighted average of the differences between the membership and non-membership value-related $(\alpha - \beta)$ cuts. The expected accuracy function value was the weighted average of the summations of the membership and non-membership value-related $(\alpha - \beta)$ cuts. In both formulas, weights were determined according to a basic unit monotonic function. Qin et al. [29] investigated the Choquet integral for the case that the measure space was an interval intuitionistic fuzzy one. The authors established the interval-valued intuitionistic fuzzy measures system to create the importance measure of attributes. With fuzzy entropy, Shapely values, and the interval-valued intuitionistic fuzzy measure, the authors prepared a theoretical background of calculating the weights of experts to aggregate the decision information of each expert. Finally, the authors employed the score function to rank their alternatives. Li and Wu [30] evaluated the solution method for a multi-criteria group decision environment in which attribute weight information was entirely unknown, and the evaluation information was stated with an interval-valued intuitionistic fuzzy number. The authors proposed a new score function based on the summation of endpoints of $(\alpha - \beta)$ cuts, the difference between the endpoints of the $(\alpha - \beta)$ cuts, and the risk factor determined by a decision-maker. The authors used the score function to compute the crisp values of each attribute and to construct an information entropy function that is used to obtain criterion weight. Xian et al. [31] extended Atanassov's intuitionistic fuzzy number and Atanassov's interval-valued intuitionistic fuzzy number concepts to generalized Atanassov's intuitionistic fuzzy number and generalized interval-valued intuitionistic fuzzy number concepts, respectively. The authors employed these concepts to state an interval-valued intuitionistic fuzzy linguistic variable. The authors used the interval-valued intuitionistic fuzzy linguistic variable concepts to construct the preference degree of each attribute. Then, the authors calculated two interval-valued intuitionistic fuzzy linguistic distance measures of each alternative from the interval-valued intuitionistic fuzzy linguistic positive ideal solution and negative ideal solution. The distance formula was the absolute mean of the differences of membership and non-membership values of the related $(\alpha - \beta)$ cuts. Meng et al. [32] developed a novel approach for group decision-making with interval-valued intuitionistic fuzzy preference relations that can deal with inconsistent and incomplete cases. To check the multiplicative consistency of interval-valued intuitionistic fuzzy preference relations, the authors stated 0–1 mixed programming models. To compute the weights of the decision-makers, the authors proposed a distance measure on interval-valued intuitionistic fuzzy preference relations. The distance is actually the average of absolute differences between two interval-valued intuitionistic fuzzy preference relations that are offered by decision-makers. Kong et al. [33] proposed an alternative way to evaluate the threat assessments of group targets. The authors suggested dealing with this problem using the interval-valued intuitionistic fuzzy multi-attribute group decision-making method. The authors employed the interval-valued intuitionistic fuzzy entropy to calculate attribute weights based on the decision-makers' decision matrix. The authors used a Shannon entropy-like formula to compute the distance between the judgment value and ideal solutions. Based on this formula, the authors stated a non-linear optimization problem and solved the problem using the improved artificial bee colony algorithm, which was proposed by the authors. Li et al. [34] proposed two operators, namely the intuitionistic fuzzy weighted induced ordered weighted averaging distance operator and the intuitionistic weighted induced ordered weighted averaging weighted average distance operator. Both operators include the ordering phase based on an ordinary intuitionistic fuzzy distance formula. The authors recommended the second operator as a solution to the limitations of the first one. In the intuitionistic fuzzy multi-attribute decision-making model, the authors used the second operator to compute alternative values to rank the alternatives. Hao and Chen [35] investigated ranking problems in multi-attribute decision-making problems with an interval-valued intuitionistic fuzzy environment. The authors proposed two aggregation operators: the interval-valued intuitionistic fuzzy composed ordered weighted arithmetic averaging operator and the interval-valued intuitionistic composed ordered weighted geometric averaging operator. These operators were used to compute the comprehensive attribute values of the alternatives. The authors suggested the maximum and minimum attribute values, similar to the positive and negative ideal solutions. Then, the authors employed the Euclidian distance-like ranking method. Alcantud [36] evaluated multi-attribute group decision-making problems in an intuitionistic fuzzy environment. In that problem's environment, experts' ratings were stated as intuitionistic fuzzy variables. The author first aggregated these intuitionistic fuzzy sets through employing a novel intuitionistic fuzzy direct weighted geometric operator, in which pre-determined weights were used to the power of the membership and non-membership values, and these powered results were multiplied. Then, aggregated intuitionistic fuzzy variables were ranked based on the score function, which was the difference between the membership and non-membership functions, and the accuracy function, which was the summation of the membership and non-membership functions. Ding and Wang [37] investigated a TOPSIS-based multi-attribute decision-making problem in which the attribute weights were unknown, and the decision information was in the form of intuitionistic fuzzy numbers. The authors proposed a similarity measure that depends on the minimal absolute differences of the membership and non-membership values. The authors introduced new score and accuracy functions. The score function consists of the summation of the difference between the membership and non-membership values and the weighted difference between the membership and non-membership values, where weights are hesitancy degrees. The accuracy function consists of the summation of the membership and non-membership values and weighted membership and weighted non-membership values, where weights are hesitancy degrees. Based on the proposed score function, the authors proposed a Shannon entropy-like entropy formula to calculate the attribute weights. To rank the alternatives, the authors calculated relative similarity measures between the positive ideal solution and the alternatives and between the negative ideal solution and the alternatives. Faizi et al. [38] evaluated multi-criteria group decision-making problems with an intuitionistic fuzzy environment. The authors modified the COMET method to employ it in an intuitionistic fuzzy environment. The authors computed characteristics objects defined by decision makers and performed pairwise comparisons of the objects by adding decision-makers' opinions. The authors employed the score function to obtain crisp numbers for the criteria. The authors finally used these crisp numbers in the inference system of COMET. Chen and Tsai [39] proposed an approach to solving multi-attribute decision-making problems by defining a new score function of interval-valued intuitionistic fuzzy values. The score function was based on the average of the square root of membership and non-membership values of interval-valued intuitionistic fuzzy values. The authors ranked alternatives in multi-attribute decision-making problems according to the proposed score function. Wang et al. [40] adopted the intuitionistic fuzzy TOPSIS method for the geo-environmental carrying capacity problem. The authors used geomorphic units as alternatives to be ranked. Using an intuitionistic fuzzy matrix and the positive and negative ideal solutions, the authors computed the weighted distances, of which the formula was very similar to the Hamming distance formula. Finally, using these distances, the authors computed the indicators to rank their alternatives. The authors implemented the approach to the Meishan City, China, data set. Yang et al. [41] investigated the Frank aggregation operators (averaging and geometric) based on the complex intuitionistic fuzzy set theory and proposed a list of averaging operators, such as the complex intuitionistic fuzzy Frank weighted averaging operator, complex intuitionistic fuzzy Frank ordered weighted averaging operator, complex intuitionistic fuzzy Frank hybrid averaging operator, complex intuitionistic fuzzy Frank weighted geometric operator, complex intuitionistic fuzzy Frank ordered weighted geometric operator, and complex intuitionistic fuzzy Frank hybrid geometric operator. The authors embedded these techniques into multi-attribute decision-making problems to measure the performances of the proposed operators. The authors used these operators to aggregate the information in the decision matrix of the multi-attribute decision-making problem. The authors preferred employing the score function to order the alternatives. Jin and Garg [42] proposed a new score function for intuitionistic fuzzy numbers based on a probabilistic perspective. The authors evaluated the value of the score function, like computing the probability of a continuous random variable. An individual's score was calculated by determining the ratio of the part more minor than the individual to the whole. The authors constructed an entropy index using their proposed score function. The entropy index was used to derive the weights of the criteria in multi-criteria decision-making problems. The authors employed the proposed score function and prospect value function to calculate dominance degrees between alternatives. The authors ranked the alternatives using the dominance degree, negative ideal solution, and positive ideal solution. The score function was similar to computing probability and available for comparison. Huang et al. [43] proposed a new ranking method based on a probabilistic dominance relationship and implemented the ranking method into multi-attribute decision-making problems with an intuitionistic fuzzy environment. In the first step, the authors transformed intuitionistic fuzzy numbers by redefining their membership and non-membership values to mitigate the uncertainty arising from hesitancy. Then, the authors computed the probabilistic dominance degree of an intuitionistic fuzzy number relative to other intuitionistic fuzzy numbers based on the joint probability density function, which concerns the relationship between the membership and non-membership functions. The authors adopted this technique to comparing objects phase of the multi-attribute decision-making problem. Zhengsen et al. [44] implemented the multi-criteria decision problem to the investment decision problem in distributed production. The authors used subjective weights that were expressed as triangular intuitionistic fuzzy numbers. The authors employed the formula to quantify triangular intuitionistic fuzzy numbers. The formula, which is evaluated as a defuzzification, was a weighted averaging of the parameters of triangular intuitionistic fuzzy numbers. The authors used λ to reflect the attitude of decision-makers to the degree of uncertainty. Feng et al. [45] proposed a new perspective to the already used definition of generalized intuitionistic fuzzy soft sets. Based on this novel perspective, some existing concepts and findings about generalized intuitionistic fuzzy soft sets were improved. The authors designed an algorithmic solution approach for multi-attribute decision-making problems by employing generalized intuitionistic fuzzy soft sets and required operators. The authors ordered the alternatives using the proposed expectation score function. The score function was computed as the sum of the constant and the average difference between the membership and non-membership functions. Feng et al. [46] evaluated the problem of ranking intuitionistic fuzzy values and its applications to decision-making problems. The authors first proposed the novel concept of the Minkowski score function. Then, the authors embedded the attitudinal parameter into the first formula to reach a more generalized score function concept. The attitudinal parameter was employed to produce weights for the membership and non-membership functions of the intuitionistic fuzzy value. The Minkowski score function was a parameter-based method that could cover various score functions by adjusting the parameter values. The authors used the Minkowski score function to rank the overall intuitionistic fuzzy preference in the multi-attribute decision-making problem. Agarwal et al. [47] extended the generalized intuitionistic fuzzy soft set by proposing the generalization parameter that was also intuitionistic fuzzy. The authors investigated the novel score and the accuracy functions to compare two intuitionistic fuzzy numbers. Both score and accuracy functions were based on the squared of the membership and non-membership functions. The authors employed these functions to rank alternatives in intuitionistic fuzzy multi-criteria decision-making problems.

In nearly all of the studies mentioned here concerning multi-criteria decision-making problems, the authors only utilized one type of tool to model uncertainty, such as trapezoidal IFN, triangular IFN, intuitionistic fuzzy linguistic variable, and so on. In real-life problems, the weights of attributes and/or the decision-makers' opinions can be stated through different IFNs. The point is that if we have generally defined and mathematically inclusive IFN, we can use all of the solution methods for multi-criteria decision-making problems. We aimed to fill in the gap with the NLPIFN. Moreover, these studies concerning multi-criteria decision-making problems can be classified according to ranking methods into two classes: (i) weighted averaging-based methods (as published by the authors of [23,26,34,38,42,43,47]) and (ii) distance-based methods (as published by the authors of [24,25,27–33,35–37,39–41,45–47]). Nearly all of the distance-based methods mentioned here were based on score and/or accuracy functions, of which the main motivation was to measure the similarity between the alternative and ideal solutions. Again, in nearly all of the distance-based methods, interval-valued intuitionistic fuzzy numbers were employed. We assume that interval-valued intuitionistic fuzzy numbers are defined in discrete space. From that point of view, the IF-WABL method is not suitable to process such numbers until a discrete version of IF-WABL is defined, which is highly possible. While we evaluated weighted averaging-based methods, IF-WABL can transform into all of them, providing that the IF-WABL parameters are chosen specially and properly.

As mentioned above, IFNs are employed in many computational areas in various fields, such as artificial intelligence, optimization, decision-making, and operations research. Consequently, the requirements for a general and inclusive mathematical definition of an IFN and a well-defined and easily applicable defuzzification method are obvious.

However, converting fuzzy decision-making problems into their equivalent crisp problems using a defuzzifier along with a decision-maker's opinion is not the only way to solve such problems [48–51]. Orazbayev et al. [48] developed a method for deriving linguistic models of fuzzyly defined objects and then proposed a heuristic method for solving the multi-criteria optimization problem in a fuzzy environment without employing any defuzzification method. The authors applied the proposed heuristic method to the problem of two-criteria optimization in the delayed petroleum coking process, which is utilized in the production of electrodes and anodes, space technology, electronics, and metallurgy, with fuzzy constraints. In another study, Orazbayev et al. [49] investigated a complex chemical engineering system of an oil refinery under uncertain conditions with respect to various types of information. To handle the aforementioned system as a whole, the authors developed models and then combined these models into a single model. After their modeling efforts, the authors produced a fuzzy optimization problem and then proposed an algorithm that does not include a defuzzification step. To obtain further information concerning the solution of fuzzy decision-making problems without applying a defuzzification method, see topics published by the author of [50].

IFNs have various application areas, making a general and inclusive mathematical definition of IFNs increasingly necessary. As the IFN possesses mathematically superior properties, a general representation can be available for modeling different problems, and it has become possible to use different types of IFNs within the same problem. In this paper, we proposed the non-linear pentagonal intuitionistic fuzzy number (NLPIFN), which has a general and inclusive mathematical definition. We showed that if a user changes the component values of an NLPIFN properly, the user can realize a very large family of IFNs, such as linear pentagonal IFNs, non-linear trapezoidal IFNs, linear trapezoidal IFNs, non-linear triangular IFNs, linear triangular IFNs, and Baloui's Generalized IFN [52]. For example, if a scientist would like to use a linear pentagonal IFN and non-linear trapezoidal IFN at the same time in their model, they can use the NLPIFN by properly adjusting the component values of the NLPIFN to acquire linear pentagonal IFNs and non-linear trapezoidal IFNs whenever required. In this study, we outlined some definitions and basic arithmetic operations for the newly defined NLPIFN. We also evaluated a flexible, well-defined, and inclusive defuzzification method called IF-WABL [53]. The main idea behind this method was to utilize all relevant information provided by an IFN. The parameters of the IF-WABL method were used to give weights to the $(\alpha - \beta)$ cuts of the IFN, the sides of the membership and non-membership functions, and the membership and non-membership functions themselves. As a result of these parameters, every piece of information provided by the IFN is injected into the defuzzification process. The IF-WABL method is also suitable due to the subjectivity of the IF theory. A user who employs the IF-WABL method can determine the parameter values of the method (according to the conditions given in the method's definition) based on their own desires and/or the nature of the problem being solved. In this study, we presented several mathematical properties of IF-WABL. We also provided a fast and easily applicable formula to compute the defuzzified value of the NLPIFN by employing the IF-WABL method. To show the usage of both the NLPIFN and its IF-WABL formula, we presented an example related to the intuitionistic fuzzy minimum spanning tree problem.

Many research papers have been presented where intuitionistic fuzzy numbers are investigated and implemented in various fields. Still, many more scopes are present to study these topics. In this paper, we aimed to develop an intuitionistic fuzzy number and its application. The possible novelties and contributions of this study can be mentioned as follows:

1. The non-linear pentagonal intuitionistic fuzzy number is defined.
2. Arithmetic operations of the NLPIFN are formulated using $(\alpha - \beta)$ cuts representation.
3. The short-cut formula of the intuitionistic fuzzy weighted averaging based on levels (IF-WABL) value of NLPIFN is derived.

4. A solution approach for the intuitionistic fuzzy minimum spanning tree (IF MST) problem based on the IF-WABL value of NLPIFN has been proposed.

In this paper, we have focused on the NLPIFN. We also have presented the arithmetic operations of NLPIFNs using $(\alpha - \beta)$ cuts representation. A modified version of Prim's algorithm was suggested to solve the (IF MST) problem, of which the edge weights can be any IFNs among the linear pentagonal IFNs, non-linear trapezoidal IFNs, linear trapezoidal IFNs, non-linear triangular IFNs, linear triangular IFNs, and Baloui's Generalized IFN. Finally, we implemented the solution approach to one numerical illustration.

The structure of the paper is as follows: The second section presents the fundamental preliminary concepts. In the third section, we introduce the NLPIFN and obtain arithmetic operations related to the number using the $(\alpha - \beta)$ cuts approach. Relations between the NLPIFN and IFNs are addressed in this section. A short-cut IF-WABL defuzzification formula is derived in Section 4. The application of NLPIFNs in the IF minimum spanning tree problem is presented in Section 5. Lastly, conclusions are given in Section 6.

2. Preliminaries

This paper sought to model uncertainty by employing different IFNs. Thus, we began with the most fundamental approach to deal with uncertainty problems and provided a definition of fuzzy sets.

Definition 1 ([1]). *Let X be a space of points (objects), with a generic element of X denoted by x. Thus, X = {x}. A fuzzy set (class) A in X is characterized by a membership (characteristic) function, $\mu_A(x)$, associated with each point in X a real number in the interval [0, 1] with the value of $\mu_A(x)$ at x representing the "grade of membership" of x in A. Thus, the nearer the value of $\mu_A(x)$ is to unity, the higher the grade of membership of x in A.*

The previous definition was extended to deal with the different types of uncertainties that are encountered in real-life problems. Thus, a new class of fuzzy sets is created called higher-order fuzzy sets. The type 2 fuzzy set [54] is one element of this new class. With a type 2 fuzzy set, a researcher can employ a fuzzy set to model the membership values of the elements in the relevant fuzzy set. Therefore, based on the novel definition, membership values are also fuzzy sets.

Definition 2 ([54]). *A Type 2 Fuzzy Set, represented as $\widetilde{A}$, is a fuzzy set described by a type 2 membership function, $0 \le \mu_{\widetilde{A}}(x,u) \le 1$, as follows:*

$$\widetilde{A} = \left\{ \left((x,u), \mu_{\widetilde{A}}(x,u) \right) \middle| \forall x \in X,\ \forall u \in J_X \subseteq [0,1] \right\}$$

where x, J_X, and u and $\mu_{\widetilde{A}}(x,u)$ denote the primary variable, the primary membership function in the [0, 1] interval, the secondary variable, and the secondary membership function at x , respectively.

Another member of the higher-order fuzzy set class is IFS. An IFS is characterized by two related functions, namely the membership function, which is the same as the fuzzy set, and the non-membership function. In this paper, we concentrated on IFSs and proposed an alternative mathematical formulation for this member. Thus, we evaluated fundamental definitions related to IFS.

Definition 3 ([2]). *An IFS A in X is defined as an object in the form of $A = \{\langle x, \mu_A(x), \nu_A(x)\rangle : x \in X\}$, where the functions $\mu_A : X \to [0,1]$ and $\nu_A : X \to [0,1]$ define the degree of membership and the degree of non-membership of the element $x \in X$, respectively, and for every $x \in X$ in A, $0 \le \mu_A(x) + \nu_A(x) \le 1$ is held.*

Definition 4 ([2]). *For every common fuzzy subset A on X, the intuitionistic fuzzy index of x in A is defined as* $\pi_A(x) = 1 - \mu_A(x) - \nu_A(x)$. *This phenomenon is also known as the degree of hesitancy or degree of uncertainty of the element x in A. For every* $x \in X, 0 \le \pi_A(x) \le 1$.

Definition 5 ([53]). *An IFN* $\tilde{A}$ *is defined as follows:*

- An intuitionistic fuzzy subset of the real line.
- Normal, that is, there is some $x_0 \in \mathcal{R}$, such that $\mu_{\underset{A}{\sim}}(x_0) = 1$ and $\nu_{\underset{A}{\sim}}(x_0) = 0$.
- Convex for the membership function $\mu_{A^*}(x)$, that is, $\mu_{\underset{A}{\sim}}(\lambda x_1 + (1-\lambda)x_2)$ $\ge \min\left(\mu_{\underset{A}{\sim}}(x_1), \mu_{\underset{A}{\sim}}(x_2)\right)$ for every $x_1, x_2 \in \mathcal{R}, \lambda \in [0,1]$.
- Concave for the non-membership function $\nu_{\underset{A}{\sim}}(x)$, that is, $\nu_{\underset{A}{\sim}}(\lambda x_1 + (1-\lambda)x_2) \le \max\left(\nu_{\underset{A}{\sim}}(x_1), \nu_{\underset{A}{\sim}}(x_2)\right)$ for every $x_1, x_2 \in \mathcal{R}, \lambda \in [0,1]$.

Definition 6 ([53]). *The support of IFN* $\tilde{A}$ *on* $\mathcal{R}$ *is the crisp set of all* $x \in \mathcal{R}$, *such that* $\mu_{\underset{A}{\sim}}(x) > 0$, $\nu_{\underset{A}{\sim}}(x) > 0$, *and* $\mu_{\underset{A}{\sim}}(x) + \nu_{\underset{A}{\sim}}(x) \le 1$.

Definition 7. $\mathcal{F}_c(\mathcal{R})$ *will denote the class of (bounded) IFNs which maps* $\mu_{\underset{A}{\sim}} : X \to [0,1]$ *and* $\nu_{\underset{A}{\sim}} : X \to [0,1]$, *such that their* α *and* β *cuts are as follows:*

- $\alpha, \beta \in [0,1]$ and $\alpha + \beta \le 1$;
- $\tilde{A}{}^{\mu}_{\alpha} = \begin{cases} \left\{x \in R : \mu_{\underset{A}{\sim}}(x) \ge \alpha\right\} & if \alpha \in (0,1] \\ cl\left\{x \in R : \mu_{\underset{A}{\sim}}(x) > 0\right\} & if \alpha = 0 \end{cases}$;
- $\tilde{A}{}^{\nu}_{\alpha} = \begin{cases} \left\{x \in R : \nu_{\underset{A}{\sim}}(x) \le \beta\right\} & if \beta \in (0,1] \\ cl\left\{x \in R : \nu_{\underset{A}{\sim}}(x) < 1\right\} & if \beta = 1 \end{cases}$.

Definition 8. *A Triangular IFN (TIFN)* $\tilde{A}$ *is an IFS in* $\mathcal{R}$ *with the membership function and non-membership function as follows:*

$$\mu_{\underset{A}{\sim}}(x) = \begin{cases} \frac{x-a_1}{a_2-a_1} & a_1 \le x \le a_2 \\ \frac{a_3-x}{a_3-a_2} & a_2 \le x \le a_3 \end{cases}$$

$$v_{\underset{A}{\sim}}(x) = \begin{cases} \frac{a_2-x}{a_2-a_1'} & a_1' \le x \le a_2 \\ \frac{x-a_2}{a_3'-a_2} & a_2 \le x \le a_3' \end{cases}$$

where $a_1' \le a_1 \le a_2 \le a_3 \le a_3'$ and the symbolic representation of TIFN is $\tilde{A}_{TIFN} = (a_2; a_1, a_3, a_1', a_3')$.

Definition 9. *A Trapezoidal IFN (TrIFN)* $\tilde{A}$ *is an IFS in* $\mathcal{R}$ *with the membership function and non-membership function as follows:*

$$\mu_{\underset{A}{\sim}}(x) = \begin{cases} \frac{x-a_1}{a_2-a_1} & a_1 \le x \le a_2 \\ 1 & a_2 \le x \le a_3 \\ \frac{a_4-x}{a_4-a_3} & a_3 \le x \le a_4 \end{cases}$$

$$v_{\underset{A}{\sim}}(x) = \begin{cases} \frac{a_2-x}{a_2-a_1'} & a_1' \le x \le a_2 \\ 0 & a_2 \le x \le a_3 \\ \frac{x-a_3}{a_4'-a_3} & a_3 \le x \le a_4' \end{cases}$$

where $a_1' \leq a_1 \leq a_2 \leq a_3 \leq a_4 \leq a_4'$. The symbolic representation of TrIFN is $\widetilde{A}_{TrIFN} = (a_2, a_3;\ a_1, a_4,\ a_1', a_4')$.

Definition 10 ([55]). *Let X denote a non-empty set. The Generalized IFS A in X is defined as an object of the form* $A = \{\langle x, \mu_A(x), \nu_A(x)\rangle : x \in X\}$, *where the functions* $\mu_A : X \to [0,1]$ *and* $\nu_A : X \to [0,1]$ *define the degree of membership and the degree of non-membership of A, respectively,* $0 \leq \mu_A(x)^{\delta} + \nu_A(x)^{\delta} \leq 1$ *for each* $x \in X$, *and* $\delta = n$ *or* $\frac{1}{n}$, $n = 1, 2, \ldots, N$.

3. Representations of the NLPIFN and Its Arithmetic Operations

In this section, we present the membership and non-membership functions of the NLPIFN, its $(\alpha - \beta)$ cuts representation, the arithmetic operations on the NLPIFN using $(\alpha - \beta)$ cuts representation, and the transition between the NLPIFN and other IFNs.

Definition 11. *An NLPIFN* $\widetilde{A}$ *is an IFS in* $\mathcal{R}$ *with a membership function and non-membership function as follows:*

$$\mu_{\widetilde{A}}(x) = \begin{cases} k\left(\frac{x-a_1}{a_2-a_1}\right)^{n_1} & a_1 \leq x \leq a_2 \\ k + (1-k)\left(\frac{x-a_2}{a_3-a_2}\right)^{n_2} & a_2 \leq x \leq a_3 \\ k + (1-k)\left(\frac{a_4-x}{a_4-a_3}\right)^{m_2} & a_3 \leq x \leq a_4 \\ k\left(\frac{a_5-x}{a_5-a_4}\right)^{m_1} & a_4 \leq x \leq a_5 \end{cases}$$

$$\nu_{\widetilde{A}}(x) = \begin{cases} k' + (1-k\prime)\left(\frac{a_2'-x}{a_2'-a_1'}\right)^{n_1'} & a_1' \leq x \leq a_2' \\ k\prime\left(\frac{a_3-x}{a_3-a_2'}\right)^{n_2'} & a_2' \leq x \leq a_3 \\ k\prime\left(\frac{x-a_3}{a_4'-a_3}\right)^{m_2'} & a_3 \leq x \leq a_4' \\ k' + (1-k\prime)\left(\frac{x-a_4'}{a_5'-a_4'}\right)^{m_1'} & a_4' \leq x \leq a_5' \end{cases}$$

where $a_1' \leq a_1 \leq a_2' \leq a_2 \leq a_3 \leq a_4 \leq a_4' \leq a_5 \leq a_5'$, $n_1 > 0$, $m_1 > 0$, $n_2 > 0$, $m_2 > 0$, $n_1' > 0$, $m_1' > 0$, $n_2' > 0$, $m_2' > 0$, $k > 0$, $k' > 0$, $k + k\prime \leq 1$, and $k > k\prime$. The symbolic representation of the NLPIFN is $\widetilde{A} = \left(a_3; a_1, a_2, a_4, a_5, a_1', a_2', a_4', a_5'\right)$. Figure 1 shows the membership and non-membership functions of $\widetilde{A} = (a_3 = 11, a_1 = 5, a_2 = 7.5, a_4 = 12, a_5 = 16, a_1' = 4$, $a_2' = 7, a_4' = 14$, and $a_5' = 17)$, $k = 0.5$, $k' = 0.45$, $n_1 = m_1 = 0.4$, and $n_2 = m_2 = 1.3$, $n_1' = m_1' = 2.1, n_2' = m_2' = 0.7$. In Figure 1, the blue curves represent the graph of membership function of the NLPIFN and the red curves represent the graph of non-membership function of the NLPIFN.

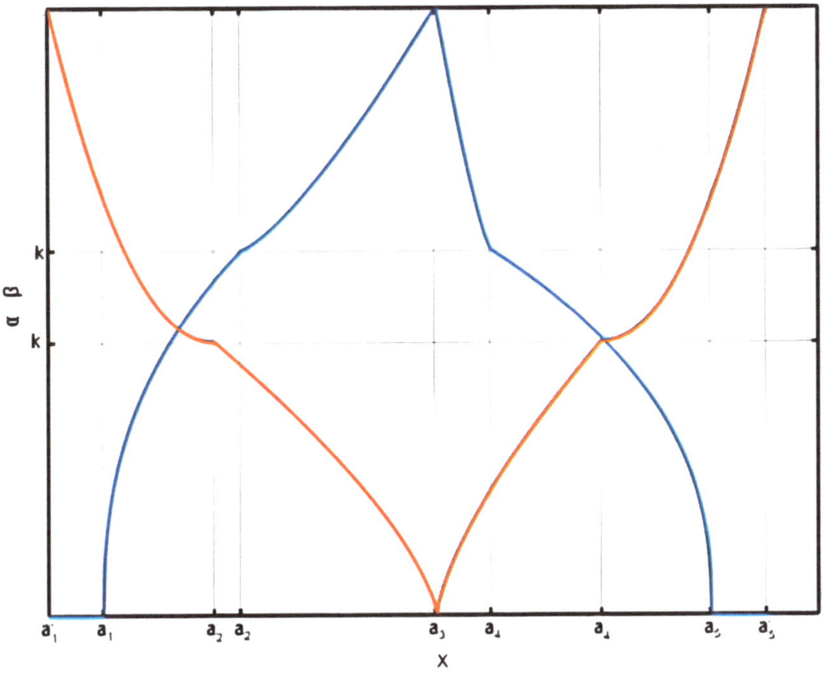

Figure 1. Graphical representation of a NLPIFN.

Lemma 1. *If the NLPIFN $\tilde{A}$ is constructed with respect to Definition 11, then $\tilde{A}$ is also an IFN.*

Proof of Lemma 1: It is clear that the condition $\mu_{\tilde{A}}(x) + \nu_{\tilde{A}}(x) \geq 0$ is always satisfied because of the definitions of the membership function and non-membership function. To prove the lemma, we must show that $\mu_{\tilde{A}}(x) + \nu_{\tilde{A}}(x) \leq 1$ is valid for all elements of $\tilde{A}$. Based on the definition of the NLPIFN, we know that the membership function increases monotonously with respect to its variable in the intervals $[a_1,\ a_2]$ and $[a_2,\ a_3]$, and decreases monotonously with respect to its variable in the intervals $[a_3,\ a_4]$ and $[a_4,\ a_5]$. In addition, the non-membership function increases monotonously with respect to its variable in the intervals $[a_3,\ a_4']$ and $[a_4',\ a_5']$, and decreases monotonously with respect to its variable in the intervals $[a_1',\ a_2']$ and $[a_2',\ a_3]$. Thus, if we show that $\mu_{\tilde{A}}(x) + \nu_{\tilde{A}}(x) \leq 1$ is valid for just the limit values of the intervals, all of the values in the intervals satisfy the necessary conditions as follows:

- For a_1', $\mu_{\tilde{A}}(a_1') = 0$ and $\nu_{\tilde{A}}(a_1') = 1.0$, so the condition is satisfied.
- For a_1, $\mu_{\tilde{A}}(a_1) = 0$ and $\nu_{\tilde{A}}(a_1) = k' + (1 - k\prime)\left(\frac{a_2'-a_1}{a_2'-a_1'}\right)^{n_1'}$. From Definition 11, we know that $\frac{a_2'-a_1}{a_2'-a_1'} < 1.0$. Based on the value of n_1', we have two possible limit values for $\nu_{\tilde{A}}(a_1)$: (i) $\lim_{n_1'\to 0^+} \nu_{\tilde{A}}(a_1) = 1$ and (ii) $\lim_{n_1'\to\infty} \nu_{\tilde{A}}(a_1) = k'$. As a result, the condition is satisfied.
- For a_2', $\mu_{\tilde{A}}(a_2') = k\left(\frac{a_2'-a_1}{a_2-a_1}\right)^{n_1}$ and $\nu_{\tilde{A}}(a_2') = k'$. From Definition 11, we know that $\frac{a_2'-a_1}{a_2-a_1} < 1.0$. Based on the value of n_1, we have two possible limit values for $\mu_{\tilde{A}}(a_2')$: (i) $\lim_{n_1\to 0^+} \mu_{\tilde{A}}(a_2') = k$ and (ii) $\lim_{n_1\to\infty} \mu_{\tilde{A}}(a_2') = 0$. As a result, the condition is satisfied.

- For a_2, $\mu_{\widetilde{A}}(a_2) = k$ and $\nu_{\widetilde{A}}(a_2) = k\prime\left(\frac{a_3-a_2}{a_3-a_2'}\right)^{n_2'}$. From Definition 11, we know that $\frac{a_3-a_2}{a_3-a_2'} < 1.0$. Based on the value of n_2', we have two possible limit values for $\nu_{\widetilde{A}}(a_2)$: (i) $\lim\limits_{n_2'\to 0^+}$ for $\nu_{\widetilde{A}}(a_2) = k\prime$ and (ii) $\lim\limits_{n_2'\to\infty}$ for $\nu_{\widetilde{A}}(a_2) = 0$. As a result, the condition is satisfied.
- For a_3, $\mu_{\widetilde{A}}(a_3) = 1.0$ and $\nu_{\widetilde{A}}(a_3) = 0$, so the condition is satisfied.
- For a_4, $\mu_{\widetilde{A}}(a_4) = k$ and $\nu_{\widetilde{A}}(a_4) = k\prime\left(\frac{a_4-a_3}{a_4'-a_3}\right)^{m_2'}$. From Definition 11, we know that $\frac{a_4-a_3}{a_4'-a_3} < 1.0$. Based on the value of m_2', we have two possible limit values for $\nu_{\widetilde{A}}(a_4)$: (i) $\lim\limits_{m_2'\to 0^+}$ for $\nu_{\widetilde{A}}(a_4) = k\prime$ and (ii) $\lim\limits_{m_2'\to\infty}$ for $\nu_{\widetilde{A}}(a_4) = 0$. As a result, the condition is satisfied.
- For a_4', $\mu_{\widetilde{A}}(a_4') = k\left(\frac{a_5-a_4'}{a_5-a_4}\right)^{m_1}$ and $\nu_{\widetilde{A}}(a_4') = k\prime$. From Definition 11, we know that $\frac{a_5-a_4'}{a_5-a_4} < 1.0$. Based on the value of m_1, we have two possible limit values for $\mu_{\widetilde{A}}(a_4')$: (i) $\lim\limits_{m_1\to 0^+}$ for $\mu_{\widetilde{A}}(a_4') = k$ and (ii) $\lim\limits_{m_1\to\infty}$ for $\mu_{\widetilde{A}}(a_4') = 0$. As a result, the condition is satisfied.
- For a_5, $\mu_{\widetilde{A}}(a_5) = 0$ and $\nu_{\widetilde{A}}(a_5) = k' + (1-k\prime)\left(\frac{x-a_4'}{a_5'-a_4'}\right)^{m_1'}$. From Definition 11, we know that $\frac{x-a_4'}{a_5'-a_4'} < 1.0$. Based on the value of m_1', we have two possible limit values for $\nu_{\widetilde{A}}(a_5)$: (i) $\lim\limits_{m_1'\to 0^+}$ for $\nu_{\widetilde{A}}(a_5) = 1$ and (ii) $\lim\limits_{m_1'\to\infty}$ for $\nu_{\widetilde{A}}(a_5) = k'$. As a result, the condition is satisfied.
- For a_5', $\mu_{\widetilde{A}}(a_5') = 0$ and $\nu_{\widetilde{A}}(a_5') = 1.0$, so the condition is satisfied. □

Definition 12. *The $(\alpha-\beta)$ cuts representation of a NLPIFN is written as follows:*

$$\inf\widetilde{A}^{\mu}_{\alpha} = \begin{cases} A_L^1(\alpha) = a_1 + (a_2-a_1)\left(\frac{\alpha}{k}\right)^{\frac{1}{n_1}} & \alpha\in(0,k] \\ A_L^2(\alpha) = a_2 + (a_3-a_2)\left(\frac{\alpha-k}{1-k}\right)^{\frac{1}{n_2}} & \alpha\in(k,1] \end{cases}$$

$$\sup\widetilde{A}^{\mu}_{\alpha} = \begin{cases} A_R^1(\alpha) = a_5 - (a_5-a_4)\left(\frac{\alpha}{k}\right)^{\frac{1}{m_1}} & \alpha\in(0,k] \\ A_R^2(\alpha) = a_4 - (a_4-a_3)\left(\frac{\alpha-k}{1-k}\right)^{\frac{1}{m_2}} & \alpha\in(k,1] \end{cases}$$

$$\inf\widetilde{A}^{\nu}_{\beta} = \begin{cases} A_L^1(\beta) = a_3 - (a_3-a_2')\left(\frac{\beta}{k\prime}\right)^{\frac{1}{n_2'}} & \beta\in(0,k\prime] \\ A_L^2(\beta) = a_2' - (a_2'-a_1')\left(\frac{\beta-k\prime}{1-k\prime}\right)^{\frac{1}{n_1'}} & \beta\in(k\prime,1] \end{cases}$$

$$\sup\widetilde{A}^{\nu}_{\beta} = \begin{cases} A_R^1(\beta) = a_3 - (a_3-a_4')\left(\frac{\beta}{k\prime}\right)^{\frac{1}{m_2'}} & \beta\in(0,k\prime] \\ A_R^2(\beta) = a_4' - (a_4'-a_5')\left(\frac{\beta-k\prime}{1-k\prime}\right)^{\frac{1}{m_1'}} & \beta\in(k\prime,1] \end{cases}$$

After these definitions, we evaluated the arithmetic operations on the NLPIFNs. Letting $\widetilde{A} = \left(a_3; a_1, a_2, a_4, a_5, a_1', a_2', a_4', a_5'\right)$ and $\widetilde{B} = \left(b_3; b_1, b_2, b_4, b_5, b_1', b_2', b_4', b_5'\right)$ represent two NLPIFNs, we assumed that k, $k\prime$, n_1, n_2, m_1, m_2, n_1', n_2', m_1', and m_2' are the same for both NLPIFNs. Employing the $(\alpha-\beta)$ cuts approach, addition and subtraction of the two NLPIFNs proceeded as follows:

$$\widetilde{C} = \widetilde{A} + \widetilde{B}$$

where

$$\inf\widetilde{C}_\alpha^\mu = \begin{cases} (a_1+b_1) + ((a_2+b_2) - (a_1+b_1))\left(\frac{\alpha}{k}\right)^{\frac{1}{n_1}} & \alpha \in (0,k] \\ (a_2+b_2) + ((a_3+b_3) - (a_2+b_2))\left(\frac{\alpha-k}{1-k}\right)^{\frac{1}{n_2}} & \alpha \in (k,1] \end{cases}$$
$$\sup\widetilde{C}_\alpha^\mu = \begin{cases} (a_5+b_5) - ((a_5+b_5) - (a_4+b_4))\left(\frac{\alpha}{k}\right)^{\frac{1}{m_1}} & \alpha \in (0,k] \\ (a_4+b_4) - ((a_4+b_4) - (a_3+b_3))\left(\frac{\alpha-k}{1-k}\right)^{\frac{1}{m_2}} & \alpha \in (k,1] \end{cases}$$
$$\inf\widetilde{C}_\beta^\nu = \begin{cases} (a_3+b_3) - ((a_3+b_3) - (a_2'+b_2'))\left(\frac{\beta}{k\prime}\right)^{\frac{1}{n_2'}} & \beta \in (0,k\prime] \\ (a_2'+b_2') - \left((a_2'+b_2') - (a_1'+b_1')\right)\left(\frac{\beta-k\prime}{1-k\prime}\right)^{\frac{1}{n_1'}} & \beta \in (k\prime,1] \end{cases}$$
$$\sup\widetilde{C}_\beta^\nu = \begin{cases} (a_3+b_3) - \left((a_3-b_3) - (a_4'+b_4')\right)\left(\frac{\beta}{k\prime}\right)^{\frac{1}{m_2'}} & \beta \in (0,k\prime] \\ (a_4'+b_4') - ((a_4'+b_4') - (a_5'+b_5'))\left(\frac{\beta-k\prime}{1-k\prime}\right)^{\frac{1}{m_1'}} & \beta \in (k\prime,1] \end{cases}$$
$$\widetilde{C} = \widetilde{A} - \widetilde{B}$$

where

$$\inf\widetilde{C}_\alpha^\mu = \begin{cases} (a_1-b_1) + ((a_2-b_2) - (a_1-b_1))\left(\frac{\alpha}{k}\right)^{\frac{1}{n_1}} & \alpha \in (0,k] \\ (a_2-b_2) + ((a_3-b_3) - (a_2-b_2))\left(\frac{\alpha-k}{1-k}\right)^{\frac{1}{n_2}} & \alpha \in (k,1] \end{cases}$$
$$\sup\widetilde{C}_\alpha^\mu = \begin{cases} (a_5-b_5) - ((a_5-b_5) - (a_4-b_4))\left(\frac{\alpha}{k}\right)^{\frac{1}{m_1}} & \alpha \in (0,k] \\ (a_4-b_4) - ((a_4-b_4) - (a_3-b_3))\left(\frac{\alpha-k}{1-k}\right)^{\frac{1}{m_2}} & \alpha \in (k,1] \end{cases}$$
$$\inf\widetilde{C}_\beta^\nu = \begin{cases} (a_3-b_3) - ((a_3-b_3) - (a_2'-b_2'))\left(\frac{\beta}{k\prime}\right)^{\frac{1}{n_2'}} & \beta \in (0,k\prime] \\ (a_2'-b_2') - \left((a_2'-b_2') - (a_1'-b_1')\right)\left(\frac{\beta-k\prime}{1-k\prime}\right)^{\frac{1}{n_1'}} & \beta \in (k\prime,1] \end{cases}$$
$$\sup\widetilde{C}_\beta^\nu = \begin{cases} (a_3-b_3) - \left((a_3-b_3) - (a_4'-b_4')\right)\left(\frac{\beta}{k\prime}\right)^{\frac{1}{m_2'}} & \beta \in (0,k\prime] \\ (a_4'-b_4') - ((a_4'-b_4') - (a_5'+b_5'))\left(\frac{\beta-k\prime}{1-k\prime}\right)^{\frac{1}{m_1'}} & \beta \in (k\prime,1] \end{cases}$$

It became simple to write the membership and non-membership functions of the resulting NLPIFNs with respect to the above $(\alpha-\beta)$ cuts. Multiplication and division of the two NLPIFNs proceeded slightly differently from the addition and subtraction operations. We applied the essentials of interval arithmetic to the $(\alpha-\beta)$ cuts representations to obtain the desired results of the aforementioned operations as follows:

$$\widetilde{C} = \widetilde{A} \times \widetilde{B}$$

where

$$\inf\widetilde{C}_\alpha^\mu = \begin{cases} min\left\{A_L^1(\alpha)B_L^1(\alpha),\ A_L^1(\alpha)B_R^1(\alpha),\ A_R^1(\alpha)B_L^1(\alpha),\ A_R^1(\alpha)B_R^1(\alpha)\right\} & \alpha \in (0,k] \\ min\left\{A_L^2(\alpha)B_L^2(\alpha),\ A_L^2(\alpha)B_R^2(\alpha),\ A_R^2(\alpha)B_L^2(\alpha),\ A_R^2(\alpha)B_R^2(\alpha)\right\} & \alpha \in (k,1] \end{cases}$$
$$\sup\widetilde{C}_\alpha^\mu = \begin{cases} max\left\{A_L^1(\alpha)B_L^1(\alpha),\ A_L^1(\alpha)B_R^1(\alpha),\ A_R^1(\alpha)B_L^1(\alpha),\ A_R^1(\alpha)B_R^1(\alpha)\right\} & \alpha \in (0,k] \\ max\left\{A_L^2(\alpha)B_L^2(\alpha),\ A_L^2(\alpha)B_R^2(\alpha),\ A_R^2(\alpha)B_L^2(\alpha),\ A_R^2(\alpha)B_R^2(\alpha)\right\} & \alpha \in (k,1] \end{cases}$$
$$\inf\widetilde{C}_\beta^\nu = \begin{cases} min\left\{A_L^1(\beta)B_L^1(\beta),\ A_L^1(\beta)B_R^1(\beta),\ A_R^1(\beta)B_L^1(\beta),\ A_R^1(\beta)B_R^1(\beta)\right\} & \beta \in (0,k\prime] \\ min\left\{A_L^2(\beta)B_L^2(\beta),\ A_L^2(\beta)B_R^2(\beta),\ A_R^2(\beta)B_L^2(\beta),\ A_R^2(\beta)B_R^2(\beta)\right\} & \beta \in (k\prime,1] \end{cases}$$
$$\sup\widetilde{C}_\beta^\nu = \begin{cases} max\left\{A_L^1(\beta)B_L^1(\beta),\ A_L^1(\beta)B_R^1(\beta),\ A_R^1(\beta)B_L^1(\beta),\ A_R^1(\beta)B_R^1(\beta)\right\} & \beta \in (0,k\prime] \\ max\left\{A_L^2(\beta)B_L^2(\beta),\ A_L^2(\beta)B_R^2(\beta),\ A_R^2(\beta)B_L^2(\beta),\ A_R^2(\beta)B_R^2(\beta)\right\} & \beta \in (k\prime,1] \end{cases}$$
$$\widetilde{C} = \widetilde{A}/\widetilde{B}$$

where

$$\inf\widetilde{C}_{\alpha}^{\mu} = \begin{cases} min\left\{\frac{A_L^1(\alpha)}{B_L^1(\alpha)}, \frac{A_L^1(\alpha)}{B_R^1(\alpha)}, \frac{A_R^1(\alpha)}{B_L^1(\alpha)}, \frac{A_R^1(\alpha)}{B_R^1(\alpha)}\right\} & \alpha \in (0,k] \\ min\left\{\frac{A_L^2(\alpha)}{B_L^2(\alpha)}, \frac{A_L^2(\alpha)}{B_R^2(\alpha)}, \frac{A_R^2(\alpha)}{B_L^2(\alpha)}, \frac{A_R^2(\alpha)}{B_R^2(\alpha)}\right\} & \alpha \in (k,1] \end{cases}$$

$$\sup\widetilde{C}_{\alpha}^{\mu} = \begin{cases} max\left\{\frac{A_L^1(\alpha)}{B_L^1(\alpha)}, \frac{A_L^1(\alpha)}{B_R^1(\alpha)}, \frac{A_R^1(\alpha)}{B_L^1(\alpha)}, \frac{A_R^1(\alpha)}{B_R^1(\alpha)}\right\} & \alpha \in (0,k] \\ max\left\{\frac{A_L^2(\alpha)}{B_L^2(\alpha)}, \frac{A_L^2(\alpha)}{B_R^2(\alpha)}, \frac{A_R^2(\alpha)}{B_L^2(\alpha)}, \frac{A_R^2(\alpha)}{B_R^2(\alpha)}\right\} & \alpha \in (k,1] \end{cases}$$

$$\inf\widetilde{C}_{\beta}^{\nu} = \begin{cases} min\left\{\frac{A_L^1(\beta)}{B_L^1(\beta)}, \frac{A_L^1(\beta)}{B_R^1(\beta)}, \frac{A_R^1(\beta)}{B_L^1(\beta)}, \frac{A_R^1(\beta)}{B_R^1(\beta)}\right\} & \beta \in (0,k\prime] \\ min\left\{\frac{A_L^2(\beta)}{B_L^2(\beta)}, \frac{A_L^2(\beta)}{B_R^2(\beta)}, \frac{A_R^2(\beta)}{B_L^2(\beta)}, \frac{A_R^2(\beta)}{B_R^2(\beta)}\right\} & \beta \in (k\prime,1] \end{cases}$$

$$\sup\widetilde{C}_{\beta}^{\nu} = \begin{cases} max\left\{\frac{A_L^1(\beta)}{B_L^1(\beta)}, \frac{A_L^1(\beta)}{B_R^1(\beta)}, \frac{A_R^1(\beta)}{B_L^1(\beta)}, \frac{A_R^1(\beta)}{B_R^1(\beta)}\right\} & \beta \in (0,k\prime] \\ max\left\{\frac{A_L^2(\beta)}{B_L^2(\beta)}, \frac{A_L^2(\beta)}{B_R^2(\beta)}, \frac{A_R^2(\beta)}{B_L^2(\beta)}, \frac{A_R^2(\beta)}{B_R^2(\beta)}\right\} & \beta \in (k\prime,1] \end{cases}$$

In this paper, we used the NLPIFN as it covers various forms of IFNs. If we specially determine the components of the NLPIFN, we obtain different IFNs. In Table 1, we outline the relationships between the NLPIFN and various forms of the IFNs.

Table 1. Forms of NLPIFNs when selecting different components.

Components of the NLPIFN	Type of IFN
$n_1 = n_2 = m_1 = m_2 = n_1' = n_2' = m_1' = m_2' = 1$	Linear Pentagonal IFN
$k = 1$, $k' = 0$	Non-linear Trapezoidal IFN
$k = 1$, $k' = 0$, $n_1 = m_1 = n_1' = m_1' = 1$	Linear Trapezoidal IFN
$k = 0$, $k' = 1$	Non-linear Triangular IFN
$k = 0$, $k' = 1$, $n_2 = m_2 = n_2' = m_2' = 1$	Linear Triangular IFN
$k = 1$, $k' = 0$, $n_1 = m_1 = n_1' = m_1' = \delta$	Baloui's Generalized IFN
$k = 0$, $k' = 1$, $n_2 = m_2 = n_2' = m_2' = \delta$	Baloui's Generalized IFN

Based on Table 1, NLPIFNs may have a variety of application areas and comprise various types of IFNs. Although we defined the corresponding arithmetic operations based on the NLPIFNs, we still require a proper defuzzification approach for the NLPIFNs to employ these numbers in real-life problems.

4. Definition of IF-WABL and Formula for NLPIFNs

The requirement for a flexible, integral, and inclusive defuzzification method for NLPIFNs is obvious. The IF-WABL [53] defuzzification method possesses these properties with the following definition.

Definition 13. *For an arbitrary IFN* $\widetilde{A}$, *the IF-WABL defuzzification method can be outlined as follows:*

$$IF - WABL\left(\widetilde{A}\right) = \theta\, I\left(\widetilde{A}_{\alpha}^{\mu}\right) + (1-\theta)\, I\left(\widetilde{A}_{\beta}^{\nu}\right)$$

where

$$I\left(\widetilde{A^{\mu}_{\alpha}}\right) = \int_0^1 \left(c^{\mu}_L\, inf\widetilde{A^{\mu}_{\alpha}} + c^{\mu}_R\, sup\widetilde{A^{\mu}_{\alpha}}\right) p(\alpha)d\alpha;$$
$$I\left(\widetilde{A^{\nu}_{\beta}}\right) = \int_0^1 \left(c^{\nu}_L\, inf\widetilde{A^{\nu}_{\beta}} + c^{\nu}_R\, sup\widetilde{A^{\nu}_{\beta}}\right) s(\beta)d\beta;$$

$\theta \in [0,1];\ c^{\mu}_L, c^{\mu}_R, c^{\nu}_L, c^{\nu}_R \geq 0;\ c^{\mu}_L + c^{\mu}_R = 1;\ c^{\nu}_L + c^{\nu}_R = 1;\ \int_0^1 p(\alpha)d\alpha = 1;\ \int_0^1 s(\beta)d\beta = 1.$

Indeed, $I\left(\widetilde{A^{\mu}_{\alpha}}\right)$ and $\mathrm{I}\left(\widetilde{\mathrm{A}^{\nu}_{\beta}}\right)$ can be understood as special defuzzified values of the membership and non-membership functions of an IFN, respectively. By employing θ, we merged these defuzzified values to obtain a defuzzified value of the IFN. In this way, θ models the user's priority related to the membership function over the non-membership function. While c^{μ}_L and c^{μ}_R are weights of the left and right sides for the membership function of the IFN, c^{ν}_L and c^{ν}_R are weights of the left and right sides for the non-membership function of the IFN, respectively. The user of the IF-WABL method determines the shape of $p(\alpha)$ to create weights to the α cuts (membership) of the IFN, and the user of the IF-WABL method designs the function $s(\beta)$ to assign weights to the β cuts (non-membership) of the IFN. All of these coefficients and functions are called IF-WABL parameters and are determined by the user of the IF-WABL method with respect to the normality and non-negativity conditions of the parameters. The advantages of using the IF-WABL method can be classified into two parts. First, a researcher employing the IF-WABL method can include all of the information contained by the IFN in the relevant process via IF-WABL parameters. IF-WABL parameters generally have two types: weights for sides of the IFN (c^{μ}_L, c^{μ}_R, c^{ν}_L, and c^{ν}_R) and weight functions for the $(\alpha - \beta)$ cuts of the IFN ($p(\alpha)$ and $s(\beta)$). Together, these weights enable the user to employ every piece of information based on the IFN. The other advantage of utilizing IF-WABL is its flexibility property. Due to its flexibility, the IF-WABL defuzzification method can mimic other defuzzification methods by adjusting the values of the IF-WABL parameters. Moreover, a researcher can design their own defuzzification method subject to the normality and non-negativity conditions of the IF-WABL parameters. This application agrees well with the spirit of the IF theory.

Beyond its flexibility and inclusiveness properties, IF-WABL has some mathematical advantages. Based on these properties, some of the arithmetic operations between the IFNs can be easily handled. Before mentioning these characteristics of the IF-WABL method, we offer a definition for the IF extension of a function.

Definition 14. *Let $f(a_1, \ldots, a_n)$ be a function. The IF extension of the function f is $\Phi : \mathcal{F}^n_c(\mathcal{R}) \to \mathcal{F}_c(\mathcal{R})$. Moreover, for IFNs $\left(\widetilde{A_1}, \ldots, \widetilde{A_n}\right)$, $\Phi\left(\widetilde{A_1}, \ldots, \widetilde{A_n}\right)$ is an IF subset and IF extension value of $f(a_1, \ldots, a_n)$. For this subset, $(\alpha - \beta)$ cuts are as follows:*

$$\Phi^{\mu}_{\alpha}\left(\widetilde{A_1}, \ldots, \widetilde{A_n}\right) = \left[inff\left(\widetilde{A^{\mu}_{1,\alpha}}, \ldots, \widetilde{A^{\mu}_{n,\alpha}}\right), sup\left(\widetilde{A^{\mu}_{1,\alpha}}, \ldots, \widetilde{A^{\mu}_{n,\alpha}}\right)\right]$$
$$\Phi^{\nu}_{\beta}\left(\widetilde{A_1}, \ldots, \widetilde{A_n}\right) = \left[inff\left(\widetilde{A^{\nu}_{1,\beta}}, \ldots, \widetilde{A^{\nu}_{n,\beta}}\right), sup\left(\widetilde{A^{\nu}_{1,\beta}}, \ldots, \widetilde{A^{\nu}_{n,\beta}}\right)\right]$$

where

$$f\left(\widetilde{A^{\mu}_{1,\alpha}}, \ldots, \widetilde{A^{\mu}_{n,\alpha}}\right) = \left\{f(a_1, \ldots, a_n) \middle| a_i \in \widetilde{A^{\mu}_{i,\alpha}}; i = 1, \ldots, n\right\};$$
$$f\left(\widetilde{A^{\nu}_{1,\beta}}, \ldots, \widetilde{A^{\nu}_{n,\beta}}\right) = \left\{f(a_1, \ldots, a_n) \middle| a_i \in \widetilde{A^{\nu}_{i,\beta}}; i = 1, \ldots, n\right\};$$
$$\mu_{\widetilde{A_i}}(a_i) + \nu_{\widetilde{A_i}}(a_i) \leq 1;\ i = 1, \ldots, n.$$

Lemma 2. *Let the IF extension of the linear function* $f(a_1,\ldots,a_n)$ *be* $\Phi\left(\tilde{A}_1,\ldots,\tilde{A}_n\right)$. *For* $\forall\,\alpha,\beta\in[0,1];\ \alpha+\beta\le 1$, *we write:*

$$\begin{aligned}
L_{\Phi(\tilde{A}_1,\ldots,\tilde{A}_n)}(\alpha) &= f\left(\overline{inf}\ \tilde{A}^{\mu}_{1,\alpha},\ldots,\overline{inf}\tilde{A}^{\mu}_{n,\alpha}\right)\\
R_{\Phi(\tilde{A}_1,\ldots,\tilde{A}_n)}(\alpha) &= f\left(\overline{sup}\ \tilde{A}^{\mu}_{1,\alpha},\ldots,\overline{sup}\tilde{A}^{\mu}_{n,\alpha}\right)\\
L_{\Phi(\tilde{A}_1,\ldots,\tilde{A}_n)}(\beta) &= f\left(\overline{inf}\ \tilde{A}^{\nu}_{1,\beta},\ldots,\overline{inf}\tilde{A}^{\nu}_{n,\beta}\right)\\
R_{\Phi(\tilde{A}_1,\ldots,\tilde{A}_n)}(\beta) &= f\left(\overline{sup}\ \tilde{A}^{\nu}_{1,\beta},\ldots,\overline{sup}\tilde{A}^{\nu}_{n,\beta}\right)
\end{aligned}$$

where

$$\overline{inf}\ \tilde{A}^{\mu}_{i,\alpha} = \begin{cases} inf\tilde{A}^{\mu}_{i,\alpha}, & f \text{ is non}-\text{increasing w.r.t. } a_i\\ sup\tilde{A}^{\mu}_{i,\alpha} & else\end{cases};$$

$$\overline{sup}\ \tilde{A}^{\mu}_{i,\alpha} = \begin{cases} sup\tilde{A}^{\mu}_{i,\alpha}, & f \text{ is non}-\text{decreasing w.r.t. } a_i\\ inf\tilde{A}^{\mu}_{i,\alpha} & else\end{cases};$$

$$\overline{inf}\ \tilde{A}^{\nu}_{i,\beta} = \begin{cases} inf\tilde{A}^{\nu}_{i,\beta}, & f \text{ is non}-\text{decreasing w.r.t. } a_i\\ sup\tilde{A}^{\nu}_{i,\beta}, & else\end{cases};$$

$$\overline{sup}\ \tilde{A}^{\nu}_{i,\beta} = \begin{cases} sup\tilde{A}^{\nu}_{i,\beta}, & f \text{ is non}-\text{increasing w.r.t. } a_i\\ inf\tilde{A}^{\nu}_{i,\beta}, & else\end{cases}.$$

Moreover, let f *be a monotone and continuous function with respect to each of its components. If* $c^{\mu}_L = c^{\mu}_R$ *and* $c^{\nu}_L = c^{\nu}_R$, *for* $\forall\,\alpha,\beta\in[0,1];\ \alpha+\beta\le 1$, *the term is valid as follows:*

$$\begin{aligned}
c^{\mu}_L\overline{inf}\ \tilde{A}^{\mu}_{i,\alpha} + c^{\mu}_R\overline{sup}\ \tilde{A}^{\mu}_{i,\alpha} &= c^{\mu}_L inf\tilde{A}^{\mu}_{i,\alpha} + c^{\mu}_R sup\tilde{A}^{\mu}_{i,\alpha};\, i=1,\ldots,n\\
c^{\nu}_L\overline{inf}\ \tilde{A}^{\nu}_{i,\beta} + c^{\nu}_R\ \overline{sup}\ \tilde{A}^{\nu}_{i,\beta} &= c^{\nu}_L inf\tilde{A}^{\nu}_{i,\beta} + c^{\nu}_R sup\tilde{A}^{\nu}_{i,\beta};\ i=1,\ldots,n
\end{aligned}$$

Proof of Lemma 2: In the first part, let f be a monotone non-decreasing function with respect to each of its components. Then, we find the following:

$$\begin{aligned}
\overline{inf}\ \tilde{A}^{\mu}_{i,\alpha} &= inf\tilde{A}^{\mu}_{i,\alpha};\, i=1,\ldots,n\\
\overline{sup}\ \tilde{A}^{\mu}_{i,\alpha} &= sup\tilde{A}^{\mu}_{i,\alpha};\, i=1,\ldots,n\\
\overline{inf}\ \tilde{A}^{\nu}_{i,\beta} &= inf\tilde{A}^{\nu}_{i,\beta};\ i=1,\ldots,n\\
\overline{sup}\ \tilde{A}^{\nu}_{i,\beta} &= sup\tilde{A}^{\nu}_{i,\beta};\ i=1,\ldots,n
\end{aligned}$$

Thus, the lemma is valid. In the second case, let f be a monotone decreasing function with respect to each of its components. Then, we can write the following:

$$\begin{aligned}
\overline{inf}\ \tilde{A}^{\mu}_{i,\alpha} &= \sup\tilde{A}^{\mu}_{i,\alpha};\, i=1,\ldots,n\\
\overline{sup}\ \tilde{A}^{\mu}_{i,\alpha} &= \inf\tilde{A}^{\mu}_{i,\alpha};\, i=1,\ldots,n\\
\overline{inf}\ \tilde{A}^{\nu}_{i,\beta} &= \sup\tilde{A}^{\nu}_{i,\beta};\ i=1,\ldots,n\\
\overline{sup}\ \tilde{A}^{\nu}_{i,\beta} &= \inf\tilde{A}^{\nu}_{i,\beta};\ i=1,\ldots,n
\end{aligned}$$

We assumed that $c_L^{\mu} = c_R^{\mu}$ and $c_L^{\nu} = c_R^{\nu}$; thus, the lemma is valid. □

Using the lemma, we can write the following theorem.

Theorem 1. *Let $f(a_1, \ldots, a_n)$ be a linear function. For the case $c_L^{\mu} = c_R^{\mu}$, $c_L^{\nu} = c_R^{\nu}$, and IFNs $\widetilde{A}_1, \ldots, \widetilde{A}_n$, we state the following:*

$$IF-WABL\left(\Phi\left(\widetilde{A}_1,\ldots,\widetilde{A}_n\right)\right) = f\left(IF-WABL\left(\widetilde{A}_1\right),\ldots,IF-WABL\left(\widetilde{A}_n\right)\right)$$

where Φ is an IF extension of the function f. Moreover, the function f is a monotone non-decreasing function; the above statement is valid when $c_L^{\mu} \neq c_R^{\mu}$ and $c_L^{\nu} \neq c_R^{\nu}$.

Proof of Theorem 1: Based on the IF-WABL definition, we can write the statement as follows:

$$IF-WABL\left(\Phi\left(\widetilde{A}_1,\ldots,\widetilde{A}_n\right)\right) = \theta I\left(\Phi_\alpha^{\mu}\left(\widetilde{A}_1,\ldots,\widetilde{A}_n\right)\right) + (1-\theta)I\left(\Phi_\beta^{\nu}\left(\widetilde{A}_1,\ldots,\widetilde{A}_n\right)\right)$$

Then, we evaluated the last equality in two pieces:

$$I\left(\Phi_\alpha^{\mu}\left(\widetilde{A}_1,\ldots,\widetilde{A}_n\right)\right) = \int_0^1 \left(c_L^{\mu} L_{\Phi(\widetilde{A}_1,\ldots,\widetilde{A}_n)}(\alpha) + c_R^{\mu} R_{\Phi(\widetilde{A}_1,\ldots,\widetilde{A}_n)}(\alpha)\right) p(\alpha) d\alpha$$

From Lemma 2, we can write the following:

$$\begin{aligned} &I\left(\Phi_\alpha^{\mu}\left(\widetilde{A}_1,\ldots,\widetilde{A}_n\right)\right) \\ &= \int_0^1 \left(c_L^{\mu} f\left(\overline{inf}\ \widetilde{A}_{1,\alpha}^{\mu},\ldots,\overline{inf}\,\widetilde{A}_{n,\alpha}^{\mu}\right)\right. \\ &\left.+c_R^{\mu} f\left(\overline{sup}\ \widetilde{A}_{1,\alpha}^{\mu},\ldots,\overline{sup}\widetilde{A}_{n,\alpha}^{\mu}\right)\right) p(\alpha) d\alpha \end{aligned}$$

where $\overline{inf}\widetilde{A}_{i,\alpha}^{\mu}$ and $\overline{sup}\widetilde{A}_{i,\alpha}^{\mu}; i = 1, \ldots, n$ are defined as in Lemma 2.

$$\begin{aligned} &I\left(\Phi_\alpha^{\mu}\left(\widetilde{A}_1,\ldots,\widetilde{A}_n\right)\right) \\ &= \int_0^1 c_L^{\mu} f\left(\overline{inf}\ \widetilde{A}_{1,\alpha}^{\mu},\ldots,\overline{inf}\widetilde{A}_{n,\alpha}^{\mu}\right) p(\alpha) d\alpha \\ &+\int_0^1 c_R^{\mu} f\left(\overline{sup}\ \widetilde{A}_{1,\alpha}^{\mu},\ldots,\overline{sup}\widetilde{A}_{n,\alpha}^{\mu}\right) p(\alpha) d\alpha \end{aligned}$$

We know that f is a linear function, so we can write the following equality:

$$\begin{aligned} &I\left(\Phi_\alpha^{\mu}\left(\widetilde{A}_1,\ldots,\widetilde{A}_n\right)\right) \\ &= f\left(\int_0^1 \left(c_L^{\mu}\overline{inf}\ \widetilde{A}_{1,\alpha}^{\mu} + c_R^{\mu}\overline{sup}\ \widetilde{A}_{1,\alpha}^{\mu}\right) p(\alpha) d\alpha, \ldots, \int_0^1 \left(c_L^{\mu}\overline{inf}\widetilde{A}_{n,\alpha}^{\mu} + c_R^{\mu}\overline{sup}\widetilde{A}_{n,\alpha}^{\mu}\right) p(\alpha) d\alpha\right) \end{aligned}$$

From the definition of IF-WABL, we know that θ is a positive number. Thus, we can write the following:

$$\theta I\left(\Phi_{\alpha}^{\mu}\left(\widetilde{A}_1,\ldots,\widetilde{A}_n\right)\right)$$
$$=\theta f\left(\int_0^1\left(c_L^{\mu}\overline{inf}\ \widetilde{A}_{1,\alpha}^{\mu}+c_R^{\mu}\overline{sup}\ \widetilde{A}_{1,\alpha}^{\mu}\right)p(\alpha)d\alpha,\ldots,\int_0^1\left(c_L^{\mu}\overline{inf}\,\widetilde{A}_{n,\alpha}^{\mu}+c_R^{\mu}\overline{sup}\widetilde{A}_{n,\alpha}^{\mu}\right)p(\alpha)d\alpha\right)$$
$$=f\left(\theta\int_0^1\left(c_L^{\mu}\overline{inf}\ \widetilde{A}_{1,\alpha}^{\mu}+c_R^{\mu}\overline{sup}\ \widetilde{A}_{1,\alpha}^{\mu}\right)p(\alpha)d\alpha,\ldots,\theta\int_0^1\left(c_L^{\mu}\overline{inf}\,\widetilde{A}_{n,\alpha}^{\mu}+c_R^{\mu}\overline{sup}\widetilde{A}_{n,\alpha}^{\mu}\right)p(\alpha)d\alpha\right)$$

Following a similar path, we obtained the statement given below for the second piece:

$$(1-\theta)I\left(\Phi_{\beta}^{\nu}\left(\widetilde{A}_1,\ldots,\widetilde{A}_n\right)\right)$$
$$=f((1-\theta)\int_0^1\left(c_L^{\nu}\overline{inf}\ \widetilde{A}_{1,\beta}^{\nu}+c_R^{\nu}\overline{sup}\ \widetilde{A}_{1,\beta}^{\nu}\right)s(\beta)d\beta,\ldots,$$
$$(1-\theta)\int_0^1\left(c_L^{\nu}\overline{inf}\,\widetilde{A}_{n,\beta}^{\nu}+c_R^{\mu}\overline{sup}\widetilde{A}_{n,\beta}^{\nu}\right)s(\beta)d\beta)$$

where f can be a monotone non-decreasing function or not. If f is not a monotone non-decreasing function, then $c_L^{\mu}=c_R^{\mu}$ and $c_L^{\nu}=c_R^{\nu}$ must be satisfied. If f is a monotone non-decreasing function, then c_L^{μ}, c_R^{μ}, c_L^{ν}, and c_R^{ν} can be determined arbitrarily. Based on these two alternatives, we can write the following statements:

$$\theta I\left(\Phi_{\alpha}^{\mu}\left(\widetilde{A}_1,\ldots,\widetilde{A}_n\right)\right)$$
$$=f(\theta\int_0^1\left(c_L^{\mu}inf\ \widetilde{A}_{1,\alpha}^{\mu}+c_R^{\mu}sup\widetilde{A}_{1,\alpha}^{\mu}\right)p(\alpha)d\alpha,\ldots,$$
$$\theta\int_0^1\left(c_L^{\mu}inf\widetilde{A}_{n,\alpha}^{\mu}+c_R^{\mu}sup\widetilde{A}_{n,\alpha}^{\mu}\right)p(\alpha)d\alpha)=f\left(\theta I\left(\widetilde{A}_{1,\alpha}^{\mu}\right),\ldots,\theta I\left(\widetilde{A}_{n,\alpha}^{\mu}\right)\right)$$

and

$$(1-\theta)I\left(\Phi_{\beta}^{\nu}\left(\widetilde{A}_1,\ldots,\widetilde{A}_n\right)\right)$$
$$=f\left((1-\theta)\int_0^1\left(c_L^{\nu}inf\widetilde{A}_{1,\beta}^{\nu}+c_R^{\nu}sup\widetilde{A}_{1,\beta}^{\nu}\right)s(\beta)d\beta,\ldots,(1-\theta)\int_0^1\left(c_L^{\nu}inf\widetilde{A}_{n,\beta}^{\nu}+c_R^{\mu}sup\widetilde{A}_{n,\beta}^{\nu}\right)s(\beta)d\beta\right)$$
$$=f\left((1-\theta)I\left(\widetilde{A}_{1,\beta}^{\nu}\right),\ldots,(1-\theta)I\left(\widetilde{A}_{n,\beta}^{\nu}\right)\right)$$

We then merged these two statements knowing that f is a linear function as follows:

$$\theta I\left(\Phi_{\alpha}^{\mu}\left(\widetilde{A}_1,\ldots,\widetilde{A}_n\right)\right)+(1-\theta)I\left(\Phi_{\beta}^{\nu}\left(\widetilde{A}_1,\ldots,\widetilde{A}_n\right)\right)$$
$$=f\left(\theta I\left(\widetilde{A}_{1,\alpha}^{\mu}\right),\ldots,\theta I\left(\widetilde{A}_{n,\alpha}^{\mu}\right)\right)+f\left((1-\theta)I\left(\widetilde{A}_{1,\beta}^{\nu}\right),\ldots,(1-\theta)I\left(\widetilde{A}_{n,\beta}^{\nu}\right)\right)$$
$$IF-WABL\left(\Phi\left(\widetilde{A}_1,\ldots,\widetilde{A}_n\right)\right)$$
$$=f\left(\theta I\left(\widetilde{A}_{1,\alpha}^{\mu}\right)+(1-\theta)I\left(\widetilde{A}_{1,\beta}^{\nu}\right),\ldots,\theta I\left(\widetilde{A}_{n,\alpha}^{\mu}\right)+(1-\theta)I\left(\widetilde{A}_{n,\beta}^{\nu}\right)\right)$$
$$IF-WABL\left(\Phi\left(\widetilde{A}_1,\ldots,\widetilde{A}_n\right)\right)=f\left(IF-WABL\left(\widetilde{A}_1\right),\ldots,IF-WABL\left(\widetilde{A}_n\right)\right)$$

□

As a result of Theorem 1, we can state following relations:

- $\mathrm{IF-WABL}\left(\gamma\widetilde{A}\right)=\gamma\mathrm{IF-WABL}\left(\widetilde{A}\right)$, where $\gamma\geq 0$ and $\gamma\in\mathrm{R}$.
- $\mathrm{IF-WABL}\left(\widetilde{A}+\widetilde{B}\right)=\mathrm{IF-WABL}\left(\widetilde{A}\right)+\mathrm{IF-WABL}\left(\widetilde{B}\right)$.

- If $\mathrm{IF}-\mathrm{WABL}\left(\widetilde{A}\right) < \mathrm{IF}-\mathrm{WABL}\left(\widetilde{B}\right)$, then $\widetilde{A} \widetilde{<} \widetilde{B}$ for IFNs $\widetilde{A}$ and $\widetilde{B}$.

These results are very useful for adopting IFNs to real-life problems. Moreover, as noted previously, the IF-WABL method is a flexible approach, as are NLPIFNs. Next, we described the defuzzification short-cut formula for NLPIFNs to merge these two flexible approaches. Based on this short-cut formula, a researcher can easily apply the defuzzification method to their own defuzzification strategy to tackle real-life problems.

Theorem 2. *Let $\widetilde{A} = \left(a_3;\ a_1, a_2, a_4, a_5,\ a_1', a_2', a_4', a_5'\right.$ be a NLPIFN, with $n_1 = m_1$ and $n_2 = m_2$ for the membership function, and $n_1' = m_1'$ and $n_2' = m_2'$ for the non-membership function. The IF-WABL defuzzified value of $\widetilde{A}$ is calculated as follows:*

$$\begin{aligned} IF-WABL\left(\widetilde{A}\right) = {} & \theta[(c_L a_2 + c_R a_4) + I_2[c_L(a_3 - a_2) - c_R(a_4 - a_3)] \\ & +[c_L(a_2 - a_1) - c_R(a_5 - a_4)](I_1 - u)] \\ & +(1-\theta)\left[(c_L a_2' + c_R a_4') + (v - J_1)\left[c_L(a_3 - a_2') - c_R(a_4' - a_3)\right]\right. \\ & \left.-J_2\left[c_L\left(a_2' - a_1'\right) - c_R\left(a_5' - a_4'\right)\right]\right] \end{aligned}$$

where

$$c_L = c_L^{\mu} = c_L^{\nu};\ c_R = c_R^{\mu} = c_R^{\nu};\ u = \int_0^k p(\alpha)d\alpha;\ I_1 = \int_0^k \left(\tfrac{\alpha}{k}\right)^{\frac{1}{n_1}} p(\alpha)d\alpha;$$
$$I_2 = \int_k^1 \left(\tfrac{\alpha-k}{1-k}\right)^{\frac{1}{n_2}} p(\alpha)d\alpha;\ v = \int_0^{k'} s(\beta)d\beta;\ J_1 = \int_0^{k'} \left(\tfrac{\beta}{k'}\right)^{\frac{1}{n_2'}} s(\beta)d\beta;$$
$$J_2 = \int_{k'}^1 \left(\tfrac{\beta-k'}{1-k'}\right)^{\frac{1}{n_1'}} s(\beta)d\beta.$$

Proof of Theorem 2: The $(\alpha - \beta)$ cuts representation of the NLPIFN $\widetilde{A}$ given in Definition 12 is written in the IF-WABL formula given in Definition 13. After the application of integral operations, we reached the formula given in Theorem 2. □

The formula outlined in Theorem 2 is a general defuzzification formula that covers all defuzzification formulas for all IFNs given in Table 1. A researcher can easily apply the IF-WABL method after adjusting the parameters of NLPIFN with respect to Table 1 and determining the IF-WABL parameters with respect to the decision-making strategy of the study. Thus, different users can obtain different defuzzified values for the same NLPIFN.

Example 1. *Let $\widetilde{A} = (11;\ 5, 7.5, 12, 16, 4, 7, 14, 17)$ be a NLPIFN with $k = 0.5$ and $k' = 0.45$; in addition, $n_1 = m_1 = 0.4$, $n_2 = m_2 = 1.3$, $n_1' = m_1' = 2.1$, and $n_2' = m_2' = 0.7$. For the same NLPIFN, we can compute various IF-WABL defuzzified values by adjusting the parameters of the IF-WABL method. For the IF-WABL parameter $s(\beta) = (l+1)\beta^l$, the chosen values set is $l = 0.45$, 0.75, 2.0, and 3.7. For the the IF-WABL parameter $p(\alpha) = (t+1)\alpha^t$, the chosen values set is $t = 0.3$, 0.6, 3.0, and 4.2. For the IF-WABL parameter c_L, the chosen values set is $c_L = 0.2$, 0.5, 0.6, and 0.9. For the IF-WABL parameter θ, $\theta = 0.35$ is chosen. Employing all of the parameter combinations, we computed various IF-WABL defuzzified values for each given NLPIFN $\widetilde{A}$ and present these values in Table 2.*

Table 2. Various defuzzified values for the NLPIFN $\tilde{A}$.

Values of Parameters		c_L=0.2 c_R=0.8	c_L=0.5 c_R=0.6	c_L=0.6 c_R=0.4	c_L=0.9 c_R=0.1
$t = 0.3$	$l = 0.45$	11.19250	9.51232	8.95226	7.27208
	$l = 0.75$	11.12610	9.38482	8.80438	7.06306
	$l = 2.0$	10.89610	9.04328	8.42566	6.57280
	$l = 3.7$	10.71070	8.82510	8.19659	6.31105
$t = 0.6$	$l = 0.45$	11.12430	9.50938	8.97107	7.35615
	$l = 0.75$	11.05800	9.38189	8.82320	7.14714
	$l = 2.0$	10.82790	9.04033	8.44447	6.65686
	$l = 3.7$	10.64250	8.82218	8.21541	6.39513
$t = 3.0$	$l = 0.45$	10.92930	9.53205	9.06630	7.66906
	$l = 0.75$	10.86290	9.40455	8.91842	7.46004
	$l = 2.0$	10.63290	9.06300	8.53969	6.96977
	$l = 3.7$	10.44740	8.84484	8.31064	6.70803
$t = 4.2$	$l = 0.45$	10.90790	9.54557	9.09146	7.72912
	$l = 0.75$	10.84160	9.41807	8.94358	7.52011
	$l = 2.0$	10.61155	9.07652	8.56485	7.02983
	$l = 3.7$	10.42610	8.85836	8.33580	6.76810

5. Application of NLPIFNs in the IF Minimum Spanning Tree Problem

In this section, we applied the NLPIFN concept and IF-WABL method to the IF minimum spanning tree problem (MSTP). The MSTP is one of the most fundamental and well-known combinatorial optimization problems in the classical graph theory. The MSTP has many application areas, such as transportation [56], logistics [57], image processing [58], statistical cluster analysis [59], wireless telecommunication networks [60], and distribution systems [61]. In a classical deterministic case, we assumed that the values of all edge weights are crisp numbers. For a deterministic case, the MSTP solution can be derived using the many algorithms in the literature. However, edge weights are not crisp values in some real-world processes. For such cases, various scientists have suggested different approaches. Gao and Lu [62] formulated a fuzzy quadratic MSTP by employing an expected value model, chance-constrained programming, and dependent-chance programming. The authors proposed a genetic algorithm approach to solve this problem. Janiak and Kasperski [63] evaluated a MSTP with fuzzy costs in a given connected graph. The authors used the possibility theory to find the solution to the problem. Nayeem and Pal [64] studied a fuzzy MSTP with constraints. By employing a version of the credibility measure, the authors formulated the problem as dependent-chance and chance-constrained programming problems. Zhou et al. [65] presented a fuzzy MST notion for a fuzzy MSTP based on a credibility measure. The authors evaluated the solutions of the problem for different types of fuzzy numbers. Dey and Pal [66] suggested using a graded mean integration representation of fuzzy numbers to compare and add fuzzy numbers. Using this representation, the authors adopted the famous Prim's algorithm into a fuzzy MSTP. Broumi et al. [67] investigated an MSTP with trapezoidal fuzzy neutrosophic edge weights. The authors proposed an algorithm using the score function of TrFN. Dey et al. [50] evaluated an MSTP with interval-type 2 fuzzy sets used to represent the arc lengths. The authors introduced a genetic algorithm for finding the solution to the MSTP. In all research [54,62–67] mentioned in this part of our study, the authors generally preferred to model the weights of edges in the network using one type of fuzzy number. The authors generally did not include the user's perspective in the solution process. On the other hand, by utilizing our approach, one can use any of the IFN types, including linear pentagonal IFNs, non-linear trapezoidal IFNs, linear trapezoidal IFNs, non-linear triangular IFNs, linear triangular IFNs, and Baloui's Generalized IFN. Moreover, by adjusting the IF-WABL parameters according to the user's perspective on the problem, the user's subjectivity can be injected into the solution process of the problem.

In this study, we proposed a version of Prim's algorithm to evaluate the IF MSTP. Here, we benefited from the flexibility properties of the NLPIFN and IF-WABL method by redefining Prim's algorithm for the IF MSTP. In our version, one can use any type of IFN (i.e., Linear Pentagonal, Non-linear Trapezoidal, Linear Trapezoidal, Non-linear Triangular, or Linear Triangular) to state the edge weights of the problem. At the very beginning stage of the problem solution process, we transformed each type of IFN into a NLPIFN by utilizing the component selection alternatives given in Table 1. Next, we employed the IF-WABL defuzzification formula given in Theorem 2 to compute the defuzzified values of the NLPIFN edge weights. In every step of Prim's algorithm, the arc that has the lowest weight among the remaining arcs must be located. Then, we extended the solution tree to realize a solution to the problem. The re-defined version of Prim's algorithm for the IF MSTP can be given as follows:

Step 0. Determine the types of IFNs used to define the edge weights and transform all of them into NLPIFNs using Table 1. Compute the IF-WABL defuzzified values of all weights by employing the formula given in Theorem 2. Define V for all nodes and E for all edges.

Step 1. Choose an arbitrary node x from V and define $V_{new} = \{x\}$. Set $E_{new} = \varnothing$.

Step 2. Find an arc (u, v) with the lowest IF-WABL defuzzified weight, such that u is in V_{new} and v is not. If there is more than one arc with the same IF-WABL defuzzified weight, arbitrarily pick one of the arcs.

Step 3. Add v to V_{new} and (u, v) to E_{new}.

Step 4. If $V_{new} = V$, then STOP, keep $E^* = E_{new}$, which describes the IFMST, and compute the total IF-WABL defuzzified values of the NLPIFN weights that belong to the chosen arcs to determine the solution for the IF MSTP. Otherwise, go to Step 2.

In Figure 2, we present a flow chart of the re-defined version of Prim's algorithm. This flowchart, illustrating the proposed approach, was designed to provide a clear overview of the entire process.

Example 2. *Suppose there are eight oil exploration platforms on the sea. Oil can be extracted from each of these platforms. All the oil obtained must be delivered to land. Laying a pipeline from each platform to the land is a very costly operation; it is a less costly operation to first connect the platforms with pipes and then connect one of the platforms to the land. The most important characteristic when connecting the platforms is the cost. Some platforms cannot be connected to each other due to the lack of suitable physical properties on the seabed. The network given in Figure 3 presents the hypothetical locations of the platforms and possible connections between them. Due to the distance between the platforms, the physical conditions of the seabed, and other natural reasons, the pipe laying costs between the platforms cannot be calculated with certainty. Therefore, these costs expressed in IFNs should be determined by engineers. Without a loss of generality, all of the weights are given as NLPIFNs and their components are given in Table 3. For all NLPIFNs in the example, some values of the components are determined as* $k = 0.61$ *and* $k' = 0.36$; $n_1 = m_1 = 1.4$, $n_2 = m_2 = 0.8$, $n'_1 = m'_1 = 2.3$, *and* $n'_2 = m'_2 = 0.6$. *Here, we sought to obtain the IFMST of the graph by applying the proposed version of Prim's algorithm. To apply the proposed approach, we must compute the defuzzified values of the given NLPIFN weights presented in Table 3. The IF-WABL parameters for this example were determined as follows:* $\theta = 0.40$; $c_L = 0.3$; $c_R = 0.7$; $p(\alpha) = 2.3\alpha^{1.3}$; *and* $s(\beta) = 4.6\beta^{3.6}$. *The defuzzified values of the NLPIFN weights are computed with respect to the given values of the IF-WABL parameters by utilizing the formula given in Theorem 2.*

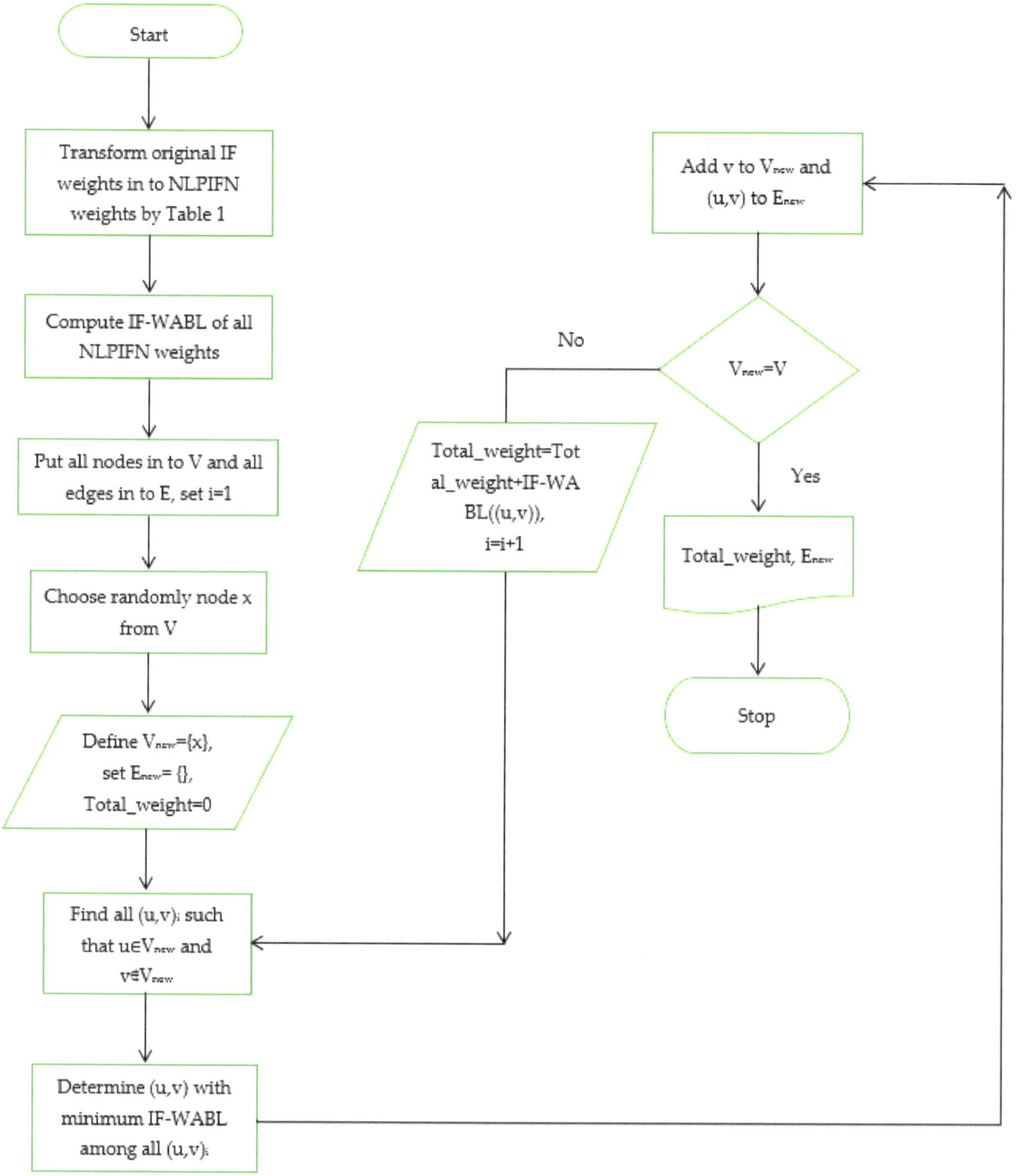

Figure 2. Flow chart of the re-defined version of Prim's algorithm.

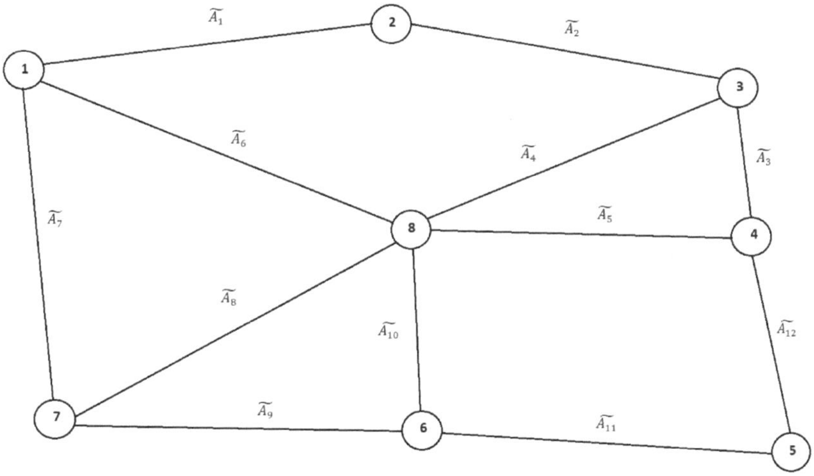

Figure 3. Graph of the IFMST problem example.

Table 3. Weights of the IFMST problem example.

Weight	a_1'	a_1	a_2'	a_2	a_3	a_4	a_4'	a_5	a_5'	IF-WABL
$\widetilde{A}_1$	10.6	11.47	11.82	12.12	12.62	12.66	12.85	13.77	13.94	12.761
$\widetilde{A}_2$	2.07	3.07	3.99	4.34	4.44	5.06	5.11	5.96	6.38	4.914
$\widetilde{A}_3$	4.91	5.52	6.10	6.31	6.72	6.89	7.72	8.21	8.52	7.151
$\widetilde{A}_4$	5.38	6.15	6.40	6.79	7.20	7.68	8.24	8.33	8.71	7.568
$\widetilde{A}_5$	6.75	7.30	7.34	7.46	7.88	8.83	9.18	9.82	9.98	8.685
$\widetilde{A}_6$	8.97	9.32	10.13	10.40	10.51	11.17	11.72	11.77	12.70	11.238
$\widetilde{A}_7$	2.93	3.83	3.88	4.36	4.49	4.51	5.27	5.81	6.68	5.081
$\widetilde{A}_8$	10.85	11.74	12.16	12.89	13.22	13.71	14.44	15.27	16.14	14.034
$\widetilde{A}_9$	8.04	8.72	9.61	9.64	10.41	10.52	10.96	11.04	11.47	10.401
$\widetilde{A}_{10}$	5.50	5.80	6.54	6.59	6.88	7.16	7.94	8.39	8.43	7.327
$\widetilde{A}_{11}$	6.10	6.55	7.42	7.77	8.17	8.58	9.29	9.82	10.00	8.616
$\widetilde{A}_{12}$	11.89	12.41	13.27	13.73	14.32	14.79	15.57	15.83	16.04	14.662

We next used the re-defined version of Prim's algorithm to solve the given IFMST problem. First, the IF-WABL values of the given NLPIFN weights were calculated. The computed IF-WABL values are presented in Table 3. Node 4 was randomly chosen as the starting point of the algorithm. After Node 4, Nodes 3, 2, 8, 6, 5, 7, and 1 were added to the IFMST. Finally, we reached the solution set of arcs $E^* = \{(4,3), (3,2), (3,8), (8,6), (6,5), (6,7),$ and $(7,1)\}$ for the problem. A graphical illustration of the final solution is given in Figure 4, where red lines are used to emphasize the chosen arcs. The total edge weight was equal to 51.099.

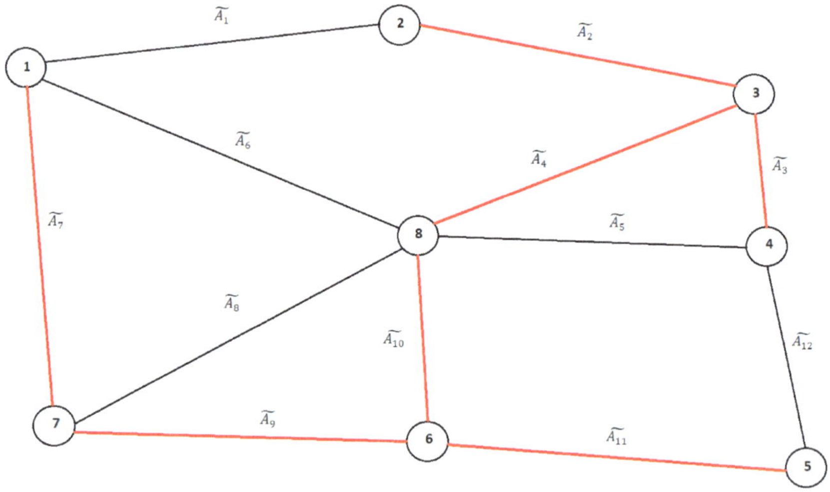

Figure 4. The solution set of arcs of the IFMST problem example.

6. Conclusions

In this paper, we proposed a mathematical definition of a new type of intuitionistic fuzzy number called the non-linear pentagonal intuitionistic fuzzy number (NLPIFN). Moreover, we presented some fundamental characteristics of NLPIFNs that demonstrate $(\alpha - \beta)$ cuts representation and arithmetic operations. We also outlined the relationship between the NLPIFN and other types of IFNs. The results show that the NLPIFN is able to model various types of IFNs, such as linear pentagonal IFNs, non-linear trapezoidal IFNs, linear trapezoidal IFNs, non-linear triangular IFNs, linear triangular IFNs, and Baloui's Generalized IFN. This property of the NLPIFN allows researchers to create much more flexible models. We also utilized a flexible, strong, and mathematically solid defuzzification method for arbitrary IFNs called IF-WABL [53]. In this study, we also described some mathematical properties of the IF-WABL method and then derived an easy-to-use formula for the IF-WABL method that could be used to defuzzy the NLPIFN. Employing the NLPIFN and IF-WABL together resulted in the following advantages: (i) the NLPIFN was able to transform into various IFNs, enabling researchers to design models that include different types of IFNs together. (ii) Owing to the flexibility of the IF-WABL method, researchers can now create different defuzzification methods that reflect their defuzzification strategies. (iii) Due to the easy-to-use IF-WABL defuzzification formula derived for the NLPIFN, users can easily adopt NLPIFNs and the IF-WABL method into their models. In the final section of the paper, we embedded the NLPIFN definition and IF-WABL method into the solution process of the IF MSTP. For this purpose, we adopted the famous and mathematically sound Prim's algorithm for the IF edge weight scenario. We also presented a numerical example for the IF MSTP. In the future, we will study the adaptation of the NLPIFN definition and IF-WABL method into multi-attribute decision-making problems. We will adjust the IF-WABL method parameters to reflect the strategic consensus of all decision-makers. Moreover, we will define a discrete version of the IF-WABL to implement the version of the IF-WABL into multi-attribute decision-making problems.

Funding: This research received no external funding.

Data Availability Statement: Not applicable.

Acknowledgments: This paper was not supported by any foundations or third parties.

Conflicts of Interest: The author declares no conflict of interest.

References

1. Zadeh, L.A. Fuzzy Sets. *Inf. Control* **1965**, *8*, 338–353. [CrossRef]
2. Atanassov, K.T. Intuitionistic Fuzzy Sets. *Fuzzy Set Syst.* **1986**, *20*, 87–96. [CrossRef]
3. Xing, Y.; Qiu, D. Solving Triangular Intuitionistic Fuzzy Matrix Game by Applying the Accuracy Function Method. *Symmetry* **2019**, *11*, 1258. [CrossRef]
4. Ghaffar, A.R.A.; Hasan, G.; Ashraf, Z.; Khan, M.F. Fuzzy Goal Programming with an Imprecise Intuitionistic Fuzzy Preference Relations. *Symmetry* **2020**, *12*, 1548. [CrossRef]
5. Büyükselçuk, E.Ç.; Sarı, Y.C. The Best Whey Protein Powder Selection via VIKOR Based on Circular Intuitionistic Fuzzy Sets. *Symmetry* **2023**, *15*, 1313. [CrossRef]
6. Baklouti, A. Multiple-Attribute Decision Making Based on the Probabilistic Dominance Relationship with Fuzzy Algebras. *Symmetry* **2023**, *15*, 1188. [CrossRef]
7. Nayagam, V.L.G.; Jeevaraj, S.; Sivaraman, G. Complete Ranking of Intuitionistic Fuzzy Numbers. *Fuzzy Inf. Eng.* **2016**, *8*, 237–254. [CrossRef]
8. Nagoorgani, A.; Ponnalagu, K. A New Approach on Solving Intuitionistic Fuzzy Linear Programming Problem. *Appl. Math. Sci.* **2012**, *6*, 3467–3474.
9. Hajek, P.; Olej, V. Defuzzification Methods in Intuitionistic Fuzzy Inference Systems of Takagi-Sugeno Type. In Proceedings of the 11th International Conference on Fuzzy Systems and Knowledge Discovery, Xiamen, China, 19–21 August 2014; pp. 232–236.
10. Grzegrorzewski, P. The hamming distance between intuitionistic fuzzy sets. In Proceedings of the IFSA 2003 World Congress, Istanbul, Turkey, 30 June–2 July 2003; pp. 35–38.
11. Iakovidis, D.K.; Papageorgiou, E. Intuitionistic Fuzzy Cognitive Maps for Medical Decision Making. *IEEE Trans. Inf. Technol. Biomed.* **2011**, *1*, 100–107. [CrossRef]
12. Akram, M.; Shahzad, S.; Butt, A.; Khaliq, A. Intuitionistic Fuzzy Logic Control for Heater Fans. *Math. Comput. Sci.* **2013**, *7*, 367–387. [CrossRef]
13. Nayagam, V.L.G.; Sivaraman, G. Ranking of Interval-Valued Intuitionistic Fuzzy Sets. *Appl. Soft Comput.* **2011**, *11*, 3368–3372. [CrossRef]
14. Dongfeng, C.; Yu, F.; Yongxue, L. Threat Assessment for Air Defense Operations Based on Intuitionistic Fuzzy Logic. *Procedia Eng.* **2012**, *29*, 3302–3306. [CrossRef]
15. Yager, R.R. Some Aspects of Intuitionistic Fuzzy Sets. *Fuzzy Optim Decis Making* **2009**, *8*, 67–90. [CrossRef]
16. Seikh, M.R.; Prasun Kumar Nayak, P.K.; Pal, M. Matrix Games with Intuitionistic Fuzzy Pay-offs. *J. Inf. Optim. Sci.* **2015**, *36*, 159–181. [CrossRef]
17. Hajek, P.; Olej, V. Interval-valued Intuitionistic Fuzzy Inference System For Supporting Corporate Financial Decisions. In Proceedings of the IEEE International Conference on Fuzzy Systems (FUZZ-IEEE), Rio de Janeiro, Brazil, 8–13 July 2018; pp. 1–7.
18. Giri, S.K.; Garai, T.; Garg, H.; Sahidul, I. Possibilistic Mean of Generalized Non-Linear Intuitionistic Fuzzy Number to Solve a Price and Quality Dependent Demand Multi-Item Inventory Model. *Comp. Appl. Math.* **2021**, *40*, 110. [CrossRef]
19. Paramanik, R.; Kumar, N.; Mahato, S.K. Solution for the Optimality of an Intuitionistic Fuzzy Redundancy Allocation Problem for Complex System Using Yager's Ranking Method of Defuzzification with Soft Computation. *Int. J. Syst. Assur. Eng. Manag.* **2022**, *13*, 615–624. [CrossRef]
20. Singh, R.B.; Kumar, R.; Kumar, B.; Kumar, T.; Gupta, V.K. C-Control Charts Using Intuitionistic Fuzzy Numbers and Weighted Defuzzification Method. *Int. J. Early Child. Spec. Educ.* **2022**, *14*, 917–924.
21. Karthick, B.; Uthayakumar, R. A Closed-Loop Supply Chain Model with Carbon Emission and Pricing Decisions under an Intuitionistic Fuzzy Environment. *Environ. Dev. Sustain.* **2022**. [CrossRef]
22. Maity, S.; Chakraborty, A.; De, S.K.; Madhumangal, P. A Study of an EOQ Model of Green Items with the Effect of Carbon Emission under Pentagonal Intuitionistic Dense Fuzzy Environment. *Soft Comput.* **2023**, *27*, 15033–15055. [CrossRef]
23. Ye, J. Expected value method for intuitionistic trapezoidal fuzzy multicriteria decision-making problems. *Expert Syst. Appl.* **2011**, *38*, 11730–11734. [CrossRef]
24. Yue, Z. Deriving Decision Maker's Weights Based on Distance Measure for Interval-Valued Intuitionistic Fuzzy Group Decision Making. *Expert Syst. Appl.* **2011**, *38*, 11665–11670. [CrossRef]
25. Wang, J.; Li, K.; Zhang, H. Interval-Valued Intuitionistic Fuzzy Multi-Criteria Decision-Making Approach Based on Prospect Score Function. *Knowl. Based Syst.* **2012**, *27*, 119–125. [CrossRef]
26. Wan, S.P.; Wang, Q.Y.; Dong, J.Y. The extended VIKOR method for multi-attribute group decision making with triangular intuitionistic fuzzy numbers. *Knowl.-Based Syst.* **2013**, *52*, 65–77. [CrossRef]
27. Meng, F.; Zhang, Q.; Cheng, H. Approaches to Multiple-Criteria Group Decision Making Based on Interval-Valued Intuitionistic Fuzzy Choquet Integral with Respect to the Generalized λ-Shapley Index. *Knowl. Based Syst.* **2013**, *37*, 237–249. [CrossRef]
28. Wu, J.; Chiclana, F. A Risk Attitudinal Ranking Method for Interval-Valued Intuitionistic Fuzzy Numbers Based on Novel Attitudinal Expected Score and Accuracy Functions. *Appl. Soft Comput.* **2014**, *22*, 272–286. [CrossRef]
29. Qin, J.; Liu, X.; Pedrycz, W. Multi-Attribute Group Decision Making Based on Choquet Integral under Interval-Valued Intuitionistic Fuzzy Environment. *Int. J. Comput. Intell. Syst.* **2016**, *9*, 133–152. [CrossRef]
30. Li, W.; Wu, C. A Multicriteria Interval-Valued Intuitionistic Fuzzy Set TOPSIS Decision-Making Approach Based on the Improved Score Function. *J. Intell. Syst.* **2016**, *25*, 239–250. [CrossRef]

31. Xian, S.; Dong, Y.; Liu, Y.; Jing, N. A Novel Approach for Linguistic Group Decision Making Based on Generalized Interval-Valued Intuitionistic Fuzzy Linguistic Induced Hybrid Operator and TOPSIS. *Int. J. Intell. Syst.* **2018**, *33*, 288–314. [CrossRef]
32. Meng, F.; Tang, J.; Wang, P.; Chen, X. A Programming-Based Algorithm for Interval-Valued Intuitionistic Fuzzy Group Decision Making. *Knowl. Based Syst.* **2013**, *144*, 122–143. [CrossRef]
33. Kong, D.; Chang, T.; Wang, Q.; Sun, H.; Dai, W. A Threat Assessment Method of Group Targets Based on Interval-Valued Intuitionistic Fuzzy Multi-Attribute Group Decision-Making. *Appl. Soft Comput.* **2018**, *67*, 350–369. [CrossRef]
34. Li, Z.; Sun, D.; Zeng, S. Intuitionistic Fuzzy Multiple Attribute Decision-Making Model Based on Weighted Induced Distance Measure and Its Application to Investment Selection. *Symmetry* **2018**, *10*, 261. [CrossRef]
35. Hao, Y.; Chen, X. Study on the Ranking Problems in Multiple Attribute Decision Making Based on Interval-Valued Intuitionistic Fuzzy Numbers. *Int J Intell Syst.* **2018**, *33*, 560–572. [CrossRef]
36. Alcantud, J.C.R. Multi-Attribute Group Decision-Making Based on Intuitionistic Fuzzy Aggregation Operators Defined by Weighted Geometric Means. *Granul. Comput.* **2023**. [CrossRef]
37. Ding, Q.; Wang, Y.M. Intuitionistic Fuzzy TOPSIS Multi-attribute Decision Making Method Based on Revised Scoring Function and Entropy Weight Method. *J. Intell. Fuzzy Syst.* **2019**, *36*, 625–635. [CrossRef]
38. Faizi, S.; Sałabun, W.; Rashid, T.; Zafar, S.; Wątróbski, J. Intuitionistic Fuzzy Sets in Multi-Criteria Group Decision Making Problems Using the Characteristic Objects Method. *Symmetry* **2020**, *12*, 1382. [CrossRef]
39. Chen, S.M.; Tsai, K.Y. Multi Attribute Decision Making Based on New Score Function of Interval-Valued Intuitionistic Fuzzy Values and Normalized Score Matrices. *Inf. Sci.* **2021**, *575*, 714–731. [CrossRef]
40. Wang, Y.; Yuan, M.; Zhou, X.; Qu, X. Evaluation of Geo-Environment Carrying Capacity Based on Intuitionistic Fuzzy TOPSIS Method: A Case Study of China. *Sustainability* **2023**, *15*, 8121. [CrossRef]
41. Yang, X.; Mahmood, T.; Ali, Z.; Hayat, K. Identification and Classification of Multi-Attribute Decision-Making Based on Complex Intuitionistic Fuzzy Frank Aggregation Operators. *Mathematics* **2023**, *11*, 3292. [CrossRef]
42. Jin, J.; Garg, H. Intuitionistic Fuzzy Three-Way Ranking-Based TOPSIS Approach with a Novel Entropy Measure and Its Application to Medical Treatment Selection. *Adv. Eng. Softw.* **2023**, *180*, 103459. [CrossRef]
43. Huang, Z.; Weng, S.; Lv, Y.; Liu, H. Ranking Method of Intuitionistic Fuzzy Numbers and Multiple Attribute Decision Making Based on the Probabilistic Dominance Relationship. *Symmetry* **2023**, *15*, 1001. [CrossRef]
44. Zhengsen, J.; Xiaoyu, Y.; Wanying, L.; Dongxiao, N. A Multi-Criteria Decision-Making Framework for Distributed Generation Projects Investment Considering the Risk of Electricity Market Trading. *J. Clean. Prod.* **2023**, *416*, 137837.
45. Feng, F.; Fujita, H.; Ali, M.I.; Yager, R.R.; Liu, X. Another View on Generalized Intuitionistic Fuzzy Soft Sets and Related Multiattribute Decision Making Methods. *IEEE Trans. Fuzzy Syst.* **2018**, *27*, 474–488. [CrossRef]
46. Feng, F.; Zheng, Y.; Alcantud, J.C.R.; Wang, Q. Minkowski Weighted Score Functions of Intuitionistic Fuzzy Values. *Mathematics* **2020**, *8*, 1143. [CrossRef]
47. Agarwal, M.; Biswas, K.K.; Hanmandlu, M. Generalized Intuitionistic Fuzzy Soft Sets with Applications in Decision-Making. *Appl. Soft Comput.* **2013**, *13*, 3552–3566. [CrossRef]
48. Orazbayev, B.; Dyussembina, E.; Uskenbayeva, G.; Shukirova, A.; Orazbayeva, K. Methods for Modeling and Optimizing the Delayed Coking Process in a Fuzzy Environment. *Processes* **2023**, *11*, 450. [CrossRef]
49. Orazbayev, B.B.; Ospanov, E.A.; Orazbayeva, K.N.; Kurmangazieva, L.T. A Hybrid Method for the Development of Mathematical Models of a Chemical Engineering System in Ambiguous Conditions. *Math. Models Comput. Simul.* **2018**, *10*, 748–758. [CrossRef]
50. Zimmermann, H.J. *Fuzzy Set Theory—And Its Applications*, 5th ed.; Springer Science+Business Media LLC.: Berlin/Heidelberg, Germany, 2018.
51. Orazbayev, B.; Zhumadillayeva, A.; Orazbayeva, K.; Iskakova, S.; Utenova, B.; Gazizov, F.; Ilyashenko, S.; Afanaseva, O. The System of Models and Optimization of Operating Modes of a Catalytic Reforming Unit Using Initial Fuzzy Information. *Energies* **2022**, *15*, 1573. [CrossRef]
52. Shabani, A.; Jamkhaneh, E.B. A new generalized intuitionistic fuzzy number. *J. Fuzzy Set Valued Anal.* **2014**, *24*, 1–10. [CrossRef]
53. Mert, A. On the WABL Defuzzification Method for Intuitionistic Fuzzy Numbers. In *Intelligent and Fuzzy Techniques in Big Data Analytics and Decision Making*, 1st ed.; Kahraman, C., Cebi, S., Onar, S.C., Oztaysi, B., Tolga, A.C., Sari, I.U., Eds.; Springer: Cham, Switzerland, 2019; Volume 1, pp. 39–47.
54. Dey, A.; Son, L.H.; Pal, A.; Long, H.V. Fuzzy Minimum Spanning Tree with Interval Type 2 Fuzzy Arc Length: Formulation and a New Genetic Algorithm. *Soft Comput.* **2020**, *24*, 3963–3974. [CrossRef]
55. Jamkhaneh, E.B.; Nadarajah, S. A new generalized intuitionistic fuzzy set. *Hacet. J. Math. Stat.* **2015**, *44*, 1537–1551. [CrossRef]
56. Majumder, S.; Kar, S.; Pal, T. Rough-fuzzy quadratic minimum spanning tree problem. *Expert Syst.* **2019**, *36*, e12364. [CrossRef]
57. Syarif, A.; Gen, M. Solving exclusionary side constrained transportation problem by using a hybrid spanning tree-based genetic algorithm. *J. Intell. Manuf.* **2003**, *14*, 389–399. [CrossRef]
58. Nithya, S.; Bhuvaneswari, S.; Senthil, S. Robust minimal spanning tree using intuitionistic fuzzy c-means clustering algorithm for breast cancer detection. *Am. J. Neural Netw. Appl.* **2019**, *5*, 12–22. [CrossRef]
59. Gao, W.; Zhang, Q.; Lu, Z.; Wu, D.; Du, X. Modelling and application of fuzzy adaptive minimum spanning tree in tourism agglomeration area division. *Knowl.-Based Sys.* **2018**, *143*, 317–326. [CrossRef]
60. Chamodrakas, I.; Martakos, D. Autility-based fuzzy topsis method for energy efficient networks election in heterogeneous wireless networks. *Appl. Soft Comput.* **2012**, *12*, 1929–1938. [CrossRef]

61. Mohanta, K.; Dey, A.; Debnath, N.C.; Pal, A. An algorithmic approach for finding minimum spanning tree in a intuitionistic fuzzy graph. In Proceedings of the 32nd International Conference on Computer Applications in Industry and Engineering, San Diego, USA, 30 September–2 October 2019; pp. 140–149.
62. Gao, J.; Lu, M. Fuzzy Quadratic Minimum Spanning Tree Problem. *Appl. Math. Comput.* **2005**, *164*, 773–788. [CrossRef]
63. Janiak, A.; Kasperski, A. The Minimum Spanning Tree Problem with Fuzzy Costs. *Fuzzy Optim. Decis. Making* **2008**, *7*, 105–118. [CrossRef]
64. Nayeem, A.; Pal, M. Diameter Constrained Fuzzy Minimum Spanning Tree Problem. *Int. J. Comput. Intell. Syst.* **2013**, *6*, 1040–1051. [CrossRef]
65. Zhou, J.; Chen, L.; Wang, K.; Yang, F. Fuzzy α-minimum Spanning Tree Problem: Definition and Solutions. *Int. J. Gen. Syst.* **2016**, *45*, 311–335. [CrossRef]
66. Dey, A.; Pal, A. Prim's Algorithm for Solving Minimum Spanning Tree Problem in Fuzzy Environment. *Ann. Fuzzy Math. Inform.* **2016**, *12*, 419–430.
67. Broumi, S.; Bakali, A.; Talea, M.; Smarandache, F.; Uluçay, V. Minimum Spanning Tree in Trapezoidal Fuzzy Neutrosophic Environment. In *Innovations in Bio-Inspired Computing and Applications*, 1st ed.; Abraham, A., Haqiq, A., Muda, A., Gandhi, N., Eds.; Springer: Cham, Switzerland, 2018; Volume 1, pp. 25–35. [CrossRef]

symmetry

MDPI

Article

Multi-Attribute Group Decision-Making Methods Based on Entropy Weights with q-Rung Picture Uncertain Linguistic Fuzzy Information

Mengran Sun [1,†], Yushui Geng [1,*,†] and Jing Zhao [1,2,†]

1 School of Computer Science and Technology, Qilu University of Technology (Shandong Academy of Sciences), Jinan 250353, China; 10431220607@stu.qlu.edu.cn (M.S.); zj@qlu.edu.cn (J.Z.)
2 Shandong Provincial Key Laboratory of Computer Networks, Shandong Fundamental Research Center for Computer Science, Jinan 250353, China
* Correspondence: gys@qlu.edu.cn
† These authors contributed equally to this work.

Abstract: This paper introduces a new concept called q-rung picture uncertain linguistic fuzzy sets (q-RPULSs). These sets provide a reliable and comprehensive method for describing complex and uncertain decision-making information. In addition, q-RPULSs help to integrate the decision maker's quantitative assessment ideas with qualitative assessment information. For the q-RPUL multi-attribute group decision-making problem with unknown weight information, an entropy-based fuzzy set method for q-rung picture uncertainty language is proposed. The method considers the interrelationships among attributes and builds a q-rung picture uncertain language model. In addition, the q-RPULMSM operator and its related properties are discussed in this paper. This operator enables the fusion of q-RPULSs and helps to reach consensus in decision-making scenarios. To demonstrate the validity of the methodology, we provide a real case study involving commodity selection. Based on this case study, the reasonableness and superiority of the method are evaluated, highlighting the practical advantages and applicability of q-RPULSs in decision-making processes.

Keywords: q-rung picture uncertain linguistic fuzzy sets; Maclaurin symmetric mean operator; multi-attribute decision-making; entropy measure

Citation: Sun, M.; Geng, Y.; Zhao, J. Multi-Attribute Group Decision-Making Methods Based on Entropy Weights with q-Rung Picture Uncertain Linguistic Fuzzy Information. *Symmetry* **2023**, *15*, 2027. https://doi.org/10.3390/sym15112027

Academic Editors: Changyou Wang, Dong Qiu, Yonghong Shen, José Carlos R. Alcantud and Sergei D. Odintsov

Received: 8 October 2023
Revised: 28 October 2023
Accepted: 1 November 2023
Published: 8 November 2023

1. Introduction

MAGDM is a vital process that involves decision makers evaluating and prioritizing alternatives while considering various attributes [1]. The goal is to select the most advantageous option from a range of available programs. This process plays a significant role in modern decision-making science and is widely applied in fields such as engineering, economics, and management. The use of mathematical models [2] based on partial differential equations allows us to model physically relevant quantities. A new method to optimize the hyperparameters was proposed by Effat Jalaeian Zaferani et al. [3]. Due to the complexity of real-world issues and the unpredictable nature of decision-making environments, traditional mathematical models based on binary logic are no longer adequate for accurately representing the attribute values associated with potential solutions during the decision-making process. Therefore, the researchers introduced some fuzzy sets.

FSs made significant progress with the pioneering work of Zadeh [4]. FSs have emerged as a crucial tool for representing imprecise and uncertain information. Ataanassov [5] further contributed to the field by building upon Zadeh's work. In addition to fuzzy sets, Zadeh introduced intuitionistic fuzzy sets, which enhance the theoretical framework by representing uncertain information and phenomena more effectively. Intuitionistic fuzzy sets incorporate both subordination and non-subordination dimensions, surpassing classical fuzzy sets in this aspect. However, it is important to note that intuitionistic fuzzy sets must satisfy the non-boundedness condition, which restricts their practical application and scope. To overcome this limitation, Yager [6] proposed Pythagorean fuzzy sets, which strictly adhere to the condition that the sum of the squares of the positive and negative ratings must not exceed 1. This breakthrough led to extensive research on solving multi-attribute group decision-making (MAGDM) problems using Pythagorean fuzzy sets. Zhang et al. [7] introduced generalized Pythagorean fuzzy Bonferroni mean operators, which are valuable in capturing the interrelationships among Pythagorean fuzzy numbers and finding practical utility in decision-making. Furthermore, Garg [8] explored the practical applications of Pythagorean fuzzy sets in MAGDM by presenting logarithmic operator laws and aggregation operators specifically tailored for them. Xu et al. [9] introduced a set of Pythagorean fuzzy intersection Muirhead averaging operators as a solution to handle the intersection between Pythagorean membership and non-membership, while also effectively capturing the interrelationships among multiple Pythagorean fuzzy numbers. Despite the abundant research conducted on Pythagorean fuzzy sets, these sets possess certain limitations, particularly when employed in complex decision problems. In certain scenarios, it is observed that the quadratic sum of the positive and negative ratings do not surpass 1, while the sum of the cubic or higher powers exceeds 1. To overcome this limitation, Yager [10] proposed q-rung orthogonal fuzzy sets. The constraint in q-rung orthogonal fuzzy sets is that the summation of the q-th powers of the positive and negative ratings should not exceed 1. Liu and Wang [11] subsequently devised straightforward weighted average operators to consolidate generalized orthogonal fuzzy numbers and successfully employed these operators in the realm of multi-attribute group decision-making (MAGDM). Liu [12] introduced the generalized orthogonal fuzzy Bonferroni mean value operator as a means to amalgamate the interrelationships among q-rung orthogonal fuzzy numbers.

However, in reality, decision-making problems can be excessively complex. We may encounter situations where human voters provide different types of answers in a poll, such as yes, no, reject, or abstain. Under such scenarios, the fuzzy set proof presented above is not sufficient. Thus, Cuong and Kreinovich [13] have made significant contributions by introducing picture fuzzy sets (PFSs). They have conducted extensive research on the fundamental operations and properties of PFSs. PFSs are distinguished by their positive, neutral, and negative degrees of membership, while adhering to the constraint that the cumulative sum of the positive evaluation, neutral evaluation, and negative evaluation must not surpass 1. Thong and Soncite [14,15] have developed various fuzzy clustering algorithms using fuzzy sets of images. These algorithms have been successfully applied to weather forecasting and project selection. However, there are limitations of these methods. For example, they are no longer used when dealing with the sum of positive, neutral, and negative ratings exceeding 1. To address this issue, Li et al. [16] proposed a new method using q-RPFSs with the constraint that the sum of the q powers of positive, neutral, and negative ratings must be equal to or less than one. This advancement in the unique constraint form of q-RPFSs effectively addresses the inherent limitations of q-level generalized orthogonal fuzzy sets and graphical fuzzy sets. Pinar et al. [17] proposed the q-RPF-KNN algorithm, which computes the distance between test instances and training instances. Comparing with other KNN algorithms, the results are more perfect. Akram et al. [18] utilized 2TLCq-RPFSs to solve the problem of optimal machine selection. Tahir et al. [19] introduced T-spherical fuzzy sets and applied them to medical diagnosis. While previous approaches are unable to comprehensively address quantitative and qualitative decision-making and the intricate relationships between multiple parameters, our proposed method and operators aim to fill this important gap. By introducing innovative methods, we aim to provide decision makers with an integrated framework that considers both quantitative and qualitative aspects of decision-making.

In certain scenarios, decision makers often prioritize quantitative decisions over qualitative ones due to constraints such as time limitations and limited expertise. This tendency to incorporate both quantitative and qualitative assessment information is particularly evident in real-world MAGDM problems. In such complex decision-making scenarios, it is crucial to consider not only the numerical values associated with the attributes but also the qualitative aspects. By recognizing the importance of both quantitative and qualitative factors, decision makers can ensure a more comprehensive and balanced assessment of options in MAGDM problems. Decision makers recognize the need to consider and integrate both types of information provided by stakeholders in order to make informed and well-rounded decisions. The utilization of linguistic variables as valuable tools in expressing the qualitative evaluations of decision makers has demonstrated its effectiveness. Li et al. [16] introduced a q-rung picture linguistic set in order to select a suitable enterprise resource planning system. Consequently, a fusion of ULVs and q-rung picture fuzzy sets has been employed to accurately capture the evaluations of decision makers. Singh et al. [20] used the LDULFPEWG operator to select the best microgrid scheme. In order to analyze the conditions of the anomalous aluminum electrolyzer, zhu et al. [21] studied the PUL-DUCG model and achieved satisfactory results. As a result, this research introduces a novel concept known as q-RPULSs. This integration enhances the representation of decision makers' evaluations, providing a comprehensive and robust framework. To illustrate, let us examine a situation in which a professor is evaluating the research capabilities of a graduate student.

Researchers have introduced a range of operators employed to aggregate the decision matrix, facilitating the derivation of comprehensive attribute values for each alternative. Subsequently, by ranking the alternatives based on the scores of the comprehensive attributes, researchers are able to identify the optimal solution. This approach enables efficient decision-making in scenarios involving multiple attributes, ensuring a comprehensive and well-informed selection process by effectively considering the correlation between any pair of input parameters. In the realm of multi-attribute decision-making, information aggregation operators hold significant prominence and have garnered considerable attention from scholars. Noteworthy operators include the Bonferroni mean (BM) operator [22], the Heronian mean (HM) operator [23,24], and the Maclaurin symmetric mean (MSM) operator [25]. The interrelationships between two input parameters are effectively captured by the Bonferroni mean (BM) operator, which was originally introduced by Bonferroni [22]. Fatma et al. [26] proposed the picture fuzzy Bonferroni mean, which was chosen to match the company's enterprise resource planning system. Liu et al. [12] proposed the q-rung orthopair fuzzy Bonferroni mean operator, which solves the project investment problem. Similarly, the HM aggregation operator, introduced by Gleb et al. [27], shares similar characteristics with the BM operator, allowing for the consideration of correlations among any pair of input parameters. Liu et al. [28] proposed a intuitionistic uncertain linguistic arithmetic Heronian mean operator and applied it to project investment. Sumera et al. [29] proposed a generalized 2-tuple linguistic bipolar fuzzy Heronian mean operator and its application to battery selection. Nevertheless, the BM operator and the HM operator do not have the ability to account for interrelationships among multiple parameters. As a consequence, this restriction may introduce biases and inaccuracies in the evaluation results when dealing with complex real-world problems. To tackle this issue, Maclaurin [25] proposed a solution by introducing the MSM operator. The MSM operator offers the capability of considering the correlation among multiple input parameters, thereby enhancing the accuracy and dependability of the evaluation outcomes. Subsequent advancements led Detemple and Robertson [30] to develop an extended version of the MSM operator. Building upon the strengths of the MSM operator, researchers have conducted extensive studies that have yielded numerous noteworthy results. Wang et al. [31] proposed the IFPMSM operator and applied it to air quality evaluation.

The above-described method focuses on scenarios where complete attribute weight information is known but, in many real-world MAGDM problems, attribute weights are often unknown. Therefore, a novel MAGDM approach is proposed for dealing with MAGDM problems under q-RPULSs with unknown weight information. This study aims to address this issue as follows: (1) Recognizing that the Maclaurin symmetric mean (MSM) operator can consider interrelationships amongst multiple attributes; introducing q-RPULSs of the MSM operator to effectively handle extreme evaluations of decision makers. (2) Proposing a new MAGDM technique for the q-RPUL multi-attribute group decision-making problem that accounts for unknown attribute weights. The rest of this paper is organized as follows: Section 2 reviews and discusses fundamental concepts and theories comprehensively. Section 3 introduces several MSM operators designed for q-rung picture uncertain linguistic sets (q-RPULSs), including the q-rung picture uncertain language Maclaurin symmetric averaging operator (q-RPULMSM) and the q-rung picture uncertain language weighted Maclaurin symmetric averaging operator (q-RPULWMSM). Furthermore, this section extensively examines the properties of these operators. Section 4 describes the aggregation method for problem-solving. Section 5 showcases the performance of the method by applying it to a real-world scenario or simulation, and provides empirical evidence of its utility. Finally, in Section 6, conclusions are drawn based on the key findings and results obtained from the study. Table 1 is provided to assist in better understanding the fuzzy sets and operators mentioned in this article.

Table 1. Fuzzy sets and operators.

Abbreviation	Full Name
MAGDM	multi-attribute group decision-making
FSs	fuzzy sets
IFSs	intuitionistic fuzzy sets
PyFSs	Pythagorean fuzzy sets
PFSs	picture fuzzy sets
q-ROFs	q-rung orthopair fuzzy sets
q-ROULSs	q-rung orthopair uncertain linguistic sets
q-RPULSs	q-rung picture uncertain linguistic sets
q-RPFSs	q-rung picture fuzzy sets
ULVs	uncertain linguistic variables
MSM	Maclaurin symmetric mean
q-RPULMSM	q-rung picture uncertain linguistic Maclaurin symmetric mean
q-RPULWMSM	q-rung picture uncertain linguistic weighted Maclaurin symmetric mean
2TLCq-RPFSs	2-tuple linguistic complex q-rung picture fuzzy sets
LDULFPEWG	linear diophantine uncertain linguistic fuzzy power Einstein-weighted geometric
TSULWA	T-spherical uncertain linguistic weighted averaging
T-SFWGMSM	T-spherical fuzzy weighted geometric Maclaurin symmetric mean
q-RPFDHM	q-rung picture fuzzy dual Heronian mean
q-RPULA	q-rung picture uncertain linguistic averaging
PULMSM	picture uncertain linguistic Maclaurin symmetric mean
q-RPULBM	q-rung picture uncertain linguistic Bonferroni mean
SPULMSM	spherical picture uncertain linguistic Maclaurin symmetric mean
RAM	random access memory

2. Preliminaries

In this section, we provide a brief introduction to various types of fuzzy sets, including ULSs, PFSs, q-ROFSs, q-RPLSs, q-ROULSs, and q-RPFSs, and their corresponding operations. In addition, we discuss in depth an important tool applicable to fuzzy set theory, namely MSM. Furthermore, we introduce the novel concept of q-RPULSs and provide scoring functions and distance measures that can be employed to evaluate q-RPULSs.

Definition 1 ([32])**.** *One can describe the representation of a PFS C_{HT} in a nonempty fixed set X as follows:*

$$C_{HT} = \{< x, u_{C_{HT}}(x), \eta_{C_{HT}}(x), v_{C_{HT}}(x) > | x \in X\} \tag{1}$$

In this context, the term "positive rating" $u_{C_{HT}}$ denotes the rating to which x belongs positively to C_{HT}, while the term "neutrality rating" $\eta_{C_{HT}}$ signifies the degree to which x has neutral association with C_{HT}. Additionally, the term "negative rating" $v_{C_{HT}}$ indicates the degree to which x has a negative association with C_{HT}. The degrees of affiliation mentioned above adhere to the following conditions: $0 \leq u_{C_{HT}}(x) + \eta_{C_{HT}}(x) + v_{C_{HT}}(x) \leq 1$. Moreover, refusal rating, denoted as $\pi_A(x)$, can be determined by $\pi_{C_{HT}}(x) = (1 - (u_{C_{HT}}(x) + \eta_{C_{HT}}(x) + v_{C_{HT}}(x)))$.

The triplets $(u_{C_{HT}}(x), \eta_{C_{HT}}(x), v_{C_{HT}}(x))$ are called picture fuzzy numbers (PFNs) and play a significant role in representing uncertainty and fuzziness in PFSs.

Definition 2 ([17])**.** *Let us define a q-ROFS on a nonempty fixed set X as follows:*

$$C_{HT} = \{< x, u_{C_{HT}}(x), v_{C_{HT}}(x) > |x \in X\} \tag{2}$$

Here, $u_{C_{HT}}$ and $v_{C_{HT}}$ represent affiliation and non-affiliation of x to C_{HT}, respectively. It is necessary for the following condition to hold for every x in X: $x \in X$: $0 \leq (u_{C_{HT}}(x)^q + v_{C_{HT}}(x)^q) \leq 1, (q \geq 1)$. Additionally, the degree of refusal rating is calculated as:

$$\pi_{C_{HT}}(x) = (1 - (u_{C_{HT}}(x)^q + v_{C_{HT}}(x)^q))^{\frac{1}{q}}. \tag{3}$$

To provide a more convenient representation, we can refer to the notation $< u_{C_{HT}}(x), v_{C_{HT}}(x) >$ as a q-ROFN.

Definition 3 ([17])**.** *We can define a q-RPFS on set of positive real numbers X in the following manner:*

$$C_{HT} = \{< x, u_{C_{HT}}(x), \eta_{C_{HT}}(x), v_{C_{HT}}(x) > |x \in X\} \tag{4}$$

In this definition, we ensure that $0 \leq (u_{C_{HT}}(x)^q + \eta_{C_{HT}}(x)^q + v_{C_{HT}}(x)^q) \leq 1$ for each element x in X. The values $u_{C_{HT}}(x), \eta_{C_{HT}}(x), v_{C_{HT}}(x)$ belong to the range [0, 1] and represent the positive, neutral, and negative ratings of x to the q-RPFS. Additionally, we can calculate the refusal rating $\pi_A(x)$using the expression $\pi_{C_{HT}}(x) = (1 - (u_{C_{HT}}(x)^q + \eta_{C_{HT}}(x)^q + v_{C_{HT}}(x)^q))^{\frac{1}{q}}$.
For simplicity, we refer to each triplet $(u_{C_{HT}}(x), \eta_{C_{HT}}(x), v_{C_{HT}}(x))$ as a q-RPFN.

Definition 4 ([16])**.** *We can define a q-RPLS C_{HT} on an ordinary fixed set X:*

$$C_{HT} = \{< x, s_{\phi(x)}, (u_{C_{HT}}(x), \eta_{C_{HT}}(x), v_{C_{HT}}(x))] > |x \in X\} \tag{5}$$

Here, the term $s_{\phi(x)}$ belongs to S and $s_{\phi(x)}$ represents the linguistic term interval in S. The triplet $u_{C_{HT}}(x), \eta_{C_{HT}}(x), v_{C_{HT}}(x)$ represents the positive, neutral, and negative ratings of the element x in the q-RPULS. These membership degrees satisfy the conditions that $0 \leq (u_{C_{HT}}(x)^q + \eta_{C_{HT}}(x)^q + v_{C_{HT}}(x)^q) \leq 1$ and $u_{C_{HT}}(x), \eta_{C_{HT}}(x), v_{C_{HT}}(x) \in [0,1]$ are within the range [0, 1]. For convenience, we can refer to the notation $< s_{\phi(x)}, (u_{C_{HT}}(x), \eta_{C_{HT}}(x), v_{C_{HT}}(x)) >$ as the q-RPLS. To simplify the notation further, we may write it as $< s_{\phi}, (u, \eta, v) >$.

Definition 5 ([33])**.** *Linguistic term set $S = \{s_0, s_1, ..., s_{t-1}\}$ is composed of k elements, where k is an odd number. Generally, t = 3, 5, 7, 9. For example, t equals 5, $S = \{s_0, s_1, s_2, s_3, s_4\} = \{verypoor, poor, good, verygood, excellent\}$.*

Definition 6 ([34])**.** *We can define a q-ROULS C_{HT} on an ordinary fixed set X:*

$$C_{HT} = \{< x, [s_{\phi(x)}, s_{\psi(x)}], (u_{C_{HT}}(x), v_{C_{HT}}(x))] > |x \in X\} \tag{6}$$

Here, the terms $s_{\phi(x)}, s_{\psi(x)}$ belong to S and $s_{\phi(x)}, s_{\psi(x)}$ represents the linguistic term interval in S. The $u_{C_{HT}}(x), v_{C_{HT}}(x)$ represents the positive and negative ratings of the element x in the q-ROULS. These membership degrees satisfy the conditions that $0 \leq (u_{C_{HT}}(x)^q + v_{C_{HT}}(x)^q) \leq 1$ and $u_{C_{HT}}(x), v_{C_{HT}}(x) \in [0,1]$ are within the range [0, 1]. For convenience, we can refer to the notation $< [s_{\phi(x)}, s_{\psi(x)}], (u_{C_{HT}}(x), v_{C_{HT}}(x)) >$ as the q-ROULS. To simplify the notation further, we may write it as $< [s_{\phi}, s_{\psi}], (u, v) >$.

Definition 7. *We can define a q-RPULS C_{HT} on an ordinary fixed set X:*

$$C_{HT} = \{< x, [s_{\phi(x)}, s_{\psi(x)}], (u_{C_{HT}}(x), \eta_{C_{HT}}(x), v_{C_{HT}}(x))] > |x \in X\} \tag{7}$$

Here, the terms $s_{\phi(x)}, s_{\psi(x)}$ belong to S and $s_{\phi(x)}, s_{\psi(x)}$ represents the linguistic term interval in S. The triplet $u_{C_{HT}}(x), \eta_{C_{HT}}(x), v_{C_{HT}}(x)$ represents the positive, neutral, and negative ratings of the element x in the q-RPULS. These membership degrees satisfy the conditions that $0 \le (u_{C_{HT}}(x)^q + \eta_{C_{HT}}(x)^q + v_{C_{HT}}(x)^q) \le 1$ and $u_{C_{HT}}(x), \eta_{C_{HT}}(x), v_{C_{HT}}(x) \in [0,1]$ are within the range [0, 1]. For convenience, we can refer to the notation $< [s_{\phi(x)}, s_{\psi(x)}], (u_{C_{HT}}(x), \eta_{C_{HT}}(x), v_{C_{HT}}(x)) >$ as the q-RPULS. To simplify the notation further, we may write it as $< [s_{\phi}, s_{\psi}], (u, \eta, v) >$.

Definition 8. *Let $a_1 =< [s_{\phi_1}, s_{\psi_1}], (u_1, \eta_1, v_1) >$ and $a_2 =< [s_{\phi_2}, s_{\psi_2}], (u_2, \eta_2, v_2) >$ be two q-RPULSs, and consider a positive real number m, where in several fundamental operations:*

1. $\alpha_1 \oplus \alpha_2 = < [s_{\phi_1+\phi_2}, s_{\psi_1+\psi_2}], ((u_1^q + u_2^q - u_1^q u_2^q)^{\frac{1}{q}}, \eta_1\eta_2, v_1 v_2) >$;
2. $\alpha_1 \otimes \alpha_2 = < [s_{\phi_1\phi_2}, s_{\psi_1\psi_2}], (u_1 u_2, (\eta_1^q + \eta_2^q - \eta_1^q\eta_2^q)^{\frac{1}{q}}, (v_1^q + v_2^q - v_1^q v_2^q)^{\frac{1}{q}}) >$;
3. $m\alpha_1 =< [s_{m\phi_1}, s_{m\psi_1}], ((1-(1-u_1^q)^m)^{\frac{1}{q}}, \eta_1^m, v_1^m) >$;
4. $\alpha_1^m =< [s_{\phi_1^m}, s_{\psi_1^m}], (u_1^m, (1-(1-\eta_1^q)^m)^{\frac{1}{q}}, (1-(1-v_1^q)^m)^{\frac{1}{q}}) >$.

By utilizing Definition 8 as a foundation, we can obtain the following rules.

Theorem 1. *Let $\Gamma_1 =< [s_{\phi_1}, s_{\psi_1}], (u_1, \eta_1, v_1) >$ and $\Gamma_2 =< [s_{\phi_2}, s_{\psi_2}], (u_2, \eta_2, v_2) >$ be two q-RPULSs, and $\lambda, \lambda_1, \lambda_2 > 0$; then:*

1. $\Gamma_1 \oplus \Gamma_2 = \Gamma_2 \oplus \Gamma_1$;
2. $\Gamma_1 \otimes \Gamma_2 = \Gamma_2 \otimes \Gamma_1$;
3. $\lambda(\Gamma_1 \oplus \Gamma_2) = \lambda\Gamma_1 \oplus \lambda\Gamma_2$
4. $(\Gamma_1 \otimes \Gamma_2)^\lambda = \Gamma_1^\lambda \otimes \Gamma_2^\lambda$
5. $\lambda_1\Gamma \oplus \lambda_2\Gamma = (\lambda_1 + \lambda_2)\Gamma$
6. $\Gamma^{\lambda_1} \otimes \Gamma^{\lambda_2} = \Gamma^{(\lambda_1+\lambda_2)}$
7. $(\Gamma^{\lambda_1})^{\lambda_2} = \Gamma^{\lambda_1\lambda_2}$

Definition 9. *Consider a q-RPULS denoted as $\Gamma =< [s_\phi, s_\psi], (u, \eta, v) >$. Let us introduce a score function $S(\Gamma)$ and an exact function $A(\Gamma)$ defined with respect to Γ.*

$$S(\Gamma) = \frac{\phi + \psi}{4} \frac{(u^q + 1 - \eta^q - v^q)}{3} \tag{8}$$

$$A(\Gamma) = \frac{\phi + \psi}{2}(u^q + \eta^q + v^q) \tag{9}$$

The comparative law for q-RPULSs is as follows:

Definition 10 ([35]). *Let $\Gamma_1 =< [s_{\phi_1}, s_{\psi_1}], (u_1, \eta_1, v_1) >$ and $\Gamma_2 =< [s_{\phi_2}, s_{\psi_2}], (u_2, \eta_2, v_2) >$ be two q-RPULSs; then:*

- *If $(\Gamma_1) < S(\Gamma_2)$, then $\Gamma_1 < \Gamma_2$;*
- *If $(\Gamma_1) > S(\Gamma_2)$, then $\Gamma_1 > \Gamma_2$;*
- *If $(\Gamma_1) = S(\Gamma_2)$, then*
  1. *If $A(\Gamma_1) < A(\Gamma_2)$, then $\Gamma_1 < \Gamma_2$;*
  2. *If $A(\Gamma_1) > A(\Gamma_2)$, then $\Gamma_1 > \Gamma_2$;*
  3. *If $A(\Gamma_1) = A(\Gamma_2)$, then $\Gamma_1 = \Gamma_2$.*

Definition 11 ([36]). *Let $\Gamma_1 =< [s_{\phi_1}, s_{\psi_1}], (u_1, \eta_1, v_1) >$ and $\Gamma_2 =< [s_{\phi_2}, s_{\psi_2}], (u_2, \eta_2, v_2) >$ be two q-RPULSs, and $q \ge 1$; then, the q-RPUL distance measure between them is defined as:*

$$\begin{aligned} d(\Gamma_1, \Gamma_2) = \frac{1}{4(t-1)} (&|u_1^q\phi_1 - u_2^q\phi_2| + |\eta_1^q\phi_1 - \eta_2^q\phi_2| + |v_1^q\phi_1 - v_2^q\phi_2| + |\pi_1^q\phi_1 - \pi_2^q\phi_2| \\ &+ |u_1^q\psi_1 - u_2^q\psi_2| + |\eta_1^q\psi_1 - \eta_2^q\psi_2| + |v_1^q\psi_1 - v_2^q\psi_2| + |\pi_1^q\psi_1 - \pi_2^q\psi_2|). \end{aligned} \tag{10}$$

Definition 12 ([37,38])**.** *Suppose we have a collection of crisp numbers represented as ζ_i (where i = 1, 2, ..., n), then the $MSM^{(k)}$ operator is the following:*

$$MSM^{(k)} = \left(\frac{\sum_{1\leq i_1<\ldots<i_k\leq n}\prod_{j=1}^{k}\zeta_{i_j}}{C_n^k}\right)^{\frac{1}{k}} \tag{11}$$

In the given context, where k is a parameter with a range of values $1, 2, \ldots, n$, and $i = 1, 2, \ldots, n$, the notation $C_n^k = \frac{n!}{k!(n-k)!}$.

Theorem 2. *The significant features of $MSM^{(k)}$ are as follows:*

1. *Idempotency. If $\sigma_i(i = 1, 2, ..., n) = \sigma$ for all i, then $MSM^{(k)} = (\sigma, \sigma, ..., \sigma) = \sigma$;*
2. *Monotonicity. If $\sigma_i \leq \zeta_i$ for all i, then $MSM^{(k)}(\sigma_1, \sigma_2, ..., \sigma_n) \leq MSM^{(k)}(\zeta_1, \zeta_2, ..., \zeta_n)$;*
3. *Boundedness. $min(\sigma_1, \sigma_2, ..., \sigma_n) \leq MSM^{(k)}(\sigma_1, \sigma_2, ..., \sigma_n) \leq max(\sigma_1, \sigma_2, ..., \sigma_n)$.*

3. The q-Rung Picture Uncertain Linguistic Set Aggregation Operators

3.1. The q-Rung Picture Uncertain Linguistic Set Aggregation Maclaurin Symmetric Mean Operators

We will discuss the development of fuzzy arithmetic aggregation operators using the concept of q-rung picture uncertain linguistic sets in this section. Some examples of these operators include the q-RPULMSM operator and the q-RPULWMSM operator.

Definition 13. *Let $h_l =< [s_{\phi_l}, s_{\varphi_l}], (u_l, \eta_l, v_l) >$ be the set of q-RPULSs, then the q-RPULMSM operator is defined as:*

$$q - RPULMSM^{(k)}(h_1, h_2, ..., h_n) = \left(\frac{\bigoplus_{1\leq l_1<\ldots<l_k\leq n}\bigotimes_{j=1}^{k} h_{l_j}}{C_n^k}\right)^{\frac{1}{k}}. \tag{12}$$

By applying the computational laws of q-RPULN, we can derive the subsequent results for the q-RPULMSM operator:

$$\begin{aligned} q - RPULMSM^{(k)}(h_1, h_2, ..., h_n) =&< [s_{\left(\frac{\sum_{1\leq l_1<\ldots<l_k\leq n}\prod_{j=1}^{k}\phi_{l_j}}{C_n^k}\right)^{\frac{1}{k}}}, s_{\left(\frac{\sum_{1\leq l_1<\ldots<l_k\leq n}\prod_{j=1}^{k}\varphi_{l_j}}{C_n^k}\right)^{\frac{1}{k}}}], \\ &((1 - \prod_{1\leq l_1<\ldots<l_k\leq n}(1 - \prod_{j=1}^{k} u_{l_j}^q)^{\frac{1}{C_n^k}})^{\frac{1}{qk}}, \\ &(1 - (1 - \prod_{1\leq l_1<\ldots<l_k\leq n}(1 - \prod_{j=1}^{k}(1 - \eta_{l_j}^q))^{\frac{1}{C_n^k}})^{\frac{1}{k}})^{\frac{1}{q}}, \\ &(1 - (1 - \prod_{1\leq l_1<\ldots<l_k\leq n}(1 - \prod_{j=1}^{k}(1 - v_{l_j}^q))^{\frac{1}{C_n^k}})^{\frac{1}{k}})^{\frac{1}{q}}). \end{aligned} \tag{13}$$

Proof. Based on the above definition, we can derive

$$\bigotimes_{j=1}^{k} h_{l_j} =< [s_{\prod_{j=1}^{k}\phi_{l_j}}, s_{\prod_{j=1}^{k}\varphi_{l_j}}], (\prod_{j=1}^{k} u_{l_j}, (1 - \prod_{j=1}^{k}(1 - \eta_{l_j}))^{\frac{1}{q}}, (1 - \prod_{j=1}^{k}(1 - v_{l_j}))^{\frac{1}{q}}) > . \tag{14}$$

Furthermore,

$$\bigoplus_{1\leq l_1<\ldots<l_k\leq n}\bigotimes_{j=1}^{k} h_{l_j} =< [s_{(\sum_{1\leq l_1<\ldots<l_k\leq n}\prod_{j=1}^{k}\phi_{l_j})^{\frac{1}{k}}}, s_{(\sum_{1\leq l_1<\ldots<l_k\leq n}\prod_{j=1}^{k}\psi_{l_j})^{\frac{1}{k}}}], \\ ((1-\prod_{1\leq l_1<\ldots<l_k\leq n}(1-\prod_{j=1}^{k}u_{l_j}^{q}))^{\frac{1}{q}}, \\ \prod_{1\leq l_1<\ldots<l_k\leq n}(1-\prod_{j=1}^{k}(1-\eta_{l_j}^{q}))^{\frac{1}{q}}, \\ \prod_{1\leq l_1<\ldots<l_k\leq n}(1-\prod_{j=1}^{k}(1-v_{l_j}^{q}))^{\frac{1}{q}}) > . \tag{15}$$

Thus,

$$\frac{\bigoplus_{1\leq l_1<\ldots<l_k\leq n}\bigotimes_{j=1}^{k} h_{l_j}}{C_n^k} =< [s_{(\frac{\sum_{1\leq l_1<\ldots<l_k\leq n}\prod_{j=1}^{k}\phi_{l_j}}{C_n^k})^{\frac{1}{k}}}, s_{(\frac{\sum_{1\leq l_1<\ldots<l_k\leq n}\prod_{j=1}^{k}\psi_{l_j}}{C_n^k})^{\frac{1}{k}}}], \\ ((1-\prod_{1\leq l_1<\ldots<l_k\leq n}(1-\prod_{j=1}^{k}u_{l_j}^{q})^{\frac{1}{C_n^k}})^{\frac{1}{q}}, \\ (\prod_{1\leq l_1<\ldots<l_k\leq n}(1-\prod_{j=1}^{k}(1-\eta_{l_j}^{q}))^{\frac{1}{C_n^k}})^{\frac{1}{q}}, \\ (\prod_{1\leq l_1<\ldots<l_k\leq n}(1-\prod_{j=1}^{k}(1-v_{l_j}^{q}))^{\frac{1}{C_n^k}})^{\frac{1}{q}}) > . \tag{16}$$

Therefore,

$$q-RPULMSM^{(k)}(h_1,h_2,\ldots,h_n) =< [s_{(\frac{\sum_{1\leq l_1<\ldots<l_k\leq n}\prod_{j=1}^{k}\phi_{l_j}}{C_n^k})^{\frac{1}{k}}}, s_{(\frac{\sum_{1\leq l_1<\ldots<l_k\leq n}\prod_{j=1}^{k}\psi_{l_j}}{C_n^k})^{\frac{1}{k}}}], \\ ((1-\prod_{1\leq l_1<\ldots<l_k\leq n}(1-\prod_{j=1}^{k}u_{l_j}^{q})^{\frac{1}{C_n^k}})^{\frac{1}{qk}}, \\ (1-(1-\prod_{1\leq l_1<\ldots<l_k\leq n}(1-\prod_{j=1}^{k}(1-\eta_{l_j}^{q}))^{\frac{1}{C_n^k}})^{\frac{1}{k}})^{\frac{1}{q}}, \\ (1-(1-\prod_{1\leq l_1<\ldots<l_k\leq n}(1-\prod_{j=1}^{k}(1-v_{l_j}^{q}))^{\frac{1}{C_n^k}})^{\frac{1}{k}})^{\frac{1}{q}}). \tag{17}$$

□

Theorem 3. *This theorem establishes that, if h_l = <$[s_{\phi l}, s_{\psi l}]$, (u_l, η_l, v_l)> (l = 1, 2, ..., n) represents a set of q-RPULNs, then the $q-RPULMSM^{(k)}$ operator possesses the following rules:*

1. *Idempotency. If all $h_l = h =< [s_\phi, s_\psi], (u, \eta, v) >$ are equal for all l, then $q-RPULMSM^{(k)}$ = $(h, h, \ldots, h) = h$.*
2. *Monotonicity. Let $h_l =< [s_{\phi_l}, s_{\psi_l}], (u_l, \eta_l, v_l) >$ and $g_j =< [s_{\phi_j}, s_{\psi_j}], (u_j, \eta_j, v_j) > (l, j = 1, 2, \ldots, n)$ be two sets of q-RPULSs; if $s_{\phi_l} \leq s_{\phi_j}, s_{\psi_l} \geq s_{\psi_j}, u_i \leq u_j, \eta_l \geq \eta_j, v_l \geq v_j$, then $q-RPULMSM^{(k)}(h_1, h_2, \ldots, h_n) \leq q-RPULMSM^{(k)}(g_1, g_2, \ldots, g_n)$.*
3. *Boundedness. Let $h_i =< [s_{\phi_i}, s_{\psi_i}], (u_i, \eta_i, v_i) > (i = 1, 2, \ldots, n)$ be a set of q-RPULNs and $h^+ = ([max(s_{\phi_i}), min(s_{\psi_i})], max(u_i), min(\eta_i), min(v_i))$, $h^- = ([min(s_{\phi_i}), max(s_{\psi_i})], min(u_i), max(\eta_i), max(v_i))$; then, $h^- \leq q-RPULMSM^{(k)}(a_1, a_2, \ldots, a_n) \leq h^+$.*

4. *Permutation Invariance. Let h_i be a permutation of h_i^* for all i; therefore,*
$q - RPULMSM^{(k)}(h_1, h_2, ..., h_n) = q - RPULMSM^{(k)}(h_1^*, h_2^*, ..., h_n^*)$

Proof 1. Let $h_l = h$ for each i; then,

$q - RPULMSM^{(k)}(h_1, h_2, ..., h_n) = (\frac{\bigoplus_{1 \leq l_1 < ... < l_k \leq n} \bigotimes_{j=1}^{k} h_{l_j}}{C_n^k})^{\frac{1}{k}} = (\frac{\bigoplus_{1 \leq l_1 < ... < l_k \leq n} \bigotimes_{j=1}^{k} h}{C_n^k})^{\frac{1}{k}} = (\frac{\bigoplus_{1 \leq l_1 < ... < l_k \leq n} h^k}{C_n^k})^{\frac{1}{k}} = (\frac{\bigoplus_{1 \leq l_1 < ... < l_k \leq n} h}{C_n^k}) = h$

Proof 2. Consider $u_l \leq u_j$; we can obtain $\prod_{m=1}^{k} u_{l_m}^q \leq \prod_{m=1}^{k} u_{j_m}^q$; then, $1 - \prod_{m=1}^{k} u_{l_m}^q \geq 1 - \prod_{m=1}^{k} u_{j_m}^q$; therefore' $1 - \prod_{1 \leq l_1 < ... < l_k \leq n}(1 - \prod_{m=1}^{k} u_{l_m}^q)^{\frac{1}{C_n^k}})^{\frac{1}{qk}} \leq 1 - \prod_{1 \leq l_1 < ... < l_k \leq n}(1 - \prod_{m=1}^{k} u_{j_m}^q)^{\frac{1}{C_n^k}})^{\frac{1}{qk}}$. $\eta_l \geq \eta_j, v_l \geq v_j$ are similar to $u_l \leq u_j$, so we omit them. Therefore, $q - RPULMSM^{(k)}(h_1, h_2, ..., h_n) \leq q - RPULMSM^{(k)}(g_1, g_2, ..., g_n)$

Proof 3. From proof 1, 2, we have
$h^- = q - RPULMSM^{(k)}(h^-, h^-, ..., h^-) \leq q - RPULMSM^{(k)}(h_1, h_2, ..., h_n)$,
$q - RPULMSM^{(k)}(h_1, h_2, ..., h_n) \leq q - RPULMSM^{(k)}(h^+, h^+, ..., h^+)$; *then,*
$h^- \leq q - RPULMSM^{(k)}(h_1, h_2, ..., h_n) \leq h^+$. *Moreover, we will delve into specific instances of the q-RPULMSM operator by considering various parameter values assigned to k and q.*

Case 1: When k = 1, the q-RPULMSM operator simplifies to the q-RPULA operator.

$$
\begin{aligned}
q - RPULMSM^{(k)}(a_1, a_2, ..., a_n) = &< [s_{(\frac{\sum_{1 \leq i_1 < ... < i_k \leq n} \prod_{j=1}^{k} \phi_{i_j}}{n})}, s_{(\frac{\sum_{1 \leq i_1 < ... < i_k \leq n} \prod_{j=1}^{k} \psi_{i_j}}{n})}], \\
&((1 - \prod_{1 \leq i_1 \leq n} (1 - \prod_{j=1}^{1} u_{i_j}^q)^{\frac{1}{C_n^1}})^{\frac{1}{q}}, \\
&(1 - (1 - \prod_{1 \leq i_1 \leq n} (1 - \prod_{j=1}^{1} (1 - \eta_{i_j}^q))^{\frac{1}{C_n^1}})^{\frac{1}{1}})^{\frac{1}{q}}, \\
&(1 - (1 - \prod_{1 \leq i_1 \leq n} (1 - \prod_{j=1}^{1} (1 - v_{i_j}^q))^{\frac{1}{C_n^1}})^{\frac{1}{1}})^{\frac{1}{q}}) > \\
&= q - RPULA(a_1, a_2, ..., a_n).
\end{aligned}
\tag{18}
$$

Case 2: When k = 2, the q-RPULMSM operator transforms into the q-RPULBM operator.

$$
\begin{aligned}
q - RPULMSM^{(k)}(a_1, a_2, \ldots, a_n) &= (\frac{\sum_{1 \leq i_1 < i_2 \leq n} \prod_{j=1}^{2} a_{i_j}}{C_n^2})^{\frac{1}{2}} = (\frac{2 \sum_{1 \leq i_1 < i_2 \leq n} \prod_{j=1}^{2} a_{i_1} a_{i_2}}{n(n-1)})^{\frac{1}{2}} \\
&= (\frac{\sum_{i,j=1, i \neq j} a_{i_1} a_{i_2}}{n(n-1)})^{\frac{1}{2}} = q - RPULBM^{1,1}(a_1, a_2, \ldots, a_n).
\end{aligned}
\tag{19}
$$

Case 3: When q = 1, the q-RPULMSM operator simplifies to the PULMSM operator.

$$
\begin{aligned}
q - RPULMSM^{(k)}(a_1, a_2, ..., a_n) = &< [s_{(\frac{\sum_{1 \leq i_1 < ... < i_k \leq n} \prod_{j=1}^{k} \phi_{i_j}}{C_n^k})^{\frac{1}{k}}}, s_{(\frac{\sum_{1 \leq i_1 < ... < i_k \leq n} \prod_{j=1}^{k} \psi_{i_j}}{C_n^k})^{\frac{1}{k}}}], \\
&((1 - \prod_{1 \leq i_1 < ... < i_k \leq n} (1 - \prod_{j=1}^{k} u_{i_j})^{\frac{1}{C_n^k}})^{\frac{1}{k}}, \\
&(1 - (1 - \prod_{1 \leq i_1 < ... < i_k \leq n} (1 - \prod_{j=1}^{k} (1 - \eta_{i_j}))^{\frac{1}{C_n^k}})^{\frac{1}{k}}), \\
&(1 - (1 - \prod_{1 \leq i_1 < ... < i_k \leq n} (1 - \prod_{j=1}^{k} (1 - v_{i_j}))^{\frac{1}{C_n^k}})^{\frac{1}{k}})) > \\
&= PULMSM^{(k)}(a_1, a_2, ..., a_n).
\end{aligned}
\tag{20}
$$

Case 4: When q = 2, the q-RPULMSM operator can be simplified to the SPULMSM operator.

$$
\begin{aligned}
q - RPULMSM^{(k)}(a_1, a_2, ..., a_n) =&< [s_{(\frac{\sum_{1\le i_1<...<i_k\le n}\prod_{j=1}^{k}\phi_{i_j}}{C_n^k})^{\frac{1}{k}}}, s_{(\frac{\sum_{1\le i_1<...<i_k\le n}\prod_{j=1}^{k}\psi_{i_j}}{C_n^k})^{\frac{1}{k}}}], \\
&((1 - \prod_{1\le i_1<...<i_k\le n}(1 - \prod_{j=1}^{k} u_{i_j}^2)^{\frac{1}{C_n^k}})^{\frac{1}{2k}}, \\
&(1 - (1 - \prod_{1\le i_1<...<i_k\le n}(1 - \prod_{j=1}^{k}(1 - \eta_{i_j}^2))^{\frac{1}{C_n^k}})^{\frac{1}{k}})^{\frac{1}{2}}, \\
&(1 - (1 - \prod_{1\le i_1<...<i_k\le n}(1 - \prod_{j=1}^{k}(1 - v_{i_j}^2))^{\frac{1}{C_n^k}})^{\frac{1}{k}})^{\frac{1}{2}}) > \\
&= SPULMSM^{(k)}(a_1, a_2, ..., a_n).
\end{aligned} \tag{21}
$$

Definition 14. *Let $a_i =< [s_{\phi_i}, s_{\psi_i}], (u_i, \eta_i, v_i) >$ be the set of q-RPULSs; $w = (w_1, w_2, ..., w_n)^T$ is a weight vector and satisfies $w_i \in [0,1]$ and $\sum_{i=1}^{n} = 1, wherek = 1, 2, ..., n$; then, the q-RPULWMSM operator is defined as:*

$$
q - RPULWMSM^{(k)}(a_1, a_2, ..., a_n) = (\frac{\bigoplus_{1\le i_1<...<i_k\le n}\bigotimes_{j=1}^{k} w_{i_j}a_{i_j}}{C_n^k})^{\frac{1}{k}}. \tag{22}
$$

We can deduce the following outcomes for the q-RPULWMSM operator by utilizing the computational laws of q-RPULN:

$$
\begin{aligned}
q - RPFWMSM^{(k)}(a_1, a_2, ..., a_n) =&< [s_{(\frac{\sum_{1\le i_1<...<i_k\le n}\prod_{j=1}^{k} w_{i_j}\phi_{i_j}}{C_n^k})^{\frac{1}{k}}}, s_{(\frac{\sum_{1\le i_1<...<i_k\le n}\prod_{j=1}^{k} w_{i_j}\psi_{i_j}}{C_n^k})^{\frac{1}{k}}}], \\
&((1 - \prod_{1\le i_1<...<i_k\le n}(1 - \prod_{j=1}^{k}(1 - (1 - u_{i_j}^q)^{w_{i_j}}))^{\frac{1}{C_n^k}})^{\frac{1}{qk}}, \\
&(1 - (1 - \prod_{1\le i_1<...<i_k\le n}(1 - \prod_{j=1}^{k}(1 - \eta_{i_j}^{qw_{i_j}}))^{\frac{1}{C_n^k}})^{\frac{1}{k}})^{\frac{1}{q}}, \\
&(1 - (1 - \prod_{1\le i_1<...<i_k\le n}(1 - \prod_{j=1}^{k}(1 - v_{i_j}^{qw_{i_j}}))^{\frac{1}{C_n^k}})^{\frac{1}{k}})^{\frac{1}{q}}) > .
\end{aligned} \tag{23}
$$

Theorem 4. *Let $h_i =< [s_{\phi_i}, s_{\psi_i}], (u_i, \eta_i, v_i) >$ be the set of q-RPULSs; then, the following properties of $q - RPULWMSM^{(k)}$ are obtained:*

1. *Idempotency. If all $h_i = h =< [s_\phi, s_\psi], (u, \eta, v) >$ are equal for all i, then $q - RPULWMSM^{(k)}$ = $(h, h, ..., h) = h$;*
2. *Monotonicity. Let $h_i =< [s_{\phi_i}, s_{\psi_i}], (u_i, \eta_i, v_i) >$ and $g_j =< [s_{\phi_j}, s_{\psi_j}], (u_j, \eta_j, v_j) > (i, j = 1, 2, ..., n)$ be two sets of q-RPULSs; if $s_{\phi_i} \le s_{\phi_j}, s_{\psi_i} \ge s_{\psi_j}, u_i \le u_j, \eta_i \ge \eta_j, v_i \ge v_j$, then $q - RPULWMSM^{(k)}(h_1, h_2, ..., h_n) \le q - RPULWMSM^{(k)}(g_1, g_2, ..., g_n)$;*
3. *Boundedness. Let $h_i =< [s_{\phi_i}, s_{\psi_i}], (u_i, \eta_i, v_i) > (i = 1, 2, ..., n)$ be a set of q-RPULNs and $h^+ = ([max(s_{\phi_i}), min(s_{\psi_i})], max(u_i), min(\eta_i), min(v_i))$, $h^- = ([min(s_{\phi_i}), max(s_{\psi_i})], min(u_i), max(\eta_i), max(v_i))$; then, $h^- \le q - RPULWMSM^{(k)}(a_1, a_2, ..., a_n) \le h^+$.*
4. *Commutativity. Let h_i be a permutation of h_i^* for all i; therefore, $q - RPULWMSM^{(k)}(h_1, h_2, ..., h_n) = q - RPULWMSM^{(k)}(h_1^*, h_2^*, ..., h_n^*)$*

The proof for the q-RPFWMSM theorem follows a similar approach to that of Theorem 3; thus, it has been excluded in this context.

3.2. A Method to Determine the Attribute Weights Based on Entropy

Definition 15. *Let q-RPULSs(X) denote the set of all q-RPULSs in the universe of discourse X. Let* $a_1 =< [s_{\phi_1}, s_{\psi_1}], (u_1, \eta_1, v_1) >$ *and* $a_2 =< [s_{\phi_2}, s_{\psi_2}], (u_2, \eta_2, v_2) >$ *be two q-RPULSs. Here are a few more properties that an entropy function G must satisfy on q-RPULSs:*

1. $G(a_1) = 0$, *if and only if* a_1 *is a crisp set;*
2. $G(a_1) = 1$ *if and only if* $s_{\phi_1} = s_{\psi_1}, u_1 = \eta_1 = v_1$;
3. $G(a_1) \le G(a_2)$, *if and only if* $u_1 \le u_2, \eta_1 \ge \eta_2$ *and* $v_1 \ge v_2$;
4. $G(a_1) = G(a_1^c)$.

Based on the given axiom, we will now introduce a measure of entropy for q-RPULSs. Let $a =< [s_\phi, s_\psi], (u, \eta, v) >$ *be a q-RPULFN; then, the entropy measure of a is defined as*

$$G(a) = 1 - d(a, a^c) \tag{24}$$

where $d(a,a^c)$ *is distance measure.*

Using the entropy measure for q-RPULSs, we propose a novel approach to ascertain the weights of aggregated q-RPULSs. Let $a_i (i = 1, 2, ..., n)$ be a collection of q-RPULSs; then, the weight of a_i is given as

$$\lambda_i = \frac{1 - E(a_i)}{n - \sum_{i=1}^{n} E(a_i)} \tag{25}$$

4. MAGDM Methods Based on q-RPULMSM Operator

This section presents techniques for solving the MAGDM problem using the q-RPULWMSM operator. For MAGDM questions, let $H = H_1, H_2, ..., H_n$ be an attribute collection; $W = w_1, w_2, ..., w_n$ is a vector of weights for attribute $L_j (j = 1, 2, ..., n)$, where $w_j \ge 0, \sum_{j=1}^{n} w_j = 1$. Suppose that $H^e = [a_{ij}^e]_{m\times n}$ is the decision matrix and that the decision maker is required to represent his/her evaluation value using a q-RPULN, which can be expressed as $a_{ij}^e =< [s_{\phi_{ij}^e}, s_{\psi_{ij}^e}], (u_{ij}^e, \eta_{ij}^e, v_{ij}^e) >$. The main steps in using the proposed operator for the MAGDM problem are as follows:

Step 1: To normalize the original decision matrix, we can utilize two attributes: a benefit attribute and a cost attribute. The normalization process follows the steps outlined below:

$$a_{ij}^e =< [s_{\phi_{ij}^e}, s_{\psi_{ij}^e}], (u_{ij}^e, \eta_{ij}^e, v_{ij}^e) >= \begin{Bmatrix} < [s_{\phi_{ij}^e}, s_{\psi_{ij}^e}], (u_{ij}^e, \eta_{ij}^e, v_{ij}^e) >, G_j \in J_1 \\ < [s_{\phi_{ij}^e}, s_{\psi_{ij}^e}], (v_{ij}^e, \eta_{ij}^e, u_{ij}^e) >, G_j \in J_2 \end{Bmatrix} \tag{26}$$

where J_1 and J_2 denote benefit-type attributes and cost-type attributes, respectively.

Step 2: Compute the $\mathrm{Sup}(a_{il}, a_{im})$ by

$$Sup(a_{il}, a_{im}) = 1 - d(a_{il}, a_{im}), \tag{27}$$

where $\mathrm{Sup}(a_{il}, a_{im})$ symbolize support values for a_{il} from $a_{im}, l, m = 1, 2, ..., n; l \ne m$.

Step 3: Compute $Q(a_{ij})$ by

$$Q(a_{ij}) = \sum_{l,m=1, l\ne m}^{n} Sup(a_{il}, a_{im}), \tag{28}$$

Step 4: Compute the weight of $L_j (j = 1, 2, ..., n)$ based on the entropy measure; the result is below:

$$\lambda_i = \frac{1 - G(a_i)}{n - \sum_{i=1}^{n} G(a_i)} \tag{29}$$

Step 5: Compute the power weights w_{ij} using the below method.

$$w_{ij} = \frac{\lambda_i (1 + Q(a_{ij}))}{\sum_{i=1}^{n} \lambda_i (1 + Q(a_{ij}))}, \tag{30}$$

Step 6: Aggregate all attribute values $a_{ij}(j = 1, 2, ..., n)$ using the q-RPULWMSM operator to obtain a composite value a_i.

$$a_i = q - RPULWMSM^{(k)}(a_{i1}, a_{i2}, ..., a_{in}) =< [s_{(\frac{\Sigma_{1\leq i_1<...<i_k\leq n}\Pi_{j=1}^{k} w_{i_j}\phi_{i_j}}{C_n^k})^{\frac{1}{k}}}, s_{(\frac{\Sigma_{1\leq i_1<...<i_k\leq n}\Pi_{j=1}^{k} w_{i_j}\psi_{i_j}}{C_n^k})^{\frac{1}{k}}}],$$
$$((1 - \prod_{1\leq i_1<...<i_k\leq n} (1 - \prod_{j=1}^{k}(1 - (1 - u_{i_j}^{q})^{w_{i_j}}))^{\frac{1}{C_n^k}})^{\frac{1}{qk}},$$
$$(1 - (1 - \prod_{1\leq i_1<...<i_k\leq n} (1 - \prod_{j=1}^{k}(1 - \eta_{i_j}^{qw_{i_j}}))^{\frac{1}{C_n^k}})^{\frac{1}{k}})^{\frac{1}{q}},$$
$$(1 - (1 - \prod_{1\leq i_1<...<i_k\leq n} (1 - \prod_{j=1}^{k}(1 - v_{i_j}^{qw_{i_j}}))^{\frac{1}{C_n^k}})^{\frac{1}{k}})^{\frac{1}{q}}) > . \quad (31)$$

where w is a vector of weights for the attribute.

Step 7: Use the value of the score function $S(a_i)$ calculated in Equation (7).

Step 8: By utilizing the sequence of the overall values to arrange alternatives, select the optimal one.

5. Numerical Example And Comparative Analysis

5.1. Evaluation Steps for the q-RPULWMSM Operator

This example is adopted from He and Zhang [39]. To verify the validity of this method, an example is used for calculation, comparison, and analysis. The annual "618" e-commerce shopping festival is the day of national consumers and the e-commerce platform of the carnival; the major e-commerce platforms launch the most favorable activities of the year. In this context, a college student plans to go to Taobao Mall to buy computers, for example, after the initial screening, but is still indecisive about four computers; respectively, A_1 is an Asus computer, A_2 is a Lenovo computer, A_3 is a Dell computer, and A_4 is an Apple computer. The student developed four selection indicators based on his preferences: C_1 is price; C_2 is range; C_3 is chip processing power; and C_4 is RAM. Each decision maker is asked to evaluate the four items in terms of the four attributes using q-RPULNs. Therefore, the decision matrix $A^e = [a_{ij}^e]_{m\times n}$ follows from Table 2:

Table 2. The q-RPULSs decision matrix.

	C_1	C_2	C_3	C_4
A_1	<[s_5, s_5], (0.5 ,0.4, 0.1)>	<[s_2, s_3], (0.8, 0.1, 0.1)>	<[s_5, s_6], (0.4, 0.3, 0.2)>	<[s_3, s_4], (0.1, 0.8, 0.1)>
A_2	<[s_4, s_5], (0.7, 0.1, 0.1)>	<[s_5, s_5], (0.1, 0.7, 0.2)>	<[s_3, s_4], (0.1, 0.7, 0.2)>	<[s_4, s_4], (0.7, 0.1, 0.1)>
A_3	<[s_3, s_4], (0.8, 0.1, 0.1)>	<[s_4, s_4], (0.1, 0.8, 0.1)>	<[s_4, s_5], (0.1, 0.8, 0.1)>	<[s_4, s_5], (0.6, 0.2, 0.1)>
A_4	<[s_6, s_6], (0.7, 0.1, 0.1)>	<[s_2, s_3], (0.7, 0.2, 0.1)>	<[s_3, s_4], (0.1, 0.7, 0.1)>	<[s_3, s_3], (0.1, 0.8, 0.1)>

Step 1: Since all attributes are benefit attributes, normalization is not required.

Step 2: Calculate the Sup(a_{il}, a_{im}) (l, m = 1, 2, 3, 4; i = 1, 2, 3, 4; $l \neq m$). Let q = 3. Therefore, the result of calculation is as follows.

$$S^{12} = S^{21} = (0.6826, 0.6990, 0.6604, 0.7064);$$
$$S^{13} = S^{31} = (0.8839, 0.7136, 0.6188, 0.5928);$$
$$S^{14} = S^{41} = (0.6297, 0.9584, 0.7794, 0.4954);$$
$$S^{23} = S^{32} = (0.5951, 0.8751, 0.9584, 0.7745);$$
$$S^{24} = S^{42} = (0.7040, 0.6888, 0.6224, 0.7754);$$
$$S^{34} = S^{43} = (0.5591, 0.7550, 0.6214, 0.9026).$$

Step 3: According to Equation (28), calculate $Q(a_{ij})$; the result is below.

$$Q = \begin{bmatrix} 2.1962 & 2.3710 & 2.0586 & 1.7946 \\ 1.9817 & 2.2629 & 2.2412 & 2.2563 \\ 2.0381 & 2.3437 & 2.1986 & 2.2699 \\ 1.8910 & 2.4022 & 2.0232 & 2.1734 \end{bmatrix}$$

Step 4: Calculate the weght of $L_j(j = 1, 2, ..., n)$ based on the entropy measure of q-RPULSs as the following formula:

According to Equation (24), we seek the entropy measure as follows:

$$G(a_{ij}) = \begin{bmatrix} 0.8967 & 0.7871 & 0.9487 & 1.0000 \\ 0.7435 & 0.9942 & 0.9959 & 0.7720 \\ 0.7019 & 1.0000 & 1.0000 & 0.8387 \\ 0.6580 & 0.8575 & 1.0000 & 1.0000 \end{bmatrix}$$

According to Equation (29), calculate the weight based on the entropy measure; the result is the following:

$$\lambda_{ij} = \begin{bmatrix} 0.2811 & 0.5793 & 0.1396 & 0.0000 \\ 0.5188 & 0.0117 & 0.0083 & 0.4612 \\ 0.6489 & 0.0000 & 0.0000 & 0.3511 \\ 0.7059 & 0.2941 & 0.0000 & 0.0000 \end{bmatrix}$$

Step 5: Calculate the power weights w_{ij}, $q = 3$ and $k = 2$; the result is the following:

$$w_{ij} = \begin{bmatrix} 0.2741 & 0.5957 & 0.1302 & 0.0000 \\ 0.4968 & 0.0123 & 0.0086 & 0.4823 \\ 0.6319 & 0.0000 & 0.0000 & 0.3680 \\ 0.6710 & 0.3289 & 0.0000 & 0.0000 \end{bmatrix}$$

Step 6: Aggregate all attribute values $a_{ij}(j = 1, 2, ..., n)$ using Equation (31) to obtain a composite value a_i; the result is the following:

$$a_1 = <[s_{2.5693}, s_{3.1356}], (0.3240, 0.0271, 0.0070)>,$$
$$a_2 = <[s_{2.8837}, s_{3.2217}], (0.2540, 0.0202, 0.0051)>,$$
$$a_3 = <[s_{2.3624}, s_{3.0498}], (0.2610, 0.0000, 0.0000)>,$$
$$a_4 = <[s_{2.3014}, s_{2.8187}], (0.3040, 0.0000, 0.0000)>.$$

Step 7: Use the value of the score function $S(a_i)$ calculated in Equation (8). The result is the following:

$$S(a_1) = 0.4916, S(a_2) = 0.5171, S(a_3) = 0.4590, S(a_4) = 0.4387.$$

Step 8: Rank the four alternative options.

$$A_2 > A_1 > A_3 > A_4.$$

Therefore, Lenovo computers A_2 best fit that college student's choices.

5.2. Comparative Analysis and Discussion

We compare our proposed method with other methods in this section. These methods consist of the TSULWA operator introduced by Wang et al. [36], the T-SFWGMSM operator proposed by Liu et al. [40], and the q-RPFDHM operator presented by He et al. [41]. The comparison results are available in Table 3.

Table 3. Compared with other methods.

Methods	Score Values	Ranking
q-RPULWMSM	$S(a_1) = 0.4916$, $S(a_2) = 0.5171$, $S(a_3) = 0.4590$, $S(a_4) = 0.4387$.	$A_2 > A_1 > A_3 > A_4$
TSULWA [36]	$S(a_1) = 0.4416$, $S(a_2) = 0.4671$, $S(a_3) = 0.4590$, $S(a_4) = 0.4364$.	$A_2 > A_3 > A_1 > A_4$
T-SFWGMSM [40]	$S(a_1) = 0.4334$, $S(a_2) = 0.4571$, $S(a_3) = 0.4532$, $S(a_4) = 0.4236$.	$A_2 > A_3 > A_1 > A_4$
q-RPFDWHM [41]	$S(a_1) = 0.4853$, $S(a_2) = 0.4951$, $S(a_3) = 0.4590$, $S(a_4) = 0.4596$.	$A_2 > A_1 > A_4 > A_3$

By examining the table, we can observe that the most favorable alternative among all the methods is represented by A_2. This outcome serves as evidence to support the validity and practicality of the method introduced. Moreover, the ranking outcomes presented in this study diverge from other methods such as [36,40,41], primarily due to the limitations of these methods. These previous methods only account for the interaction between two parameters and overlook the correlation between multiple parameters. Operators such as q-RPULWMSM have the following characteristics:

- Q-rung picture uncertain linguistic sets (q-RPULSs) incorporate qualitative and quantitative aspects of decision-making, while also utilizing linguistic terms that are easily comprehensible and relatable to people's perception.
- The MSM operator provides a powerful tool to account for the interdependence of multiple input parameters, resulting in the improved accuracy and reliability of evaluation results.
- A novel solution is put forward for the issue of MAGDM with unknown attribute weights.

The parameter q is a key factor in determining the final rankings of alternative goods. To evaluate the influence of the parameter q on the experimental outcomes, we conducted the aforementioned example using different values of q (starting from $k = 2$). The resulting rankings for various q values are depicted in Figure 1.

Figure 1 illustrates that employing the q-RPULWMSM operator yields distinct scores for different q values. However, despite the variability in scores, the final outcome consistently favors alternative A_2. In practical decision-making scenarios, selecting an optimal q value depends on the decision maker's personal preferences and judgment. The q value in the q-RPULWMSM operator allows the decision maker to customize the weighting of attributes and their interactions according to their individual priorities and the specific context of the decision. This flexibility empowers the decision maker to adjust the level of significance assigned to the relationship between attributes and fine-tune the evaluation process to better reflect their preferences and requirements. By having the freedom to choose the q value, the decision maker can tailor the decision model to their unique needs, resulting in more effective and personalized decision outcomes. Through thorough analysis, it is evident that the method introduced in this paper exhibits remarkable adaptability and effectiveness when compared to existing problem-solving approaches.

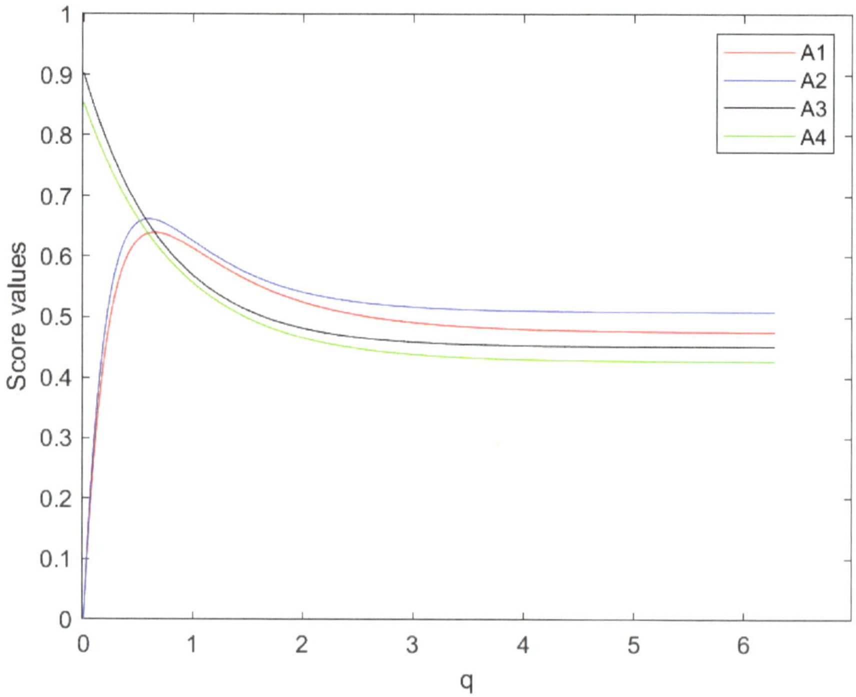

Figure 1. Score values of the alternative when $q \in (0, 6)$ based on the q-RPULWMSM operator.

6. Conclusions

This paper introduces a new approach to address the MAGDM problem. It combines the q-RPULSs method with the MSM operator, resulting in the q-RPULMSM operator. This operator not only considers qualitative and quantitative decision-making but also captures comprehensive information, avoids information loss, and considers the neutrality of the decision maker and the interrelationships among multiple attributes. To handle the issue of unknown attribute weights, the entropy measure is employed. Consequently, we propose a comprehensive approach to solve the MAGDM problem, and provide a numerical example to demonstrate its superiority and accuracy.

While our proposed method has several advantages over existing approaches, it also has limitations. One drawback is its reliance on limited decision-maker data. In real-world scenarios, there may be more attributes involved, requiring the use of multiple methods and metrics for evaluation. Therefore, future research will focus on integrating complex decision-making problems with big data to overcome these limitations.

Author Contributions: Conceptualization, M.S. and Y.G.; methodology, M.S.; validation, M.S. and Y.G.; formal analysis, Y.G.; investigation, M.S.; resources, J.Z.; data curation, M.S.; writing—original draft preparation, M.S.; writing—review and editing, Y.G.; visualization, J.Z.; supervision, Y.G.; project administration, Y.G. All authors have read and agreed to the published version of the manuscript.

Funding: This work is supported in part by Shandong Natural Science Foundation—Joint Fund, ZR2022LZH008, The 20 Planned Projects in Jinan (No. 2021GXRC046).

Institutional Review Board Statement: Not applicable.

Informed Consent Statement: Not applicable.

Data Availability Statement: Not applicable.

Acknowledgments: We would like to thank the editor and anonymous reviewers for their valuable comments and suggestions for improving the paper.

Conflicts of Interest: The authors declare no conflict of interest.

References

1. Mardani, A.; Jusoh, A.; Zavadskas, E.K. Fuzzy multiple criteria decision-making techniques and applications—Two decades review from 1994 to 2014. *Expert Syst. Appl.* **2015**, *42*, 4126–4148. [CrossRef]
2. Khodadadian, A.; Parvizi, M.; Teshnehlab, M.; Heitzinger, C. Rational design of field-effect sensors using partial differential equations, Bayesian inversion, and artificial neural networks. *Sensors* **2022**, *22*, 4785. [CrossRef] [PubMed]
3. Jalaeian Zaferani, E.; Teshnehlab, M.; Khodadadian, A.; Heitzinger, C.; Vali, M.; Noii, N.; Wick, T. Hyper-parameter optimization of stacked asymmetric auto-encoders for automatic personality traits perception. *Sensors* **2022**, *22*, 6206. [CrossRef]
4. Zadeh, L.A. Fuzzy sets. *Inf. Control.* **1965**, *8*, 338–353. [CrossRef]
5. Atanassov, K.T.; Atanassov, K.T. *Intuitionistic Fuzzy Sets*; Springer: Berlin/Heidelberg, Germany, 1999.
6. Yager, R.R. Pythagorean membership grades in multicriteria decision making. *IEEE Trans. Fuzzy Syst.* **2013**, *22*, 958–965. [CrossRef]
7. Zhang, R.; Wang, J.; Zhu, X.; Xia, M.; Yu, M. Some generalized Pythagorean fuzzy Bonferroni mean aggregation operators with their application to multiattribute group decision-making. *Complexity* **2017**, *2017*, 5937376. [CrossRef]
8. Garg, H. New logarithmic operational laws and their aggregation operators for Pythagorean fuzzy set and their applications. *Int. J. Intell. Syst.* **2019**, *34*, 82–106. [CrossRef]
9. Xu, Y.; Shang, X.; Wang, J. Pythagorean fuzzy interaction Muirhead means with their application to multi-attribute group decision-making. *Information* **2018**, *9*, 157. [CrossRef]
10. Yager, R.R. Generalized orthopair fuzzy sets. *IEEE Trans. Fuzzy Syst.* **2016**, *25*, 1222–1230. [CrossRef]
11. Liu, P.; Wang, P. Some q-rung orthopair fuzzy aggregation operators and their applications to multiple-attribute decision making. *Int. J. Intell. Syst.* **2018**, *33*, 259–280. [CrossRef]
12. Liu, P.; Liu, J. Some q-rung orthopai fuzzy Bonferroni mean operators and their application to multi-attribute group decision making. *Int. J. Intell. Syst.* **2018**, *33*, 315–347. [CrossRef]
13. Cuong, B.C.; Kreinovich, V. Picture fuzzy sets-a new concept for computational intelligence problems. In Proceedings of the 2013 Third World Congress on Information and Communication Technologies (WICT 2013), Hanoi, Vietnam, 15–18 December 2013; pp. 1–6.
14. Son, L.H. Dpfcm. *Expert Syst. Appl. Int. J.* **2015**, *42*, 51–66. [CrossRef]
15. Thong, P.H.; Son, L.H. A new approach to multi-variable fuzzy forecasting using picture fuzzy clustering and picture fuzzy rule interpolation method. In Proceedings of the Knowledge and Systems Engineering: Proceedings of the Sixth International Conference KSE 2014, Hanoi, Vietnam, 9–11 October 2014; Springer: Berlin/Heidelberg, Germany, 2015; pp. 679–690.
16. Li, L.; Zhang, R.; Wang, J.; Shang, X.; Bai, K. A novel approach to multi-attribute group decision-making with q-rung picture linguistic information. *Symmetry* **2018**, *10*, 172. [CrossRef]
17. Pinar, A.; Boran, F.E. A novel distance measure on q-rung picture fuzzy sets and its application to decision making and classification problems. *Artif. Intell. Rev.* **2022**, *55*, 1317–1350. [CrossRef]
18. Akram, M.; Khan, A.; Ahmad, U.; Alcantud, J.C.R.; Al-Shamiri, M.M.A. A new group decision-making framework based on 2-tuple linguistic complex *q*-rung picture fuzzy sets. *Math. Biosci. Eng.* **2022**, *19*, 11281–11323. [CrossRef] [PubMed]
19. Mahmood, T.; Ullah, K.; Khan, Q.; Jan, N. An approach toward decision-making and medical diagnosis problems using the concept of spherical fuzzy sets. *Neural Comput. Appl.* **2019**, *31*, 7041–7053. [CrossRef]
20. Singh, S.; Kanwar, N.; Zindani, D. Linear diophantine uncertain linguistic-based prospect theory approach for performance evaluation of islanded microgrid-system scenarios. *Clean Energy* **2023**, *7*, 263–282. [CrossRef]
21. Zhu, Y.J.; Guo, W.; Liu, H.C. Knowledge representation and reasoning with an extended dynamic uncertain causality graph under the Pythagorean uncertain linguistic environment. *Appl. Sci.* **2022**, *12*, 4670. [CrossRef]
22. Bonferroni, C. Sulle medie multiple di potenze. *Boll. Dell'Unione Mat. Ital.* **1950**, *5*, 267–270.
23. Wei, G.; Gao, H.; Wei, Y. Some q-rung orthopair fuzzy Heronian mean operators in multiple attribute decision making. *Int. J. Intell. Syst.* **2018**, *33*, 1426–1458. [CrossRef]
24. Chen, Y.; Liu, P. Multi-attribute decision-making approach based on intuitionistic trapezoidal fuzzy generalized heronian OWA operator. *J. Intell. Fuzzy Syst.* **2014**, *27*, 1381–1392. [CrossRef]
25. Maclaurin, C. A second letter to Martin Folkes, Esq.; concerning the roots of equations, with demonstration of other rules of algebra. *Philos. Trans. R. Soc. Lond. Ser. A* **1729**, *1729*, 59–96.
26. Ateş, F.; Akay, D. Some picture fuzzy Bonferroni mean operators with their application to multicriteria decision making. *Int. J. Intell. Syst.* **2020**, *35*, 625–649. [CrossRef]
27. Gleb, B.; Ana, P.; Tomasa, C. *Aggregation Functions: A Guide for Practitioners*; Springer: Berlin/Heidelberg, Germany, 2010; pp. 139–141.
28. Liu, P.; Liu, Z.; Zhang, X. Some intuitionistic uncertain linguistic Heronian mean operators and their application to group decision making. *Appl. Math. Comput.* **2014**, *230*, 570–586. [CrossRef]

29. Naz, S.; Akram, M.; Al-Shamiri, M.M.A.; Khalaf, M.M.; Yousaf, G. A new MAGDM method with 2-tuple linguistic bipolar fuzzy Heronian mean operators. *Math. Biosci. Eng.* **2022**, *19*, 3843–3878. [CrossRef] [PubMed]
30. DeTemple, D.W.; Robertson, J.M. *On Generalized Symmetric Means of Two Variables*; Serija Matematika i Fizika; Publikacije Elektrotehničkog Fakulteta: New York, NY, USA, 1979; pp. 236–238.
31. Liu, P.; Chen, S.M.; Wang, Y. Multiattribute group decision making based on intuitionistic fuzzy partitioned Maclaurin symmetric mean operators. *Inf. Sci.* **2020**, *512*, 830–854. [CrossRef]
32. Cuong, B.C.; Kreinovich, V. Picture fuzzy sets. *J. Comput. Sci. Cybern.* **2014**, *30*, 409–420.
33. Herrera, F.; Herrera-Viedma, E. Linguistic decision analysis: Steps for solving decision problems under linguistic information. *Fuzzy Sets Syst.* **2000**, *115*, 67–82. [CrossRef]
34. Yang, Z.; Garg, H. Interaction power partitioned maclaurin symmetric mean operators under q-rung orthopair uncertain linguistic information. *Int. J. Fuzzy Syst.* **2022**, *24*, 1079–1097. [CrossRef]
35. Wang, J.; Zhang, R.; Li, L.; Zhu, X.; Shang, X. A novel approach to multi-attribute group decision making based on q-rung orthopair uncertain linguistic information. *J. Intell. Fuzzy Syst.* **2019**, *36*, 5565–5581. [CrossRef]
36. Wang, H.; Ullah, K. T-spherical uncertain linguistic MARCOS method based on generalized distance and Heronian mean for multi-attribute group decision-making with unknown weight information. *Complex Intell. Syst.* **2023**, *9*, 1837–1869. [CrossRef]
37. Wang, J.q.; Yang, Y.; Li, L. Multi-criteria decision-making method based on single-valued neutrosophic linguistic Maclaurin symmetric mean operators. *Neural Comput. Appl.* **2018**, *30*, 1529–1547. [CrossRef]
38. Wei, G.; Wei, C.; Wang, J.; Gao, H.; Wei, Y. Some q-rung orthopair fuzzy maclaurin symmetric mean operators and their applications to potential evaluation of emerging technology commercialization. *Int. J. Intell. Syst.* **2019**, *34*, 50–81. [CrossRef]
39. Akram, M.; Shahzadi, G.; Alcantud, J.C.R. Multi-attribute decision-making with q-rung picture fuzzy information. In *Granular Computing*; Springer: Berlin/Heidelberg, Germany, 2022; pp. 1–19.
40. Liu, P.; Zhu, B.; Wang, P. A multi-attribute decision-making approach based on spherical fuzzy sets for Yunnan Baiyao's R&D project selection problem. *Int. J. Fuzzy Syst.* **2019**, *21*, 2168–2191.
41. He, J.; Wang, X.; Zhang, R.; Li, L. Some q-rung picture fuzzy Dombi Hamy Mean operators with their application to project assessment. *Mathematics* **2019**, *7*, 468. [CrossRef]

symmetry

MDPI

Article

Special Discrete Fuzzy Numbers on Countable Sets and Their Applications

Na Qin [1,2] and Zengtai Gong [2,*]

1 College of Computer Science and Engineering, Northwest Normal University, Lanzhou 730070, China; qinna@nwnu.edu.cn
2 College of Mathematics and Statistics, Northwest Normal University, Lanzhou 730070, China
* Correspondence: gongzt@nwnu.edu.cn

Abstract: There are some drawbacks to arithmetic and logic operations of general discrete fuzzy numbers, which limit their application. For example, the result of the addition operation of general discrete fuzzy numbers defined by the Zadeh's extension principle may not satisfy the condition of becoming a discrete fuzzy number. In order to solve these problems, special discrete fuzzy numbers on countable sets are investigated in this paper. Since the representation theorem of fuzzy numbers is the basic tool of fuzzy analysis, two kinds of representation theorems of special discrete fuzzy numbers on countable sets are studied first. Then, the metrics of special discrete fuzzy numbers on countable sets are defined, and the relationship between these metrics and the uniform Hausdorff metric (i.e., supremum metric) of general fuzzy numbers is discussed. In addition, the triangular norm and triangular conorm operations (t-norm and t-conorm for short) of special discrete fuzzy numbers on countable sets are presented, and the properties of these two operators are proven. We also prove that these two operators satisfy the basic conditions for closure of operation and present some examples. Finally, the applications of special discrete fuzzy numbers on countable sets in image fusion and aggregation of subjective evaluation are proposed.

Keywords: discrete fuzzy number; countable set; aggregation; image fusion; subjective evaluation

Citation: Qin, N.; Gong, Z. Special Discrete Fuzzy Numbers on Countable Sets and Their Applications. *Symmetry* **2024**, *16*, 264. https://doi.org/10.3390/sym16030264

Academic Editor: László T. Kóczy

Received: 19 January 2024
Revised: 17 February 2024
Accepted: 18 February 2024
Published: 21 February 2024

1. Introduction

Parameter uncertainty is often involved in the process of information system representation and modeling and is usually described as a fuzzy number [1]. The general fuzzy numbers are triangular, trapezoidal, and Gaussian fuzzy numbers, etc. The most commonly used fuzzy number in engineering applications is the symmetrical triangular fuzzy number. The theoretical and mathematical modeling process of continuous fuzzy numbers and symmetric fuzzy numbers have been investigated extensively. As a powerful tool to characterize and process discrete uncertain information, discrete fuzzy numbers [2] have important theoretical value and a strong application background in fuzzy information processing [3], image interpretation [4], multiple-attribute group decision making [5,6], fuzzy transformation, and inversion.

In 2001, William Voxman [2] first put forward the discrete fuzzy numbers and constructed two kinds of canonical representations of general discrete fuzzy numbers. In 2005, the level set representation theorem of discrete fuzzy numbers was proven by Wang Guixiang et al. [7]. On this basis, the addition and multiplication operations of discrete fuzzy number space were defined. Using similar methods, Casasnovas and Riera [8,9] researched the problem of the maximum and minimum values of discrete fuzzy numbers and studied the triangular norms and triangular conorms to discrete fuzzy numbers in 2011. In the same year, Riera and Torrens [10] defined fuzzy implication functions on sets of discrete fuzzy numbers. Using the above operations, Riera and Torrens [11] defined an integration operator for discrete fuzzy numbers in 2012. Furthermore, Riera and Torrens investigated the coimplications [12] and residual implications [13] of discrete fuzzy number space. The two scholars further defined a pair of discrete aggregation functions on discrete fuzzy numbers sets and applied them to language decision models [14]. In 2015, Riera et al. [15,16] presented a fuzzy decision model and used discrete fuzzy numbers to model complete and incomplete qualitative information; then, they gave an aggregation method for this information.

In recent years, many achievements have been made in the theoretical and application research of discrete fuzzy numbers. In 2019, Zhao Meng et al. [17] proposed a sort method based on shape similarity, which used symbolic representation to construct the shape of discrete fuzzy membership function and describe the subjective language preference evaluation of experts. Ma Xiaoyu et al. [18] presented a semantic computing model based on discrete fuzzy numbers and measured the group decision results based on the model in order to reach a consensus. In 2021, Gong Zengtai et al. [4] defined the concept of the three-dimensional generalized discrete fuzzy number (3-GDFN) and the similarity of 3-GDFNs, which were applied to color image interpretation and color mathematical morphology. Riera et al. [19] discussed the application of an admissible order of discrete fuzzy number sets in decision problems in the same year. A new denoising method for color images based on three-dimensional discrete fuzzy number was proposed by Qin Na and Gong Zengtai [20] in 2023.

However, the general discrete fuzzy numbers have defects in arithmetic operations and logical operations, such as the addition and multiplication operations defined by the Zadeh's extension principle [21] as the membership function of discrete fuzzy numbers may not satisfy the closure. The difference operation and the measurement of discrete fuzzy numbers especially cannot be reasonably defined, which limits the application of discrete fuzzy numbers in some aspects.

In order to solve these problems, scholars have proposed extended addition and multiplication operations that maintain the closure of discrete fuzzy numbers sets. The discrete fuzzy numbers whose support set was an arithmetic sequence on the set of natural numbers were defined in [22,23]. A closed-keeping addition operation for general discrete fuzzy numbers was presented in [7]. Then, the concepts of generalized discrete fuzzy numbers [24] and fuzzy integers [25] were proposed. In 2008, Wang Guixiang et al. [26] defined a discrete fuzzy number on a fixed set whose support set was a countable set. When the addition and subtraction operations on this countable set remained closed, the corresponding addition and subtraction operations on discrete fuzzy number spaces were also closed. Based on the definition of a special discrete fuzzy number proposed in [26], the related conceptions and application of special discrete fuzzy numbers on countable sets are researched in this article. The main contributions of this article are as follows:

1. The endpoints function representation theorem of special discrete fuzzy numbers on countable sets is proven.
2. Two metrics of special discrete fuzzy numbers on countable sets are defined and compared.
3. The definitions and properties of t-norm operator and t-conorm operator of special discrete fuzzy numbers on countable sets are proposed and proven. In addition, these two operators are used in the practical application of image fusion and subjective evaluation.

The rest of the article is organized as follows: In Section 2, we review some basic concepts about discrete fuzzy numbers. In Section 3, the definition and representation theorem of the special discrete fuzzy numbers on countable sets are investigated and proven. In Section 4, we research the metrics of special discrete fuzzy numbers on countable sets and compare them with the uniform Hausdorff metric of general fuzzy numbers. The definitions of the t-norm operator and t-conorm operator of special discrete fuzzy numbers on countable sets are presented in Section 5. In Section 6, the pixel values of gray-scale images are represented by special discrete fuzzy numbers on countable sets. Furthermore, the application of the t-norm operator and t-conorm operator defined in Section 5 in gray image fusion is presented. The application of special discrete fuzzy numbers on countable sets in aggregation of subjective evaluation is proposed in Section 7. Finally, the conclusions are described in Section 8.

2. Preliminaries

The conception and theorem related to discrete fuzzy numbers are briefly introduced in this section. Firstly, the definition of fuzzy set [21] is given.

Let $\mathbb{R}$ be the Euclidean space; a fuzzy set of $\mathbb{R}$ is a mapping $u : \mathbb{R} \to [0,1]$. Let $[u]^r = \{x \in \mathbb{R} : u(x) \geq r\}$ for any $r \in (0,1]$ be its r-level set. With the notation supp u, we denote the support of u, i.e., supp $u = \{x \in \mathbb{R} : u(x) > 0\}$. In addition, we denote the closure of supp u with $[u]^0$, i.e., $[u]^0 = \overline{\{x \in \mathbb{R} : u(x) > 0\}}$.

As a generalization of the concepts of real numbers and interval numbers, the discrete fuzzy numbers are special fuzzy sets that satisfy certain conditions.

Definition 1 ([2]). *A fuzzy set $u : \mathbb{R} \to [0,1]$ is called a discrete fuzzy number if the support of u is finite, i.e., there exist $x_1, x_2, \ldots, x_n \in \mathbb{R}$ with $x_1 < x_2 < \cdots < x_n$ such that $[u]^0 = \{x_1, x_2, \ldots, x_n\}$, and there exist the natural numbers s, t with $1 \leq s \leq t \leq n$ such that*

(1) $u(x_i) = 1$ *for any natural number i with $s \leq i \leq t$;*
(2) $u(x_i) \leq u(x_j)$ *for any natural numbers i, j with $1 \leq i \leq j \leq s$;*
(3) $u(x_i) \geq u(x_j)$ *for any natural numbers i, j with $t \leq i \leq j \leq n$.*

We denote the collection of all discrete fuzzy numbers with $\mathcal{F}_\mathcal{D}$.

Remark 1. *If the fuzzy set u is a discrete fuzzy number, then the support of u coincides with its closure, i.e., supp $u = [u]^0$.*

The representation theorem of discrete fuzzy numbers is an important tool for the theoretical study of fuzzy analysis.

Theorem 1 ([7]). *Let $u \in \mathcal{F}_\mathcal{D}$. Then, the following statements (1)–(4) hold:*

(1) *$[u]^r$ is a nonempty finite subset of $\mathbb{R}$ for any $r \in [0,1]$;*
(2) *$[u]^{r_2} \subset [u]^{r_1}$ for any $r_1, r_2 \in [0,1]$ with $r_1 \leq r_2$;*
(3) *For any $r_1, r_2 \in [0,1]$ with $0 \leq r_1 \leq r_2 \leq 1$, if $x \in [u]^{r_1} \setminus [u]^{r_2}$, we have $x < y$ for all $y \in [u]^{r_2}$, or $x > y$ for all $y \in [u]^{r_2}$;*
(4) *For any $r_0 \in (0,1]$, there exists a real number r_0' with $0 < r_0' < r_0$ such that $[u]^{r_0'} = [u]^{r_0}$ (i.e., $[u]^r = [u]^{r_0}$ for any $r \in [r_0', r_0]$).*

Conversely, if for any $r \in [0,1]$ there exists $A_r \subset \mathbb{R}$, satisfying the following conditions (i)–(iv):

(i) *A_r is nonempty and finite for any $r \in [0,1]$;*
(ii) *$A_{r_2} \subset A_{r_1}$ for any $r_1, r_2 \in [0,1]$ with $r_1 \leq r_2$;*
(iii) *For any $r_1, r_2 \in [0,1]$ with $0 \leq r_1 \leq r_2 \leq 1$, if $x \in A_{r_1} \setminus A_{r_2}$, then $x < y$ for all $y \in A_{r_2}$, or $x > y$ for all $y \in A_{r_2}$;*
(iv) *For any $r_0 \in (0,1]$, there exists a real number r_0' with $0 < r_0' < r_0$ such that $A_{r_0'} = A_{r_0}$ (i.e., $A_r = A_{r_0}$ for any $r \in [r_0', r_0]$),*

then, there exists a unique $u \in \mathcal{F}_\mathcal{D}$ such that $[u]^r = A_r$ for any $r \in [0,1]$.

Establishing proper measurement on discrete fuzzy number space $\mathcal{F}_\mathcal{D}$ is the basic starting point of using fuzzy mathematics theory to analyze and deal with practical problems. The definition of the supremum metric on $\mathcal{F}_\mathcal{D}$ space is proposed.

Definition 2. *Let $u, v \in \mathcal{F}_\mathcal{D}$, for any $r \in [0,1]$, the mapping $D : \mathcal{F}_\mathcal{D} \times \mathcal{F}_\mathcal{D} \to [0, +\infty)$ is defined as follow:*

$$D(u,v) = \sup_{r \in [0,1]} \max\{| \underline{u}(r) - \underline{v}(r) |, | \overline{u}(r) - \overline{v}(r) |\}. \quad (1)$$

Obviously, $(\mathcal{F}_{\mathcal{D}}, D)$ is a metric space with respect to this supremum metric D.

3. Special Discrete Fuzzy Numbers on Countable Sets

In 2008, the conception of discrete fuzzy numbers with finite support sets on fixed sets was proposed by Wang Guixiang et al. [26]. The following definitions and discussion in this paper are carried out on the countable subset C of the real number field R.

Definition 3 ([26]). *Let C be a countable subset of real number field R. If a fuzzy set $u : R \to [0,1]$ satisfies the following conditions:*

(1) $[u]^0 \subset C$ *and* $[u]^0$ *is finite;*
(2) *There exists* $x_0 \in C$ *such that* $u(x_0) = 1$;
(3) *For any* $x_s, x_t \in C$ *with* $x_s \leq x_t \leq x_0$, $u(x_s) \leq u(x_t)$ *is tenable;*
(4) *For any* $x_s, x_t \in C$ *with* $x_0 \leq x_s \leq x_t$, $u(x_s) \geq u(x_t)$ *is tenable.*

Then, u is a discrete fuzzy number on C, and we denote the collection of all discrete fuzzy numbers with $\mathcal{F}_{\mathcal{D}C}$. Obviously, $\mathcal{F}_{\mathcal{D}C} \subset \mathcal{F}_{\mathcal{D}}$.

Let C be a countable subset of real number field R; for any $x', y' \in R$ with $x' \leq y'$, we denote

$$[x', y']_C = \{z \in C : x' \leq z \leq y'\}.$$

The representation theorem of fuzzy numbers plays an important role in the basic theory of fuzzy analysis. In order to study the operation of discrete fuzzy numbers, the level sets representation theorem of discrete fuzzy numbers on a countable set C is presented in [26].

Theorem 2 ([26]). *Let C be a countable subset of real number field R and $u \in \mathcal{F}_{\mathcal{D}C}$. Then,*

(1) *For any* $r \in [0,1]$, *there exist* $x_r, y_r \in C$ *with* $x_r \leq y_r$, *such that* $[u]^r = [x_r, y_r]_C$, *and* $[x_0, y_0]_C$ *is finite;*
(2) *For any* $r_1, r_2 \in [0,1]$ *with* $0 \leq r_1 \leq r_2 \leq 1$, $[u]^{r_2} \subset [u]^{r_1}$ *is tenable;*
(3) *For any* $r_0 \in (0,1]$, *there exists a real number* r_0' *with* $0 < r_0' < r_0$, *such that* $[u]^{r_0'} = [u]^{r_0}$, *i.e., for any* $r \in [r_0', r_0]$, $[u]^r = [u]^{r_0}$ *is tenable.*

Conversely, if for any $r \in [0,1]$, there exists $A_r \subset R$ satisfying

(i) *There exist* $x_r, y_r \in C$ *with* $x_r \leq y_r$, *such that* $A_r = [x_r, y_r]_C$ *and* $[x_0, y_0]_C$ *is finite;*
(ii) *For any* $r_1, r_2 \in [0,1]$ *with* $0 \leq r_1 \leq r_2 \leq 1$, $A_{r_2} \subset A_{r_1}$ *is tenable;*
(iii) *For any* $r_0 \in (0,1]$, *there exists a real number* r_0' *with* $0 < r_0' < r_0$, *such that* $A_{r_0'} = A_{r_0}$, *i.e., for any* $r \in [r_0', r_0]$, $A_r = A_{r_0}$ *is tenable.*

Then, there exists a unique $u \in \mathcal{F}_{\mathcal{D}C}$ such that $[u]^r = A_r$ for any $r \in [0,1]$.

By means of Theorem 2, a discrete fuzzy number on countable sets can be regarded as a family of nonempty closed intervals satisfying some specific conditions. Next, let us prove the endpoints function representation theorem of special discrete fuzzy numbers on the countable set C. For any $u \in \mathcal{F}_{\mathcal{D}C}$, u can be represented by two real-valued functions on the interval [0,1] that satisfy certain conditions. We denote $\underline{u}(r) = \min[u]^r$ and $\overline{u}(r) = \max[u]^r$; then, $\underline{u}(r)$ and $\overline{u}(r)$ have the following properties:

Theorem 3. *If $u \in \mathcal{F}_{\mathcal{D}C}$, then $\underline{u}(r)$ and $\overline{u}(r)$ are two functions on $[0,1]$, and they satisfy the following conditions:*

(1) $\underline{u}(r)$ *is monotone nondecreasing left continuous;*
(2) $\overline{u}(r)$ *is monotone nonincreasing left continuous;*
(3) $\underline{u}(r) \leq \overline{u}(r)$ *for all* $r \in [0,1]$;
(4) $\underline{u}(r)$ *and* $\overline{u}(r)$ *are right continuous at* $r = 0$.

Conversely, if for any $r \in [0,1]$, $X(r)$ and $Y(r)$ are two functions on $[0,1]$, and they satisfy the following conditions:

(i) $X(r)$ *is monotone nondecreasing left continuous;*
(ii) $Y(r)$ *is monotone nonincreasing left continuous;*
(iii) $X(r) \leq Y(r)$ *for all* $r \in [0,1]$;
(iv) $X(r)$ *and* $Y(r)$ *are right continuous at* $r = 0$.

Then, there exists a unique $u \in \mathcal{F}_{DC}$ *such that* $\underline{u}(r) = X(r), \overline{u}(r) = Y(r)$ *for any* $r \in [0,1]$.

Proof. At first, we prove that $u \in \mathcal{F}_{DC}$ implies conditions (1)–(4) of this theorem.

Because $u \in \mathcal{F}_{DC}$, let $[u]^0 = \{x_1, x_2, \cdots, x_n\} \subset C, x_1 < x_2 < \cdots < x_n$, there exists $1 \leq k \leq n$ such that $u(x_k) = 1$. When $1 \leq i \leq j \leq k$, $u(x_i) \leq u(x_j)$ is tenable, when $k \leq i \leq j \leq n$, $u(x_i) \geq u(x_j)$ is tenable.

From the definitions of $\underline{u}(r)$ and $\overline{u}(r)$, the $\underline{u}(r)$ and $\overline{u}(r)$ can only be taken on $[u]^0$, and the set $[u]^0$ is finite, so $\underline{u}(r)$ and $\overline{u}(r)$ are the functions on $[0,1]$.

Let $r_1, r_2 \in [0,1]$ and $r_1 < r_2$. From Theorem 2 of the discrete fuzzy numbers on countable sets, $[u]^{r_1} \supset [u]^{r_2}$ is tenable, so we have $\underline{u}(r_1) = \min[u]^{r_1} \leq \min[u]^{r_2} = \underline{u}(r_2)$ and $\overline{u}(r_1) = \max[u]^{r_1} \geq \max[u]^{r_2} = \overline{u}(r_2)$; then, $\underline{u}(r)$ is a monotone nondecreasing function and $\overline{u}(r)$ is a monotone nonincreasing function. Next, we prove that $\underline{u}(r)$ and $\overline{u}(r)$ are left continuous.

We denote $A_i = u(x_i), i = 1, 2, \cdots, k$ for any $r_0 \in (0,1]$, if $r_0 \leq A_1$, and because $\underline{u}(r) = \min[u]^r$, we know that when $r \in [0, r_0]$, $\underline{u}(r) = A_1$ holds. Therefore, $\underline{u}(r)$ is left continuous at r_0. If $r_0 > A_1$, then $\{A_i \geq r_0 : i = 1, 2, \cdots, k\}$, and $\{A_i < r_0 : i = 1, 2, \cdots, k\}$ are nonempty, so we set $a = \min\{A_i \geq r_0 : i = 1, 2, \cdots, k\}, b = \max\{A_i < r_0 : i = 1, 2, \cdots, k\}$. Obviously, there exists $b < r_0 \leq a$. Then, from $\underline{u}(r) = \min[u]^r$, when $r \in (b, r_0]$, $\underline{u}(r) = a$ holds; therefore, $\underline{u}(r)$ is left continuous at r_0.

We denote $B_i = u(x_i), i = k, k+1, \cdots, n$ for any $r_0 \in (0,1]$, if $r_0 \leq B_n$, and because $\overline{u}(r) = \max[u]^r$, we know that when $r \in [0, r_0]$, $\overline{u}(r) = B_n$ holds. Therefore, $\overline{u}(r)$ is left continuous at r_0. If $r_0 > B_n$, then $\{B_i \geq r_0 : i = 1, 2, \cdots, k\}$ and $\{B_i < r_0 : i = 1, 2, \cdots, k\}$ are nonempty. So, we set $c = \min\{B_i \geq r_0 : i = k, k+1, \cdots, n\}, d = \max\{B_i < r_0 : i = k, k+1, \cdots, n\}$. Obviously, there exists $d < r_0 \leq c$. Then, from $\overline{u}(r) = \max[u]^r$, when $r \in (d, r_0]$, $\overline{u}(r) = c$ holds; therefore, $\overline{u}(r)$ is left continuous at r_0.

For any $r \in [0,1]$, $\underline{u}(r) \leq \underline{u}(1) = \min[u]^1 \leq \max[u]^1 = \overline{u}(1) \leq \overline{u}(r)$; then, $\underline{u}(r) \leq \overline{u}(r)$ is tenable.

Then, because $\underline{u}(r) = A_1$ is tenable when $r \in [0, A_1]$, therefore $\underline{u}(r)$ is right continuous at $r = 0$. Because $\overline{u}(r) = B_n$ is tenable when $r \in [0, B_n]$, therefore $\overline{u}(r)$ is right continuous at $r = 0$.

The proof of the first part of this theorem is completed. Secondly, we prove the next part of the theorem.

Let $M_r = \{X(h) : r \leq h \leq 1\} \bigcup \{Y(h) : r \leq h \leq 1\}$ for any $r \in [0,1]$. Because $X(r)$ and $Y(r)$ are two functions on $[0,1]$, M_r is nonempty and finite for any $r \in [0,1]$. So, M_r satisfies condition (i) of Theorem 2. According to the definition of M_r, it also satisfies condition (ii) of Theorem 2.

Next, we prove that M_r satisfies condition (iii) of Theorem 2.

Let $r_0 \in (0,1]$. Because $X(r)$ is a function on $[0,1]$ and left continuous, there exists $r_0' \in (0, r_0)$ such that when $r \in [r_0', r_0]$, $X(r) = X(r_0)$ is tenable. Similarly, $Y(r)$ is a function on $[0,1]$ and left continuous, so there exists $r_0'' \in (0, r_0)$ such that when $r \in [r_0'', r_0]$, $Y(r) = Y(r_0)$ is tenable.

Let $h_0 = \min(r_0', r_0'')$, when $r \in [h_0, r_0]$, we have $X(r) = X(r_0)$ and $Y(r) = Y(r_0)$. So, when $r \in [h_0, r_0]$,

$$\begin{aligned} M_r &= \{X(h) : r \leq h \leq 1\} \bigcup \{Y(h) : r \leq h \leq 1\} \\ &= \{X(h) : r_0 \leq h \leq 1\} \bigcup \{Y(h) : r_0 \leq h \leq 1\} \\ &= M_{r_0}, \end{aligned}$$

then, M_r satisfies condition (iii) of the Theorem 2.

According to the Theorem 2, there is a unique $u \in \mathcal{F}_{\mathcal{D}C}$ such that $[u]^r = M_r$ is tenable for any $r \in [0,1]$, i.e.,

$$\begin{aligned} \underline{u}(r) &= \min[u]^r = \min M_r \\ &= \min(\{X(h) : r \leq h \leq 1\} \bigcup \{Y(h) : r \leq h \leq 1\}) \\ &= \min(\{X(h) : r \leq h \leq 1\}) \\ &= X(r), \end{aligned}$$

$$\begin{aligned} \overline{u}(r) &= \max[u]^r = \max M_r \\ &= \max(\{X(h) : r \leq h \leq 1\} \bigcup \{Y(h) : r \leq h \leq 1\}) \\ &= \max(\{Y(h) : r \leq h \leq 1\}) \\ &= Y(r). \end{aligned}$$

We completed the proof of this theorem. □

According to the level set representation theorem of the general discrete fuzzy numbers in [7] and the Theorem 2 of the discrete fuzzy numbers on countable sets, the following theorem can be obtained directly.

Theorem 4 ([26])**.** *Let C be a countable subset of real number field R, and $u, v \in \mathcal{F}_{\mathcal{D}C}$, $k \in R$. Then, for any $r \in [0,1]$,*

(1) $[u+v]^r = [u]^r + [v]^r$;
(2) $[ku]^r = k[u]^r$;
(3) $[uv]^r = [u]^r[v]^r$.

The conditions of closure operations on $\mathcal{F}_{\mathcal{D}C}$ space are proven in Theorem 5; these conditions cannot be omitted, and the corresponding example can be found in Example 3.1 and Remark 3.2 of [26].

Theorem 5 ([26])**.** *Let C be a countable subset of real number field R. If $u, v \in \mathcal{F}_{\mathcal{D}C}, k \in R$, then*

(1) $ku \in \mathcal{F}_{\mathcal{D}C}$ *if C satisfies $kx \in C$ for any $x \in C$;*
(2) $u + v \in \mathcal{F}_{\mathcal{D}C}$ *if C preserves the closeness of the operations of addition and difference.*

4. Metrics of Special Discrete Fuzzy Numbers on Countable Sets

Fuzzy numbers play an important role in applications in the fields of approximate reasoning, fuzzy control, and fuzzy decision [6]. In order to solve problems in practical application, it is necessary to research the properties of measurement in fuzzy number space and analyze the relationship between various measurements. Likewise, the measurement in fuzzy number space is also an important part of fuzzy analysis theory. In order to develop and perfect the theory of fuzzy analysis, the measurement of special discrete fuzzy numbers on countable sets is investigated in this section.

Because $(\mathcal{F}_{\mathcal{D}}, D)$ is a metric space and $\mathcal{F}_{\mathcal{D}C} \subset \mathcal{F}_{\mathcal{D}}$, D is also a metric on $\mathcal{F}_{\mathcal{D}C}$ space. Considering the particularity of $\mathcal{F}_{\mathcal{D}C}$ space and the investigation on this space-related theories and applications, two other definitions of metric on $\mathcal{F}_{\mathcal{D}C}$ space are proposed.

Definition 4. *Let the mapping $\dot{D} : \mathcal{F}_{\mathcal{D}C} \times \mathcal{F}_{\mathcal{D}C} \to [0, +\infty)$ be defined as follows:*
if $[u]^0 = [v]^0$, then

$$\begin{aligned} \dot{D} : \mathcal{F}_{\mathcal{D}C} \times \mathcal{F}_{\mathcal{D}C} &\to [0, +\infty) \\ (u, v) &\to \dot{D}(u, v) = \sup_{x \in C} \mid u(x) - v(x) \mid . \end{aligned} \quad (2)$$

Definition 5. *Let the mapping $\hat{D} : \mathcal{F}_{\mathcal{D}C} \times \mathcal{F}_{\mathcal{D}C} \to [0, +\infty)$ be defined as follows:*

$$\begin{aligned} \hat{D} : \mathcal{F}_{\mathcal{D}C} \times \mathcal{F}_{\mathcal{D}C} &\to [0, +\infty) \\ (u, v) &\to \hat{D}(u, v) = \sup_{r \in [0,1]} \left(\frac{| \underline{u}(r) - \underline{v}(r) | + | \overline{u}(r) - \overline{v}(r) |}{2} \right). \end{aligned} \tag{3}$$

Next, the basic properties of the two metrics defined in Definitions 4 and 5 are proven.

Theorem 6. *For any $u, v, w \in \mathcal{F}_{\mathcal{D}C}$, $k \in R$, then $\dot{D}$ and $\hat{D}$ satisfy:*

(1) $\dot{D}(u, v) = \dot{D}(v, u), \hat{D}(u, v) = \hat{D}(v, u)$;
(2) $\dot{D}(u, v) \geq 0, \hat{D}(u, v) \geq 0$;
(3) $\dot{D}(u, v) = 0 \Leftrightarrow u = v, \hat{D}(u, v) = 0 \Leftrightarrow u = v$;
(4) $\dot{D}(u, v) \leq \dot{D}(u, w) + \dot{D}(w, v)$, $\hat{D}(u, v) \leq \hat{D}(u, w) + \hat{D}(w, v)$;
(5) $\dot{D}(u + w, v + w) = \dot{D}(u, v), \hat{D}(u + w, v + w) = \hat{D}(u, v)$;
(6) $\dot{D}(ku, kv) = |k|\dot{D}(u, v), \hat{D}(ku, kv) = |k|\hat{D}(u, v)$.

Proof. Obviously, (1) and (2) of the theorem are true. Then, prove (3) of the theorem, $\dot{D}(u, v) = 0 \Leftrightarrow u = v$ is tenable.

$$\begin{aligned} & \hat{D}(u, v) = 0 \\ \Leftrightarrow\ & \sup_{r \in [0,1]} \left(\frac{| \underline{u}(r) - \underline{v}(r) | + | \overline{u}(r) - \overline{v}(r) |}{2} \right) = 0 \\ \Leftrightarrow\ & | \underline{u}(r) - \underline{v}(r) | = 0 \ \ and \ \ | \overline{u}(r) - \overline{v}(r) | = 0 \\ \Leftrightarrow\ & \underline{u}(r) = \underline{v}(r) \ \ and \ \ \overline{u}(r) = \overline{v}(r) \\ \Leftrightarrow\ & [\underline{u}(r), \overline{u}(r)]_C = [\underline{v}(r), \overline{v}(r)]_C \\ \Leftrightarrow\ & [u]^r = [v]^r \\ \Leftrightarrow\ & u = v. \end{aligned}$$

The proof of (4) of the theorem is as follows:
If $[u]^0 = [v]^0 = [w]^0$,

$$\begin{aligned} \dot{D}(u, v) &= \sup_{x \in C} | u(x) - v(x) | \\ &= \sup_{x \in C} | u(x) - w(x) + w(x) - v(x) | \\ &\leq \sup_{x \in C} \{| u(x) - w(x) | + | w(x) - v(x) |\} \\ &\leq \sup_{x \in C} | u(x) - w(x) | + \sup_{x \in C} | w(x) - v(x) | \\ &= \dot{D}(u, w) + \dot{D}(w, v). \end{aligned}$$

For any $u, v, w \in \mathcal{F}_{\mathcal{D}C}$,

$$\begin{aligned} \hat{D}(u, v) &= \sup_{r \in [0,1]} \left(\frac{| \underline{u}(r) - \underline{v}(r) | + | \overline{u}(r) - \overline{v}(r) |}{2} \right) \\ &= \sup_{r \in [0,1]} \left(\frac{| \underline{u}(r) - \underline{w}(r) + \underline{w}(r) - \underline{v}(r) | + | \overline{u}(r) - \overline{w}(r) + \overline{w}(r) - \overline{v}(r) |}{2} \right) \\ &\leq \sup_{r \in [0,1]} \left(\frac{| \underline{u}(r) - \underline{w}(r) | + | \underline{w}(r) - \underline{v}(r) | + | \overline{u}(r) - \overline{w}(r) | + | \overline{w}(r) - \overline{v}(r) |}{2} \right) \\ &\leq \sup_{r \in [0,1]} \left(\frac{| \underline{u}(r) - \underline{w}(r) | + | \underline{w}(r) - \underline{v}(r) |}{2} \right) + \sup_{r \in [0,1]} \left(\frac{| \overline{u}(r) - \overline{w}(r) | + | \overline{w}(r) - \overline{v}(r) |}{2} \right) \\ &= \hat{D}(u, w) + \hat{D}(w, v). \end{aligned}$$

The proof of (5) of the theorem is as follows:
If $[u]^0 = [v]^0 = [w]^0$,

$$\begin{aligned}\dot{D}(u+w, v+w) &= \sup_{x\in C} \mid (u+w)(x) - (v+w)(x) \mid \\ &= \sup_{x\in C} \mid (u(x)+w(x)) - (v(x)+w(x)) \mid \\ &= \sup_{x\in C} \mid (u)(x) - (v)(x) \mid \\ &= \dot{D}(u,v).\end{aligned}$$

For any $u, v, w \in \mathcal{F}_{\mathcal{D}C}$,

$$\begin{aligned}\hat{D}(u+w, v+w) &= \sup_{r\in[0,1]} \left(\frac{\mid \underline{(u+w)}(r) - \underline{(v+w)}(r) \mid + \mid \overline{(u+w)}(r) - \overline{(v+w)}(r) \mid}{2}\right) \\ &= \sup_{r\in[0,1]} \left(\frac{\mid \underline{u}(r) + \underline{w}(r) - \underline{v}(r) - \underline{w}(r) \mid + \mid \overline{u}(r) + \overline{w}(r) - \overline{v}(r) - \overline{w}(r) \mid}{2}\right) \\ &= \sup_{r\in[0,1]} \left(\frac{\mid \underline{u}(r) - \underline{v}(r) \mid + \mid \overline{u}(r) - \overline{v}(r) \mid}{2}\right) \\ &= \hat{D}(u,v).\end{aligned}$$

Finally, the proof of (6) of the theorem is as follows:

$$\begin{aligned}\dot{D}(ku, kv) &= \sup_{x\in C} \mid ku(x) - kv(x) \mid \\ &= \sup_{x\in C} |k| \mid u(x) - v(x) \mid \\ &= |k| \sup_{x\in C} \mid u(x) - v(x) \mid \\ &= |k|\dot{D}(u,v).\end{aligned}$$

$$\begin{aligned}\hat{D}(ku, kv) &= \sup_{r\in[0,1]} \left(\frac{\mid \underline{ku}(r) - \underline{kv}(r) \mid + \mid \overline{ku}(r) - \overline{kv}(r) \mid}{2}\right) \\ &= \sup_{r\in[0,1]} \left(\frac{|k| \mid \underline{u}(r) - \underline{v}(r) \mid + |k| \mid \overline{u}(r) - \overline{v}(r) \mid}{2}\right) \\ &= |k| \sup_{r\in[0,1]} \left(\frac{\mid \underline{u}(r) - \underline{v}(r) \mid + \mid \overline{u}(r) - \overline{v}(r) \mid}{2}\right) \\ &= |k|\hat{D}(u,v).\end{aligned}$$

The proof of the theorem is complete. □

Then, the relationship between the metric $\hat{D}$ and D is proven. The metric D is introduced in Definition 2. D is also a metric on $\mathcal{F}_{\mathcal{D}C}$ space because of $\mathcal{F}_{\mathcal{D}C} \subset \mathcal{F}_{\mathcal{D}}$.

Theorem 7. *For any $u, v \in \mathcal{F}_{\mathcal{D}C}$, the metric $\hat{D}$ and D satisfy $\frac{1}{2}D \le \hat{D} \le D$, i.e.,*

$$\frac{1}{2}D(u,v) \le \hat{D}(u,v) \le D(u,v).$$

Proof. For any $u, v \in \mathcal{F}_{\mathcal{D}C}$ and $r \in [0,1]$, from the definitions of $\hat{D}$ and D, we have the following equation:

$$
\begin{aligned}
\frac{1}{2}D(u,v) &= \frac{1}{2}\sup_{r\in[0,1]} \max\{\mid \underline{u}(r)-\underline{v}(r)\mid, \mid \overline{u}(r)-\overline{v}(r)\mid\} \\
&= \frac{1}{2}\sup_{r\in[0,1]} \left(\frac{\mid \underline{u}(r)-\underline{v}(r)\mid + \mid \overline{u}(r)-\overline{v}(r)\mid + \mid (\mid \underline{u}(r)-\underline{v}(r)\mid - \mid \overline{u}(r)-\overline{v}(r)\mid)\mid}{2}\right) \\
&\leq \sup_{r\in[0,1]} \frac{1}{4}(\mid \underline{u}(r)-\underline{v}(r)\mid + \mid \overline{u}(r)-\overline{v}(r)\mid + \mid \underline{u}(r)-\underline{v}(r)\mid + \mid \overline{u}(r)-\overline{v}(r)\mid) \\
&= \sup_{r\in[0,1]} \frac{1}{2}(\mid \underline{u}(r)-\underline{v}(r)\mid + \mid \overline{u}(r)-\overline{v}(r)\mid) \\
&= \hat{D}(u,v) \\
&\leq \frac{1}{2}(2\max\{\mid \underline{u}(r)-\underline{v}(r)\mid, \mid \overline{u}(r)-\overline{v}(r)\mid\}) \\
&= D(u,v).
\end{aligned}
$$

From that, we can directly obtain the fact that for any $u,v \in \mathcal{F}_{\mathcal{DC}}$, $\frac{1}{2}D(u,v) \leq \hat{D}(u,v) \leq D(u,v)$ is tenable.

The proof of the theorem is complete. □

5. The Triangular Norm and Triangular Conorm Operations of Special Discrete Fuzzy Numbers on Countable Sets

Propositional logic refers to a formula representing a "proposition" formed by a logical operator combined with an atomic proposition [27]. In fuzzy logic, a logical proposition is connected by fuzzy logic conjunctive words. In the process of a numerical operation, the logical connectives' "conjunctions" are realized by a triangular norm operator, while the logical connectives' "disjunction" are realized by a triangular conorm operator. In this section, we mainly investigate the triangular norm and triangular conorm operations of special discrete fuzzy numbers on countable sets and their properties. Firstly, some definitions and results of the triangular norm and triangular conorm operations on posets are reviewed; then, the discrete triangular norm operator $\mathbb{T}$ and triangular conorm operator $\mathbb{S}$ on $\mathcal{F}_{\mathcal{DC}}$ space are defined.

Let $(P, \leq)$ be a nontrivial bounded partially ordered set with a maximum element "m" and a minimum element "e".

If T (or S) is a triangular norm operator on the bounded countable set $C \subset R$, then we can define the binary operation $\mathbb{T}$ (or $\mathbb{S}$) on the $\mathcal{F}_{\mathcal{DC}}$ space. The following theorems illustrate the fundamental properties of the triangular norm operator and the triangular conorm operator.

Definition 6 ([28]). *Let the triangular norm operator $T : P \times P \to P$ be a binary operation on the poset P; for any $x, y, z, x', y' \in P$, the following axioms are satisfied:*

(1) *Commutativity: $T(x,y) = T(y,x)$;*
(2) *Associativity: $T(T(x,y),z) = T(x,T(y,z))$;*
(3) *Monotonicity: $T(x,y) \leq T(x',y')$ when $x \leq x', y \leq y'$;*
(4) *Boundary condition: $T(x,m) = x$.*

Definition 7 ([28]). *Let the triangular conorm operator $S : P \times P \to P$ be a binary operation on the poset P; for any $x, y, z, x', y' \in P$, the following axioms are satisfied:*

(1) *Commutativity: $S(x,y) = S(y,x)$;*
(2) *Associativity: $S(S(x,y),z) = S(x,S(y,z))$;*
(3) *Monotonicity: $S(x,y) \leq S(x',y')$ when $x \leq x', y \leq y'$;*
(4) *Boundary condition: $T(x,e) = x$.*

Generally speaking, when the algebraic operation or lattice operation is extended to the fuzzy number space, the membership function of the fuzzy number can be directly used for calculation based on the Zadeh expansion principle [21] or the equivalent level set representation can be used for calculation. However, the result of the calculation may not be a discrete fuzzy number in $\mathcal{F}_D$ space [9].

Now, we consider the $\mathcal{F}_{DC}$ space of special discrete fuzzy numbers on countable sets; for any $u, v \in \mathcal{F}_{DC}$, there exist $x_u^r, y_u^r, x_v^r, y_v^r \in C$ and $x_u^r \leq y_u^r$, $x_v^r \leq y_v^r$ such that $[u]^r = [x_u^r, y_u^r]_C$, $[v]^r = [x_v^r, y_v^r]_C$.

Definition 8. *For any $r \in [0,1]$, let us consider the set*

$$\begin{aligned} T([u]^r, [v]^r) &= \{T(x,y) \mid x \in [u]^r,\ y \in [v]^r\} \\ &= \{T(x,y) \mid x \in [x_u^r, y_u^r]_C,\ y \in [x_v^r, y_v^r]_C\}, \end{aligned}$$

where $[u]^0 = \text{supp } u$, $[v]^0 = \text{supp } v$.

Proposition 1. *For any $r \in [0,1]$, if any $x, y \in C$ satisfy $T(x,y) \in C$, then $T([u]^r, [v]^r)$ satisfies conditions (1), (2), and (3) in Theorem 2.*

Proof. (1) For any $r \in [0,1]$, $[u]^r$ and $[v]^r$ are nonempty and finite, then $T([u]^r, [v]^r)$ is nonempty and finite, and $T([u]^0, [v]^0)$ is finite.

(2) For any $r_1, r_2 \in [0,1]$ and $0 \leq r_1 \leq r_2 \leq 1$, $[u]^{r_2} \subset [u]^{r_1}$ and $[v]^{r_2} \subset [v]^{r_1}$ are tenable; therefore, $x_u^{r_1} \leq x_u^{r_2}, y_u^{r_2} \leq y_u^{r_1}, x_v^{r_1} \leq x_v^{r_2}, y_v^{r_2} \leq y_v^{r_1}$, because T satisfies monotonicity,

$$\begin{aligned} T(x_u^{r_1}, x_v^{r_1}) &\leq T(x_u^{r_2}, x_v^{r_2}), \\ T(y_u^{r_2}, y_v^{r_2}) &\leq T(y_u^{r_1}, y_v^{r_1}), \\ T(x_u^{r_2}, x_v^{r_2}) &\leq T(y_u^{r_2}, y_v^{r_2}). \end{aligned}$$

These three inequalities are combined:

$$T(x_u^{r_1}, x_v^{r_1}) \leq T(x_u^{r_2}, x_v^{r_2}) \leq T(y_u^{r_2}, y_v^{r_2}) \leq T(y_u^{r_1}, y_v^{r_1}).$$

Therefore,

$$T([u]^{r_2}, [v]^{r_2}) \subset T([u]^{r_1}, [v]^{r_1}).$$

(3) Because $u, v \in \mathcal{F}_{DC}$, then for any $r_0 \in [0,1]$, there exist $r_1', r_2' \in R$ that satisfy $0 < r_1' < r_0$ and $0 < r_2' < r_0$ such that $[u]^{r_1'} = [u]^{r_0}$ and $[v]^{r_2'} = [v]^{r_0}$ are tenable, i.e., $[u]^{\alpha_1} = [u]^{r_0}$ is tenable for any $\alpha_1 \in [r_1', r_0]$, and $[u]^{\alpha_2} = [u]^{r_0}$ is tenable for any $\alpha_2 \in [r_2', r_0]$. Therefore, if $\alpha = \alpha_1 \vee \alpha_2$ then

$$T([u]^{\alpha}, [v]^{\alpha}) = T([u]^{r_0}, [v]^{r_0}).$$

The proof of the theorem is complete. □

Theorem 8. *There exists a unique discrete fuzzy number on countable set C denoted $\mathbb{T}(u,v)$ such that for any $r \in [0,1]$, the r-level set $[\mathbb{T}(u,v)]^r$ is defined by $T([u]^r, [v]^r)$, and*

$$\mathbb{T}(u,v)(z) = \sup\{r \in [0,1] \mid\ z \in T([u]^r, [v]^r)\}$$

is tenable.

Proof. Derived from Proposition 1 and Theorem 2. □

Similarly, the following propositions and theorems can be proven.

Definition 9. *For any $r \in [0,1]$, let us consider the set*

$$\begin{aligned} S([u]^r,[v]^r) &= \{S(x,y) \mid x \in [u]^r, y \in [v]^r\} \\ &= \{S(x,y) \mid x \in [x_u^r, y_u^r]_C, y \in [x_v^r, y_v^r]_C\}, \end{aligned}$$

where $[u]^0 = \text{supp}\, u$, $[v]^0 = \text{supp}\, v$.

Proposition 2. *For any $r \in [0,1]$, if any $x, y \in C$ satisfy $S(x,y) \in C$, then $S([u]^r,[v]^r)$ satisfies conditions (1), (2), and (3) in Theorem 2.*

Theorem 9. *There exist unique discrete fuzzy numbers on countable sets denoted by $\mathbb{S}(u,v)$, whose r-level set $[\mathbb{S}(u,v)]^r$ is defined by $S([u]^r,[v]^r)$ for any $r \in [0,1]$, and*

$$\mathbb{S}(u,v)(z) = \sup\{r \in [0,1] \mid z \in S([u]^r,[v]^r)\}$$

is tenable.

Remark 2. *According to the above results, if T is a triangular norm operator on the bounded countable set $C \subset R$, then we can define the binary operation $\mathbb{T}$ on the $\mathcal{F}_{DC}$ space,*

$$\begin{aligned} \mathbb{T} : \mathcal{F}_{DC} \times \mathcal{F}_{DC} &\rightarrow \mathcal{F}_{DC} \\ (u,v) &\rightarrow \mathbb{T}(u,v). \end{aligned}$$

The $\mathbb{T}$ is called the triangular norm operator of discrete fuzzy numbers on $\mathcal{F}_{DC}$.
Similarly, we define the triangular conorm operator of discrete fuzzy numbers, denoted as $\mathbb{S}$.

Remark 3. *Generally speaking, the condition "for any $x, y \in C$ satisfy $T(x,y) \in C$" in Proposition 1 and the condition "for any $x, y \in C$ satisfy $S(x,y) \in C$" in Proposition 2 cannot be omitted. The following examples can be used to illustrate.*

Example 1. *Let $C = \{0,2,3,4,5\}$. $u, v \in \mathcal{F}_{DC}$ are defined by*

$$u = \{0.2/0, 0.5/2, 1/3, 0.8/5\},$$

$$v = \{0.8/3, 1/4, 0.6/5\}.$$

The Lukasiewicz triangular norm operator is $T_L = \max\{0, x+y-5\}$; according to the above definition and theorem, $\mathbb{T}_L(u,v)$ can be calculated as follows:

(1) *When $r = 0.2$, $[u]^{0.2} = \{0,2,3,5\}$, and $[v]^{0.2} = \{3,4,5\}$, then $T_L([u]^{0.2},[v]^{0.2}) = \{0,1,2,3,4,5\}$,*
(2) *When $r = 0.5$, $[u]^{0.5} = \{2,3,5\}$, and $[v]^{0.5} = \{3,4,5\}$, then $T_L([u]^{0.5},[v]^{0.5}) = \{0,1,2,3,4,5\}$,*
(3) *When $r = 0.6$, $[u]^{0.6} = \{3,5\}$, and $[v]^{0.6} = \{3,4,5\}$, then $T_L([u]^{0.6},[v]^{0.6}) = \{1,2,3,4,5\}$,*
(4) *When $r = 0.8$, $[u]^{0.8} = \{3,5\}$, and $[v]^{0.8} = \{3,4\}$, then $T_L([u]^{0.8},[v]^{0.8}) = \{1,2,3,4\}$,*
(5) *When $r = 1$, $[u]^1 = \{3\}$, and $[v]^1 = \{4\}$, then $T_L([u]^1,[v]^1) = \{2\}$.*

Finally, we obtain

$$\mathbb{T}_L(u,v) = \{0.5/0, 0.8/1, 1/2, 0.8/3, 0.8/4, 0.6/5\},$$

then $[\mathbb{T}_L(u,v)]^0$ is not a subset of C. According to Theorem 2, $\mathbb{T}_L(u,v) \notin \mathcal{F}_{DC}$, and it is not a discrete fuzzy number on the countable set C. So, the condition "for any $x, y \in C$ satisfy $T(x,y) \in C$" in Proposition 1 cannot be omitted.

Now, some examples of operations using discrete triangular norm and triangular conorm operator are presented.

Example 2. *Let* $C = \{0, 1, 2, 3, 4, 5\}$. $u, v \in \mathcal{F}_{\mathcal{D}C}$ *are defined by:*

$$u = \{0.2/0, 0.5/2, 1/3, 0.8/5\},$$

$$v = \{0.1/1, 0.8/3, 1/4, 0.6/5\}.$$

The Lukasiewicz triangular norm operator $T_L = \max\{0, x + y - 5\}$, *according to the above definition and theorem:*

$$\mathbb{T}_L(u, v) = \{0.5/0, 0.8/1, 1/2, 0.8/3, 0.8/4, 0.6/5\},$$

then $\mathbb{T}_L(u, v) \in \mathcal{F}_{\mathcal{D}C}$.

Example 3. *Let* $C = \{0, 1, 2, 3, 4, 5\}$. $u, v \in \mathcal{F}_{\mathcal{D}C}$ *are defined by:*

$$u = \{0.2/0, 0.5/2, 1/3, 0.8/5\},$$

$$v = \{0.1/1, 0.8/3, 1/4, 0.6/5\}.$$

The Lukasiewicz triangular conorm operator $S_L = \min\{5, x + y\}$, *according to the above definition and theorem:*

$$\mathbb{S}_L(u, v) = \{0.1/1, 0.1/2, 0.2/3, 0.2/4, 1/5\},$$

then $\mathbb{S}_L(u, v) \in \mathcal{F}_{\mathcal{D}C}$.

Example 4. *Let* $C = \{0, 1, 2, 3, 4, 5\}$. $u, v \in \mathcal{F}_{\mathcal{D}C}$ *are defined by:*

$$u = \{0.2/0, 0.5/2, 1/3, 0.8/5\},$$

$$v = \{0.1/1, 0.8/3, 1/4, 0.6/5\}.$$

The Min triangular norm operator $T_{Min} = \min\{x, y\}$, *according to the above definition and theorem:*

$$\mathbb{T}_{Min}(u, v) = \{0.2/0, 0.2/1, 0.5/2, 1/3, 0.8/4, 0.6/5\},$$

then $\mathbb{T}_{Min}(u, v) \in \mathcal{F}_{\mathcal{D}C}$.

Example 5. *Let* $C = \{0, 1, 2, 3, 4, 5\}$. $u, v \in \mathcal{F}_{\mathcal{D}C}$ *are defined by:*

$$u = \{0.2/0, 0.5/2, 1/3, 0.8/5\},$$

$$v = \{0.1/1, 0.8/3, 1/4, 0.6/5\}.$$

The Max triangular conorm operator $S_{Max} = \max\{x, y\}$, *according to the above definition and theorem:*

$$\mathbb{S}_{Max}(u, v) = \{0.1/1, 0.1/2, 0.8/3, 1/4, 0.6/5\},$$

then $\mathbb{S}_{Max}(u, v) \in \mathcal{F}_{\mathcal{D}C}$.

Some properties of the triangular norm and triangular conorm of special discrete fuzzy numbers on countable sets are investigated below.

Proposition 3. *Let the triangular norm* $T : P \times P \to P$ *and the triangular conorm* $S : P \times P \to P$ *be binary operators on poset* P*; for any* $x, y, z \in P$*, the following properties hold:*

(1) Commutativity:

$$T(x, y) = T(y, x),$$

$$S(x, y) = S(y, x).$$

(2) *Associativity:*

$$T(T(x,y),z) = T(x,T(y,z)),$$
$$S(S(x,y),z) = S(x,S(y,z)).$$

Proof. Straightforward. It can be obtained directly from the definitions of the triangular norm T and the triangular conorm S. □

Theorem 10. *Let $\mathbb{T} : \mathcal{F}_{\mathcal{D}C} \times \mathcal{F}_{\mathcal{D}C} \to \mathcal{F}_{\mathcal{D}C}$ be a triangular norm operator and $\mathbb{S} : \mathcal{F}_{\mathcal{D}C} \times \mathcal{F}_{\mathcal{D}C} \to \mathcal{F}_{\mathcal{D}C}$ be a triangular conorm operator; for any $u, v, w \in \mathcal{F}_{\mathcal{D}C}$, the following properties hold:*

(1) *Commutativity:*

$$\mathbb{T}(u,v) = \mathbb{T}(v,u),$$
$$\mathbb{S}(u,v) = \mathbb{S}(v,u).$$

(2) *Associativity:*

$$\mathbb{T}(\mathbb{T}(u,v),w) = \mathbb{T}(u,\mathbb{T}(v,w)),$$
$$\mathbb{S}(\mathbb{S}(u,v),w) = \mathbb{S}(u,\mathbb{S}(v,w)).$$

Proof. We only prove the property of $\mathbb{T}$; the proof of $\mathbb{S}$ is similar.

Let the r-level sets of $u, v, w \in \mathcal{F}_{\mathcal{D}C}$ be $[u]^r = [x_u^r, y_u^r]_C$, $[v]^r = [x_v^r, y_v^r]_C$, $[w]^r = [x_w^r, y_w^r]_C$ for any $r \in [0,1]$, respectively.

(1) In order to prove $\mathbb{T}(u,v) = \mathbb{T}(v,u)$, we need to prove that for any $r \in [0,1]$, both sides of the equation have the same r-level set.

$$\begin{aligned} [\mathbb{T}(u,v)]^r &= T([u]^r,[v]^r) \\ &= \{T(x,y) \mid x \in [u]^r, y \in [v]^r\} \\ &= \{T(y,x) \mid y \in [v]^r, x \in [u]^r\} \\ &= T([v]^r,[u]^r) \\ &= [\mathbb{T}(v,u)]^r. \end{aligned}$$

(2) In order to prove $\mathbb{T}(\mathbb{T}(u,v),w) = \mathbb{T}(u,\mathbb{T}(v,w))$, we need to prove that for any $r \in [0,1]$, both sides of the equation have the same r-level set.

$$\begin{aligned} [\mathbb{T}(\mathbb{T}(u,v),w)]^r &= T([\mathbb{T}(u,v)]^r,[w]^r) \\ &= T(T([u]^r,[v]^r),[w]^r) \\ &= \{T(T(x,y),z) \mid x \in [u]^r, y \in [v]^r, z \in [w]^r\} \\ &= \{T(x,T(y,z)) \mid x \in [u]^r, y \in [v]^r, z \in [w]^r\} \\ &= T([u]^r,T([v]^r,[w]^r)) \\ &= [\mathbb{T}(u,\mathbb{T}(v,w))]^r. \end{aligned}$$

The proof of the theorem is complete. □

6. Application to Image Fusion

In this section, we apply the above-investigated special discrete fuzzy numbers on countable sets in the image fusion field [29–31]. Firstly, an interpretation of a gray image as a special discrete fuzzy numbers on countable sets is introduced.

The gray image is modeled as functions $f : D_f \subset R^2 \to \tau \subset R$, where D_f is the domain of the gray image, and τ is the corresponding gray-scale value space. We normalize the corresponding gray-scale value to the value in the interval [0,1].

6.1. Interpretation of Gray Image as Special Discrete Fuzzy Numbers on Countable Sets

After the following steps, a gray image is represented by the special discrete fuzzy numbers on countable sets.

(1) Let a gray image with 256 grayscale levels, i.e., $\{0,1,\ldots,255\}$, be I, and the size of I is $M \times N$. $I(x,y)$ represents a gray-scale value of (x,y) in I, where $x \in \{1,2,\ldots,M\}, y \in \{1,2,\ldots,N\}$.

(2) We take a point $(x_0,y_0), x_0 \in \{2,3,\ldots,M-1\}, y_0 \in \{2,3,\ldots,N-1\}$ in I as the center and use the neighboring pixels around (x_0,y_0) to form a rectangle, we call this rectangle W. The size of W is $n_W \times n_W$. When $n_W = 3$, the points of W are represented as $(x_0+i, y_0+j), i,j = \{-1,0,1\}$ and the corresponding pixel value can be expressed as $I(x_0+i,y_0+j), i,j = \{-1,0,1\}$.

(3) In order to represent the gray-scale pixel value, the mean value $\overline{W}$ and standard deviation $\overline{S}$ of W are calculated.

$$\overline{W} = \frac{\sum_{i=-1}^{1}\sum_{j=-1}^{1} I(x_0+i,y_0+j)}{3\times 3}, \tag{4}$$

$$\overline{S} = \sqrt{\frac{\sum_{i=-1}^{1}\sum_{j=-1}^{1}(I(x_0+i,y_0+j)-\overline{W})^2}{3\times 3-1}}. \tag{5}$$

(4) We construct Gaussian discrete fuzzy numbers for $I(x_0,y_0)$.
$u : R \to [0,1]$ is defined by:

$$u(I(x,y)) = \begin{cases} \exp(-\frac{(I(x,y)-\overline{W})^2}{2\overline{S}^2}), & \text{if } (x,y) \in W \\ 0, & \text{otherwise.} \end{cases} \tag{6}$$

Then, u is the special discrete fuzzy numbers on countable sets with $[u]^0 = \{I(x_0+i,y_0+j) : i,j = \{-1,0,1\}\}$. In this case, the countable set is $C = \{0,1,\ldots,255\}$.

The above steps are shown in Figure 1.

In different gray image processing environments, the other sizes and shapes of W can be selected to construct special discrete fuzzy numbers on countable sets.

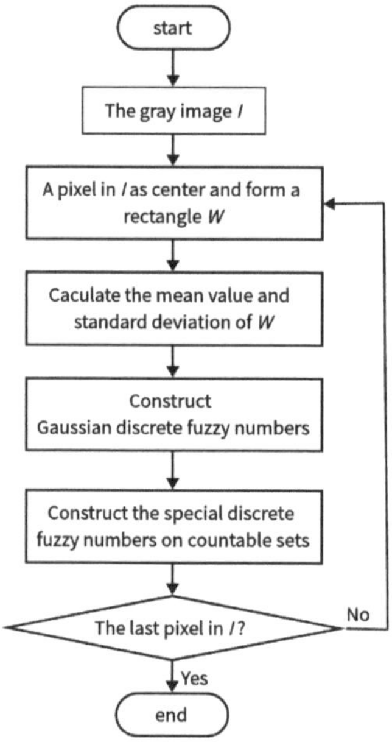

Figure 1. The steps of using the special discrete fuzzy numbers on countable sets to represent pixel value of gray images.

Example 6. *Let image I be a gray image with 256 grayscale levels, i.e.,* $\{0,1,\ldots,255\}$. *Let the point* (x_0, y_0) *be a center and take its eight neighboring pixels to form a rectangle W. The size of W is* $n_W \times n_W$ *and* $n_W = 3$. *The different objects I,* $I(x_0, y_0)$ *and the corresponding special discrete fuzzy numbers on countable sets are shown in Figure 2. When* $I(x_0, y_0) = 122$, *its special discrete fuzzy numbers on countable set representation is shown in Figure 2.*

In this case, the countable set is $C = \{0,1,\ldots,255\}$ *and u is the special discrete fuzzy numbers on countable sets with* $[u]^0 = \{83,109,110,111,117,122,132,137,148\}$. *The corresponding membership degree is expressed as follows:*

$$u = \{0.17/83, 0.88/109, 0.90/110, 0.92/111, 1.00/117, 0.98/122, 0.78/132, 0.63/137, 0.31/148\}.$$

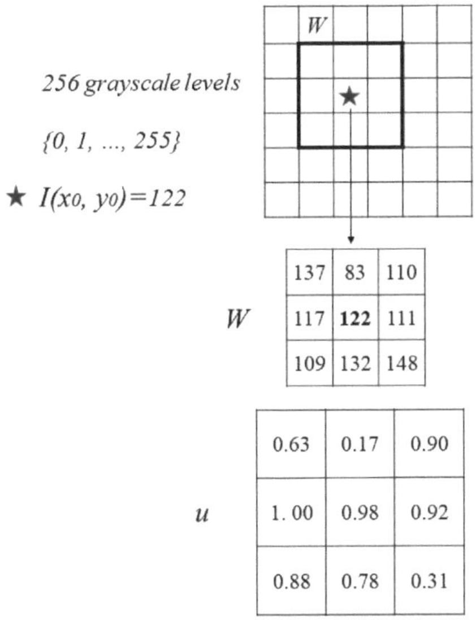

Figure 2. Using the special discrete fuzzy numbers on countable sets to represent pixel value of gray images.

6.2. Gray Image Fusion by Means of the Triangular Norm and Triangular Conorm Operations of Special Discrete Fuzzy Numbers on Countable Sets

In order to construct the fusion algorithm of two gray-scale images, we first give a definition of the mass center of special discrete fuzzy numbers on countable sets.

Definition 10. *Let w be a special discrete fuzzy number on countable sets,* $[w]^0 = \{x_1, x_2, \ldots, x_n\}$. *The mass center of w is defined as follows:*

$$\overline{M}(w) = \frac{\sum_{i=1}^{n} w(x_i)x_i}{\sum_{i=1}^{n} w(x_i)}. \quad (7)$$

The mass center of special discrete fuzzy numbers on countable sets is a crisp number. When we use the special discrete fuzzy numbers on countable sets to represent the pixel value of gray images, the mass center is an approximation of the corresponding pixel value of gray images.

The image fusion algorithm of two gray-scale images will be given below. Let the two gray images be f and g with same size, and the size of them is $M \times N$. $f(x,y)$ is used to express the pixel gray value at the point (x,y) in f, and $g(x',y')$ is used to express the pixel gray value at the point (x',y') in f, where $x \in \{1,\ldots,M\}, x' \in \{1,\ldots,M\}, y \in \{1,\ldots,N\}$, $y' \in \{1,\ldots,N\}$.

(1) Let the point (x, y) of f be the center and interpret it as special discrete fuzzy numbers on countable sets; this discrete fuzzy number is denoted as $u(f(x, y))$. Similarly, let the point (x', y') of g be the center and interpret it as special discrete fuzzy numbers on countable sets; this discrete fuzzy number is denoted as $v(g(x', y'))$.

(2) By using the triangular norm $\mathbb{T}$ or triangular conorm $\mathbb{S}$ defined in Section 5, two discrete fuzzy numbers $u(f(x, y))$ and $v(g(x', y'))$ at corresponding positions are operated, and a new discrete fuzzy number $\mathbb{T}(u, v)$ or $\mathbb{S}(u, v)$ is obtained.

(3) The mass center of the new discrete fuzzy number is calculated according to Equation (7) as the pixel gray value of the fused image.

(4) Change the points (x, y) and (x', y') to the same position and skip to step (1) until the points (x, y) and (x', y') traverse the image f and g, respectively.

After the above steps, images f and g are fused into a new image. The flowchart of the gray-scale image fusion algorithm is shown in Figure 3.

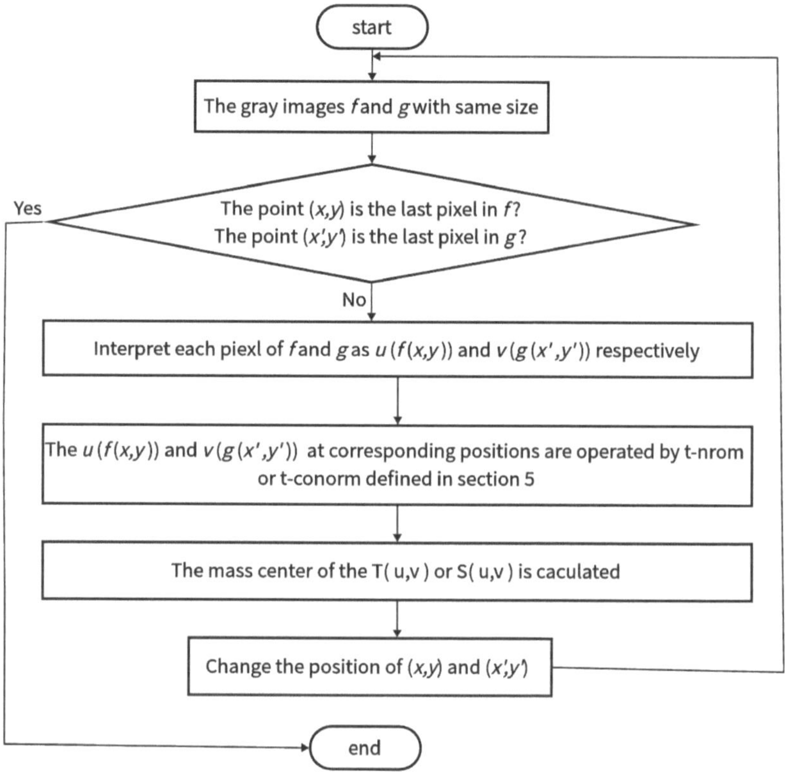

Figure 3. The flowchart of gray-scale image fusion algorithm.

To demonstrate the effectiveness of the above algorithm, an example of the fusion of the thermal image and the visible light image is presented. We conducted the experiments with the TNO Image Fusion Dataset the original thermal image and visible light image are shown in Figure 4.

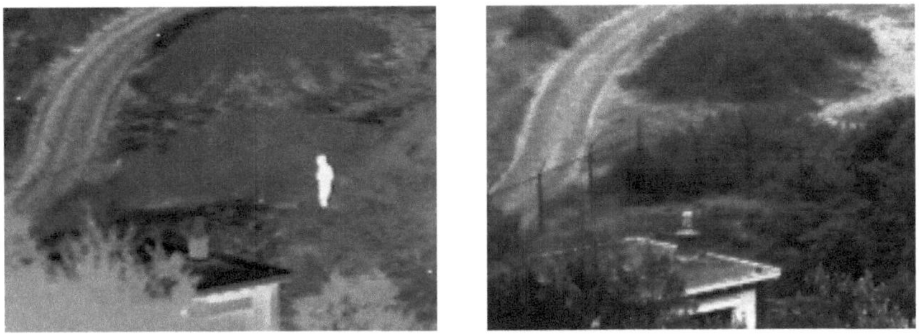

(a) (b)

Figure 4. The original images. (**a**) The thermal image. (**b**) The visible light image.

The fusion of the thermal image and the visible light image can not only reflect the military target but also have a certain ability of texture expression [32]. The corresponding experimental results are given in Figure 5. The software environment is Microsoft Windows 10 Home Edition and MATLAB R2018a. The hardware environment is a PC with an Intel(R) Core(TM)i5-8250U@1.60GHz CPU and 8.00 GB dual-channel DDR4 RAM.

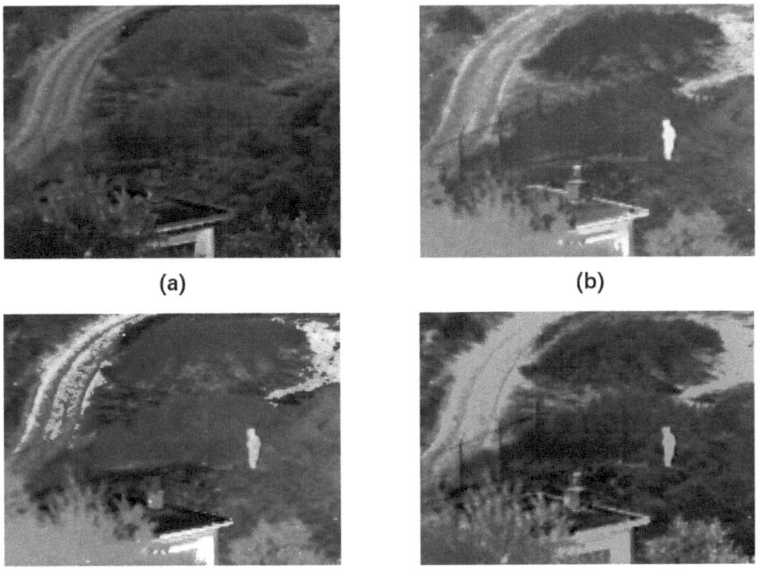

(a) (b) (c) (d)

Figure 5. The results of the fusion of thermal image and visible light image. (**a**) $\mathbb{T}_{Min}$. (**b**) $\mathbb{S}_{Max}$. (**c**) $\mathbb{T}_L$. (**d**) $\mathbb{S}_L$.

According to the experimental results in Figure 5, the different image fusion effects can be obtained by means of different aggregation operators defined in Section 5. For example, in Figure 5a, the texture and details of the road and leaves are clearer, while the outline of the pedestrian and roof is more pronounced in Figure 5b. In Figure 5c, the position of the person is more prominently displayed. The texture of the fence and grass in Figure 5d is more clearly distinguishable. Furthermore, the results of Figure 5a,b show that the aggregate result of the $\mathbb{T}_{Min}$ operator makes the overall image brightness low, while the aggregate result of $\mathbb{S}_{Max}$ operator has relatively high image brightness, which is consistent with the basic characteristics of these two operators. In practical applications, different aggregation operators can be selected according to different image fusion requirements.

7. Application to Aggregation of Subjective Evaluation

Scholars use discrete fuzzy numbers to describe human fuzzy language information, which can be applied to the realistic scenes such as group decision making, expert evaluation, or intelligent recommendation. The application of special discrete fuzzy numbers on countable sets to aggregation of subjective evaluation is proposed in this section. The specific steps of how to aggregate the subjective evaluations of multiple experts into a decision result are as follows:

The first step is to consider the semantic model $L = \{VB, B, MB, F, MG, G, VG\}$ where the letters refer to the linguistic terms "Very Bad", "Bad", "More or Less Bad", "Fair", "More or Less Good", "Good", and "Very Good"; they are arranged in ascending order:

$$VB \prec B \prec MB \prec F \prec MG \prec G \prec VG.$$

In order to facilitate the representation and operation of the special discrete fuzzy numbers on countable sets, the semantic pattern $L = \{VB, B, MB, F, MG, G, VG\}$ can be represented as the countable set $C = \{0, 1, 2, 3, 4, 5, 6\}$. In this case, the elements of set C correspond in a one-to-one manner with the elements of set L.

In the second step, the experts give subjective evaluation results based on the semantic pattern L. E_i is used to represent the subjective evaluation results of each expert, where $i = 1, 2, 3$. Each E_i is a special discrete fuzzy number on countable sets with semantic pattern L as its support set. Moreover, let us consider the importance of each expert and use the weight $\omega_1, \omega_2, \omega_3 \in \mathcal{F}_{DC}$ to describe. $E_1, E_2, E_3, \omega_1, \omega_2, \omega_3 \in \mathcal{F}_{DC}$ are defined as follows:

$$E_1 = \{0.3/1, 0.4/2, 0.7/3, 1/4, 0.8/5, 0.6/6\},$$

$$E_2 = \{0.2/0, 0.4/1, 1/2, 0.4/3, 0.2/4\},$$

$$E_3 = \{0.5/2, 0.6/3, 0.7/4, 1/5, 0.7/6\},$$

$$\omega_1 = \{0.6/1, 0.8/2, 1/3, 0.7/4\},$$

$$\omega_2 = \{0.4/2, 0.6/3, 1/4, 0.8/5\},$$

$$\omega_3 = \{0.4/3, 0.6/4, 1/5, 0.8/6\}.$$

In the third step, based on triangular norm and triangular conorm operations of special discrete fuzzy numbers on countable sets defined before, let us aggregate the subjective evaluations of multiple experts into a decision result. The final group consensus subjective evaluation results are still represented by special discrete fuzzy numbers on countable sets and can be interpreted directly.

Example 7. *Let $C = \{0, 1, 2, 3, 4, 5, 6\}$, $E_1, E_2, E_3, \omega_1, \omega_2, \omega_3 \in \mathcal{F}_{DC}$, the Lukasiewicz triangular norm operator $T_L = \max\{0, x + y - 6\}$, and Lukasiewicz triangular conorm operator $S_L = \min\{6, x + y\}$; according to the above definition and theorem in Section 5, we can calculate:*

$$b_1 = \mathbb{T}_L(E_1, \omega_1) = \{0.8/0, 1/1, 0.8/2, 0.7/3, 0.6/4\},$$

$$b_2 = \mathbb{T}_L(E_2, \omega_2) = \{1/0, 0.8/1, 0.4/2, 0.2/3\},$$

$$b_3 = \mathbb{T}_L(E_3, \omega_3) = \{0.5/0, 0.6/1, 0.6/2, 0.7/3, 1/4, 0.8/5, 0.7/6\},$$

then, $b_1, b_2, b_3 \in \mathcal{F}_{DC}$.

Next, we calculate the $\mathbb{S}_L$ for b_1, b_2, b_3,

$$\mathbb{S}_L(b_1, \mathbb{S}_L(b_2, b_3)) = \{0.5/0, 0.6/1, 0.6/2, 0.7/3, 0.8/4, 1/5, 0.8/6\}.$$

$\mathbb{S}_L(b_1, \mathbb{S}_L(b_2, b_3))$ *are discrete fuzzy numbers on countable set C. According to the semantic pattern* $L = \{VB, B, MB, F, MG, G, VG\}$*, the membership of "Very Bad" is 0.5, the membership of "Bad" is 0.6, the membership of "More or Less Bad" is 0.6, the membership of "Fair" is 0.7, the membership of "More or Less Good" is 0.8, the membership of "Good" is 1, and the membership of "Very Good" is 0.8. Therefore, the final group consensus subjective evaluation result is "Good".*

Example 8. *Let* $C = \{0, 1, 2, 3, 4, 5, 6\}$*,* $E_1, E_2, E_3, \omega_1, \omega_2, \omega_3 \in \mathcal{F}_{DC}$*. The triangular norm operator* $T_{Min} = \min\{x, y\}$ *and triangular conorm operator* $S_{Max} = \max\{x, y\}$*,*

$$d_1 = \mathbb{T}_{Min}(E_1, \omega_1) = \{0.6/1, 0.8/2, 1/3, 0.7/4\},$$

$$d_2 = \mathbb{T}_{Min}(E_2, \omega_2) = \{0.2/0, 0.4/1, 1/2, 0.4/3, 0.2/4\},$$

$$d_3 = \mathbb{T}_{Min}(E_3, \omega_3) = \{0.5/2, 0.6/3, 0.7/4, 1/5, 0.7/6\},$$

then $d_1, d_2, d_3 \in \mathcal{F}_{DC}$*.*

Next, we calculate the $\mathbb{S}_{Max}$ *for* d_1, d_2, d_3*,*

$$\mathbb{S}_{Max}(d_1, \mathbb{S}_{Max}(d_2, d_3)) = \{0.5/2, 0.6/3, 0.7/4, 1/5, 0.7/6\}.$$

Similarly, the final group consensus subjective evaluation result is still "Good".

8. Conclusions

In order to solve the problem in which the arithmetic operations and logic operations of general discrete fuzzy numbers do not satisfy the closure, a representation theorem in the form of endpoint functions of discrete fuzzy numbers defined on countable sets is proven in this paper. To overcome the defect that it is hard to define the measure of discrete fuzzy numbers reasonably in practical application, two different metrics are defined, and the relationship between them and the supremum metric (also called the uniform Hausdorff metric) of general fuzzy numbers is discussed. Further, the triangular norm and triangular conorm operations for discrete fuzzy numbers on countable sets are presented, and the properties of these two operators are investigated. We point out the conditions for maintaining the closure on $\mathcal{F}_{DC}$ space of these two operators, which is a good property in specific applications. Finally, application examples of image fusion and group consensus opinion based on triangular norm and triangular conorm operations of special discrete fuzzy numbers on countable sets are given. In the near future, we want to extend to multi-dimensional discrete fuzzy numbers on countable sets and investigate their applications in the modeling and processing of multi-dimensional discrete uncertain data.

Author Contributions: Conceptualization, Z.G.; methodology, Z.G. and N.Q.; software, N.Q.; validation, Z.G., N.Q.; formal analysis, Z.G., N.Q.; investigation, Z.G., N.Q.; resources, N.Q.; data curation, N.Q.; writing—original draft preparation, Z.G., N.Q.; writing—review and editing, Z.G., N.Q.; visualization, Z.G., N.Q.; supervision, Z.G. All authors have read and agreed to the published version of the manuscript.

Funding: This research was funded by the National Natural Science Foundation of China number "12061067". This research was supported by Northwest Normal University Young Teachers Research Ability Enhancement Program number "NWNU-LKQN2022-03".

Data Availability Statement: Data are contained within the article.

Acknowledgments: We would like to express our gratitude to the editors and anonymous reviewers who have contributed to improving our article.

Conflicts of Interest: The authors declare no conflicts of interest.

References

1. Chang, S.; Zadeh, L.A. On Fuzzy Mapping and Control. *IEEE Trans. Syst. Man Cybern.* **1972**, *2*, 30–34. [CrossRef]
2. Voxman, W. Canonical representations of discrete fuzzy numbers. *Fuzzy Sets Syst.* **2001**, *118*, 457–466. [CrossRef]
3. Gong, Z.; Qin, N.; Zhang, G. Visible watermarking in document images using two-stage fuzzy inference system. *Vis. Comput.* **2022**, *38*, 707–718. [CrossRef]
4. Gong, Z.; Qin, N.; Zhang, G. Three-Dimensional Generalized Discrete Fuzzy Number and Applications in Color Mathematical Morphology. *IEEE Access* **2021**, *9*, 25405–25421. [CrossRef]
5. Yu, Q. Hamacher Operations for Complex Cubic q-Rung Orthopair Fuzzy Sets and Their Application to Multiple-Attribute Group Decision Making. *Symmetry* **2023**, *15*, 2118. [CrossRef]
6. Li, X.; Liu, Z.; Han, X.; Liu, N.; Yuan, W. An Intuitionistic Fuzzy Version of Hellinger Distance Measure and Its Application to Decision-Making Process. *Symmetry* **2023**, *15*, 500. [CrossRef]
7. Wang, G.; Wu, C.; Zhao, C. Representation and Operations of discrete fuzzy numbers. *Southeast Asian Bull. Math.* **2005**, *29*, 1003–1010.
8. Casasnovas, J.; Riera, J.V. Maximum and minimum of discrete fuzzy numbers. *Front. Artif. Intell. Appl. Artif. Intell. Res. Dev.* **2007**, *163*, 273–280.
9. Casasnovas, J.; Riera, J.V. Extension of discrete t-norms and t-conorms to discrete fuzzy numbers. *Fuzzy Sets Syst.* **2011**, *167*, 65–81. [CrossRef]
10. Riera, J.V.; Torrens, J. Fuzzy implications defined on the set of discrete fuzzy numbers. In Proceedings of the EUSFLAT-LFA 2011, Aix-les-Bains, France, 18–22 July 2011.
11. Riera, J.V.; Torrens, J. Aggregation of subjective evaluations based on discrete fuzzy numbers. *Fuzzy Sets Syst.* **2012**, *191*, 21–40. [CrossRef]
12. Clapés, J.V.; Torrens, J. *Coimplications in the Set of Discrete Fuzzy Numbers*; Atlantis Press: Amsterdam, The Netherlands, 2013; pp. 207–214.
13. Riera, J.V.; Torrens, J. Residual implications on the set of discrete fuzzy numbers. *Inf. Sci.* **2013**, *247*, 131–143. [CrossRef]
14. Riera, J.V.; Torrens, J. Aggregation functions on the set of discrete fuzzy numbers defined from a pair of discrete aggregations. *Fuzzy Sets Syst.* **2014**, *241*, 76–93. [CrossRef]
15. Riera, J.V.; Massanet, S.; Herrera-Viedma, E.; Torrens, J. Some interesting properties of the fuzzy linguistic model based on discrete fuzzy numbers to manage hesitant fuzzy linguistic information. *Appl. Soft Comput.* **2015**, *36*, 383–391. [CrossRef]
16. Riera, J.V.; Torrens, J. Using discrete fuzzy numbers in the aggregation of incomplete qualitative information. *Fuzzy Sets Syst.* **2015**, *264*, 121–137. [CrossRef]
17. Zhao, M.; Liu, M.; Su, J.; Liu, T. A shape similarity-based ranking method of hesitant fuzzy linguistic preference relations using discrete fuzzy number for group decision making. *Soft Comput. Fusion Found. Methodol. Appl.* **2019**, *23*, 13569–13589. [CrossRef]
18. Ma, X.; Zhao, M.; Zou, X. Measuring and reaching consensus in group decision making with the linguistic computing model based on discrete fuzzy numbers. *Appl. Soft Comput.* **2019**, *77*, 135–154. [CrossRef]
19. Clapés, J.V.R.; Massanet, S.; Sola, H.; Fernandez, J. On Admissible Orders on the Set of Discrete Fuzzy Numbers for Application in Decision Making Problems. *Mathematics* **2021**, *9*, 1–16.
20. Qin, N.; Gong, Z. Color image denoising by means of three-dimensional discrete fuzzy numbers. *Vis. Comput.* **2023**, *39*, 2051–2063. [CrossRef]
21. Zadeh, L.A. Fuzzy sets. *Inf. Control.* **1965**, *8*, 338–353. [CrossRef]
22. Casasnovas, J.; Riera, J.V. On the addition of discrete fuzzy numbers. *WSEAS Trans. Math.* **2006**, 549–554. Available online: https://dl.acm.org/doi/abs/10.5555/1974762.1974848 (accessed on 18 January 2024).
23. Casasnovas, J.; Riera, J.V. Discrete fuzzy numbers defined on a subset of natural numbers. In *Theoretical Advances and Applications of Fuzzy Logic and Soft Computing: Advances in Soft Computing*; Springer: Berlin/Heidelberg, Germany, 2007; pp. 573–582.
24. Wang, G.; Wang, J. Generalized Discrete Fuzzy Number and Application in Risk Evaluation. *Int. J. Fuzzy Syst.* **2015**, *17*, 531–543. [CrossRef]
25. Wang, G.; Nan, Q.; Li, J. Fuzzy integers and methods of constructing them to represent uncertain or imprecise integer information. *Int. J. Innov. Comput. Inf. Control.* **2015**, *11*, 1483–1494.
26. Wang, G.; Zhang, Q.; Cui, X. The discrete fuzzy numbers on a fixed set with finite support set. In Proceedings of the IEEE Conference on Cybernetics and Intelligent Systems, Chengdu, China, 21–24 September 2008.
27. Peter, K.E.; Radko, M.; Endre, P. *Triangular Norms*; Springer Science and Business Media: Berlin/Heidelberg, Germany, 2000.
28. Zhang, D. Triangular norms on partially ordered sets. *Fuzzy Sets Syst.* **2005**, *153*, 195–209. [CrossRef]
29. Paramanandham, N.; Rajendiran, K. Multi sensor image fusion for surveillance applications using hybrid image fusion algorithm. *Multimed. Tools Appl.* **2018**, *77*, 12405–12436. [CrossRef]
30. Tian, Y.; Yang, W.; Wang, J. Image fusion using a multi-level image decomposition and fusion method. *Appl. Opt.* **2021**, *60*, 7466–7479. [CrossRef] [PubMed]

31. Wang, C.; Ma, R.; Yan, D.; Cao, H.; Shen, C. Polarization image fusion method with image enhancement. *Phys. Scr.* **2024**, *99*, 026003. [CrossRef]
32. Liu, Z.; Blasch, E.; Xue, Z.; Wu, W. Objective Assessment of Multiresolution Image Fusion Algorithms for Context Enhancement in Night Vision: A Comparative Study. *IEEE Trans. Pattern Anal. Mach. Intell.* **2012**, *34*, 94–109. [CrossRef] [PubMed]

symmetry

MDPI

Article

Two Extensions of the Sugeno Class and a Novel Constructed Method of Strong Fuzzy Negation for the Generation of Non-Symmetric Fuzzy Implications

Maria N. Rapti, Avrilia Konguetsof * and Basil K. Papadopoulos

Section of Mathematics and Informatics, Department of Civil Engineering, School of Engineering, Democritus University of Thrace, 67100 Xanthi, Greece; marapti@civil.duth.gr (M.N.R.); papadob@civil.duth.gr (B.K.P.)
* Correspondence: akogkets@civil.duth.gr; Tel.: +30-2541079741

Abstract: In this paper, we present two new classes of fuzzy negations. They are an extension of a well-known class of fuzzy negations, the Sugeno Class. We use it as a base for our work for the first two construction methods. The first method generates rational fuzzy negations, where we use a second-degree polynomial with two parameters. We investigate which of these two conditions must be satisfied to be a fuzzy negation. In the second method, we use an increasing function instead of the parameter δ of the Sugeno class. In this method, using an arbitrary increasing function with specific conditions, fuzzy negations are produced, not just rational ones. Moreover, we compare the equilibrium points of the produced fuzzy negation of the first method and the Sugeno class. We use the equilibrium point to present a novel method which produces strong fuzzy negations by using two decreasing functions which satisfy specific conditions. We also investigate the convexity of the new fuzzy negation. We give some conditions that coefficients of fuzzy negation of the first method must satisfy in order to be convex. We present some examples of the new fuzzy negations, and we use them to generate new non-symmetric fuzzy implications by using well-known production methods of non-symmetric fuzzy implications. We use convex fuzzy negations as decreasing functions to construct an Archimedean copula. Finally, we investigate the quadratic form of the copula and the conditions that the coefficients of the first method and the increasing function of the second method must satisfy in order to generate new copulas of this form.

Keywords: Sugeno class; fuzzy negation; rational function; fuzzy implication; copula; convex function

Citation: Rapti, M.N.; Konguetsof, A.; Papadopoulos, B.K. Two Extensions of the Sugeno Class and a Novel Constructed Method of Strong Fuzzy Negation for the Generation of Non-Symmetric Fuzzy Implications. *Symmetry* **2024**, *16*, 317. https://doi.org/10.3390/sym16030317

Academic Editors: László T. Kóczy and Sergei D. Odintsov

Received: 26 January 2024
Revised: 20 February 2024
Accepted: 29 February 2024
Published: 6 March 2024

1. Introduction

In recent years, there has been a growing body of research on fuzzy sets, systems, and fuzzy logic and their applications in practice, as well as the construction of new fuzzy negations, implications, and copulas. The production of a new fuzzy implication and copula is required. Fuzzy implications are the generalization of classical (Boolean) inference in the interval of [0, 1]. They are widely known to play an important role in the fields of fuzzy logic, decision theory, and fuzzy control. For this reason, the generation of new fuzzy implications has created the need to generate new fuzzy negations. Extensive research has been conducted in the literature on the production of fuzzy negations [1–6]. We know that we can generate fuzzy implications from aggregation functions and fuzzy negations [7–15]. Other methods of generating fuzzy implications can be achieved using additive generating functions or by some initial implications [16–22]. Thus, fuzzy implications are useful in fuzzy relational equations and fuzzy mathematical morphology, fuzzy measures and image processing [23], data mining [24], and computing with words and fuzzy partitions. On the other hand, functions with two variables, named copulas, have attracted the interest of many researchers because they are used in many fields. Copulas [25–28] are functions of two variables with specific properties based on probability theory and are often used in statistics and economics. In recent decades, the interest of many researchers in copulas has been very intense, as is evident from the large number of different copula constructions. Moreover, copulas introduce a new way to model multivariable data by considering the type of structure of these variables.

Although they come from different backgrounds, copulas and fuzzy implications have much in common with each other. The literature testifies that there have been many in-depth studies analyzing the relationship aggregation functions in general, and references have been made to them [29,30]. In recent years, new ways of constructing implications and copula functions have appeared, and their properties have been extensively studied. Fuzzy implications are studied in many areas. The construction of new fuzzy implications requires the construction of new fuzzy negations. The goal of this paper is to continue to construct rational fuzzy functions and, this time, fuzzy negations.

This paper is partially inspired by Sugeno-class fuzzy implication. Here, we present two new classes of fuzzy negations, the first of which generates rational fuzzy negations and the second of which generates rational negations assuming that the function g is polynomial. The first one is a parametric, with two parameters γ, δ which satisfy various conditions. We kept parameter δ from the Sugeno class and added another parameter γ just to generalize it to a second-degree polynomial. The second method is fuzzy negation, which is a generalization of the well-known fuzzy negation Sugeno class, replacing the parameter δ with an increasing function g. Some conditions, like $\delta > -1$, turn into $g(x) > -1$. Compared to previous works, herein, a new function is used in place of the parameter δ, and this creates a large range of fuzzy negations where the choice of an appropriate function creates new implications that satisfy specific conditions. Imagine that g can be any polynomial function of any degree, which means that the denominator can have a degree higher than two, as the first method has. On the other hand, g can be also any other type of function, and the produced negation is a composition of trigonometric functions or a root function. Using all these new fuzzy negations and in combination with known methods of constructing fuzzy implications, many new implications are produced.

A new method which produces strong fuzzy negations is presented. Strong negations produce S-implications and satisfy some basic properties of fuzzy implications, like the exchange principle, ordering property, and identity principle. We generalize an old method by using the equilibrium point ε of the new fuzzy negation and two decreasing functions f, g with specific conditions. We compare the equilibrium points of the new negations of the two first methods. Also, we investigate which conditions the coefficients of the produced negation of the first method and the function g of the second method must satisfy in order to be convex. We use this convexity to produce Archimedean copulas using a well-known method. Finally, we investigate another category of copula, the quadratic section, which has the form $C(x,y) = a(y)x^2 + (y - a(y))x$. We give another proof of condition $-1 \leq \frac{\partial a(y)}{\partial y} \leq 1$ that the function a must satisfy. Function $a(x)$ has at least two roots: the numbers 0 and 1. Using root *1*, and because it is also a root of the fuzzy negations, we can give it the following form: $a(x) = x \cdot N(x)$, where N is a fuzzy negation. Choosing the Sugeno class or its extension of the second method, we investigate which conditions the parameter δ or the function g must satisfy in order for the function a to be the appropriate for the quadratic section of the copula. With the help of fuzzy negations, we produce fuzzy implications which we can customize into an application. They fit better because, here, we use a function in place of a parameter δ. Thus, we can choose an appropriate inference. We have a plethora of implications, and, therefore, we can choose the most appropriate implication to simulate the data we have.

The paper is organized as follows. In Section 2, we recall the basic concepts and definitions used in the paper. In Section 3, we study the newly constructed methods of fuzzy negations, strong fuzzy negations, and their convexity. We present many examples of the produced negations. Also, we give some examples of the new fuzzy implications that are produced when two or more new negations are combined. Finally, we investigate the quadratic form of the copula, and we combine the new fuzzy negations, giving extra conditions to produce the copula. We present examples of the quadratic form of the copula and Archimedean copulas.

2. Preliminaries

To help the reader to become familiar with the theory, here, we outline some of the concepts and results employed in the rest of the paper.

Definition 1. (see [30] Definition 1.4.1). *The function* $N : [0,1] \to [0,1]$ *is a fuzzy negation if the following properties are applied:*

$$N(0) = 1\ ,\ N(1) = 0 \tag{1}$$

$$N\text{: is decreasing.} \tag{2}$$

Definition 2. (see [30] Definition 1.4.2 (i)). *A fuzzy negation N is called strict if the following properties are applied:*

$$N \text{ is strictly decreasing.} \tag{3}$$

$$N \text{ is continuous.} \tag{4}$$

Definition 3. (see [30] Definition 1.4.2 (ii)). *A fuzzy negation N is called strong if*

$$N(N(x)) = x \tag{5}$$

Definition 4. (see [30] Definition 1.4.2 (ii)). *The solution of the equation $N(x) = x$ is called the equilibrium point of N. If the function N is continuous, the equilibrium point is unique.*

Table 1 below shows some basic fuzzy negations used in this article.

Table 1. Examples of basic fuzzy negations.

Name	Fuzzy Negations
Threshold class	$N^t(x) = \begin{cases} 1, & if\ x < t \\ 1 \acute{\eta}\ 0, & if\ x = t,\ t \in (0,1) \\ 0, & if\ x > t \end{cases}$
Standard negation	$\mathrm{N(x)} = 1 - \mathrm{x}$
The least fuzzy negation	$N_{D1}(x) = \begin{cases} 1, & if\ x = 0 \\ 0, & if\ x \in (0,1] \end{cases}$
The greatest fuzzy negation	$N_{D2}(x) = \begin{cases} 0, & if\ x = 1 \\ 1, & if\ x \in [0,1) \end{cases}$
Yager class	$N^w(x) = (1 - x^w)^{\frac{1}{w}}\ ,\ \ w > 0$
Sugeno class	$N_\delta(x) = \frac{1-x}{1+\delta x},\ \delta > -1$

Fuzzy implications have probably become the most important operations in fuzzy logic, approximate reasoning, and fuzzy control. These operators not only model fuzzy conditionals, but also make inferences in any fuzzy rule-based system. These operators are defined as follows.

Definition 5. (see [30] Definition 1.1.1). *A function* $I : [0,1]^2 \to [0,1]$ *is called a fuzzy implication, if it satisfies, for all* $x, x_1,\ x_2,\ y,\ y_1, y_2 \in [0,1]$, *the following conditions:*

$$x_1 \le x_2 \Leftrightarrow I(x_1, y) \ge I(x_2, y), \text{ i.e., } I(\cdot, y) \text{ is decreasing.} \tag{6}$$

$$y_1 \leq y_2 \Leftrightarrow I(x,\ y_1) \leq\ I(x,\ y_2),\ \text{i.e.,}\ I(x,\cdot)\ \text{is increasing.} \tag{7}$$

$$I(0,0) = 1 \tag{8}$$

$$I(1,1) = 1 \tag{9}$$

$$I(1,0) = 0 \tag{10}$$

Definition 6. (see [30] Definition 1.4.15 (ii)). *If I is a fuzzy implication, then the function* $N_I : [0,1] \to [0,1]$ *with the form*

$$N_I(x) = I(x,0) \tag{11}$$

is called a natural negation of I.

Definition 7. (see [30] Definitions 1.3.1, 1.5.1). *A fuzzy implication I is said to satisfy:*

i. *the left neutrality property if:*

$$I(1,y) = y,\ y \in [0,1] \tag{12}$$

ii. *the exchange principle if:*

$$I(x, I(y,z)) = I(y, I(x,z)),\ x,y,z\ \in [0,1] \tag{13}$$

iii. *the identity principle if:*

$$I(x,x) = 1,\ x \in [0,1] \tag{14}$$

iv. *the ordering property if:*

$$I(x,y) = 1\ \Leftrightarrow x \leq y,\ x,y \in [0,1] \tag{15}$$

v. *the law of contraposition with respect to N if:*

$$I(x,y) = I(N(y), N(x))\ ,\ x,y\ \in [0,1] \tag{16}$$

vi. *the law of left contraposition with respect to N if:*

$$I(N(x),y) = I(N(y),x),\ x,y\ \in [0,1] \tag{17}$$

vii. *the law of right contraposition with respect to N if:*

$$I(x, N(y)) = I(y, N(x)),\ x,y\ \in [0,1] \tag{18}$$

Definition 8. *Let I be a nonempty interval of R. A function f from I to R is convex if and only if*

$$\frac{\partial^2 f}{\partial x^2} \geq 0 \tag{19}$$

Definition 9. ([28]). *A function* $C : [0,1]^2 \to [0,1]$ *is called a copula if it satisfies the following properties:*

$$C(0,t) = C(t,0) = 0\ \text{for each}\ 0 \leq t \leq 1 \tag{20}$$

$$C(1,t) = C(t,1) = t\ \text{for each}\ 0 \leq t \leq 1 \tag{21}$$

The C-volume of a rectangle must be not negative, e.g.,

$$V_H = C(x_1,y_1) - C(x_1,y_2) - C(x_2,y_1) + C(x_1,y_1) \geq 0 \tag{22}$$

for each $x_1 \leq x_2$ *and* $y_1 \leq y_2$ *where* $0 \leq x_1, x_2, y_1, y_2 \leq 1$.

Definition 10. ([28]). *If the function C is a copula, then the function in form*

$$C^*(x,y) = x + y - 1 + C(1-x, 1-y) \tag{23}$$

for each $0 \leq x, y \leq 1$ *is also a copula, and it is called a survival copula.*

Definition 11. ([30]). *If f is a decreasing function where* $f(1) = 0$*, then we define the pseudo-inverse of function f as:*

$$\text{given by } f^{[-1]} = \begin{cases} f^{-1}(x),\ if\ 0 \leq x \leq f(0) \\ 0\ ,if\ f(0) \leq x \leq \infty \end{cases} \tag{24}$$

Definition 12. ([30]). *Let* $f : [0,1] \to [0,\infty]$ *be a continuous, strictly decreasing, and convex function such that* $f(1) = 0$*, and let* $f^{[-1]}$ *be the pseudo-inverse. Let* $C : [0,1] \to [0,1]$*, defined by:*

$$C(x,y) = f^{[-1]}(f(x) + f(y)) \tag{25}$$

Then, C is an Archimedean copula.

3. Results

In this section, we give definitions and proofs of the newly generated fuzzy negations. The utility of fuzzy negations is known because, with the help of a new negation, we can construct a family of fuzzy implications. Also, we give examples of the new negations and the new fuzzy implications that are produced. Using the above equilibrium points and generalizing a known formula, we construct the branching functions and we generate strong fuzzy negations. Moreover, we combine the new fuzzy negations with the quadratic form of the copula.

3.1. New Fuzzy Negations

Theorem 1. *The function* $N : [0,1] \to [0,1]$*, with the following form:*

$$N_{\gamma,\delta}(x) = \frac{1-x}{\gamma x^2 + \delta x + 1}, \tag{26}$$

is a fuzzy negation if the condition $\frac{\gamma - |\gamma|}{2} + \delta + 1 > 0$ *is satisfied, where* $\gamma \in \mathbb{R} - \{0\}$ *and* $\delta \in \mathbb{R}$.

Proof. The boundary conditions (1) are satisfied:$(0) = 1$ $N(1) = 0$.

Also, the monotony condition (2):

$$\frac{\partial N_{\gamma,\delta}(x)}{\partial x} = \frac{\gamma x^2 - 2\gamma x - \delta - 1}{(\gamma x^2 + \delta \chi + 1)^2} = \frac{\gamma(x-1)^2 - \gamma - \delta - 1}{(\gamma x^2 + \delta \chi + 1)^2} = \frac{\gamma(x-1)^2 - (\gamma + \delta + 1)}{(\gamma x^2 + \delta \chi + 1)^2} \overset{\gamma \neq 0}{=} \frac{\gamma\left[(x-1)^2 - \frac{(\gamma+\delta+1)}{\gamma}\right]}{(\gamma x^2 + \delta \chi + 1)^2}$$

If $\gamma < 0$ and $\gamma + \delta + 1 > 0$, then $\gamma \cdot \left[(x-1)^2 - \frac{(\gamma+\delta+1)}{\gamma}\right] < 0$, so the monotony condition $\frac{\partial N_{\gamma,\delta}(x)}{\partial x} < 0$ is satisfied.

If $\gamma > 0$ and $\delta + 1 > 0$, then $\frac{\partial N_{\gamma,\delta}(x)}{\partial x} < 0$

$$x \in [0,1] \Leftrightarrow (x-1)^2 \leq 1 \Leftrightarrow (x-1)^2 - \frac{\gamma + \delta + 1}{\gamma} \leq 1 - \frac{\gamma + \delta + 1}{\gamma} = \frac{-\delta - 1}{\gamma} < 0$$

□

Proposition 1. *The fuzzy negation of the Theorem 1 is strong if and only if* $\gamma = 0$*, which means it is the Sugeno class.*

Remark 1. *If* $\gamma = 0$*, then the produced negation is the well-known Sugeno class* $N_\delta(x) = \frac{1-x}{\delta x+1}$*, where* $\delta > -1$*.*

Remark 2. *If* $\gamma = \delta = 0$*, then the produced negation is the well-known classical (standard) fuzzy negation.*

Remark 3. *The fuzzy negation of Theorem 1 is a strict fuzzy negation.*

Theorem 2. *Let* $g : \mathbb{R} \to [-1, +\infty)$*, an increasing function. Then, the function* $N^g : [0,1] \to [0,1]$*, with the following form:*

$$N^g(x) = \frac{1-x}{x \cdot g(x) + 1} \tag{27}$$

is a fuzzy negation.

Proof. Boundary conditions (1) are satisfied: $N^g(0) = 1$ $N^g(1) = 0$.

Monotony condition (2):

$$\frac{\partial N^g(x)}{\partial x} = -\frac{\frac{\partial g(x)}{\partial x} \cdot x \cdot (1-x) + (g(x)+1)}{(x \cdot g(x) + 1)^2} < 0$$

□

Because g is an increasing function, $\frac{\partial g(x)}{\partial x} \geq 0$ for every $x \in [0,1]$, and $g(x) \geq -1$.

Remark 4. *The function of Theorem 2 is a strict fuzzy negation.*

Remark 5. *The function of Theorem 2 is an evolution if and only if g is a constant function.*

Remark 6. *If we choose* $g(x) = -\frac{1}{x+1}$*, then the fuzzy negation that is produced from Theorem 2 is a well-known* $N^g(x) = 1 - x^2$*.*

Proposition 2. *Let* $g : \mathbb{R} \to (-1, +\infty)$*, the increasing function of the Theorem 2. We define the following increasing function,* $K : \mathbb{R} \to (-1, +\infty)$*, given by:*

$$K(x) = x \cdot g(x) \tag{28}$$

If K is a concave function, then the fuzzy negation N^g *of the Theorem 2 is a convex function.*

Proof. If K is an increasing function, then $\frac{\partial K(x)}{\partial x} = g(x) + x \cdot \frac{\partial g(x)}{\partial x} \geq 0$. If K is a concave function, then $\frac{\partial^2 K}{\partial x^2} \leq 0$. We will calculate the second partial derivate of K.

$$\frac{\partial^2 K(x)}{\partial x^2} = \frac{\partial\left(\frac{\partial K(x)}{\partial x}\right)}{\partial x^2} = \frac{\partial g(x)}{\partial x} + \frac{\partial g(x)}{\partial x} + x \cdot \frac{\partial^2 g(x)}{\partial x^2} = 2 \cdot \frac{\partial g(x)}{\partial x} + x \cdot \frac{\partial^2 g(x)}{\partial x^2} \leq 0$$

We know from Theorem 3 that N^g is a strictly decreasing function, so:

$$\frac{\partial N^g(x)}{\partial x} = \frac{\frac{\partial g(x)}{\partial x} \cdot (x^2 - x) - (g(x)+1)}{(x \cdot g(x) + 1)^2} < 0 \Leftrightarrow \frac{\partial g(x)}{\partial x} \cdot \left(x^2 - x\right) - (g(x)+1) < 0$$

$$\frac{\partial^2 N^g(x)}{\partial x^2} = \frac{\left[\frac{\partial^2 g(x)}{\partial x^2}(x^2-x)+2(x-1)\cdot\frac{\partial g(x)}{\partial x}\right]\cdot(x\cdot g(x)+1)-2\cdot\left(g(x)+x\cdot\frac{\partial g(x)}{\partial x}\right)\cdot\left[\frac{\partial g(x)}{\partial x}\cdot(x^2-x)-(g(x)+1)\right.}{(x\cdot g(x)+1)^3} =$$

$$= \frac{(x-1)\cdot\left(x\cdot\frac{\partial^2 g(x)}{\partial x^2}+2\frac{\partial g(x)}{\partial x}\right)(x\cdot g(x)+1)-2\cdot\left(g(x)+x\cdot\frac{\partial g(x)}{\partial x}\right)\cdot\left[\frac{\partial g(x)}{\partial x}\cdot(x^2-x)-(g(x)+1)\right]}{(x\cdot g(x)+1)^3} \geq 0$$

$$\left.\begin{array}{c} x-1\leq 0\,,\ x\in[0,1] \\ x\cdot\frac{\partial^2 g(x)}{\partial x^2}+2\frac{\partial g(x)}{\partial x}\leq 0 \\ x\cdot g(x)+1\geq 0 \\ g(x)+x\cdot\frac{\partial g(x)}{\partial x}\geq 0 \\ \frac{\partial g(x)}{\partial x}\cdot(x^2-x)-(g(x)+1)\leq 0 \end{array}\right\} \Longrightarrow \frac{\partial^2 N^g(x)}{\partial x^2}\geq 0$$

□

Proposition 3. *If* $\gamma \geq 0$ *and* $\varepsilon_1, \varepsilon_2$ *are the equilibrium points of* $N_{\gamma,\delta}$, N_δ, *respectively, then*

$$\varepsilon_1 \leq \varepsilon_2 \tag{29}$$

Proof. If $\gamma \geq 0$, then $\gamma x^2 + \delta x + 1 \geq \delta \chi + 1 \overset{x\in[0,1]}{\Leftrightarrow} \frac{1-x}{\gamma x^2+\delta x+1} \leq \frac{1-x}{\delta \chi+1} \Leftrightarrow N_{\gamma,\delta}(x) \leq N_\delta(x)$. Let $\varepsilon_1, \varepsilon_2$ be the equilibrium points of $N_{\gamma,\delta}$ and N_δ, respectively. Suppose that $\varepsilon_2 < \varepsilon_1$, then $N_{\gamma,\delta}(\varepsilon_2) > N_{\gamma,\delta}(\varepsilon_1) \Leftrightarrow N_{\gamma,\delta}(\varepsilon_2) > \varepsilon_1 \Leftrightarrow \varepsilon_1 < N_{\gamma,\delta}(\varepsilon_2) < N_\delta(\varepsilon_2) = \varepsilon_2$, which is a contradiction. Therefore, $\varepsilon_1 < \varepsilon_2$. □

Example 1. *In Figure 1 we present the graphs of three functions,* $N_{3,5}(x) = \frac{1-x}{3x^2+5x+1}$ *(the black one),* $N_5(x) = \frac{1-x}{1+5x}$ *(the green one), and the identity function* $f(x) = x$. *(the blue one).* $N_{3,5}$ *belongs to fuzzy negations of Theorem 1 and* N_5 *belongs to fuzzy negation* N_δ *of the Table 1.*

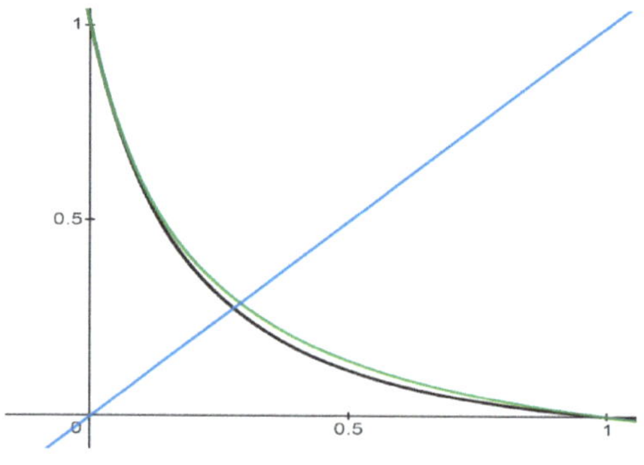

Figure 1. Fuzzy negations of Example 1.

As we can see, the equilibrium point of $N_{\gamma,\delta}$ ($\gamma = 3 > 0$) is to the left of the point of the N_δ function.

The distance between these two equilibrium points is $\sqrt{2}\cdot|\varepsilon_1 - \varepsilon_2|$, where $\varepsilon_1, \varepsilon_2$ are the equilibrium points of functions N_γ, N_δ, respectively.

We can produce strong branching fuzzy negations [1] where one branch is a rational function. If N is a fuzzy negation, which is not necessary, there is a strong negation, and $N(\varepsilon) = \varepsilon$, where ε is the equilibrium point of N. Thus, if N is any continuous fuzzy negation in the interval [0, 1], then the following form [12] produces strong fuzzy negations N_1, and, in our case, rational fuzzy negations.

Below, in Figure 2 we present the graph of the function N_1

$$N_1(x) = \begin{cases} N(x)\,,\ x \in [0, \varepsilon] \\ \\ N^{-1}(x)\,,\ x \in (\varepsilon, 1] \end{cases} \tag{30}$$

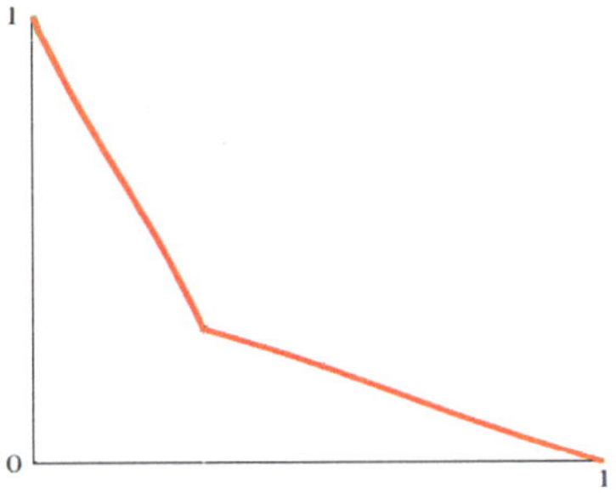

Figure 2. Fuzzy negation N_1.

We will generalize the above formula using two decreasing functions, f, g.

Theorem 3. *Let ε be the equilibrium point of N_s. $f : \mathbb{R} \to (-\infty, 1]$ and $g : \mathbb{R} \to [0, +\infty)$, two decreasing functions with the following conditions:*
$f^{-1} = g$, $f(0) = 1$ and $g(1) = 0$. Then the following form is a strong fuzzy negation:

$$N_s(x) = \begin{cases} f\left(\frac{g(\varepsilon)\cdot x}{\varepsilon}\right)\,,\ x \le \varepsilon \\ \\ \frac{g(x)\cdot\varepsilon}{g(\varepsilon)}\,, x > \varepsilon \end{cases} \tag{31}$$

Proof. For $x \le \varepsilon$, we have $N_s(x) = f\left(\frac{g(\varepsilon)\cdot x}{\varepsilon}\right)$

$$N_s(0) = f\left(\frac{g(\varepsilon)\cdot 0}{\varepsilon}\right) = f(0) = 1$$

For $x > \varepsilon$, we have $N_s(x) = \frac{g(x)\cdot\varepsilon}{g(\varepsilon)}$

$$N_s(1) = \frac{g(1)\cdot\varepsilon}{g(\varepsilon)} = 0$$

Monotony condition:
For $x \le \varepsilon$, we have $N_s(x) = f\left(\frac{g(\varepsilon)\cdot x}{\varepsilon}\right)$
For every $x_1, x_2 \in [0, \varepsilon]$ where $x_1 \le x_2 \overset{g>0}{\Leftrightarrow} \frac{g(\varepsilon)}{\varepsilon}\cdot x_1 \le \frac{g(\varepsilon)}{\varepsilon}\cdot x_2 \overset{f\searrow}{\Leftrightarrow}$

$$f\left(\frac{g(\varepsilon)}{\varepsilon}\cdot x_1\right) \ge f\left(\frac{g(\varepsilon)}{\varepsilon}\cdot x_2\right) \Leftrightarrow N_s(x_1) \ge N_s(x_2)$$

Thus, we conclude that N_s is decreasing when $x \le \varepsilon$.
For $x > \varepsilon$, we have $N_s(x) = \frac{g(x)\cdot\varepsilon}{g(\varepsilon)}$
For every $x_1, x_2 \in [0, \varepsilon]$ where $x_1 \le x_2 \overset{g\searrow}{\Leftrightarrow} g(x_1) \ge g(x_2) \overset{g>0}{\Leftrightarrow} \frac{g(x_1)\cdot\varepsilon}{g(\varepsilon)} \ge \frac{g(x_2)\cdot\varepsilon}{g(\varepsilon)} \Leftrightarrow$ $N_s(x_1) \ge N_s(x_2)$
Thus, we conclude that N_s is decreasing when $x > \varepsilon$. □

Now, we will present some examples of new fuzzy negations. We will define some values for parameters γ and δ of Theorem 1, and we will produce new fuzzy negations.

Example 2. *If we define* $\gamma = 1,\ \delta = 0$, *the produced negation is* $N_{1,0}(x) = \frac{1-x}{x^2+1}$ *(the green graph), and the inverse function is* $N_{1,0}{}^{-1}(x) = \dfrac{-1+\sqrt{1+4x(1-x)}}{2x}$ *(the black one).*

In Figure 3 we present the graphs of the function $N_{1,0}$, $N_{1,0}{}^{-1}$.

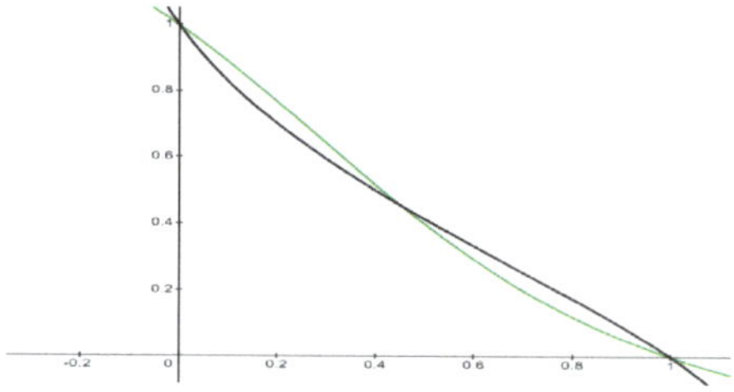

Figure 3. Fuzzy negations $N_{1,0}$ and $N_{1,0}{}^{-1}$.

Then, the produced strong fuzzy negation has the following form and graph:

$$N^s(x) = \begin{cases} \frac{1-x}{x^2+1},\ x \in \left[0,\ \sqrt[3]{\sqrt{\frac{59}{108}} + \frac{1}{2}} - \sqrt[3]{\sqrt{\frac{59}{108}} - \frac{1}{2}}\right] \\ \dfrac{-1+\sqrt{1+4x(1-x)}}{2x}, x \in \left[\sqrt[3]{\sqrt{\frac{59}{108}} + \frac{1}{2}} - \sqrt[3]{\sqrt{\frac{59}{108}} - \frac{1}{2}}\ ,\ 1\right] \end{cases} \tag{32}$$

where $\varepsilon = \sqrt[3]{\sqrt{\frac{59}{108}} + \frac{1}{2}} - \sqrt[3]{\sqrt{\frac{59}{108}} - \frac{1}{2}}$ *is the equilibrium point of* N^s.

In the Figure 4 we present the graph of function N^s. *Particularly, the black graph is the first branch of* N^s *and the green graph is the second branch of* N^s.

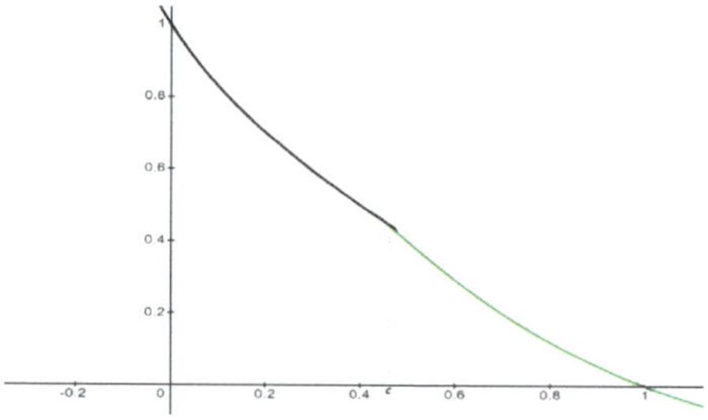

Figure 4. Fuzzy negation N^s.

Example 3. *For* $\gamma = -3,\ \delta = 4$, *the produced negation is*

$$N_{-3,4}(x) = \frac{1-x}{-3x^2+4x+1} \tag{33}$$

In the Figure 5 the graph of function $N_{-3,4}$ *is presented.*

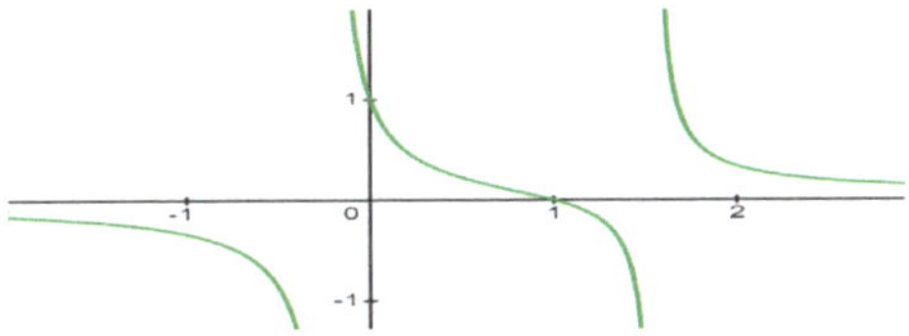

Figure 5. Fuzzy negation $N_{-3,4}$.

3.2. Fuzzy Implications Generated from Fuzzy Negations of Theorems 1 and 2

Fuzzy negations are very useful in the construction of both fuzzy implications and copulas. Firstly, we will use fuzzy negations that were generated from the above methods for the construction of fuzzy implications.

Example 4. *According to the formula [8]* $I(x,y) = N_2\left(\frac{d(x)}{d(1)} \blacktriangledown N_1(y)\right)$, N_1, N_2 *are two fuzzy negations and* $d : [0,1] \to [0,\infty)$ *is an increasing and continuous function with* $g(0) = 0$*. From Theorem 1, if we set* $\gamma = 1, \delta = 1$*, and from Theorem 3, if* $g(x) = x^2$*, then the produced negations are* $N_{1,1}(x) = \frac{1-x}{x^2+x+1}$ *and* $N^g(x) = \frac{1-x}{x^3+1}$*. If we set* $N_1 = N_{1,1}$, $N_2 = N^g$*, and* $d(x) = \sqrt{x}$*, we generate the following fuzzy implication:*

$$I(x,y) = \frac{1 - \frac{\sqrt{x}(1-y)}{y^2+y+1}}{\left(\frac{\sqrt{x}(1-y)}{y^2+y+1}\right)^3 + 1} \tag{34}$$

And its natural negation is

$$I(x,0) = N_I(x) = \frac{1-\sqrt{x}}{\sqrt{x}+1} \tag{35}$$

Moreover, we can construct parametric fuzzy implications using the produced fuzzy negations of Theorems 1 and 2.

Remark 7. *If we choose a strong fuzzy negation from relation (32), then the produced fuzzy implication satisfies the neutrality property.*

Proposition 4. *Let* $N_{\gamma,\delta}$ *,* N^g *be two fuzzy negations of Theorems 1, 2 with the form* $N_{\gamma,\delta}(x) = \frac{1-x}{\gamma x^2+\delta x+1}$ $N^g(x) = \frac{1-x}{x \cdot g(x)+1}$*. If we set* $N_1 = N_{\gamma,\delta}$, $N_2 = N^g$*, then, according to formula [8],* $I(x,y) = N_2\left(\frac{d(x)}{d(1)} \blacktriangledown N_1(y)\right)$*, and the produced implication has the form:*

$$I(x,y) = I^g_{\gamma,\delta}(x,y) = \frac{1 - \frac{d(x)}{d(1)} \cdot \frac{1-y}{\gamma y^2 + \delta y + 1}}{\frac{d(x)}{d(1)} \cdot \frac{1-y}{\gamma y^2 + \delta y + 1} \cdot g\left(\frac{d(x)}{d(1)} \cdot \frac{1-y}{\gamma y^2 + \delta y + 1}\right) + 1} \tag{36}$$

Proof. Proof is obvious. □

With this combination, we can make many rational fuzzy implications. We can make a family of them. Also, we can use fuzzy negations as decreasing functions to construct copulas. The following form helps us to understand this.

In the literature, various methods of manufacturing copulas have been presented. Here, we will deal with the Archimedean copulas.

Example 5. *According to Theorem 1, if we choose for $\gamma = -3$, $\delta = 7$, then we take the fuzzy negation:*

$$N_{-3,7}(x) = \frac{1-x}{-3x^2+7x+1} \tag{37}$$

Fuzzy negation $N_{-3,7}$ is strict and convex. Its inverse function has the form:

$$N_{-3,7}^{-1}(x) = \begin{cases} \frac{7x+1-\sqrt{61x^2+2x+1}}{2x}, \; 0 < x \leq 1 \\ 1, \; x = 0 \end{cases} \tag{38}$$

And its pseudoinverse has the form:

$$N_{-3,7}^{[-1]}(x) = \begin{cases} N_{-3,7}^{-1}(x), \; if \; 0 \leq x \leq 1 \\ 0, \; x > 1 \end{cases} \tag{39}$$

If we define:

$$h_1(x) = 7\cdot\left(\frac{1-x}{-3x^2+7x+1} + \frac{1-y}{-3y^2+7y+1}\right) + 1$$

$$h_2(x) = \sqrt{61\cdot\left(\frac{1-x}{-3x^2+7x+1} + \frac{1-y}{-3y^2+7y+1}\right)^2 + 2\cdot\left(\frac{1-x}{-3x^2+7x+1} + \frac{1-y}{-3y^2+7y+1}\right) + 1}$$

$$h_3(x) = 2\cdot\left(\frac{1-x}{-3x^2+7x+1} + \frac{1-y}{-3y^2+7y+1}\right)$$

then, by the form (18), a new copula is generated.

$$C(x,y) = \begin{cases} \frac{h_1(x) - h_2(x)}{h_3(x)}, \; 0 \leq x, y \leq 1 \\ 0, \; N_{-3,7}(x) + N_{-3,7}(y) > 1 \\ 1, \; x = y = 1 \end{cases} \tag{40}$$

Proposition 5. *If $\gamma < 0$ and $2\gamma + \delta > 0$ or $\gamma > 0$ and $\delta^2 + \delta - \gamma > 0$, then the fuzzy negation $N^{\gamma,\delta}$ of Theorem 1 is a convex function.*

Proof. If we calculate the second derivate of $N_{\gamma,\delta}$, we have the following: $\frac{\partial^2 N_{\gamma,\delta}(x)}{\partial x^2} = \frac{-\gamma^2x^3+3\gamma^2x^2+3\gamma x+3\gamma\delta x+\delta^2+\delta-\gamma}{(\gamma x^2+\delta\chi+1)^3}$.

We define $f(x) = -\gamma^2x^3 + 3\gamma^2x + 3\gamma x + 3\gamma\delta x + \delta^2 + \delta - \gamma$; then:

$$\frac{\partial f(x)}{\partial x} = -3\gamma^2x^2 + 6\gamma^2x + 3\gamma + 3\gamma\delta$$

And the discriminant of the polynomial

$$\Delta = 36\gamma^4 + 36\gamma^3(1+\delta) = 36\gamma^4 + 36\gamma^3(1+\delta+\gamma-\gamma) = 36\gamma^3(1+\delta+\gamma)$$

If we examine the case, $\gamma < 0$ and $2\gamma + \delta > 0$; then, $\Delta = 36\gamma^3(1+\delta+\gamma) < 0$, which means that $\frac{\partial f(x)}{\partial x} < 0 \Leftrightarrow f(x)$ is a decreasing function, so we have $f(x) > f(1) \Leftrightarrow f(x) > (\gamma+\delta+1)(2\gamma+\delta) > 0$.

In this case ($\gamma < 0$), we already know that $\gamma + \delta + 1 > 0$. So, $\frac{\partial^2 N_{\gamma,\delta}(x)}{\partial x^2} > 0 \Leftrightarrow (2\gamma + \delta)(\gamma + \delta + 1) > 0 \Leftrightarrow 2\gamma + \delta > 0$.

In the case that $\gamma > 0$ and $\delta^2 + \delta - \gamma > 0$, we have the following:

$$\Delta = 36\gamma^3(1+\delta+\gamma) > 0 \Leftrightarrow x_{1,2} = \frac{-6\gamma^2 \pm \sqrt{36\gamma^3(1+\delta+\gamma)}}{-6\gamma^2} = \frac{-6\gamma^2 \pm 6\gamma\sqrt{\gamma(1+\delta+\gamma)}}{-6\gamma^2} = \frac{\gamma \pm \sqrt{\gamma(1+\delta+\gamma)}}{\gamma}$$

$x_1, x_2 \notin [0,1]$, which means that $\frac{\partial f(x)}{\partial x} > 0$, for all $x \in [0,1] \Leftrightarrow \frac{\partial N_{\gamma,\delta}(x)}{\partial x}$, is an increasing function. Thus, $\frac{\partial N_{\gamma,\delta}(x)}{\partial x} > \frac{\partial N_{\gamma,\delta}(0)}{\partial x} = \delta^2 + \delta - \gamma > 0$. □

3.3. Copulas with Quadratic Sections

We will analyze one of the linear sections of copulas, the quadratic form of the copula. In the book of Nelsen [28], we can find the quadratic and cubic sections of copulas.

The quadratic section of the copula is defined by the form:

$$C(x,y) = a(y)x^2 + b(y)x + c(y)$$

And the cubic section of the copula is defined by the form:

$$C(x,y) = a(y)x^3 + b(y)x^2 + c(y)x + d(y)$$

Before that, we present a proof of the equivalency $\frac{\partial^2 C(x,y)}{\partial xy} \geq 0$ and the last condition of the copula. We will use the main value theorem twice.

Proposition 6. *We know that, for a function to be 2-increasing, it must satisfy the inequality* $C(x_1,y_1) + C(x_2,y_2) - C(x_1,y_2) - C(x_2,y_1) \geq 0$. *This inequality is equivalent to*

$$\frac{\partial^2 C(x,y)}{\partial xy} \geq 0 \tag{41}$$

when C is a differentiable function.

Proof. We apply the mean value theorem for the function $C(x,y_1)$ in the interval $[x_1,x_2]$:

$$\exists\, \xi_1 \in (x_1,x_2): \frac{\partial C(\xi_1, y_1)}{\partial x} = \frac{C(x_2,y_1) - C(x_1,y_1)}{x_2 - x_1}$$

We apply the mean value theorem for the function $C(x,y_2)$ in the interval $[x_1,x_2]$:

$$\exists\, \xi_1 \in (x_1,x_2): \frac{\partial C(\xi_1, y_2)}{\partial x} = \frac{C(x_2,y_2) - C(x_1,y_2)}{x_2 - x_1}$$

Let us suppose that $C(x_1,y_1) + C(x_2,y_2) - C(x_1,y_2) - C(x_2,y_1) \geq 0$, then:

$$\frac{\partial C(\xi_1, y_2)}{\partial x} - \frac{\partial C(\xi_1, y_1)}{\partial x} \geq 0 \Leftrightarrow \frac{\partial^2 C(x,y)}{\partial xy} \geq 0$$

The other implication is analogous, but proceeds in reverse order. □

Proposition 7. *Function* $C : [0,\ 1]^2 \to [0,\ 1]$ *with quadratic form*

$$C(x,y) = a(y)x^2 + b(y)x + c(y) \tag{42}$$

is a copula if $a(0) = b(0) = 0$, $a(1) = 0$, $b(1) = 1$ *and* $\left|\frac{\partial a(y)}{\partial y}\right| \leq 1$.

Proof. Employing the boundary conditions, we have the following:

$$C(0,y) = c(y) = 0$$

$$C(x,0) = a(0)x^2 + b(0)x = 0 \Leftrightarrow a(0) = b(0) = 0$$
$$C(1,y) = a(y) + b(y) = y \Leftrightarrow b(y) = y - a(y)$$

$$C(x,1) = a(1)x^2 + b(1)x = x \Leftrightarrow \ a(1) = 0, \ b(1) = 1$$

After the boundary conditions, the quadratic form of the copula takes the following form

$$C(x,y) = a(y)x^2 + (\ y - a(y))x \tag{43}$$

We know that, in order for a function to be 2-increasing, it must satisfy the following inequality:

$$C(x_1,y_1) + C(x_2,y_2) - C(x_1,y_2) - C(x_2,y_1) \geq 0$$

This inequality is equivalent to $\frac{\partial^2 C(x)}{\partial xy} \geq 0$ when the function C is differentiable. We will use this inequality to set some conditions for the function $a(y)$.

$$\frac{\partial C(x,y)}{\partial x} = 2xa(y) + y - a(y)$$

$$\frac{\partial^2 C(x)}{\partial xy} = 2x\frac{\partial a(y)}{\partial y} + 1 - \frac{\partial a(y)}{\partial y} \Leftrightarrow \frac{\partial^2 C(x)}{\partial xy} = 1 + \frac{\partial a(y)}{\partial y}(2x-1) \geq 0$$

In the case of $\frac{\partial a(y)}{\partial y} \geq 0$, we have:

$$0 \leq x \leq 1 \Leftrightarrow -1 \leq 2x - 1 \leq 1 \Leftrightarrow -\frac{\partial a(y)}{\partial y} \leq \frac{\partial a(y)}{\partial y}(2x-1) \leq \frac{\partial a(y)}{\partial y} \Leftrightarrow$$

$$1 - \frac{\partial a(y)}{\partial y} \leq 1 + \frac{\partial a(y)}{\partial y}(2x-1) \leq 1 + \frac{\partial a(y)}{\partial y} \Leftrightarrow$$

$$1 - \frac{\partial a(y)}{\partial y} \leq \frac{\partial^2 C(x)}{\partial xy} \leq 1 + \frac{\partial a(y)}{\partial y} \Leftrightarrow \frac{\partial^2 C(x)}{\partial xy} \geq 0 \Leftrightarrow 1 - \frac{\partial a(y)}{\partial y} \geq 0 \Leftrightarrow \frac{\partial a(y)}{\partial y} \leq 1$$

In the case of $\frac{\partial a(y)}{\partial y} \leq 0$, we have:

$$1 + \frac{\partial a(y)}{\partial y} \leq \frac{\partial^2 C(x)}{\partial xy} \leq 1 - \frac{\partial a(y)}{\partial y} \Leftrightarrow \frac{\partial^2 C(x)}{\partial xy} \geq 0 \Leftrightarrow 1 + \frac{\partial a(y)}{\partial y} \geq 0 \Leftrightarrow \frac{\partial a(y)}{\partial y} \geq -1$$

We conclude that the function $a(y)$ must satisfy the following condition:

$$-1 \leq \frac{\partial a(y)}{\partial y} \leq 1 \Leftrightarrow \left|\frac{\partial a(y)}{\partial y}\right| \leq 1 \tag{44}$$

□

Function $a(y)$ has at least two roots: the numbers 0 and 1. Using root 1, and because it is also a root of the fuzzy negations, we can give it the following form: $a(y) = y{\cdot}N(y)$, where N is a fuzzy negation. Here, we can make combinations with the above generated fuzzy negations. If we choose the Sugeno fuzzy negation, we will study what conditions must be satisfied by coefficient δ.

Theorem 4. *Let $N_\delta : [0,1] \to [0,1]$, the Sugeno class fuzzy negation $N_\delta(x) = \frac{1-x}{\delta\chi+1}$, and $a : [0,\ 1] \to \mathbb{R}$ with the form $a(y) = y{\cdot}N_\delta(y)$.*

$$If\ \delta \geq 0, then -1 \leq \frac{\partial a(y)}{\partial y} \leq 1 \tag{45}$$

Proof.

$$a(y) = y{\cdot}N_\delta(y) = \frac{y{\cdot}(1-y)}{\delta y+1} \Leftrightarrow \frac{\partial a(y)}{\partial y} = \frac{-\delta y^2 - 2y + 1}{(\delta y+1)^2}$$

Function $a(y)$ must satisfy the inequality $-1 \leq \frac{\partial a(y)}{\partial y} \leq 1$.

For $\frac{\partial a(y)}{\partial y} \leq 1$, we have $\frac{-\delta y^2-2y+1}{(\delta y+1)^2} \leq 1 \Leftrightarrow y(\delta+1)(\delta y+2) \geq 0 \Leftrightarrow$, which is always true.

For $\frac{\partial a(y)}{\partial y} \geq -1$, we have $\frac{-\delta y^2-2y+1}{(\delta y+1)^2} \geq -1 \Leftrightarrow \delta(\delta-1)y^2 + 2(\delta-1)y + 2 \geq 0$.

If we set $f(y) = \delta(\delta-1)y^2 + 2(\delta-1)y + 2$, then $\frac{\partial f(y)}{\partial y} = 2\delta(\delta-1)y + 2(\delta-1) = 2(\delta-1)(\delta y+1)$.

If $\delta \geq 1$, then $\frac{\partial f(y)}{\partial y} \geq 0$. Thus, $f(y) \geq f(0) = 2 > 0$, (6) is true.

If $-1 < \delta \leq 1$, then $\frac{\partial f(y)}{\partial y} \leq 0$. Thus, $.f(y) \geq f(1) = \delta(\delta-1) + 2(\delta-1) + 2 = \delta^2 + \delta = \delta(\delta+1) \geq 0 \Leftrightarrow \delta \geq 0$.

We therefore conclude that inequality is satisfied when $\delta \geq 0$. □

As follows, if we choose the fuzzy negation of Theorem 2, $N^g(x) = \frac{1-x}{x{\cdot}g(x)+1}$, we will study what conditions must be established by the function g in order to satisfy the inequality $-1 \leq \frac{\partial a(y)}{\partial y} \leq 1$. We recall that the function g is an increasing function and $g(x) > -1$.

Theorem 5. *Let $N^g : [0,1] \to [0,1]$, the fuzzy negation of the Theorem 2 and function $a : [0,\ 1] \to \mathbb{R}$ defined by $a(y) = yN^g(y)$.*

$$If\ g(y) \geq 0\ and\ \frac{\partial g(y)}{\partial y} \leq 2\ then -1 \leq \frac{\partial a(y)}{\partial y} \leq 1 \tag{46}$$

Proof.

$$a(y) = yN^g(x) = \frac{y-y^2}{yg(y)+1} \Leftrightarrow \frac{\partial a(y)}{\partial y} = \frac{-y^2 g(y) + y^2\frac{\partial g(y)}{\partial y}(y-1) + 1 - 2y}{(yg(y)+1)^2}$$

Function $a(y)$ must satisfy the inequality $-1 \leq \frac{\partial a(y)}{\partial y} \leq 1$.

For $\frac{\partial a(y)}{\partial y} \leq 1$

$$\Leftrightarrow \frac{-y^2 g(y) + y^2\frac{\partial g(y)}{\partial y}(y-1) + 1 - 2y}{(yg(y)+1)^2} \leq 1 \Leftrightarrow$$

$$y^2\frac{\partial g(y)}{\partial y}(y-1) - yg(y){\cdot}(y + y{\cdot}g(y) + 2) \leq 0\ when\ g(y) \geq 0$$

For $\frac{\partial a(y)}{\partial y} \geq -1$

$$\frac{-y^2 g(y) + y^2 \frac{\partial g(y)}{\partial y}(y-1) + 1 - 2y}{\left(yg(y)+1\right)^2} \geq -1 \Leftrightarrow$$

$$yg(y)[(yg(y)+1)+(1-y)] + (1-y)\left(2 - y^2 \cdot \frac{\partial g(y)}{\partial y}\right) \geq 0 \Leftrightarrow \frac{\partial g(y)}{\partial y} \leq 2$$

□

Example 6. *If we take the quadratic section of the copula* $C(x,y) = a(y)x^2 + (y - a(y))x$ *for* $\delta = 2$ *we can set* $a(y) = y \cdot N_\delta(y) = \frac{y \cdot (1-y)}{2y+1}$*, then the produced copula is:*

$$C(x,y) = \frac{y \cdot (1-y)}{2y+1} \cdot x^2 + \left(y - \frac{y \cdot (1-y)}{2y+1}\right) \cdot x \tag{47}$$

The survival copula (15) is defined by:

$$C(x,y) = x + y - 1 + C(1-x, 1-y) =$$

$$x + y - 1 + \frac{y \cdot (1-y)}{3-2y} \cdot (1-x)^2 + \left((1-y) - \frac{y \cdot (1-y)}{3-2y}\right)(1-x) \tag{48}$$

Example 7. *If we choose* $g(x) = x^2 \Leftrightarrow \frac{\partial g(x)}{\partial x} = 2x \leq \frac{2}{x^2} \Leftrightarrow 2x^3 \leq 2$, *which is true for every* $x \in [0,\ 1]$. *Thus, we can produce another copula if we set* $a(y) = yN^g(y) \overset{g(y)=y^2}{=} \frac{y-y^2}{y^3+1}$. *Then, the produced copula is*

$$C(x,y) = \frac{y - y^2 \cdot x^2}{y^3+1} + \left(y - \frac{y-y^2}{y^3+1}\right) \cdot x \tag{49}$$

The survival copula is defined by:

$$C(x,y) = x + y - 1 + C(1-x, 1-y) =$$

$$x + y - 1 + \frac{(1-y) - (1-y)^2 \cdot \left(1-x\right)^2}{(1-y)^3 + 1} + \left(y - \frac{1 - y - (1-y)^2}{(1-y)^3+1}\right) \cdot (1-x) \tag{50}$$

3.4. A Presentation of a Hypothetical Scenario

Let X, Y represented linguistic variables, i.e., fuzzy sets. Let us also suppose that $X \Rightarrow Y$. For each, $x \in X$ and $y \in Y$ correspond to a value pair (x_i, y_i). If we collect a "good sample" (x_i, y_i), $i = 1, \ldots, n$, then we have:

$$x_1 \Rightarrow y_1$$

$$x_2 \Rightarrow y_2$$

$$\vdots$$

$$x_n \Rightarrow y_n$$

But since we have a "good sample",

$$x_1 \Rightarrow y_1 = 1$$

$$x_2 \Rightarrow y_2 = 1$$

$$\vdots$$

$$x_n \Rightarrow y_n = 1$$

Then, using our implication, which is produced by a convex negation with a parameter a, we have the parametric implication $J(x, y, a)$.

Thus, we have:

$$x_1 \Rightarrow y_1 = J(x_1, y_1, a)$$

$$x_2 \Rightarrow y_2 = J(x_2, y_2, a)$$

$$\vdots$$

$$x_n \Rightarrow y_n = J(x_n, y_n, a)$$

Now, we can select the "best implication" as that which has the shortest distance from *1*. That is, we see this when the number

$$(1 - J(x_1, y_1, a))^2 + (1 - J(x_2, y_2, a))^2 + \ldots + (1 - J(x_n, y_n, a))^2 \tag{51}$$

becomes the minimum.

For further reading and other research applications, the development method in [31,32] could also be applied.

4. Conclusions

The main goal of our construction of fuzzy negations is the generation of fuzzy implications. The symmetry or lack thereof of the generated fuzzy implications plays a key role in the application. For example, if the generated implications are symmetric, then the cause and the causality are mixed. In our construction, the cause and the causality are distinct. Moreover, new fuzzy implications give us new copulas. In this work, we have proposed some novel construction methods of fuzzy negations. Firstly, we presented a new class of rational fuzzy negations inspired by the Sugeno class fuzzy negation. Secondly, we replaced the parameter δ of the Sugeno class with an increasing function g with specific conditions. We generalized a form which generates strong fuzzy negations by using two decreasing functions f, g. Also, we gave some extra conditions so that the new fuzzy negations would be convex and we gave many examples of the new generated fuzzy negations (see Figures 1–5). Finally, we dealt with the quadratic section of the copula, trying to find the appropriate function $a(x)$ using the new fuzzy negations of the Theorems 1 and 2. As a future work, we can investigate some other methods that produce copulas. We will produce parametric copulas and research what conditions the coefficients must satisfy. At this point, we must emphasize the fact that our suggested method could also be applied by using a method that is amazing, in our opinion, on the cubic section of the copula:

$$C(x, y) = a(y)x^3 + b(y)x^2 + c(y)x + d(y) \tag{52}$$

which we can find in the book of Nelsen [28]. With this method, the case of the cubic section of the copula, which has two functions, a and b, with common roots of the numbers *0* and *1*, is investigated. Using the new fuzzy negation of the first method, we can find which conditions its coefficients must satisfy in order to produce a copula. We could accomplish the same result using the extension of the Sugeno class. In this class, we investigate a function g in which we must determinate properties to be satisfied such that a cubic copula can be produced. On the other hand, we can continue to extend other well-known fuzzy negations by using appropriate functions instead of parameters. In addition to this, we can investigate the extension of the Yager class of fuzzy negation, where instead of the parameter w, we can use a function with the appropriate properties.

The more new negations are produced, the more fuzzy implications and copulas can be generated. In research, we need many such functions of two variables in order to be able to choose the best one for each case every time.

Author Contributions: Conceptualization, M.N.R. and B.K.P.; methodology, M.N.R. and B.K.P.; software, M.N.R.; validation, M.N.R., A.K. and B.K.P.; formal analysis, M.N.R. and A.K.; investigation, M.N.R., A.K. and B.K.P.; resources, M.N.R. and A.K.; data curation, M.N.R.; writing—original draft preparation, M.N.R.; writing—review and editing, M.N.R. and A.K.; visualization, M.N.R.; supervision, A.K and B.K.P.; project administration, A.K. and B.K.P. All authors have read and agreed to the published version of the manuscript.

Funding: This research received no external funding.

Data Availability Statement: No new data were created or analyzed in this study.

Acknowledgments: The authors would like to thank the anonymous referees for their valuable comments and suggestions.

Conflicts of Interest: The authors declare no conflict of interest.

References

1. Bustince, H.; Campión, M.J.; De Miguel, L.; Induráin, E. Strong negations and restricted equivalence functions revisited: An analytical and topological approach. *Fuzzy Sets Syst.* **2022**, *441*, 110–129. [CrossRef]
2. Bedregal, B.C. On interval fuzzy negations. *Fuzzy Sets Syst.* **2010**, *161*, 2290–2313. [CrossRef]
3. Gupta, V.K.; Massanet, S.; Vemuri, N.R. Novel construction methods of interval-valued fuzzy negations and aggregation functions based on admissible orders. *Fuzzy Sets Syst.* **2023**, *473*, 108722. [CrossRef]
4. Grabowski, A. On Fuzzy Negations Generated by Fuzzy Implications. *Formaliz. Math.* **2020**, *28*, 121–128. [CrossRef]
5. De Lima, A.A.; Bedregal, B.; Mezzomo, I. *Ordinal Sums of the Main Classes of Fuzzy Negations and the Natural Negations of t-Norms, t-Conorms and Fuzzy Implications*; Elsevier: Amsterdam, The Netherlands, 2020; Volume 116, pp. 19–32.
6. Grabowski, A. On Fuzzy Negations and Laws of Contraposition. Lattice of Fuzzy Negations. *Formaliz. Math.* **2023**, *31*, 151–159. [CrossRef]
7. Baczynski, M.; Jayaram, B. QL-implications: Some properties and intersections. *Fuzzy Sets Syst.* **2010**, *161*, 158–188. [CrossRef]
8. Baczynski, M.; Jayaram, B. (U, N)-implications and their characterizations. *Fuzzy Sets Syst.* **2009**, *160*, 2049–2062. [CrossRef]
9. Durante, F.; Klement, E.P.; Meriar, R.; Sempi, C. Conjunctors and their residual implicators: Characterizations and construction methods. *Mediterr. J. Math.* **2007**, *4*, 343–356. [CrossRef]
10. Massanet, S.; Torrens, J. An Overview of Construction Methods of Fuzzy Implications. In *Advances in Fuzzy Implication Functions*; Studies in Fuzziness and Soft Computing; Springer: Berlin/Heidelberg, Germany, 2013; Volume 300, pp. 1–30. [CrossRef]
11. Rapti, M.; Papadopoulos, B. A Method of Generating Fuzzy Implications from n Increasing Functions and n + 1 Negations. *Mathematics* **2020**, *8*, 886. [CrossRef]
12. Baczynski, M.; Jayaram, B.; Massanet, S.; Torrens, J. Fuzzy implications: Past, present, and future. In *Springer Handbook of Computational Intelligence. Springer Handbooks*; Springer: Berlin/Heidelberg, Germany, 2015; pp. 183–202. [CrossRef]
13. Sainio, E.; Turunen, E.; Mesiar, R. A characterization of fuzzy implications generated by generalized quantifiers. *Fuzzy Sets Syst.* **2008**, *159*, 491–499. [CrossRef]
14. Baczynski, M.; Jayaram, B. On the characterization of (S, N)-implications. *Fuzzy Sets Syst.* **2007**, *158*, 1713–1727. [CrossRef]
15. Massanet, S.; Torrens, J. Threshold generation method of construction of a new implication from two given ones. *Fuzzy Sets Syst.* **2012**, *205*, 50–75. [CrossRef]
16. Balasubramanian, J. Yager's new class of implications J_f and some classical tautologies. *Inf. Sci.* **2007**, *177*, 930–946. [CrossRef]
17. Daniilidou, A.; Konguetsof, A.; Souliotis, G.; Papadopoulos, B. Generator of Fuzzy Implications. *Algorithms* **2023**, *16*, 569. [CrossRef]
18. Massanet, S.; Vicente, J.; Clapes, R.; Aguilera, D.R. On fuzzy polynomials implications. In Proceedings of the 2015 Conference of the International Fuzzy Systems Association and the European Society for Fuzzy Logic and Technology (IFSA-EUSFLAT-15), Montpellier, France, 15–19 July 2014. [CrossRef]
19. Torrens, S.M.J. A new method of generating fuzzy implications from given ones. In Proceedings of the 7th Conference of the European Society for Fuzzy Logic and Technology (EUSFLAT-11), Aix-les-Bains, France, 18–22 July 2011.

20. Mas, M.; Monserrat, M.; Torrens, J.; Trillas, E. A survey on fuzzy implication functions. *IEEE Trans. Fuzzy Syst.* **2007**, *15*, 1107–1121. [CrossRef]
21. Grzerorzewski, P. Probabilistic Implications. In Proceedings of the 7th Conference of the European Society for Fuzzy Logic and Technology (EUSFLAT-11), Aix-les-Bains, France, 18–22 July 2011. [CrossRef]
22. Bustince, H.; Pagola, M.; Barrenechea, E. Construction of fuzzy indices from fuzzy DIsubsethood measures: Application to the global comparison of images. *Inf. Sci.* **2007**, *177*, 906–929. [CrossRef]
23. Chaira, T. Fuzzy Measures in Image Processing. In *Fuzzy Sets and Their Extensions: Representation, Aggregation and Models*; Springer: Berlin/Heidelberg, Germany, 2008.
24. Jayaram, B.; Mesiar, R. I-fuzzy equivalence relations and i-fuzzy partitions. *Inf. Sci.* **2009**, *179*, 1278–1297. [CrossRef]
25. Morillas, P.M. A method to obtain new copulas from a given one. *Metrika* **2005**, *61*, 169–184. [CrossRef]
26. Mesiar, R.; Kolesarova, A. Copulas and fuzzy implications. *Int. J. Approx. Reason.* **2020**, *117*, 52–59. [CrossRef]
27. Durante, F.; Sempi, C. *Principles of Copula Theory*; Chapman and Hall/CRC: New York, NY, USA, 2015. [CrossRef]
28. Nelsen, R.B. *An Introduction to Copulas*, 2nd ed.; Springer: New York, NY, USA, 2006.
29. Baczynski, M.; Jayaram, B. (S, N)-and R-implications; a state-of-the-art survey. *Fuzzy Sets Syst.* **2008**, *159*, 1836–1859. [CrossRef]
30. Baczynski, M.; Jayaram, B. *Fuzzy Implications*; Springer: Berlin/Heidelberg, Germany, 2008. [CrossRef]
31. Javadpour, A.; Sangaiah, A.K.; Zaviyeh, H.; Ja'fari, F. Enhancing Energy Efficiency in IoT Networks Through Fuzzy Clustering and Optimization. In *Mobile Networks and Applications*; Springer: Berlin/Heidelberg, Germany, 2023. [CrossRef]
32. Botzoris, G.N.; Papadopoulos, K.; Papadopoulos, B.K. A method for the evaluation and selection of an appropriate fuzzy implication by using statistical data. *Fuzzy Econ.* **2015**, *20*, 19–29. [CrossRef]

symmetry

MDPI

Article

Enhancing Integer Time Series Model Estimations through Neural Network-Based Fuzzy Time Series Analysis

Mohammed H. El-Menshawy [1], Mohamed S. Eliwa [2,3], Laila A. Al-Essa [4], Mahmoud El-Morshedy [5,6,*] and Rashad M. EL-Sagheer [1,7]

1 Mathematics Department, Faculty of Science, Al-Azhar University, Naser City, Cairo 11884, Egypt; m.h.elmenshawy@azhar.edu.eg (M.H.E.-M.); rashadmath@azhar.edu.eg (R.M.E.-S.)
2 Department of Statistics and Operations Research, College of Science, Qassim University, Buraydah 51482, Saudi Arabia; m.eliwa@qu.edu.sa
3 Department of Mathematics, Faculty of Science, Mansoura University, Mansoura 35516, Egypt
4 Department of Mathematical Sciences, College of Science, Princess Nourah bint Abdulrahman University, P.O. Box 84428, Riyadh 11671, Saudi Arabia
5 Department of Mathematics, College of Science and Humanities in Al-Kharj, Prince Sattam Bin Abdulaziz University, Al-Kharj 11942, Saudi Arabia
6 Department of Statistics and Computer Science, Faculty of Science, Mansoura University, Mansoura 35516, Egypt
7 High Institute of Computer and Management Information System, First Statement, Cairo 11865, Egypt
* Correspondence: m.elmorshedy@psau.edu.sa

Abstract: This investigation explores the effects of applying fuzzy time series (FTSs) based on neural network models for estimating a variety of spectral functions in integer time series models. The focus is particularly on the skew integer autoregressive of order one (NSINAR(1)) model. To support this estimation, a dataset consisting of NSINAR(1) realizations with a sample size of n = 1000 is created. These input values are then subjected to fuzzification via fuzzy logic. The prowess of artificial neural networks in pinpointing fuzzy relationships is harnessed to improve prediction accuracy by generating output values. The study meticulously analyzes the enhancement in smoothing of spectral function estimators for NSINAR(1) by utilizing both input and output values. The effectiveness of the output value estimates is evaluated by comparing them to input value estimates using a mean-squared error (MSE) analysis, which shows how much better the output value estimates perform.

Keywords: neural network; time series; NSINAR(1); spectrum; bispectrum; computer simulation; Daniell lag window; fuzzy inference; statistics and numerical data

Citation: El-Menshawy, M.H.; Eliwa, M.S.; Al-Essa, L.A.; El-Morshedy, M.; EL-Sagheer, R.M. Enhancing Integer Time Series Model Estimations through Neural Network-Based Fuzzy Time Series Analysis. *Symmetry* **2024**, *16*, 660. https://doi.org/10.3390/sym16060660

Academic Editors: Jian-Qiang Wang, Hsien-Chung Wu and Sergei D. Odintsov

Received: 17 March 2024
Revised: 26 April 2024
Accepted: 15 May 2024
Published: 27 May 2024

1. Introduction

In recent years, a variety of FTS methodologies have emerged in the literature. FTSs can be defined as employing fuzzy sets to represent its observations. Ref. [1] provided the initial description of FTSs and outlined its fundamental definitions. Fundamentally, an FTS is comprised of three consecutive steps: fuzzification, fuzzy relationship formation, and defuzzification. Numerous studies that have investigated these processes [2–5] have focused solely on the most recent process. Additionally, because the formation of fuzzy links is directly related to predicting, numerous studies have concentrated on it [6–10]. Artificial neural networks appear to be quite good at figuring out fuzzy relationships that increase the forecasting performance's accuracy. Generally, artificial neural network techniques have shown success in a wide range of applications as in [11–13], and researchers often employ neural networks to build fuzzy relationships of the FTS. Over time, there have been notable breakthroughs in the field of modeling integer-valued time series due to the substantial attention given to this topic. The integer autoregressive (INAR) model is one of the best among them for modeling counting series. In recent years, researchers have been striving to improve the INAR model's capacity to accurately reproduce observed data. This effort has involved modifications to various aspects of INAR models, including adjustments to the marginal distribution (see [14–17]), others the ranking of the models as [18,19], and yet others, the thinning operators as [20–27]. Ref. [28] investigates certain statistical metrics for a number of INAR(1) models. To match specific data and more accurately characterize it, [29] provided an INAR(1) model based on two thinning operators. The fuzzy logic employed in [30] enhanced the estimation of all density functions. Ref. [31] conducted research on the FTS technique to enhance periodograms while keeping their statistical characteristics. Ref. [32] investigates a few statistical properties and all density functions for the ZTPINAR(1) process. Ref. [33] applies the FTS based on the Chen method to smoothing estimates for the DCGINAR(1) process. Ref. [34] used a novel technique of FTSs to improve the estimation of stationary processes' unknown parameters by traditional methods. Ref. [35] employed a fuzzy Markov chain to enhance the estimates of density functions with respect to the MCGINAR(1) process.

Since it focuses on building fuzzy relationships that lead to forecasting, [36] was the first to apply neural networks to FTS predictions. Ref. [37] proposes a novel method for handling high-order multivariate fuzzy time series that is based on artificial neural networks. Ref. [38] develops a fuzzy time series model based on neural networks to enhance the forecasting of observations. Ref. [39] provides a brand-new hybrid fuzzy time series technique that uses artificial neural networks for defuzzification and a fuzzy c-means (FCM) method for fuzzification. Ref. [40] creates and develops precise statistical forecasting models to predict the monthly API and assesses these models to track the state of the air quality. In a unique method, [41] created a PSNN to create fuzzy associations in high-order FTSs and modified PSO to train the network's weights. By combining a convectional neural network and FTS method, [42] suggested short-term load forecasting. Ref. [43] employed various techniques to forecast the air pollution index (API) of Kuala Lumpur, Malaysia, for the year 2017. These techniques included the use of artificial neural networks (ANNs), autoregressive integrated moving average (ARIMA), trigonometric regressors, Box–Cox transformation, ARMA errors, trend and seasonality (TBATS), and multiple fuzzy time series (FTS) models. Ref. [44] built an LSTM recurrent neural network based on trend fuzzy granulation for long-term time series forecasting. A unique multi-functional recurrent fuzzy neural network (MFRFNN) for time series prediction was developed in [45]. Ref. [46] suggested a shallow and deep neural network model for demand forecasting fuzzy time series pharmaceutical data.

The purpose of this research is to present fuzzy time series (FTSs), which are based on neural network models [36], and is intended to enhance estimates of density functions for integer time series. These functions are spectral, bispectral, and normalized bispectral density functions. The NSINAR(1) model is used in this strategy. All spectrum functions and their smoothed estimations for NSINAR(1) are computed for this purpose. We use neural network-based FTSs and forecast realizations to generate the output values for NSINAR(1) observational "input values". All density functions are estimated with input and output values. The contribution of the output values of neural network-based FTSs to smoothing of these estimations is investigated by contrasting the two cases using the results.

2. Developing the Forecasting Models

The following are the procedures for establishing a forecasting model: data preparation, evaluation, and selection; neural network construction (in terms of input variable selection, transfer function, structure, etc. [47].

2.1. Preparing Data

A number of crucial decisions, including data preparation, input variable selection, network type and design, the transfer function, training methodology, and model validation, assessment, and selection, must be made by the neural network forecaster. Some of these choices can be made while building the model, but others must be carefully thought through before beginning any modeling work. Given that neural networks operate on data-driven principles, data preparation emerges as a pivotal initial step in crafting an effective neural network model. Indeed, the creation of a practical and predictive neural network model heavily relies on the availability of a robust, sufficient, and representative dataset. Consequently, the quality of the data significantly influences the reliability of neural network models. Moreover, ample data are indispensable for the training process of neural networks. Numerous studies have utilized a practical ratio ranging from 70%:30% to 90%:10% for distinguish between in-samples and out-of-samples [47]. As a result, we use NSINAR(1) to construct a series of size n=1000. For our estimation (the in-sample), we chose the data from the first observation to the 800th, and for our forecast (the out-of-sample), we used the data from the 801st and 1000th. In other words, the ratio is around $\frac{800}{1000} : \frac{200}{1000} = 80\% : 20\%$ falling among the two categories of samples.

2.2. Setup of a Neural Network

The model used in forecasting the most is a multilayer feedforward structure [48]. As a result, backpropagation [49] was selected as the model, and *PC Neuron Institutional*, a backpropagation software package, was selected as the method for creating the forecasting model. In the setup, our goal was to first build (or train) the fuzzy associations between each FLR before forecasting. An FLR is a 1-1 relationship. Hence, there is one input layer and one output layer with one node each. The majority of forecasting applications have employed only one hidden layer and a suitable number of hidden nodes, even if there are several criteria for selecting the number of hidden layers and hidden nodes in each layer [50–52]. A minimal neural network was used [53] to avoid over-fitting. As a result, we employed two hidden nodes and one hidden layer. As a result, we created the neural network structure shown in Figure 1. Figure 2 shows the purpose of each node in the hidden and output layers. The previous layer's node(t) r, like X_r in the diagram, provides input(t) to the node s. A weight, Wrs, which represents the strength of the connection between each connection from node r to s, is attached to each one. The following formula is used to calculate node s'output, Y_t [30].

$$Y_t = f(\sum W_{rs} \times X_r - \theta_r), \tag{1}$$

$$f(z) = \frac{1}{1 + exp(-z)}, \tag{2}$$

where f(z) is a sigmoid function.

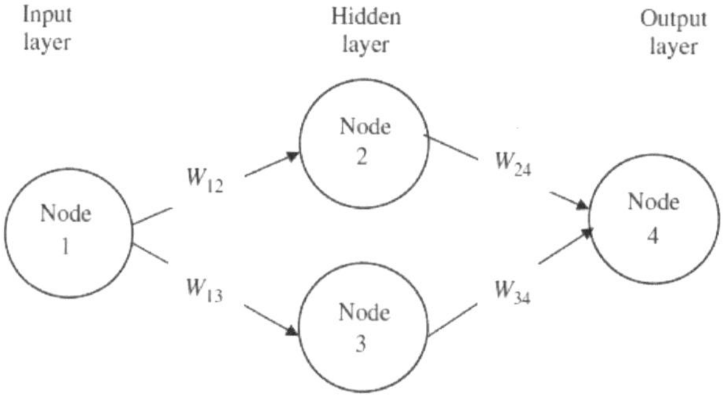

Figure 1. Neural network structure.

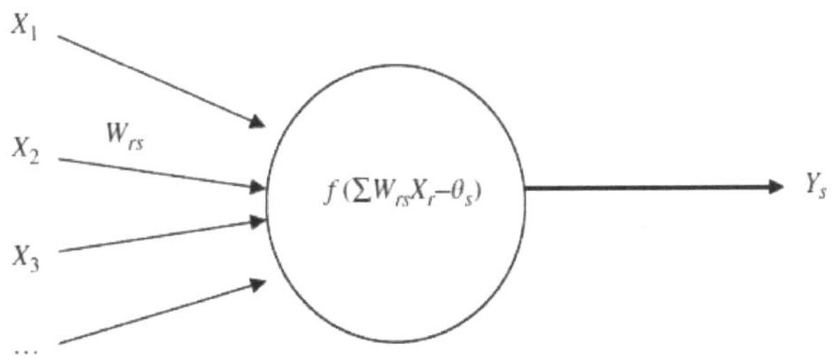

Figure 2. A node in a neural network.

2.3. Model Selection and Evaluation

A pertinent study [54] states that no single approach has proven to be consistently best for all kinds of applications, including neural network applications. Thus, we used a simple model, as well as a hybrid one. An in-sample and an out-of-sample category were created for the observations. A further division into known and unknown patterns was made for the out-of-sample observations. In contrast to the unidentified patterns that constituted the majority of the data outside of the sample, the observations that were present in both outside of the sample and inside the sample were regarded as established patterns. With regard to their respective original functions, we used the mean-squared error (MSE) to compare the performance of the three estimators in each of the three scenarios. For details on the calculation of the MSE, please refer to [32,33], which results in a different evaluation of the three different types of observations.

3. Fuzzy Time Series Models Utilizing Neural Networks

This study applied a backpropagation neural network to forecast the fuzzy observations with respect to the FTS of NSINAR(1). There are six steps in this study, which can be reported as follows:

1. Defining and partitioning the universe of discourse: According to the problem domain of NSINAR(1)′ series, the universe of discourse for observations, U =[starting, ending], is defined. After the length of the intervals, l, is determined, U can be partitioned into equal-length intervals $u_1, u_2, u_3, \ldots, u_b, b = 1, \ldots$ and their corresponding midpoints $m_1, m_2, m_3, \ldots, m_b$: respectively.

$$u_b = [starting + (b-1) \times l_a, starting + b \times l_a], \tag{3}$$

$$m_b = \frac{1}{2} \times [starting + (b-1) \times l_a, starting + b \times l_a]. \tag{4}$$

2. Defining fuzzy sets for observations: Each linguistic observation, A_i, can be defined by the intervals $u_1, u_2, u_3, \ldots, u_b$, where $A_i = f_{Ai}(u_1)/u_1 + f_{Ai}(u_2)/u_2 + \ldots + f_{Ai}(u_b)/u_b$.
3. Fuzzifying the observations: A fuzzy set is created by fuzzifying each observation. An observation is fuzzified to A_i if its greatest degree of membership is in A_i, just as in [6,55].
4. Establishing the fuzzy relationship (neural network training): The fuzzy associations in these **FLR**s were built (or trained) using a backpropagation neural network. Index i served as the input, and index j served as the appropriate output for each FLR, $A_i \to A_j$. These **FLR**s became the input and output patterns for neural network training.
5. Forecasting: A description of the hybrid and basic models can be found below. The basic model uses a neural network methodology to forecast each piece of data, while the hybrid model uses the same neural network approach to forecast the known patterns together with a simple strategy to anticipate the unknown patterns.

Model 1 (basic mode): Assume $F(t-1) = A_{i'}$. We chose i' as the forecast input in order to make the calculations easier. Assume that j' is the neural network's output. The hazy forecast is $A_{j'}$, we say. In other words,

$$F(t) = A_{j'}. \tag{5}$$

Model 2 (hybrid mode): Assume $F(t-1) = A_{i'}$. If $A_{i'}$ is a recognized pattern, the basic model is used to obtain the fuzzy forecast. If $A_{i'}$ is an unknown pattern, then we merely take Ai as the fuzzily predicted value for $F(t)$, in accordance with Chen's model [6]. That is,

$$F(t) = A_{i'}. \tag{6}$$

6. Defuzzifying: No matter whatever model is used, the defuzzified forecast is always equal to the fuzzy forecast's midpoint. Assume $A_{k'}$ is the fuzzy prediction for F(t). The forecast that has been defuzzed corresponds to $A_{k'}$'s middle, i.e.,

$$forecast_t = m_{k'}. \tag{7}$$

For additional details on this methodology, see [36]. Therefore, the forecast observations that were obtained from the generated realizations from the NSINAR(1) process—known as the "input values"—are the "output values" of this approach.

4. The New Skew INAR(1) Model

The NSINAR(1) process was first defined by [56]. These model, also known as true integer autoregressive models, have become necessary for the modeling of count data with positive and negative values. It defines the NSINAR(1) as

$$X_t = \beta \star X_{t-1} + \eta_t \tag{8}$$

where $\beta \star X_{t-1} \overset{d}{=} \beta * A_{t-1} - \beta \circ B_{t-1}$ is the difference between the negative binomial thinning and binomial thinning operators, where the counting series $\beta * A_{t-1}$ and $\beta \circ B_{t-1}$ are independent random variables. $\beta * A = \sum_{i=0}^{A} W_i$ and $\beta \circ B = \sum_{i=0}^{B} U_i$, where W_i is a sequence of *i.i.d* geometric random variables and U_i is a sequence of *i.i.d.* Bernoulli random variables independent of W_i, $X_t = A_t - B_t$, where $A_t \sim$ geometric$(\frac{\gamma}{1+\gamma})$, $B_t \sim$ Poisson(λ), $\{X_t\}$ is a sequence of random variables having a geometric-Poisson (γ, λ), and η_t has the distribution of $\epsilon_t - \varepsilon_t$, where $\{\epsilon_t\}$ and $\{\varepsilon_t\}$ are independent r.v.s and X_t and η_{t-l} are independent for all $l \geq 1$. ε_t are i.i.d. r.v.s with a common Poisson$(\lambda(1-\beta))$ distribution, and ϵ_t is a mixture of two random variables with geometric $\gamma/(1+\gamma)$ and geometric$(\beta/(1+\beta))$ distributions. The condition of the stationarity of the process $\{X_t\}$ is $0 \leq \beta \leq \gamma/(1+\gamma)$, and the condition of the non-stationarity of the process $\{X_t\}$ is $\gamma/(1+\gamma) \leq \beta \leq 1$. Here, our study is restricted to the stationary case. Some properties of X_t are introduced:

The mean $\gamma_X = \gamma - \lambda$, the variance $\sigma_X^2 = \gamma(\gamma+1) + \lambda$, the second-order central moment $R_2(s) = \beta^s(\gamma^2 + \gamma + \lambda) = \beta^s R_2(0)$, and the third-order central moment are calculated as $R_3(0,0) = 2\gamma^3 + 3\gamma^2 + \gamma - \lambda$, $R_3(0,s) = \beta^s(2\gamma^3 + 3\gamma^2 + \gamma - \lambda) = \beta^s R_3(0,0)$, and $R_3(s,s) = \beta^{2s} R_3(0,0) - \beta R_2(0) \frac{\beta^s - \beta^{2s}}{(1-\beta)}$. Refer to [23] and [56] for detailed information on the thinning operator $\star$ and the NSINAR(1) model, respectively.

5. Spectral and Bispectral Density Functions

In time series analysis, statistical spectral analysis plays a number of roles, including the estimate, hypothesis testing, data reduction, and description. It is quite helpful to examine a time series in both the time and frequency domains when performing an analysis. The Fourier transform, which converts the time series from the time domain to the frequency domain, is the fundamental tool of spectral analysis. This field frequently contains a wealth of important information that requires additional research to locate. Second-order spectra have played a very important role in the analysis of linear and Gaussian time series data and in signal processing. When the process is Gaussian, the second-order spectra contain all the necessary and useful information about the process, and we do not need to consider higher order spectra. Before analyzing the time series data, in most cases, we assume that the series is generated from a linear process and even from a Gaussian process for further simplified analysis. But, in reality, this is not the case for every process. The reason behind assuming the linearity of the process is that it is very easy to fit a linear model in comparison to fitting the actual non-linear model. In order to study non-linear and non-Gaussian processes, one needs to consider higher order spectra. Theoretically, it is possible to compute the spectrum of any order, but computationally, it is very costly. Hence, we will consider only the bispectrum, the simplest higher order spectrum. So, we can say that the second-order spectra will not adequately characterize the series (unless it is Gaussian), and hence, there is a need for higher order spectral analysis. The simplest type of higher order spectral analysis is the bispectral analysis. This leads us to the bispectral density function, which gives us important details regarding the process' nonlinearity. The normalized bispectrum's modulus for continuous non-Gaussian time series is flat.

The spectral density function "SDF", bispectral density function "BDF", and normalized bispectral density function "NBDF" of NSINAR(1) are provided in this section.

Theorem 1. *If (8) is satisfied by $\{X_t\}$, then the SDF, denoted by $g(w)$, is computed as Let $\{X_t\}$ satisfy (8), then the SDF, represented by $g(w)$ is calculated as*

$$g(w) = \frac{(1-\beta^2)(\gamma^2+\gamma+\lambda)}{2\pi(1+\beta^2-2\beta\cos w)}, \quad -\pi \le w \le \pi. \tag{9}$$

Proof.

$$\begin{aligned} g(w) &= \frac{1}{2\pi}\sum_{t=-\infty}^{\infty} R_2(t)exp(-iwt) = \frac{1}{2\pi}[R_2(0) + \sum_{t=1}^{\infty}\beta^t R_2(0)exp(-iwt) + \sum_{t=1}^{\infty}\beta^t R_2(0)exp(iwt)] \\ &= \frac{R_2(0)}{2\pi}[1 + \frac{\beta exp(-iw)}{1-\beta exp(-iw)} + \frac{\beta exp(iw)}{1-\beta exp(iw)}] = \frac{R_2(0)[1-\beta^2]}{2\pi(1+\beta^2-2\beta cos w)}. \end{aligned}$$

□

Theorem 2. *If (8) is satisfied by $\{X_t\}$, then the BDF, denoted by $g(w_1, w_2)$, are computed as*

$$\begin{aligned} g(w_1,w_2) =& \frac{1}{(2\pi)^2}\Bigg[R_3(0,0)\{1+F_1(-w_1)+F_1(-w_2)+F_1(w_1+w_2)+\left(R_3(0,0)+\frac{\beta^2R_2(0)}{\beta(1-\beta)}\right)\{F_2(w_1) \\ &+F_2(w_2)+F_2(-w_1-w_2)\}-\left(\frac{\beta^2R_2(0)}{\beta(1-\beta)}\right)\{F_1(w_1)+F_1(w_2)+F_1(-w_1-w_2)\} \\ &+F_1(-w_1)\{[F_2(-w_1-w_2)+F_2(w_2)](R_3(0,0)+\frac{\beta^2R_2(0)}{\beta(1-\beta)})-[F_1(-w_1-w_2) \\ &+F_1(w_2)]\frac{\beta^2R_2(0)}{\beta(1-\beta)}\}+F_1(-w_2)\{[F_2(-w_1-w_2)+F_2(w_1)](R_3(0,0)+\frac{\beta^2R_2(0)}{\beta(1-\beta)}) \\ &-[F_1(-w_1-w_2)+F_1(w_1)]\frac{\beta^2R_2(0)}{\beta(1-\beta)}\}+F_1(w_1+w_2)\{[F_2(w_1)+F_2(w_2)](R_3(0,0) \\ &+\frac{\beta^2R_2(0)}{\beta(1-\beta)})-[F_1(w_1)+F_1(w_2)]\frac{\beta^2R_2(0)}{\beta(1-\beta)}\}\Bigg], \quad -\pi \le w_1,w_2 \le \pi, \end{aligned} \tag{10}$$

where $F_1(w_k) = \frac{\beta exp(iw_k)}{1-\beta exp(iw_k)}$ *and* $F_2(w_k) = \frac{\beta^2 exp(iw_k)}{1-\beta^2 exp(iw_k)}, k = 1,2.$

Proof. We can write $g(w_1, w_2)$ as (see [17]) in the following formulae:

$$g(w_1,w_2) = \frac{1}{(2\pi)^2}[\sum_{t_1=0}^{\infty}\sum_{t_2=t_1}^{\infty} R_3(t_1,t_2)exp(-i(t_1w_1+t_2w_2)) + \sum_{t_2=0}^{\infty}\sum_{t_1=t_2+1}^{\infty} R_3(t_2,t_1)exp(-i(t_1w_1+t_2w_2))$$
$$+\sum_{t_1=0}^{\infty}\sum_{t_2=-\infty}^{-1} R_3(-t_2,t_1-t_2)exp(-i(t_1w_1+t_2w_2)) + \sum_{t_1=-\infty}^{-1}\sum_{t_2=-\infty}^{t_1-1} R_3(t_1-t_2,-t_2)exp(-i(t_1w_1+t_2w_2))$$
$$+\sum_{t_2=-\infty}^{-1}\sum_{t_1=-\infty}^{-t_2} R_3(t_2-t_1,-t_1)exp(-i(t_1w_1+t_2w_2)) + \sum_{t_1=-\infty}^{-1}\sum_{t_2=0}^{\infty} R_3(-t_1,t_2-t_1)exp(-i(t_1w_1+t_2w_2))].$$

Applying the symmetry characteristics of the third-order cumulants (see [57]), then

$$g(w_1,w_2) = \frac{1}{(2\pi)^2}[R_3(0,0) + \sum_{\tau=1}^{\infty} R_3(0,\tau)\{exp(-i\tau w_1) + exp(-i\tau w_2) + exp(i\tau(w_1+w_2))\}$$
$$+\sum_{\tau=1}^{\infty} R_3(\tau,\tau)\{exp(i\tau w_1) + exp(i\tau w_2) + exp(-i\tau(w_1+w_2))\}$$
$$+\sum_{t=1}^{\infty}\sum_{\tau=1}^{\infty} R_3(t,t+\tau)\{exp(-itw_1 - i(t+\tau)w_2) + exp(-itw_2 - i(t+\tau)w_1)$$
$$+exp(itw_1 - i\tau w_2)exp(itw_2 - i\tau w_1) + exp(i\tau w_1 + i(t+\tau)w_2) + exp(i\tau w_2 + i(t+\tau)w_1)\}].$$

Using the expressions of $R_3(0,\tau)$, $R_3(\tau,\tau)$ and $R_3(s,s+\tau)$, we obtain

$$g(w_1,w_2) = \frac{1}{(2\pi)^2}[R_3(0,0) + \sum_{\tau=1}^{\infty} \beta^{\tau} R_3(0,0)\{exp(-i\tau w_1) + exp(-i\tau w_2) + exp(i\tau(w_1+w_2))\}$$
$$+\sum_{\tau=1}^{\infty}(\beta^{2\tau}R_3(0,0) - \beta^2 R_2(0)\frac{\beta^{\tau}-\beta^{2\tau}}{\beta(1-\beta)})\{exp(i\tau w_1) + exp(i\tau w_2) + exp(-i\tau(w_1+w_2))\}$$
$$+\sum_{t=1}^{\infty}\sum_{\tau=1}^{\infty}\beta^{\tau}[\beta^{2t}R_3(0,0) - \beta^2 R_2(0)\frac{\beta^{t}-\beta^{2t}}{\beta(1-\beta)}]\{exp(-itw_1 - i(t+\tau)w_2) + exp(-itw_2 - i(t+\tau)w_1)$$
$$+exp(itw_1 - i\tau w_2)exp(itw_2 - i\tau w_1) + exp(i\tau w_1 + i(t+\tau)w_2) + exp(i\tau w_2 + i(t+\tau)w_1)\}].$$

All these summations can be evaluated as follows, for example

$$\sum_{\tau=1}^{\infty}(\beta^{\tau}exp(-i\tau w_1)) = \sum_{\tau=1}^{\infty}(\beta exp(-iw_1))^{\tau} = \frac{\beta exp(-iw_1)}{1-\beta exp(-iw_1)} = F_1(-w_1),$$

Hence, following a few computations and summations, we have

$$
\begin{aligned}
g(w_1,w_2) = & \frac{1}{(2\pi)^2}[R_3(0,0) + R_3(0,0)\{\frac{\beta exp(-iw_1)}{1-\beta exp(-iw_1)} + \frac{\beta exp(-iw_2)}{1-\beta exp(-iw_2)} + \frac{\beta exp(i(w_1+w_2))}{1-\beta exp(i(w_1+w_2))}\} \\
& + (R_3(0,0) + \frac{\beta^2 R_2(0)}{\beta-\beta^2})\{\frac{\beta^2 exp(iw_1)}{1-\beta^2 exp(iw_1)} + \frac{\beta^2 exp(iw_2)}{1-\beta^2 exp(iw_2)} + \frac{\beta^2 exp(-i(w_1+w_2))}{1-\beta^2 exp(-i(w_1+w_2))}\} \\
& - \frac{\beta^2 R_2(0)}{\beta-\beta^2}\{\frac{\beta exp(iw_1)}{1-\beta exp(iw_1)} + \frac{\beta exp(iw_2)}{1-\beta exp(iw_2)} + \frac{\beta exp(-i(w_1+w_2))}{1-\beta exp(-i(w_1+w_2))}\} + (R_3(0,0) \\
& + \frac{\beta^2 R_2(0)}{\beta-\beta^2}\{\frac{\beta^2 exp(-i(w_1+w_2))}{1-\beta^2 exp(-i(w_1+w_2))}\frac{\beta exp(-iw_2)}{1-\beta exp(-iw_2)} + \frac{\beta^2 exp(-i(w_1+w_2))}{1-\beta^2 exp(-i(w_1+w_2))}\frac{\beta exp(-iw_1)}{1-\beta exp(-iw_1)} \\
& + \frac{\beta^2 exp(iw_1)}{1-\beta^2 exp(iw_1)}\frac{\beta exp(-iw_2)}{1-\beta exp(-iw_2)} + \frac{\beta^2 exp(iw_2)}{1-\beta^2 exp(iw_2)}\frac{\beta exp(-iw_1)}{1-\beta exp(-iw_1)} \\
& + \frac{\beta^2 exp(iw_1)}{1-\beta^2 exp(iw_1)}\frac{\beta exp(i(w_1+w_2))}{1-\beta exp(i(w_1+w_2))} + \frac{\beta^2 exp(iw_2)}{1-\beta^2 exp(iw_2)}\frac{\beta exp(i(w_1+w_2))}{1-\beta exp(i(w_1+w_2))}\} \\
& + \frac{\beta^2 R_2(0)}{\beta-\beta^2}\{\frac{\beta exp(-i(w_1+w_2))}{1-\beta^{-i(w_1+w_2)}}\frac{\beta exp(-iw_2)}{1-\beta exp(-iw_2)} + \frac{\beta exp(-i(w_1+w_2))}{1-\beta exp(-i(w_1+w_2))}\frac{\beta exp(-iw_1)}{1-\beta exp(-iw_1)} \\
& + \frac{\beta exp(iw_1)}{1-\beta exp(iw_1)}\frac{\beta exp(-iw_2)}{1-\beta exp(-iw_2)} + \frac{\beta exp(iw_2)}{1-\beta exp(iw_2)}\frac{\beta exp(-iw_1)}{1-\beta exp(-iw_1)} \\
& + \frac{\beta exp(iw_1)}{1-\beta exp(iw_1)}\frac{\beta exp(i(w_1+w_2))}{1-\beta exp(i(w_1+w_2))} + \frac{\beta exp(iw_2)}{1-\beta exp(iw_2)}\frac{\beta exp(i(w_1+w_2))}{1-\beta exp(i(w_1+w_2))}\}],
\end{aligned}
$$

and by taking, $F_1(w_k) = \frac{\beta exp(iw_k)}{1-\beta exp(iw_k)}$ and $F_2(w_k) = \frac{\beta^2 exp(iw_k)}{1-(\beta^2 exp(iw_k))}, k = 1,2.$, the proof is complete. The NBDF, represented by $f(w_1,w_2)$, is calculated as

$$
f(w_1,w_2) = \frac{g(w_1,w_2)}{\sqrt{g(w_1)g(w_2)g(w_1+w_2)}}, \tag{11}
$$

where $g(w_1,w_2)$ and $g(w)$ are obtained by (11) and (9), respectively. □

Figure 3 illustrates the generated observations from the NSINAR(1) process at $\lambda = 3$, $\beta = 0.25$, and $\gamma = 5$. Figures 4, 5, and 6 show, respectively, the SDF, BDF, and NBDF of NSINAR(1) at $\lambda = 3, \beta = 0.25$, and $\gamma = 5$. We infer that the model is linear from Figures 5 and 6 and the results in Tables 1 and 2, since the NBDF values, which fall between (0.73, 0.78), are flatter (constant, very tightly spaced apart) than the BDF values, which fall between (5, 20). The simulated series of the forecasted NSINAR(1) observations of the neural network-based FTS in both the basic model and the hybrid model are shown in Figure 7. Figure 7 shows that the shape and properties of the time series are maintained by the forecasted observations. From Figures 3 and 7, one can deduce that the series is stationary and its values are positive- and negative-valued, and this agrees with the definition of the NSINAR(1) model.

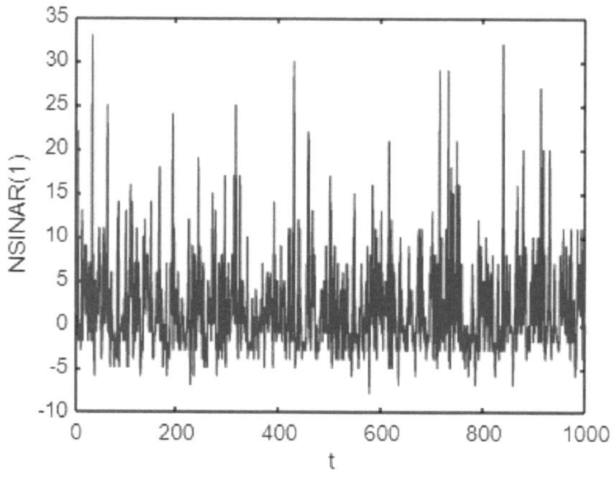

Figure 3. NSINAR(1) model simulations using $\lambda = 0.3, \beta = 0.25$, and $\gamma = 5$.

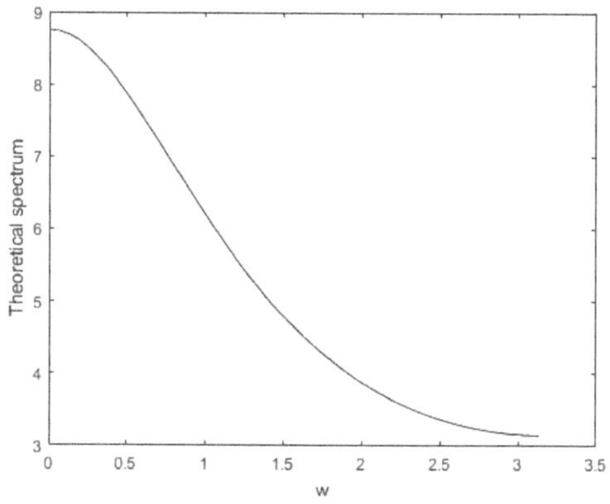

Figure 4. SDF of NSINAR(1) using $\lambda = 0.3$, $\beta = 0.25$, and $\gamma = 5$.

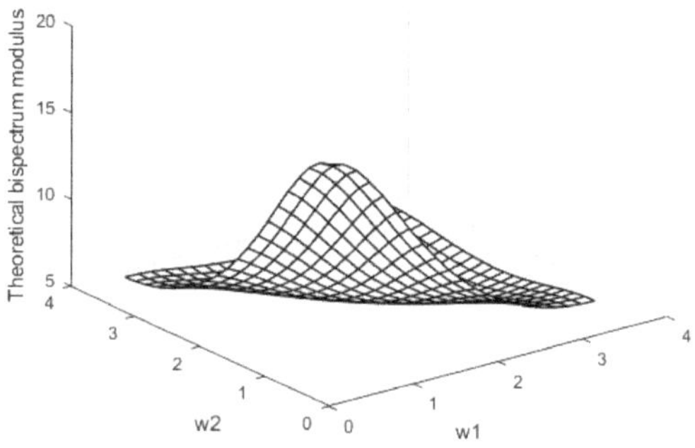

Figure 5. BDF of NSINAR(1) using $\lambda = 0.3, \beta = 0.25$, and $\gamma = 5$.

Table 1. The BDF of NSINAR(1) using $\lambda = 0.3, \beta = 0.25$, and $\gamma = 5$.

w_1 \ w_2	0.00 π	0.05 π	0.10 π	0.15 π	0.20 π	0.25 π	0.30 π	0.35 π	0.40 π	0.45 π	0.50 π	0.55 π	0.60 π	0.65 π	0.70 π	0.75 π	0.80 π	0.85 π	0.90 π	0.95 π	π
0.00 π	18.956	18.759	18.196	17.344	16.301	15.167	14.024	12.932	11.925	11.022	10.228	9.541	8.954	8.459	8.049	7.715	7.451	7.252	7.112	7.030	7.002
0.05 π	18.759	18.379	17.672	16.726	15.642	14.508	13.397	12.354	11.405	10.562	9.827	9.194	8.657	8.208	7.839	7.542	7.312	7.144	7.034	6.979	6.979
0.10 π	18.196	17.672	16.874	15.890	14.814	13.721	12.671	11.697	10.821	10.047	9.376	8.802	8.317	7.915	7.587	7.328	7.132	6.995	6.914	6.887	6.914
0.15 π	17.344	16.726	15.890	14.918	13.888	12.864	11.893	11.001	10.203	9.502	8.897	8.382	7.950	7.594	7.308	7.085	6.923	6.816	6.763	6.763	6.816
0.20 π	16.301	15.642	14.814	13.888	12.929	11.990	11.106	10.300	9.582	8.954	8.414	7.956	7.574	7.263	7.016	6.829	6.698	6.621	6.595	6.621	6.698
0.25 π	15.167	14.508	13.721	12.864	11.990	11.141	10.347	9.625	8.984	8.425	7.946	7.542	7.207	6.938	6.728	6.574	6.473	6.423	6.423	6.473	6.574
0.30 π	14.024	13.397	12.671	11.893	11.106	10.347	9.638	8.996	8.427	7.932	7.509	7.154	6.863	6.632	6.457	6.334	6.261	6.237	6.261	6.334	6.457
0.35 π	12.932	12.354	11.697	11.001	10.300	9.625	8.996	8.426	7.922	7.485	7.113	6.803	6.552	6.356	6.212	6.118	6.071	6.071	6.118	6.212	6.356
0.40 π	11.925	11.405	10.821	10.203	9.582	8.984	8.427	7.922	7.476	7.091	6.764	6.495	6.280	6.116	6.001	5.932	5.909	5.932	6.001	6.116	6.280
0.45 π	11.022	10.562	10.047	9.502	8.954	8.425	7.932	7.485	7.091	6.751	6.465	6.232	6.049	5.914	5.825	5.781	5.781	5.825	5.914	6.049	6.232
0.50 π	10.228	9.827	9.376	8.897	8.414	7.946	7.509	7.113	6.764	6.465	6.216	6.015	5.861	5.753	5.688	5.667	5.688	5.753	5.861	6.015	6.216
0.55 π	9.541	9.194	8.802	8.382	7.956	7.542	7.154	6.803	6.495	6.232	6.015	5.843	5.716	5.632	5.590	5.590	5.632	5.716	5.843	6.015	6.232
0.60 π	8.954	8.657	8.317	7.950	7.574	7.207	6.863	6.552	6.280	6.049	5.861	5.716	5.613	5.551	5.531	5.551	5.613	5.716	5.861	6.049	6.280
0.65 π	8.459	8.208	7.915	7.594	7.263	6.938	6.632	6.356	6.116	5.914	5.753	5.632	5.551	5.511	5.511	5.551	5.632	5.753	5.914	6.116	6.356
0.70 π	8.049	7.839	7.587	7.308	7.016	6.728	6.457	6.212	6.001	5.825	5.688	5.590	5.531	5.511	5.531	5.590	5.688	5.825	6.001	6.212	6.457
0.75 π	7.715	7.542	7.328	7.085	6.829	6.574	6.334	6.118	5.932	5.781	5.667	5.590	5.551	5.551	5.590	5.667	5.781	5.932	6.118	6.334	6.574
0.80 π	7.451	7.312	7.132	6.923	6.698	6.473	6.261	6.071	5.909	5.781	5.688	5.632	5.613	5.632	5.688	5.781	5.909	6.071	6.261	6.473	6.698
0.85 π	7.252	7.144	6.995	6.816	6.621	6.423	6.237	6.071	5.932	5.825	5.753	5.716	5.716	5.753	5.825	5.932	6.071	6.237	6.423	6.621	6.816
0.90 π	7.112	7.034	6.914	6.763	6.595	6.423	6.261	6.118	6.001	5.914	5.861	5.843	5.861	5.914	6.001	6.118	6.261	6.423	6.595	6.763	6.914
0.95 π	7.030	6.979	6.887	6.763	6.621	6.473	6.334	6.212	6.116	6.049	6.015	6.015	6.049	6.116	6.212	6.334	6.473	6.621	6.763	6.887	6.979
π	7.002	6.979	6.914	6.816	6.698	6.574	6.457	6.356	6.280	6.232	6.216	6.232	6.280	6.356	6.457	6.574	6.698	6.816	6.914	6.979	7.002

Table 2. The NBDF of NSINAR(1) using $\lambda = 0.3, \beta = 0.25$, and $\gamma = 5$.

w_1 \ w_2	0.00 π	0.05 π	0.10 π	0.15 π	0.20 π	0.25 π	0.30 π	0.35 π	0.40 π	0.45 π	0.50 π	0.55 π	0.60 π	0.65 π	0.70 π	0.75 π	0.80 π	0.85 π	0.90 π	0.95 π	π
0.00 π	0.7319	0.7322	0.7332	0.7346	0.7363	0.7381	0.7399	0.7417	0.7433	0.7447	0.7460	0.7471	0.7480	0.7488	0.7494	0.7499	0.7503	0.7507	0.7509	0.7510	0.7510
0.05 π	0.7322	0.7329	0.7340	0.7356	0.7373	0.7392	0.7410	0.7426	0.7442	0.7455	0.7467	0.7477	0.7485	0.7492	0.7498	0.7503	0.7507	0.7509	0.7511	0.7512	0.7512
0.10 π	0.7332	0.7340	0.7353	0.7369	0.7387	0.7405	0.7422	0.7438	0.7453	0.7465	0.7476	0.7485	0.7493	0.7500	0.7505	0.7509	0.7512	0.7515	0.7516	0.7516	0.7516
0.15 π	0.7346	0.7356	0.7369	0.7386	0.7403	0.7420	0.7437	0.7452	0.7465	0.7477	0.7487	0.7496	0.7503	0.7509	0.7514	0.7517	0.7520	0.7522	0.7523	0.7523	0.7522
0.20 π	0.7363	0.7373	0.7387	0.7403	0.7419	0.7436	0.7451	0.7466	0.7478	0.7489	0.7499	0.7507	0.7514	0.7519	0.7523	0.7527	0.7529	0.7530	0.7531	0.7530	0.7529
0.25 π	0.7381	0.7392	0.7405	0.7420	0.7436	0.7451	0.7466	0.7479	0.7491	0.7502	0.7511	0.7518	0.7524	0.7529	0.7533	0.7536	0.7538	0.7539	0.7539	0.7538	0.7536
0.30 π	0.7399	0.7410	0.7422	0.7437	0.7451	0.7466	0.7480	0.7493	0.7504	0.7514	0.7522	0.7529	0.7535	0.7539	0.7543	0.7545	0.7546	0.7547	0.7546	0.7545	0.7543
0.35 π	0.7417	0.7426	0.7438	0.7452	0.7466	0.7479	0.7493	0.7505	0.7515	0.7525	0.7532	0.7539	0.7544	0.7548	0.7551	0.7553	0.7554	0.7554	0.7553	0.7551	0.7548
0.40 π	0.7433	0.7442	0.7453	0.7465	0.7478	0.7491	0.7504	0.7515	0.7525	0.7534	0.7542	0.7548	0.7552	0.7556	0.7559	0.7560	0.7561	0.7560	0.7559	0.7556	0.7552
0.45 π	0.7447	0.7455	0.7465	0.7477	0.7489	0.7502	0.7514	0.7525	0.7534	0.7542	0.7549	0.7555	0.7559	0.7563	0.7565	0.7566	0.7566	0.7565	0.7563	0.7559	0.7555
0.50 π	0.7460	0.7467	0.7476	0.7487	0.7499	0.7511	0.7522	0.7532	0.7542	0.7549	0.7556	0.7561	0.7565	0.7568	0.7570	0.7570	0.7570	0.7568	0.7565	0.7561	0.7556
0.55 π	0.7471	0.7477	0.7485	0.7496	0.7507	0.7518	0.7529	0.7539	0.7548	0.7555	0.7561	0.7566	0.7569	0.7572	0.7573	0.7573	0.7572	0.7569	0.7566	0.7561	0.7555
0.60 π	0.7480	0.7485	0.7493	0.7503	0.7514	0.7524	0.7535	0.7544	0.7552	0.7559	0.7565	0.7569	0.7573	0.7574	0.7575	0.7574	0.7573	0.7569	0.7565	0.7559	0.7552
0.65 π	0.7488	0.7492	0.7500	0.7509	0.7519	0.7529	0.7539	0.7548	0.7556	0.7563	0.7568	0.7572	0.7574	0.7576	0.7576	0.7574	0.7572	0.7568	0.7563	0.7556	0.7548
0.70 π	0.7494	0.7498	0.7505	0.7514	0.7523	0.7533	0.7543	0.7551	0.7559	0.7565	0.7570	0.7573	0.7575	0.7576	0.7575	0.7573	0.7570	0.7565	0.7559	0.7551	0.7543
0.75 π	0.7499	0.7503	0.7509	0.7517	0.7527	0.7536	0.7545	0.7553	0.7560	0.7566	0.7570	0.7573	0.7574	0.7574	0.7573	0.7570	0.7566	0.7560	0.7553	0.7545	0.7536
0.80 π	0.7503	0.7507	0.7512	0.7520	0.7529	0.7538	0.7546	0.7554	0.7561	0.7566	0.7570	0.7572	0.7573	0.7572	0.7570	0.7566	0.7561	0.7554	0.7546	0.7538	0.7529
0.85 π	0.7507	0.7509	0.7515	0.7522	0.7530	0.7539	0.7547	0.7554	0.7560	0.7565	0.7568	0.7569	0.7569	0.7568	0.7565	0.7560	0.7554	0.7547	0.7539	0.7530	0.7522
0.90 π	0.7509	0.7511	0.7516	0.7523	0.7531	0.7539	0.7546	0.7553	0.7559	0.7563	0.7565	0.7566	0.7565	0.7563	0.7559	0.7553	0.7546	0.7539	0.7531	0.7523	0.7516
0.95 π	0.7510	0.7512	0.7516	0.7523	0.7530	0.7538	0.7545	0.7551	0.7556	0.7559	0.7561	0.7561	0.7559	0.7556	0.7551	0.7545	0.7538	0.7530	0.7523	0.7516	0.7512
π	0.7510	0.7512	0.7516	0.7522	0.7529	0.7536	0.7543	0.7548	0.7552	0.7555	0.7556	0.7555	0.7552	0.7548	0.7543	0.7536	0.7529	0.7522	0.7516	0.7512	0.7510

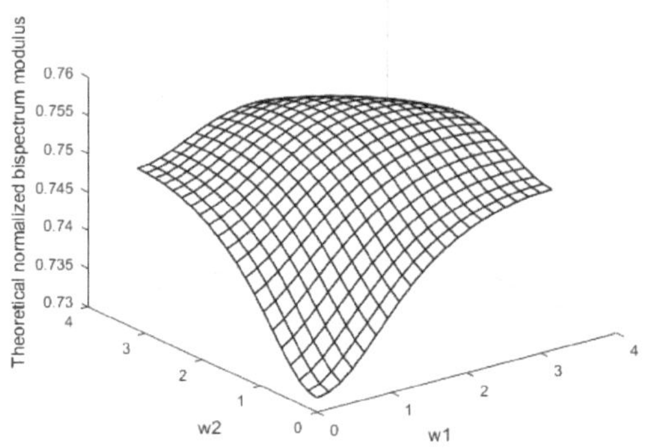

Figure 6. NBDF of NSINAR(1) using $\lambda = 0.3, \beta = 0.25$, and $\gamma = 5$.

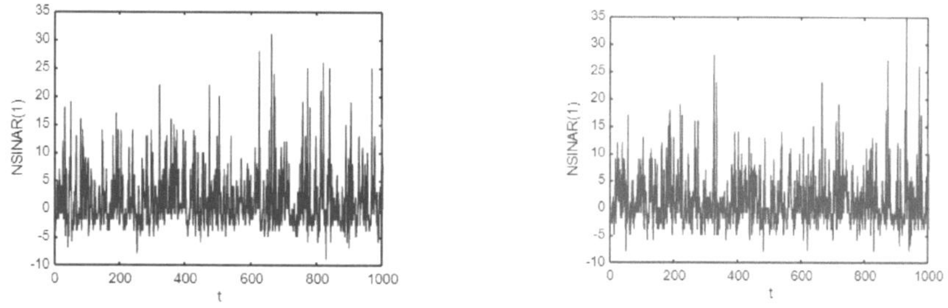

(**a**) Basic model (**b**) Hybrid model

Figure 7. The simulated series of the forecasted NSINAR(1) observations of neural network-based FTS.

6. Estimations of SDF, BDF, and NBDF

The smoothed periodogram technique by the lag window is utilized to estimate the spectral density functions. The lag window is one-dimensional in the case of the SDF and two-dimensional lag in the case of the BDF. Generally, if $X_1, X_2, \ldots, X_N$ is the realizations of a real-valued third-order stationary process $\{X_t\}$ with mean γ, autocovariance $R_2(s)$, and third cumulant $R_3(s_1, s_2)$, the smoothed spectrum, smoothed bispectrum, and smoothed normalized bispectrum are, respectively, given by (see [28])

$$\begin{aligned} \hat{g}(w) &= \frac{1}{2\pi} \sum_{s=-(N-1)}^{N-1} \Phi(s)\hat{R}_2(s)\exp(-isw) \\ &= \frac{1}{2\pi} \sum_{s=-(N-1)}^{N-1} \Phi(s)\hat{R}_2(s)cosws, \end{aligned} \tag{12}$$

$$\hat{g}(w_1, w_2) = \frac{1}{4\pi^2} \sum_{s_1=-(N-1)}^{N-1} \sum_{s_2=-(N-1)}^{N-1} \Phi(s_1, s_2)\hat{R}_3(s_1, s_2)\exp(-is_1w_1 - is_2w_2), \tag{13}$$

$$\hat{f}(w_1, w_2) = \frac{\hat{g}(w_1, w_2)}{\sqrt{\hat{g}(w_1)\hat{g}(w_2)\hat{g}(w_1 + w_2)}}, \tag{14}$$

where $\hat{R}_2(t)$ and $\hat{R}_3(t_1, t_2)$, the natural estimators for $R_2(t)$ and $R_3(t_1, t_2)$ are, respectively, given by

$$\hat{R}_2(s) = \frac{1}{N-s} \sum_{t=1}^{N-|s|} (X_t - \bar{X})(X_{t+|s|} - \bar{X}), \tag{15}$$

$$\bar{X} = \frac{1}{N} \sum_{t=1}^{N} X_t,$$

$$\hat{R}_3(s_1, s_2) = \frac{1}{N} \sum_{t=1}^{N-\beta} (X_t - \bar{X})(X_{t+s_1} - \bar{X})(X_{t+s_2} - \bar{X}), \tag{16}$$

where $s_1, s_2 \geq 0, \beta = max(0, s_1, s_2), s = 0, \pm 1, \pm 2, ..., \pm(N-1), -\pi \leq w_1, w_2 \leq \pi,$ "$\Phi(s)$" is a one-dimensional lag window and "$\Phi(s_1, s_2)$" $= \Phi(s_1 - s_2)\Phi(s_1)\Phi(s_2)$ is a two-dimensional lag window given by [58]. This section calculates estimates of the SDF, BDF, and NBDF by employing a smoothed periodogram approach that depends on the lag windows. The Daniell [59] window was chosen with a different number of frequencies M = 7 and M = 9. These estimates are calculated for three scenarios: (i) the generated realizations from NSINAR(1), which serve as the FTS's "input values", and (ii) and (iii), the forecasted observations, which serve as the output values of the FTS, which is based on a neural network.

Figures 8 and 9 illustrate the estimated SDF for the input and output values of the FTS using Daniell lag windows at M = 7 and M = 9, respectively. Figures 10 and 11 illustrate the estimated BDF for the input and output values of the FTS using Daniell lag windows at M = 7 and M = 9, respectively. Figures 12 and 13 illustrate the estimated NBDF for the input and output values of the FTS using Daniell lag windows at M = 7 and M = 9, respectively. Tables 3–5 display the estimated BDF obtained with the Daniell window when M = 7 for the input values for the FTS, as well as the output values of the FTS, which depend on a neural network (in the case of the basic and hybrid models).

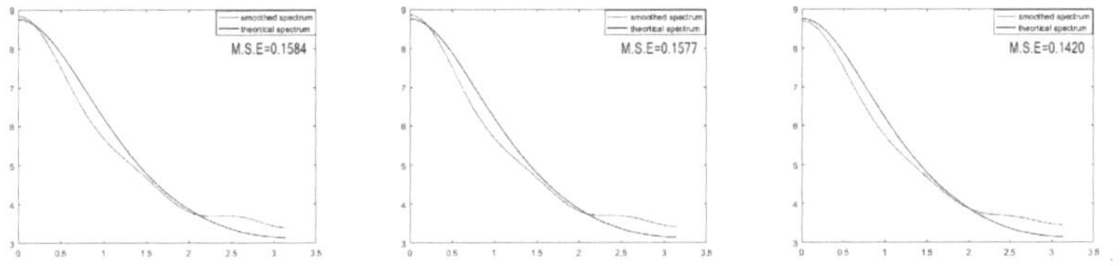

(**i**) input values (**ii**) output values "Model 1" (**iii**) output values "Model 2"

Figure 8. The SDF and estimated SDF obtained with the Daniell window when M = 7, both in the case of the input and output values of the FTS.

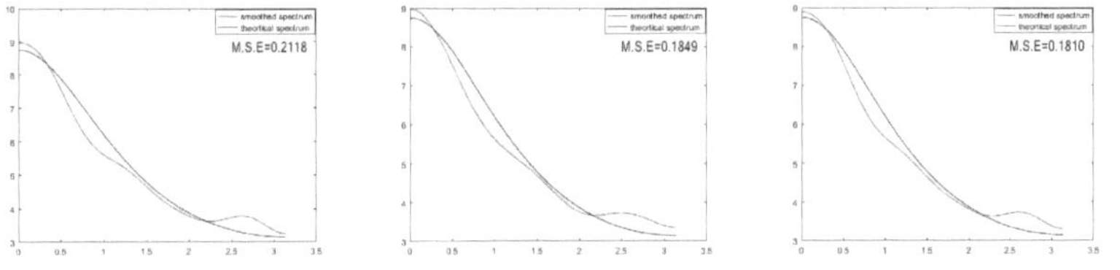

(**i**) input values (**ii**) output values "Model 1" (**iii**) output values "Model 2"

Figure 9. The SDF and estimated SDF obtained with the Daniell window when M = 9, both in the case of the input and output values.

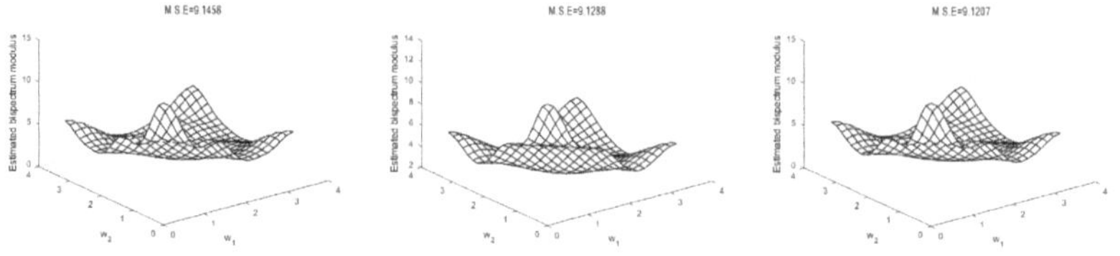

(**i**) input values (**ii**) output values "Model 1" (**iii**) output values "Model 2"

Figure 10. Estimated BDF obtained with the Daniell window when M = 7, both in the case of the input and output values.

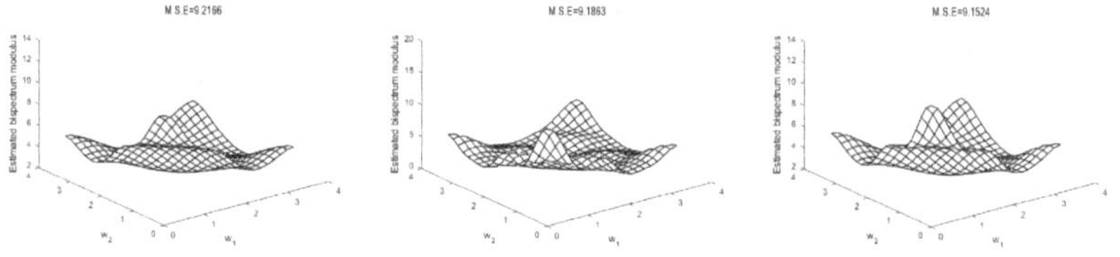

(**i**) input values (**ii**) output values "Model 1" (**iii**) output values "Model 2"

Figure 11. Estimated BDF obtained with the Daniell window when M = 9 both in the case of the input and output values.

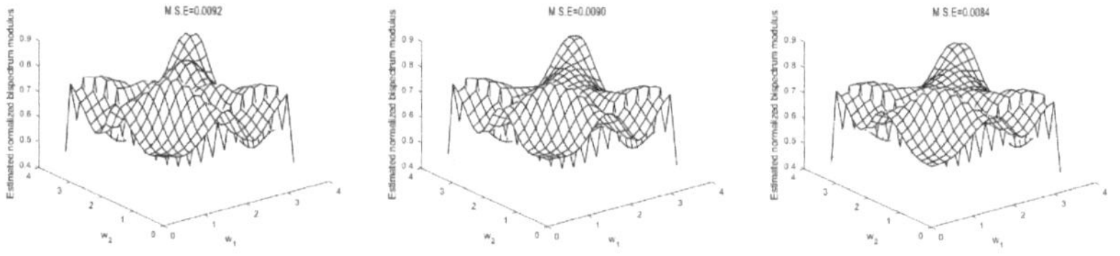

(**i**) input values (**ii**) output values "Model 1" (**iii**) output values "Model 2"

Figure 12. Estimated NBDF obtained with the Daniell window when M = 7 both in the case of the input and output values.

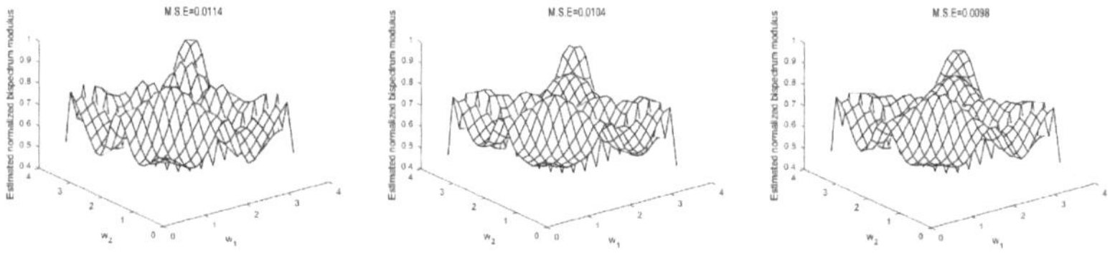

(**i**) input values (**ii**) output values "Model 1" (**iii**) output values "Model 2"

Figure 13. Estimated NBDF obtained with the Daniell window when M = 9 both in the case of the input and output values.

Table 3. Estimated BDF of NSINAR(1) using the Daniell window at M=7 by the input values of the FTS.

w_1 \ w_2	0.00 π	0.05 π	0.10 π	0.15 π	0.20 π	0.25 π	0.30 π	0.35 π	0.40 π	0.45 π	0.50 π	0.55 π	0.60 π	0.65 π	0.70 π	0.75 π	0.80 π	0.85 π	0.90 π	0.95 π	π
0.0 π	19.583	19.380	18.624	17.139	15.161	13.305	12.036	11.269	10.580	9.750	8.976	8.532	8.359	8.102	7.505	6.668	5.878	5.307	4.935	4.700	4.613
0.05 π	19.380	18.903	17.784	16.010	13.980	12.286	11.214	10.534	9.863	9.142	8.610	8.375	8.205	7.779	7.041	6.217	5.544	5.074	4.751	4.568	4.568
0.10 π	18.624	17.784	16.357	14.430	12.406	10.813	9.867	9.322	8.859	8.459	8.238	8.106	7.807	7.213	6.457	5.758	5.207	4.770	4.445	4.317	4.445
0.15 π	17.139	16.010	14.430	12.495	10.627	9.291	8.593	8.258	8.025	7.872	7.772	7.552	7.083	6.444	5.816	5.277	4.777	4.301	3.980	3.980	4.301
0.20 π	15.161	13.980	12.406	10.627	9.132	8.228	7.808	7.575	7.379	7.221	7.012	6.629	6.103	5.587	5.149	4.704	4.175	3.675	3.462	3.675	4.175
0.25 π	13.305	12.286	10.813	9.291	8.228	7.688	7.376	7.040	6.670	6.314	5.922	5.473	5.060	4.745	4.439	4.001	3.464	3.076	3.076	3.464	4.001
0.30 π	12.036	11.214	9.867	8.593	7.808	7.376	6.947	6.374	5.752	5.187	4.709	4.352	4.135	3.970	3.699	3.270	2.852	2.681	2.852	3.270	3.699
0.35 π	11.269	10.534	9.322	8.258	7.575	7.040	6.374	5.551	4.733	4.081	3.671	3.487	3.420	3.303	3.035	2.690	2.457	2.457	2.690	3.035	3.303
0.40 π	10.580	9.863	8.859	8.025	7.379	6.670	5.752	4.733	3.842	3.253	2.995	2.948	2.930	2.805	2.561	2.319	2.220	2.319	2.561	2.805	2.930
0.45 π	9.750	9.142	8.459	7.872	7.221	6.314	5.187	4.081	3.253	2.811	2.679	2.676	2.638	2.491	2.269	2.099	2.099	2.269	2.491	2.638	2.676
0.50 π	8.976	8.610	8.238	7.772	7.012	5.922	4.709	3.671	2.995	2.679	2.587	2.555	2.467	2.288	2.092	2.008	2.092	2.288	2.467	2.555	2.587
0.55 π	8.532	8.375	8.106	7.552	6.629	5.473	4.352	3.487	2.948	2.676	2.555	2.463	2.314	2.138	2.032	2.032	2.138	2.314	2.463	2.555	2.676
0.60 π	8.359	8.205	7.807	7.083	6.103	5.060	4.135	3.420	2.930	2.638	2.467	2.314	2.162	2.089	2.084	2.089	2.162	2.314	2.467	2.638	2.930
0.65 π	8.102	7.779	7.213	6.444	5.587	4.745	3.970	3.303	2.805	2.491	2.288	2.138	2.089	2.130	2.130	2.089	2.138	2.288	2.491	2.805	3.303
0.70 π	7.505	7.041	6.457	5.816	5.149	4.439	3.699	3.035	2.561	2.269	2.092	2.032	2.084	2.130	2.084	2.032	2.092	2.269	2.561	3.035	3.699
0.75 π	6.668	6.217	5.758	5.277	4.704	4.001	3.270	2.690	2.319	2.099	2.008	2.032	2.089	2.089	2.032	2.008	2.099	2.319	2.690	3.270	4.001
0.80 π	5.878	5.544	5.207	4.777	4.175	3.464	2.852	2.457	2.220	2.099	2.092	2.138	2.162	2.138	2.092	2.099	2.220	2.457	2.852	3.464	4.175
0.85 π	5.307	5.074	4.770	4.301	3.675	3.076	2.681	2.457	2.319	2.269	2.288	2.314	2.314	2.288	2.269	2.319	2.457	2.681	3.076	3.675	4.301
0.90 π	4.935	4.751	4.445	3.980	3.462	3.076	2.852	2.690	2.561	2.491	2.467	2.463	2.467	2.491	2.561	2.690	2.852	3.076	3.462	3.980	4.445
0.95 π	4.700	4.568	4.317	3.980	3.675	3.464	3.270	3.035	2.805	2.638	2.555	2.555	2.638	2.805	3.035	3.270	3.464	3.675	3.980	4.317	4.568
π	4.613	4.568	4.445	4.301	4.175	4.001	3.699	3.303	2.930	2.676	2.587	2.676	2.930	3.303	3.699	4.001	4.175	4.301	4.445	4.568	4.613

Table 4. Estimated BDF of NSINAR(1) using the Daniell window at M=7 by the output values of the neural network-based FTS "Model 1".

w_1 \ w_2	0.00 π	0.05 π	0.10 π	0.15 π	0.20 π	0.25 π	0.30 π	0.35 π	0.40 π	0.45 π	0.50 π	0.55 π	0.60 π	0.65 π	0.70 π	0.75 π	0.80 π	0.85 π	0.90 π	0.95 π	π
0.0 π	19.523	19.160	18.115	16.535	14.695	12.941	11.551	10.610	10.005	9.545	9.109	8.679	8.274	7.859	7.350	6.701	5.983	5.344	4.906	4.685	4.624
0.05 π	19.160	18.460	17.165	15.475	13.672	12.054	10.835	10.043	9.534	9.133	8.746	8.367	7.987	7.547	6.980	6.295	5.604	5.054	4.721	4.581	4.581
0.10 π	18.115	17.165	15.785	14.150	12.455	10.948	9.839	9.162	8.774	8.489	8.206	7.895	7.528	7.060	6.465	5.795	5.171	4.713	4.459	4.382	4.459
0.15 π	16.535	15.475	14.150	12.630	11.061	9.701	8.761	8.251	7.995	7.800	7.565	7.263	6.879	6.396	5.820	5.208	4.664	4.280	4.089	4.089	4.280
0.20 π	14.695	13.672	12.455	11.061	9.678	8.573	7.884	7.531	7.315	7.082	6.786	6.437	6.042	5.590	5.077	4.544	4.079	3.765	3.655	3.765	4.079
0.25 π	12.941	12.054	10.948	9.701	8.573	7.773	7.296	6.975	6.640	6.245	5.835	5.456	5.103	4.730	4.303	3.854	3.476	3.261	3.261	3.476	3.854
0.30 π	11.551	10.835	9.839	8.761	7.884	7.296	6.865	6.400	5.838	5.265	4.797	4.465	4.207	3.929	3.586	3.230	2.967	2.873	2.967	3.230	3.586
0.35 π	10.610	10.043	9.162	8.251	7.531	6.975	6.400	5.692	4.926	4.279	3.861	3.637	3.483	3.280	3.008	2.751	2.605	2.605	2.751	3.008	3.280
0.40 π	10.005	9.534	8.774	7.995	7.315	6.640	5.838	4.926	4.084	3.494	3.194	3.075	2.982	2.813	2.592	2.412	2.346	2.412	2.592	2.813	2.982
0.45 π	9.545	9.133	8.489	7.800	7.082	6.245	5.265	4.279	3.494	3.026	2.831	2.760	2.666	2.494	2.294	2.164	2.164	2.294	2.494	2.666	2.760
0.50 π	9.109	8.746	8.206	7.565	6.786	5.835	4.797	3.861	3.194	2.831	2.678	2.586	2.450	2.263	2.096	2.028	2.096	2.263	2.450	2.586	2.678
0.55 π	8.679	8.367	7.895	7.263	6.437	5.456	4.465	3.637	3.075	2.760	2.586	2.440	2.274	2.120	2.029	2.029	2.120	2.274	2.440	2.586	2.760
0.60 π	8.274	7.987	7.528	6.879	6.042	5.103	4.207	3.483	2.982	2.666	2.450	2.274	2.145	2.084	2.070	2.084	2.145	2.274	2.450	2.666	2.982
0.65 π	7.859	7.547	7.060	6.396	5.590	4.730	3.929	3.280	2.813	2.494	2.263	2.120	2.084	2.105	2.105	2.084	2.120	2.263	2.494	2.813	3.280
0.70 π	7.350	6.980	6.465	5.820	5.077	4.303	3.586	3.008	2.592	2.294	2.096	2.029	2.070	2.105	2.070	2.029	2.096	2.294	2.592	3.008	3.586
0.75 π	6.701	6.295	5.795	5.208	4.544	3.854	3.230	2.751	2.412	2.164	2.028	2.029	2.084	2.084	2.029	2.028	2.164	2.412	2.751	3.230	3.854
0.80 π	5.983	5.604	5.171	4.664	4.079	3.476	2.967	2.605	2.346	2.164	2.096	2.120	2.145	2.120	2.096	2.164	2.346	2.605	2.967	3.476	4.079
0.85 π	5.344	5.054	4.713	4.280	3.765	3.261	2.873	2.605	2.412	2.294	2.263	2.274	2.274	2.263	2.294	2.412	2.605	2.873	3.261	3.765	4.280
0.90 π	4.906	4.721	4.459	4.089	3.655	3.261	2.967	2.751	2.592	2.494	2.450	2.440	2.450	2.494	2.592	2.751	2.967	3.261	3.655	4.089	4.459
0.95 π	4.685	4.581	4.382	4.089	3.765	3.476	3.230	3.008	2.813	2.666	2.586	2.586	2.666	2.813	3.008	3.230	3.476	3.765	4.089	4.382	4.581
π	4.624	4.581	4.459	4.280	4.079	3.854	3.586	3.280	2.982	2.760	2.678	2.760	2.982	3.280	3.586	3.854	4.079	4.280	4.459	4.581	4.624

Table 5. Estimated BDF of NSINAR(1) using the Daniell window at M=7 by the outputvalues of the neural network-based FTS "Model 2".

w_1 \ w_2	**0.00 π**	**0.05 π**	**0.10 π**	**0.15 π**	**0.20 π**	**0.25 π**	**0.30 π**	**0.35 π**	**0.40 π**	**0.45 π**	**0.50 π**	**0.55 π**	**0.60 π**	**0.65 π**	**0.70 π**	**0.75 π**	**0.80 π**	**0.85 π**	**0.90 π**	**0.95 π**	π
0.0 π	18.710	18.588	18.004	16.674	14.807	13.023	11.736	10.844	10.064	9.349	8.834	8.526	8.245	7.834	7.284	6.648	5.975	5.355	4.914	4.701	4.649
0.05 π	18.588	18.230	17.235	15.555	13.638	12.054	10.975	10.179	9.473	8.909	8.563	8.322	7.991	7.502	6.907	6.259	5.609	5.064	4.728	4.595	4.595
0.10 π	18.004	17.235	15.819	13.965	12.165	10.802	9.884	9.213	8.695	8.369	8.182	7.944	7.532	6.986	6.389	5.775	5.187	4.722	4.453	4.371	4.453
0.15 π	16.674	15.555	13.965	12.212	10.688	9.585	8.839	8.313	7.976	7.804	7.643	7.323	6.836	6.294	5.759	5.220	4.698	4.283	4.058	4.058	4.283
0.20 π	14.807	13.638	12.165	10.688	9.495	8.648	8.043	7.600	7.321	7.131	6.864	6.444	5.957	5.504	5.071	4.602	4.125	3.757	3.618	3.757	4.125
0.25 π	13.023	12.054	10.802	9.585	8.648	7.969	7.422	6.970	6.613	6.277	5.870	5.424	5.032	4.706	4.359	3.935	3.513	3.249	3.249	3.513	3.935
0.30 π	11.736	10.975	9.884	8.839	8.043	7.422	6.856	6.316	5.800	5.295	4.821	4.447	4.190	3.963	3.660	3.287	2.972	2.851	2.972	3.287	3.660
0.35 π	10.844	10.179	9.213	8.313	7.600	6.970	6.316	5.624	4.940	4.342	3.908	3.655	3.501	3.319	3.048	2.757	2.573	2.573	2.757	3.048	3.319
0.40 π	10.064	9.473	8.695	7.976	7.321	6.613	5.800	4.940	4.161	3.585	3.255	3.101	2.991	2.824	2.598	2.398	2.320	2.398	2.598	2.824	2.991
0.45 π	9.349	8.909	8.369	7.804	7.131	6.277	5.295	4.342	3.585	3.108	2.873	2.764	2.661	2.503	2.316	2.185	2.185	2.316	2.503	2.661	2.764
0.50 π	8.834	8.563	8.182	7.643	6.864	5.870	4.821	3.908	3.255	2.873	2.686	2.583	2.468	2.305	2.143	2.073	2.143	2.305	2.468	2.583	2.686
0.55 π	8.526	8.322	7.944	7.323	6.444	5.424	4.447	3.655	3.101	2.764	2.583	2.463	2.324	2.160	2.048	2.048	2.160	2.324	2.463	2.583	2.764
0.60 π	8.245	7.991	7.532	6.836	5.957	5.032	4.190	3.501	2.991	2.661	2.468	2.324	2.178	2.072	2.040	2.072	2.178	2.324	2.468	2.661	2.991
0.65 π	7.834	7.502	6.986	6.294	5.504	4.706	3.963	3.319	2.824	2.503	2.305	2.160	2.072	2.060	2.060	2.072	2.160	2.305	2.503	2.824	3.319
0.70 π	7.284	6.907	6.389	5.759	5.071	4.359	3.660	3.048	2.598	2.316	2.143	2.048	2.040	2.060	2.040	2.048	2.143	2.316	2.598	3.048	3.660
0.75 π	6.648	6.259	5.775	5.220	4.602	3.935	3.287	2.757	2.398	2.185	2.073	2.048	2.072	2.072	2.048	2.073	2.185	2.398	2.757	3.287	3.935
0.80 π	5.975	5.609	5.187	4.698	4.125	3.513	2.972	2.573	2.320	2.185	2.143	2.160	2.178	2.160	2.143	2.185	2.320	2.573	2.972	3.513	4.125
0.85 π	5.355	5.064	4.722	4.283	3.757	3.249	2.851	2.573	2.398	2.316	2.305	2.324	2.324	2.305	2.316	2.398	2.573	2.851	3.249	3.757	4.283
0.90 π	4.914	4.728	4.453	4.058	3.618	3.249	2.972	2.757	2.598	2.503	2.468	2.463	2.468	2.503	2.598	2.757	2.972	3.249	3.618	4.058	4.453
0.95 π	4.701	4.595	4.371	4.058	3.757	3.513	3.287	3.048	2.824	2.661	2.583	2.583	2.661	2.824	3.048	3.287	3.513	3.757	4.058	4.371	4.595
π	4.649	4.595	4.453	4.283	4.125	3.935	3.660	3.319	2.991	2.764	2.686	2.764	2.991	3.319	3.660	3.935	4.125	4.283	4.453	4.595	4.649

6.1. Discussion of Results

In contrast to the input values for the FTS and the output values of the FTS, which depend on a neural network (in the case of the basic and hybrid models), and depending on the M.S.E at the top of each image, we discover the following:

- Figures 8–13 illustrate the preference for the hybrid model, followed by the basic model, over the input values in estimating the SDF, BDF, and NBDF, as the hybrid model's outputs had the lowest mean-squared error (refer to [32] and [33] to find out how to compute the MSE). In general, this indicates that the neural network-based FTS (whether used with the basic model or the hybrid model) significantly improved the smoothing of density functions' estimates.
- The Daniell window at M = 7 performs better than that at M = 9 in estimating the SDF for all three situations (input values and output values for the basic and hybrid models), according to a comparison of Figures 8 and 9.
- The Daniell window at M = 7 performs better than that at M = 9 in estimating the BDF for all three situations (input values and output values for the basic and hybrid models), according to a comparison of Figures 10 and 11.
- The Daniell window at M = 7 performs better than that at M = 9 in estimating the NBDF for all three situations (input values and output values for the basic and hybrid models), according to a comparison of Figures 12 and 13.

6.2. Empirical Analysis

To create a series with size n = 1000, we employed NSINAR(1). Data ranging from the first observation to the 800th were utilized for our estimation (the in-sample), whereas data spanning the 801st and 1000th were used for our forecast (the out-of-sample). These observations were generated from NSINAR(1) fifteen times, and thus, fifteen time series are available. The proposed method is applied to each time series generated from NSINAR(1). In the following scenarios, the estimators of the spectral density functions were found: for the observations produced by the NSINAR(1) model and for the observations estimated by the basic and hybrid models using the suggested methodology. The MSE was used to compare these estimators in the three scenarios. The input values were compared to the respective performances of the two models. Based on the mean-squared errors (MSEs) of each of the fifteen series, we discovered that the hybrid model outperformed the basic model in terms of performance. When comparing all the series, the hybrid model outperformed the input values in 12 out of the 15 series, while the basic model outperformed the input values in 9 out of the 15 series.

7. Conclusions

More precise smoothing estimates of the SDF, BDF, and NBDF for the INAR(1) models were suggested using a unique strategy. A neural network-based FTS was employed in this method. Consequently, the SDF, BDF, and NBDF for a recognized process (NSINAR(1)) were computed. The observations produced by this process served as the FTS input values. In order to anticipate the observations of NSINAR(1)'s observations, two models were employed: the basic and hybrid models, both applying neural networks. These forecasted observations served as the output values of the neural network-based FTS. Both the input and output values were used for calculating the estimates of the SDF, BDF, and NBDF of NSINAR(1). A definite improvement in the estimation for the hybrid model over the basic model, as well as the input values was discovered by comparing all density functions with their estimations in each scenario. As a result, the neural network-based FTS (either via the basic model or the hybrid model) helped further improve the smoothing of the INAR(1) estimates. Future research will attempt to improve the aforementioned technique using pi-sigma artificial neural networks, despite the fact that this requires far more work than this method to achieve the best estimate smoothing when compared to the findings reached here.

Author Contributions: Methodology, M.E.-M., M.S.E. and R.M.E.-S.; Software, M.E.-M. and M.H.E.-M.; Validation, M.S.E. and M.H.E.-M.; Formal analysis, M.S.E. and R.M.E.-S.; Investigation, M.E., M.E.-M. and L.A.A.-E.; Resources, M.E.-M. and L.A.A.-E.; Data curation, M.H.E.-M., M.S.E. and M.E.-M.; Writing—original draft, M.E.-M.; Writing—review & editing, M.S.E. and R.M.E.-S.; Visualization, M.H.E.-M., M.S.E., L.A.A.-E. and M.E.-M.; Project administration, M.E.-M and R.M.E.-S.; Funding acquisition, L.A.A.-E. All authors have read and agreed to the published version of the manuscript.

Funding: Princess Nourah bint Abdulrahman University Researchers Supporting Project number (PNURSP2024R443), Princess Nourah bint Abdulrahman University, Riyadh, Saudi Arabia. This study is supported via funding from Prince sattam bin Abdulaziz University project number (PSAU/2024/R/1445).

Data Availability Statement: Data are contained within the article.

Conflicts of Interest: The authors declare no conflicts of interest.

References

1. Song, Q.; Chissom, B.S. Fuzzy time series and its models. *Fuzzy Sets Syst.* **1993**, *54*, 269–277. [CrossRef]
2. Huarng, K. Effective lengths of intervals to improve forecasting in fuzzy time series. *Fuzzy Sets Syst.* **2001**, *123*, 387–394. [CrossRef]
3. Yu, T.H. A refined fuzzy time-series model for forecasting. *Phys. A Stat. Mech. Its Appl.* **2005**, *346*, 657–681. [CrossRef]
4. Huarng, K.; Yu, T.H. Ratio-based lengths of intervals to improve enrollment forecasting. In Proceedings of the Ninth International Conference on Fuzzy Theory and Technology, Cary, NC, USA, 23 September 2003.
5. Huarng, K.; Yu, T.H. A dynamic approach to adjusting lengths of intervals in fuzzy time series forecasting. *Intell. Data Anal.* **2004**, *8*, 3–27. [CrossRef]
6. Chen, S.M. Forecasting enrollments based on fuzzy time series. *Fuzzy Sets Syst.* **1996**, *81*, 311–319. [CrossRef]
7. Chen, S.M. Forecasting enrollments based on high-order fuzzy time series. *Cybern. Syst.* **2002**, *33*, 1–16. [CrossRef]
8. Hwang, J.R.; Chen, S.M.; Lee, C.H. Handling forecasting problems using fuzzy time series. *Fuzzy Sets Syst.* **1998**, *100*, 217–228. [CrossRef]
9. Song, Q.; Chissom, B.S. Forecasting enrollments with fuzzy time series-Part II. *Fuzzy Sets Syst.* **1994**, *62*, 1–8. [CrossRef]
10. Huarng, K. Heuristic models of fuzzy time series for forecasting. *Fuzzy Sets Syst.* **2001**, *123*, 369–386. [CrossRef]
11. Kitchens, F.L.; Johnson, J.D.; Gupta, J.N. Predicting automobile insurance losses using artificial neural networks. In *Neural Networks in Business: Techniques and Applications*; IGI Global: Hershey, PA, USA, 2002; pp. 167–187.
12. Widrow, B.; Rumelhart, D.E.; Lehr, M.A. Neural networks: Applications in industry, business and science. *Commun. ACM* **1994**, *37*, 93–106. [CrossRef]
13. Zhang, G.; Patuwo, B.E.; Hu, M.Y. Forecasting with artificial neural networks: The state of the art. *Int. J. Forecast.* **1998**, *14*, 35–62. [CrossRef]
14. McKenzie, E. Autoregressive moving-average processes with negative-binomial and geometric marginal distributions. *Adv. Appl. Probab.* **1986**, *18*, 679–705. [CrossRef]
15. Al-Osh, M.A.; Aly, E.A.A. First order autoregressive time series with negative binomial and geometric marginals. *Commun. Stat.-Theory Methods* **1992**, *21*, 2483–2492. [CrossRef]
16. Alzaid, A.; Al-Osh, M. First-order integer-valued autoregressive (INAR(1)) process: Distributional and regression properties. *Stat. Neerl.* **1988**, *42*, 53–61. [CrossRef]
17. Bakouch, H.S.; Ristić, M.M. Zero truncated Poisson integer-valued AR(1) model. *Metrika* **2010**, *72*, 265–280. [CrossRef]
18. Alzaid, A.A.; Al-Osh, M.A. Some autoregressive moving average processes with generalized Poisson marginal distributions. *Ann. Inst. Stat. Math.* **1993**, *45*, 223–232. [CrossRef]
19. Jin-Guan, D.; Yuan, L. The integer-valued autoregressive (INAR(p)) model. *J. Time Ser. Anal.* **1991**, *12*, 129–142. [CrossRef]
20. Aly, E.A.A.; Bouzar, N. Explicit stationary distributions for some Galton-Watson processes with immigration. *Stoch. Model.* **1994**, *10*, 499–517. [CrossRef]
21. Ristić, M.M.; Nastić, A.S.; Miletić, A.V. A geometric time series model with dependent Bernoulli counting series. *J. Time Ser. Anal.* **2013**, *34*, 466–476. [CrossRef]
22. Latour, A. Existence and stochastic structure of a non-negative integer-valued autoregressive process. *J. Time Ser. Anal.* **1998**, *19*, 439–455. [CrossRef]
23. Ristić, M.M.; Bakouch, H.S.; Nastić, A.S. A new geometric first-order integer-valued autoregressive (NGINAR(1)) process. *J. Stat. Plan. Inference* **2009**, *139*, 2218–2226. [CrossRef]
24. Ristić, M.M.; Nastić, A.S.; Bakouch, H.S. Estimation in an integer-valued autoregressive process with negative binomial marginals (NBINAR(1)). *Commun. Stat.-Theory Methods* **2012**, *41*, 606–618. [CrossRef]
25. Ristić, M.M.; Nastić, A.S.; Jayakumar, K.; Bakouch, H.S. A bivariate INAR(1) time series model with geometric marginals. *Appl. Math. Lett.* **2012**, *25*, 481–485. [CrossRef]

26. Nastić, A.S.; Ristić, M.M. Some geometric mixed integer-valued autoregressive (INAR) models. *Stat. Probab. Lett.* **2012**, *82*, 805–811. [CrossRef]
27. Nastić, A.S.; Ristić, M.M.; Bakouch, H.S. A combined geometric INAR(p) model based on negative binomial thinning. *Math. Comput. Model.* **2012**, *55*, 1665–1672. [CrossRef]
28. Gabr, M.M.; El-Desouky, B.S.; Shiha, F.A.; El-Hadidy, S.M. Higher Order Moments, Spectral and Bispectral Density Functions for INAR(1). *Int. J. Comput. Appl.* **2018**, *182*, 0975–8887.
29. Miletić, A.V.; Ristić, M.M.; Nastić, A.S.; Bakouch, H.S. An INAR(1) model based on a mixed dependent and independent counting series. *J. Stat. Comput. Simul.* **2018**, *88*, 290–304. [CrossRef]
30. Teamah, A.A.M.; Faied, H.M.; El-Menshawy, M.H. Using the Fuzzy Time Series Technique to Improve the Estimation of the Spectral Density Function. *J. Stat. Adv. Theory Appl.* **2018**, *19*, 151–170. [CrossRef]
31. Teamah, A.A.M.; Faied, H.M.; El-Menshawy, M.H. Effect of Fuzzy Time Series Technique on Estimators of Spectral Analysis. *Recent Adv. Math. Res. Comput. Sci.* **2022**, *6*, 29–38.
32. El-menshawy, M.H.; Teamah, A.A.M.; Abu-Youssef, S.E.; Faied, H.M. Higher Order Moments, Cumulants, Spectral and Bispectral Density Functions of the ZTPINAR(1) Process. *Appl. Math* **2022**, *16*, 213–225.
33. El-Morshedy, M.; El-Menshawy, M.H.; Almazah, M.M.A.; El-Sagheer, R.M.; Eliwa, M.S. Effect of fuzzy time series on smoothing estimation of the INAR(1) process. *Axioms* **2022**, *11*, 423. [CrossRef]
34. Alqahtani, K.M.; El-Menshawy, M.H.; Eliwa, M.S.; El-Morshedy, M.; EL-Sagheer, R.M. Fuzzy Time Series Inference for Stationary Linear Processes: Features and Algorithms With Simulation. *Appl. Math* **2023**, *17*, 405–416.
35. El-Menshawy, M.H.; Teamah, A.E.M.A.; Eliwa, M.S.; Al-Essa, L.A.; El-Morshedy, M.; EL-Sagheer, R.M. A New Statistical Technique to Enhance MCGINAR (1) Process Estimates under Symmetric and Asymmetric Data: Fuzzy Time Series Markov Chain and Its Characteristics. *Symmetry* **2023**, *15*, 1577. [CrossRef]
36. Huarng, K.; Yu, T.H. The application of neural networks to forecast fuzzy time series. *Phys. A Stat. Mech. Its Appl.* **2006**, *363*, 481–491. [CrossRef]
37. Egrioglu, E.; Aladag, C.H.; Yolcu, U.; Uslu, V.R.; Basaran, M.A. A new approach based on artificial neural networks for high order multivariate fuzzy time series. *Expert Syst. Appl.* **2009**, *36*, 10589–10594. [CrossRef]
38. Yu, T.H.K.; Huarng, K.H. A neural network-based fuzzy time series model to improve forecasting. *Expert Syst. Appl.* **2010**, *37*, 3366–3372. [CrossRef]
39. Egrioglu, E.; Aladag, C.H.; Yolcu, U. Fuzzy time series forecasting with a novel hybrid approach combining fuzzy c-means and neural networks. *Expert Syst. Appl.* **2013**, *40*, 854–857. [CrossRef]
40. Rahman, N.H.A.; Lee, M.H.; Suhartono; Latif, M.T. Artificial neural networks and fuzzy time series forecasting: An application to air quality. *Qual. Quant.* **2015**, *49*, 2633–2647. [CrossRef]
41. Bas, E.; Grosan, C.; Egrioglu, E.; Yolcu, U. High order fuzzy time series method based on pi-sigma neural network. *Eng. Appl. Artif. Intell.* **2018**, *72*, 350–356. [CrossRef]
42. Sadaei, H.J.; Silva, P.C.; Guimaraes, F.G.; Lee, M.H. Short-term load forecasting by using a combined method of convolutional neural networks and fuzzy time series. *Energy* **2019**, *175*, 365–377. [CrossRef]
43. Koo, J.W.; Wong, S.W.; Selvachandran, G.; Long, H.V.; Son, L.H. Prediction of Air Pollution Index in Kuala Lumpur using fuzzy time series and statistical models. *Air Qual. Atmos. Health* **2020**, *13*, 77–88. [CrossRef]
44. Tang, Y.; Yu, F.; Pedrycz, W.; Yang, X.; Wang, J.; Liu, S. Building trend fuzzy granulation-based LSTM recurrent neural network for long-term time-series forecasting. *IEEE Trans. Fuzzy Syst.* **2021**, *30*, 1599–1613. [CrossRef]
45. Nasiri, H.; Ebadzadeh, M.M. MFRFNN: Multi-functional recurrent fuzzy neural network for chaotic time series prediction. *Neurocomputing* **2022**, *507*, 292–310. [CrossRef]
46. Rathipriya, R.; Abdul Rahman, A.A.; Dhamodharavadhani, S.; Meero, A.; Yoganandan, G. Demand forecasting model for time-series pharmaceutical data using shallow and deep neural network model. *Neural Comput. Appl.* **2023**, *35*, 1945–1957. [CrossRef] [PubMed]
47. Zhang, G.P. Business forecasting with artificial neural networks: An overview. In *Neural Networks in Business Forecasting*;2004; pp. 1–22.
48. Indro, D.C.; Jiang, C.X.; Patuwo, B.; Zhang, G. Predicting mutual fund performance using artificial neural networks. *Omega* **1999**, *27*, 373–380. [CrossRef]
49. Rumelhart, D.E.; McClelland, J.L.; Parallel Distributed Processing Research Group, C. *Parallel Distributed Processing: Explorations in the Microstructure of Cognition, Vol. 1: Foundations*; MIT Press: Cambridge, MA, USA, 1986.
50. Cybenko, G. Approximation by superpositions of a sigmoidal function. *Math. Control Signals Syst.* **1989**, *2*, 303–314. [CrossRef]
51. Hornik, K. Approximation capabilities of multilayer feedforward networks. *Neural Netw.* **1991**, *4*, 251–257. [CrossRef]
52. Hornik, K. Some new results on neural network approximation. *Neural Netw.* **1993**, *6*, 1069–1072. [CrossRef]
53. Armstrong, J.S. *Principles of Forecasting: A Handbook for Researchers and Practitioners*; Springer: Berlin/Heidelberg, Germany, 2001; Volume 30.
54. Zhang, G.P. *Neural Networks in Business Forecasting*; IGI Global: Hershey, PA, USA, 2004.
55. Song, Q.; Chissom, B.S. Forecasting enrollments with fuzzy time series—Part I. *Fuzzy Sets Syst.* **1993**, *54*, 1–9. [CrossRef]
56. Bourguignon, M.; Vasconcellos, K.L. A new skew integer valued time series process. *Stat. Methodol.* **2016**, *31*, 8–19. [CrossRef]

57. Eduarda Da Silva, M.; Oliveira, V.L. Difference equations for the higher-order moments and cumulants of the INAR (1) model. *J. Time Ser. Anal.* **2010**, *25*, 317–333. [CrossRef]
58. Rao, T.S.; Gabr, M.M. *An Introduction to Bispectral Analysis and Bilinear Time Series Models;* Springer Science & Business Media: Berlin/Heidelberg, Germany, 1984; Volume 24.
59. Daniell, P.J. Discussion on symposium on autocorrelation in time series. *J. R. Stat. Soc.* **1946**, *8*, 88–90.

symmetry

MDPI

Article

Introducing Fixed-Point Theorems and Applications in Fuzzy Bipolar *b*-Metric Spaces with ψ_α- and $\mathcal{F}_\eta$- Contractive Maps

Salam Alnabulsi [1], Wael Mahmoud Mohammad Salameh [2] and Mohammad H. M. Rashid [3,*]

1 Department of Mathematics, Faculty of Science, University of Jordan, Amman 11942, Jordan; s.alnabulsi@ju.edu.jo
2 Faculty of Information Technology, Abu Dhabi University, Abu Dhabi 59911, United Arab Emirates; wael.salameh@adu.ac.ae
3 Department of Mathematics & Statistics, Faculty of Science, Mutah University, P.O. Box 7, Alkarak 61710, Jordan
* Correspondence: mrash@mutah.edu.jo; Tel.: +962-795516301

Abstract: In this study, we introduce novel concepts within the framework of fuzzy bipolar *b*-metric spaces, focusing on various mappings such as ψ_α-contractive and $\mathcal{F}_\eta$-contractive mappings, which are essential for quantifying distances between dissimilar elements. We establish fixed-point theorems for these mappings, demonstrating the existence of invariant points under certain conditions. To enhance the credibility and applicability of our findings, we provide illustrative examples that support these theorems and expand the existing knowledge in this field. Furthermore, we explore practical applications of our research, particularly in solving integral equations and fractional differential equations, showcasing the robustness and utility of our theoretical advancements. Symmetry, both in its traditional sense and within the fuzzy context, is fundamental to our study of fuzzy bipolar *b*- metric spaces. The introduced contractive mappings and fixed-point theorems expand the theoretical framework and offer robust tools for addressing practical problems where symmetry is significant.

Keywords: fixed points; fuzzy *b*-metric space; fuzzy bipolar *b*-metric space; *b*-triangular property; integral equations; fractional differential equation

Citation: Alnabulsi, S.; Salameh, W.M.M.; Rashid, M.H.M. Introducing Fixed-Point Theorems and Applications in Fuzzy Bipolar *b*-Metric Spaces with ψ_α- and $\mathcal{F}_\eta$- Contractive Maps. *Symmetry* **2024**, *16*, 777. https://doi.org/10.3390/sym16060777

Academic Editor: Ioan Rașa

Received: 22 May 2024
Revised: 13 June 2024
Accepted: 17 June 2024
Published: 20 June 2024

1. Introduction

Fixed-point theory is very important in many fields, such as engineering, optimization, physics, economics, and mathematics. The Banach fixed-point theorem, introduced by Banach [1], greatly strengthened this theory and sparked extensive research in both mathematics and science.

In 1975, Kramosil and Michalek [2] introduced the innovative idea of fuzzy metric spaces. This concept built on the continuous *t*-norm introduced by Schweizer and Sklar in 1960 [3] and the foundational fuzzy set theory proposed by L.A. Zadeh in 1965 [4]. George and Veeramani [5] expanded this idea by incorporating the Hausdorff topology and adapting classical metric space theorems. This expansion led to significant discoveries in fuzzy metric spaces and their generalizations [6–11]. In a recent mathematical breakthrough, Mutlu and Gürdal [12] introduced bipolar metric spaces. Unlike traditional metric spaces, which focus on distances within a single set, bipolar metric spaces consider distances between points from two distinct sets. Researchers [7,12,13] have since explored fixed-point theorems in bipolar metric spaces, discovering various applications. Building on this, Bartwal et al. [14] introduced fuzzy bipolar metric spaces, extending the principles of fuzzy metric spaces. They proposed a unique way to measure distances between points in different sets, leading to significant advancements in fixed-point results for fuzzy bipolar metric spaces [12,15]. Kumer et al. [9] introduced the concept of contravariant $(\alpha - \psi)$ Meir–Keeler contractive mappings by defining α-orbital admissible mappings and covariant

Meir–Keeler contraction in bipolar metric spaces. They proved fixed-point theorems for these contractions and provided some corollaries of their main results. In 2016, Mutlu et al. [12] introduced a new type of metric space called bipolar metric spaces. Since then, researchers have established several fixed-point theorems using various contractive conditions within the context of bipolar metric spaces (see [10]).

This study aims to address a gap in research by introducing new concepts such as ψ_α-contractive type covariant mappings, contravariant mappings, and $\digamma_\eta$-contractive type covariant mappings within fuzzy bipolar metric spaces. We establish fixed-point theorems in this context. Our main goal is to extend the criteria for self-mappings by introducing control functions and admissibility while considering the triangular property of induced fuzzy bipolar metrics. Although existing literature provides valuable insights into fixed-point theory and fuzzy bipolar metric spaces, the study of control functions and admissible self-mappings within fuzzy bipolar metric spaces remains unexplored. Our paper addresses a key research gap by advancing the theoretical foundations of generalized fuzzy metric spaces and enhancing the understanding of fixed-point theory. By integrating a control function and admissible self-mappings with the triangular property, our expanded framework provides a versatile foundation applicable to various fields.

In fuzzy bipolar b-metric spaces, symmetry is essential for defining the structure and properties of the space. A b-metric space generalizes a metric space by relaxing the symmetry requirement, and in the fuzzy context, distances are represented by fuzzy sets instead of exact values, allowing for a more nuanced representation of uncertainty. The ψ_α-contractive and $\digamma_\eta$-contractive mappings introduced in this study can exhibit symmetry properties based on their definitions.

A mapping T is ψ_α-contractive if it satisfies a condition involving a function ψ_α, which can include symmetric or asymmetric terms. Similarly, $\digamma_\eta$-contractive mappings involve a function $\digamma_\eta$ that can also reflect symmetry considerations. These mappings ensure the existence of fixed points in fuzzy bipolar b-metric spaces, with symmetry influencing the nature and uniqueness of these fixed points. The fixed-point theorems for ψ_α-contractive and $\digamma_\eta$-contractive mappings often depend on symmetry conditions, which simplify the proofs of existence and uniqueness.

Examples in the study highlight the importance of these symmetry conditions in practical applications, such as solving integral equations and fractional differential equations, where symmetric structures like kernel functions or boundary conditions are involved. In conclusion, symmetry, both in its traditional sense and within the fuzzy context, is fundamental to our study of fuzzy bipolar b-metric spaces. The introduced contractive mappings and fixed-point theorems expand the theoretical framework and provide robust tools for addressing practical problems where symmetry plays a crucial role.

In this study, we thoroughly explore the fundamental concepts of fuzzy bipolar b-metric spaces in Section 2. In Section 3, we establish key results about the existence and uniqueness of fixed points within these spaces by introducing ψ_α-contractive mappings. These results leverage a unique property of fuzzy bipolar b-metric spaces, explained with the help of a control function. In Section 4, we introduce another type of mapping called $\digamma_\eta$-contractive mappings and present additional fixed-point results. Finally, in Section 5, we demonstrate the practical applications of our findings by showing how they can be used to solve nonlinear integral equations. Our work provides valuable insights for both theoretical understanding and real-world applications, enhancing the use of fixed-point theory in fuzzy bipolar b-metric spaces.

2. Preliminaries

In order to demonstrate our main findings, it is necessary to introduce several fundamental definitions drawn from the existing literature, outlined below:

Definition 1 ([16]). *A binary operation $* : [0,1] \times [0,1] \to [0,1]$ is said to be a continuous τ-norm if $([0,1], *)$ is a topological monoid with unit 1, such that $\xi * \zeta \le \gamma * \delta$ whenever $\xi \le \gamma, \zeta \le \delta$ for all $\xi, \zeta, \gamma, \delta \in [0,1]$.*

Definition 2 ([14]). *Let $\mathscr{A}$ and $\mathscr{B}$ be two nonempty sets. A quadruple $(\mathscr{A}, \mathscr{B}, \mathscr{F}_v, *)$ is called a fuzzy bipolar metric space (FBMS), where $*$ and $\mathscr{F}_v$ are a continuous τ-norm and a fuzzy set on $\mathscr{A} \times \mathscr{B} \times (0, \infty)$, respectively, such that for all $\tau, \rho, \nu > 0$:*

(FBMS1) $\mathscr{F}_v(\omega, \xi, \tau) > 0$ *for all* $(\omega, \xi) \in \mathscr{A} \times \mathscr{B}$;
(FBMS2) $\mathscr{F}_v(\omega, \xi, \tau) = 1$ *if and only if* $\omega = \xi$ *for* $\omega \in \mathscr{A}$ *and* $\xi \in \mathscr{B}$;
(FBMS3) $\mathscr{F}_v(\omega, \xi, \tau) = \mathscr{F}_v(\xi, \omega, \tau)$ *for all* $\omega, \xi \in \mathscr{A} \cap \mathscr{B}$;
(FBMS4) $\mathscr{F}_v(\omega_1, \xi_2, \tau + \rho + \nu) \ge \mathscr{F}_v(\omega_1, \xi_1, \tau) * \mathscr{F}_v(\omega_2, \xi_1, \rho) * \mathscr{F}_v(\omega_2, \xi_2, \nu)$ *for all* $\omega_1, \omega_2 \in \mathscr{A}$ *and* $\xi_1, \xi_2 \in \mathscr{B}$;
(FBMS5) $\mathscr{F}_v(\omega, \xi, \cdot) : [0, \infty) \to [0,1]$ *is left continuous;*
(FBMS6) $\mathscr{F}_v(\omega, \xi, \cdot)$ *is non-decreasing for all* $\omega \in \mathscr{A}$ *and* $\xi \in \mathscr{B}$.

Definition 3 ([17]). *Let $\mathscr{A}$ be a non-empty set and let $\theta \ge 1$ be a given real number. A function $\varrho : \mathscr{A} \times \mathscr{A} \to [0, \infty)$ is said to be a b-metric space if for all $x, y, z \in \mathscr{A}$ the following conditions hold:*

(BM1) $\varrho(x, y) = 0$ *if and only if* $x = y$;
(BM2) $\varrho(x, y) = \varrho(y, x)$;
(BM3) $\varrho(x, z) \le \theta[\varrho(x, y) + \varrho(y, z)]$.

The pair $(\mathscr{A}, \varrho)$ is a b-metric space.

Remark 1 ([18]). *It is important to discuss that every b-metric space is not necessarily a metric space. With $\theta = 1$, every b-metric space is a metric space.*

Definition 4 ([10]). *Let $\mathscr{A}$ and $\mathscr{B}$ be two non-empty sets, and and let $\theta \ge 1$ be a given real number. Function $\varrho : \mathscr{A} \times \mathscr{A} \to [0, \infty)$ satisfies the following conditions:*

(BBM1) $\varrho(x, y) = 0$ *if and only if* $x = y$ *for all* $(x, y) \in \mathscr{A} \times \mathscr{B}$;
(BBM2) $\varrho(x, y) = \varrho(y, x)$ *for all* $x, y \in \mathscr{A} \cap \mathscr{B}$;
(BBM3) $\varrho(x_1, y_2) \le \theta[\varrho(x_1, y_1) + \varrho(x_2, y_1) + \varrho(x_2, y_2, w)]$ *for all* $x_1, x_2 \in \mathscr{A}$ *and* $y_1, y_2 \in \mathscr{B}$.

Then, ϱ is a b-bipolar metric and $(\mathscr{A}, \mathscr{B}, \varrho)$ is a b-bipolar metric space. If $\mathscr{A} \cap \mathscr{B} = \emptyset$, then the space is called a disjoint; otherwise, it is called a joint. Set $\mathscr{A}$ is the left pole and set $\mathscr{B}$ is the right pole of $(\mathscr{A}, \mathscr{B}, \varrho)$. The elements of $\mathscr{A}$, $\mathscr{B}$, and $\mathscr{A} \cap \mathscr{B}$ are the left, right, and central elements, respectively.

Definition 5 ([10]). *Let $\mathscr{A}$ and $\mathscr{B}$ be two non-empty sets and $\theta \ge 1$. A five tuple $(\mathscr{A}, \mathscr{B}, \mathscr{F}_v, \theta, *)$ is called a fuzzy bipolar b-metric space (FBBMS), where $*$ and $\mathscr{F}_v$ are the continuous τ-norm and the fuzzy set on $\mathscr{A} \times \mathscr{B} \times (0, \infty)$, respectively, such that for all $\tau, \rho, \nu > 0$, the following is applicable:*

(FBMS1) $\mathscr{F}_v(\omega, \xi, \tau) > 0$ *for all* $(\omega, \xi) \in \mathscr{A} \times \mathscr{B}$;
(FBMS2) $\mathscr{F}_v(\omega, \xi, \tau) = 1$ *if and only if* $\omega = \xi$ *for* $\omega \in \mathscr{A}$ *and* $\xi \in \mathscr{B}$;
(FBMS3) $\mathscr{F}_v(\omega, \xi, \tau) = \mathscr{F}_v(\xi, \omega, \tau)$ *for all* $\omega, \xi \in \mathscr{A} \cap \mathscr{B}$;
(FBMS4) $\mathscr{F}_v(\omega_1, \xi_2, \theta(\tau + \rho + \nu)) \ge \mathscr{F}_v(\omega_1, \xi_1, \tau) * \mathscr{F}_v(\omega_2, \xi_1, \rho) * \mathscr{F}_v(\omega_2, \xi_2, \nu)$ *for all* $\omega_1, \omega_2 \in \mathscr{A}$ *and* $\xi_1, \xi_2 \in \mathscr{B}$;
(FBMS5) $\mathscr{F}_v(\omega, \xi, \cdot) : [0, \infty) \to [0,1]$ *is left continuous;*
(FBMS6) $\mathscr{F}_v(\omega, \xi, \cdot)$ *is non-decreasing for all* $\omega \in \mathscr{A}$ *and* $\xi \in \mathscr{B}$.

Definition 6 ([10]). *Let $(\mathscr{A}, \mathscr{B}, \mathscr{F}_v, \theta, *)$ be a fuzzy bipolar b-metric space.*

(S1) *Point $\omega \in \mathscr{A} \cup \mathscr{B}$ is called the left, right, and central point if $\omega \in \mathscr{A}$, $\omega \in \mathscr{B}$, and both hold. Similarly, sequence $\{\omega_\beta\}$, ξ_β on set $\mathscr{A}, \mathscr{B}$ is said to be a left and right sequence, respectively.*
(S2) *Sequence $\{\omega_\beta\}$ is convergent to point ω if and only if $\{\omega_\beta\}$ is a left sequence, ω is a right point, and $\lim_{\beta \to \infty} \mathscr{F}_v(\omega_\beta, \theta, *) = 1$ for $\tau > 0$, or ω_β is a right sequence, ω is a left point, and $\mathscr{F}_v(\omega, \omega_\beta, \tau) = 1$ for $\tau > 0$.*

Definition 7 ([10]). *In an FBBMS, sequence* $(\{\omega_n\}, \{\xi_n\})$ *is called a bisequence on* $\mathscr{A} \times \mathscr{B}$ *and it is said to be convergent if both* $\{\omega_n\}$ *and* $\{\xi_n\}$ *are convergent. If both sequences converge to a common point q, then* $(\{\omega_n\}, \{\xi_n\})$ *is a biconvergent.*

The bisequence $(\{\omega_n\}, \{\xi_n\})$ *in a FBBMS* $\mathscr{F}_v(\omega_\beta, \theta, *)$ *is called a Cauchy bisequence if, for any* $\delta > 0$*, there exist a number* $\gamma \in \mathbb{N}$ *such that for all* $w, g \geq \delta$ *and* $w, g \in \mathbb{N}$*, we have*

$$\mathscr{F}_v(\omega_w, \xi_g, \tau) > 1 - \delta, \qquad \text{for all } \tau > 0.$$

In other words, $(\{\omega_n\}, \{\xi_n\})$ *is a Cauchy bisequence if*

$$\lim_{w,g \to \infty} \mathscr{F}_v(\omega_w, \xi_g, \tau) = 1, \qquad \text{for all } \tau > 0.$$

Lemma 1. *In an FBBMS* $(\mathscr{A}, \mathscr{B}, \mathscr{F}_v, \theta, *)$*, the limit* $\gamma \in \mathscr{A} \cap \mathscr{B}$ *of a bisequence is always unique.*

Lemma 2 ([19]). *In an FBBMS* $(\mathscr{A}, \mathscr{B}, \mathscr{F}_v, \theta, *)$*, if a Cauchy bisequence is convergent, it is biconvergent.*

Lemma 3 ([19]). *An FBBMS* $(\mathscr{A}, \mathscr{B}, \mathscr{F}_v, \theta, *)$ *is considered complete if every Cauchy bisequence within* $\mathscr{A} \times \mathscr{B}$ *converges within it.*

Definition 8 ([10]). *Let* $(\mathscr{A}_1, \mathscr{B}_1, \mathscr{F}_v, \theta, *)$ *and* $(\mathscr{A}_2, \mathscr{B}_2, \mathscr{M}_\varsigma, \theta, *)$ *be two FBBMSs and a function* $\phi : \mathscr{A}_1 \cup \mathscr{B}_1 \to \mathscr{A}_2 \cup \mathscr{B}_2$*. Then, the following is applicable:*

(i) *If* $\phi(\mathscr{A}_1) \subseteq \mathscr{B}_2$ *and* $\phi(\mathscr{B}_1) \subseteq \mathscr{A}_2$*, then* ϕ *is a contravariant from* $(\mathscr{A}_1, \mathscr{B}_1, \mathscr{F}_v, \theta, *)$ *to* $(\mathscr{A}_2, \mathscr{B}_2, \mathscr{M}_\varsigma, \theta, *)$ *and it is denoted by* $\phi : (\mathscr{A}_1, \mathscr{B}_1, \mathscr{F}_v, \theta, *) \leftrightarrows (\mathscr{A}_2, \mathscr{B}_2, \mathscr{M}_\varsigma, \theta, *)$.

(ii) *If* $\phi(\mathscr{A}_1) \subseteq \mathscr{A}_2$ *and* $\phi(\mathscr{B}_1) \subseteq \mathscr{B}_2$*, then* ϕ *is a covariant from* $(\mathscr{A}_1, \mathscr{B}_1, \mathscr{F}_v, \theta, *)$ *to* $(\mathscr{A}_2, \mathscr{B}_2, \mathscr{M}_\varsigma, \theta, *)$ *and it is denoted by* $\phi : (\mathscr{A}_1, \mathscr{B}_1, \mathscr{F}_v, \theta, *) \rightrightarrows (\mathscr{A}_2, \mathscr{B}_2, \mathscr{M}_\varsigma, \theta, *)$.

We establish the continuity of covariant and contravariant mappings within fuzzy bipolar b-metric spaces.

Definition 9. *Let* $(\mathscr{A}_1, \mathscr{B}_1, \mathscr{F}_v, \theta, *)$ *and* $(\mathscr{A}_2, \mathscr{B}_2, \mathscr{M}_\varsigma, \theta, *)$ *be two FBBMSs.*

(a) *Mapping* $\phi : (\mathscr{A}_1, \mathscr{B}_1, \mathscr{F}_v, \theta, *) \rightrightarrows (\mathscr{A}_2, \mathscr{B}_2, \mathscr{M}_\varsigma, \theta, *)$ *is said to be left-continuous at a particular point* $a_0 \in \mathscr{A}_1$ *if for any given* $\varepsilon > 0$ *there exists* $\delta > 0$*; such that, for all* $b \in \mathscr{B}_1$*, conditions* $\mathscr{F}_v(a_0, b, \tau) < \delta$ *and* $\mathscr{M}_\varsigma(f(a_0), f(b), \tau) < \varepsilon$ *hold.*

(b) *Mapping* $\phi : (\mathscr{A}_1, \mathscr{B}_1, \mathscr{F}_v, \theta, *) \rightrightarrows (\mathscr{A}_2, \mathscr{B}_2, \mathscr{M}_\varsigma, \theta, *)$ *is said to be left-continuous at a particular point* $b_0 \in \mathscr{B}_1$ *if for any given* $\varepsilon > 0$ *there exists* $\delta > 0$*; such that, for all* $a \in \mathscr{A}_1$*, conditions* $\mathscr{F}_v(a, b_0, \tau) < \delta$ *and* $\mathscr{M}_\varsigma(f(a), f(b_0), \tau) < \varepsilon$ *hold.*

(c) *Mapping* ϕ *is said to be continuous if it is left-continuous at every point* $a \in \mathscr{A}_1$ *and right-continuous at each point* $b \in \mathscr{B}_1$.

(d) *Contravariant* $\phi : \phi : (\mathscr{A}_1, \mathscr{B}_1, \mathscr{F}_v, \theta, *) \leftrightarrows (\mathscr{A}_2, \mathscr{B}_2, \mathscr{M}_\varsigma, \theta, *)$ *is continuous if and only if it is continuous when considered as a covariant mapping* $\phi : (\mathscr{A}_1, \mathscr{B}_1, \mathscr{F}_v, \theta, *) \rightrightarrows (\mathscr{A}_2, \mathscr{B}_2, \mathscr{M}_\varsigma, \theta, *)$.

Definition 10 ([10]). *Let* $(\mathscr{A}, \mathscr{B}, \mathscr{F}_v, \theta, *)$ *be a fuzzy bipolar b-metric space. The fuzzy bipolar b-metric space* $\mathscr{F}_v$ *is b-triangular (BT) if the following is applicable:*

$$\begin{aligned}\frac{1}{\mathscr{F}_v(\omega_1, \xi_2, \tau)} - 1 \;\leq\;& \theta\left(\frac{1}{\mathscr{F}_v(\omega_1, \xi_1, \tau)} - 1\right) + \theta\left(\frac{1}{\mathscr{F}_v(\omega_2, \xi_1, \tau)} - 1\right) \\ +\;& \theta\left(\frac{1}{\mathscr{F}_v(\omega_2, \xi_2, \tau)} - 1\right).\end{aligned}$$

Lemma 4. *Let $(\mathscr{A}, \mathscr{B}, \mathscr{F}_v, \theta, *)$ be a fuzzy bipolar b-metric space, where $*$ is a continuous τ-norm and $\mathscr{F}_v : \mathscr{A} \times \mathscr{B} \times (0, \infty) \to [0, 1]$ is defined as*

$$\mathscr{F}_v(\omega, \xi, \tau) = \frac{\tau}{\tau + \phi(\omega, \xi)},$$

where $\phi(\omega, \xi)$ is a bipolar b-metric space on $\mathscr{A} \times \mathscr{B}$. Then, the FBBMS is b-triangular.

Proof. For any $\omega_1, \omega_2 \in \mathscr{A}$ and $\xi_1, \xi_2 \in \mathscr{B}$, we have the following:

$$\begin{aligned}
\frac{1}{\mathscr{F}_v(\omega_1, \xi_2, \tau)} - 1 &= \frac{\phi(\omega_1, \xi_2)}{\tau} \\
&\leq \theta\frac{\phi(\omega_1, \xi_1)}{\tau} + \theta\frac{\phi(\omega_2, \xi_1)}{\tau} + \theta\frac{\phi(\omega_2, \xi_2)}{\tau} \\
&\leq \theta\left(\frac{1}{\mathscr{F}_v(\omega_1, \xi_1, \tau)} - 1\right) + \theta\left(\frac{1}{\mathscr{F}_v(\omega_2, \xi_1, \tau)} - 1\right) \\
&+ \theta\left(\frac{1}{\mathscr{F}_v(\omega_2, \xi_2, \tau)} - 1\right).
\end{aligned}$$

Hence, $\mathscr{F}_v$ is b-triangular. □

Example 1. *Let $(\mathscr{A}, \mathscr{B}, \mathscr{F}_v, \theta, *)$ be a fuzzy bipolar b-metric space, where $*$ is a continuous τ-norm defined by $w * q = \min\{w, q\}$ and $\mathscr{F}_v : \mathscr{A} \times \mathscr{B} \times (0, \infty) \to [0, 1]$ defined by*

$$\mathscr{F}_v(\omega, \xi, \tau) = \frac{\tau}{\tau + d_b(\omega, \xi)},$$

where d_b is a b-metric space. Then, the FBBMS is b-triangular.

Proof. For any $\omega_1, \omega_2 \in \mathscr{A}$ and $\xi_1, \xi_2 \in \mathscr{B}$, we have the following:

$$\begin{aligned}
\frac{1}{\mathscr{F}_v(\omega_1, \xi_2, \tau)} - 1 &= \frac{d_p(\omega_1, \xi_2)}{\tau} \\
&\leq \theta\frac{d_p(\omega_1, \xi_1)}{\tau} + \theta\frac{d_p(\omega_2, \xi_1)}{\tau} + \theta\frac{d_p(\omega_2, \xi_2)}{\tau} \\
&\leq \theta\left(\frac{1}{\mathscr{F}_v(\omega_1, \xi_1, \tau)} - 1\right) + \theta\left(\frac{1}{\mathscr{F}_v(\omega_2, \xi_1, \tau)} - 1\right) \\
&+ \theta\left(\frac{1}{\mathscr{F}_v(\omega_2, \xi_2, \tau)} - 1\right), \qquad \text{for } \tau > 0.
\end{aligned}$$

Consequently, the FBBMS is b-triangular. □

Definition 11. *Let $(\mathscr{A}, \mathscr{B}, \mathscr{F}_v, \theta, *)$ be a complete FBBSM with a constant $\theta \geq 1$, where $*$ is a continuous τ-norm and mapping $\psi : \mathscr{A} \cup \mathscr{B} \to \mathscr{A} \cup \mathscr{B}$ is called a fuzzy b-contraction if there exists $\gamma \in (0, \frac{1}{\theta})$, such that*

$$\frac{1}{\mathscr{F}_v(\psi(\omega), \psi(\xi), \tau)} - 1 \leq \gamma\left(\frac{1}{\mathscr{F}_v(\omega, \xi, \tau)} - 1\right) \tag{1}$$

for all $\omega \in \mathscr{A}, \xi \in \mathscr{B}$, and $\tau > 0$, such that $\theta\gamma < 1$.

3. ψ_α-Contraction Mappings and Fixed-Point Results

Definition 12. *Let Ψ_θ be the family of all right-continuous and non-decreasing functions $\psi : [0, \infty) \to [0, \infty)$ such that $\sum_{n=1}^{\infty} \psi^n(t) < \infty$ for all $t > 0$, where ψ^n is the n-th iterate of ψ, satisfying the following conditions:*

(Q1) $\psi(0) = 0$;

(Q2) $\psi(\kappa) < \kappa$ *for all* $\kappa > 0$;
(Q3) $\lim_{n\to\infty} \psi^n(\kappa) = 0$ *for all* $\kappa > 0$, *where* $\psi^n(\kappa)$ *is the n-th iteration of* ψ *at* κ.

Remark 2. *For our purpose, for* $\theta \geq 1$, *we define the following:*

$$\Psi_\theta := \{\psi : [0,\infty) \to [0,\infty), \psi \text{ is non-decreasing, right-continuous, and } \textstyle\sum_{n=1}^{\infty} \theta^n \psi^n(t) < \infty\}.$$

It is clear that, with the help of conditions (Q1)-(Q3), if $\psi \in \Psi_\theta$, *then* $\lim_{n\to\infty} \theta^n \psi^n(t) = 0$ *for all* $t > 0$; *hence,* $\psi(t) < t$.

Definition 13. *Let* $(\mathscr{A}, \mathscr{B}, \mathscr{F}_v, \theta, *)$ *be an FBBMS. Mapping*

$$\phi : (\mathscr{A}, \mathscr{B}, \mathscr{F}_v, \theta, *) \rightrightarrows (\mathscr{A}, \mathscr{B}, \mathscr{F}_v, \theta, *)$$

is purported to be an ψ_α*-contractive covariant mapping if for the functions* $\alpha : \mathscr{A} \times \mathscr{B} \times (0,\infty) \to [0,\infty)$, $\psi \in \Psi_\theta$, *and* $\gamma \in (0, \frac{1}{\theta})$, *the below condition holds:*

$$\alpha(a,b,\tau)\left(\frac{1}{\mathscr{F}_v(\phi(a),\phi(b),\tau)} - 1\right) \leq \gamma\psi\left(\frac{1}{\mathscr{F}_v(a,b,\tau)} - 1\right) \tag{2}$$

for all $a \in \mathscr{A}, b \in \mathscr{B}$ *and* $\tau > 0$, *such that* $\theta\gamma < 1$.

Definition 14. *Let* $(\mathscr{A}, \mathscr{B}, \mathscr{F}_v, \theta, *)$ *be an FBBMS. Mapping*

$$\phi : (\mathscr{A}, \mathscr{B}, \mathscr{F}_v, \theta, *) \rightleftarrows (\mathscr{A}, \mathscr{B}, \mathscr{F}_v, \theta, *)$$

is purported to be an ψ_α*-contractive contravariant mapping for the functions* $\alpha : \mathscr{A} \times \mathscr{B} \times (0,\infty) \to [0,\infty)$, $\psi \in \Psi_\theta$, *and* $\gamma \in (0, \frac{1}{\theta})$, *such that the below condition holds:*

$$\alpha(a,b,\tau)\left(\frac{1}{\mathscr{F}_v(\phi(b),\phi(a),\tau)} - 1\right) \leq \gamma\psi\left(\frac{1}{\mathscr{F}_v(a,b,\tau)} - 1\right) \tag{3}$$

for all $a \in \mathscr{A}, b \in \mathscr{B}$ *and* $\tau > 0$, *such that* $\theta\gamma < 1$.

Definition 15. *Let* $(\mathscr{A}, \mathscr{B}, \mathscr{F}_v, \theta, *)$ *be an FBBMS. Mapping*

$$\phi : (\mathscr{A}, \mathscr{B}, \mathscr{F}_v, \theta, *) \rightrightarrows (\mathscr{A}, \mathscr{B}, \mathscr{F}_v, \theta, *)$$

is purported to be a covariant that is α*-admissible if there exists a function* $\alpha : \mathscr{A} \times \mathscr{B} \times (0,\infty) \to [0,\infty)$ *such that, for all* $a \in \mathscr{A}, b \in \mathscr{B}$ *and* $\tau > 0$,

$$\alpha(a,b,\tau) \geq 1 \quad \text{implies} \quad \alpha(\phi(a),\phi(b),\tau) \geq 1.$$

Definition 16. *Let* $(\mathscr{A}, \mathscr{B}, \mathscr{F}_v, \theta, *)$ *be an FBBMS. Mapping*

$$\phi : (\mathscr{A}, \mathscr{B}, \mathscr{F}_v, \theta, *) \leftrightarrows (\mathscr{A}, \mathscr{B}, \mathscr{F}_v, \theta, *)$$

is purported to be a contravariant that is α*-admissible if there exists a function* $\alpha : \mathscr{A} \times \mathscr{B} \times (0,\infty) \to [0,\infty)$ *such that, for all* $a \in \mathscr{A}, b \in \mathscr{B}$ *and* $\tau > 0$,

$$\alpha(a,b,\tau) \geq 1 \quad \text{implies} \quad \alpha(\phi(b),\phi(a),\tau) \geq 1.$$

Theorem 1. *Let* $(\mathscr{A}, \mathscr{B}, \mathscr{F}_v, \theta, *)$ *be a complete FBBMS. Assume that* $\phi : (\mathscr{A}, \mathscr{B}, \mathscr{F}_v, \theta, *) \rightrightarrows (\mathscr{A}, \mathscr{B}, \mathscr{F}_v, \theta, *)$ *is an* ψ_α*-contractive covariant mapping satisfying the following conditions:*

(i) ϕ *is continuous.*
(ii) ϕ *is* α*-admissible.*
(iii) There exists $a_0 \in \mathscr{A}$, $b_0 \in \mathscr{B}$ *such that* $\alpha(a_0, b_0, \tau) \geq 1$, $\alpha(a_0, \phi(b_0), \tau) \geq 1$ *for all* $\tau > 0$.

Under these conditions, ϕ admits a fixed point. That is, $\phi(\mu) = \mu$ for some $\mu \in \mathscr{A} \cap \mathscr{B}$.

Proof. Fix $a_0 \in \mathscr{A}$ and $b_0 \in \mathscr{B}$ such that $\alpha(a_0, \phi(b_0), \tau) \geq 1$ for all $\tau > 0$. Define $\phi(a_n) = a_{n+1}$ and $\phi(b_n) = b_{n+1}$ for all $n \in \mathbb{N} \cup \{0\}$. Then, $(\{a_n\}, \{b_n\})$ is a bisequence in $(\mathscr{A}, \mathscr{B}, \mathscr{F}_v, \theta, *)$.

For any $\tau > 0$, from condition (3) and the α-admissibility of covariant mapping ϕ, we obtain the following:

$$\begin{aligned} \alpha(a_0, b_0, \tau) \geq 1 &\Rightarrow \alpha(\phi(a_0), \phi(b_0), \tau) \geq 1, \\ \alpha(a_0, b_1, \tau) = \alpha(a_0, \phi(b_0), \tau) \geq 1 &\Rightarrow \alpha(\phi(a_0), \phi(b_1), \tau) = \alpha(a_1, b_2, \tau) \geq 1, \\ \alpha(a_1, b_1, \tau) = \alpha(\phi(a_0), \phi(b_0), \tau) \geq 1 &\Rightarrow \alpha(\phi(a_1), \phi(b_1), \tau) = \alpha(a_2, b_2, \tau) \geq 1, \\ \alpha(a_1, b_2, \tau) = \alpha(a_1, \phi(b_1), \tau) \geq 1 &\Rightarrow \alpha(\phi(a_1), \phi(b_1), \tau) = \alpha(a_2, b_2, \tau) \geq 1, \\ \alpha(a_2, b_2, \tau) = \alpha(\phi(a_1), \phi(b_1), \tau) \geq 1 &\Rightarrow \alpha(\phi(a_2), \phi(b_2), \tau) = \alpha(a_3, b_3, \tau) \geq 1. \end{aligned}$$

By repeating this process, we obtain the following:

$$\alpha(a_{n+1}, b_{n+1}, \tau) \geq 1 \text{ and } \alpha(a_n, b_{n+1}, \tau) \geq 1, \quad \text{for all } n \in \mathbb{N}. \tag{4}$$

Using conditions (2) and (4) for $a = a_n$ and $b = b_n$, we obtain the following:

$$\begin{aligned} \frac{1}{\mathscr{F}_v(a_{n+1}, b_{n+1}, \tau)} - 1 &= \frac{1}{\mathscr{F}_v(\phi(a_n), \phi(b_n), \tau)} - 1 \\ &\leq \alpha(a_n, b_n, \tau)\left(\frac{1}{\mathscr{F}_v(\phi(a_n), \phi(b_n), \tau)} - 1\right) \\ &\leq \gamma\psi\left(\frac{1}{\mathscr{F}_v(\phi(a_n), \phi(b_n), \tau)} - 1\right), \end{aligned}$$

and for $a = a_{n-1}$ and $b = b_n$, we obtain

$$\begin{aligned} \frac{1}{\mathscr{F}_v(a_n, b_{n+1}, \tau)} - 1 &= \frac{1}{\mathscr{F}_v(\phi(a_{n-1}), \phi(b_n), \tau)} - 1 \\ &\leq \alpha(a_{n-1}, b_n, \tau)\left(\frac{1}{\mathscr{F}_v(\phi(a_{n-1}), \phi(b_n), \tau)} - 1\right) \\ &\leq \gamma\psi\left(\frac{1}{\mathscr{F}_v(a_n, b_n, \tau)} - 1\right). \end{aligned}$$

By the process of induction, we can obtain

$$\frac{1}{\mathscr{F}_v(a_{n+1}, b_{n+1}, \tau)} - 1 \leq \gamma^{n+1}\psi^{n+1}\left(\frac{1}{\mathscr{F}_v(a_0, b_0, \tau)} - 1\right)$$

and

$$\frac{1}{\mathscr{F}_v(a_n, b_{n+1}, \tau)} - 1 \leq \gamma^n\psi^n\left(\frac{1}{\mathscr{F}_v(a_0, b_1, \tau)} - 1\right).$$

Now, for $m > n$, $m, n \in \mathbb{N}$, using the properties of ψ and b-triangularity of $\mathscr{F}_v$, we obtain the following:

$$\begin{aligned}
\frac{1}{\mathscr{F}_v(a_n, b_m, \tau)} - 1 &\leq \theta\left(\frac{1}{\mathscr{F}_v(a_n, b_n, \tau)} - 1\right) + \theta\left(\frac{1}{\mathscr{F}_v(a_{n+1}, b_n, \tau)} - 1\right) \\
&+ \theta\left(\frac{1}{\mathscr{F}_v(a_{n+1}, b_m, \tau)} - 1\right) \\
&\vdots \\
&\leq \theta\left(\frac{1}{\mathscr{F}_v(a_n, b_n, \tau)} - 1\right) + \theta\left(\frac{1}{\mathscr{F}_v(a_{n+1}, b_m, \tau)} - 1\right) \\
&+ \cdots + \theta^m\left(\frac{1}{\mathscr{F}_v(a_{m-1}, b_{m-1}, \tau)} - 1\right) + \theta^m\left(\frac{1}{\mathscr{F}_v(a_m, b_{m-1}, \tau)} - 1\right) \\
&+ \theta^m\left(\frac{1}{\mathscr{F}_v(a_m, b_m, \tau)} - 1\right) \\
&\leq \theta\gamma^n\psi^n\left(\frac{1}{\mathscr{F}_v(a_0, b_0, \tau)} - 1\right) + \theta\gamma^n\psi^n\left(\frac{1}{\mathscr{F}_v(a_1, b_0, \tau)} - 1\right) \\
&+ \cdots + \theta^m\gamma^{m-1}\psi^{m-1}\left(\frac{1}{\mathscr{F}_v(a_0, b_0, \tau)} - 1\right) \\
&+ \theta^m\gamma^m\psi^m\left(\frac{1}{\mathscr{F}_v(a_1, b_0, \tau)} - 1\right) + \theta^m\gamma^m\psi^m\left(\frac{1}{\mathscr{F}_v(a_0, b_0, \tau)} - 1\right) \\
&\leq \theta\gamma^n\left(1 + \theta\gamma + \theta^2\gamma^2 + \cdots + \theta^{m-1}\gamma^{m-n}\right)\psi^n\left(\frac{1}{\mathscr{F}_v(a_0, b_0, \tau)} - 1\right) \\
&+ \theta\gamma^n\left(1 + \theta\gamma + \theta^2\gamma^2 + \cdots + \theta^{m-1}\gamma^{m-n}\right)\psi^n\left(\frac{1}{\mathscr{F}_v(a_1, b_0, \tau)} - 1\right) \\
&\leq \frac{\theta\gamma^n}{1 - \theta\gamma}\psi^n\left(\frac{1}{\mathscr{F}_v(a_0, b_0, \tau)} - 1\right) + \frac{\theta\gamma^n}{1 - \theta\gamma}\psi^n\left(\frac{1}{\mathscr{F}_v(a_1, b_0, \tau)} - 1\right).
\end{aligned}$$

Also, for $n > m$, $n, m \in \mathbb{N}$, we obtain the following:

$$\begin{aligned}
\frac{1}{\mathscr{F}_v(a_n, b_m, \tau)} - 1 &\leq \theta\left(\frac{1}{\mathscr{F}_v(a_m, b_m, \tau)} - 1\right) + \theta\left(\frac{1}{\mathscr{F}_v(a_{m+1}, b_m, \tau)} - 1\right) \\
&+ \theta\left(\frac{1}{\mathscr{F}_v(a_{m+1}, b_n, \tau)} - 1\right) \\
&\vdots \\
&\leq \theta\left(\frac{1}{\mathscr{F}_v(a_m, b_m, \tau)} - 1\right) + \theta\left(\frac{1}{\mathscr{F}_v(a_{m+1}, b_n, \tau)} - 1\right) \\
&+ \cdots + \theta^n\left(\frac{1}{\mathscr{F}_v(a_{n-1}, b_{n-1}, \tau)} - 1\right) + \theta^n\left(\frac{1}{\mathscr{F}_v(a_n, b_{n-1}, \tau)} - 1\right) \\
&+ \theta^n\left(\frac{1}{\mathscr{F}_v(a_n, b_n, \tau)} - 1\right) \\
&\leq \theta\gamma^m\psi^m\left(\frac{1}{\mathscr{F}_v(a_0, b_0, \tau)} - 1\right) + \theta\gamma^m\psi^m\left(\frac{1}{\mathscr{F}_v(a_1, b_0, \tau)} - 1\right) \\
&+ \cdots + \theta^n\gamma^{n-1}\psi^{n-1}\left(\frac{1}{\mathscr{F}_v(a_0, b_0, \tau)} - 1\right) \\
&+ \theta^n\gamma^n\psi^n\left(\frac{1}{\mathscr{F}_v(a_1, b_0, \tau)} - 1\right) + \theta^n\gamma^n\psi^n\left(\frac{1}{\mathscr{F}_v(a_0, b_0, \tau)} - 1\right)
\end{aligned}$$

$$\begin{aligned}
&\leq \theta\gamma^m\Big(1+\theta\gamma+\theta^2\gamma^2+\cdots+\theta^{n-1}\gamma^{n-m}\Big)\psi^m\left(\frac{1}{\mathscr{F}_v(a_0,b_0,\tau)}-1\right)\\
&+ \theta\gamma^m\Big(1+\theta\gamma+\theta^2\gamma^2+\cdots+\theta^{n-1}\gamma^{n-m}\Big)\psi^m\left(\frac{1}{\mathscr{F}_v(a_1,b_0,\tau)}-1\right)\\
&\leq \frac{\theta\gamma^m}{1-\theta\gamma}\psi^m\left(\frac{1}{\mathscr{F}_v(a_0,b_0,\tau)}-1\right)+\frac{\theta\gamma^m}{1-\theta\gamma}\psi^m\left(\frac{1}{\mathscr{F}_v(a_1,b_0,\tau)}-1\right).
\end{aligned}$$

Since $\theta\gamma < 1$, and letting $m, n \to \infty$ in the above cases, we obtain

$$\lim_{n,m\to\infty} \mathscr{F}_v(a_n, b_m, \tau) = 1, \quad \tau > 0.$$

Thus, we conclude that $(\{a_n\}, \{b_n\})$ is a Cauchy bisequence in $(\mathscr{A}, \mathscr{B}, \mathscr{F}_v, \theta, *)$. Due to the completeness of FBBMS $(\mathscr{A}, \mathscr{B}, \mathscr{F}_v, \theta, *)$, $(\{a_n\}, \{b_n\})$ is a convergent bisequence; hence, through Lemma 2 it biconverges to a point $\mu \in \mathscr{A} \cap \mathscr{B}$, i.e., $\{a_n\} \to \mu$ and $\{b_n\} \to \mu$.

Now, we show that μ is a fixed point of ϕ. Using the properties of ϕ and b-triangularity of $\mathscr{F}_v$, we obtain the following:

$$\begin{aligned}
\frac{1}{\mathscr{F}_v(\phi(\mu),\mu,\tau)}-1 &\leq \leq \theta\left(\frac{1}{\mathscr{F}_v(\phi(\mu),\phi(a_n),\tau)}-1\right)+\theta\left(\frac{1}{\mathscr{F}_v(\phi(a_n),\phi(b_n),\tau)}-1\right)\\
&+ \theta\left(\frac{1}{\mathscr{F}_v(\phi(b_n),\mu,\tau)}-1\right)\\
&\leq \theta\gamma\psi\left(\frac{1}{\mathscr{F}_v(\mu,b_n,\tau)}-1\right)+\theta\gamma\psi\left(\frac{1}{\mathscr{F}_v(a_n,b_n,\tau)}-1\right)\\
&+ \theta\gamma\psi\left(\frac{1}{\mathscr{F}_v(\mu,b_n,\tau)}-1\right).
\end{aligned}$$

By continuity of ϕ , $\phi(a_n) \to \phi(\mu)$ and $\phi(b_n) \to \phi(\mu)$. Hence, by letting $n \to \infty$, we obtain $\mathscr{F}_v(\phi(\mu), \mu, \tau) = 1, \tau > 0$. So, $\phi(\mu) = \mu$. □

Example 2. *Let* $\mathscr{A} = [-1, 1]$ *and* $\mathscr{B} = (\mathbb{N} \cup \{0\}) \setminus \{1\}$ *equipped with a continuous* τ*-norm. Define* $\mathscr{F}_v(a, b, \tau) = \frac{\tau}{\tau+|a-b|^2}$ *for all* $a \in \mathscr{A}, b \in \mathscr{B}$ *and* $\tau > 0$*. Clearly,* $(\mathscr{A}, \mathscr{B}, \mathscr{F}_v, \theta, *)$ *is a complete FBBMS. Define* $\alpha(a, b, \tau) = 1$ *for all* $a \in \mathscr{A}, b \in \mathscr{B}$ *and* $\tau > 0$*. Suppose* $\phi : \mathscr{A} \cup \mathscr{B} \rightrightarrows \mathscr{A} \cup \mathscr{B}$ *can be defined by* $\phi(s) = \sin(\frac{s}{5})$*. Consider* $\psi(w) = \frac{w}{3}$ *for all* $w \in [0, \infty)$*. Then, it is easy to verify that* ψ *is right-continuous and non-decreasing and satisfies all conditions stated in Definition 12.*

Now, for $a \in \mathscr{A}$ *and* $b \in \mathscr{B}$*,* $a \neq b$*, we can obtain the following:*

$$\begin{aligned}
\alpha(a,b,\tau)\left(\frac{1}{\mathscr{F}_v(\phi(a),\phi(b),\tau)}-1\right) &= \frac{|\phi(a)-\phi(b)|}{\tau}\\
&= \frac{\left|\sin(\frac{a}{5})-\sin\left(\frac{b}{5}\right)\right|^2}{\tau}\\
&\leq \frac{1}{25}\frac{|a-b|^2}{\tau}\\
&\leq \frac{1}{9}\frac{|a-b|^2}{\tau}\\
&= \frac{1}{3}\psi\left(\frac{1}{\mathscr{F}_v(a,b,\tau)}-1\right).
\end{aligned}$$

Thus, $\phi : \mathscr{A} \cup \mathscr{B} \rightrightarrows \mathscr{A} \cup \mathscr{B}$ *is continuous and satisfies the following condition:*

$$\alpha(a,b,\tau)\left(\frac{1}{\mathscr{F}_v(\phi(a),\phi(b),\tau)}-1\right) \leq \gamma\psi\left(\frac{1}{\mathscr{F}_v(a,b,\tau)}-1\right)$$

for all $a \in \mathscr{A}, b \in \mathscr{B}$ *with* $a \neq b$ *and* $\tau > 0$*.*

So, all axioms of Theorem 1 are satisfied with $\gamma = \frac{1}{3}$*, and consequently,* ϕ *has a unique fixed point, i.e.,* $\mu = 1$.

Theorem 2. *Let* $(\mathscr{A}, \mathscr{B}, \mathscr{F}_v, \theta, *)$ *be a complete FBBMS. Assume that* $\phi : (\mathscr{A}, \mathscr{B}, \mathscr{F}_v, \theta, *) \leftrightarrows (\mathscr{A}, \mathscr{B}, \mathscr{F}_v, \theta, *)$ *is an* ψ_α*-contractive contravariant mapping satisfying the following conditions:*

(i) ϕ *is continuous;*
(ii) ϕ *is* α*-admissible;*
(iii) There exists $a_0 \in \mathscr{A}$, $b_0 \in \mathscr{B}$ *such that* $\alpha(a_0, b_0, \tau) \geq 1$, $\alpha(a_0, \phi(b_0), \tau) \geq 1$ *for all* $\tau > 0$.

Under these conditions, ϕ *admits a fixed point. That is,* $\phi(\mu) = \mu$ *for* $\mu \in \mathscr{A} \cap \mathscr{B}$.

Proof. Fix $a_0 \in \mathscr{A}$ and $b_0 \in \mathscr{B}$ such that $\alpha(a_0, \phi(b_0), \tau) \geq 1$ for all $\tau > 0$. Define $\phi(a_n) = b_n$ and $\phi(b_n) = a_{n+1}$ for all $n \in \mathbb{N} \cup \{0\}$. Then, $(\{a_n\}, \{b_n\})$ is a bisequence in $(\mathscr{A}, \mathscr{B}, \mathscr{F}_v, \theta, *)$.

For any $\tau > 0$, from condition (3) and the α-admissibility of covariant mapping ϕ, we obtain the following:

$$\begin{aligned}
\alpha(a_0, b_0, \tau) \geq 1 \quad &\Rightarrow \quad \alpha(\phi(b_0), \phi(a_0), \tau) = \alpha(a_1, b_0, \tau) \geq 1 \\
\alpha(a_1, b_0, \tau) \geq 1 \quad &\Rightarrow \quad \alpha(\phi(b_0), \phi(a_1), \tau) = \alpha(a_1, b_1, \tau) \geq 1 \\
\alpha(a_1, b_1, \tau) \geq 1 \quad &\Rightarrow \quad \alpha(\phi(b_1), \phi(a_1), \tau) = \alpha(a_2, b_1, \tau) \geq 1 \\
\alpha(a_2, b_1, \tau) \geq 1 \quad &\Rightarrow \quad \alpha(\phi(b_1), \phi(a_2), \tau) = \alpha(a_2, b_2, \tau) \geq 1 \\
\alpha(a_2, b_2, \tau) \geq 1 \quad &\Rightarrow \quad \alpha(\phi(b_2), \phi(a_2), \tau) = \alpha(a_3, b_2, \tau) \geq 1.
\end{aligned}$$

By repeating this process, we obtain

$$\alpha(a_n, b_n, \tau) \geq 1 \text{ and } \alpha(a_{n+1}, b_n, \tau) \geq 1, \quad \text{for all } n \in \mathbb{N}. \tag{5}$$

Employing the conditions (3) and (5) for $a = a_n$ and $b = b_{n-1}$, we obtain

$$\begin{aligned}
\frac{1}{\mathscr{F}_v(a_n, b_n, \tau)} - 1 &= \frac{1}{\mathscr{F}_v(\phi(b_{n-1}), \phi(a_n), \tau)} - 1 \\
&\leq \alpha(a_n, b_{n-1}, \tau)\left(\frac{1}{\mathscr{F}_v(\phi(b_{n-1}), \phi(a_n), \tau)} - 1\right) \\
&\leq \gamma\psi\left(\frac{1}{\mathscr{F}_v(\phi(a_n), \phi(b_{n-1}), \tau)} - 1\right),
\end{aligned}$$

and for $a = a_{n+1}$ and $b = b_n$, we obtain

$$\begin{aligned}
\frac{1}{\mathscr{F}_v(a_{n+1}, b_n, \tau)} - 1 &= \frac{1}{\mathscr{F}_v(\phi(b_n), \phi(a_n), \tau)} - 1 \\
&\leq \alpha(a_n, b_n, \tau)\left(\frac{1}{\mathscr{F}_v(\phi(b_n), \phi(a_n), \tau)} - 1\right) \\
&\leq \gamma\psi\left(\frac{1}{\mathscr{F}_v(a_n, b_n, \tau)} - 1\right).
\end{aligned}$$

By the process of induction, we can obtain

$$\frac{1}{\mathscr{F}_v(a_n, b_n, \tau)} - 1 \leq \gamma^{2n-1}\psi^{2n-1}\left(\frac{1}{\mathscr{F}_v(a_0, b_1, \tau)} - 1\right)$$

and

$$\frac{1}{\mathscr{F}_v(a_{n+1}, b_n, \tau)} - 1 \leq \gamma^{2n+1}\psi^{2n+1}\left(\frac{1}{\mathscr{F}_v(a_0, b_0, \tau)} - 1\right).$$

Now, for $m > n$, $m, n \in \mathbb{N}$, using the properties of ψ and b-triangularity of $\mathscr{F}_v$, we obtain the following:

$$\begin{aligned}
\frac{1}{\mathscr{F}_v(a_n, b_m, \tau)} - 1 &\leq \theta\left(\frac{1}{\mathscr{F}_v(a_n, b_n, \tau)} - 1\right) + \theta\left(\frac{1}{\mathscr{F}_v(a_n, b_{n+1}, \tau)} - 1\right) \\
&+ \theta\left(\frac{1}{\mathscr{F}_v(a_{n+1}, b_m, \tau)} - 1\right) \\
&\vdots \\
&\leq \theta\left(\frac{1}{\mathscr{F}_v(a_n, b_n, \tau)} - 1\right) + \theta\left(\frac{1}{\mathscr{F}_v(a_n, b_{n+1}, \tau)} - 1\right) \\
&+ \theta\left(\frac{1}{\mathscr{F}_v(a_{n+1}, b_{n+1}, \tau)} - 1\right) \\
&+ \cdots + \theta^m\left(\frac{1}{\mathscr{F}_v(a_{m-1}, b_{m-1}, \tau)} - 1\right) + \theta^m\left(\frac{1}{\mathscr{F}_v(a_{m-1}, b_m, \tau)} - 1\right) \\
&+ \theta^m\left(\frac{1}{\mathscr{F}_v(a_m, b_m, \tau)} - 1\right) \\
&\leq \theta\gamma^n\psi^n\left(\frac{1}{\mathscr{F}_v(a_0, b_0, \tau)} - 1\right) + \theta\gamma^n\psi^n\left(\frac{1}{\mathscr{F}_v(a_0, b_1, \tau)} - 1\right) \\
&+ \theta\gamma^{n+1}\psi^{n+1}\left(\frac{1}{\mathscr{F}_v(a_0, b_0, \tau)} - 1\right) \\
&+ \cdots + \theta^m\gamma^{m-1}\psi^{m-1}\left(\frac{1}{\mathscr{F}_v(a_0, b_0, \tau)} - 1\right) \\
&+ \theta^m\gamma^{m-1}\psi^{m-1}\left(\frac{1}{\mathscr{F}_v(a_0, b_1, \tau)} - 1\right) \\
&+ \theta^m\gamma^m\psi^m\left(\frac{1}{\mathscr{F}_v(a_0, b_0, \tau)} - 1\right) \\
&\leq \theta\gamma^n\left(1 + \theta\gamma + \cdots + \theta^{m-1}\gamma^{m-1}\right)\psi^n\left(\frac{1}{\mathscr{F}_v(a_0, b_0, \tau)} - 1\right) \\
&+ \theta\gamma^n\left(1 + \theta\gamma + \cdots + \theta^{m-1}\gamma^{m-1}\right)\psi^n\left(\frac{1}{\mathscr{F}_v(a_0, b_1, \tau)} - 1\right) \\
&\leq \frac{\theta\gamma^n}{1 - \theta\gamma}\psi^n\left(\frac{1}{\mathscr{F}_v(a_0, b_0, \tau)} - 1\right) + \frac{\theta\gamma^n}{1 - \theta\gamma}\psi^n\left(\frac{1}{\mathscr{F}_v(a_0, b_1, \tau)} - 1\right).
\end{aligned}$$

Also, for $n > m$, $n, m \in \mathbb{N}$, we obtain the following:

$$\begin{aligned}
\frac{1}{\mathscr{F}_v(a_n, b_m, \tau)} - 1 &\leq \theta\left(\frac{1}{\mathscr{F}_v(a_m, b_m, \tau)} - 1\right) + \theta\left(\frac{1}{\mathscr{F}_v(a_m, b_{m+1}, \tau)} - 1\right) \\
&+ \theta\left(\frac{1}{\mathscr{F}_v(a_{m+1}, b_n, \tau)} - 1\right) \\
&\vdots \\
&\leq \theta\left(\frac{1}{\mathscr{F}_v(a_m, b_m, \tau)} - 1\right) + \theta\left(\frac{1}{\mathscr{F}_v(a_m, b_{m+1}, \tau)} - 1\right) \\
&+ \theta\left(\frac{1}{\mathscr{F}_v(a_{m+1}, b_{m+1}, \tau)} - 1\right) \\
&+ \cdots + \theta^n\left(\frac{1}{\mathscr{F}_v(a_{n-1}, b_{n-1}, \tau)} - 1\right) + \theta^n\left(\frac{1}{\mathscr{F}_v(a_{n-1}, b_n, \tau)} - 1\right) \\
&+ \theta^n\left(\frac{1}{\mathscr{F}_v(a_n, b_n, \tau)} - 1\right)
\end{aligned}$$

$$
\begin{aligned}
&\leq \theta\gamma^m\psi^m\left(\frac{1}{\mathscr{F}_v(a_0,b_0,\tau)}-1\right)+\theta\gamma^m\psi^m\left(\frac{1}{\mathscr{F}_v(a_0,b_1,\tau)}-1\right)\\
&+ \theta\gamma^{m+1}\psi^{m+1}\left(\frac{1}{\mathscr{F}_v(a_0,b_0,\tau)}-1\right)\\
&+ \cdots+\theta^n\gamma^{n-1}\psi^{n-1}\left(\frac{1}{\mathscr{F}_v(a_0,b_0,\tau)}-1\right)+\theta^n\gamma^{n-1}\psi^{n-1}\left(\frac{1}{\mathscr{F}_v(a_0,b_1,\tau)}-1\right)\\
&+ \theta^n\gamma^n\psi^n\left(\frac{1}{\mathscr{F}_v(a_0,b_0,\tau)}-1\right)\\
&\leq \theta\gamma^m\left(1+\theta\gamma+\cdots+\theta^{n-1}\gamma^{n-1}\right)\psi^m\left(\frac{1}{\mathscr{F}_v(a_0,b_0,\tau)}-1\right)\\
&+ \theta\gamma^n\left(1+\theta\gamma+\cdots+\theta^{m-1}\gamma^{m-1}\right)\psi^n\left(\frac{1}{\mathscr{F}_v(a_0,b_1,\tau)}-1\right)\\
&\leq \frac{\theta\gamma^m}{1-\theta\gamma}\psi^m\left(\frac{1}{\mathscr{F}_v(a_0,b_0,\tau)}-1\right)+\frac{\theta\gamma^m}{1-\theta\gamma}\psi^m\left(\frac{1}{\mathscr{F}_v(a_0,b_1,\tau)}-1\right).
\end{aligned}
$$

Since $\theta\gamma < 1$, and letting $m, n \to \infty$ in the above cases, we obtain

$$
\lim_{n,m\to\infty} \mathscr{F}_v(a_n, b_m, \tau) = 1, \quad \tau > 0.
$$

Thus, we conclude that $(\{a_n\},\{b_n\})$ is a Cauchy bisequence in $(\mathscr{A},\mathscr{B},\mathscr{F}_v,\theta,*)$. Due to the completeness of FBBMS $(\mathscr{A},\mathscr{B},\mathscr{F}_v,\theta,*)$, $(\{a_n\},\{b_n\})$ is a convergent bisequence; hence, through Lemma 2, it biconverges to a point $\mu \in \mathscr{A}\cap\mathscr{B}$, i.e., $\{a_n\}\to\mu$ and $\{b_n\}\to\mu$.

Now, we show that μ is a fixed point of ϕ. Using the properties of ϕ and b-triangularity of $\mathscr{F}_v$, we obtain

$$
\begin{aligned}
\frac{1}{\mathscr{F}_v(\phi(\mu),\mu,\tau)}-1 &\leq \leq\theta\left(\frac{1}{\mathscr{F}_v(\phi(\mu),\phi(a_n),\tau)}-1\right)+\theta\left(\frac{1}{\mathscr{F}_v(\phi(a_n),\phi(b_n),\tau)}-1\right)\\
&+ \theta\left(\frac{1}{\mathscr{F}_v(\phi(b_n),\mu,\tau)}-1\right).
\end{aligned}
$$

By continuity of ϕ , $\phi(a_n)\to\phi(\mu)$ and $\phi(b_n)\to\phi(\mu)$. Hence, by letting $n\to\infty$, we obtain $\mathscr{F}_v(\phi(\mu),\mu,\tau)=1$, $\tau>0$. So, $\phi(\mu)=\mu$. □

Theorem 3. *Let $(\mathscr{A},\mathscr{B},\mathscr{F}_v,\theta,*)$ be a complete FBBMS, and let*

$$
\phi : (\mathscr{A},\mathscr{B},\mathscr{F}_v,\theta,*) \rightrightarrows (\mathscr{A},\mathscr{B},\mathscr{F}_v,\theta,*)
$$

be an ψ_α-contractive covariant mapping satisfying the following conditions:

1. *For bisequence $(\{a_n\},\{b_n\})$, if $\alpha(a_n,b_n,\tau)\geq 1$ for all $n\in\mathbb{N}$, $\{a_n\}\to\mu$, $\{b_n\}\to\mu$ as $n\to\infty$ for $\mu\in\mathscr{A}\cap\mathscr{B}$, then $\alpha(\mu,b_n,\tau)\geq 1$ for all $\tau>0$ and $n\in\mathbb{N}$;*
2. *ϕ is α-admissible;*
3. *There exists $a_0\in\mathscr{A}$, $b_0\in\mathscr{B}$ such that $\alpha(a_0,b_0,\tau)\geq 1$, $\alpha(a_0,\phi(b_0),\tau)\geq 1$.*

Under these assumptions, ϕ admits a fixed point. That is, $\phi(\mu)=\mu$ for some $\mu\in\mathscr{A}\cap\mathscr{B}$.

Proof. By proving Theorem 1, we derived a bisequence $(\{a_n\},\{b_n\})$, which exhibits Cauchy properties within the context of a complete FBBMS $(\mathscr{A},\mathscr{B},\mathscr{F}_v,\theta,*)$. This bisequence, denoted by $(\{a_n\},\{b_n\})$, biconverges to a point $\mu\in\mathscr{A}\cap\mathscr{B}$, implying that both $\{a_n\}$ and $\{b_n\}$ converge to μ as n tends to infinity.

Now, through condition (1) and (4), we obatin the following:

$$
\alpha(\mu,b_n,\tau)\geq 1 \quad \text{for all } n\in\mathbb{N} \text{ and } \tau>0. \tag{6}
$$

Once more, employing conditions (2) and (6), along with the b-triangular property of $\mathscr{F}_v$, we achieve the following:

$$\left(\frac{1}{\mathscr{F}_v(\phi(\mu),\mu,\tau)}-1\right) \leq \theta\left(\frac{1}{\mathscr{F}_v(\phi(\mu),\phi(b_n),\tau)}-1\right)+\theta\left(\frac{1}{\mathscr{F}_v(\phi(a_n),\phi(b_n),\tau)}-1\right)$$

$$\begin{aligned}
&+ \theta\left(\frac{1}{\mathscr{F}_v(\phi(a_n),\mu,\tau)}-1\right)\\
&\leq \alpha(\mu,b_n,\tau)\theta\left(\frac{1}{\mathscr{F}_v(\phi(\mu),\phi(b_n),\tau)}-1\right)+\alpha(a_n,b_n,\tau)\theta\left(\frac{1}{\mathscr{F}_v(\phi(a_n),\phi(b_n),\tau)}-1\right)\\
&+ \theta\left(\frac{1}{\mathscr{F}_v(\phi(a_{n+1}),\phi(\mu),\tau)}-1\right) \qquad (7)\\
&\leq \theta\gamma\psi\left(\frac{1}{\mathscr{F}_v(\mu,b_n,\tau)}-1\right)+\theta\gamma\psi\left(\frac{1}{\mathscr{F}_v(a_n,b_n,\tau)}-1\right)+\theta\left(\frac{1}{\mathscr{F}_v(a_{n+1},\mu,\tau)}-1\right)\\
&\leq \theta\gamma\psi\left(\frac{1}{\mathscr{F}_v(\mu,b_n,\tau)}-1\right)+\theta\gamma\psi\left[\left(\frac{1}{\mathscr{F}_v(\phi(a_n),\mu,\tau)}-1\right)+\theta\left(\frac{1}{\mathscr{F}_v(\mu,\mu,\tau)}-1\right)\right.\\
&\left.+\theta\left(\frac{1}{\mathscr{F}_v(\mu,b_n,\tau)}-1\right)\right]+\theta\left(\frac{1}{\mathscr{F}_v(a_{n+1},\mu,\tau)}-1\right).
\end{aligned}$$

Letting $n \to \infty$ in (7), and using the continuity of ψ, we obtain

$$\mathscr{F}_v(\phi(\mu),\mu,\tau) = 1 \quad \text{for all } \tau > 0,$$

which yields to $\phi(\mu) = \mu$. □

Theorem 4. *Let $(\mathscr{A},\mathscr{B},\mathscr{F}_v,\theta,*)$ be a complete FBBMS, and let*

$$\phi : (\mathscr{A},\mathscr{B},\mathscr{F}_v,\theta,*) \leftrightarrows (\mathscr{A},\mathscr{B},\mathscr{F}_v,\theta,*)$$

be an ψ_α-contractive contravariant mapping satisfying the following conditions:

1. *For bisequence $(\{a_n\},\{b_n\})$, if $\alpha(a_n,b_n,\tau) \geq 1$ for all $n \in \mathbb{N}$, $\{a_n\} \to \mu$, $\{b_n\} \to \mu$ as $n \to \infty$ for $\mu \in \mathscr{A} \cap \mathscr{B}$, then $\alpha(\mu,b_n,\tau) \geq 1$ for all $\tau > 0$ and $n \in \mathbb{N}$;*
2. *ϕ is α-admissible;*
3. *There exists $a_0 \in \mathscr{A}$, $b_0 \in \mathscr{B}$ such that $\alpha(a_0,b_0,\tau) \geq 1$, $\alpha(a_0,\phi(b_0),\tau) \geq 1$.*

Under these assumptions, ϕ admits a fixed point. That is, $\phi(\mu) = \mu$ for some $\mu \in \mathscr{A} \cap \mathscr{B}$.

Proof. By proving Theorem 2, we derived a bisequence $(\{a_n\},\{b_n\})$, which exhibits Cauchy properties within the context of a complete FBBMS $(\mathscr{A},\mathscr{B},\mathscr{F}_v,\theta,*)$. This bisequence, denoted by $(\{a_n\},\{b_n\})$, biconverges to point $\mu \in \mathscr{A} \cap \mathscr{B}$, implying that both $\{a_n\}$ and $\{b_n\}$ converge to μ as n tends to infinity.

Now, through condition (1) and (5), we obtain the following:

$$\alpha(a_n,\mu,\tau) \geq 1 \quad \text{for all } n \in \mathbb{N} \text{ and } \tau > 0. \qquad (8)$$

Once more, employing conditions (3) and (8), along with the b-triangular property of $\mathscr{F}_v$, we achieve the following:

$$
\begin{aligned}
&\left(\frac{1}{\mathscr{F}_v(\phi(\mu),\mu,\tau)}-1\right) \leq \theta\left(\frac{1}{\mathscr{F}_v(\phi(\mu),\phi(a_n),\tau)}-1\right)+\theta\left(\frac{1}{\mathscr{F}_v(\phi(b_n),\phi(a_n),\tau)}-1\right)\\
+\ &\theta\left(\frac{1}{\mathscr{F}_v(\phi(b_n),\mu,\tau)}-1\right)\\
\leq\ &\alpha(a_n,\mu,\tau)\theta\left(\frac{1}{\mathscr{F}_v(\phi(\mu),\phi(a_n),\tau)}-1\right)+\alpha(a_n,b_n,\tau)\theta\left(\frac{1}{\mathscr{F}_v(\phi(b_n),\phi(a_n),\tau)}-1\right)\\
+\ &\theta\left(\frac{1}{\mathscr{F}_v(\phi(a_{n+1}),\phi(\mu),\tau)}-1\right)\\
\leq\ &\theta\gamma\psi\left(\frac{1}{\mathscr{F}_v(a_n,\mu,\tau)}-1\right)+\theta\gamma\psi\left(\frac{1}{\mathscr{F}_v(a_n,b_n,\tau)}-1\right)+\theta\left(\frac{1}{\mathscr{F}_v(a_{n+1},\mu,\tau)}-1\right)\\
\leq\ &\theta\gamma\psi\left(\frac{1}{\mathscr{F}_v(a_n,\mu,\tau)}-1\right)+\theta\gamma\psi\left[\left(\frac{1}{\mathscr{F}_v(\phi(a_n),\mu,\tau)}-1\right)+\theta\left(\frac{1}{\mathscr{F}_v(\mu,\mu,\tau)}-1\right)\right.\\
&\left.+\theta\left(\frac{1}{\mathscr{F}_v(\mu,b_n,\tau)}-1\right)\right]+\theta\left(\frac{1}{\mathscr{F}_v(a_{n+1},\mu,\tau)}-1\right).
\end{aligned}
\tag{9}
$$

Letting $n \to \infty$ in (9), and using the continuity of ψ, we obtain

$$\mathscr{F}_v(\phi(\mu),\mu,\tau) = 1 \quad \text{for all } \tau > 0,$$

which yields to $\phi(\mu) = \mu$. □

Theorem 5. *Under the assumption of Theorem 1 or Theorem 3 (or Theorem 2 or Theorem 4), and if there exists a point $\rho \in \mathscr{A} \cap \mathscr{B}$ such that $\alpha(a,\rho,\tau) \geq 1$ and $\alpha(\rho,b,\tau) \geq 1$ for all $\tau > 0$, $a \in \mathscr{A}$ and $b \in \mathscr{B}$, then the ψ_α-contractive covariant mapping $\phi : (\mathscr{A},\mathscr{B},\mathscr{F}_v,\theta,*) \rightrightarrows (\mathscr{A},\mathscr{B},\mathscr{F}_v,\theta,*)$ (the ψ_α-contractive contravariant mapping $\phi : (\mathscr{A},\mathscr{B},\mathscr{F}_v,\theta,*) \leftrightarrows (\mathscr{A},\mathscr{B},\mathscr{F}_v,\theta,*)$) has a unique fixed point.*

Proof. In order to show the uniqueness of a fixed point of the mapping $\phi : (\mathscr{A},\mathscr{B},\mathscr{F}_v,\theta,*) \rightrightarrows (\mathscr{A},\mathscr{B},\mathscr{F}_v,\theta,*)$ (or,$\phi : (\mathscr{A},\mathscr{B},\mathscr{F}_v,\theta,*) \leftrightarrows (\mathscr{A},\mathscr{B},\mathscr{F}_v,\theta,*)$). Suppose, on the contrary, that λ is another fixed point of ϕ. Using the assumption, there exists a point $\rho \in \mathscr{A} \cap \mathscr{B}$, such that

$$\alpha(\mu,\rho,\tau) \geq 1 \quad \text{and} \quad \alpha(\rho,\lambda,\tau) \geq 1 \quad \text{for all } \tau > 0. \tag{10}$$

Utilizing the condition (10) and α-admissibility of ϕ, we obtain

$$\alpha(\mu,\phi^n(\rho),\tau) \geq 1 \quad \text{and} \quad \alpha(\phi^n(\rho),\lambda,\tau) \geq 1 \quad \text{for all } n \in \mathbb{N} \text{ and } \tau > 0. \tag{11}$$

Also, using conditions (2) and (11), we obtain the following:

$$
\begin{aligned}
\frac{1}{\mathscr{F}_v(\mu,\phi^n(\rho),\tau)-1} &= \frac{1}{\mathscr{F}_v(\phi(\mu),\phi(\phi^{n-1}(\rho)),\tau)-1}\\
&\leq \alpha\left(\mu,\phi^{n-1}(\rho),\tau\right)\left(\frac{1}{\mathscr{F}_v(\phi(\mu),\phi(\phi^{n-1}(\rho)),\tau)-1}\right)\\
&\leq \gamma\psi\left(\frac{1}{\mathscr{F}_v(\mu,\phi^{n-1}(\rho),\tau)-1}\right).
\end{aligned}
$$

Repeating this process, we obtain

$$\frac{1}{\mathscr{F}_v(\mu,\phi^n(\rho),\tau)-1} \leq \gamma^n\psi^n\left(\frac{1}{\mathscr{F}_v(\mu,\rho,\tau)-1}\right) \quad \text{for all } n \in \mathbb{N} \text{ and } \tau > 0. \tag{12}$$

In the same way, we can also obtain

$$\frac{1}{\mathscr{F}_v(\phi^n(\rho),\lambda,\tau)-1} \leq \gamma^n \psi^n\left(\frac{1}{\mathscr{F}_v(\rho,\lambda,\tau)-1}\right) \quad \text{for all } n \in \mathbb{N} \text{ and } \tau > 0. \tag{13}$$

Letting $n \to \infty$ in (12) and (13) provides

$$\phi^n(\rho) \to \mu \quad \text{and} \quad \phi^n(\rho) \to \lambda,$$

which contradicts the uniqueness of the limit. Hence, $\mu = \lambda \in \mathscr{A} \cap \mathscr{B}$. Therefore, ϕ admits a unique fixed point in $(\mathscr{A}, \mathscr{B}, \mathscr{F}_v, \theta, *)$. □

Example 3. *Let $\mathscr{A} = (-\infty, 0]$ and $\mathscr{B} = [0, \infty)$ equipped with a continuous τ-norm. Let $d : \mathscr{A} \times \mathscr{B} \to [0, \infty$ be defined as $d(x,y) = |x-y|^2$. Define $\mathscr{F}_v(a,b,\tau) = \frac{\tau}{\tau + d(a,b)}$ for all $a \in \mathscr{A}, b \in \mathscr{B}$ and $\tau > 0$. Clearly, $(\mathscr{A}, \mathscr{B}, \mathscr{F}_v, \theta, *)$ is a complete FBBMS. Define $\phi : \mathscr{A} \cup \mathscr{B} \leftrightarrows \mathscr{A} \cup \mathscr{B}$ by $\phi(x) = -\frac{x}{3}$ for all $x \in \mathscr{A} \cup \mathscr{B}$ and $\psi(t) = \frac{1}{2}t$, $\alpha(a,b,\tau) = 1$ for all $(a,b) \in \mathscr{A} \times \mathscr{B}$. Then, $\phi([0,\infty)) \subset [0,\infty)$ and $\phi([0,\infty)) \subset (-\infty, 0]$. It is clear that ϕ is continuous contravariant mapping.*

As $x \in (-\infty, 0]$, there exists $a \in [0,\infty)$, such that $x = -a$.

Now,

$$\begin{aligned} \frac{1}{\mathscr{F}_v(\phi(a),\phi(b),\tau)} - 1 &= \frac{|\phi(a)-\phi(b)|^2}{\tau} \\ &= \frac{\left|-\frac{a}{3}+\frac{b}{3}\right|}{\tau} \\ &= \frac{1}{9}\frac{|a-b|^2}{\tau} \\ &\leq \frac{1}{3} \times \frac{1}{2}\frac{|a-b|^2}{\tau} \\ &= \frac{1}{3}\psi\left(\frac{1}{\mathscr{F}_v(a,b,\tau)} - 1\right) \end{aligned}$$

for all $a \in \mathscr{A}, b \in \mathscr{B}$ with $a \neq b$ and $\tau > 0$.

So, all the axioms of Theorem 5 are satisfied with $\gamma = \frac{1}{3}$, and consequently, ϕ has a unique fixed point, i.e., $\mu = 0$.

4. F_η-Contractive Mappings and Fixed Point Results

In this section, we present the notion of F_η-contractive mappings and η-admissible mappings within the framework of FBBMS.

Definition 17. *Let Υ_θ be the family of all left-continuous non-decreasing functions $F : [0,1] \to [0,1]$ satisfying the following conditions:*

(F1) $F(1) = 1$;

(F2) $F(v) > v$ *for all* $v \in [0,1]$;

(F3) $\lim_{n\to\infty} F^n(v) = 1$ *for all* $v \in [0,1]$, *where* $F^n(v)$ *is the n-th iteration of* F *at* v.

Definition 18. *Let $(\mathscr{A}, \mathscr{B}, \mathscr{F}_v, \theta, *)$ be an FBBMS. Mapping*

$$\phi : (\mathscr{A}, \mathscr{B}, \mathscr{F}_v, \theta, *) \rightrightarrows (\mathscr{A}, \mathscr{B}, \mathscr{F}_v, \theta, *)$$

is said to be covariant η-admissible if there exists a function $\eta : \mathscr{A} \times \mathscr{B} \times (0,\infty) \to [0,\infty)$ such that, for all $a \in \mathscr{A}$, $b \in \mathscr{B}$ and $\tau > 0$

$$\eta(a,b,\tau) \leq 1 \text{ implies } \eta(\phi(a),\phi(b),\tau) \leq 1.$$

Definition 19. *Let $(\mathscr{A}, \mathscr{B}, \mathscr{F}_v, \theta, *)$ be an FBBMS. Mapping*

$$\phi : (\mathscr{A}, \mathscr{B}, \mathscr{F}_v, \theta, *) \rightrightarrows (\mathscr{A}, \mathscr{B}, \mathscr{F}_v, \theta, *)$$

is said to be $\digamma_\eta$-contractive covariant mapping if for the functions $\eta : \mathscr{A} \times \mathscr{B} \times (0, \infty) \to [0, \infty)$ and $\digamma \in \Upsilon$ the following condition holds:

$$\mathscr{F}_v(a, b, \tau) > 0 \text{ implies } \eta(a, b, \tau)\mathscr{F}_v(\phi(a), \phi(b), \tau) \geq \theta\digamma(\mathscr{F}_v(a, b, \tau)) \tag{14}$$

for all $a \in \mathscr{A}, b \in \mathscr{B}, a \neq b$ and $\tau > 0$.

Theorem 6. *Let $(\mathscr{A}, \mathscr{B}, \mathscr{F}_v, \theta, *)$ be a complete FBBMS. Assume that $\phi : (\mathscr{A}, \mathscr{B}, \mathscr{F}_v, \theta, *) \rightrightarrows (\mathscr{A}, \mathscr{B}, \mathscr{F}_v, \theta, *)$ is $\digamma_\eta$-contractive covariant mapping satisfying the following conditions:*

(i) *ϕ is η-admissible;*

(ii) *For bisequence $(\{a_n\}, \{b_n\})$, if $\eta(a_n, b_n, \tau) \leq 1$ for all $n \in \mathbb{N}$, $\{a_n\} \to \mu$, $\{b_n\} \to \mu$ as $n \to \infty$ for $\mu \in \mathscr{A} \cap \mathscr{B}$, then $\eta(\mu, a_n, \tau) \leq 1$ and $n \in \mathbb{N}$;*

(iii) *There exists $a_0 \in \mathscr{A}, b_0 \in \mathscr{B}$ such that $\eta(a_0, b_0, \tau) \leq 1$, $\eta(a_0, \phi(b_0), \tau) \leq 1$ for $\tau > 0$.*

Under these axioms, ϕ admits a fixed point. That is, $\phi(\mu) = \mu$ for some $\mu \in \mathscr{A} \cap \mathscr{B}$.

Proof. Fix $a_0 \in \mathscr{A}$ and $b_0 \in \mathscr{B}$ such that $\phi(a_0, \phi(b_0), \tau) \leq 1$. Define $\phi(a_n) = a_{n+1}$ and $\phi(b_n) = b_{n+1}$ for all $n \in \mathbb{N} \cup \{0\}$. Then, $(\{a_n\}, \{b_n\})$ is a bisequence in $(\mathscr{A}, \mathscr{B}, \mathscr{F}_v, \theta, *)$. For any $\tau > 0$, from the axiom (iii) and η-admissibility of covariant mapping ϕ, we obtain the following:

$$\begin{aligned}
\eta(a_0, b_0, \tau) \leq 1 &\Rightarrow \eta(\phi(a_0), \phi(b_0), \tau) \leq 1 \\
\eta(a_0, b_1, \tau) = \eta(a_0, \phi(b_0), \tau) \leq 1 &\Rightarrow \eta(\phi(a_0), \phi(b_1), \tau) = \eta(a_1, b_2, \tau) \leq 1 \\
\eta(a_1, b_1, \tau) = \eta(\phi(a_0), \phi(b_0), \tau) \leq 1 &\Rightarrow \eta(\phi(a_1), \phi(b_1), \tau) = \eta(a_2, b_2, \tau) \leq 1 \\
\eta(a_1, b_2, \tau) = \eta(a_1, \phi(b_1), \tau) \leq 1 &\Rightarrow \eta(\phi(a_1), \phi(b_2), \tau) = \eta(a_2, b_3, \tau) \leq 1 \\
\eta(a_2, b_2, \tau) = \eta(\phi(a_1), \phi(b_1), \tau) \leq 1 &\Rightarrow \eta(\phi(a_2), \phi(b_2), \tau) = \eta(a_3, b_3, \tau) \leq 1.
\end{aligned}$$

By repeating this process, we obtain

$$\eta(a_{n+1}, b_{n+1}, \tau) \leq 1 \text{ and } \eta(a_n, b_{n+1}, \tau) \leq 1 \text{ for all} n \in \mathbb{N}. \tag{15}$$

Using conditions (14) and (15), for $a = a_n$ and $b = b_n$, we obtain

$$\begin{aligned}
\mathscr{F}_v(a_{n+1}, b_{n+1}, \tau) &= \mathscr{F}_v(\phi(a_n), \phi(b_n), \tau) \\
&\geq \eta(a_n, b_n, \tau)\mathscr{F}_v(\phi(a_n), \phi(b_n), \tau) \\
&\geq \frac{1}{\theta}\digamma(a_n, b_n, \tau),
\end{aligned}$$

and for $a = a_{n-1}$ and $b = b_n$, we obtain

$$\begin{aligned}
\mathscr{F}_v(a_n, b_{n+1}, \tau) &= \mathscr{F}_v(\phi(a_{n-1}), \phi(b_n), \tau) \\
&\geq \eta(a_{n-1}, b_n, \tau)\mathscr{F}_v(\phi(a_{n-1}), \phi(b_n), \tau) \\
&\geq \theta\digamma(a_{n-1}, b_n, \tau).
\end{aligned}$$

By the process of induction, we can obtain the following:

$$\begin{aligned}
\mathscr{F}_v(a_{n+1}, b_{n+1}, \tau) &\geq \theta^{n+1}\digamma^{n+1}\mathscr{F}_v(a_0, b_0, \tau) \text{ and} \\
\mathscr{F}_v(a_n, b_{n+1}, \tau) &\geq \theta^n\digamma^n\mathscr{F}_v(a_0, b_1, \tau).
\end{aligned}$$

Now, for $m > n$, $m \in \mathbb{N}$, using the properties of $\digamma$ and b-triangularity of $\mathscr{F}_v$, we obtain the following:

$$\begin{aligned}
\mathscr{F}_v(a_n, b_m, \tau) &\geq \mathscr{F}_v(a_n, b_n, \tau) * \mathscr{F}_v(a_n, b_{n+1}, \tau) * \mathscr{F}_v(a_{n+1}, b_m, \tau) \\
&\vdots \\
&\geq \mathscr{F}_v(a_n, b_n, \tau) * \mathscr{F}_v(a_{n+1}, b_{n+1}, \tau) * \cdots * \mathscr{F}_v(a_{m-1}, b_{m-1}, \tau) \\
&\quad * \mathscr{F}_v(a_{m-1}, b_m, \tau) * \mathscr{F}_v(a_m, b_m, \tau) \\
&\geq \theta^n \digamma^n(\mathscr{F}_v(a_0, b_0, \tau)) * \theta^n \digamma^n(\mathscr{F}_v(a_0, b_1, \tau)) * \theta^{n+1} \digamma^{n+1}(\mathscr{F}_v(a_0, b_0, \tau)) \\
&\quad * \theta^{n+1} \digamma^{n+1}(\mathscr{F}_v(a_0, b_1, \tau)) * \cdots * \theta^{m-1} \digamma^{m-1}(\mathscr{F}_v(a_0, b_1, \tau)) * \\
&\quad \theta^m (\digamma^m \mathscr{F}_v(a_0, b_0, \tau)) \\
&\geq \theta^m (\digamma^m(\mathscr{F}_v(a_0, b_0, \tau)) * \digamma^m(\mathscr{F}_v(a_0, b_1, \tau)) * \cdots * \digamma^m(\mathscr{F}_v(a_0, b_0, \tau))) \\
&\geq \digamma^m(\mathscr{F}_v(a_0, b_0, \tau)) * \digamma^m(\mathscr{F}_v(a_0, b_1, \tau)) * \cdots * \digamma^m(\mathscr{F}_v(a_0, b_0, \tau)).
\end{aligned}$$

Letting $n, m \to \infty$ and using the properties of $\digamma$, we obtain

$$\lim_{n,m \to \infty} \mathscr{F}_v(a_n, b_m, \tau) = 1 * 1 * \cdots * 1 = 1 \text{ for all } \tau > 0.$$

Thus, we conclude that $(\{a_n\}, \{b_n\})$ is a Cauchy bisequence in $(\mathscr{A}, \mathscr{B}, \mathscr{F}_v, \theta, *)$. Due to the completeness of FBBMS $(\mathscr{A}, \mathscr{B}, \mathscr{F}_v, \theta, *)$, $(\{a_n\}, \{b_n\})$ is a convergent bisequence; hence, through Lemma 1, it biconverges to a point $\mu \in \mathscr{A} \cap \mathscr{B}$ i.e., $\{a_n\} \to \mu$ and $\{b_n\} \to \mu$.

Finally, we show that μ is a fixed point of ϕ. Using properties of $\digamma$ and conditions (14) and (15), we obtain the following:

$$\begin{aligned}
\mathscr{F}_v(\phi(\mu), \mu, \tau) &\geq \mathscr{F}_v(\phi(\mu), \phi(b_n), \tau) * \mathscr{F}_v(\phi(a_n), \phi(b_n), \tau) * \mathscr{F}_v(\phi(a_n), \mu, \tau) \\
&\geq \eta(\mu, b_n, \tau) \mathscr{F}_v(\phi(\mu), \phi(b_n), \tau) * \eta(a_n, b_n, \tau) \mathscr{F}_v(\phi(a_n), \phi(b_n), \tau) \\
&* \mathscr{F}_v(a_{n+1}, \mu, \tau) \\
&\geq \theta \digamma(\mathscr{F}_v(\mu, b_n, \tau)) * \theta \digamma(\mathscr{F}_v(a_n, b_n, \tau)) * \mathscr{F}_v(a_{n+1}, \mu, \tau) \\
&\geq \digamma(\mathscr{F}_v(\mu, b_n, \tau)) * \digamma(\mathscr{F}_v(a_n, b_n, \tau)) * \mathscr{F}_v(a_{n+1}, \mu, \tau).
\end{aligned}$$

As $n \to \infty$, through right-continuity of $\digamma$, we obtain

$$\mathscr{F}_v(\phi(\mu), \mu, \tau) = 1 \text{ for } \tau > 0.$$

Consequently, $\phi(\mu) = \mu$. □

Theorem 7. *Under the conditions stipulated in Theorem 6, and with the additional assumption that*

(P) *there exists a point* $\rho \in \mathscr{A} \cap \mathscr{B}$ *such that* $\eta(a, \rho, \tau) \leq 1$ *and* $\eta(\rho, b, \tau) \leq 1$ *for all* $\tau > 0$, *where* $a \in \mathscr{A}$ *and* $b \in \mathscr{B}$,

then the covariant mapping ϕ, *being* $\digamma_\eta$*-contractive, possesses a unique fixed point.*

Proof. We demonstrate the distinctiveness of the fixed point within the mapping

$$\phi : (\mathscr{A}, \mathscr{B}, \mathscr{F}_v, \theta, *) \rightrightarrows (\mathscr{A}, \mathscr{B}, \mathscr{F}_v, \theta, *).$$

If we assume otherwise, considering λ as another fixed point of ϕ apart from μ, then according to condition (P), there exists a point $\rho \in \mathscr{A} \cap \mathscr{B}$

$$\eta(\mu, \rho, \tau) \leq 1 \text{ and } \eta(\rho, \lambda, \tau) \leq 1 \text{ for all } \tau > 0. \quad (16)$$

By employing condition (16) alongside the η-admissibility of ϕ, we obtain

$$\eta(\mu, \phi^n(\rho), \tau) \leq 1 \text{ and } \eta(\phi^n(\rho), \lambda, \tau) \leq 1 \text{ for all } n \in \mathbb{N} \text{ and } \tau > 0. \quad (17)$$

Also, using conditions (14) and (17), we obtain the following:

$$\begin{aligned} \mathscr{F}_v(\mu, \phi^n(\rho), \tau) &= \mathscr{F}_v(\phi(\mu), \phi(\phi^{n-1}(\rho)), \tau) \\ &\geq \eta(\mu, \phi^{n-1}(\rho), \tau)\mathscr{F}_v(\phi(\mu), \phi(\phi^{n-1}(\rho)), \tau) \\ &\geq \theta F\left(\mathscr{F}_v\left(\mu, \phi^{n-1}(\rho), \tau\right)\right). \end{aligned}$$

Repeating this process, we obtain

$$\mathscr{F}_v(\mu, \phi^n(\rho), \tau) \geq \theta^n F(\mathscr{F}_v(\mu, \rho, \tau)) \geq F(\mathscr{F}_v(\mu, \rho, \tau)) \text{ for all } n \in \mathbb{N} \text{ and } \tau > 0. \tag{18}$$

In the same way, we can also deduce

$$\mathscr{F}_v(\phi^n(\rho), \lambda, \tau) \geq \theta^n F(\mathscr{F}_v(\rho, \lambda, \tau)) \geq F(\mathscr{F}_v(\rho, \lambda, \tau)) \text{ for all } n \in \mathbb{N} \text{ and } \tau > 0. \tag{19}$$

Letting $n \to \infty$ in (18) and (19) provides

$$\phi^n(\rho) \to \mu \text{ and } \phi^n(\rho) \to \lambda,$$

which contradicts the uniqueness of the limit. Hence, $\mu = \lambda \in \mathscr{A} \cap \mathscr{B}$. Consequently, ϕ admits a unique fixed point in $(\mathscr{A}, \mathscr{B}, \mathscr{F}_v, \theta, *)$. □

5. Applications

5.1. Integral Equation

This subsection is devoted to illustrating how the existence and uniqueness of a solution for nonlinear integral equations are demonstrated by employing established findings concerning covariant mappings.

Consider the integral equation in the form:

$$\Phi(t) = \mathfrak{F}(t) + \omega \int_0^q \Theta(t,s)\Phi(s)\, ds, \tag{20}$$

where $\omega > 0$, $\mathfrak{F}(t)$ is a fuzzy function of $s \in [0,q]$, and $\Theta : [0,q] \times [0,q] \times \mathbb{R} \to \mathbb{R}$ is an integral kernel (see [20]). Our aim is to demonstrate the existence and uniqueness of the solution of Equation (20) by utilizing Theorem 5. We consider $C([0,q],\mathbb{R})$ as a collection of all real-valued continuous functions defined on the set $[0,q]$. The induced metric $\mathscr{D}$: $C([0,q],\mathbb{R}) \times C([0,q],\mathbb{R}) \to \mathbb{R}^+$ is defined as $\mathscr{D}(A,B) = \|A - B\|$, $A, B \in C([0,q],\mathbb{R})$.

Now, define a binary relation $*$ as a continuous τ-norm and $\mathscr{F}_v : C([0,q],\mathbb{R}) \times C([0,q],\mathbb{R}) \times (0,\infty) \to [0,1]$ as

$$\mathscr{F}_v(A,B,\tau) = \frac{\tau}{\tau + \mathscr{D}(A,B)}$$

for $A, B \in C([0,q],\mathbb{R})$ and $\tau > 0$. Then, $\mathscr{F}_v$ is b-triangular and the quadruple $(C([0,q],\mathbb{R}),$ $C([0,q],\mathbb{R}), \mathscr{F}_v, \theta, \tau)$ forms a complete fuzzy bipolar b-metric space.

Theorem 8. *Suppose that for all $A, B \in C([0,q],\mathbb{R})$, the following condition holds:*

$$\|\phi(A) - \phi(B)\| \leq \frac{\gamma^2}{\theta}\|A - B\|, \tag{21}$$

where $\phi : C([0,q],\mathbb{R}) \to C([0,q],\mathbb{R})$, $\gamma \in (0,1)$, and $\theta \geq 1$. Then, the integral Equation (20) has a unique solution in $C([0,q],\mathbb{R})$.

Proof. Define $\phi : C([0,q],\mathbb{R}) \to C([0,q],\mathbb{R})$ by

$$(\phi B)(t) = \mathfrak{F}(t) + \omega \int_0^q \Theta(t,s)B(s)\, ds. \tag{22}$$

Let ϕ be well defined. It is worth noting that ϕ possesses a unique fixed point in $C([0,q],\mathbb{R})$ if and only if the integral Equation (20) admits a unique solution. Let $\alpha(B,A,\tau)=1$ for all $A,B \in C([0,q],\mathbb{R})$ and $\tau > 0$, and $\psi(\nu)=\frac{\gamma}{\theta}\nu$ for all $\nu \in [0,\infty)$. It is straightforward to confirm that ψ is right-continuous and fulfills the properties outlined in Definition 12. By employing (21) and (22), for $A,B \in C([0,q],\mathbb{R})$, we can establish the following:

$$\begin{aligned}
\alpha(B,A,\tau)\left(\frac{1}{\mathscr{F}_v(\phi(B),\phi(A),\tau)}-1\right) &= \frac{\mathscr{D}(\phi(B),\phi(A))}{\tau} \\
&= \frac{\|\phi(B)-\phi(A)\|}{\tau} \\
&\leq \frac{\gamma^2}{\theta}\frac{\|B-A\|}{\tau} \\
&\leq \gamma\frac{\gamma}{\theta}\left(\frac{\|B-A\|}{\tau}\right) \\
&= \gamma\psi\left(\frac{1}{\mathscr{F}_v(B,A,\tau)}-1\right).
\end{aligned}$$

Hence, we obtain

$$\alpha(B,A,\tau)\left(\frac{1}{\mathscr{F}_v(\phi(B),\phi(A),\tau)}-1\right) \leq \psi\left(\frac{1}{\mathscr{F}_v(B,A,\tau)}-1\right)$$

for all $B,A \in C([0,q],\mathbb{R})$.

Therefore, the integral operator ϕ satisfies all the conditions specified in Theorem 5. Consequently, according to Theorem 5, there exists a unique fixed point in $C([0,q],\mathbb{R})$ for the operator ϕ. This implies the existence of a unique solution to Problem (20) in $C([0,q],\mathbb{R})$. □

Example 4. *Let* $E = C([0,1],\mathbb{R})$. *Consider the integral equation*

$$B(t) = e^{-3t} + \omega\int_0^1 e^{-(t+s)}B(s)\,ds, \tag{23}$$

where $|\omega| \leq \frac{\gamma}{3}$, $\gamma \in (0,1)$. *Then, for* $A,B \in E$, *we obtain the following:*

$$\begin{aligned}
\|(\phi(B))(y)-(\phi(A))(y)\| &= \left\| e^{-3y}+\omega\int_0^1 e^{-(y+s)}B(s)\,ds \right.\\
&\quad \left. -\left(e^{-3y}+\omega\int_0^1 e^{-(y+s)}A(s)\,ds\right)\right\| \\
&= |\omega|\left\|\int_0^1 e^{-(y+s)}B(s)\,ds-\int_0^1 e^{-(y+s)}A(s)\,ds\right\| \\
&= |\omega|\left\|\int_0^1 e^{-(y+s)}(B(s)-A(s))\,ds\right\| \\
&\leq |\omega|\int_0^1 e^{-(y+s)}\|B(s)-A(s)\|\,ds \\
&\leq \frac{2}{3}\|B(s)-A(s)\| \\
&\leq \gamma\|B(s)-A(s)\|.
\end{aligned}$$

All the conditions specified in Theorem 8 are satisfied. Hence, there exists a unique solution to the nonlinear integral problem (23) in the space $C([0,1],\mathbb{R})$.

Consider the integral equation as follows.

Theorem 9. *Let us consider the integral equation*

$$\Theta(\kappa) = \mathfrak{F}(\kappa) + \int_{\mathscr{E}_1 \cup \mathscr{E}_2} \mathscr{G}(\kappa, s, \Theta(s))\, ds, \quad \kappa \in \mathscr{E}_1 \cup \mathscr{E}_2, \tag{24}$$

where $\mathscr{E}_1 \cup \mathscr{E}_2$ *is a Lebesgue measurable set and* $\mathfrak{F}(\kappa)$ *is a fuzzy function of* $\kappa \in [0, p]$. *Suppose that*

(H1) $\mathscr{G} : (\mathscr{E}_1^2 \cup \mathscr{E}_2^2) \times [0, \infty) \to [0, \infty)$ *and* $\Theta \in L^\infty(\mathscr{E}_1) \cup L^\infty(\mathscr{E}_2)$;

(H2) There is a continuous function $\phi : \mathscr{E}_1^2 \cup \mathscr{E}_2^2 \to [0, \infty)$ *and* $\gamma \in (0, 1)$ *satisfying*

$$|\mathscr{G}(\kappa, s, a(s)) - \mathscr{G}(\kappa, s, b(s))| \le \sqrt{\frac{\gamma^2}{\theta}\Theta(\kappa, s)}|a(\kappa) - b(\kappa)|,$$

for $\kappa, s \in \mathscr{E}_1^2 \cup \mathscr{E}_2^2$, $\gamma \in (0, 1)$ *and* $\theta \ge 1$;

(H3) $\int_{\mathscr{E}_1 \cup \mathscr{E}_2} \Theta(\kappa, s)\, ds \le 1$.

Then, the integral Equation (24) has a unique solution in $\Theta \in L^\infty(\mathscr{E}_1) \cup L^\infty(\mathscr{E}_2)$.

Proof. Let $\mathscr{A} = L^\infty(\mathscr{E}_1)$ and $\mathscr{B} = L^\infty(\mathscr{E}_2)$ be two normed linear space, where $\mathscr{E}_1, \mathscr{E}_2$ are Lebesgue measurable sets and $m(\mathscr{E}_1 \cup \mathscr{E}_2) < \infty$.

Let $\mathscr{F}_v : \mathscr{A} \times \mathscr{B} \times (0, \infty) \to [0, 1]$ given by

$$\mathscr{F}_v(a, b, \tau) = \frac{\tau}{\tau + |a - b|^2}$$

for all $a \in \mathscr{A}, b \in \mathscr{B}$ and $\tau > 0$. Then, $(\mathscr{A}, \mathscr{B}, \mathscr{F}_v, \theta, *)$ is a complete FBBMS.

Let $\alpha(a, b, \tau) = 1$ for all $a \in \mathscr{A}, b \in \mathscr{B}$ and $\tau > 0$ and $\psi(m) = \frac{\gamma}{\theta} m$ for all $m \in [0, \infty)$. Then, it is easy to verify that ψ is right-continuous and satisfies the properties stated in Definition 12.

Define $\phi : L^\infty(\mathscr{E}_1) \cup L^\infty(\mathscr{E}_2) \rightrightarrows L^\infty(\mathscr{E}_1) \cup L^\infty(\mathscr{E}_2)$ provided by

$$\phi(\Theta(\kappa)) = \mathfrak{F}(\kappa) + \omega \int_{\mathscr{E}_1 \cup \mathscr{E}_2} \mathscr{G}(\kappa, s, \Theta(s))\, ds, \quad \kappa \in \mathscr{E}_1 \cup \mathscr{E}_2.$$

Now,

$$\begin{aligned}
\frac{1}{\mathscr{F}_v(\phi(a(\kappa)), \phi(b(\kappa)), \tau)} - 1 &= \frac{|\phi(a(\kappa)) - \phi(b(\kappa))|^2}{\tau} \\
&= \frac{\left|\mathfrak{F}(\kappa) + \int_{\mathscr{E}_1 \cup \mathscr{E}_2} \mathscr{G}(\kappa, s, a(s))\, ds - \left(\mathfrak{F}(\kappa) + \int_{\mathscr{E}_1 \cup \mathscr{E}_2} \mathscr{G}(\kappa, s, b(s))\, ds\right)\right|^2}{\tau} \\
&= \frac{\omega\left|\int_{\mathscr{E}_1 \cup \mathscr{E}_2} (\mathscr{G}(\kappa, s, a(s)) - \mathscr{G}(\kappa, s, b(s)))ds\right|^2}{\tau} \\
&\le \frac{\int_{\mathscr{E}_1 \cup \mathscr{E}_2} \gamma \Theta(\kappa, s)|a(\kappa) - b(\kappa)|^2\, ds}{\tau} \\
&\le \frac{\gamma^2 |a(\kappa) - b(\kappa)|^2}{\theta\tau} \\
&\le \gamma\psi\left(\frac{1}{\mathscr{F}_v(a(\kappa), b(\kappa), \tau)} - 1\right).
\end{aligned}$$

Hence, all hypotheses of Theorem 1 are verified, and consequently, the integral Equation (24) has a unique solution. □

5.2. Fractional Differential Equations

We recall many important definitions from fractional calculus theory [21,22]. For a function $\Theta \in C[0,1]$, the order $\nu > 0$ of the Riemann—Liouville fractional derivative is

$$\frac{1}{\Gamma(\vartheta - \nu)} \frac{d^{\vartheta}}{d\kappa^{\vartheta}} \int_0^{\kappa} \frac{\Theta(s)}{(\kappa - s)^{\nu - \vartheta + 1}} ds = \mathcal{D}^{\nu}\Theta(\kappa). \tag{25}$$

From (25), the right-hand side is pointwise defined as $[0,1]$, where $[\nu]$ and Γ are the integer part of the number ν and the Euler gamma function.

Consider the following fractional differential equation:

$$\begin{aligned} {}^{s}\mathcal{D}^{\varsigma}\Theta(\kappa) \quad + \quad \mathcal{G}(\kappa, \Theta(\kappa)) = 0, \quad 0 \le \kappa \le 1, \varsigma \in [1,2] \\ \Theta(0) = \Theta(1) = 0, \end{aligned}$$

where $\mathcal{G} : [0,1] \times \mathbb{R} \to \mathbb{R}$ is a continuous function and ${}^{s}\mathcal{D}^{\varsigma}$ represents the Caputo fractional derivative of order ς, which is defined by

$${}^{s}\mathcal{D}^{\varsigma} = \frac{1}{\Gamma(\vartheta - \varsigma)} \int_0^{\delta} \frac{\Theta^{\vartheta}(s)\, ds}{(\kappa - s)^{\varsigma - \vartheta + 1}}.$$

Let

$$\begin{aligned} \mathcal{A} &= (C[0,1], [0,\infty)) = \{f : [0,1] \to [0,\infty) : f \text{ is continuous function}\} \text{ and} \\ \mathcal{B} &= (C[0,1], (-\infty,0]) = \{f : [0,1] \to (-\infty,0] : f \text{ is continuous function}\}. \end{aligned}$$

Consider $\mathcal{F}_v : \mathcal{A} \times \mathcal{B} \times (0,\infty) \to \mathbb{R}^+$ given by

$$\mathcal{F}_v(a,b,\tau) = \frac{\tau}{\tau + \sup_{\kappa \in [0,1]} |a(\kappa) - b(\kappa)|^2}$$

for all $(a,b) \in \mathcal{A} \times \mathcal{B}$. Then, $(\mathcal{A}, \mathcal{B}, \mathcal{F}_v, \theta, *)$ is a complete FBBMS.

Theorem 10. *Consider the nonlinear fractional differential Equation (25). Suppose that the following hypotheses are held:*

(H1) We can determine $\gamma \in (0,1), \theta \ge 1$ *and* $(a,b) \in \mathcal{A} \times \mathcal{B}$ *such that*

$$|\mathcal{G}(\kappa, a) - \mathcal{G}(\kappa, b)| \le \sqrt{\frac{\gamma^2}{\theta}} |a(\kappa) - b(\kappa)|; \tag{26}$$

(H2) $\sup_{\kappa \in (0,1)} \int_0^1 |\mathcal{Q}(\kappa, s)|\, ds \le 1.$

Then, the FDE (25) has a unique solution in $\mathcal{A} \cup \mathcal{B}$.

Proof. The given FDE (25) is equivalent to the following integral equation

$$a(\kappa) = \int_0^1 \mathcal{Q}(\kappa, s) \mathcal{G}(a, b(s))\, ds, \tag{27}$$

where

$$\mathcal{Q}(\kappa, s) = \begin{cases} \frac{[\kappa(1-s)]^{\varsigma-1} - (\kappa - s)^{\varsigma - 1}}{\Gamma(\varsigma)}, & \text{if } 0 \le s \le \kappa \le 1; \\ \frac{[\kappa(1-s)]^{\varsigma-1}}{\Gamma(\varsigma)}, & \text{if } 0 \le \kappa \le s \le 1. \end{cases}$$

Define $\phi : \mathcal{A} \cup \mathcal{B} \to \mathcal{A} \cup \mathcal{B}$ by

$$\phi(a(\kappa)) = \int_0^1 \mathcal{Q}(\kappa, s) \mathcal{G}(\phi(a), b(s))\, ds,$$

and taking $\psi(m) = \frac{\gamma}{\theta}m$. Now,

$$\begin{aligned} |\phi(a(\kappa)) - \phi(b(\kappa))| &= \left| \int_0^1 \mathscr{Q}(\kappa,s)\mathscr{G}(\phi(a),a(s))\,ds - \int_0^1 \mathscr{Q}(\kappa,s)\mathscr{G}(\phi(b),b(s))\,ds \right| \\ &\leq \int_0^1 |\mathscr{Q}(\kappa,s)|^2\,ds \times \int_0^1 |\mathscr{G}(\phi(a),a(s)) - \mathscr{G}(\phi(b),b(s))|^2\,ds \\ &\leq \frac{\gamma^2}{\theta}|a(\kappa) - b(\kappa)|^2. \end{aligned}$$

Taking the supremum on both sides, we obtain the following:

$$\mathscr{F}_v(\phi(a),\phi(b),\tau) \leq \gamma\psi(\mathscr{F}_v(a,b,\tau)) \quad \text{for all } \tau > 0.$$

Therefore,

$$\begin{aligned} \frac{1}{\mathscr{F}_v(\phi(a),\phi(b),\tau)} - 1 &= \frac{\sup_{\kappa\in[0,1]}|\phi(a(\kappa)) - \phi(b(\kappa))|^2}{\tau} \\ &\leq \frac{\sup_{\kappa\in[0,1]}|a(\kappa) - b(\kappa)|^2}{\tau} \\ &= \gamma\psi\left(\frac{1}{\mathscr{F}_v(a(\kappa),b(\kappa),\tau)} - 1\right). \end{aligned}$$

As a result, all the hypotheses of Theorem 5 are fulfilled, and consequently, the fractional differential Equation (25) has a unique solution. □

6. Conclusions and Future Work

This study introduces new concepts in the field of fuzzy bipolar b-metric spaces. We investigate various types of mappings, including ψ_α-contractive and $\digamma_\eta$-contractive mappings, which are crucial for measuring distances between different entities. The paper also establishes fixed-point theorems for these mappings, demonstrating the existence of stationary points under certain conditions. We validate these theorems through examples, adding to the existing knowledge in this area. Additionally, we highlight the practical applications of these concepts, particularly in solving integral equations, thereby enhancing the reliability and usefulness of our research findings.

In future research, there is potential to expand upon the innovative concepts presented in this study within fuzzy bipolar b-metric spaces. This could involve a deeper exploration of ψ_α-contractive and $\digamma_\eta$-contractive mappings to gain further insights and applications. Key areas for investigation include broadening the conditions for generalized fixed-point theorems, discovering new types of contractive mappings, and enlarging the categories of fuzzy bipolar b-metric spaces. Furthermore, the development of efficient algorithms for practical fixed-point computation will improve the theoretical results in computational scenarios. These mappings can be applied to complex systems like multi-dimensional fractional differential equations and nonlinear integral equations. Moreover, exploring their utility in diverse fields such as optimization, machine learning, and network theory will enhance their applicability. Finally, empirical validation of these theoretical advancements in real-world problems will ensure their robustness and reliability. By pursuing these avenues, future research has the potential to significantly expand both the theoretical understanding and practical applications of fuzzy bipolar b-metric spaces.

Author Contributions: Conceptualization, S.A. and M.H.M.R.; Software, M.H.M.R.; Validation, W.M.M.S. and M.H.M.R.; Formal analysis, S.A., W.M.M.S., and M.H.M.R.; Investigation, W.M.M.S. and M.H.M.R.; Resources, M.H.M.R.; Data curation, M.H.M.R.; Writing—original draft, S.A. and M.H.M.R.; Writing—review & editing, S.A., W.M.M.S., and M.H.M.R.; Visualization, S.A., W.M.M.S., and M.H.M.R.; Supervision, M.H.M.R.; Project administration, W.M.M.S. and M.H.M.R.; Funding acquisition, W.M.M.S. All authors have read and agreed to the published version of the manuscript.

Funding: This research received no external funding.

Data Availability Statement: Data are contained within the article.

Conflicts of Interest: The authors declare no conflict of interest.

References

1. Banach, S. Sur les opérations dans les ensembles abstraits et leur application aux équations intégrales. *Fundam. Math.* **1922**, *3*, 133–181. [CrossRef]
2. Kramosil, I.; Michálek, J. Fuzzy metrics and statistical metric spaces. *Kybernetika* **1975**, *11*, 336–344.
3. Schweizer, B.; Sklar, A. Statistical metric spaces. *Pacific J. Math.* **1960**, *10*, 313–334. [CrossRef]
4. Zadeh, L.A. Fuzzy sets. *Inf. Control.* **1965**, *8*, 338–353. [CrossRef]
5. George, A.; Veeramani, P. On some results in fuzzy metric spaces. *Fuzzy Sets Syst.* **1994**, *64*, 395–399. [CrossRef]
6. Fang, J.X. On fixed point theorems in fuzzy metric spaces. *Fuzzy Sets Syst.* **1992**, *46*, 107–113. [CrossRef]
7. Gaba, Y.U.; Aphane, M.; Aydi, H. (α, BK)-Contractions in Bipolar Metric Spaces. *J. Math.* **2021**, *2021*, 1–6.
8. Gupta, V. Banach contraction theorem on fuzzy cone *b*-metric space. *J. Appl. Res. Technol.* **2020**, *18*, 154–160.
9. Kumar, M.; Kumar, P.; Ramaswamy, R.; Abdelnaby, O.A.A.; Elsonbaty, A.; Radenović, S. $(\alpha - \psi)$- Meir–Keeler Contractions in Bipolar Metric Spaces. *Mathematics* **2023**, *11*, 1310. [CrossRef]
10. Ramalingam, B.; Ege, O.; Aloqaily, A.; Mlaiki, N. Fixed-Point Theorems on Fuzzy Bipolar *b*-Metric Spaces. *Symmetry* **2023**, *15*, 1831. [CrossRef]
11. Shen, Y.; Qium, D.; Chen, W. Fixed point theorems in fuzzy metric spaces. *Appl. Math. Lett.* **2012**, *25*, 138–141. [CrossRef]
12. Mutlu, A.; Gürdal, U. Bipolar metric spaces and some fixed point theorems. *J. Nonlinear Sci. Appl.* **2016**, *9*, 5362–5373. [CrossRef]
13. Gaba, Y.U.; Aphane, M.; Sihag, V. On two Banach-type fixed points in bipolar metric spaces. *Abstr. Appl. Anal.* **2021**, *2021*, 1–10. [CrossRef]
14. Bartwal, A.; Dimri, R.C.; Prasad, G. Some fixed point theorems in fuzzy bipolar metric spaces. *J. Nonlinear Sci. Appl.* **2020**, *13*, 196–204. [CrossRef]
15. Rao, N.S.; Kalyani, K.; Mitiku, B. Fixed point theorems for nonlinear contractive mappings in ordered *b*-metric space with auxiliary function. *BMC Res. Notes* **2020**, *13*, 451. [CrossRef] [PubMed]
16. Schweizer, B.; Sklar, A. *Probabilistical Metric Spaces*; Dover Publications: New York, NY, USA, 2005.
17. Aydi, H.; Bota, M.F.; Karapınar, E.; Mitrovic, S. A fixed point theorem for set-valued quasi-contractions in b-metric spaces. *Fixed Point Theory Appl.* **2012**, *2012*, 88. . [CrossRef]
18. Singh, S.L.; Prasad, B. Some coincidence theorems and stability of iterative procedures. *Comput. Math. Appl.* **2008**, *55*, 2512–2520. [CrossRef]
19. Kumar, S.; Sharma, M. A Fixed Point Result In Bipolar Metric Spaces. *Neuroquantology* **2022**, *20*, 312.
20. Mani, G.; Gnanaprakasam, A.J.; Haq, A.U.; Jarad, F.; Baloch, I.A. Solving an integral equation by using fixed point approach in fuzzy bipolar metric spaces. *J. Funct. Spaces* **2021** , *2021*, 9129992. [CrossRef]
21. Kilbas, A.A.; Srivastava, H.M.; Trujillo, J.J. Theory and Applications of Fractional Differential Equations. In *North-Holland Mathematics Studies*; Elsevier: Amsterdam, The Netherlands, 2006; Volume 204.
22. Samko, S.G.; Kilbas, A.A.; Marichev, O.I. *Fractional Integrals and Derivatives: Theory and Applications*; Gordon and Breach Science Publishers: Basel, Switzerland, 1993.

symmetry

MDPI

Article

Fuzzy Reasoning Symmetric Quintuple-Implication Method for Mixed Information and Its Application

Ning Yao, Hao Chen, Ruirui Zhao and Minxia Luo *

Department of Information and Computing Science, China Jiliang University, Hangzhou 310018, China; ningyao@cjlu.edu.cn (N.Y.); s22080701001@cjlu.edu.cn (H.C.); ruiruizhao@cjlu.edu.cn (R.Z.)
* Correspondence: mxluo@cjlu.edu.cn; Tel.: +86-571-8687-5634

Abstract: Rule-based reasoning with different kinds of uncertain information has been identified in numerous applications within the real world. Any reasoning method must be able to coherently obtain the inference result by composing the given if–then rule with the assertion of the given input. The symmetric quintuple-implication principle was established by introducing symmetry into the five implication operators included. For example, the first, third and fifth implication operators exhibit symmetric properties, i.e., the three implication operators are taken as the same kind of operator and the second and fourth implication operators satisfy symmetry, that is, the two implication operators take the same kind of operator. So, the reasoning method induced by this principle possesses significant advantages in terms of its logical foundation and reductivity. This paper derives and studies reasoning methods for the mixture of fuzzy information and intuitionistic fuzzy information based on the symmetric quintuple-implication principle where all five implication operators satisfy symmetry (also called the quintuple-implication principle). Such reasoning methods are based on the ideas that the input and the given if–then rule can be combined for calculation only when their information representations exhibit consistency. An inconsistent given if–then rule with two different representations should be regarded as the composition of two different consistent given if–then rules with their own unique representations. This paper then elaborates on the methods by employing the possibility and necessity operators and the quintuple-implication principle from the perspective of whether the representation of rule antecedent and rule consequent is consistent or not. The reductivity of all the proposed reasoning methods is also analyzed in detail. This paper mainly contributes to the development of a novel mixed information reasoning framework, along with the introduction of the quintuple-implication principle into reasoning with mixed information. The proposed methods have also been applied to pattern recognition, and several experiments demonstrate that the mixed information reasoning methods based on the quintuple-implication principle are superior to the corresponding methods based on the triple I principle.

Keywords: fuzzy sets; intuitionistic fuzzy sets; mixed information; quintuple-implication principle; reductivity

Academic Editor: Marek T. Malinowski

Received: 14 January 2025
Revised: 24 February 2025
Accepted: 25 February 2025
Published: 28 February 2025

Citation: Yao, N.; Chen, H.; Zhao, R.; Luo, M. Fuzzy Reasoning Symmetric Quintuple-Implication Method for Mixed Information and Its Application. *Symmetry* **2025**, *17*, 369. https://doi.org/10.3390/sym17030369

1. Introduction

The main pattern of reasoning is to draw conclusions from given if–then rules and uncertain information. In actuality, the types of information are complex and diverse. For example, Zadeh [1] proposed the concept of a fuzzy set (FS) to describe the ambiguity and uncertainty of information. As a generalization of the fuzzy set concept, Atanassov [2] proposed the concept of an intuitionistic fuzzy set (IFS), which utilizes both the membership function and the non-membership function to elaborate on the uncertainty of information more precisely. When it comes to reasoning based on if–then rules and the input information, there could exist circumstances where the information representation in the input is inconsistent with the information representation in the rules. However, different information representations correspond to different reasoning mechanisms. Fuzzy set-based reasoning methods and intuitionistic fuzzy set-based reasoning methods will not be able to solve the inference problem with mixed information. It is hoped that in a hybrid information representation environment, the obtained conclusions will be still valid and interpretable. Therefore, the core of this paper is to study reasoning methods when the problem of interest is filled with mixed information, specifically information represented by a mixture of fuzzy sets and intuitionistic fuzzy sets. This inference problem can also be interpreted as an extended version of modus ponens (MP) with a mixture of fuzzy information and intuitionistic fuzzy information. Here, the rule antecedent and rule consequent can be expressed by fuzzy sets or by intuitionistic fuzzy sets or by the mixture of fuzzy sets and intuitionistic fuzzy sets; the input can be expressed by fuzzy sets or by intuitionistic fuzzy sets. This leads to the following inference problem: Given a nonempty universe of discourse X as the input space, a nonempty universe of discourse Y as the output space, and for all $x \in X$ and $y \in Y$,

The given rule:	If	x is $\mathbb{A}$,	then	y is $\mathbb{B}$
Input:		x is $\mathbb{A}^*$		
Output:				y is ?

where $\mathbb{A}$ and $\mathbb{A}^*$ may be fuzzy sets or intuitionistic fuzzy sets of universe X, and $\mathbb{B}$ may be a fuzzy set or an intuitionistic fuzzy set of universe Y.

1.1. The Inference Method Within the Fuzzy Environment

On the basis of fuzzy sets, Wang [3] gave the inference problem, called fuzzy modus ponens (FMP), that is, the inference problem related to the given rule "if x is A, then y is B" and the input "x is A^*", where A and A^* are fuzzy sets of the universe X, B is a fuzzy set of the universe Y and the output B^* is also a fuzzy set of Y. For solving the FMP, Zadeh [4] introduced a compositional rule of inference (CRI). Although it is widely employed in engineering and other fields, the CRI lacks a logical foundation and it fails to satisfy reductivity. Therefore, the results derived from the CRI are not always consistent with human intuition. To overcome this deficiency, Wang [3,5] proposed the triple I principle, which interprets the inference result B^* as the solution most supported by the given if–then rule, providing a rigorous logical basis for fuzzy reasoning. Pei [6] put forward a triple I method based on all residuated implications induced by left continuous t-norms. In the reasoning processes of the CRI and the triple I method, the degree to which A^* is similar to A is not taken into account. This may give rise to circumstances in which calculations are either meaningless or yield misleading outcomes. Hence, Zhou et al. [7] proposed the quintuple-implication principle for fuzzy reasoning. So far, the quintuple-implication principle has been studied by many scholars. Luo et al. [8] laid down a rigorous logical foundation for the quintuple-implication principle of fuzzy reasoning. Li et al. [9] analyzed the performance of a fuzzy system that satisfies the quintuple-implication principle and studied the robustness and general approximation ability of quintuple-implication reasoning methods under different implications, such as R-implication, S-implication and QL-implication.

1.2. The Inference Method Within the Intuitionistic Fuzzy Environment

An intuitionistic fuzzy modus ponens (IFMP) is a generalization of the FMP from fuzzy sets to intuitionistic fuzzy sets, namely, combining the given rule "if x is $\mathcal{A}$, then y is $\mathcal{B}$" with an input "x is $\mathcal{A}^*$" in order to obtain a new output "y is $\mathcal{B}^*$", where $\mathcal{A}$ and $\mathcal{A}^*$ are intuitionistic fuzzy sets of the universe X, and $\mathcal{B}$ and $\mathcal{B}^*$ are intuitionistic fuzzy sets of the universe Y. Cornelis et al. [10] proffered the residual intuitionistic-implication operator and undertook an in-depth exploration of the CRI for intuitionistic fuzzy reasoning. Zheng et al. [11] generalized the triple I method to intuitionistic fuzzy systems and investigated the reductivity of the triple I method for the IFMP. Li et al. [12] investigated the intuitionistic residual implications and the intuitionistic given if–then rule. Moreover, the approximation properties of the intuitionistic Mamdani, the intuitionistic Larsen and the intuitionistic triple I fuzzy systems are obtained. Duan et al. [13] explored four kinds of intuitionistic similarity and utilized them to analyze the robustness for the triple I method of intuitionistic fuzzy reasoning. Zeng et al. [14] discussed the quintuple-implication principle of intuitionistic fuzzy reasoning by using the intuitionistic t-norm generated by the left continuous t-norm.

1.3. Motivation

The research goal of this paper is to propose a new perspective on solving mixed information reasoning problems to make up for the shortcomings of the existing mixed information reasoning methods and to enrich the research on mixed information reasoning. Specifically, this paper attempts to build a novel framework for reasoning with a mixture of fuzzy information and intuitionistic fuzzy information and then develops the corresponding mixed information reasoning methods under this framework. Concerning reasoning with if–then rules under mixed information types of fuzzy sets and intuitionistic fuzzy sets, there are several reasons supporting this study.

The first comes from the construction of reasoning methods that are closely related to the given rule as well as the way information is represented. Obviously, the FMP and IFMP belong to the case in which the representations of rule antecedent $\mathbb{A}$ and rule consequent $\mathbb{B}$ in the given if–then rule are consistent, either by fuzzy sets or by intuitionistic fuzzy sets. Since the input $\mathbb{A}^*$ is expressed in the same way with the representations of $\mathbb{A}$ and $\mathbb{B}$, the induced inference methods are constructed in fuzzy systems with a unique representation according to the existing reasoning principles, such as the triple-implication principle and the quintuple-implication principle. However, the representation of $\mathbb{A}^*$ may be different from those of $\mathbb{A}$ and $\mathbb{B}$, or the representations of $\mathbb{A}$ and $\mathbb{B}$ may not be the same. In these cases, reasoning methods based on fuzzy sets or on intuitionistic fuzzy sets cannot directly reach reasonable and effective conclusions.

The second reason comes from the given if–then rules. It has been found that there are eight types of mixture scenarios that can arise, summarized in Table 1 with regard to the issue whether the representation of information in the given rules is consistent. Here, it is assumed that the information types of $\mathbb{A}$, $\mathbb{A}^*$ and $\mathbb{B}$ can be arbitrarily set to be fuzzy or intuitionistic fuzzy. Accordingly, the quality of the inference result depends largely on how to use the given if–then rules to design the inference method that will inevitably involve the conversion between different information types. In designing an inference procedure, it is natural to let the given rules speak for themselves. In other words, the information conversion of the given rule will be carried out only when the given rule itself has a mixed representation, in which case a given if–then rule with mixed information types will consist of two given if–then rules with different single information types.

Table 1. The mixed information inference problems.

Type	The Given Rule	Rule Antecedent	Rule Consequent	Input	Output
1	Consistent	FS	FS	FS	FS
2		IFS	IFS	IFS	IFS
3		FS	FS	IFS	?
4		IFS	IFS	FS	?
5	Inconsistent	FS	IFS	FS	?
6		IFS	FS	IFS	?
7		FS	IFS	IFS	?
8		IFS	FS	FS	?

Note: "?" indicates the unknown information type.

The third reason comes from the current research status on mixed information reasoning problems and the conversion between different information types. In terms of converting intuitionistic fuzzy sets to fuzzy sets, Atanassov suggested in [2] the possibility operator and the necessity operator to characterize this conversion. Ref. [15] has used this conversion operation from intuitionistic fuzzy sets to fuzzy sets, as well as a simple conversion operation from fuzzy sets to intuitionistic fuzzy sets by setting the non-membership degree as 1-membership degree, to explore the reasoning methods for a fuzzy and intuitionistic fuzzy information mixture on the basis of the triple-implication principle. But in some cases, the inference results given by this reasoning principle are often meaningless, without considering the connection between rule antecedent and input. The application examples described at the end of this paper also illustrate this point. Moreover, the work on mixed information reasoning is currently limited. It merits further investigation to tackle mixed information inference problems based on the quintuple-implication principle for the sake of overcoming the defects of existing methods.

On the basis of the aforementioned analysis, a new class of mixed information reasoning methods is proposed in this paper based on the quintuple-implication principle for the FMP in [7] and for the IFMP in [14]. The proposed methods are grounded in the conversion operators between fuzzy sets and intuitionistic fuzzy sets as presented in [2], starting from whether the given rules are consistent, so as to address the issues listed in Table 1. Moreover, in view of the limited available datasets on mixed information reasoning, this paper collected the datasets represented by fuzzy sets or intuitionistic fuzzy sets from the relevant literature in the field of fuzzy reasoning and constructed the corresponding datasets suitable for the mixed information inference problems studied. These constructed datasets were used to test the effectiveness of the reasoning methods built in this paper. Considering that the pattern recognition problem can be easily solved by transforming it into an inference problem, the datasets constructed in this paper belong to the application scope of pattern recognition, with each dataset containing both fuzzy set and intuitionistic fuzzy set representations. The proposed reasoning methods were compared with the methods in [15] on these constructed datasets.

To end this section, the contribution and structure of this paper are exhibited. The present paper is devoted to the study of solving the inference problems using information that is a hybrid between two different representation forms in a more reasonable way. The main contribution of this work is summarized as below:

1. A new perspective for addressing the mixed information reasoning problem is offered, as well as the corresponding inference framework designed based on whether the representation of the given if–then rules is consistent;
2. Using the quintuple-implication principle in fuzzy reasoning and the conversion operation between fuzzy sets and intuitionistic fuzzy sets, the details of the specific methods for all types of mixed information inference models are developed under the

established inference framework, accompanied by the discussion of the reductivity of all the methods;

3. Several pattern recognition tasks with a mixture of fuzzy information and intuitionistic fuzzy information are built to test the proposed reasoning methods, which indicates that these new methods overcome problems with the triple-implication principle and possess a significant advantage in addressing mixed information reasoning tasks.

The structure of this paper is as follows. Section 2 gives some necessary definitions and conclusions. In Section 3, the quintuple-implication reasoning methods to reason with mixed information are constructed from two directions of consistency and inconsistency for the expression of the given if–then rules. Section 4 discusses the reductivity of the proposed methods. In Section 5, four pattern recognition experiments are given to verify that the work presented in this paper is reasonable and effective. The last part is the conclusion.

2. Preliminaries

This section provides some important definitions and conclusions that will be utilized in the sequel.

Definition 1 ([1]). *A fuzzy set A on a universe of discourse X is characterized by a membership function $A : X \longrightarrow [0,1]$ with the form $A = \{\langle x, A(x)\rangle | x \in X\}$, where for each element x of X, a number $A(x)$ in the interval $[0,1]$ is interpreted as the degree of membership of x in A. If A satisfies the condition that $\exists x_0 \in X, A(x_0) = 1$, then A is called normal. The set of all fuzzy sets on universe X is denoted as $FS(X)$.*

Definition 2 ([2]). *An intuitionistic fuzzy set $\mathcal{A}$ on a universe of discourse X is defined by a membership function $\mathcal{A}_t : X \longrightarrow [0,1]$ and a non-membership function $\mathcal{A}_f : X \longrightarrow [0,1]$ under the condition that $\mathcal{A}_t(x) + \mathcal{A}_f(x) \in [0,1]$ for all $x \in X$. Here, write $\mathcal{A} = \{\langle x, \mathcal{A}_t(x), \mathcal{A}_f(x)\rangle | x \in X\}$ and $\mathcal{A}(x) = \langle \mathcal{A}_t(x), \mathcal{A}_f(x)\rangle$. If $\mathcal{A}$ satisfies the condition that $\exists x_0 \in X, \mathcal{A}(x_0) = \langle 1, 0\rangle$, then $\mathcal{A}$ is called normal. The set of all intuitionistic fuzzy sets on X is denoted as $IFS(X)$. The intuitionistic fuzzy set $\mathcal{A}$ degenerates into fuzzy sets if and only if $\mathcal{A}_t(x) + \mathcal{A}_f(x) = 1$ for all $x \in X$.*

Moreover, an intuitionistic fuzzy number α is denoted by $\alpha = \langle \alpha_t, \alpha_f\rangle$, where $\alpha_t, \alpha_f \in [0,1]$ and $\alpha_t + \alpha_f \leq 1$. The set of all intuitionistic fuzzy numbers is denoted as $\mathcal{I}^*$. A partial order $\preceq$ on $\mathcal{I}^*$ can be defined as $\alpha_1 \preceq \alpha_2$ if and only if $\alpha_{1t} \leq \alpha_{2t}$ and $\alpha_{1f} \geq \alpha_{2f}$ for all $\alpha_1, \alpha_2 \in \mathcal{I}^*$. Intuitionistic fuzzy sets $\mathcal{A}_1 = \mathcal{A}_2$ if and only if $\mathcal{A}_{1t}(x) = \mathcal{A}_{2t}(x)$ and $\mathcal{A}_{1f}(x) = \mathcal{A}_{2f}(x)$ for all $\mathcal{A}_1, \mathcal{A}_2 \subseteq IFS(X)$.

Definition 3 ([2]). *Let $\mathcal{A} = \{\langle x, \mathcal{A}_t(x), \mathcal{A}_f(x)\rangle | x \in X\}$ be an intuitionistic fuzzy set. Then, the necessity operator is a mapping $\natural$: $IFS(X) \longrightarrow FS(X)$ such that $\natural\mathcal{A} = \{\langle x, \mathcal{A}_t(x)\rangle | x \in X\}$; the possibility operator is a mapping $\sharp$: $IFS(X) \longrightarrow FS(X)$ such that $\sharp\mathcal{A} = \{\langle x, \mathcal{A}_{-f}(x)\rangle | x \in X\}$, where $\mathcal{A}_{-f}(x) = 1 - \mathcal{A}_f(x)$.*

Proposition 1 ([2]). *Let $\P$: $FS(X) \longrightarrow IFS(X)$ be a mapping and $A = \{\langle x, A(x)\rangle | x \in X\}$ be a fuzzy set. Then, the set $\P A = \{\langle x, A(x), 1 - A(x)\rangle | x \in X\}$ is an intuitionistic fuzzy set.*

Definition 4 ([16]). *A t-norm is a binary function $\otimes : [0,1] \times [0,1] \longrightarrow [0,1]$, which is commutative, associative, increasing in each variable and contains neutral element 1 such that $x \otimes 1 = x$ for all $x \in [0,1]$. A t-conorm is a binary function $\oplus : [0,1] \times [0,1] \longrightarrow [0,1]$, which is commutative, associative, increasing in each variable and contains neutral element 0 such that $x \oplus 0 = x$ for all $x \in [0,1]$. The t-conorm $\oplus$ given by $a \oplus b = 1 - (1 - a) \otimes (1 - b)$ is said to be the dual t-conorm of $\otimes$, with the pair $(\otimes, \oplus)$ as a dual pair. Analogously, the t-norm $\otimes$ defined by $a \otimes b = 1 - (1 - a) \oplus (1 - b)$ is called the dual t-norm of $\oplus$, with the pair $(\otimes, \oplus)$ as a dual pair.*

Definition 5 ([16]). *A binary function* $\rightarrow: [0,1] \times [0,1] \longrightarrow [0,1]$ *is called a residual implication (R-implication) if there exists a left-continuous t-norm* $\otimes$ *such that* $a \rightarrow b = \bigvee\{x \in [0,1] | x \otimes a \leq b\}$ *for all* $a, b \in [0,1]$. *Further,* $\otimes$ *and* $\rightarrow$ *form an adjoint pair* $(\otimes, \rightarrow)$ *and satisfy the residuation property, i.e.,* $c \otimes a \leq b$ *if and only if* $c \leq a \rightarrow b$ *for all* $a, b, c \in [0,1]$.

Example 1 ([16]). *The Łukasiewicz t-norm* $\otimes_{Łu}$ *and the corresponding Łukasiewicz implication* $\rightarrow_{Łu}$ *are expressed as follows:* $a \otimes_{Łu} b = (a + b - 1) \vee 0$, $a \rightarrow_{Łu} b = (1 - a + b) \wedge 1$ *for all* $a, b \in [0,1]$.

Definition 6 ([11]). *A binary function* $\otimes_{\mathcal{I}^*} : \mathcal{I}^* \times \mathcal{I}^* \longrightarrow \mathcal{I}^*$ *is called an intuitionistic t-norm induced from t-norm* $\otimes$, *if it satisfies* $\alpha \otimes_{\mathcal{I}^*} \beta = \langle \alpha_t \otimes \beta_t, \alpha_f \oplus \beta_f \rangle$ *for all* $\alpha = \langle \alpha_t, \alpha_f \rangle$, $\beta = \langle \beta_t, \beta_f \rangle \in \mathcal{I}^*$.

A binary function $\oplus_{\mathcal{I}^*} : \mathcal{I}^* \times \mathcal{I}^* \longrightarrow \mathcal{I}^*$ *is called an intuitionistic t-conorm induced from t-conorm* $\oplus$, *if it satisfies* $\alpha \oplus_{\mathcal{I}^*} \beta = \langle \alpha_t \oplus \beta_t, \alpha_f \otimes \beta_f \rangle$ *for all* $\alpha = \langle \alpha_t, \alpha_f \rangle, \beta = \langle \beta_t, \beta_f \rangle \in \mathcal{I}^*$, *where* $\oplus$ *is the dual t-conorm of the t-norm* $\otimes$.

Definition 7 ([11]). *A binary operator* $\rightarrow_{\mathcal{I}^*}: \mathcal{I}^* \times \mathcal{I}^* \longrightarrow \mathcal{I}^*$ *is called an intuitionistic residual implication (intuitionistic R-implication) if there exists a left-continuous intuitionistic t-norm* $\otimes_{\mathcal{I}^*}$ *such that* $\alpha \rightarrow_{\mathcal{I}^*} \beta = \bigvee\{\theta \in \mathcal{I}^* | \theta \otimes_{\mathcal{I}^*} \alpha \preceq \beta\}$, $\forall \alpha, \beta \in \mathcal{I}^*$. *Further,* $\otimes_{\mathcal{I}^*}$ *and* $\rightarrow_{\mathcal{I}^*}$ *form an adjoint pair* $(\otimes_{\mathcal{I}^*}, \rightarrow_{\mathcal{I}^*})$ *and satisfy the residuation property, i.e.,* $\forall \alpha, \beta, \gamma \in \mathcal{I}^*$, $\gamma \otimes_{\mathcal{I}^*} \alpha \preceq \beta$ *if and only if* $\gamma \preceq \alpha \rightarrow_{\mathcal{I}^*} \beta$.

Example 2 ([11]). *The intuitionistic Łukasiewicz t-norm* $\otimes_{\mathcal{I}^*_{Łu}}$ *and the corresponding intuitionistic R-implication* $\rightarrow_{\mathcal{I}^*_{Łu}}$ *are expressed as follows:* $\alpha \otimes_{\mathcal{I}^*_{Łu}} \beta = \langle (\alpha_t + \beta_t - 1) \vee 0, (\alpha_f + \beta_f) \wedge 1 \rangle$, $\alpha \rightarrow_{\mathcal{I}^*_{Łu}} \beta = \langle (1 - \alpha_t + \beta_t) \wedge (1 - \alpha_f + \beta_f) \wedge 1, (\beta_f - \alpha_f) \vee 0 \rangle$ *for all* $\alpha, \beta \in \mathcal{I}^*$.

Quintuple-Implication Principle for FMP ([7]). *Let* $\rightarrow$ *be an R-implication derived from a left-continuous t-norm* $\otimes$ *and then* B^* *is the smallest fuzzy subset on* Y *such that there is the following:*

$$(A(x) \rightarrow B(y)) \rightarrow ((A^*(x) \rightarrow A(x)) \rightarrow (A^*(x) \rightarrow B^*(y))) = 1 \text{ for all } x \in X, y \in Y,$$

where A, A^* *are fuzzy sets on* X, *and* B *is fuzzy sets on* Y.

Theorem 1 ([7]). *Let* $\rightarrow$ *be an R-implication derived from a left-continuous t-norm* $\otimes$ *and then the quintuple-implication solution* $B^* = \{\langle y, B^*(y) \rangle | y \in Y\}$ *for the FMP problem is presented as follows:*

$$B^*(y) = \bigvee_{x \in X} \{A^*(x) \otimes ((A^*(x) \rightarrow A(x)) \otimes (A(x) \rightarrow B(y)))\}, y \in Y. \quad (1)$$

Quintuple-Implication Principle for IFMP ([14]). *Let* $\rightarrow_{\mathcal{I}^*}$ *be an intuitionistic R-implication derived from a left-continuous intuitionistic t-norm* $\otimes_{\mathcal{I}^*}$ *and then* $\mathcal{B}^*$ *is the smallest intuitionistic fuzzy subset on* Y *such that there is the following:*

$$(\mathcal{A}(x) \rightarrow_{\mathcal{I}^*} \mathcal{B}(y)) \rightarrow_{\mathcal{I}^*} ((\mathcal{A}^*(x) \rightarrow_{\mathcal{I}^*} \mathcal{A}(x)) \rightarrow_{\mathcal{I}^*} (\mathcal{A}^*(x) \rightarrow_{\mathcal{I}^*} \mathcal{B}^*(y))) = \langle 1, 0 \rangle \text{ for all } x \in X, y \in Y,$$

where $\mathcal{A}, \mathcal{A}^*$ *are intuitionistic fuzzy sets on* X, *and* $\mathcal{B}$ *is intuitionistic fuzzy sets on* Y.

Theorem 2 ([14]). *Let* $\rightarrow_{\mathcal{I}^*}$ *be an intuitionistic R-implication derived from a left-continuous intuitionistic t-norm* $\otimes_{\mathcal{I}^*}$ *and then the quintuple-implication solution* $\mathcal{B}^* = \{\langle y, \mathcal{B}^*_t(y), \mathcal{B}^*_f(y) \rangle | y \in Y\}$ *for the IFMP problem is presented as follows:*

$$\mathcal{B}^*(y) = \bigvee_{x \in X} \{\mathcal{A}^*(x) \otimes_{\mathcal{I}^*} ((\mathcal{A}^*(x) \rightarrow_{\mathcal{I}^*} \mathcal{A}(x)) \otimes_{\mathcal{I}^*} (\mathcal{A}(x) \rightarrow_{\mathcal{I}^*} \mathcal{B}(y)))\}, y \in Y, \quad (2)$$

and

$$\begin{aligned} \mathcal{B}_t^*(y) = \bigvee_{x \in X} \{&\mathcal{A}_t^*(x) \otimes (((\mathcal{A}_t^*(x) \rightarrow \mathcal{A}_t(x)) \wedge (\mathcal{A}_{-f}^*(x) \rightarrow \mathcal{A}_{-f}(x))) \\ &\otimes ((\mathcal{A}_t(x) \rightarrow \mathcal{B}_t(y)) \wedge (\mathcal{A}_{-f}(x) \rightarrow \mathcal{B}_{-f}(y))))\}, y \in Y, \\ \mathcal{B}_f^*(y) = \bigwedge_{x \in X} \{&\mathcal{A}_f^*(x) \oplus ((1 - \mathcal{A}_{-f}^*(x) \rightarrow \mathcal{A}_{-f}(x)) \oplus (1 - \mathcal{A}_{-f}(x) \rightarrow \mathcal{B}_{-f}(y)))\}, y \in Y, \end{aligned}$$

where $\mathcal{A}_{-f} = 1 - \mathcal{A}_f$, $\mathcal{A}_{-f}^* = 1 - \mathcal{A}_f^*$ *and* $\mathcal{B}_{-f} = 1 - \mathcal{B}_f$, *and* $\oplus$ *is the dual t-conorm of t-norm* $\otimes$.

3. The Quintuple-Implication Fuzzy Reasoning Method with Mixed Information

For reasoning with given if–then rules of mixed information, since there may exist the mismatch between the representation of the input and that of the given rules of the knowledge base in real life, the ability of a quintuple-implication reasoning method based on single information is limited. From Table 1, it is easy to find that the information types in both rule antecedent and rule consequent are consistent in Types 1–4, whereas they exhibit inconsistency in Types 5–8. Considering this analysis, in this section, we will delve into the quintuple-implication principle for reasoning with mixed information from these two distinct perspectives of the given if–then rules.

The reasoning framework to solve inference problems Type 1–Type 8

As for the inference models with consistent given if–then rules (Types 1–4), the input information first needs to be consistent with the information representation in the given rules. For example, as for Type 3, the input $\mathcal{A}^*$ has the priority to be converted into the same information type A^* as the given rule "if x is A, then y is B"; as for Type 4, the input A^* has the priority to be converted into an intuitionistic fuzzy set $\mathcal{A}^*$, same as the representation of the given rule "if x is $\mathcal{A}$, then y is $\mathcal{B}$". Then, the subsequent inference steps can be performed to obtain the output with the same representation as the rule, together with the inference result consistent with the representation of the input by employing the reciprocal conversion formula between fuzzy sets and intuitionistic fuzzy sets. Figure 1 shows the processing framework of the first four types of inference models.

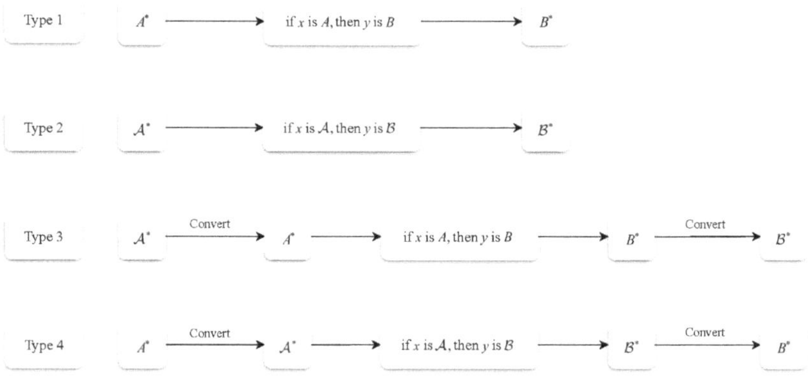

Figure 1. Mixed information reasoning with consistent rules.

Regarding the inference model Types 5–8 with an inconsistency in the representation of rule antecedent and rule consequent, a given rule containing mixed information needs to be initially converted into a set of two distinct given rules, each having different single information representation through the corresponding conversion operations. For example, as for Types 5 and 7, the inconsistent given rule "if x is A, then y is $\mathcal{B}$" is considered to consist of two consistent given rules "if x is A, then y is B" with B converted from $\mathcal{B}$ and "if x is $\mathcal{A}$, then y is $\mathcal{B}$" with $\mathcal{A}$ converted from A; as for Types 6 and 8, the inconsistent given rule "if x is $\mathcal{A}$, then y is B" is viewed as being composed of two consistent given rules "if x is A, then y is B" with A converted from $\mathcal{A}$ and "if x is $\mathcal{A}$, then y is $\mathcal{B}$" with $\mathcal{B}$ converted from B. Next, the input is combined with each of these two given rules, respectively, to carry out the subsequent inference process. At this stage, the two directions will yield their own outputs and the processing in both directions will be found to be partially similar to the reasoning scheme based on consistent given if–then rules. Ultimately, these outputs are aggregated to produce a final inference result that can be expressed in a form consistent with the rule consequent or in alignment with the input. The processing scheme for reasoning under inconsistent given if–then rules is exhibited in Figure 2.

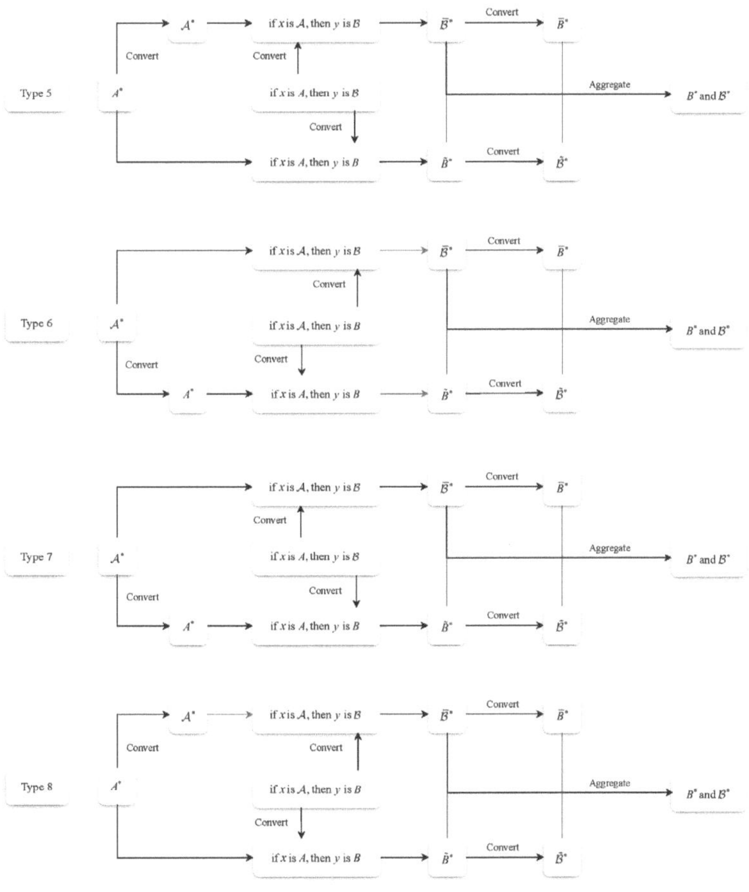

Figure 2. Mixed information reasoning with inconsistent rules.

3.1. The Quintuple-Implication Fuzzy Reasoning Method with Mixed Information of Consistent Rules

To address the problems in reasoning under consistent rules, we first discuss the mixed information inference problem of Type 4, described as follows:

The given rule:	If x is $\mathcal{A}$,	then	y is $\mathcal{B}$
Input:	x is A^*		
Output:			y is ?

where $\mathcal{A}$ is an intuitionistic fuzzy set on the universe X, $\mathcal{B}$ is an intuitionistic fuzzy set on the universe Y and A^* is a fuzzy set on the universe X. We aim to derive an output based on the referential rule "if x is $\mathcal{A}$, then y is $\mathcal{B}$" and the given input "x is A^*" by utilizing the quintuple-implication principle.

The method to reasoning with Type 4 mixed information

Step 1: Convert the fuzzy set A^* into the intuitionistic fuzzy set $\mathcal{A}^* = \{\langle x, A^*(x), 1 - A^*(x)\rangle | x \in X\}$ via Proposition 1 in [2], which hence leads to the following problem:

The given rule:	If x is $\mathcal{A}$,	then	y is $\mathcal{B}$
Input:	x is $\mathcal{A}^*$		
Output:			y is $\bar{\mathcal{B}}^*$

where $\mathcal{A}$ and $\mathcal{A}^*$ are intuitionistic fuzzy sets defined on the universe X, and $\mathcal{B}$ and $\bar{\mathcal{B}}^*$ are intuitionistic fuzzy sets on the universe Y.

Step 2: Solve the inference problem in Step 1 and obtain the solution $\bar{\mathcal{B}}^* = \{\langle y, \bar{\mathcal{B}}_t^*(y), \bar{\mathcal{B}}_f^*(y)\rangle | y \in Y\}$ by applying Theorem 2 in [14] (i.e., quintuple-implication method for Type 2):

$$\bar{\mathcal{B}}^*(y) = \bigvee_{x\in X} \{\mathcal{A}^*(x) \otimes_{\mathcal{I}^*} ((\mathcal{A}^*(x) \rightarrow_{\mathcal{I}^*} \mathcal{A}(x)) \otimes_{\mathcal{I}^*} (\mathcal{A}(x) \rightarrow_{\mathcal{I}^*} \mathcal{B}(y)))\}, y \in Y, \tag{3}$$

$$\begin{aligned}\bar{\mathcal{B}}_t^*(y) &= \bigvee_{x\in X} \{A^*(x) \otimes (((A^*(x) \rightarrow \mathcal{A}_t(x)) \wedge (A^*(x) \rightarrow \mathcal{A}_{-f}(x)) \\ &\quad \otimes ((\mathcal{A}_t(x) \rightarrow \mathcal{B}_t(y)) \wedge (\mathcal{A}_{-f}(x) \rightarrow \mathcal{B}_{-f}(y))))\} \\ &= \bigvee_{x\in X} \{A^*(x) \otimes ((A^*(x) \rightarrow \mathcal{A}_t(x)) \otimes ((\mathcal{A}_t(x) \rightarrow \mathcal{B}_t(y)) \\ &\quad \wedge (\mathcal{A}_{-f}(x) \rightarrow \mathcal{B}_{-f}(y))))\}, y \in Y, \end{aligned} \tag{4}$$

$$\begin{aligned}\bar{\mathcal{B}}_f^*(y) &= \bigwedge_{x\in X} \{(1 - A^*(x)) \oplus ((1 - A^*(x) \rightarrow \mathcal{A}_{-f}(x)) \oplus (1 - \mathcal{A}_{-f}(x) \rightarrow \mathcal{B}_{-f}(y)))\} \\ &= 1 - \bigvee_{x\in X} \{A^*(x) \otimes ((A^*(x) \rightarrow \mathcal{A}_{-f}(x)) \otimes (\mathcal{A}_{-f}(x) \rightarrow \mathcal{B}_{-f}(y)))\}, y \in Y, \end{aligned} \tag{5}$$

where $\rightarrow_{\mathcal{I}^*}$ is an intuitionistic R-implication derived from a left-continuous intuitionistic t-norm $\otimes_{\mathcal{I}^*}$, $\rightarrow$ is an R-implication derived from a left-continuous t-norm $\otimes$ and $\oplus$ is the dual of $\otimes$.

Step 3: The solution of the Type 4 inference problem is given, as presented in Table 2.

According to the rule "if x is $\mathcal{A}$, then y is $\mathcal{B}$", the output can be obtained in the form of intuitionistic fuzzy sets, denoted as $\mathcal{B}^* = \{\langle y, \mathcal{B}_t^*(y), \mathcal{B}_f^*(y)\rangle | \mathcal{B}_t^*(y) = \bar{\mathcal{B}}_t^*(y), \mathcal{B}_f^*(y) = \bar{\mathcal{B}}_f^*(y), y \in Y\}$. Furthermore, to ensure consistency with the information type of the input "x is A^*", we also present via Definition 3 in [2] the solution in the form of fuzzy sets, i.e., $B^* = \{\langle y, B^*(y)\rangle | B^*(y) \in [\bar{\mathcal{B}}_t^*(y), 1 - \bar{\mathcal{B}}_f^*(y)], y \in Y\}$.

Table 2. The solutions for the mixed information inference problem of Type 4.

The Given Rule	Input	Output	
If x is $\mathcal{A}$, then y is $\mathcal{B}$	x is A^*	FS	$B^* = \{\langle y, B^*(y)\rangle \mid B^*(y) \in [\bar{\mathcal{B}}_t^*(y), 1 - \bar{\mathcal{B}}_f^*(y)], y \in Y\}$
		IFS	$\mathcal{B}^* = \{\langle y, \mathcal{B}_t^*(y), \mathcal{B}_f^*(y)\rangle \mid \mathcal{B}_t^*(y) = \bar{\mathcal{B}}_t^*(y), \mathcal{B}_f^*(y) = \bar{\mathcal{B}}_f^*(y), y \in Y\}$

Note: $\bar{\mathcal{B}}_t^*(y) = \bigvee_{x\in X}\{A^*(x) \otimes ((A^*(x) \to \mathcal{A}_t(x)) \otimes ((\mathcal{A}_t(x) \to \mathcal{B}_t(y)) \wedge (\mathcal{A}_{-f}(x) \to \mathcal{B}_{-f}(y))))\}, y \in Y$, $\bar{\mathcal{B}}_f^*(y) = 1 - \bigvee_{x\in X}\{A^*(x) \otimes ((A^*(x) \to \mathcal{A}_{-f}(x)) \otimes (\mathcal{A}_{-f}(x) \to \mathcal{B}_{-f}(y)))\}, y \in Y$.

Analogously, the inference problem of Type 3 can also be addressed:

The given rule:	If x is A,	then y is B
Input:	x is $\mathcal{A}^*$	
Output:		y is ?

where A and B represent two fuzzy sets on X and Y, respectively, and $\mathcal{A}^*$ is an intuitionistic fuzzy set on X.

The method to reasoning with Type 3 mixed information

Step 1: Convert the intuitionistic fuzzy sets $\mathcal{A}^*$ into fuzzy set $A^* = \{\langle x, A^*(x)\rangle \mid x \in X\}$ by using the possibility and necessity operators stated in Definition 3 in [2], where $A^*(x) \in [\mathcal{A}_t^*(x), \mathcal{A}^*_{-f}(x)]$. Since the fuzzy set A^* converted from the input $\mathcal{A}^*$ is determined by two fuzzy sets $\mathcal{A}_t^* = \natural\mathcal{A}^*$ and $\mathcal{A}^*_{-f} = \sharp\mathcal{A}^*$, to solve the Type 3 inference problem, the following two FMP problems need to be addressed in advance:

The given rule:	If x is A,	then y is B
Input:	x is $\mathcal{A}_t^*$	
Output:		y is $\tilde{B}_1^*$

The given rule:	If x is A,	then y is B
Input:	x is $\mathcal{A}^*_{-f}$	
Output:		y is $\tilde{B}_2^*$

where $\mathcal{A}_t^*, \mathcal{A}^*_{-f}$ are fuzzy sets transformed from intuitionistic fuzzy set $\mathcal{A}^*$ on X, and A and B represent two fuzzy sets on X and Y, respectively.

Step 2: Obtain the solutions to the above two inference problems. According to Theorem 1 in [7] (i.e., quintuple-implication method for Type 1),

$$\tilde{B}_1^*(y) = \bigvee_{x\in X}\{\mathcal{A}_t^*(x) \otimes ((\mathcal{A}_t^*(x) \to A(x)) \otimes (A(x) \to B(y)))\}, y \in Y, \tag{6}$$

$$\tilde{B}_2^*(y) = \bigvee_{x\in X}\{\mathcal{A}^*_{-f}(x) \otimes ((\mathcal{A}^*_{-f}(x) \to A(x)) \otimes (A(x) \to B(y)))\}, y \in Y. \tag{7}$$

where $\to$ is an R-implication derived from a left-continuous t-norm $\otimes$.

Step 3: The solution of the Type 3 inference problem is derived, as presented in Table 3.

The fuzzy output $B^* = \{\langle y, B^*(y)\rangle \mid y \in Y\}$ will be acquired via Equations (6) and (7) with the same information representation as the rule "if x is A, then y is B", where $B^*(y) \in [\tilde{B}_1^*(y) \wedge \tilde{B}_2^*(y), \tilde{B}_1^*(y) \vee \tilde{B}_2^*(y)]$. By combining Equations (6) and (7) with Definition 3 in [2], the intuitionistic fuzzy output $\mathcal{B}^* = \{\langle y, \mathcal{B}_t^*(y), \mathcal{B}_f^*(y)\rangle \mid y \in Y\}$ of the same type as the input "x is $\mathcal{A}$" can likewise be provided, where $\mathcal{B}_t^*(y) = \tilde{B}_1^*(y) \wedge \tilde{B}_2^*(y)$, $\mathcal{B}_f^*(y) = 1 - \tilde{B}_1^*(y) \vee \tilde{B}_2^*(y)$.

Table 3. The solutions for the mixed information inference problem of Type 3.

The Given Rule	Input	Output	
If x is A, then y is B	x is $\mathcal{A}^*$	FS	$B^* = \{\langle y, B^*(y)\rangle \mid B^*(y) \in [\tilde{B}_1^*(y) \wedge \tilde{B}_2^*(y), \tilde{B}_1^*(y) \vee \tilde{B}_2^*(y)], y \in Y\}$
		IFS	$\mathcal{B}^* = \{\langle y, \mathcal{B}_t^*(y), \mathcal{B}_f^*(y)\rangle \mid \mathcal{B}_t^*(y) = \tilde{B}_1^*(y) \wedge \tilde{B}_2^*(y), \mathcal{B}_f^*(y) = 1 - \tilde{B}_1^*(y) \vee \tilde{B}_2^*(y), y \in Y\}$

Note: $\tilde{B}_1^*(y) = \bigvee_{x\in X} \{\mathcal{A}_t^*(x) \otimes ((\mathcal{A}_t^*(x) \to A(x)) \otimes (A(x) \to B(y)))\}, y \in Y$, $\tilde{B}_2^*(y) = \bigvee_{x\in X} \{\mathcal{A}_{-f}^*(x) \otimes ((\mathcal{A}_{-f}^*(x) \to A(x)) \otimes (A(x) \to B(y)))\}, y \in Y$.

According to Equations (4)–(7), the following proposition is presented when the t-norm is Łukasiewicz t-norm $\otimes_{Łu}$.

Proposition 2. *(1) For the Type 4 inference problem,*

$$\begin{aligned}
\mathcal{B}_t^*(y) = \bigvee_{x\in X} \{(\mathcal{A}^*(x) + ((1 - \mathcal{A}^*(x) + \mathcal{A}_t(x)) \wedge 1 + (1 - \mathcal{A}_t(x) + \mathcal{B}_t(x)) \\
\wedge (1 - \mathcal{A}_{-f}(x) + \mathcal{B}_{-f}(x)) \wedge 1 - 1) \vee 0) - 1) \vee 0\}, y \in Y, \quad (8)
\end{aligned}$$

$$\begin{aligned}
\mathcal{B}_f^*(y) = 1 - \bigvee_{x\in X} \{(\mathcal{A}^*(x) + ((1 - \mathcal{A}^*(x) + \mathcal{A}_{-f}(x)) \wedge 1 + (1 - \mathcal{A}_{-f}(x) \\
+ \mathcal{B}_{-f}(y)) \wedge 1 - 1) \vee 0 - 1) \vee 0\}, y \in Y. \quad (9)
\end{aligned}$$

(2) For the Type 3 inference problem,

$$\begin{aligned}
\tilde{B}_1^*(y) = \bigvee_{x\in X} \{(\mathcal{A}_t^*(x) + ((1 - \mathcal{A}_t^*(x) + A(x)) \wedge 1 + (1 - A(x) + B(y)) \wedge 1 - 1) \\
\vee 0 - 1) \vee 0\}, y \in Y, \quad (10)
\end{aligned}$$

$$\begin{aligned}
\tilde{B}_2^*(y) = \bigvee_{x\in X} \{(\mathcal{A}_{-f}^*(x) + ((1 - \mathcal{A}_{-f}^*(x) + A(x)) \wedge 1 + (1 - A(x) + B(y)) \wedge 1 - 1) \\
\vee 0 - 1) \vee 0\}, y \in Y. \quad (11)
\end{aligned}$$

3.2. The Quintuple-Implication Fuzzy Reasoning Method with Mixed Information of Inconsistent Rules

To reason with inconsistent if–then rules (Types 5–8 mixed information inference problems), it is essential to first gain a precise and comprehensive understanding of the inconsistent rules, conceptualizing one inconsistent rule as comprising two distinct consistent rules, each containing unique information representation.

By this analysis, for each of the Types 5–8 inference problems, the input will be combined with the two consistent rules to conduct the inference process in their respective directions. Further, the conclusions in these two directions will be aggregated to obtain the final inference result for each type, as depicted in Figure 2. The final inference result will be expressed according to the representation of the input and rule consequent. When the representation of the input and rule consequent is the same, the final inference result will also be written with full consideration in the form that is different from the representation of the two, in addition to giving the final result with the same representation as the two.

Consider the Type 6 inference problem:

The given rule:	If	x is $\mathcal{A}$,	then	y is B
Input:		x is $\mathcal{A}^*$		
Output:				y is ?

where $\mathcal{A}$ and $\mathcal{A}^*$ represent two intuitionistic fuzzy sets, respectively, defined on the universe X, and B is a fuzzy set on the universe Y.

The method to reasoning with Type 6 mixed information

Step 1: Determine the output given the intuitionistic fuzzy if–then rule and the input. The following IFMP problem (i.e., Type 2 inference problem) needs to be addressed:

The given rule:	If x is $\mathcal{A}$,	then	y is $\mathcal{B}$
Input:	x is $\mathcal{A}^*$		
Output:			y is $\bar{\mathcal{B}}^*$

where $\mathcal{B} = \{\langle y, B(y), 1 - B(y)\rangle | y \in Y\}$ is an intuitionistic fuzzy set on the universe Y converted from fuzzy set $B = \{\langle y, B(y)\rangle | y \in Y\}$, and A and $\mathcal{A}^*$ represent two intuitionistic fuzzy sets, respectively, defined on the universe X.

Theorem 2 in [14] is utilized to obtain the intuitionistic fuzzy output $\bar{\mathcal{B}}^* = \{\langle y, \bar{\mathcal{B}}^*_t(y), \bar{\mathcal{B}}^*_f(y)\rangle | \, y \in Y\}$:

$$\bar{\mathcal{B}}^*(y) = \bigvee_{x \in X} \{\mathcal{A}^*(x) \otimes_{\mathcal{I}^*} ((\mathcal{A}^*(x) \rightarrow_{\mathcal{I}^*} \mathcal{A}(x)) \otimes_{\mathcal{I}^*} (\mathcal{A}(x) \rightarrow_{\mathcal{I}^*} \mathcal{B}(y)))\}, y \in Y. \tag{12}$$

where $\rightarrow_{\mathcal{I}^*}$ is an intuitionistic R-implication derived from a left-continuous intuitionistic t-norm $\otimes_{\mathcal{I}^*}$, and further,

$$\begin{aligned} \bar{\mathcal{B}}^*_t(y) = & \bigvee_{x \in X} \{\mathcal{A}^*_t(x) \otimes (((\mathcal{A}^*_t(x) \rightarrow \mathcal{A}_t(x)) \wedge (\mathcal{A}^*_{-f}(x) \rightarrow \mathcal{A}_{-f}(x))) \\ & \otimes (\mathcal{A}_{-f}(x) \rightarrow B(y)))\}, y \in Y \end{aligned} \tag{13}$$

$$\begin{aligned} \bar{\mathcal{B}}^*_f(y) = & \bigwedge_{x \in X} \{(1 - \mathcal{A}^*_{-f}(x)) \oplus ((1 - \mathcal{A}^*_{-f}(x) \rightarrow \mathcal{A}_{-f}(x)) \oplus (1 - \mathcal{A}_{-f}(x) \rightarrow B(y)))\} \\ = & 1 - \bigvee_{x \in X} \{\mathcal{A}^*_{-f}(x) \otimes ((\mathcal{A}^*_{-f}(x) \rightarrow \mathcal{A}_{-f}(x)) \otimes (\mathcal{A}_{-f}(x) \rightarrow B(y)))\}, y \in Y \end{aligned} \tag{14}$$

where $\rightarrow$ is an R-implication derived from a left-continuous t-norm $\otimes$ and $\oplus$ is the dual t-conorm of $\otimes$. In order to obtain the final inference result (Step 3), here, the fuzzy output $\bar{B}^* = \{\langle y, \bar{B}^*(y)\rangle | \bar{B}^*(y) \in [\bar{\mathcal{B}}^*_t(y), \bar{\mathcal{B}}^*_{-f}(y)], y \in Y\}$ is also given, where $\bar{\mathcal{B}}^*_{-f}(y) = 1 - \bar{\mathcal{B}}^*_f(y)$.

Step 2: Determine the output given the fuzzy if–then rule and the input $\mathcal{A}^*$.

Having considered that this inference issue overlaps with the Type 3 inference problem, the following two FMP problems will be addressed:

The given rule:	If x is $\mathcal{A}_t$,	then	y is B
Input:	x is $\mathcal{A}^*_t$		
Output:			y is $\tilde{B}^*_1$
The given rule:	If x is $\mathcal{A}_{-f}$,	then	y is B
Input:	x is $\mathcal{A}^*_{-f}$		
Output:			y is $\tilde{B}^*_2$

where $\mathcal{A}_t$ and $\mathcal{A}_{-f}$ are fuzzy sets on X converted from intuitionistic fuzzy set $\mathcal{A}$; $\mathcal{A}^*_t$ and $\mathcal{A}^*_{-f}$ are fuzzy sets on X converted from intuitionistic fuzzy set $\mathcal{A}^*$; and B represents a fuzzy set on Y. The above reasoning problems are solved according to Theorem 1 in [7]:

$$\tilde{B}^*_1(y) = \bigvee_{x \in X} \{\mathcal{A}^*_t(x) \otimes ((\mathcal{A}^*_t(x) \rightarrow \mathcal{A}_t(x)) \otimes (\mathcal{A}_t(x) \rightarrow B(y)))\}, y \in Y, \tag{15}$$

$$\tilde{B}^*_2(y) = \bigvee_{x \in X} \{\mathcal{A}^*_{-f}(x) \otimes ((\mathcal{A}^*_{-f}(x) \rightarrow \mathcal{A}_{-f}(x)) \otimes (\mathcal{A}_{-f}(x) \rightarrow B(y)))\}, y \in Y, \tag{16}$$

where $\rightarrow$ is an R-implication derived from a left-continuous t-norm $\otimes$.

Thus, from Equations (15) and (16), we can obtain the fuzzy output $\tilde{B}^* = \{\langle y, \tilde{B}^*(y)\rangle | y \in Y\}$, $\tilde{B}^*(y) \in [\tilde{B}_1^*(y) \wedge \tilde{B}_2^*(y), \tilde{B}_1^*(y) \vee \tilde{B}_2^*(y)]$ and the intuitionistic fuzzy output $\tilde{\mathcal{B}}^* = \{\langle y, \tilde{\mathcal{B}}_t^*(y), \tilde{\mathcal{B}}_f^*(y)\rangle | y \in Y\}$, $\tilde{\mathcal{B}}_t^*(y) = \tilde{B}_1^*(y) \wedge \tilde{B}_2^*(y)$, $\tilde{\mathcal{B}}_f^*(y) = 1 - \tilde{B}_1^*(y) \vee \tilde{B}_2^*(y)$.

Step 3: Obtain the final result of the Type 6 inference problem by consolidating the outcomes of Steps 1 and 2, as presented in Table 4.

It is easy to prove the following: by combining $\bar{B}^*$ and $\tilde{B}^*$, we obtain the fuzzy $B^* = \{\langle y, B^*(y)\rangle | B^*(y) \in [\bar{\mathcal{B}}_t^*(y) \wedge \tilde{B}_1^*(y) \wedge \tilde{B}_2^*(y), \bar{\mathcal{B}}_{-f}^*(y)) \vee \tilde{B}_1^*(y) \vee \tilde{B}_2^*(y)], y \in Y\}$; from $\bar{\mathcal{B}}^*$ and $\tilde{\mathcal{B}}^*$, we obtain the intuitionistic fuzzy $\mathcal{B}^* = \{\langle y, \mathcal{B}_t^*(y), \mathcal{B}_f^*(y)\rangle | \mathcal{B}_t^*(y) = \bar{\mathcal{B}}_t^*(y) \wedge \tilde{B}_1^*(y) \wedge \tilde{B}_2^*(y), \mathcal{B}_f^*(y) = 1 - \bar{\mathcal{B}}_{-f}^*(y) \vee \tilde{B}_1^*(y) \vee \tilde{B}_2^*(y), y \in Y\}$; moreover, there exists $\bar{\mathcal{B}}_{-f}^*(y) = 1 - \bar{\mathcal{B}}_f^*(y) = \tilde{B}_2^*(y)$ by referring to Equations (14) and (16).

Table 4. The solutions for the mixed information inference problem of Type 6.

The Given Rule	Input	Output	
if x is $\mathcal{A}$, then y is B	x is $\mathcal{A}^*$	FS	$B^* = \{\langle y, B^*(y)\rangle | B^*(y) \in [\bar{\mathcal{B}}_t^*(y) \wedge \tilde{B}_1^*(y) \wedge \tilde{B}_2^*(y), \bar{\mathcal{B}}_{-f}^*(y) \vee \tilde{B}_1^*(y) \vee \tilde{B}_2^*(y)], y \in Y\}$
		IFS	$\mathcal{B}^* = \{\langle y, \mathcal{B}_t^*(y), \mathcal{B}_f^*(y)\rangle | \mathcal{B}_t^* = \bar{\mathcal{B}}_t^*(y) \wedge \tilde{B}_1^*(y) \wedge \tilde{B}_2^*(y), \mathcal{B}_f^* = 1 - \tilde{B}_1^*(y) \vee \tilde{B}_2^*(y), y \in Y\}$

Note: $\bar{\mathcal{B}}_t^*(y) = \bigvee_{x \in X} \{\mathcal{A}_t^*(x) \otimes (((\mathcal{A}_t^*(x) \rightarrow \mathcal{A}_t(x)) \wedge (\mathcal{A}_{-f}^*(x) \rightarrow \mathcal{A}_{-f}(x))) \otimes (\mathcal{A}_{-f}(x) \rightarrow B(y)))\}, y \in Y$, $\bar{\mathcal{B}}_f^*(y) = 1 - \bigvee_{x \in X} \{\mathcal{A}_{-f}^*(x) \otimes ((\mathcal{A}_{-f}^*(x) \rightarrow \mathcal{A}_{-f}(x)) \otimes (\mathcal{A}_{-f}(x) \rightarrow B(y)))\}, y \in Y$, $\tilde{B}_1^*(y) = \bigvee_{x \in X} \{\mathcal{A}_t^*(x) \otimes ((\mathcal{A}_t^*(x) \rightarrow \mathcal{A}_t(x)) \otimes (\mathcal{A}_t(x) \rightarrow B(y)))\}, y \in Y$, $\tilde{B}_2^*(y) = \bigvee_{x \in X} \{\mathcal{A}_{-f}^*(x) \otimes ((\mathcal{A}_{-f}^*(x) \rightarrow \mathcal{A}_{-f}(x)) \otimes (\mathcal{A}_{-f}(x) \rightarrow B(y)))\}, y \in Y$.

Similar to the Type 6 inference problem, the solutions of Types 5, 7 and 8 are shown in Table 5.

Table 5. The solutions for the mixed information inference problem of Types 5, 7 and 8.

Type	The Given Rule	Input	Output	
Type 5	if x is A, then y is $\mathcal{B}$	x is A^*	FS	$B^* = \{\langle y, B^*(y)\rangle | B^*(y) \in [\tilde{B}_1^*(y), \tilde{B}_2^*(y)], y \in Y\}$
			IFS	$\mathcal{B}^* = \{\langle y, \mathcal{B}_t^*(y), \mathcal{B}_f^*(y)\rangle | \mathcal{B}_t^* = \tilde{B}_1^*(y), \mathcal{B}_f^* = 1 - \tilde{B}_2^*(y), y \in Y\}$
Type 7	if x is A, then y is $\mathcal{B}$	x is $\mathcal{A}^*$	FS	$B^* = \{\langle y, B^*(y)\rangle | B^*(y) \in [\bar{\mathcal{B}}_t^*(y) \wedge \tilde{B}_1^*(y) \wedge \tilde{B}_2^*(y), \tilde{B}_1^*(y) \vee \tilde{B}_2^*(y)], y \in Y\}$
			IFS	$\mathcal{B}^* = \{\langle y, \mathcal{B}_t^*(y), \mathcal{B}_f^*(y)\rangle | \mathcal{B}_t^* = \bar{\mathcal{B}}_t^*(y) \wedge \tilde{B}_1^*(y) \wedge \tilde{B}_2^*(y), \mathcal{B}_f^* = 1 - \tilde{B}_1^*(y) \vee \tilde{B}_2^*(y), y \in Y\}$
Type 8	if x is $\mathcal{A}$, then y is B	x is A^*	FS	$B^* = \{\langle y, B^*(y)\rangle | B^*(y) \in [\bar{\mathcal{B}}_t^*(y) \wedge \tilde{B}_1^*(y) \wedge \tilde{B}_2^*(y), \tilde{B}_1^*(y) \vee \tilde{B}_2^*(y)], y \in Y\}$
			IFS	$\mathcal{B}^* = \{\langle y, \mathcal{B}_t^*(y), \mathcal{B}_f^*(y)\rangle | \mathcal{B}_t^* = \bar{\mathcal{B}}_t^*(y) \wedge \tilde{B}_1^*(y) \wedge \tilde{B}_2^*(y), \mathcal{B}_f^* = 1 - \tilde{B}_1^*(y) \vee \tilde{B}_2^*(y), y \in Y\}$

Note: In Type 5, $\bar{\mathcal{B}}_t^*(y) = \bigvee_{x \in X} \{A^*(x) \otimes ((A^*(x) \rightarrow A(x)) \otimes (A(x) \rightarrow \mathcal{B}_t(y)))\}, y \in Y$, $\bar{\mathcal{B}}_f^*(y) = 1 - \bigvee_{x \in X} \{A^*(x) \otimes ((A^*(x) \rightarrow A(x)) \otimes (A(x) \rightarrow \mathcal{B}_{-f}(y)))\}, y \in Y$, $\tilde{B}_1^*(y) = \bigvee_{x \in X} \{A^*(x) \otimes ((A^*(x) \rightarrow A(x)) \otimes (A(x) \rightarrow \mathcal{B}_t(y)))\}, y \in Y$, $\tilde{B}_2^*(y) = \bigvee_{x \in X} \{A^*(x) \otimes ((A^*(x) \rightarrow A(x)) \otimes (A(x) \rightarrow \mathcal{B}_{-f}(y)))\}, y \in Y$. Note: In Type 7, $\bar{\mathcal{B}}_t^*(y) = \bigvee_{x \in X} \{\mathcal{A}_t^*(x) \otimes ((\mathcal{A}_{-f}^*(x) \rightarrow A(x)) \otimes (A(x) \rightarrow \mathcal{B}_t(y)))\}, y \in Y$, $\bar{\mathcal{B}}_f^*(y) = 1 - \bigvee_{x \in X} \{\mathcal{A}_{-f}^*(x) \otimes ((\mathcal{A}_{-f}^*(x) \rightarrow A(x)) \otimes (A(x) \rightarrow \mathcal{B}_{-f}(y)))\}, y \in Y$, $\tilde{B}_1^*(y) = \bigvee_{x \in X} \{\mathcal{A}_t^*(x) \otimes ((\mathcal{A}_t^*(x) \rightarrow A(x)) \otimes (A(x) \rightarrow \mathcal{B}_t(y)))\}, y \in Y$, $\tilde{B}_2^*(y) = \bigvee_{x \in X} \{\mathcal{A}_{-f}^*(x) \otimes ((\mathcal{A}_{-f}^*(x) \rightarrow A(x)) \otimes (A(x) \rightarrow \mathcal{B}_{-f}(y)))\}, y \in Y$. Note: In Type 8, $\bar{\mathcal{B}}_t^*(y) = \bigvee_{x \in X} \{A^*(x) \otimes ((A^*(x) \rightarrow \mathcal{A}_t(x)) \otimes (\mathcal{A}_{-f}(x) \rightarrow B(y)))\}, y \in Y$, $\bar{\mathcal{B}}_f^*(y) = 1 - \bigvee_{x \in X} \{A^*(x) \otimes ((A^*(x) \rightarrow \mathcal{A}_{-f}(x)) \otimes (\mathcal{A}_{-f}(x) \rightarrow B(y)))\}, y \in Y$, $\tilde{B}_1^*(y) = \bigvee_{x \in X} \{A^*(x) \otimes ((A^*(x) \rightarrow \mathcal{A}_t(x)) \otimes (\mathcal{A}_t(x) \rightarrow B(y)))\}, y \in Y$, $\tilde{B}_2^*(y) = \bigvee_{x \in X} \{A^*(x) \otimes ((A^*(x) \rightarrow \mathcal{A}_{-f}(x)) \otimes (\mathcal{A}_{-f}(x) \rightarrow B(y)))\}, y \in Y$.

Proposition 3. *For the Type 6 inference problem, if the t-norm is Łukasiewicz t-norm* $\otimes_{\mathcal{I}_{Łu}^*}$*, Equations (13)–(16) can be rewritten as*

$$\bar{\mathcal{B}}_t^*(y) = \bigvee_{x \in X} \{(\mathcal{A}_t^*(x) + ((1 - \mathcal{A}_t^*(x) + \mathcal{A}_t(x)) \wedge 1 + (1 - \mathcal{A}_t(x) + B(y)) \wedge 1 - 1) \vee 0) - 1) \vee 0\}, y \in Y, \tag{17}$$

$$\bar{\mathcal{B}}_f^*(y) = 1 - \bigvee_{x \in X} \{(\mathcal{A}_{-f}^*(x) + ((1 - \mathcal{A}_{-f}^*(x) + \mathcal{A}_{-f}(x)) \wedge 1 + (1 - \mathcal{A}_{-f}(x) + B(y)) \wedge 1 - 1) \vee 0 - 1) \vee 0\}, y \in Y, \tag{18}$$

$$\tilde{B}_1^*(y) = \bigvee_{x \in X} \{(\mathcal{A}_t^*(x) + ((1 - \mathcal{A}_t^*(x) + \mathcal{A}_t(x)) \wedge 1 + (1 - \mathcal{A}_t(x) + B(y)) \wedge 1 - 1) \vee 0 - 1) \vee 0\}, y \in Y, \tag{19}$$

$$\tilde{B}_2^*(y) = \bigvee_{x \in X} \{(\mathcal{A}_{-f}^*(x) + ((1 - \mathcal{A}_{-f}^*(x) + \mathcal{A}_{-f}(x)) \wedge 1 + (1 - \mathcal{A}_{-f}(x) + B(y)) \wedge 1 - 1) \vee 0 - 1) \vee 0\}, y \in Y. \tag{20}$$

4. Reductivity Analysis

Reductivity is an important property frequently employed as a criterion for evaluating the efficacy of reasoning methods. A reasoning method for the FMP or IFMP (with a unique information type) is considered to be reductive if the equality of the input to the rule antecedent implies that the output is equal to the rule consequent. When discussing the reductivity of methods for resolving inference problems in Table 1 that involve a mixture of information types, how to define the reductivity is a critical issue.

As to methods developed specifically for addressing the Types 3-8 inference problems, there are two representation options for the output, either in the form of fuzzy sets or in the form of intuitionistic fuzzy sets. Having considered the inconsistency of the representations among the input, rule antecedent and rule consequent, several findings are mentioned below:

1. It is possible to make the input and the antecedent of the rule equal when the representation types of the input and the antecedent of the rule are consistent;
2. It is possible to make the input and the antecedent of the rule equal by using the conversion formula from intuitionistic fuzzy sets to fuzzy sets when the input $\mathcal{A}^*$ is an intuitionistic fuzzy set and the antecedent A of the rule is a fuzzy set;
3. When the input A^* is a fuzzy set and the antecedent of the rule $\mathcal{A}$ is an intuitionistic fuzzy set (in which $\mathcal{A}_t \neq 1 - \mathcal{A}_f$), the equality between the input and the antecedent of the rule cannot be realized at this time according to the conversion formula from fuzzy sets to intuitionistic fuzzy sets.

Thus, the reductivity, to our knowledge, can be interpreted in the way that for each of Types 3, 5, 6 and 7, when the equality between the input and the antecedent of the rule is achieved, the method is called reductive if the output of this method with the same representation as the rule consequent is proved to be equal to the rule consequent. As for Types 4 and 8, the discussion of reductivity is not applicable to the methods for these two inference problems because it is not feasible to make the input and the antecedent of the rule equal.

Definition 8. *(1) For Type 3, the method is called reductive if the assumption that the input A^* converted from $\mathcal{A}^*$ is equal to the rule antecedent A implies that the fuzzy output B^* is equal to the rule consequent B.*

(2) For Type 5, the method is called reductive if the assumption that the input A^* is equal to the rule antecedent A implies that the intuitionistic fuzzy output $\mathcal{B}^*$ is equal to the rule consequent $\mathcal{B}$.

(3) For Type 6, the method is called reductive if the assumption that the input $\mathcal{A}^*$ is equal to the rule antecedent A implies that the fuzzy output B^* is equal to the rule consequent B.

(4) For Type 7, the method is called reductive if the assumption that the input A^* converted from $\mathcal{A}^*$ is equal to the rule antecedent A implies that the intuitionistic fuzzy output $\mathcal{B}^*$ is equal to the rule consequent $\mathcal{B}$.

Theorem 3. *If A is normal, then the proposed method for the Type 3 mixed information inference problem is reductive.*

Proof. If $A^* = A$ and A is normal, i.e., $A(x_0) = 1, x_0 \in X$, then there are

$$\begin{aligned} B(y) \geq & \tilde{B}_1^*(y) \\ & = \bigvee_{x \in X} \{\mathcal{A}_t^*(x) \otimes ((\mathcal{A}_t^*(x) \to A(x)) \otimes (A(x) \to B(y)))\} \\ & \geq A(x_0) \otimes ((A(x_0) \to A(x_0)) \otimes (A(x_0) \to B(y))) = B(y), \end{aligned}$$

$$\begin{aligned} B(y) \geq & \tilde{B}_2^*(y) \\ & = \bigvee_{x \in X} \{\mathcal{A}_{-f}^*(x) \otimes ((\mathcal{A}_{-f}^*(x) \to A(x)) \otimes (A(x) \to B(y)))\} \\ & \geq A(x_0) \otimes ((A(x_0) \to A(x_0)) \otimes (A(x_0) \to B(y))) = B(y). \end{aligned}$$

Then, $\tilde{B}_1^* = \tilde{B}_2^* = B$ can be obtained, and there exists the fuzzy output $B^* = \{\langle y, B^*(y) \in [\tilde{B}_1^*(y) \wedge \tilde{B}_2^*(y), \tilde{B}_1^*(y) \vee \tilde{B}_2^*(y)]\rangle | y \in Y\} = \{\langle y, B^*(y) \in [B(y), B(y)]\rangle | y \in Y\} = \{\langle y, B(y)\rangle | y \in Y\} = B$. Thus, the reductivity of the method proposed for Type 3 is proved. □

Theorem 4. *If $\mathcal{A}$ or A is normal, then the proposed methods for the Types 5–7 mixed information inference problems are reductive.*

Proof. In Type 6, if $\mathcal{A}^* = \mathcal{A}$ and $\mathcal{A}$ is normal, i.e., $\mathcal{A}(x_0) = \langle 1, 0\rangle, x_0 \in X$, then

$$\begin{aligned} \mathcal{B}(y) = & \mathcal{A}(x_0) \otimes_{\mathcal{I}^*} ((\mathcal{A}(x_0) \to_{\mathcal{I}^*} \mathcal{A}(x_0)) \otimes_{\mathcal{I}^*} (\mathcal{A}(x_0) \to_{\mathcal{I}^*} \mathcal{B}(y))) \\ = & \mathcal{A}^*(x_0) \otimes_{\mathcal{I}^*} ((\mathcal{A}^*(x_0) \to_{\mathcal{I}^*} \mathcal{A}(x_0)) \otimes_{\mathcal{I}^*} (\mathcal{A}(x_0) \to_{\mathcal{I}^*} \mathcal{B}(y))) \\ \preceq & \bigvee_{x \in X} \{\mathcal{A}^*(x) \otimes_{\mathcal{I}^*} ((\mathcal{A}^*(x) \to_{\mathcal{I}^*} \mathcal{A}(x)) \otimes_{\mathcal{I}^*} (\mathcal{A}(x) \to_{\mathcal{I}^*} \mathcal{B}(y)))\} \\ = & \bar{\mathcal{B}}^*(y) \preceq \mathcal{B}(y), \end{aligned}$$

where $\mathcal{B}$ is an intuitionistic fuzzy set converted from fuzzy set B by Proposition 1. Thus, $\bar{\mathcal{B}}^* = \{\langle y, \bar{\mathcal{B}}_t^*(y), \bar{\mathcal{B}}_f^*(y)\rangle | y \in Y\}$ is equivalent to $\mathcal{B} = \{\langle y, B(y), 1 - B(y)\rangle | y \in Y\}$. In addition, there are

$$\begin{aligned} B(y) \geq & \tilde{B}_1^*(y) \\ & = \bigvee_{x \in X} \{\mathcal{A}_t^*(x) \otimes ((\mathcal{A}_t^*(x) \to \mathcal{A}_t(x)) \otimes (\mathcal{A}_t(x) \to B(y)))\} \\ & \geq \mathcal{A}_t(x_0) \otimes ((\mathcal{A}_t(x_0) \to \mathcal{A}_t(x_0)) \otimes (\mathcal{A}_t(x_0) \to B(y))) = B(y), \\ B(y) \geq & \tilde{B}_2^*(y) \\ & = \bigvee_{x \in X} \{\mathcal{A}_{-f}^*(x) \otimes ((\mathcal{A}_{-f}^*(x) \to \mathcal{A}_{-f}(x)) \otimes (\mathcal{A}_{-f}(x) \to B(y)))\} \\ & \geq \mathcal{A}_{-f}(x_0) \otimes ((\mathcal{A}_{-f}(x_0) \to \mathcal{A}_{-f}(x_0)) \otimes (\mathcal{A}_{-f}(x_0) \to B(y))) = B(y). \end{aligned}$$

Through the above analysis, it can be obtained that $\tilde{B}_1^* = \tilde{B}_2^* = B$. Therefore, the fuzzy output $B^* = \{\langle y, B^*(y) \in [\bar{\mathcal{B}}_t^*(y) \wedge \tilde{B}_1^*(y) \wedge \tilde{B}_2^*(y), \bar{\mathcal{B}}_{-f}^*(y)) \vee \tilde{B}_1^*(y) \vee \tilde{B}_2^*(y)]\rangle | y \in Y\} = \{\langle y, B^*(y) \in [B(y), B(y)]\rangle | y \in Y\} = \{\langle y, B(y)\rangle | y \in Y\} = B$. It is proved that the method proposed for Type 6 is reductive.

Likewise, it can be proven that the methods proposed for Types 5 and 7 are reductive. □

5. Application in Pattern Recognition

Observe that pattern recognition problems involving a mixture of fuzzy and intuitionistic fuzzy information in real life can be solved by first transforming these practical problems into corresponding mixed information inference problems and then applying reasoning methods to yield the recognition results. The proposed reasoning methods were evaluated on four pattern recognition tasks with a mixture of fuzzy information and intuitionistic fuzzy information: the pattern recognition task was accompanied by a comparison with other existing reasoning methods for fuzzy and intuitionistic fuzzy-mixed information. Figure 3 depicts how to solve practical problems using the methods established in Section 3 for reasoning with mixed information.

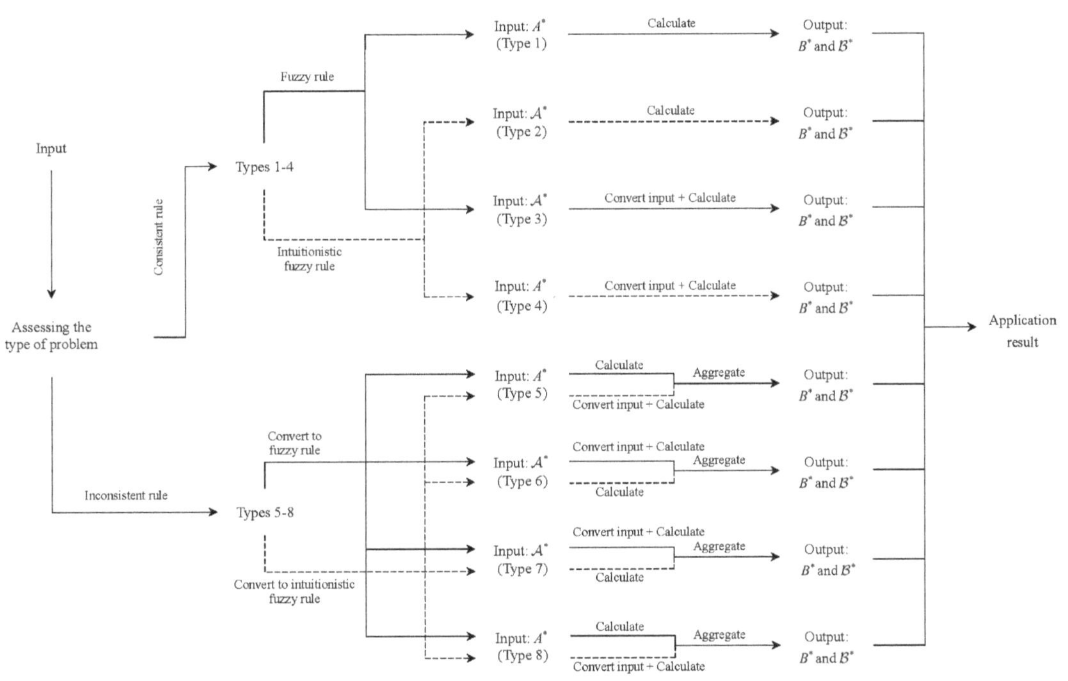

Figure 3. Process of using the presented reasoning methods to address the practical problem with the mixture of fuzzy information and intuitionistic fuzzy information.

Since the partial order $\preceq$ is unable to order all intuitionistic fuzzy numbers, a total order $\preceq_{Xu}$ based on the score function SF and the accuracy function AF is provided.

Definition 9 ([17]). *Let $\alpha = \langle \alpha_t, \alpha_f \rangle \in \mathcal{I}^*$ be an intuitionistic fuzzy number. $SF(\alpha) = \alpha_t - \alpha_f$ is called a score function and $AF(\alpha) = \alpha_t + \alpha_f$ is called an accuracy function.*

$\alpha \preceq_{Xu} \beta$ holds for the two intuitionistic fuzzy numbers $\alpha = \langle \alpha_t, \alpha_f \rangle$ and $\beta = \langle \beta_t, \beta_f \rangle$ if and only if (i) $SF(\alpha) < SF(\beta)$ and (ii) $SF(\alpha) = SF(\beta)$ and $AF(\alpha) \leq AF(\beta)$.

5.1. Method for Pattern Recognition

Let $K = \{K_1, K_2, \cdots, K_n\}$ be a set of patterns and $X = \{x_1, x_2, \cdots, x_m\}$ be a set of attributes. $\mathbb{A}_i(x_j)$ $(i = 1, 2, \cdots, n$ and $j = 1, 2, \cdots, m)$ is the value of the attributes x_j, and $\mathbb{B}_i(y)$ denote the evaluation value of ith known patterns. Both $\mathbb{A}_i(x_j)$ and $\mathbb{B}_i(y)$ are depicted by a fuzzy number or an intuitionistic fuzzy number, as indicated in Table 6.

$\mathbb{A}^*(x_j)$ represents the value of the test sample G with respect to attribute x_j, and it is also depicted by a fuzzy number or an intuitionistic fuzzy number, as shown in Table 7. The goal of this study is to recognize the sample G into these n distinct patterns.

Table 6. The relationship between the patterns and their attributes.

	x_1	x_2	$\cdots$	x_m
$\mathbb{B}_1(y)$	$\mathbb{A}_1(x_1)$	$\mathbb{A}_1(x_2)$	$\cdots$	$\mathbb{A}_1(x_m)$
$\mathbb{B}_2(y)$	$\mathbb{A}_2(x_1)$	$\mathbb{A}_2(x_2)$	$\cdots$	$\mathbb{A}_2(x_m)$
$\vdots$	$\vdots$	$\vdots$	$\vdots$	$\vdots$
$\mathbb{B}_n(y)$	$\mathbb{A}_n(x_1)$	$\mathbb{A}_n(x_2)$	$\cdots$	$\mathbb{A}_n(x_m)$

Table 7. The relationship between the test sample and its attributes.

	x_1	x_2	$\cdots$	x_m
G	$\mathbb{A}^*(x_1)$	$\mathbb{A}^*(x_2)$	$\cdots$	$\mathbb{A}^*(x_m)$

Step 1: Determine which type of mixed information inference problem this pattern recognition problem belongs to, as in Table 1. The data presented in Table 6 can be interpreted as the if–then rules within the inference problem, and the data in Table 7 can be viewed as the input within the inference problem. Then, the following n inference problems will be resolved:

$$\begin{array}{llll}
\text{The given rule:} & \text{If } x_1 \text{ is } \mathbb{A}_i, x_2 \text{ is } \mathbb{A}_i, \cdots, x_m \text{ is } \mathbb{A}_i, & \text{then } y \text{ is } \mathbb{B}_i & \\
\text{Input:} & x_1 \text{ is } \mathbb{A}^*, x_2 \text{ is } \mathbb{A}^*, \cdots, x_m \text{ is } \mathbb{A}^* & & (i = 1, 2, \cdots, n) \\
\hline
\text{Output:} & & y \text{ is } \mathbb{B}_i^* &
\end{array}$$

Step 2: Calculate the outputs $\mathbb{B}_i^*(y)$ using the proposed reasoning methods in Tables 2–5.

Step 3: Select the largest $\mathbb{B}_i^*(y)$ as the final result, and the test sample G is recognized as the pattern K_i.

Note that the choice of representation form (fuzzy sets or intuitionistic fuzzy sets) for $\mathbb{B}_i^*$ depends on the user. When $\mathbb{B}_i^*$ is expressed as fuzzy sets $B_i^* = \{\langle y, B_i^*(y)\rangle | y \in Y\}$, there exist $B_i^*(y) \in [a, b]$, $a \leq b$ and $a, b \in [0, 1]$ according to the solution representations provided in Tables 2–5. (The left endpoint a and the right endpoint b represent the minimum and maximum numbers of $B_i^*(y)$, respectively.) For the convenience of comparison, $B_i^*(y)$ is taken as a, and the $B_i^*(y)$ can be sorted by the order $\leq$. Then, the pattern K_i corresponding to the largest value of $B_i^*(y)$ is the pattern to which the test sample G belongs. When $\mathbb{B}_i^*$ is expressed as intuitionistic fuzzy sets $\mathcal{B}_i^*$, the order $\preceq_{Xu}$ is used for comparison and the pattern K_i corresponding to the largest $\mathcal{B}_i^*(y)$ is identified as the pattern to which the test sample G belongs.

5.2. Application in Pattern Recognition with Mixed Information

For the following recognition problems, the R-implication involved takes the Łukasiewicz implication $\rightarrow_{\text{Łu}}$ induced by the Łukasiewicz t-norm $\otimes_{\text{Łu}}$, and the intuitionistic R-implication takes the intuitionistic Łukasiewicz implication $\rightarrow_{\mathcal{I}^*_{\text{Łu}}}$ induced by the intuitionistic Łukasiewicz t-norm $\otimes_{\mathcal{I}^*_{\text{Łu}}}$. The Łukasiewicz t-norm and the Łukasiewicz implication are typical t-norms and R-implications, so this paper uses them for pattern recognition applications. The proposed methods are also applicable to other t-norms and their corresponding induced R-implications. Since research on mixed information reasoning methods is relatively limited, and few methods can directly address applications in pattern recognition involving mixed information of fuzzy and intuitionistic fuzzy, only the methods discussed in [15] are considered for the comparison analysis. In the future, we will try to broaden the range of methods that can be used for comparative analysis.

5.2.1. Application in Type 4 Mixed Information Pattern Recognition

Example 3. *There is a set of patterns* $K = \{K_1, K_2, K_3\}$ *and a set of attributes* $X = \{x_1, x_2, \cdots x_6\}$. *The relationships* $\mathcal{A}_i(x_j)$ $(i = 1, 2, 3, j = 1, 2, \cdots, 6)$ *between the three known patterns and their attributes from [18,19], as well as the evaluation values* $B_i(y)$ *of known patterns, are presented by intuitionistic fuzzy numbers in Table 8. Now, determine which the unknown pattern G described by fuzzy numbers in Table 9 belongs to.*

It can be determined that this pattern recognition belongs to the Type 4 mixed information inference problem according to the rules provided in Table 8 and the input given in Table 9. Using the reasoning method to the Type 4 mixed information inference problem in Table 2, the fuzzy outputs $B_i^*(y)$ associated with the unknown G are shown in Table 10 and the intuitionistic fuzzy outputs $\mathcal{B}_i^*(y)$ associated with G are given in Table 11. By borrowing the order $\leq$ for $B_i^*(y)$ in Table 10 and the order $\preceq_{Xu}$ for $\mathcal{B}_i^*(y)$ in Table 11, there exist the maximum $B_1^*(y) = 0.76$ and the maximum $\mathcal{B}_1^*(y) = \langle 0.76, 0.15 \rangle$, which implies that the unknown pattern G belongs to the known pattern K_1.

Table 8. The relationships of known patterns K_1, K_2, K_3 and their attributes in Example 3.

	$\mathcal{B}_i(y)$	x_1	x_2	x_3	x_4	x_5	x_6
K_1	⟨0.87,0.05⟩	⟨0.94,0.00⟩	⟨0.88,0.00⟩	⟨0.82,0.00⟩	⟨0.78,0.02⟩	⟨0.75,0.05⟩	⟨0.72,0.08⟩
K_2	⟨0.81,0.18⟩	⟨0.86,0.07⟩	⟨0.92,0.04⟩	⟨0.98,0.01⟩	⟨0.98,0.00⟩	⟨0.95,0.00⟩	⟨0.92,0.00⟩
K_3	⟨0.85,0.12⟩	⟨0.66,0.14⟩	⟨0.72,0.08⟩	⟨0.78,0.02⟩	⟨0.84,0.00⟩	⟨0.90,0.00⟩	⟨0.96,0.00⟩

Table 9. The attributes of the unknown pattern G in Example 3.

	x_1	x_2	x_3	x_4	x_5	x_6
G	0.83	0.76	0.79	0.82	0.85	0.78

Table 10. The fuzzy outputs $B_i^*(y)$ and recognition result in Example 3.

Method	K_1	K_2	K_3	Recognition Result
ETIM [15]	**0.85**	0.72	0.83	K_1
DTIM [15]	**0.85**	0.72	0.83	K_1
The proposed method	**0.76**	0.72	0.73	K_1

Note: Bold indicates the maximum present in that group of data.

Table 11. The intuitionistic fuzzy outputs $\mathcal{B}_i^*(y)$ and recognition result in Example 3.

Method	K_1	K_2	K_3	Recognition Result
ETIM [15]	**⟨0.85,0.15⟩**	⟨0.72,0.28⟩	⟨0.83,0.17⟩	K_1
DTIM [15]	**⟨0.85,0.15⟩**	⟨0.72,0.28⟩	⟨0.83,0.17⟩	K_1
The proposed method	**⟨0.76,0.15⟩**	⟨0.72,0.28⟩	⟨0.73,0.17⟩	K_1

Note: Bold indicates the maximum present in that group of data.

Example 4. *There is a patient G, and the symptoms of the disease are described over the feature space* $X = \{x_1, x_2, \cdots, x_5\}$, *including Temperature, Headache, Stomachache, Cough and Chest Pain.* $K = \{K_1, K_2, \cdots, K_5\}$ *describes five possible diseases, Viral Fever, Malaria, Typhoid, Stomach Problem and Heart Problem, from which the patient may suffer. Table 12 displays the symptoms* $\mathcal{A}_i(x_j)$ $(i = 1, 2, \cdots, 5, j = 1, 2, \cdots, 5)$ *for each disease as in [20–22], and the assessment value* $\mathcal{B}_i$, *all represented by intuitionistic fuzzy numbers. Table 13 exhibits the symptoms of the patient G using fuzzy numbers. The goal is to determine which of the known five diseases the patient has.*

Solving this pattern recognition problem is similar to Example 3. The fuzzy results $B_i^*(y)$ and the intuitionistic fuzzy results $\mathcal{B}_i^*(y)$ are presented in Tables 14 and 15, respectively. It can be concluded that patient G most likely suffers from Malaria.

Tables 10 and 11 respectively and Tables 14 and 15 also, respectively, display the fuzzy outcomes and the intuitionistic fuzzy outcomes of Examples 3 and 4 derived from ETIM and DTIM in [15].

The proposed method obtained the same results in Example 3 as ETIM and DTIM, demonstrating that the proposed method is feasible and effective. But ETIM and DTIM obtained the same solutions in Example 4, whereas the proposed method can provide effective results, indicating that the proposed method is superior to ETIM and DTIM.

Table 12. Symptoms characteristic for the diagnoses in Example 4.

	$\mathcal{B}_i(y)$	x_1	x_2	x_3	x_4	x_5
Viral Fever	⟨0.75,0.05⟩	⟨0.40,0.00⟩	⟨0.30,0.50⟩	⟨0.10,0.70⟩	⟨0.40,0.30⟩	⟨0.10,0.70⟩
Malaria	⟨0.75,0.05⟩	⟨0.70,0.00⟩	⟨0.20,0.60⟩	⟨0.00,0.90⟩	⟨0.70,0.00⟩	⟨0.10,0.80⟩
Typhoid	⟨0.75,0.05⟩	⟨0.30,0.30⟩	⟨0.60,0.10⟩	⟨0.20,0.70⟩	⟨0.20,0.60⟩	⟨0.10,0.90⟩
Stomach Problem	⟨0.75,0.05⟩	⟨0.10,0.70⟩	⟨0.20,0.40⟩	⟨0.80,0.00⟩	⟨0.20,0.70⟩	⟨0.20,0.70⟩
Heart Problem	⟨0.75,0.05⟩	⟨0.10,0.80⟩	⟨0.00,0.80⟩	⟨0.20,0.80⟩	⟨0.20,0.80⟩	⟨0.80,0.10⟩

Table 13. Symptoms characteristic for the patient G in Example 4.

	Temperature	Headache	Stomachache	Cough	Chest Pain
G	0.80	0.80	0.10	0.20	0.10

Table 14. The fuzzy outputs $B_i^*(y)$ and the disease of the patient G in Example 4.

Method	Viral Fever	Malaria	Typhoid	Stomach Problem	Heart Problem	Recognition Result
ETIM [15]	**0.80**	**0.80**	**0.80**	**0.80**	**0.80**	–
DTIM [15]	**0.80**	**0.80**	**0.80**	**0.80**	**0.80**	–
The proposed method	0.35	**0.65**	0.60	0.20	0.20	Malaria

Note: "–" indicates that the result was not identified, and bold indicates the maximum present in that group of data.

Table 15. The intuitionistic fuzzy outputs $\mathcal{B}_i^*(y)$ and the disease of the patient G in Example 4.

Method	Viral Fever	Malaria	Typhoid	Stomach Problem	Heart Problem	Recognition Result
ETIM [15]	⟨**0.80,0.20**⟩	⟨**0.80,0.20**⟩	⟨**0.80,0.20**⟩	⟨**0.80,0.20**⟩	⟨**0.80,0.20**⟩	–
DTIM [15]	⟨**0.80,0.20**⟩	⟨**0.80,0.20**⟩	⟨**0.80,0.20**⟩	⟨**0.80,0.20**⟩	⟨**0.80,0.20**⟩	–
The proposed method	⟨0.35,0.25⟩	⟨**0.65,0.25**⟩	⟨0.60,0.20⟩	⟨0.20,0.40⟩	⟨0.20,0.80⟩	Malaria

Note: "–" indicates that the result was not identified, and bold indicates the maximum present in that group of data.

5.2.2. Application in Type 6 Mixed Information Pattern Recognition

Example 5. *Consider a mineral identification task.* $X = \{x_1, x_2, \cdots, x_6\}$ *represents the six characteristics that a mineral possesses, and* $K_1, K_2, \cdots, K_5$*, respectively, represent five typical mineral-producing areas. The data in Tables 16 and 17 from [23] present the characteristic values* $\mathcal{A}_i(x_j)$ $(i = 1, 2, \cdots, 5, j = 1, 2, \cdots, 6)$ *for the five known minerals and the characteristic values* $\mathcal{A}^*(x_j)$ *for the unknown mineral G, written in the form of intuitionistic fuzzy sets. The evaluated value* $B_i(y)$ *of the corresponding production area for each mineral in Table 16 is given in the form of fuzzy sets. The goal is to ascertain the specific mineral area among the five from which the mineral G originates.*

Observe that the rules are represented in the mixed form of fuzzy sets and intuitionistic fuzzy sets, and the input is expressed by intuitionistic fuzzy sets with the same representation type as the rule antecedents. Therefore, this mineral identification problem is a Type 6 mixed information inference problem. Using the reasoning method to the Type 6 mixed information inference problem in Table 4, the fuzzy outputs $B_i^*(y)$ associated with the unknown mineral G are shown in Table 18 and the intuitionistic fuzzy outputs $\mathcal{B}_i^*(y)$ associated with G are given in Table 19. By choosing the maximum of the five possible values in Tables 18 and 19, it can draw a conclusion that the production area of the mineral G is K_5.

Table 16. The characteristics of five minerals from the corresponding known areas in Example 5.

	$B_i(y)$	x_1	x_2	x_3	x_4	x_5	x_6
K_1	0.75	⟨0.7390,0.1250⟩	⟨0.0330,0.8180⟩	⟨0.1880,0.6260⟩	⟨0.4920,0.3580⟩	⟨0.0200,0.6280⟩	⟨0.7390,0.1250⟩
K_2	0.75	⟨0.1240,0.6650⟩	⟨0.0300,0.8250⟩	⟨0.0480,0.8000⟩	⟨0.1360.0.6480⟩	⟨0.0190,0.8230⟩	⟨0.3930,0.6530⟩
K_3	0.75	⟨0.4490,0.3870⟩	⟨0.6620,0.2980⟩	⟨1.0000,0.0000⟩	⟨1.0000,0.0000⟩	⟨1.0000,0.0000⟩	⟨1.0000,0.0000⟩
K_4	0.75	⟨0.2800,0.7150⟩	⟨0.5210,0.3680⟩	⟨0.4700,0.4230⟩	⟨0.2950,0.6580⟩	⟨0.1880,0.8060⟩	⟨0.7350,0.1180⟩
K_5	0.75	⟨0.3260,0.4520⟩	⟨1.0000,0.0000⟩	⟨0.1820,0.7250⟩	⟨0.1560,0.7650⟩	⟨0.0490,0.8960⟩	⟨0.6750,0.2630⟩

Table 17. The characteristic of a mineral G to be identified in Example 5.

	x_1	x_2	x_3	x_4	x_5	x_6
G	⟨0.6290,0.3030⟩	⟨0.5240,0.3560⟩	⟨0.2100,0.6890⟩	⟨0.2180,0.7530⟩	⟨0.0690,0.8760⟩	⟨0.6580,0.2560⟩

Table 18. The fuzzy outputs $B_i^*(y)$ and recognition result in Example 5.

Method	K_1	K_2	K_3	K_4	K_5	Recognition Result
ETIM [15]	0.5330	**0.6580**	0.6290	0.6290	**0.6580**	−
DTIM [15]	**0.6580**	**0.6580**	0.6290	**0.6580**	**0.6580**	−
The proposed method	0.5330	0.2610	0.3560	0.5260	**0.6510**	K_5

Note: "−" indicates that the result was not identified, and bold indicates the maximum present in that group of data.

Table 19. The intuitionistic fuzzy outputs $\mathcal{B}_i^*(y)$ and recognition result in Example 5.

Method	K_1	K_2	K_3	K_4	K_5	Recognition Result
ETIM [15]	⟨0.5330,0.3560⟩	⟨**0.6580,0.2560**⟩	⟨0.6290,0.3030⟩	⟨0.6290.0.3030⟩	⟨**0.6580,0.2560**⟩	−
DTIM [15]	⟨0.6580,0.3560⟩	⟨**0.6580,0.2560**⟩	⟨0.6290,0.3030⟩	⟨0.6580,0.3030⟩	⟨**0.6580,0.2560**⟩	−
The proposed method	⟨0.5330,0.3420⟩	⟨0.2610,0.6070⟩	⟨0.5240,0.3560⟩	⟨0.5260,0.3420⟩	⟨**0.6510,0.2630**⟩	K_5

Note: "−" indicates that the result was not identified, and bold indicates the maximum present in that group of data.

Example 6. *The Indian government has released a global tender proposal to strengthen infrastructure construction and now hopes to pick a contractor from six different contractors: Jaihind Road Builders P. L. (K_1), J.K. Construction (K_2), Build Quick Infrastructure P. L. (K_3), Relcon Infra Projects L. (K_4), Tata Infrastructure L. (K_5) and Birla P. L. (K_6). These contractors are assessed based on the following four attributes x_1, x_2, x_3, x_4, namely, tender price, completion time, technical capability and background experience. The attribute values $\mathcal{A}_i(x_j)$ $(i = 1, 2, \cdots, 6, j = 1, 2, 3, 4)$ for each contractor are presented in Table 20 with the form of intuitionistic fuzzy sets. The evaluated value B_i for each contractor is given in Table 20 with the form of fuzzy sets. The attribute values $\mathcal{A}^*$ of the ideal contractor have been given by the government in Table 21 with the form of intuitionistic fuzzy sets. Now, the task is to select the appropriate contractor to undertake this project.*

Solving this pattern recognition problem is similar to Example 5. The fuzzy results $B_i^*(y)$ and the intuitionistic fuzzy results $\mathcal{B}_i^*(y)$ are presented in Tables 22 and 23, respectively. It can be concluded that the appropriate contractor is K_3.

Tables 18, 19, 22 and 23 also, respectively, display the fuzzy outcomes and the intuitionistic fuzzy outcomes of Examples 5 and 6 derived from ETIM and DTIM in [15].

By comparing the results in Examples 5 and 6, it can be observed that ETIM and DTIM did not yield reliable outcomes. This is due to the fact that the triple-implication principle used by ETIM and DTIM does not take into account the connection between the input and rule antecedents, which is what the quintuple-implication principle is good at. Therefore, the results obtained by the proposed method are more reasonable.

Table 20. The relationships of six contractors and their attributes in Example 6.

	$B_i(y)$	Tender Price	Completion Time	Technical Capability	Background Experience
K_1	0.90	⟨0.81,0.19⟩	⟨0.90,0.10⟩	⟨0.81,0.28⟩	⟨0.67,0.20⟩
K_2	0.80	⟨0.84,0.10⟩	⟨0.81,0.11⟩	⟨0.60,0.20⟩	⟨0.72.0.19⟩
K_3	0.92	⟨0.67,0.13⟩	⟨0.78,0.21⟩	⟨0.92,0.05⟩	⟨0.81,0.12⟩
K_4	0.85	⟨0.77,0.12⟩	⟨0.83,0.11⟩	⟨0.74,0.24⟩	⟨0.71,0.20⟩
K_5	0.86	⟨0.84,0.15⟩	⟨0.69,0.20⟩	⟨0.71,0.20⟩	⟨0.72,0.27⟩
K_6	0.77	⟨0.79,0.02⟩	⟨0.81,0.17⟩	⟨0.66,0.30⟩	⟨0.78,0.10⟩

Table 21. The characteristic of the ideal standards G in Example 6.

	Tender Price	Completion Time	Technical Capability	Background Experience
Ideal Standards	⟨0.72,0.22⟩	⟨0.84,0.04⟩	⟨0.92,0.08⟩	⟨0.85,0.13⟩

Table 22. The fuzzy outputs $B_i^*(y)$ and the ideal contractor in Example 6.

Method	K_1	K_2	K_3	K_4	K_5	K_6	Recognition Result
ETIM [15]	**0.92**	**0.92**	0.89	**0.92**	**0.92**	**0.92**	–
DTIM [15]	**0.92**	**0.92**	**0.92**	**0.92**	**0.92**	**0.92**	–
The proposed method	0.78	0.71	**0.89**	0.74	0.72	0.66	K_3

Note: "–" indicates that the result was not identified, and bold indicates the maximum present in that group of data.

Table 23. The intuitionistic fuzzy outputs $\mathcal{B}_i^*(y)$ and the ideal contractor in Example 6.

Method	K_1	K_2	K_3	K_4	K_5	K_6	Recognition Result
ETIM [15]	**⟨0.92,0.04⟩**	⟨0.92,0.08⟩	⟨0.85,0.04⟩	⟨0.92,0.08⟩	**⟨0.92,0.04⟩**	⟨0.92,0.08⟩	–
DTIM [15]	**⟨0.92,0.04⟩**	⟨0.92,0.08⟩	**⟨0.92,0.04⟩**	⟨0.92,0.08⟩	**⟨0.92,0.04⟩**	⟨0.92,0.08⟩	–
The proposed method	⟨0.78,0.16⟩	⟨0.71,0.20⟩	**⟨0.89,0.11⟩**	⟨0.74,0.17⟩	⟨0.72,0.28⟩	⟨0.66,0.23⟩	K_3

Note: "–" indicates that the result was not identified, and bold indicates the maximum present in that group of data.

5.3. Comparison Analysis

In the following, the pattern recognition problems provided in Examples 3–6 will be utilized to conduct a comprehensive analysis of the existing and proposed inference methods with mixed information. Table 24 summarizes the recognition outcomes of existing reasoning methods with mixed information in various pattern recognition instances. Examples 3 and 4 belong to Type 4 (inference problems with mixed information of consistent rules), while Examples 5 and 6 belong to Type 6 (inference problems with mixed information of inconsistent rules). According to Example 3, the same results for ETIM, DTIM and the method in this paper are achieved, indicating that all of these methods can be used to some extent to solve pattern recognition problems. In contrast, from the results of Examples 4–6, the patterns to which the test samples belong in these data cannot be provided by ETIM and DTIM. The rationale lies in that (1) the relationship between the input and rule antecedents is taken into account in the quintuple-implication principle as opposed to the triple-implication principle and (2), for mixed information reasoning problem with inconsistent rules, the method proposed herein comprehensively integrates the two information conversion modes, from fuzzy sets to intuitionistic fuzzy sets and from intuitionistic fuzzy sets to fuzzy sets, instead of considering the two conversion modes separately as in [15]. All these results in Examples 3–6 justify the use of the methods in this paper over the methods in [15].

Table 24. Summary of existing reasoning methods with mixed information for processing pattern recognition examples.

Method	Type 4		Type 6	
	Example 3	Example 4	Example 5	Example 6
	Can solve?			
ETIM [15]	✓	×	×	×
DTIM [15]	✓	×	×	×
The proposed method	✓	✓	✓	✓

Note: "✓" indicates that the reasoning method with mixed information can solve the pattern recognition problem, and "×" indicates that the reasoning method with mixed information cannot solve the pattern recognition problem.

It is evident that the datasets in Examples 3–6 are not derived from the real world. Considering the fact that datasets from the real world can be directly used for mixed information reasoning are relatively few and the construction process of these datasets is complex, the test of the proposed methods on the real-world datasets will be one of future research work.

Regarding the computational complexity of the methods built in this paper, this is mainly related to the specific type of mixed information inference problem. The less information needs to be converted, the lower the computational complexity. When solving the mixed information inference problems of Type 3 and Type 4, only the inputs need to be converted into the same information type as the rule, and the computational complexity is lower. And for Types 5–8 mixed information inference problems, due to the inconsistency between the representations of rule antecedent and rule consequent, it is necessary to consider the directions from fuzzy sets to intuitionistic fuzzy sets and from intuitionistic fuzzy sets to fuzzy sets at the same time, and aggregate the results obtained from the two directions, so the computational complexity is higher. Although the methods proposed in this paper are comparatively more intricate than those presented in [15], they can yield significantly more compelling outcomes in practical applications.

To summarize, the constructed mixed information reasoning methods in this paper are mainly based on the quintuple-implication principle, which has a sound logical foundation. They can be regarded as the extension of the quintuple-implication reasoning method based on fuzzy sets [7] or the extension of the quintuple-implication reasoning method based on intuitionistic fuzzy sets [14]. Furthermore, compared to the existing mixed information reasoning methods based on the triple I principle proposed in [15], the reasoning methods developed in this paper employ the same conversion operators between fuzzy sets and intuitionistic fuzzy sets as those used in [15]. Meanwhile, these two kinds of methods exhibit reductive properties in the inference problems of Types 3, 5, 6 and 7 but are not appropriate to discuss reductivity in the inference problems of Type 4 and Type 8. In addition, when designing the inference process and calculating the inference results, the mixed information reasoning methods in this paper comprehensively consider the inference results in both the direction of converting fuzzy sets into intuitionistic fuzzy sets and the direction of converting intuitionistic fuzzy sets into fuzzy sets for the inference problems with the given inconsistent rules. Compared with the methods those consider only a single conversion direction in [15], the final inference results from our methods are more advantageous. When the inference problem involves the mixture of fuzzy information and intuitionistic fuzzy information, no matter what the mixture type is, the mixed information reasoning methods constructed in this paper can directly give reasonable inference results. These analyses imply that the methods constructed in this paper provide more technical support for solving mixed information reasoning problems and have great potential and broad prospect in practical applications. In view of the fact that the methods proposed in this paper are capable of deriving more insightful conclusions and trends from the data, they can assist managers in making more informed and rational judgments and decisions in complex environments with the mixture of fuzzy information and intuitionistic fuzzy information.

6. Conclusions

A new scheme in this paper has been described to solve inference problems that are infused with various combinations of fuzzy information and intuitionistic fuzzy information. This scheme was based on the idea that the key to the rule-based reasoning is the precise use of the given if–then rules. For Type 3 and Type 4 inference problems characterized by consistent if–then rules, only the representation type of the input was adjusted to match that of the rule for building the reasoning method while maintaining the invariability of the consistent rule. For Types 5–8 inference problems with inconsistent if–then rules, a mixed representation rule was reinterpreted as two distinct single representation rules to construct specific reasoning methods. Therefore, the mixed rule needed to be converted differently twice, where each converted object involves only one of rule antecedent and rule consequent, and the input representation must be consistent with the representation of the converted rule. Subsequently, guided by the possibility and necessity operators as well as the quintuple-implication principle, the methods tailored to each type were developed, alongside the outputs in both fuzzy set representation and intuitionistic fuzzy set representation. The reductivity of the proposed methods for mixed information inference problems of Types 3–8 was also studied in detail. In addition, the proposed methods demonstrated significant effectiveness over the mixed information reasoning methods under the triple-implication principle and the same conversion operators in the multiple recognition tasks studied.

This paper primarily addresses the inference problem associated with mixed fuzzy and intuitionistic fuzzy information. When it comes to other types of hybrid information, the methods constructed in this paper will not work directly. Moreover, the methods in this paper are related to the conversion operators between fuzzy sets and intuitionistic fuzzy sets, and only the relatively simple conversion operations between the two are used, so the methods proposed in this paper have room for improvement. Possible directions for future work would be to study the mixed information reasoning methods induced by other conversion operators between fuzzy sets and intuitionistic fuzzy sets to overcome the limitations of the conversion operators employed in this paper, or to study the reasoning methods under the mixture of fuzzy and picture fuzzy information or the mixture of intuitionistic fuzzy and picture fuzzy information, leading to more interesting results.

Author Contributions: Conceptualization, N.Y., R.Z. and M.L.; Methodology, N.Y., R.Z. and M.L.; Validation, H.C.; Formal Analysis, N.Y., R.Z. and M.L.; Data Curation, H.C. and R.Z.; Writing—Original Draft and Editing, H.C.; Writing—Review and Editing, N.Y. and M.L.; Project Administration, M.L. All the authors have read and agreed to the published version of this manuscript.

Funding: This research was supported by the National Natural Science Foundation of China (Grant No. 12171445).

Data Availability Statement: Data is contained within the article.

Acknowledgments: The authors would like to thank the anonymous reviewers and editors for suggesting improvements for the article.

Conflicts of Interest: The authors declare no conflicts of interest.

References

1. Zadeh, L.A. Fuzzy sets. *Inf. Control* **1965**, *8*, 338–353. [CrossRef]
2. Atanassov, K.T. Intuitionistic fuzzy sets. *Fuzzy Sets Syst.* **1986**, *20*, 87–96. [CrossRef]
3. Wang, G.J. Full implicational triple I method for fuzzy reasoning. *Sci. China (Ser. E)* **1999**, *29*, 43–53.
4. Zadeh, L.A. Outline of a new approach to the analysis of complex systems and decision processes. *IEEE Trans. Syst. Man. Cybern* **1973**, *SMC-3*, 28–44. [CrossRef]
5. Wang, G.J. On the logic foundation of fuzzy reasoning. *Inf. Sci.* **1999**, *117*, 47–88. [CrossRef]
6. Pei, D.W. Unified full implication algorithms of fuzzy reasoning. *Inf. Sci.* **2008**, *178*, 520–530. [CrossRef]
7. Zhou, B.K.; Xu, G.Q.; Li, S.J. The quintuple implication principle of fuzzy reasoning. *Inf. Sci.* **2015**, *297*, 202–215. [CrossRef]
8. Luo, M.X.; Zhou, K.Y. Logical foundation of the quintuple implication inference methods. *Int. J. Approx. Reason.* **2018**, *101*, 1–9. [CrossRef]
9. Li, D.C.; Qin, S.J. Performance analysis of fuzzy systems based on quintuple implications method. *Int. J. Approx. Reason.* **2018**, *96*, 20–35. [CrossRef]
10. Cornelis, C.; Deschrijver, G.; Kerre, E.E. Implication in intuitionistic fuzzy and interval-valued fuzzy set theory: Construction, classification, application. *Int. J. Approx. Reason.* **2004**, *35*, 55–95. [CrossRef]
11. Zheng, M.C.; Shi, Z.K.; Liu, Y. Triple I method of approximate reasoning on Atanassov's intuitionistic fuzzy sets. *Int. J. Approx. Reason.* **2014**, *55*, 1369–1382. [CrossRef]
12. Li, J.S.; Gong, Z.T. SISO Intuitionistic Fuzzy Systems: IF- t -Norm, IF- R -Implication, and Universal Approximators. *IEEE Access* **2019**, *7*, 70265–70278. [CrossRef]
13. Duan, J.Y.; Li, X.Y. Similarity of intuitionistic fuzzy sets and its applications. *Int. J. Approx. Reason.* **2021**, *137*, 166–180. [CrossRef]
14. Zeng, S.L.; Lei, L.X. Quintuple implication principle on intuitionistic fuzzy sets. *Advanc. Artif. Intel. Secur.* **2022**, 575–589. [CrossRef]
15. Zheng, M.C.; Liu, Y. Fuzzy reasoning for mixture of fuzzy/intuitionistic fuzzy information based on Triple I method. *Symmetry* **2022**, *14*, 2184. [CrossRef]
16. Klement, E.P.; Mesiar, R.; Pap, E. *Triangular Norms*; Kluwer Academic Publishers: Dordrecht, The Netherlands, 2000.
17. Xu, Z.S. Intuitionistic Fuzzy Aggregation Operators. *IEEE T. Fuzzy Syst.* **2007**, *15*, 1179–1187. [CrossRef]
18. Iancu, I. Intuitionistic fuzzy similarity measures based on Frank t-norms family. *Pattern Recogn. Lett.* **2014**, *42*, 128–136. [CrossRef]
19. Kumar, R.; Kumar, S. An extended combined compromise solution framework based on novel intuitionistic fuzzy distance measure and score function with applications in sustainable biomass crop selection. *Expert Sys. Appl.* **2024**, *239*, 122345. [CrossRef]
20. De, S.K.; Biswas, R.; Roy, A.R. An application of intuitionistic fuzzy sets in medical diagnosis. *Fuzzy Sets Syst.* **2001**, *117*, 209–213. [CrossRef]
21. Vlachos, I.K.; Sergiadis, G.D. Intuitionistic fuzzy information—Applications to pattern recognition. *Pattern Recogn. Lett.* **2007**, *28*, 197–206. [CrossRef]
22. Luo, M.X.; Zhao, R.R.; Liang, J.J. Fuzzy reasoning full implication algorithms based on a class of interval-valued t-norms and its applications. *Eng. Appl. Artif. Intel.* **2024**, *133*, 108545. [CrossRef]
23. Wang, W.Q.; Xin, X.L. Distance measure between intuitionistic fuzzy sets. *Pattern Recogn. Lett.* **2005**, *26*, 2063–2069. [CrossRef]

Article

General Trapezoidal-Type Inequalities in Fuzzy Settings

Muhammad Amer Latif

Department of Mathematics, Faculty of Sciences, King Faisal University, Hofuf 31982, Saudi Arabia; mlatif@kfu.edu.sa

Abstract: In this study, trapezoidal-type inequalities in fuzzy settings have been investigated. The theory of fuzzy analysis has been discussed in detail. The integration by parts formula of analysis of fuzzy mathematics has been employed to establish an equality. Trapezoidal-type inequality for functions with values in the fuzzy number-valued space is proven by applying the proven equality together with the properties of a metric defined on the set of fuzzy number-valued space and Höler's inequality. The results proved in this research provide generalizations of the results from earlier existing results in the field of mathematical inequalities. An example is designed by defining a function that has values in fuzzy number-valued space and validated the results numerically using the software Mathematica (latest v. 14.1). The p-levels of the defined fuzzy number-valued mapping have been shown graphically for different values of $p \in [0, 1]$.

Keywords: trapezoidal inequality; fuzzy real number; fuzzy trapezoidal-type inequality; Banach spaces; gH-differentiable function

MSC: 26D15; 26A51

Citation: Latif, M.A. General Trapezoidal-Type Inequalities in Fuzzy Settings. *Mathematics* **2024**, 12, 3112. https://doi.org/10.3390/math12193112

Academic Editors: Changyou Wang, Dong Qiu and Yonghong Shen

Received: 16 August 2024
Revised: 19 September 2024
Accepted: 24 September 2024
Published: 4 October 2024

Copyright: © 2024 by the author. Licensee MDPI, Basel, Switzerland. This article is an open access article distributed under the terms and conditions of the Creative Commons Attribution (CC BY) license (https://creativecommons.org/licenses/by/4.0/).

1. Introduction

Mathematical inequalities play an important role in proving several results in different areas of pure and applied mathematics. That is why this topic has emerged as an important topic in mathematics over the past several years, and mathematicians have successfully applied this subject to provide new generalizations, refine existing results, and even prove new results.

In classical analysis, a trapezoidal-type inequality is an inequality that provides upper and/or lower bounds for the quantity:

$$\frac{\nu(k) + \nu(\ell)}{2}(\ell - k) - \int_k^\ell \nu(t)dt, \tag{1}$$

that is the error in approximating the integral by a trapezoidal rule, for various classes of integrable functions ν defined on the compact interval $[k, \ell]$.

Cerone et al. obtained trapezoidal-type inequalities for functions of bounded variation in [1].

Theorem 1 ([1]). *Let $\nu : [k, \ell] \to \mathbb{C}$ be a function of bounded variation. We have the inequality*

$$\left| \int_k^\ell \nu(t) dt - \frac{\nu(k) + \nu(\ell)}{2}(\ell - k) \right| \leq \frac{1}{2}(\ell - k) \bigvee_k^\ell (\nu), \tag{2}$$

where $\bigvee_k^\ell (\nu)$ denotes the total variation of ν on the interval $[k, \ell]$. The constant $\frac{1}{2}$ is the best possible one.

If the mapping ν is Lipschitzian, then the following result holds as well [2].

Theorem 2 ([2]). *Let $\nu : [k,\ell] \to \mathbb{C}$ be an L-Lipschitzian function on $[k,\ell]$, i.e., ν satisfies the condition:*

$$|\nu(t) - \nu(s)| \leq L|t-s|^{u}$$

for all $t, s \in [k,\ell], L > 0$. Then, we have the inequality:

$$\left| \int_k^\ell \nu(t)dt - \frac{\nu(k)+\nu(\ell)}{2}(\ell - k) \right| \leq \frac{1}{4}(\ell - k)^2 L. \tag{3}$$

The constant $\frac{1}{4}$ is best in (3).

With the assumption of absolute continuity for the function ν, then the following estimates in terms of the Lebesgue norms of the derivative ν' hold [3] (p. 93).

Theorem 3 ([3]). *Let $\nu : [k,\ell] \to \mathbb{C}$ be an absolutely continuous function on $[k,\ell]$. Then, we have*

$$\left| \int_k^\ell \nu(t)dt - \frac{\nu(k)+\nu(\ell)}{2}(\ell - k) \right| \leq \begin{cases} \frac{1}{4}(\ell-k)^2 \|\nu'\|_\infty, & \text{if } \nu' \in L_\infty[k,\ell], \\ \frac{1}{2(r+1)^{\frac{1}{r}}}(\ell-k)^{1+\frac{1}{r}} \|\nu'\|_w, & \text{if } \nu' \in L_w[k,\ell], \\ \frac{1}{2}(\ell-k)\|\nu'\|_1, & \end{cases} \tag{4}$$

where $w, r > 1$ with $\frac{1}{w} + \frac{1}{r} = 1$ and $\|\cdot\|_w$ ($w \in [1,\infty]$) are the Lebesgue norms, i.e.,

$$\|\nu'\|_\infty = ess \sup_{s\in[k,\ell]} |\nu'(s)|$$

and

$$\|\nu'\|_w := \left(\int_k^\ell |\nu'(s)|^w ds \right)^{\frac{1}{w}}, w \geq 1.$$

The next is a result on trapezoidal-type inequalities for operator convex functions.

Definition 1 ([4]). *A continuous function $\nu : I \to \mathbb{R}$ is operator convex on the interval I if*

$$\nu((1-t)A + tB) \leq (1-t)\nu(A) + t\nu(B) \tag{5}$$

holds in the operator order, for all $t \in [0,1]$, where A and B are self-adjoint operators in a Hilbert space $(H, \langle\cdot,\cdot\rangle)$ with spectra $Sp(A), Sp(B) \subset I$.

Theorem 4 ([4]). *Let $\nu : C \subset E \to F$ (E, F are Banach spaces and C is an open subset of E) be an operator convex function on I and $A, B, A \neq B$, self-adjoint operators on H with $Sp(A), Sp(B) \subset I$. If ν is Gâteaux differentiable on $V = [A,B] := \{(1-t)A + tB, t \in [0,1]\}$ and $\varphi : [0,1] \to [0,\infty)$ is Lebesgue integrable and symmetric about $\frac{1}{2}$, that is $\varphi(1-t) = \varphi(t)$ for all $t \in [0,1]$, then*

$$\begin{aligned} 0 &\leq \left(\int_0^1 \varphi(t)dt \right) \frac{\nu(A)+\nu(B)}{2} - \int_0^1 \varphi(t)\nu((1-t)A + tB)dt \\ &\leq \frac{1}{2} \int_0^1 \left(\frac{1}{2} - \left| t - \frac{1}{2} \right| \right) \varphi(t)dt [\nabla\nu_B(B-A) - \nabla\nu_A(B-A)], \end{aligned} \tag{6}$$

where $\nabla\nu_B(V)$ is the Gâteaux derivative over C in the direction V connecting the operators A and B.

A particular result of the above result can be obtained by taking for $\varphi \equiv 1$. Hence, for $\varphi \equiv 1$, we obtain

$$0 \leq \frac{\nu(A)+\nu(B)}{2} - \int_0^1 \nu((1-t)A+tB)dt \leq \frac{1}{8}[\nabla\nu_B(B-A) - \nabla\nu_A(B-A)]. \quad (7)$$

For some trapezoid operator inequalities in Hilbert spaces, see [5–8].

Definition 2 ([9]). *Let X be a complex Banach space. We say that the vector valued function $\nu : [k,\ell] \to X$ is strongly differentiable on the interval (k,ℓ) if the limit*

$$\nu'(t) = \lim_{h\to 0} \frac{\nu(t+h)-\nu(t)}{h}$$

exists in the norm topology for all $t \in (k,\ell)$.

The following weighted version of generalized trapezoid inequality involving two functions with one function that contains values in Banach spaces was proven in Dragomir [9].

Theorem 5 ([10]). *Assume that $\varphi : [k,\ell] \to \mathbb{C}$ and $\nu : [k,\ell] \to X$ are continuous and ν is strongly differentiable on (k,ℓ), then for all $\lambda \in [k,\ell]$, then we have the following inequality:*

$$\left\| \left(\int_\lambda^\ell \varphi(s)ds\right)\nu(\ell) + \left(\int_k^\lambda \varphi(s)ds\right)\nu(k) - \int_k^\ell \varphi(t)\nu(t)dt \right\| \leq C(\varphi,\nu,\lambda), \quad (8)$$

where

$$C(\varphi,\nu,\lambda) := \int_\lambda^\ell \left(\int_\lambda^t |\varphi(s)|ds\right) \|\nu'(t)\|dt + \int_k^\lambda \left(\int_t^\lambda |\varphi(s)|ds\right) \|\nu'(t)\|dt.$$

Moreover, the following bounds for $C(\varphi,\nu,\lambda)$ hold:

$$C(\varphi,\nu,\lambda) \leq \begin{cases} \left(\int_\lambda^\ell |\varphi(s)|ds\right)\left(\int_\lambda^\ell \|\nu'(t)\|dt\right) + \left(\int_k^\lambda |\varphi(s)|ds\right)\left(\int_k^\lambda \|\nu'(t)\|dt\right), \\[2mm] \left[\int_\lambda^\ell \left(\int_\lambda^t |\varphi(s)|ds\right)^w dt\right]^{\frac{1}{w}} \left(\int_\lambda^\ell \|\nu'(t)\|^r dt\right)^{\frac{1}{r}} \\ \quad + \left[\int_k^\lambda \left(\int_t^\lambda |\varphi(s)|ds\right)^w dt\right]^{\frac{1}{w}} \left(\int_k^\lambda \|\nu'(t)\|^r dt\right)^{\frac{1}{r}}, \\[2mm] \left[\int_\lambda^\ell \left(\int_\lambda^t |\varphi(s)|ds\right)dt\right] \sup_{t\in[\lambda,\ell]} \|\nu'(t)\| \\ \quad + \left[\int_k^\lambda \left(\int_t^\lambda |\varphi(s)|ds\right)dt\right] \sup_{t\in[k,\lambda]} \|\nu'(t)\|, \end{cases} \quad (9)$$

where $w,r > 1$ with $\frac{1}{w} + \frac{1}{r} = 1$.

A dual result for Theorem 5 is given as follows:

Theorem 6 ([9]). *Assume that $\varphi : [k,\ell] \to \mathbb{C}$ and $\nu : [k,\ell] \to X$ are continuous and φ is continuously differentiable on (k,ℓ), then for all $\lambda \in [k,\ell]$ the inequality*

$$\left\| \left(\int_\lambda^\ell \nu(s)ds\right)\varphi(\ell) + \left(\int_k^\lambda \nu(s)ds\right)\varphi(k) - \int_k^\ell \varphi(t)\nu(t)dt \right\| \leq \tilde{C}(\varphi,\nu,\lambda), \quad (10)$$

where
$$\tilde{C}(\varphi,\nu,\lambda) \leq \int_\lambda^\ell \left(\int_\lambda^t \|\nu(s)\|ds\right)|\varphi'(t)|dt + \int_k^\lambda \left(\int_t^\lambda \|\nu(s)\|ds\right)|\varphi'(t)|dt$$

The following bounds hold for $\tilde{C}(\varphi,\nu,\lambda)$*:*

$$\tilde{C}(\varphi,\nu,\lambda) \leq \begin{cases} \int_\lambda^\ell \|\nu(s)\|ds \int_\lambda^\ell |\varphi'(t)|dt + \int_k^\lambda |\nu(s)|ds \int_k^\lambda |\varphi'(t)|dt, \\ \left[\int_\lambda^\ell \left(\int_\lambda^t \|\nu(s)\|ds\right)^w dt\right]^{\frac{1}{w}} \left(\int_\lambda^\ell |\varphi'(t)|^r dt\right)^{\frac{1}{r}} \\ \quad + \left[\int_k^\lambda \left(\int_t^\lambda \|\nu(s)\|ds\right)^w dt\right]^{\frac{1}{w}} \left(\int_k^\lambda |\varphi'(t)|^r dt\right)^{\frac{1}{r}}, \\ \sup\limits_{t\in[\lambda,\ell]} |\varphi'(s)| \int_\lambda^\ell \left(\int_\lambda^t \|\nu(s)\|ds\right)dt \\ \quad + \sup\limits_{t\in[k,\lambda]} |\varphi'(s)| \int_k^\lambda \left(\int_t^\lambda \|\nu(s)\|ds\right)dt, \end{cases} \quad (11)$$

where $w, r > 1$ *with* $\frac{1}{w} + \frac{1}{r} = 1$.

This study contains trapezoidal-type inequalities for fuzzy number-valued functions that can be seen as the most general inequalities of the trapezoidal type in this field so far. The inequalities proven in this paper not only generalize the earlier studies for trapezoidal-type inequalities for functions having values in the set of real numbers but also extend those studies that have been established for functions with values in Banach spaces. The results of this paper extend the results of Theorems 5 and 6 to fuzzy settings and hence also generalize the results of Theorem 3. The novelty of the results presented in this study is that they have not been previously investigated in any studies related to fuzzy environments. The researchers can uncover significant extensions and numerous applications in the mathematical sciences and other areas of science related to fuzzy mathematics. More recent studies on Ostrowski-, trapezoidal-, and midpoint-type inequalities can be explored in [11–20] and the references cited in these researches.

The next section is devoted to the basic definitions and results of fuzzy numbers and fuzzy number-valued functions.

2. Preliminaries

In this section we point out some basic definitions and results which would help us in the sequel of this paper, we begin with the following:

Definition 3 ([21])**.** *Let us denote by* $\mathbb{R}_\mathcal{F}$ *the class of fuzzy subsets of real axis* $\mathbb{R}$ *(i.e.,* $\alpha : \mathbb{R} \longrightarrow [0,1]$*), satisfying the following properties:*

(i) $\forall \alpha \in \mathbb{R}_\mathcal{F}$*,* α *is normal, i.e., with* $\alpha(\tau) = 1$ *for some* $\tau \in \mathbb{R}$*.*
(ii) $\forall \alpha \in \mathbb{R}_\mathcal{F}$*,* α *is convex fuzzy set, i.e.,*

$$\alpha(t\tau + (1-t)\overline{\tau}) \geq \min\{\alpha(\tau), \alpha(\overline{\tau})\}, \forall t \in [0,1], \forall \tau, \overline{\tau} \in \mathbb{R}.$$

(iii) $\forall\ \alpha \in \mathbb{R}_\mathcal{F}$*,* α *is upper semi-continuous on* $\mathbb{R}$*.*
(iv) $\overline{\{\tau \in \mathbb{R} : \alpha(\tau) > 0\}}$ *is compact.*
The set $\mathbb{R}_\mathcal{F}$ *is called the space of fuzzy real numbers.*

Remark 1. *It is clear that* $\mathbb{R} \subset \mathbb{R}_\mathcal{F}$*, because any real number* $\tau_0 \in \mathbb{R}$*, can be described as the fuzzy number whose value is 1 for* $\tau = \tau_0$ *and zero otherwise.*

It is clear that $\mathbb{R} \subset \mathbb{R}_{\mathcal{F}}$, because any real number $\tau_0 \in \mathbb{R}$, can be described as the fuzzy number whose value is 1 for $\tau = \tau_0$ and zero otherwise. We will collect some further definitions and notations as needed in the sequel [22].

For $0 < p \leq 1$ and $\alpha \in \mathbb{R}_F$, we define

$$[\alpha]^p = \{\tau \in \mathbb{R} : \alpha(\tau) \geq p\}$$

and

$$[\alpha]^0 = \overline{\{\tau \in \mathbb{R} : \alpha(\tau) > 0\}}.$$

Now, it is well known that for each $p \in [0,1]$, $[\alpha]^p$, is a bounded closed interval. For $\alpha, \gamma \in \mathbb{R}_{\mathcal{F}}$ and $\lambda \in \mathbb{R}$, we have the sum $\alpha \oplus \gamma$ and the product $\lambda \odot \alpha$ are defined by $[\alpha \oplus \gamma]^p = [\alpha]^p + [\gamma]^p$, $[\lambda \odot \alpha]^p = \lambda[\alpha]^p$, $\forall p \in [0,1]$, where $[\alpha]^p + [\gamma]^p$ means the usual addition of two intervals as subsets of $\mathbb{R}$ and $\lambda[\alpha]^p$ means the usual product between a scalar and a subset of $\mathbb{R}$. It should be noted that the intervals $[\alpha \oplus \gamma]^p$ and $[\lambda \odot \alpha]^p$ uniquely determine the sum $\alpha \oplus \gamma$ of fuzzy numbers α and γ, and the product $\lambda \odot \alpha$ of a real number λ and a fuzzy number α.
Now, we define $\mathcal{D} : \mathbb{R}_{\mathcal{F}} \times \mathbb{R}_{\mathcal{F}} \longrightarrow \mathbb{R} \cup \{0\}$ by

$$\mathcal{D}(\alpha, \gamma) = \sup_{p \in [0,1]} \left(\max\left\{ \left|\alpha_-^p - \gamma_-^p\right|, \left|\alpha_+^p - \gamma_+^p\right| \right\} \right),$$

where $[\alpha]^p = \left[\alpha_-^p, \alpha_+^p\right]$, $[\gamma]^p = \left[\gamma_-^p, \gamma_+^p\right]$, then $(\mathcal{D}, \mathbb{R}_{\mathcal{F}})$ is a metric space and it possesses the following properties:

(i) $\mathcal{D}(\alpha \oplus \beta, \gamma \oplus \beta) = \mathcal{D}(\alpha, \gamma), \forall \alpha, \gamma, \beta \in \mathbb{R}_{\mathcal{F}}$.
(ii) $\mathcal{D}(\lambda \odot \alpha, \lambda \odot \gamma) = \lambda \mathcal{D}(\alpha, \gamma), \forall \alpha, \gamma \in \mathbb{R}_{\mathcal{F}}, \forall \lambda \in \mathbb{R}$.
(iii) $\mathcal{D}(\alpha \oplus \gamma, \beta \oplus e) \leq \mathcal{D}(\alpha, \beta) + \mathcal{D}(\gamma, e), \forall \alpha, \gamma, \beta, e \in \mathbb{R}_{\mathcal{F}}$

Moreover, it is well known that $(\mathbb{R}_{\mathcal{F}}, \mathcal{D})$ is a complete metric space.
Also we have the following theorem:

Theorem 7 ([23]). *We have the following properties of a fuzzy number:*

(i) *If we denote* $\tilde{o} = \mathcal{X}_{\{0\}}$, *then* $\tilde{o} \in \mathbb{R}_{\mathcal{F}}$ *is neutral element with respect to* $\oplus$, *i.e.,* $\alpha \oplus \tilde{o} = \tilde{o} \oplus \alpha$, *for all* $\alpha \in \mathbb{R}_{\mathcal{F}}$.
(ii) *With respect to* $\tilde{0}$ *none of* $\alpha \in \mathbb{R}_{\mathcal{F}} \backslash \mathbb{R}$ *has opposite in* $\mathbb{R}_{\mathcal{F}}$ *with respect to* $\oplus$.
(iii) *For any* $k, \ell \in \mathbb{R}$ *with* $k, \ell \geq 0$ *or* $k, \ell \leq 0$, *any* $\alpha \in \mathbb{R}_{\mathcal{F}}$, *we have* $(k + \ell) \odot \alpha = k \odot \alpha \oplus \ell \odot \alpha \forall k, \ell \in \mathbb{R}$ *the above property does not hold.*
(iv) *For any* $\lambda \in \mathbb{R}$ *and any* $\alpha, \gamma \in \mathbb{R}_{\mathcal{F}}$, *we have* $\lambda \odot (\alpha \oplus \gamma) = \lambda \odot \alpha \oplus \lambda \odot \gamma$.
(v) *For any* $\lambda, \mu \in \mathbb{R}$ *and any* $\alpha \in \mathbb{R}_{\mathcal{F}}$, *we have* $\lambda \odot (\mu \odot \gamma) = (\lambda \cdot \mu) \odot \gamma$.
(vi) *If we denote* $\|\alpha\|_{\mathcal{F}} = \mathcal{D}(\alpha, \tilde{o})$, $\forall \alpha \in \mathbb{R}_{\mathcal{F}}$ *then* $\|.\|_{\mathcal{F}}$ *has the properties of a usual norm on* $\mathbb{R}_{\mathcal{F}}$, *i.e.,* $\|\alpha\|_{\mathcal{F}} = 0$ *if and only if* $\alpha = \tilde{o}$, $\|\lambda \odot \alpha\|_{\mathcal{F}} = |\lambda| \cdot \|\alpha\|_{\mathcal{F}}$ *and* $\|\alpha \oplus \gamma\|_{\mathcal{F}} \leq \|\alpha\|_{\mathcal{F}} + \|\gamma\|_{\mathcal{F}}, |\|\alpha\|_{\mathcal{F}} - \|\gamma\|_{\mathcal{F}}| \leq \mathcal{D}(\alpha, \gamma)$.

Remark 2. *The propositions (ii) and (iii) in theorem show us that* $(\mathbb{R}_{\mathcal{F}}, \oplus, \odot)$ *is not a vector space over* $\mathbb{R}$ *and consequently* $(\mathbb{R}_{\mathcal{F}}, \|\cdot\|_{\mathcal{F}})$ *cannot be a normed space. However, the properties of D and those in theorem (iv)–(vi), have the effect that most of the metric properties of functions defined as* $\mathbb{R}$ *with values in a Banach space can be extended to functions* $v : \mathbb{R} \longrightarrow \mathbb{R}_{\mathcal{F}}$, *called fuzzy number-valued functions.*

In this paper, for the ranking concept, we will use a partial ordering which was introduced in [24].

Definition 4 ([24]). *Let the partial ordering $\preccurlyeq$ in $\mathbb{R}_{\mathcal{F}}$ by $\alpha \preccurlyeq \gamma$ if and only if $\alpha_-^p \leq \gamma_-^p$ and $\alpha_+^p \leq \gamma_+^p$, $\forall p \in [0,1]$, and the strict inequality $\prec$ in $\mathbb{R}_{\mathcal{F}}$ is defined by $\alpha \prec \gamma$ if and only if $\alpha_-^p < \gamma_-^p$ and $\alpha_+^p < \gamma_+^p$, $\forall p \in [0,1]$, where $[\alpha]^p = \left[\alpha_-^p, \alpha_+^p\right], [\gamma]^p = \left[\gamma_-^p, \gamma_+^p\right]$.*

Definition 5 ([25]). *Let $\tau, \overline{\tau} \in \mathbb{R}_{\mathcal{F}}$. If there exists a $z \in \mathbb{R}_{\mathcal{F}}$ such that $\tau = \overline{\tau} \oplus z$, then we call z the H-difference of τ and $\overline{\tau}$, denoted by $z = \tau \ominus \overline{\tau}$.*

Definition 6 ([26]). *Given two fuzzy numbers $\alpha, \gamma \in \mathbb{R}_{\mathcal{F}}$, the generalized Hukuhara difference (φH-difference for short) is the fuzzy number β, if it exists, such that*

$$\alpha \ominus_{\varphi H} \gamma = \beta \Longleftrightarrow \begin{cases} (i)\ \alpha = \gamma \oplus \beta, \\ \\ or\ (ii)\ \alpha = \gamma \oplus (-1)\beta. \end{cases}$$

Remark 3. *It is easy to show that (i) and (ii) are both valid if and only if β is a crisp number.*

In terms of p-levels, we have

$$\left[\alpha \ominus_{\varphi H} \gamma\right]^p = \left[\min\left\{\alpha_-^p - \gamma_-^p, \alpha_+^p - \gamma_+^p\right\}, \max\left\{\alpha_-^p - \gamma_-^p, \alpha_+^p - \gamma_+^p\right\}\right],$$

and the conditions for the existence of $\beta = \alpha \ominus_{\varphi H} \gamma \in \mathbb{R}_{\mathcal{F}}$ are as follows:

$$\text{Case (i)} \begin{cases} \beta_-^p = \alpha_-^p - \gamma_-^p \text{ and } \beta_+^p = \alpha_+^p - \gamma_+^p\ \forall p \in [0,1], \\ \\ \text{with } \beta_-^p \text{ increasing w.r.t } p,\ \beta_+^p \text{ decreasing w.r.t } p,\ \beta_-^p \leq \beta_+^p. \end{cases}$$

$$\text{Case (ii)} \begin{cases} \beta_+^p = \alpha_+^p - \gamma_+^p \text{ and } \beta_-^p = \alpha_-^p - \gamma_-^p\ \forall p \in [0,1], \\ \\ \text{with } \beta_-^p \text{ increasing w.r.t } p,\ \beta_+^p \text{ decreasing w.r.t } p,\ \beta_-^p \leq \beta_+^p. \end{cases}$$

If the φH-difference $\alpha \ominus_{\varphi H} \gamma$ does not define a proper fuzzy number, the nested property can be used for p-levels and obtain a proper fuzzy number by

$$\left[\alpha \ominus_{\varphi} \gamma\right]^p = \overline{\bigcup_{p_0 \geq p} \left([\alpha]^{p_0} \ominus_{\varphi H} [\gamma]^{p_0}\right)}, p \in [0,1],$$

where $\alpha \ominus_{\varphi} \gamma$ defines the generalized difference of two fuzzy numbers $\alpha, \gamma \in \mathbb{R}_{\mathcal{F}}$ defined in [25], and extended and studied in [26].

Remark 4. *Throughout this paper, we assume that if $\alpha, \gamma \in \mathbb{R}_{\mathcal{F}}$, then $\alpha \ominus_{\varphi H} \gamma \in \mathbb{R}_{\mathcal{F}}$.*

Proposition 1 ([27]). *For $\alpha, \gamma \in \mathbb{R}_{\mathcal{F}}$, we have*

$$\mathcal{D}\left(\alpha \ominus_{\varphi H} \gamma, \widetilde{o}\right) \leq \mathcal{D}(\alpha, \gamma).$$

Proposition 2 ([25]). *Let $\alpha, \gamma \in \mathbb{R}_{\mathcal{F}}$. If $\alpha \ominus_{\varphi H} \gamma$ exists in the sense of Definition 6, it is unique and has the following properties ($\widetilde{o}$ denotes the crisp set $\{0\}$):*

(i) $\alpha \ominus_{\varphi H} \alpha = \widetilde{o}$.
(ii) *(a)* $(\alpha \oplus \gamma) \ominus_{\varphi H} \gamma = \alpha$, *(b)* $\alpha \ominus_{\varphi H} (\alpha \ominus \gamma) = \gamma$.
(iii) *If $\alpha \ominus_{\varphi H} \gamma$ exists then also $(-\gamma) \ominus_{\varphi H} (-\alpha)$ does and $\widetilde{o} \ominus_{\varphi H} (\alpha \ominus_{\varphi H} \gamma) = (-\gamma) \ominus_{\varphi H} (-\alpha)$.*
(iv) *If $\alpha \ominus_{\varphi H} \gamma$ exists, then $\gamma \ominus_{\varphi H} \alpha$ exists and $\alpha \ominus_{\varphi H} \gamma = -\left(\gamma \ominus_{\varphi H} \alpha\right)$.*
(v) *$\alpha \ominus_{\varphi H} \gamma$ exists if and only if $\gamma \ominus_{\varphi H} \alpha$ and $(-\gamma) \ominus_{\varphi H} (-\alpha)$ exist and $\alpha \ominus_{\varphi H} \gamma = (-\gamma) \ominus_{\varphi H} (-\alpha) = -\left(\gamma \ominus_{\varphi H} \alpha\right)$.*
(vi) *$\alpha \ominus_{\varphi H} \gamma = \gamma \ominus_{\varphi H} \alpha = \beta$ if and only if $\beta = -\beta$ (in particular $\beta = \widetilde{o}$ if and only if $\alpha = \gamma$).*

(vii) *If* $\gamma \ominus_{\varphi H} \alpha$ *exists then either* $\alpha \oplus (\gamma \ominus_{\varphi H} \alpha) = \alpha$ *or* $\gamma \ominus (\gamma \ominus_{\varphi H} \alpha) = \alpha$ *and if both equalities hold then* $\gamma \ominus_{\varphi H} \alpha$ *is a crisp set* $\widetilde{o}$.

Definition 7 ([25])**.** *Let* $\alpha, \gamma \in \mathbb{R}_{\mathcal{F}}$ *have p-levels* $[\alpha]^p = \left[\alpha_-^p, \alpha_+^p\right], [\gamma]^p = \left[\gamma_-^p, \gamma_+^p\right]$, *with* $\widetilde{o} \notin [\gamma]^p, \forall p \in [0,1]$. *The* φH*-division* $\div_{\varphi H}$ *is the operation that calculates the fuzzy number (if it exists)* $\beta = \alpha \div_{\varphi H} \gamma \in \mathbb{R}_{\mathcal{F}}$ *defining by*

$$\alpha \div \varphi H \gamma = \beta \Leftrightarrow \begin{cases} (i)\ \alpha = \gamma \odot \beta, \\ or\ (ii)\ \gamma = \alpha \odot \beta^{-1}, \end{cases}$$

provided that β *is a proper fuzzy number.*

Proposition 3 ([25])**.** *Let* $\alpha, \gamma \in \mathbb{R}_{\mathcal{F}}$ *(here* 1 *is the same as* $\{1\}$*). We have the following:*

(i) *If* $\widetilde{o} \notin [\alpha]^p, \forall p$, *then* $\alpha \div_{\varphi H} \alpha = 1$.
(ii) *If* $\widetilde{o} \notin [\gamma]^p, \forall p$, *then* $\alpha\gamma \div_{\varphi H} \gamma = \alpha$.
(iii) *If* $\widetilde{o} \notin [\gamma]^p, \forall p$, *then* $1 \div_{\varphi H} \gamma = \gamma^{-1}$ *and* $1 \div_{\varphi H} \gamma^{-1} = \gamma$.
(iv) *If* $\gamma \div_{\varphi H} \alpha$ *exists then either* $\alpha(\gamma \div_{\varphi H} \alpha) = \gamma$ *or* $\gamma(\gamma \div_{\varphi H} \alpha)^{-1} = \alpha$ *and both equalities hold if and only if* $\gamma \div_{\varphi H} \alpha$ *is a crisp set.*

Remark 5. *Let* $\nu : [k, \ell] \to \mathbb{R}_{\mathcal{F}}$ *be a fuzzy-valued function. Then, the p-level representation of* ν *given by* $\nu(\tau; p) = [\underline{\nu}(\tau; p), \overline{\nu}(\tau; p)]$, $\tau \in [k, \ell], p \in [0,1]$. *Here,* $\underline{\nu}(\tau; p)$ *and* $\overline{\nu}(\tau; p)$ *are the lower and upper p-level representations for all* $\tau \in [k, \ell]$ *and* $p \in [0,1]$.

Definition 8 ([28])**.** *Let* $\nu : [k, \ell] \to \mathbb{R}_{\mathcal{F}}$ *be a fuzzy-valued function and* $\tau_0 \in [k, \ell]$. *If* $\forall \varepsilon > 0$, $\exists$ $\delta > 0$, *such that* $\forall\ \tau$

$$0 < |\tau - \tau_0| < \delta \Rightarrow \mathcal{D}(\nu(\tau), L) < \varepsilon,$$

then we say that $L \in \mathbb{R}_{\mathcal{F}}$ *is limit of* ν *in* τ_0, *which is denoted by* $\lim\limits_{\tau \to \tau_0} \nu(\tau) = L$.

Definition 9 ([28])**.** *A function* $\nu : \mathbb{R} \longrightarrow \mathbb{R}_{\mathcal{F}}$ *is said to be continuous at* $\tau_0 \in \mathbb{R}$ *if for every* $\varepsilon > 0$ *we can find* $\delta > 0$ *such that* $\mathcal{D}(\nu(\tau), \nu(\tau_0)) < \varepsilon$, *whenever* $|\tau - \tau_0| < \delta$. ν *is said to be continuous on* $\mathbb{R}$ *if it is continuous at every* $\tau_0 \in \mathbb{R}$. *We say that* ν *is continuous at each* $\tau_0 \in [k, \ell]$ *if it is continuous at each* $\tau_0 \in (k, \ell)$ *such that the continuity of* ν *is one-sided at end points* k, ℓ.

Lemma 1 ([29])**.** *For any* $k, \ell \in \mathbb{R}$, $k, \ell \geq 0$ *and* $\alpha \in \mathbb{R}_{\mathcal{F}}$, *we have*

$$\mathcal{D}(k \odot \alpha, \ell \odot \alpha) \leq |k - \ell| \mathcal{D}(\alpha, \widetilde{o}),$$

where $\widetilde{o} \in \mathbb{R}_{\mathcal{F}}$ *is defined by* $\widetilde{o} := \mathcal{X}_{\{0\}}$.

Definition 10 ([26])**.** *Let* $\tau_0 \in (k, \ell)$ *and* h *be such that* $\tau_0 + h \in (k, \ell)$, *then the* φH*-derivative of a function* $\nu : (k, \ell) \to \mathbb{R}_{\mathcal{F}}$ *at* τ_0 *is defined as*

$$\nu'_{\varphi H}(\tau_0) = \lim_{h \to 0^+} \frac{\nu(\tau_0 + h) \ominus_{\varphi H} \nu(\tau_0)}{h}$$

If $\nu'_{\varphi H}(\tau_0) \in \mathbb{R}_{\mathcal{F}}$ *in the sense of Definition 3, we say that* ν *is generalized Hukuhara differentiable (*φH*-differentiable for short) at* τ_0.

Definition 11 ([26])**.** *Let* $\nu : [k, \ell] \to \mathbb{R}_{\mathcal{F}}$ *and* $\tau_0 \in (k, \ell)$, *with* $\underline{\nu}(\tau; p)$ *and* $\overline{\nu}(\tau; p)$ *both differentiable at* τ_0, *where* $\underline{\nu}(\tau; p)$ *and* $\overline{\nu}(\tau; p)$ *are p-level representations of* $\nu(\tau; p)$ *for* $p \in [0,1]$. *Then the function* $\nu(\tau; p)$ *is* φH*-differentiable at a fixed* $\tau_0 \in (k, \ell)$ *if and only if one of the following two cases holds:*

(i) $(\underline{\nu})'(\tau_0; p)$ is increasing and $(\overline{\nu})'(\tau_0; p)$ is decreasing as functions of r and

$$(\underline{\nu})'(\tau_0; p) \leq (\overline{\nu})'(\tau_0; p), 0 \leq p \leq 1 \text{ or} \tag{12}$$

(ii) $(\overline{\nu})'(\tau_0; p)$ is increasing and $(\underline{\nu})'(\tau_0; p)$ is decreasing as functions of p and

$$(\overline{\nu})'(\tau_0; p) \leq (\underline{\nu})'(\tau_0; p), 0 \leq p \leq 1. \tag{13}$$

Moreover, for all $p \in [0, 1]$

$$(\nu)'_{\varphi H}(\tau_0; p) = \Big[\min\Big\{(\underline{\nu})'(\tau_0; p), (\overline{\nu})'(\tau_0; p)\Big\}, \max\Big\{(\underline{\nu})'(\tau_0; p) \leq (\overline{\nu})'(\tau_0; p)\Big\}\Big].$$

Definition 12 ([27]). *We say that a point* $\tau_0 \in (k, \ell)$, *is a switching point for the differentiability of* ν, *if in any neighborhood* V *of* τ_0 *there exist points* $\tau_1 < \tau_0 < \tau_2$ *such that*

type (i): at τ_1 (12) holds while (13) does not hold and at τ_2 (13) holds and (12) does not hold, or
type (ii): at τ_1 (13) holds while (12) does not hold and at τ_2 (12) holds and (13) does not hold.

Definition 13 ([28]). *Let* $\nu : (k, \ell) \to \mathbb{R}_{\mathcal{F}}$ *be* φH*-differentiable at* $c \in (k, \ell)$. *Then* ν *is fuzzy continuous at* c.

Theorem 8 ([28]). *Let* I *be closed interval in* $\mathbb{R}$. *Let* $\varphi : I \to \phi := \varphi(I) \subseteq \mathbb{R}$ *be differentiable at* τ, *and* $\nu : \phi \to \mathbb{R}_{\mathcal{F}}$ *be* φH*-differentiable* $\alpha = \varphi(\tau)$. *Assume that* φ *is strictly increasing on* I. *Then,* $(\nu \circ \varphi)'_{\varphi H}(\tau)$ *exists and*

$$(\nu \circ \varphi)'_{\varphi H}(\tau) = \nu'_{\varphi H}(\varphi(\tau)) \odot \varphi'(\tau), \forall \tau \in I.$$

Definition 14 ([22]). *Let* $\nu : [k, \ell] \longrightarrow \mathbb{R}_{\mathcal{F}}$. *We say that* ν *is a fuzzy Riemann integrable if the* $\sum^*(\gamma - \alpha) \odot \nu(\xi)$ *converges to* $I \in \mathbb{R}_{\mathcal{F}}$ *in the metric topology* $\mathcal{D}$ *of* $\mathbb{R}_{\mathcal{F}}$ *for any division* $P = \{[\alpha, \gamma]; \xi\}$ *of* $[k, \ell]$, *that is,* ν *is fuzzy Riemann integrable for every* $\varepsilon > 0$, *there exists* $\delta > 0$ *such that for any division* $P = \{[\alpha, \gamma]; \xi\}$ *of* $[k, \ell]$ *with the norms* $\Delta(P) < \delta$, *we have*

$$\mathcal{D}\left(\sum_P^*(\gamma - \alpha) \odot \nu(\xi), I\right) < \varepsilon,$$

where $\sum_P^*$ *denotes the fuzzy summation. We choose to write*

$$I := (FR)\int_k^\ell \nu(\tau)d\tau.$$

We also call a ν *as above* (FR)*-integrable.*

Theorem 9 ([30]). *Let* $\nu : [k, \ell] \longrightarrow \mathbb{R}_{\mathcal{F}}$ *be integrable and* $c \in [k, \ell]$. *Then,*

$$\int_k^\ell \nu(\tau)d\tau = \int_k^c \nu(\tau)d\tau \oplus \int_c^\ell \nu(\tau)d\tau.$$

Corollary 1 ([22]). *If* $\nu \in C([k, \ell], \mathbb{R}_{\mathcal{F}})$ *then* ν *is* (FR)*-integrable.*

Lemma 2 ([31]). *If* $\nu, \varphi : [k, \ell] \subseteq \mathbb{R} \longrightarrow \mathbb{R}_{\mathcal{F}}$ *are fuzzy continuous (with respect to the metric* $\mathcal{D}$*), then the function* $F : [k, \ell] \longrightarrow \mathbb{R}_+ \cup \{0\}$ *defined by* $F(\tau) := \mathcal{D}(\nu(\tau), \varphi(\tau))$ *is continuous on* $[k, \ell]$, *and*

$$\mathcal{D}\left((FR)\int_k^\ell \nu(\alpha)d\alpha, (FR)\int_k^\ell \varphi(\alpha)d\alpha\right) \leq \int_k^\ell \mathcal{D}(\nu(\tau), \varphi(\tau))d\tau.$$

Lemma 3 ([31]). *Let $\nu : [k,\ell] \subseteq \mathbb{R} \longrightarrow \mathbb{R}_{\mathcal{F}}$ be fuzzy continuous. Then,*

$$(FR)\int_k^\tau \nu(t)dt$$

is fuzzy continuous function w.r.t. $\tau \in [k,\ell]$.

Proposition 4 ([32]). *Let $F(t) := t^n \odot \alpha$, $t \geq 0$, $n \in \mathbb{N}$ and $\alpha \in \mathbb{R}_{\mathcal{F}}$ be fixed. The (the φH-derivative)*

$$F'(t) = nt^{n-1} \odot \alpha.$$

In particular when $n = 1$ then $F'(t) = \alpha$.

Theorem 10 ([33]). *Let I be an open interval of $\mathbb{R}$ and let $\nu : I \longrightarrow \mathbb{R}_{\mathcal{F}}$ be φH-fuzzy differentiable, $c \in \mathbb{R}$. Then, $(c \odot \nu)'_{\varphi H}$ exist and $(c \odot \nu(\tau))'_{\varphi H} = c \odot \nu'_{\varphi H}(\tau)$.*

Theorem 11 ([32]). *Let $\nu : [k,\ell] \longrightarrow \mathbb{R}_{\mathcal{F}}$ be fuzzy differentiable function on $[k,\ell]$ with φH-derivative ν' which is assumed to be fuzzy continuous. Then,*

$$\mathcal{D}(\nu(d), \nu(c)) \leq (d-c) \sup_{t\in[c,d]} \mathcal{D}(\nu'(t), \tilde{o}),$$

for any $c, d \in [k,\ell]$ with $d \geq c$.

Theorem 12 ([26]). *If ν is φH-differentiable with no switching point in the interval $[k,\ell]$, then we have*

$$\int_k^\ell \nu'_{\varphi H}(\tau)d\tau = \nu(\ell) \ominus_{\varphi H} \nu(k).$$

Theorem 13 ([28]). *Let $\nu : [k,\ell] \to \mathbb{R}_{\mathcal{F}}$ be a continuous fuzzy-valued function. Then,*

$$F(t) = \int_k^t \nu(\tau)d\tau, t \in [k,\ell]$$

is φH-differentiable and $F'_{\varphi H}(t) = \nu(t)$.

Theorem 14 ([33]). *Let $\nu : [k,\ell] \to \mathbb{R}_{\mathcal{F}}$ and $\varphi : [k,\ell] \to \mathbb{R}^+$ be two differentiable functions (ν is φH-differentiable), then*

$$\int_k^\ell \nu'_{\varphi H}(\tau) \odot \varphi(\tau)d\tau = (\nu(\ell) \odot \varphi(\ell)) \ominus_{\varphi H} (\nu(k) \odot \varphi(k)) \ominus_{\varphi H} \int_k^\ell \nu(\tau) \odot \varphi'(\tau)d\tau.$$

Theorem 15 ([33]). *Let $\nu : [k,\ell] \to \mathbb{R}_{\mathcal{F}}$ and $\varphi : [k,\ell] \to \mathbb{R}^+$ are two differentiable functions (ν is φH-differentiable), then*

$$\int_k^\tau \nu'_{\varphi H}(\tau) \odot \varphi(\tau)d\tau = (\nu(\tau) \odot \varphi(\tau)) \ominus_{\varphi H} \int_k^\tau \nu(\tau) \odot \varphi'(\tau)d\tau.$$

3. Main Results

Since fuzziness is a natural reality different from randomness and determinism, Anastassiou [14] extended Ostrowski's result [34] to the context of a fuzzy setting in 2003. In fact, Anastassiou [14] proved important results for fuzzy Hölder and fuzzy differentiable functions, respectively. Those inequalities where shown to be sharp, as equalities are attained by the choice of simple fuzzy number-valued functions. For further details on these inequalities, we refer interested readers to [14].

We begin with the following result which generalizes Theorem 6.

Theorem 16. *Suppose that $\varphi : [k,\ell] \to \mathbb{R}^+$ and $\nu : [k,\ell] \to \mathbb{R}_{\mathcal{F}}$ are continuous and ν, φ are differentiable on (k,ℓ) (ν is φH-differentiable), then for all $\lambda \in [k,\ell]$ the inequality*

$$\mathcal{D}\left(\left(\int_\lambda^\ell \varphi(s)ds\right) \odot \nu(\ell) \ominus_{\varphi H} \left(-\int_k^\lambda \varphi(s)ds\right) \odot \nu(k) \ominus_{\varphi H} \int_k^\ell \varphi(t) \odot \nu(t)dt, \tilde{0}\right) \leq B(\varphi,\nu,\lambda), \quad (14)$$

holds, where

$$B(\varphi,\nu,\lambda) := \int_\lambda^\ell \left(\int_t^\ell \varphi(s)ds\right)\mathcal{D}\left(\nu'_{\varphi H}(t),\tilde{0}\right)dt + \int_k^\lambda \left(\int_k^t \varphi(s)ds\right)\mathcal{D}\left(\nu'_{\varphi H}(t),\tilde{0}\right)dt.$$

We have the following bounds for $B(\varphi,\nu,\lambda)$:

$$B(\varphi,\nu,\lambda) \leq \begin{cases} \int_\lambda^\ell \varphi(s)ds \int_\lambda^\ell \mathcal{D}\left(\nu'_{\varphi H}(t),\tilde{0}\right)dt \\ + \int_k^\lambda \varphi(s)ds \int_k^\lambda \mathcal{D}\left(\nu'_{\varphi H}(t),\tilde{0}\right)dt \\ \\ \left[\int_\lambda^\ell \left(\int_\lambda^t [\varphi(s)]^w ds\right)dt\right]^{\frac{1}{w}} \left(\int_\lambda^\ell \left[\mathcal{D}\left(\nu'_{\varphi H}(t),\tilde{0}\right)\right]^r dt\right)^{\frac{1}{r}} \\ + \left[\int_k^\lambda \left(\int_t^\lambda [\varphi(s)]^w ds\right)dt\right]^{\frac{1}{w}} \left(\int_k^\lambda \left[\mathcal{D}\left(\nu'_{\varphi H}(t),\tilde{0}\right)\right]^r dt\right)^{\frac{1}{r}}, \\ \\ \sup_{t\in[\lambda,\ell]} \mathcal{D}\left(\nu'_{\varphi H}(t),\tilde{0}\right) \int_\lambda^\ell \left(\int_t^\ell \varphi(s)ds\right)dt \\ + \sup_{t\in[k,\lambda]} \mathcal{D}\left(\nu'_{\varphi H}(t),\tilde{0}\right) \int_k^\lambda \left(\int_k^t \varphi(s)ds\right)dt. \end{cases} \quad (15)$$

Proof. Let $\lambda \in [k,\ell]$. Using the integration by parts formula given in Theorem 14, we have

$$\begin{aligned} &\int_k^\ell \left(\int_k^t \varphi(s)ds - \int_k^\lambda \varphi(s)ds\right) \odot \nu'_{\varphi H}(t)dt \\ &= \left(\int_k^\ell \varphi(s)ds - \int_k^\lambda \varphi(s)ds\right) \odot \nu(\ell) \ominus_{\varphi H} \left(\int_k^k \varphi(s)ds - \int_k^\lambda \varphi(s)ds\right) \odot \nu(k) \\ &\qquad \ominus_{\varphi H} \int_k^\ell \varphi(t) \odot \nu(t)dt \\ &= \left(\int_\lambda^\ell \varphi(s)ds\right) \odot \nu(\ell) \ominus_{\varphi H} \left(-\int_k^\lambda \varphi(s)ds\right) \odot \nu(k) \ominus_{\varphi H} \int_k^\ell \varphi(t) \odot \nu(t)dt. \end{aligned} \quad (16)$$

We also noticed that

$$\begin{aligned} &\int_k^\ell \left(\int_k^t \varphi(s)ds - \int_k^\lambda \varphi(s)ds\right) \odot \nu'_{\varphi H}(t)dt \\ &= \int_k^\lambda \left(\int_k^t \varphi(s)ds - \int_k^\lambda \varphi(s)ds\right) \odot \nu'_{\varphi H}(t)dt \oplus \int_\lambda^\ell \left(\int_k^t \varphi(s)ds - \int_k^\lambda \varphi(s)ds\right) \odot \nu'_{\varphi H}(t)dt \\ &= \int_k^\lambda \left(\int_\lambda^t \varphi(s)ds\right) \odot \nu'_{\varphi H}(t)dt \oplus \int_\lambda^\ell \left(-\int_t^\lambda \varphi(s)ds\right) \odot \nu'_{\varphi H}(t)dt. \end{aligned} \quad (17)$$

Hence

$$\begin{aligned} &\left(\int_\lambda^\ell \varphi(s)ds\right) \odot \nu(\ell) \ominus_{\varphi H} \left(-\int_k^\lambda \varphi(s)ds\right) \odot \nu(k) \ominus_{\varphi H} \int_k^\ell \varphi(t) \odot \nu(t)dt \\ &= \int_k^\lambda \left(\int_\lambda^t \varphi(s)ds\right) \odot \nu'_{\varphi H}(t)dt \oplus \int_\lambda^\ell \left(-\int_t^\lambda \varphi(s)ds\right) \odot \nu'_{\varphi H}(t)dt \end{aligned} \quad (18)$$

The equality (18) implies that

$$\begin{aligned}
&\mathcal{D}\Big(\Big(\int_\lambda^\ell \varphi(s)ds\Big) \odot \nu(\ell) \ominus_{\varphi H} \Big(-\int_k^\lambda \varphi(s)ds\Big) \odot \nu(k) \ominus_{\varphi H} \int_k^\ell \varphi(t) \odot \nu(t)dt, \tilde{0}\Big) \\
&\quad = \mathcal{D}\Big(\int_k^\lambda \Big(\int_\lambda^t \varphi(s)ds\Big) \odot \nu'_{\varphi H}(t)dt \oplus \int_\lambda^\ell \Big(-\int_t^\lambda \varphi(s)ds\Big) \odot \nu'_{\varphi H}(t)dt, \tilde{0}\Big) \\
&\quad = \Big\| \int_k^\lambda \Big(\int_\lambda^t \varphi(s)ds\Big) \odot \nu'_{\varphi H}(t)dt \oplus \int_\lambda^\ell \Big(-\int_t^\lambda \varphi(s)ds\Big) \odot \nu'_{\varphi H}(t)dt \Big\|_{\mathcal{F}} \\
&\quad \leq \Big\| \int_k^\lambda \Big(\int_\lambda^t \varphi(s)ds\Big) \odot \nu'_{\varphi H}(t)dt \Big\|_{\mathcal{F}} + \Big\| \int_\lambda^\ell \Big(-\int_t^\lambda \varphi(s)ds\Big) \odot \nu'_{\varphi H}(t)dt \Big\|_{\mathcal{F}} \\
&\quad = \Big| \int_k^\lambda \Big(\int_u^t \varphi(s)ds\Big) \Big| \Big\| \nu'_{\varphi H}(t) \Big\|_{\mathcal{F}} dt + \Big| \int_\lambda^\ell \Big(-\int_t^\lambda \varphi(s)ds\Big) \Big| \Big\| \nu'_{\varphi H}(t)dt \Big\|_{\mathcal{F}} dt \\
&\quad \leq \int_k^\lambda \Big(\int_\lambda^t \varphi(s)ds\Big) \Big\| \nu'_{\varphi H}(t)dt \Big\|_{\mathcal{F}} dt + \int_\lambda^\ell \Big(\int_t^\lambda \varphi(s)ds\Big) \Big\| \nu'_{\varphi H}(t)dt \Big\|_{\mathcal{F}} dt \\
&\qquad\qquad = \int_\lambda^\ell \Big(\int_t^\ell \varphi(s)ds\Big) \mathcal{D}\Big(\nu'_{\varphi H}(t)dt, \tilde{0}\Big)dt \\
&\qquad\qquad\qquad + \int_k^\lambda \Big(\int_k^t \varphi(s)ds\Big) \mathcal{D}\Big(\nu'_{\varphi H}(t)dt, \tilde{0}\Big)dt. \qquad (19)
\end{aligned}$$

Hence the inequality (14) is established.

Applying the Hölder's inequality and properties of supremum, we obtain for $w, r > 1$ with $\frac{1}{w} + \frac{1}{r} = 1$, that

$$\begin{aligned}
&\int_u^\ell \Big(\int_t^\ell \varphi(s)ds\Big) \mathcal{D}\Big(\nu'_{\varphi H}(t)dt, \tilde{0}\Big)dt \\
&\qquad \leq \begin{cases} \sup\limits_{t\in[\lambda,\ell]} \Big(\int_u^t \varphi(s)ds\Big) \int_\lambda^\ell \mathcal{D}\Big(\nu'_{\varphi H}(t)dt, \tilde{0}\Big)dt, \\ \Big[\int_u^\ell \Big(\int_\lambda^t [\varphi(s)]^w ds\Big)dt\Big]^{\frac{1}{w}} \Big(\int_\lambda^\ell \Big[\mathcal{D}\Big(\nu'_{\varphi H}(t)dt, \tilde{0}\Big)\Big]^r dt\Big)^{\frac{1}{r}}, \\ \sup\limits_{t\in[\lambda,\ell]} \mathcal{D}\Big(\nu'_{\varphi H}(t)dt, \tilde{0}\Big) \int_\lambda^\ell \Big(\int_u^t \varphi(s)ds\Big)dt, \end{cases} \\
&\qquad\qquad = \begin{cases} \int_\lambda^\ell \varphi(s)ds \int_\lambda^\ell \mathcal{D}\Big(\nu'_{\varphi H}(t)dt, \tilde{0}\Big)dt, \\ \Big[\int_\lambda^\ell \Big(\int_\lambda^t [\varphi(s)]^w ds\Big)dt\Big]^{\frac{1}{w}} \Big(\int_\lambda^\ell \Big[\mathcal{D}\Big(\nu'_{\varphi H}(t)dt, \tilde{0}\Big)\Big]^r dt\Big)^{\frac{1}{r}}, \\ \sup\limits_{t\in[\lambda,\ell]} \mathcal{D}\Big(\nu'_{\varphi H}(t)dt, \tilde{0}\Big) \int_\lambda^\ell \Big(\int_u^t \varphi(s)ds\Big)dt, \end{cases} \qquad (20)
\end{aligned}$$

and

$$\int_k^\lambda \Big(\int_t^\lambda \varphi(s)ds\Big) \mathcal{D}\Big(\nu'_{\varphi H}(t)dt, \tilde{0}\Big)dt$$

$$\leq \begin{cases} \sup\limits_{t\in[k,\lambda]} \left(\int_t^\lambda \varphi(s)ds\right) \int_k^\lambda \mathcal{D}\left(\nu'_{\varphi H}(t)dt, \tilde{0}\right)dt, \\ \left[\int_k^\lambda \left(\int_t^\lambda [\varphi(s)]^w ds\right)dt\right]^{\frac{1}{w}} \left(\int_k^\lambda \left[\mathcal{D}\left(\nu'_{\varphi H}(t)dt, \tilde{0}\right)\right]^r dt\right)^{\frac{1}{r}}, \\ \sup\limits_{t\in[k,\lambda]} \mathcal{D}\left(\nu'_{\varphi H}(t)dt, \tilde{0}\right) \int_k^\lambda \left(\int_t^\lambda \varphi(s)ds\right)dt. \end{cases}$$

$$= \begin{cases} \int_k^\lambda \varphi(s)ds \int_k^\lambda \mathcal{D}\left(\nu'_{\varphi H}(t)dt, \tilde{0}\right)dt, \\ \left[\int_k^\lambda \left(\int_t^\lambda [\varphi(s)]^w ds\right)dt\right]^{\frac{1}{w}} \left(\int_k^\lambda \left[\mathcal{D}\left(\nu'_{\varphi H}(t)dt, \tilde{0}\right)\right]^r dt\right)^{\frac{1}{r}}, \\ \sup\limits_{t\in[k,\lambda]} \mathcal{D}\left(\nu'_{\varphi H}(t)dt, \tilde{0}\right) \int_k^\lambda \left(\int_t^\lambda \varphi(s)ds\right)dt. \end{cases} \quad (21)$$

Substituting (20) and (21) in (19), we obtain the inequality (14). □

The immediate consequence of Theorem 16 is the following corollary.

Corollary 2. *Suppose that the assumptions of Theorem 16 are satisfied, then the inequalities*

$$\mathcal{D}\left(\left(\int_\lambda^\ell \varphi(s)ds\right) \odot \nu(\ell) \ominus_{\varphi H} \left(-\int_k^\lambda \varphi(s)ds\right) \odot \nu(k) \ominus_{\varphi H} \int_k^\ell \varphi(t) \odot \nu(t)dt, \tilde{0}\right)$$
$$\leq \int_\lambda^\ell \varphi(s)ds \int_\lambda^\ell \mathcal{D}\left(\nu'_{\varphi H}(t)dt, \tilde{0}\right)dt + \int_k^\lambda \varphi(s)ds \int_k^\lambda \mathcal{D}\left(\nu'_{\varphi H}(t)dt, \tilde{0}\right)dt$$
$$\leq \begin{cases} \max\left\{\int_k^\lambda \varphi(s)ds, \int_\lambda^\ell \varphi(s)ds\right\} \int_k^\ell \mathcal{D}\left(\nu'_{\varphi H}(t)dt, \tilde{0}\right)dt \\ \max\left\{\int_k^\lambda \mathcal{D}\left(\nu'_{\varphi H}(t)dt, \tilde{0}\right)dt, \int_\lambda^\ell \mathcal{D}\left(\nu'_{\varphi H}(t)dt, \tilde{0}\right)dt\right\} \int_k^\ell \varphi(s)ds \end{cases}$$
$$\leq \int_k^\ell \varphi(s)ds \int_k^\ell \mathcal{D}\left(\nu'_{\varphi H}(t)dt, \tilde{0}\right)dt \quad (22)$$

for all $\lambda \in [k, \ell]$.

Proof. Proof follows from the first part of the inequality in (14) and by using the properties of the max function. □

Remark 6. *If $m \in (k, \ell)$ is such that*

$$\int_k^m \varphi(s)ds = \int_m^\ell \varphi(s)ds = \frac{1}{2}\int_k^\ell \varphi(s)ds,$$

then (22) becomes the following inequality

$$\mathcal{D}\left(\left(\int_m^\ell \varphi(s)ds\right) \odot \nu(\ell) \ominus_{\varphi H} \left(-\int_k^m \varphi(s)ds\right) \odot \nu(k) \ominus_{\varphi H} \int_k^\ell \varphi(t) \odot \nu(t)dt, \tilde{0}\right)$$
$$\leq \frac{1}{2}\int_k^\ell \varphi(s)ds \int_k^\ell D\left(\nu'_{\varphi H}(t)dt, \tilde{0}\right)dt. \quad (23)$$

Corollary 3. *With the assumptions of Theorem 16, we have*

$$\mathcal{D}\bigg(\bigg(\int_\lambda^\ell \varphi(s)ds\bigg) \odot \nu(\ell) \ominus_{\varphi H} \bigg(-\int_k^\lambda \varphi(s)ds\bigg) \odot \nu(k) \ominus_{\varphi H} \int_k^\ell \varphi(t) \odot \nu(t)dt, \tilde{0}\bigg)$$
$$\leq \sup_{t\in[k,\ell]} \mathcal{D}\Big(\nu'_{\varphi H}(t)dt, \tilde{0}\Big)\bigg[\int_\lambda^\ell (\ell - t)\varphi(t)dt + \int_k^\lambda (t-k)\varphi(t)dt\bigg] \quad (24)$$

for all $\lambda \in [k, \ell]$.

Proof. From the third part in the bounds (14), we have

$$\mathcal{D}\bigg(\bigg(\int_\lambda^\ell \varphi(s)ds\bigg) \odot \nu(\ell) \ominus_{\varphi H} \bigg(-\int_k^\lambda \varphi(s)ds\bigg) \odot \nu(k) \ominus_{\varphi H} \int_k^\ell \varphi(t) \odot \nu(t)dt, \tilde{0}\bigg)$$
$$\leq \sup_{t\in[\lambda,\ell]} \mathcal{D}\Big(\nu'_{\varphi H}(t)dt, \tilde{0}\Big) \int_\lambda^\ell \bigg(\int_\lambda^t \varphi(s)ds\bigg)dt$$
$$+ \sup_{t\in[k,\lambda]} \mathcal{D}\Big(\nu'_{\varphi H}(t)dt, \tilde{0}\Big) \int_k^\lambda \bigg(\int_t^\lambda \varphi(s)ds\bigg)dt$$
$$\leq \sup_{t\in[k,\ell]} \mathcal{D}\Big(\nu'_{\varphi H}(t)dt, \tilde{0}\Big)\bigg[\int_\lambda^\ell \bigg(\int_u^t \varphi(s)ds\bigg)dt + \int_k^\lambda \bigg(\int_t^\lambda \varphi(s)ds\bigg)dt\bigg]. \quad (25)$$

Using integration by parts, we have for $\lambda \in [k, \ell]$ that

$$\int_\lambda^\ell \bigg(\int_\lambda^t \varphi(s)ds\bigg)dt = t\int_u^t \varphi(s)ds\bigg|_u^\ell - \int_\lambda^\ell t\varphi(t)dt$$
$$= \ell\int_\lambda^\ell \varphi(t)dt - \int_\lambda^\ell t\varphi(t)dt = \int_\lambda^\ell (\ell - t)\varphi(t)dt$$

and

$$\int_k^\lambda \bigg(\int_t^\lambda \varphi(s)ds\bigg)dt = t\int_t^\lambda \varphi(s)ds\bigg|_k^u + \int_k^\lambda t\varphi(t)dt$$
$$= -k\int_k^\lambda \varphi(t)dt + \int_k^\lambda t\varphi(t)dt = \int_k^\lambda (t-k)\varphi(t)dt.$$

Thus

$$\int_k^\lambda \bigg(\int_t^\lambda \varphi(s)ds\bigg)dt + \int_\lambda^\ell \bigg(\int_\lambda^t \varphi(s)ds\bigg)dt = \int_k^\lambda (t-k)\varphi(t)dt + \int_\lambda^\ell (\ell - t)\varphi(t)dt. \quad (26)$$

Using (26) in (14), we derive (22). □

Corollary 4. *Under the assumptions of Theorem 16, we have the following non-commutative trapezoidal-type inequalities for functions with values in the space of fuzzy real numbers*

$$\mathcal{D}\bigg(\bigg(\int_\lambda^\ell \varphi(s)ds\bigg) \odot \nu(\ell) \ominus_{\varphi H} \bigg(-\int_k^\lambda \varphi(s)ds\bigg) \odot \nu(k) \ominus_{\varphi H} \int_k^\ell \varphi(t) \odot \nu(t)dt, \tilde{0}\bigg)$$

$$\leq \sup_{t\in[k,\ell]} \mathcal{D}\left(\nu'_{\varphi H}(t)dt,\tilde{0}\right) \times \begin{cases} \left[\frac{1}{2}(\ell-k)+\left|u-\frac{k+\ell}{2}\right|\right] \int_k^\ell \varphi(t)dt, \\ \left[\frac{(u-k)^{r+1}+(\ell-\lambda)^{r+1}}{(r+1)^{\frac{1}{r}}}\right]^{\frac{1}{r}} \left(\int_k^\ell (\varphi(t))^w dt\right)^{\frac{1}{w}}, \\ \left[\frac{1}{4}(\ell-k)^2+\left(u-\frac{k+\ell}{2}\right)^2\right] \sup_{t\in[k,\ell]} \varphi(t) \end{cases} \tag{27}$$

for all $\lambda \in [k,\ell]$.

Proof. By applying the Hölder's inequality for $w, r > 1$ with $\frac{1}{w}+\frac{1}{r}=1$, we obtain

$$\int_\lambda^\ell (\ell-t)\varphi(t)dt \leq \begin{cases} \sup_{t\in[\lambda,\ell]} (\ell-t) \int_\lambda^\ell \varphi(t)dt, \\ \left(\int_\lambda^\ell (\ell-t)^r dt\right)^{\frac{1}{r}} \left(\int_\lambda^\ell (\varphi(t))^w dt\right)^{\frac{1}{w}}, \\ \sup_{t\in[\lambda,\ell]} \varphi(t) \int_\lambda^\ell (\ell-t)dt, \end{cases}$$

$$= \begin{cases} (\ell-\lambda) \int_\lambda^\ell \varphi(t)dt, \\ \frac{(\ell-\lambda)^{1+\frac{1}{r}}}{(r+1)^{\frac{1}{r}}} \left(\int_\lambda^\ell (\varphi(t))^w dt\right)^{\frac{1}{w}}, \\ \frac{1}{2}(\ell-\lambda)^2 \sup_{t\in[\lambda,\ell]} \varphi(t). \end{cases}$$

Similarly, we also have

$$\int_k^\lambda (t-k)\varphi(t)dt \leq \begin{cases} (u-k) \int_k^\lambda \varphi(t)dt, \\ \frac{(u-k)^{1+\frac{1}{r}}}{(r+1)^{\frac{1}{r}}} \left(\int_k^\lambda (\varphi(t))^w dt\right)^{\frac{1}{w}}, \\ \frac{1}{2}(u-k)^2 \sup_{t\in[k,\lambda]} \varphi(t). \end{cases}$$

Hence, we obtain

$$\mathcal{D}\left(\left(\int_\lambda^\ell \varphi(s)ds\right) \odot \nu(\ell) \ominus_{\varphi H} \left(-\int_k^\lambda \varphi(s)ds\right) \odot \nu(k) \ominus_{\varphi H} \int_k^\ell \varphi(t) \odot \nu(t)dt, \tilde{0}\right)$$

$$\leq \sup_{t\in[k,\ell]} \mathcal{D}\left(\nu'_{\varphi H}(t)dt,\tilde{0}\right) \times \begin{cases} (u-k) \int_k^\lambda \varphi(t)dt + (\ell-\lambda) \int_\lambda^\ell \varphi(t)dt, \\ \frac{(u-k)^{1+\frac{1}{r}} \left(\int_k^\lambda (\varphi(t))^w dt\right)^{\frac{1}{w}} + (\ell-\lambda)^{1+\frac{1}{r}} \left(\int_\lambda^\ell (\varphi(t))^w dt\right)^{\frac{1}{w}}}{(r+1)^{\frac{1}{r}}}, \\ \frac{1}{2}(u-k)^2 \sup_{t\in[k,\lambda]} \varphi(t) + \frac{1}{2}(\ell-\lambda)^2 \sup_{t\in[\lambda,\ell]} \varphi(t) \end{cases} \tag{28}$$

for all $\lambda \in [k,\ell]$.

Since

$$(u-k)\int_k^{\lambda}\varphi(t)dt+(\ell-\lambda)\int_{\lambda}^{\ell}\varphi(t)dt=\max\{u-k,\ell-\lambda\}\left[\int_k^{\lambda}\varphi(t)dt+\int_{\lambda}^{\ell}\varphi(t)dt\right]$$
$$=\left[\frac{1}{2}(\ell-k)+\left|u-\frac{k+\ell}{2}\right|\right]\int_k^{\ell}\varphi(t)dt. \quad (29)$$

By using the elementary inequality (see [35] (p. 129)):

$$k\ell+cd\le(k^w+c^w)^{\frac{1}{w}}(\ell^r+d^r)^{\frac{1}{r}}$$

for $k,\ell,c,d\ge0$ and $w,r>1$ with $\frac{1}{w}+\frac{1}{r}=1$, we obtain

$$(u-k)^{1+\frac{1}{r}}\left(\int_k^{\lambda}(\varphi(t))^w dt\right)^{\frac{1}{w}}+(\ell-\lambda)^{1+\frac{1}{r}}\left(\int_{\lambda}^{\ell}(\varphi(t))^w dt\right)^{\frac{1}{w}}$$
$$\le\left(\left[(u-k)^{1+\frac{1}{r}}\right]^r+\left[(\ell-\lambda)^{1+\frac{1}{r}}\right]^r\right)^{\frac{1}{r}}$$
$$\times\left[\left[\left(\int_k^{\lambda}(\varphi(t))^w dt\right)^{\frac{1}{w}}\right]^w+\left[\left(\int_{\lambda}^{\ell}(\varphi(t))^w dt\right)^{\frac{1}{w}}\right]^w\right]^{\frac{1}{w}}$$
$$=\left[(u-k)^{r+1}+(\ell-\lambda)^{r+1}\right]^{\frac{1}{r}}\left[\int_k^{\lambda}(\varphi(t))^w dt+\int_{\lambda}^{\ell}(\varphi(t))^w dt\right]^{\frac{1}{w}}$$
$$=\left[(u-k)^{r+1}+(\ell-\lambda)^{r+1}\right]^{\frac{1}{r}}\left[\int_k^{\ell}(\varphi(t))^w dt\right]^{\frac{1}{w}} \quad (30)$$

Moreover, we also observe that

$$\frac{1}{2}(\lambda-k)^2\sup_{t\in[k,\lambda]}\varphi(t)+\frac{1}{2}(\ell-\lambda)^2\sup_{t\in[\lambda,\ell]}\varphi(t)\le\frac{(u-k)^2+(\ell-\lambda)^2}{2}\sup_{t\in[k,\ell]}\varphi(t)$$
$$=\left[\frac{1}{4}(\ell-k)^2+\left(u-\frac{k+\ell}{2}\right)^2\right]\sup_{t\in[k,\ell]}\varphi(t). \quad (31)$$

Then, by applying (29)–(31) in (28), we derive (27). □

One more interesting consequence of Theorem 16 is the following result.

Corollary 5. *Suppose that the assumptions of Theorem 16 are satisfied, then the following inequalities can be obtained:*

$$\mathcal{D}\left(\left(\int_{\lambda}^{\ell}\varphi(s)ds\right)\odot\nu(\ell)\ominus_{\varphi H}\left(-\int_k^{\lambda}\varphi(s)ds\right)\odot\nu(k)\ominus_{\varphi H}\int_k^{\ell}\varphi(t)\odot\nu(t)dt,\tilde{0}\right)$$
$$\le\left[\left(\int_{\lambda}^{\ell}\varphi(t)dt\right)^w(\ell-\lambda)+\left(\int_k^{\lambda}\varphi(t)dt\right)^w(u-k)\right]^{\frac{1}{w}}\left(\int_k^{\ell}\left[\mathcal{D}\left(\nu'_{\varphi H}(t)dt,\tilde{0}\right)\right]^r dt\right)^{\frac{1}{r}}$$
$$\le(\ell-k)^{\frac{1}{w}}\left[\left(\int_{\lambda}^{\ell}\varphi(t)dt\right)^w+\left(\int_k^{\lambda}\varphi(t)dt\right)^w\right]^{\frac{1}{w}}\left(\int_k^{\ell}\left[\mathcal{D}\left(\nu'_{\varphi H}(t)dt,\tilde{0}\right)\right]^r dt\right)^{\frac{1}{r}} \quad (32)$$

for all $\lambda\in[k,\ell]$.

Proof. By using the inequality (see [35] (p. 129)):

$$(k\ell+cd)\le(k^w+c^w)^{\frac{1}{w}}(\ell^r+d^r)^{\frac{1}{r}}$$

for $k, \ell, c, d > 0$ and $w, r > 1$with $\frac{1}{w} + \frac{1}{r} = 1$, we have

$$\left(\int_k^\lambda \left(\int_t^\lambda \varphi(s)ds\right)^w dt\right)^{\frac{1}{w}} \left(\int_k^\lambda \left[\mathcal{D}\left(\nu'_{\varphi H}(t)dt, \tilde{0}\right)\right]^r dt\right)^{\frac{1}{r}}$$
$$+ \left(\int_\lambda^\ell \left(\int_u^t \varphi(s)ds\right)^w dt\right)^{\frac{1}{w}} \left(\int_\lambda^\ell \left[\mathcal{D}\left(\nu'_{\varphi H}(t)dt, \tilde{0}\right)\right]^r dt\right)^{\frac{1}{r}}$$
$$\leq \left[\int_k^\lambda \left(\int_t^\lambda \varphi(s)ds\right)^w dt + \int_\lambda^\ell \left(\int_\lambda^t \varphi(s)ds\right)^w dt\right]^{\frac{1}{w}}$$
$$\times \left[\int_k^\lambda \left[\mathcal{D}\left(\nu'_{\varphi H}(t)dt, \tilde{0}\right)\right]^r dt + \int_\lambda^\ell \left[\mathcal{D}\left(\nu'_{\varphi H}(t)dt, \tilde{0}\right)\right]^r dt\right]^{\frac{1}{r}}$$
$$= \left[\int_k^\lambda \left(\int_t^\lambda \varphi(s)ds\right)^w dt + \int_\lambda^\ell \left(\int_u^t \varphi(s)ds\right)^w dt\right]^{\frac{1}{w}} \left[\int_k^\ell \left[\mathcal{D}\left(\nu'_{\varphi H}(t)dt, \tilde{0}\right)\right]^r dt\right]^{\frac{1}{r}}$$
$$\leq \left[\left(\int_k^\lambda \varphi(s)ds\right)^w \int_k^\lambda dt + \left(\int_\lambda^\ell \varphi(s)ds\right)^w \int_\lambda^\ell dt\right]^{\frac{1}{w}} \left[\int_k^\ell \left[\mathcal{D}\left(\nu'_{\varphi H}(t)dt, \tilde{0}\right)\right]^r dt\right]^{\frac{1}{r}}$$
$$= \left[\left(\int_k^\lambda \varphi(s)ds\right)^w (u-k) + \left(\int_\lambda^\ell \varphi(s)ds\right)^w (\ell - \lambda)\right]^{\frac{1}{w}} \left[\int_k^\ell \left[\mathcal{D}\left(\nu'_{\varphi H}(t)dt, \tilde{0}\right)\right]^r dt\right]^{\frac{1}{r}}$$
$$\leq (\ell - k)^{\frac{1}{w}} \left[\left(\int_k^\lambda \varphi(s)ds\right)^w + \left(\int_\lambda^\ell \varphi(s)ds\right)^w\right]^{\frac{1}{w}} \left[\int_k^\ell \left[\mathcal{D}\left(\nu'_{\varphi H}(t)dt, \tilde{0}\right)\right]^r dt\right]^{\frac{1}{r}}$$

which proves the inequality (32). □

Remark 7. *If $m \in (k, \ell)$ is such that*

$$\int_k^m \varphi(s)ds = \int_m^\ell \varphi(s)ds = \frac{1}{2}\int_k^\ell \varphi(s)ds,$$

then from (32), we obtain

$$\mathcal{D}\left(\left(\int_m^\ell \varphi(s)ds\right) \odot \nu(\ell) \ominus_{\varphi H} \left(-\int_k^m \varphi(s)ds\right) \odot \nu(k) \ominus_{\varphi H} \int_k^\ell \varphi(t) \odot \nu(t)dt, \tilde{0}\right)$$
$$\leq \frac{1}{2}(\ell - k)^{\frac{1}{w}} \left(\int_k^\ell \varphi(t)dt\right) \left(\int_k^\ell \left[\mathcal{D}\left(\nu'_{\varphi H}(t)dt, \tilde{0}\right)\right]^r dt\right)^{\frac{1}{r}}. \quad (33)$$

Remark 8. *Suppose that the assumptions of Theorem 16 are fulfilled, then we obtain the following inequalities:*

$$\mathcal{D}\left(\left(\int_{\frac{k+\ell}{2}}^\ell \varphi(s)ds\right) \odot \nu(\ell) \ominus_{\varphi H} \left(-\int_k^{\frac{k+\ell}{2}} \varphi(s)ds\right) \odot \nu(k) \ominus_{\varphi H} \int_k^\ell \varphi(t) \odot \nu(t)dt, \tilde{0}\right)$$
$$\leq M(\varphi, \nu), \quad (34)$$

where

$$M(\varphi, \nu) := \int_{\frac{k+\ell}{2}}^\ell \left(\int_t^\ell \varphi(s)ds\right) \mathcal{D}\left(\nu'_{\varphi H}(t)dt, \tilde{0}\right)dt + \int_k^{\frac{k+\ell}{2}} \left(\int_k^t \varphi(s)ds\right) \mathcal{D}\left(\nu'_{\varphi H}(t)dt, \tilde{0}\right)dt.$$

We have the following bounds for $M(\varphi,\nu)$:

$$M(\varphi,\nu) \leq \begin{cases} \left(\int_{\frac{k+\ell}{2}}^{\ell} \varphi(s)ds\right) \int_{\frac{k+\ell}{2}}^{\ell} \mathcal{D}\left(\nu'_{\varphi H}(t)dt,\tilde{0}\right)dt \\ +\left(\int_{k}^{\frac{k+\ell}{2}} \varphi(s)ds\right) \int_{k}^{\frac{k+\ell}{2}} \mathcal{D}\left(\nu'_{\varphi H}(t)dt,\tilde{0}\right)dt \\ \\ \left[\int_{\frac{k+\ell}{2}}^{\ell}\left(\int_{\frac{k+\ell}{2}}^{t} \varphi(s)ds\right)dt\right]^{\frac{1}{w}} \left(\int_{\frac{k+\ell}{2}}^{\ell}\left[\mathcal{D}\left(\nu'_{\varphi H}(t)dt,\tilde{0}\right)\right]^{r}dt\right)^{\frac{1}{r}} \\ +\left[\int_{k}^{\frac{k+\ell}{2}}\left(\int_{t}^{\frac{k+\ell}{2}} \varphi(s)ds\right)dt\right]^{\frac{1}{w}} \left(\int_{k}^{\frac{k+\ell}{2}}\left[\mathcal{D}\left(\nu'_{\varphi H}(t)dt,\tilde{0}\right)\right]^{r}dt\right)^{\frac{1}{r}}, \\ \\ \sup\limits_{t\in\left[\frac{k+\ell}{2},\ell\right]} \mathcal{D}\left(\nu'_{\varphi H}(t)dt,\tilde{0}\right) \int_{\frac{k+\ell}{2}}^{\ell}\left(\int_{\frac{k+\ell}{2}}^{t} \varphi(s)ds\right)dt \\ +\sup\limits_{t\in\left[k,\frac{k+\ell}{2}\right]} \mathcal{D}\left(\nu'_{\varphi H}(t)dt,\tilde{0}\right) \int_{k}^{\frac{k+\ell}{2}}\left(\int_{t}^{\frac{k+\ell}{2}} \varphi(s)ds\right)dt. \end{cases} \tag{35}$$

From (22), we obtain that

$$\begin{aligned} &\mathcal{D}\left(\left(\int_{\frac{k+\ell}{2}}^{\ell} \varphi(s)ds\right)\odot\nu(\ell)\ominus_{\varphi H}\left(-\int_{k}^{\frac{k+\ell}{2}} \varphi(s)ds\right)\odot\nu(k)\ominus_{\varphi H}\int_{k}^{\ell}\varphi(t)\odot\nu(t)dt,\tilde{0}\right) \\ &\leq \int_{\frac{k+\ell}{2}}^{\ell}\varphi(s)ds\int_{\frac{k+\ell}{2}}^{\ell}\mathcal{D}\left(\nu'_{\varphi H}(t)dt,\tilde{0}\right)dt+\int_{k}^{\frac{k+\ell}{2}}\varphi(s)ds\int_{k}^{\frac{k+\ell}{2}}\mathcal{D}\left(\nu'_{\varphi H}(t)dt,\tilde{0}\right)dt \\ &\leq \begin{cases} \max\left\{\int_{k}^{\frac{k+\ell}{2}}\varphi(s)ds,\int_{\frac{k+\ell}{2}}^{\ell}\varphi(s)ds\right\}\int_{k}^{\ell}\mathcal{D}\left(\nu'_{\varphi H}(t)dt,\tilde{0}\right)dt \\ \\ \max\left\{\int_{k}^{\frac{k+\ell}{2}}D\left(\nu'_{\varphi H}(t)dt,\tilde{0}\right)dt,\int_{\frac{k+\ell}{2}}^{\ell}\mathcal{D}\left(\nu'_{\varphi H}(t)dt,\tilde{0}\right)dt\right\}\int_{k}^{\ell}\varphi(s)ds \end{cases} \\ &\leq \int_{k}^{\ell}\varphi(s)ds\int_{k}^{\ell}\mathcal{D}\left(\nu'_{\varphi H}(t)dt,\tilde{0}\right)dt. \end{aligned} \tag{36}$$

From (27) we derive the non-commutative mid-point type inequalities forfunctions with values in space of fuzzy real numbers

$$\begin{aligned} &\mathcal{D}\left(\left(\int_{\frac{k+\ell}{2}}^{\ell} \varphi(s)ds\right)\odot\nu(\ell)\ominus_{\varphi H}\left(-\int_{k}^{\frac{k+\ell}{2}} \varphi(s)ds\right)\odot\nu(k)\ominus_{\varphi H}\int_{k}^{\ell}\varphi(t)\odot\nu(t)dt,\tilde{0}\right) \\ &\leq \sup_{t\in[k,\ell]}\mathcal{D}\left(\nu'_{\varphi H}(t)dt,\tilde{0}\right)\times\begin{cases} \frac{1}{2}(\ell-k)\int_{k}^{\ell}\varphi(t)dt, \\ \\ \frac{(\ell-k)^{1+\frac{1}{r}}}{2(r+1)^{\frac{1}{r}}}\left(\int_{k}^{\ell}(\varphi(t))^{w}dt\right)^{\frac{1}{w}}, \\ \\ \frac{1}{4}(\ell-k)^{2}\sup\limits_{t\in[k,\ell]}\varphi(t). \end{cases} \end{aligned} \tag{37}$$

From (32), we can obtain

$$\begin{aligned} &D\left(\left(\int_{\frac{k+\ell}{2}}^{\ell} \varphi(s)ds\right)\odot\nu(\ell)\ominus_{\varphi H}\left(-\int_{k}^{\frac{k+\ell}{2}} \varphi(s)ds\right)\odot\nu(k)\ominus_{\varphi H}\int_{k}^{\ell}\varphi(t)\odot\nu(t)dt,\tilde{0}\right) \\ &\leq \left(\frac{\ell-k}{2}\right)^{\frac{1}{w}}\left[\left(\int_{\frac{k+\ell}{2}}^{\ell}\varphi(t)dt\right)^{w}+\left(\int_{k}^{\frac{k+\ell}{2}}\varphi(t)dt\right)^{w}\right]^{\frac{1}{w}} \end{aligned}$$

$$\times\left(\int_k^\ell\left[D\left(\nu'_{\varphi H}(t)dt,\tilde{0}\right)\right]^r dt\right)^{\frac{1}{r}}. \quad (38)$$

If we consider the case when $\varphi(t)=1$, $t\in[k,\ell]$, then by (14) we obtain

$$\mathcal{D}\left((\ell-\lambda)\odot\nu(\ell)\ominus_{\varphi H}(-(\lambda-k))\odot\nu(k)\ominus_{\varphi H}\int_k^\ell\nu(t)dt,\tilde{0}\right)\le B(\nu,\lambda), \quad (39)$$

where

$$B(\nu,\lambda):=\int_\lambda^\ell(t-u)\mathcal{D}\left(\nu'_{\varphi H}(t)dt,\tilde{0}\right)dt+\int_k^\lambda(u-t)\mathcal{D}\left(\nu'_{\varphi H}(t)dt,\tilde{0}\right)dt.$$

The bounds of $B(\nu,\lambda)$ are given by

$$B(\nu,\lambda)\le\begin{cases}(\ell-\lambda)\int_\lambda^\ell\mathcal{D}\left(\nu'_{\varphi H}(t)dt,\tilde{0}\right)dt\\+(\lambda-k)\int_k^\lambda\mathcal{D}\left(\nu'_{\varphi H}(t)dt,\tilde{0}\right)dt\\ \\ \frac{(\ell-\lambda)^{1+\frac{1}{w}}}{(w+1)^{\frac{1}{w}}}\left(\int_\lambda^\ell\left[\mathcal{D}\left(\nu'_{\varphi H}(t)dt,\tilde{0}\right)\right]^r dt\right)^{\frac{1}{r}}\\+\frac{(\lambda-k)^{1+\frac{1}{w}}}{(w+1)^{\frac{1}{w}}}\left(\int_k^\lambda\left[\mathcal{D}\left(\nu'_{\varphi H}(t)dt,\tilde{0}\right)\right]^r dt\right)^{\frac{1}{r}},\\ \\ \frac{1}{2}(\ell-\lambda)^2\sup_{t\in[\lambda,\ell]}\mathcal{D}\left(\nu'_{\varphi H}(t)dt,\tilde{0}\right)\\+\frac{1}{2}(k-\lambda)^2\sup_{t\in[\lambda,u]}\mathcal{D}\left(\nu'_{\varphi H}(t)dt,\tilde{0}\right)\end{cases} \quad (40)$$

for all $\lambda\in[k,\ell]$ for $w,r>1$ and $\frac{1}{w}+\frac{1}{r}=1$.

From the first inequality in (22), we obtain

$$\mathcal{D}\left((\ell-\lambda)\odot\nu(\ell)\ominus_{\varphi H}(-(\lambda-k))\odot\nu(k)\ominus_{\varphi H}\int_k^\ell\nu(t)dt,\tilde{0}\right)$$
$$\le\left[\frac{1}{2}(\ell-k)+\left|\lambda-\frac{k+\ell}{2}\right|\right]\int_k^\ell\mathcal{D}\left(\nu'_{\varphi H}(t)dt,\tilde{0}\right)dt \quad (41)$$

for all $\lambda\in[k,\ell]$.

From (27), we alsohave the following Ostrowski-type inequality

$$\mathcal{D}\left((\ell-\lambda)\odot\nu(\ell)\ominus_{\varphi H}(-(\lambda-k))\odot\nu(k)\ominus_{\varphi H}\int_k^\ell\nu(t)dt,\tilde{0}\right)$$
$$\le(\ell-k)^{\frac{1}{w}}\left[(\lambda-k)^{w+1}+(\ell-\lambda)^{w+1}\right]^{\frac{1}{w}}\left(\int_k^\ell\mathcal{D}\left(\nu'_{\varphi H}(t)dt,\tilde{0}\right)dt\right)^{\frac{1}{r}} \quad (42)$$

for all $\lambda\in[k,\ell]$.

A dual result can be stated as follows:

Theorem 17. *Suppose that $\varphi:[k,\ell]\to\mathbb{R}^+$ and $\nu:[k,\ell]\to\mathbb{R}_{\mathcal{F}}$ are continuous and ν, φ are differentiable on (k,ℓ) (ν is φH-differentiable), then for all $\lambda\in[k,\ell]$ the inequality*

$$\mathcal{D}\left(\left(\int_k^\ell\varphi(t)\odot\nu(t)dt\right)\ominus_{\varphi H}\left(-\varphi(\ell)\odot\int_\lambda^\ell\nu(s)ds\right)\right.$$
$$\left.\ominus_{\varphi H}\left(\varphi(k)\odot\int_k^\lambda\nu(s)ds\right),\tilde{0}\right)\le\tilde{B}(\varphi,\nu,\lambda), \quad (43)$$

where

$$\tilde{B}(\varphi,\nu,\lambda) := \int_{\lambda}^{\ell} \varphi'(t)\left(\int_{\lambda}^{t} \mathcal{D}(\nu(s),\tilde{0})ds\right)dt + \int_{k}^{\lambda} \varphi'(t)\left(\int_{t}^{\lambda} \mathcal{D}(\nu(s),\tilde{0})ds\right)dt.$$

We have the following bounds for $B(\varphi,\nu,\lambda)$*:*

$$\tilde{B}(\varphi,\nu,\lambda) \leq \begin{cases} \left(\int_{\lambda}^{\ell} \varphi'(t)dt\right)\left(\int_{\lambda}^{\ell} \mathcal{D}(\nu(s),\tilde{0})ds\right) \\ +\left(\int_{k}^{\lambda} \varphi'(t)dt\right)\left(\int_{k}^{\lambda} \mathcal{D}(\nu(s),\tilde{0})ds\right) \\ \\ \left[\int_{\lambda}^{\ell}\left(\int_{\lambda}^{t} \mathcal{D}(\nu(s)dt,\tilde{0})ds\right)^{w} dt\right]^{\frac{1}{w}} \left[\int_{\lambda}^{\ell}\left(\varphi'(t)\right)^{r} dt\right]^{\frac{1}{r}} \\ +\left[\int_{k}^{\lambda}\left(\int_{t}^{\lambda} \mathcal{D}(\nu(s)dt,\tilde{0})ds\right)^{w} dt\right]^{\frac{1}{w}} \left[\int_{k}^{\lambda}\left(\varphi'(t)\right)^{r} dt\right]^{\frac{1}{r}}, \\ \\ \int_{\lambda}^{\ell}\left(\int_{\lambda}^{t} \mathcal{D}(\nu(s)dt,\tilde{0})ds\right)dt \sup_{t\in[\lambda,\ell]} \varphi(t) \\ + \int_{k}^{\lambda}\left(\int_{t}^{\lambda} \mathcal{D}(\nu(s)dt,\tilde{0})ds\right)dt \sup_{t\in[k,\lambda]} \varphi(t) \end{cases} \tag{44}$$

for $w, r > 1$ *with* $\frac{1}{w} + \frac{1}{r} = 1$.

Proof. Using integration by parts given by Theorem 14, we obtain

$$\int_{\lambda}^{\ell} \varphi'(t) \odot \left(\int_{\lambda}^{t} \nu(s)ds\right)dt = \varphi(\ell) \odot \int_{\lambda}^{\ell} \nu(s)ds \ominus_{\varphi H} \tilde{0} \ominus_{\varphi H} \int_{\lambda}^{\ell} \varphi(t) \odot \nu(t)dt \tag{45}$$

and

$$\begin{aligned} &\int_{k}^{\lambda} \varphi'(t) \odot \left(\int_{t}^{\lambda} \nu(s)ds\right)dt \\ &\quad = -\tilde{0} \ominus_{\varphi H} \varphi(k) \odot \int_{k}^{\lambda} \nu(s)ds \ominus_{\varphi H} \left(-\int_{k}^{\lambda} \varphi(t) \odot \nu(t)dt\right) \\ &\quad = \left(-\int_{k}^{\lambda} \varphi(t) \odot \nu(t)dt\right) \ominus_{\varphi H} \left(\varphi(k) \odot \int_{k}^{\lambda} \nu(s)ds\right). \end{aligned} \tag{46}$$

Hence, by using (iii), (iv) and (v) of Proposition 2, we obtain from (45) and (46) that

$$\begin{aligned} &\int_{\lambda}^{\ell} \varphi'(t) \odot \left(\int_{u}^{t} \nu(s)ds\right)dt \ominus_{\varphi H} \int_{k}^{\lambda} \varphi'(t) \odot \left(\int_{t}^{\lambda} \nu(s)ds\right)dt \\ &\quad = \left(\varphi(\ell) \odot \int_{\lambda}^{\ell} \nu(s)ds\right) \ominus_{\varphi H} \tilde{0} \ominus_{\varphi H} \left(\int_{\lambda}^{\ell} \varphi(t) \odot \nu(t)dt\right) \\ &\quad \ominus_{\varphi H} \left(-\int_{k}^{\lambda} \varphi(t) \odot \nu(t)dt\right) \ominus_{\varphi H} \left(\varphi(k) \odot \int_{k}^{\lambda} \nu(s)ds\right) \\ &\quad = \tilde{0} \ominus_{\varphi H} \left(-\varphi(\ell) \odot \int_{\lambda}^{\ell} \nu(s)ds\right) \ominus_{\varphi H} \left(\int_{\lambda}^{\ell} \varphi(t) \odot \nu(t)dt\right) \\ &\quad \ominus_{\varphi H} \left(-\int_{k}^{\lambda} \varphi(t) \odot \nu(t)dt\right) \ominus_{\varphi H} \left(\varphi(k) \odot \int_{k}^{\lambda} \nu(s)ds\right) \\ &\quad = \left(\int_{\lambda}^{\ell} \varphi(t) \odot \nu(t)dt\right) \ominus_{\varphi H} \left((-1)\int_{k}^{\lambda} \varphi(t) \odot \nu(t)dt\right) \\ &\quad \ominus_{\varphi H} \left(-\varphi(\ell) \odot \int_{\lambda}^{\ell} \nu(s)ds\right) \ominus_{\varphi H} \left(\varphi(k) \odot \int_{k}^{\lambda} \nu(s)ds\right) \end{aligned}$$

$$= \int_k^\ell \varphi(t) \odot \nu(t)dt \ominus_{\varphi H} \left(-\varphi(\ell) \odot \int_\lambda^\ell \nu(s)ds\right) \ominus_{\varphi H} \varphi(k) \odot \int_k^\lambda \nu(s)ds. \quad (47)$$

Thus from (47), using the properties of the metric D and the norm$\|\cdot\|_{\mathcal{F}}$ induced by the metric D, we have

$$\begin{aligned}
&D\Big(\int_k^\ell \varphi(t) \odot \nu(t)dt \ominus_{\varphi H} \left(-\varphi(\ell) \odot \int_\lambda^\ell \nu(s)ds\right) \ominus_{\varphi H} \left(\varphi(k) \odot \int_k^\lambda \nu(s)ds\right), \tilde{0}\Big) \\
&= D\Big(\int_\lambda^\ell \left(\varphi'(t) \odot \int_\lambda^t \nu(s)ds\right)dt \ominus_{\varphi H} \int_k^\lambda \left(\varphi'(t) \odot \int_t^\lambda \nu(s)ds\right)dt, \tilde{0}\Big) \\
&\leq D\Big(\int_\lambda^\ell \varphi'(t) \odot \left(\int_u^t \nu(s)ds\right)dt, \int_k^\lambda \varphi'(t) \odot \left(\int_t^\lambda \nu(s)ds\right)dt\Big) \\
&= D\Big(\int_\lambda^\ell \varphi'(t) \odot \left(\int_\lambda^t \nu(s)ds\right)dt \oplus \tilde{0}, \tilde{0} \oplus \int_k^\lambda \varphi'(t) \odot \left(\int_t^\lambda \nu(s)ds\right)dt\Big) \\
&\leq D\Big(\int_\lambda^\ell \varphi'(t) \odot \left(\int_u^t \nu(s)ds\right)dt, \tilde{0}\Big) + D\Big(\tilde{0}, \int_k^\lambda \varphi'(t) \odot \left(\int_t^\lambda \nu(s)ds\right)dt\Big) \\
&= D\Big(\int_\lambda^\ell \varphi'(t) \odot \left(\int_\lambda^t \nu(s)ds\right)dt, \tilde{0}\Big) + D\Big(\int_k^\lambda \varphi'(t) \odot \left(\int_t^\lambda \nu(s)ds\right)dt, \tilde{0}\Big) \\
&\leq \int_\lambda^\ell \varphi'(t)\left(\int_u^t \|\nu(s)\|_{\mathcal{F}}ds\right)dt + \int_k^\lambda \varphi'(t)\left(\int_t^\lambda \|\nu(s)\|_{\mathcal{F}}ds\right)dt.
\end{aligned}$$

The inequality (43) is thus established. □

Example 1. *Consider the fuzzy number-valued mapping ν: $[2,3] \to \mathbb{R}_{\mathcal{F}}$ defined by*

$$\nu(t)(\theta) = \begin{cases} \frac{\theta - 2 + t^{\frac{1}{2}}}{1 - t^{\frac{1}{2}}}, & \theta \in \left[2 - t^{\frac{1}{2}}, 3\right] \\ \frac{2 + t^{\frac{1}{2}} - \theta}{t^{\frac{1}{2}} - 1}, & \theta \in \left(3, 2 + t^{\frac{1}{2}}\right] \\ 0, & \text{otherwise.} \end{cases}$$

Then, for each $p \in [0,1]$, we have

$$\nu^p(t) = \left[(1-p)\left(2 - t^{\frac{1}{2}}\right) + 3p, (1-p)\left(2 + t^{\frac{1}{2}}\right) + 3p\right] = \left[\nu_-^p(t), \nu_+^p(t)\right].$$

We also define a mapping $\varphi : [2,3] \to \mathbb{R}^+$ by $\varphi(t) = t^2$. Then, according to the metric $\mathcal{D} : \mathbb{R}_{\mathcal{F}} \times \mathbb{R}_{\mathcal{F}} \longrightarrow \mathbb{R}^+ \cup \{0\}$ as defined in the beginning of Section 2 with $\lambda = \frac{5}{2} \in [2,3]$ and $w = 4, r = \frac{4}{3}$, then the inequality (14) takes the following form:

$$\mathcal{D}\Big(\left(\int_{\frac{5}{2}}^3 \varphi(s)ds\right) \odot \nu(3) \ominus_{\varphi H} \left(-\int_2^{\frac{5}{2}} \varphi(s)ds\right) \odot \nu(2) \ominus_{\varphi H} \int_2^3 \varphi(t) \odot \nu(t)dt, \tilde{0}\Big) \leq B\left(\varphi, \nu, \frac{5}{2}\right). \quad (48)$$

We now calculate the left hand side in (48) as follows:

$$\begin{aligned}
&\mathcal{D}\Big(\left(\int_{\frac{5}{2}}^3 \varphi(s)ds\right) \odot \nu(3) \ominus_{\varphi H} \left(-\int_2^{\frac{5}{2}} \varphi(s)ds\right) \odot \nu(2) \ominus_{\varphi H} \int_2^3 \varphi(t) \odot \nu(t)dt, \tilde{0}\Big) \\
&= \mathcal{D}\Big(\left(\int_{\frac{5}{2}}^3 s^2 ds\right) \odot \nu(3) - \left(-\int_2^{\frac{5}{2}} s^2 ds\right) \odot \nu(2) - \int_2^3 t^2 \odot \nu(t)dt, \tilde{0}\Big)
\end{aligned}$$

$$
\begin{aligned}
&= \left(2+3^{\frac{1}{2}}\right)\left(\int_{\frac{5}{2}}^{3} s^2 ds\right) + \left(2+2^{\frac{1}{2}}\right)\left(\int_{2}^{\frac{5}{2}} s^2 ds\right) - \int_{2}^{3} t^2\left(2+t^{\frac{1}{2}}\right)dt \\
&= \frac{61}{24}\left(\sqrt{2}+2\right) + \frac{91}{24}\left(\sqrt{3}+2\right) + \frac{1}{168}\left(384\sqrt{2} - 375\sqrt{10} - 854\right) = 0.0327721.
\end{aligned}
$$

where

$$
B\left(\varphi, \nu, \frac{5}{2}\right) := \int_{\frac{5}{2}}^{3}\left(\int_{t}^{3} \varphi(s)ds\right)\mathcal{D}\left(\nu'_{\varphi H}(t), \tilde{0}\right)dt + \int_{2}^{\frac{5}{2}}\left(\int_{2}^{t} \varphi(s)ds\right)\mathcal{D}\left(\nu'_{\varphi H}(t), \tilde{0}\right)dt.
$$

Now, we calculate the bounds for $B\left(\varphi, \nu, \frac{5}{2}\right)$ *as follows:*

$$
B\left(\varphi, \nu, \frac{5}{2}\right) \leq \begin{cases}
\int_{\frac{5}{2}}^{3} s^2 ds \int_{\frac{5}{2}}^{3} \frac{1}{2\sqrt{t}}dt + \int_{2}^{\frac{5}{2}} s^2 ds \int_{2}^{\frac{5}{2}} \frac{1}{2\sqrt{t}}dt \\
\left[\int_{\frac{5}{2}}^{3}\left(\int_{\frac{5}{2}}^{t} s^8 ds\right)dt\right]^{\frac{1}{4}}\left(\int_{\frac{5}{2}}^{3}\left[\frac{1}{2\sqrt{t}}\right]^{\frac{4}{3}}dt\right)^{\frac{3}{4}} \\
+\left[\int_{2}^{\frac{5}{2}}\left(\int_{t}^{\frac{5}{2}} s^8 ds\right)dt\right]^{\frac{1}{4}}\left(\int_{2}^{\frac{5}{2}}\left[\frac{1}{2\sqrt{t}}\right]^{\frac{4}{3}}dt\right)^{\frac{3}{4}}, \\
\frac{1}{2}\sqrt{\frac{2}{5}}\int_{\frac{5}{2}}^{3}\left(\int_{t}^{3} s^2 ds\right)dt + \frac{1}{2\sqrt{2}}\int_{2}^{\frac{5}{2}}\left(\int_{2}^{t} s^2 ds\right)dt.
\end{cases}
$$

We use the software Mathematica to evaluate the above integrals as follows:

$$
\begin{aligned}
&\int_{\frac{5}{2}}^{3} s^2 ds \int_{\frac{5}{2}}^{3} \frac{1}{2\sqrt{t}}dt + \int_{2}^{\frac{5}{2}} s^2 ds \int_{2}^{\frac{5}{2}} \frac{1}{2\sqrt{t}}dt \\
&\qquad = \frac{91}{24}\left(\sqrt{3} - \sqrt{\frac{5}{2}}\right) + \frac{61\left(\sqrt{5}-2\right)}{24\sqrt{2}} = 0.996476,
\end{aligned}
$$

$$
\begin{aligned}
&\left[\int_{\frac{5}{2}}^{3}\left(\int_{2}^{t} s^8 ds\right)dt\right]^{\frac{1}{4}}\left(\int_{\frac{5}{2}}^{3}\left[\frac{1}{2\sqrt{t}}\right]^{\frac{4}{3}}dt\right)^{\frac{3}{4}} \\
&\qquad + \left[\int_{2}^{\frac{5}{2}}\left(\int_{t}^{3} s^8 ds\right)dt\right]^{\frac{1}{4}}\left(\int_{2}^{\frac{5}{2}}\left[\frac{1}{2\sqrt{t}}\right]^{\frac{4}{3}}dt\right)^{\frac{3}{4}} \\
&= \frac{1}{16}\left(\sqrt[3]{6} - \sqrt[3]{5}\right)^{3/4}\sqrt[4]{\frac{144{,}237{,}333}{5}} + \frac{1}{16}\sqrt[4]{\frac{10{,}228{,}879}{10}}\left(3\left(\sqrt[3]{10}-2\right)\right)^{3/4} = 1.97398
\end{aligned}
$$

and

$$
\frac{1}{2}\sqrt{\frac{2}{5}}\int_{\frac{5}{2}}^{3}\left(\int_{t}^{3} s^2 ds\right)dt + \frac{1}{2\sqrt{2}}\int_{2}^{\frac{5}{2}}\left(\int_{2}^{t} s^2 ds\right)dt = \frac{83}{192}\sqrt{\frac{5}{2}} + \frac{165}{128\sqrt{2}} = 1.59502.
$$

Hence, it can be observed from the above calculations of that the inequality (14) of Theorem 16 is valid for the above choices of functions over the interval $[2,3]$ *Figure 1.*

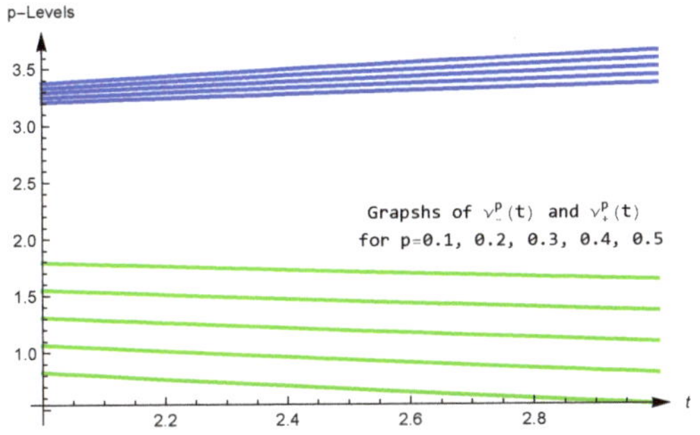

Figure 1. Graphs of p-levels of $v_-^p(t)$ are shown in green and those of $v_+^p(t)$ are shown in blue.

4. Concluding Remarks

In the last forty years, there has been significant growth in the field of mathematical inequalities. Many researchers have published a plethora of articles using innovative approaches. Within the extensive literature on mathematical inequalities, trapezoidal-type inequalities stand out as important. These inequalities are utilized to estimate the absolute deviation of the average value of a function's values at the end points of a closed interval of the real line from its integral mean.

Mathematicians have established various generalizations of trapezoidal-type inequalities, such as those for functions of bounded variation, Lipschitzian mappings, absolutely continuous functions, operator convex functions, and those involving two functions with values in Banach spaces. One of the notable studies on the generalizations of trapezoidal-type inequalities is highlighted in the paper [9].

In the present study, a more general result of the trapezoidal-type in the fuzzy context is proven, which generalizes not only the results from [9] but also extends the results from [1,2,4,7,8]. In order to obtain the results, a number of novel results from the theory of calculus of fuzzy number-valued functions were used. An identity has been proven by using the integration by parts, the properties of space of fuzzy numbers, and by employing the Hölder inequality to prove several new and novel inequalities of the trapezoidal-type for functions that have values in the space of fuzzy numbers. A numerical example is given to exhibit the validity of the obtained results. The results of this study can be a good source to obtain more new results for the researchers working in the field of mathematical inequalities in fuzzy number-valued calculus.

Funding: This work is supported by the Deanship of Scientific Research, King Faisal University under the Ambitious Researcher Track (Grant No. KFU241925).

Data Availability Statement: No data have been used in the manuscript.

Acknowledgments: The author would be very thankful to all the anonymous referees for their very useful and constructive comments in order to improve the paper.

Conflicts of Interest: The author declares no conflicts of interest.

References

1. Cerone, P.; Dragomir, S.S.; Pearce, C.E.M. A generalised trapezoid inequality for functions of bounded variation. *Turk. J. Math.* **2000**, *24*, 147–163.
2. Dragomir, S.S. On the trapezoid quadrature formula for Lipschitzian mappings and applications. *Tamkang J. Math.* **1999**, *30*, 133–138. [CrossRef]
3. Cerone, P.; Dragomir, S.S. Trapezoidal-type rules from an inequalities point of view. In *Handbook of Analytic-Computational Methods in Applied Mathematics*; Anastassiou, G.A., Ed.; Chapman & Hall/CRC Press: New York, NY, USA, 2000; pp. 65–134.
4. Dragomir, S.S. Reverses of operator Féjer's inequalities. *Tokyo J. Math.* **2021**, *44*, 351–366. [CrossRef]
5. Dragomir, S.S. Operator Inequalities of Ostrowski and Trapezoidal Type. In *Springer Briefs in Mathematics*; Springer: New York, NY, USA, 2012; p. x+112, ISBN 978-1-4614-1778-1.

6. Dragomir, S.S. *Riemann–Stieltjes Integral Inequalities for Complex Functions Defined on Unit Circle with Applications to Unitary Operators in Hilbert Spaces*; CRC Press: Boca Raton, FL, USA, 2019; 160p, ISBN 9780367337100.
7. Dragomir, S.S. Generalised trapezoid-type inequalities for complex functions defined on unit circle with applications for unitary operators in Hilbert spaces. *Mediterr. J. Math.* **2015**, *12*, 573–591. [CrossRef]
8. Dragomir, S.S. Trapezoid type inequalities for complex functions defined on the unit circle with applications for unitary operators in Hilbert spaces. *Georgian Math. J.* **2016**, *23*, 199–210. [CrossRef]
9. Dragomir, S.S. Generalized trapezoid type inequalities for functions with values in Banach spaces. *J. Iran. Math. Soc.* **2021**, *2*, 17–38.
10. Barnett, N.S.; Buşe, C.; Cerone, P.; Dragomir, S.S. On weighted Ostrowski type inequalities for operators and vector-valued functions. *J. Inequal. Pure Appl. Math.* **2002**, *3*, 12.
11. Latif, M.A. More general Ostrowski type inequalities in the fuzzy context. *Mathematics* **2024**, *12*, 500. 12030500. [CrossRef]
12. Anastassiou, G.A. Ostrowski type inequalities. *Proc. Am. Math. Soc.* **1995**, *123*, 3775–3791. [CrossRef]
13. Ahmadini, A.A.H.; Afzal, W.; Abbas, M.; Aly, E.S. Weighted Fejér, Hermite–Hadamard, and Trapezium-Type Inequalities for (h_1, h_2)–Godunova–Levin Preinvex Function with Applications and Two Open Problems. *Mathematics* **2024**, *12*, 382. [CrossRef]
14. Anastassiou, G.A. Fuzzy Ostrowski type inequalities. *J. Comput. Appl. Math.* **2003**, *22*, 279–292. [CrossRef]
15. Anastassiou, G.A. Ostrowski and Landau inequalities for Banach space valued functions. *Math. Comput. Model.* **2012**, *55*, 312–329. [CrossRef]
16. Hezenci, F.; Budak, H. Novel results on trapezoid-type inequalities for conformable fractional integrals. *Turk. J. Math.* **2023**, *47*, 425–438. [CrossRef]
17. Dragomir, S.S. A refinement of Ostrowski's inequality for absolutely continuous functions whose derivatives belong to L_∞ and applications. *Lib. Math.* **2002**, *22*, 49–63.
18. Latif, M.A.; Almutairi, O.B. Ostrowski-Type Inequalities for Functions of Two Variables in Banach Spaces. *Mathematics* **2024**, *12*, 2748. [CrossRef]
19. Niu, Y.; Ali, R.S.; Talib, N.; Mubeen, S.; Rahman, G.; Yildiz, C.; Awwad, F.A.; Ismail, E.A.A. Exploring Advanced Versions of Hermite-Hadamard and Trapezoid-Type Inequalities by Implementation of Fuzzy Interval-Valued Functions. *J. Funct. Spaces* **2024**, *2024*, 1988187. [CrossRef]
20. Stojiljković, V.; Mirkov, N.; Radenović, S. Variations in the Tensorial Trapezoid Type Inequalities for Convex Functions of Self-Adjoint Operators in Hilbert Spaces. *Symmetry* **2024**, *16*, 121. [CrossRef]
21. Wu, C.; Gong, Z. On Henstock integral of fuzzy number valued functions (I). *Fuzzy Sets Syst.* **2001**, *120*, 523–532. [CrossRef]
22. Congxin, W.; Ming, M. On embedding problem of fuzzy number space: Part 3. *Fuzzy Sets Syst.* **1992**, *16*, 281–286. [CrossRef]
23. Anastassiou, G.A.; Gal, S. On a fuzzy trigonometric approximation theorem of Weierstrass-type. *J. Fuzzy Math.* **2001**, *9*, 701–708.
24. Kaleva, O.; Seikkala, S. On fuzzy metric spaces. *Fuzzy Sets Syst.* **1984**, *12*, 215–229. [CrossRef]
25. Stefanini, L. A generalization of Hukuhara difference and division for interval and fuzzy arithmetic. *Fuzzy Sets Syst.* **2010**, *161*, 1564–1584. [CrossRef]
26. Bede, B.; Stefanini, L. Generalized differentiability of fuzzy-valued functions. *Fuzzy Sets Syst.* **2013**, *230*, 119–141. [CrossRef]
27. Stefanini, L.; Bede, B. Generalized Hukuhara differentiability of interval-valued functions and interval differential equations. *Nonlinear Anal.* **2009**, *71*, 1311–1328. [CrossRef]
28. Anastassiou, G.A. Fuzzy Mathematics: Approximation Theory. In *Studies in Fuzziness and Soft Computing*; Springer: Berlin/Heidelberg, Germany, 2010.
29. Gouyandeh, Z.; Allahviranloo, T.; Abbasbandy, S.; Armand, A. A fuzzy solution of heat equation under generalized Hukuhara differentiability by fuzzy Fourier transform. *Fuzzy Sets Syst.* **2017**, *309*, 81–97. [CrossRef]
30. Kaleva, O. Fuzzy differential equations. *Fuzzy Sets Syst.* **1987**, *24*, 301–317. [CrossRef]
31. Anastassiou, G.A. Rate of convergence of Fuzzy neural network operators, univariate case. *J. Fuzzy Math.* **2002**, 755–780.
32. Anastassiou, G.A. On H-fuzzy differentiation. *Math. Balk.* **2002**, *16*, 153–193.
33. Armand, A.; Allahviranloo, T.; Gouyandeh, Z. Some fundamental results on fuzzy calculus. *Iran. J. Fuzzy Syst.* **2018**, *15*, 27–46.
34. Ostrowski, A. Über die Absolutabweichung einer differentiebaren Funktion von ihrem Integralmittelwert. *Comment. Math. Helv.* **1937**, *10*, 226–227. [CrossRef]
35. Matić, M.; Barnes, E.S.; Marsh, D.C.B.; Radok, J.R.M. *Elementary Inequalities*; P. Noordhoff Ltd.: Groningen, The Netherlands, 1964.

information

Article

Simulation-Enhanced MQAM Modulation Identification in Communication Systems: A Subtractive Clustering-Based PSO-FCM Algorithm Study

Zhi Quan, Hailong Zhang, Jiyu Luo and Haijun Sun *

School of Electrical and Information Engineering, Zhengzhou University, Zhengzhou 450001, China; iezquan@zzu.edu.cn (Z.Q.); zhl1820827289@163.com (H.Z.)
* Correspondence: iehjsun@zzu.edu.cn

Abstract: Signal modulation recognition is often reliant on clustering algorithms. The fuzzy c-means (FCM) algorithm, which is commonly used for such tasks, often converges to local optima. This presents a challenge, particularly in low-signal-to-noise-ratio (SNR) environments. We propose an enhanced FCM algorithm that incorporates particle swarm optimization (PSO) to improve the accuracy of recognizing M-ary quadrature amplitude modulation (MQAM) signal orders. The process is a two-step clustering process. First, the constellation diagram of the received signal is used by a subtractive clustering algorithm based on SNR to figure out the initial number of clustering centers. The PSO-FCM algorithm then refines these centers to improve precision. Accurate signal classification and identification are achieved by evaluating the relative sizes of the radii around the cluster centers within the MQAM constellation diagram and determining the modulation order. The results indicate that the SC-based PSO-FCM algorithm outperforms the conventional FCM in clustering effectiveness, notably enhancing modulation recognition rates in low-SNR conditions, when evaluated against a variety of QAM signals ranging from 4QAM to 64QAM.

Keywords: modulation recognition; fuzzy c-means algorithm; constellation diagram; particle swarm optimization algorithm; MQAM signal

Citation: Quan, Z.; Zhang, H.; Luo, J.; Sun, H. Simulation-Enhanced MQAM Modulation Identification in Communication Systems: A Subtractive Clustering-Based PSO-FCM Algorithm Study. *Information* **2024**, *15*, 42. https://doi.org/10.3390/info15010042

Academic Editor: Giuseppe Psaila

Received: 25 November 2023
Revised: 7 January 2024
Accepted: 8 January 2024
Published: 12 January 2024

1. Introduction

The recognition of modulation type in an unknown signal holds significant importance as it provides essential insights into its structure, origin, and properties. Automatic modulation classification serves various purposes, including spectrum surveillance and management, interference identification, military threat evaluation, electronic countermeasures, source identification, and numerous others. For instance, identifying the modulation type of an intercepted signal allows for more efficient jamming by focusing available resources on vital signal parameters. This is particularly relevant in wireless communications, where different services follow established modulation standards.

Modulation recognition is a crucial aspect of signal processing, entailing the determination of a signal's modulation mode without prior knowledge. M-ary quadrature amplitude modulation (MQAM) is a widely used digital modulation technology employed in satellite communication and cable networks due to its commendable spectrum efficiency and robust interference resistance. The lack of prior information, such as signal parameters at the receiving end, can make it hard to figure out the modulation order of the QAM signal in non-cooperative communication situations, especially when the signal-to-noise ratio (SNR) is low [1].

Digital modulation identification algorithms can be categorized into two main groups: maximum likelihood hypothesis-based methods rooted in decision theory and statistical pattern recognition techniques relying on feature extraction [2,3]. These techniques are particularly valuable in uncooperative channel environments, and pattern recognition algorithms are often preferred in practical applications due to the absence of prior knowledge about received modulation signals [4]. Higher-order constellation (HOC)-based techniques are well-known pattern recognition methods that perform well at classifying digital modulation signals when the signal-to-noise ratio (SNR) is low. However, they might not work well for classifying higher-order MQAM modulation formats [5]. The constellation diagram varies between different modulation signal types and serves as a robust signature. Researchers have employed algorithms that utilize constellation diagram to identify the order of MQAM [6–9]. It is possible to recognize modulation in MQAM signals by putting together the constellation diagram using clustering algorithms [10].

The subtractive clustering (SC) algorithm constitutes a significant focus in the field of MQAM signal constellation reconstruction [11]. This algorithm considers each data point as a potential cluster center and calculates it based on the density index of the signal's data points. Lu et al. [12] predefined the optimal clustering radius for MQAM signals and employed the SC algorithm to reconstruct the MQAM signal's constellation diagram. However, this approach demands significant computational resources and exhibits poor clustering performance in low signal-to-noise ratio conditions. Cheng et al. [13] extracted characteristic parameters from the signal's constellation diagram using the SC algorithm and compared them with those from the standard constellation diagram to figure out what kind of modulation it was. However, the method showed limited noise resilience and lacked a standardized approach for selecting clustering radii.

To improve the accuracy of clustering center coordinates within the signal's constellation diagram, some studies integrate the fuzzy c-means (FCM) algorithm for secondary clustering. FCM is a clustering algorithm that assesses the degree to which each data point belongs to a specific cluster through a membership relationship [14,15]. However, FCM is sensitive to the values that are chosen at the start for the cluster centers, and its results often get stuck in local optima, making it harder to find the globally optimal clustering centers. To address this challenge, stochastic techniques such as particle swarm optimization (PSO) are employed to increase the likelihood of locating the global optimum [16]. Implementing PSO in the FCM algorithm has been successful in various areas, including image processing and engineering [17–20].

This paper introduces a PSO-FCM algorithm for the reconstruction of the MQAM modulation constellation diagram. This algorithm combines the FCM and PSO algorithms into a three-step process: initial cluster center computation using the subtractive clustering (SC) algorithm based on the signal-to-noise ratio (SN-SC); subsequent utilization of the PSO-FCM algorithm, leveraging the initially obtained cluster centers; and the combined benefits of FCM and PSO for improved cluster center accuracy. The PSO-FCM algorithm avoids getting stuck in local minima by utilizing the PSO global search method to find candidate solutions. The modulation type of the signal constellation can be found by finding the ratio of the largest and smallest cluster center radius.

The subsequent sections of this paper are organized as follows: Section 2 outlines the signal model employed; Section 3 provides a detailed explanation of the methodology used in this study, which includes the signal-to-noise ratio-based subtractive clustering (SN-SC) algorithm and the particle swarm optimization with fuzzy c-means (PSO-FCM) algorithm; Section 4 illustrates the simulation results; and Section 5 concludes the work.

2. Signal Model

In the receiver system, the sampled signal, denoted as y_i, is represented as follows:

$$y_i = \alpha e^{j2\pi f_o i t_s} s_i + w_i, \quad (1)$$

where s_i denotes the baseband signal, shaped using a root-raised cosine pulse with a random roll-off factor. The sampling duration is represented by the variable t_s, while the complex-valued channel fading gain, capturing the flat fading experienced by the signal, is represented by α. The methodology that we have developed is specifically designed to be effective for narrowband signals, which have a bandwidth smaller than the coherence bandwidth of the channel. By narrowband, we refer to signals whose frequency span falls within a range where the channel exhibits consistent characteristics and a limited range of frequency-related variations. In this scenario, each frequency component undergoes the same block-fading coefficient, allowing for simplified representation using a single-tap channel filter α. The term f_o accounts for the carrier frequency offset, arising from a discrepancy between the RF signal frequency and local oscillator frequency. The term w_i denotes zero mean Gaussian noise. The carrier frequency offset (CFO) in the received signal y_i is estimated using an eighth-order non-linearity and corrected using the method proposed in [11]. After that, the signal that has been corrected for the CFO is resampled to an integer multiple of the estimated symbol rate for matched filtering. The system accommodates for the presence of additive white Gaussian noise (AWGN) and factors in slow and flat fading channels. The received symbol x_i is expressed as

$$x_i = \alpha h_i + w_i', \tag{2}$$

where h_i represents the extracted symbol from one of the considered modulation schemes, and w_i' is Gaussian noise. The signal-to-noise ratio (SNR) for symbols with unit power can be defined as:

$$SNR = 10 \log_{10} \frac{P_s}{\sigma_{w'}^2}, \tag{3}$$

where $P_s = \frac{1}{N} \sum_{i=0}^{N-1} |x_i|^2$.

3. Methodology

Our proposed methodology (Figure 1) offers an approach for classifying single-carrier QAM modulations. This technique integrates two distinct algorithms: SN-SC and PSO-FCM. It focuses on the analysis of constellation shapes within the in-phase and quadrature (I-Q) diagrams associated with QAM modulations. To ensure a precise classification process, the methodology follows a systematic procedure. Initially, phase correction is applied to received signals. After that, the SN-SC algorithm quickly goes through the corrected constellation points to find and identify the cluster centers in each I-Q diagram. By utilizing the cluster centers obtained from the SN-SC block, the integration of PSO and FCM algorithms further refines the received signals, resulting in an accurate classification of the QAM modulation order.

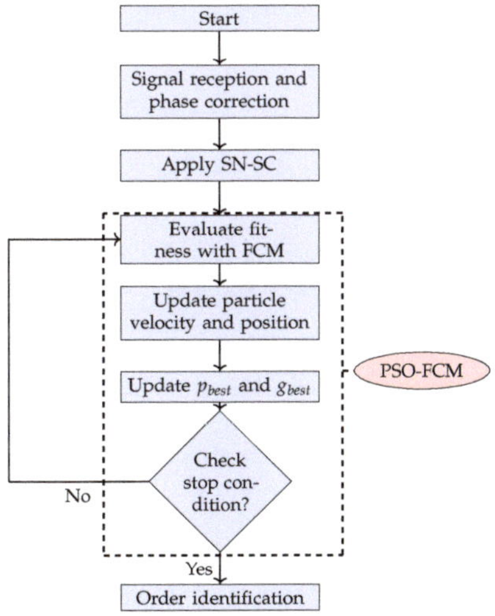

Figure 1. Block diagram of the subtractive-clustering-based PSO-FCM algorithm.

3.1. Signal-to-Noise-Ratio-Based Subtractive Clustering Algorithm (SN-SC)

The SN-SC algorithm introduces a clustering approach that integrates considerations of both local density and SNR, as outlined in Algorithm 1. In the SN-SC method, each data point is considered a potential cluster center with the maximum local density, where the density measure D_i is calculated as follows:

$$D_i = \sum_{k=1}^{N} \exp\left(-\frac{\|x_i - x_k\|^2}{K_a \cdot {r_a}^2}\right), i = 1, 2, \cdots, N. \tag{4}$$

The SN-SC algorithm relies on the 'density' metric to identify initial cluster centers within a neighbourhood radius (r_a), which is defined as $\sqrt{\frac{\frac{1}{N}\sum_{i=0}^{N-1}|x_i|^2}{\mathrm{SNR}+1}}$. r_a also represents the average noise power amplitude. If the radius is too small, potential data points near the cluster center may be overlooked. Conversely, setting the radius too high increases the contribution of all potential data points, including noise, which can distort the modulated signal and affect the density radius parameter of the constellation diagram. The coefficient K_a represents the adjustment weighting of different types of modulated signals. Choosing an appropriate scaling factor, K_a, enables the algorithm to attain a relatively stable density metric across the entire SNR range. Determining the optimal value of K_a in practical engineering often involves conducting multiple experiments.

Algorithm 1 SN-SC Algorithm

Step	**Operation**
	Input: x, λ, SNR
	Output: z
	Initialization
	$cl = 1, \mathrm{Flag} = 0,$
1	$r_a = \frac{P_s}{\mathrm{SNR}+1}$
	for $i = 1 : N$
2	$D_i = \sum_{k=1}^{N} \exp\left(-\frac{\|x_i - x_k\|^2}{k_a \cdot r_a}\right)$
	end
3	$D_{cl} = \max\{\mathbf{D}\}, z_{cl} = x_{cl}$
	while Flag $= 0$
4	for each i data point $D_i = D_i - D_{cl} \cdot \exp\left(\frac{\|x_i - z_{cl}\|^2}{k_b \cdot r_a}\right)$
5	$cl = cl + 1$
6	repeat step 3
7	if $D_{cl} < \lambda D_1$, Flag $= 1$
8	return z

Each data point updates its density based on the obtained center for the lth cluster (x_{cl}) as follows:

$$D_i = D_i - D_{cl} \cdot \exp\left(\frac{\|x_i - x_{cl}\|^2}{K_b \cdot r_a}\right), \tag{5}$$

where D_{cl} represents the density of the data point (x_{cl}), and K_b is a value greater than one to avoid obtaining closely spaced centers. The algorithm selects the data point with the maximum density as the new center of the cluster, denoted as x_{cl+1}. The algorithm repeats the process until it meets the condition $D_{cl+1} < \lambda D_1$, signaling the termination of the cluster center decision. In this condition, λ is a given parameter ($0 < \lambda < 1$).

3.2. Proposed Integration of PSO and FCM Algorithms

In this section, we will provide a brief description of the FCM and PSO algorithms, followed by an introduction to the new version of the hybrid clustering method based on FCM and PSO integration.

3.2.1. FCM

Fuzzy c-means (FCM) is a clustering algorithm that assigns each data point to clusters with varying membership degrees. This approach effectively groups data into fuzzy subsets, which is crucial for applications in pattern recognition or data analysis. Notably, FCM requires a predefined cluster count to perform optimally, which is obtained from the cluster centers determined by the SN-SC algorithm.

Let $\mathbf{x} = \{x_1, \cdots, x_i, \cdots, x_N\}$ represent a clustering dataset of N objects indexed by i, with each x_i represented by a vector of quantitative variables. $\mathbf{z} = \{z_1, \cdots, z_C\}$ denotes the set of centers of C clusters listed by j and $U = [u_{ij}]_{N \times C}$ as a fuzzy partition matrix, where u_{ij} indicates the membership of the ith object to the jth cluster. The constraints on u_{ij} are as follows: $u_{ij} \in [0,1], \sum_{j=1}^{C} u_{ij} = 1$, and $0 < \sum_{i=1}^{N} u_{ij} < N$. The FCM algorithm aims to minimize an objective function by finding the optimal cluster centers and their corresponding membership degrees, as defined in the following equation:

$$J = \sum_{i=1}^{N} \sum_{j=1}^{C} (u_{ij})^m d_{ij}^2, \tag{6}$$

where $m(m > 1)$ is the fuzzy weighting exponent and $d_{ij} = \|x_i - z_j\|$ represents the Euclidean distance. The dissimilarity between data x_i and cluster center z_j is indicated. To minimize J, clustering center z_j and the membership degree u_{ij} are updated according to:

$$z_j = \frac{\sum_i^N u_{ij}^m x_i}{\sum_{i=1}^N u_{ij}^m} \qquad j \in \{1, 2, \cdots, C\} \tag{7}$$

and

$$u_{ij} = \frac{1}{\sum_{k=1}^{C} (\frac{d_{ij}}{d_{ik}})^{\frac{2}{m-1}}}. \tag{8}$$

The update stops when the cluster centers from the previous iteration closely approximate those generated in the current iteration.

3.2.2. PSO

Inspired by the collective behavior of birds seeking food, the PSO algorithm is a population-based optimization technique. Potential solutions, termed particles, traverse the problem space by following the best particles. The fitness value referred to as p_{best} assesses each particle's coordinates in the problem space associated with the best solution achieved so far. The swarm progresses toward the best solution, the global best, denoted as g_{best}. The search for p_{best} and g_{best} follows:

$$x_i^{(t)} = v_i^{(t-1)} + x_i^{(t-1)}, \tag{9}$$

where

$$\begin{aligned} v_i^{(t)} &= \omega \cdot v_i^{(t-1)} + c_1 \cdot r_1^{(t-1)} \cdot (p_{best\,i} - x_i^{(t-1)}) \\ &+ c_2 \cdot r_2^{(t-1)} \cdot (g_{best} - x_i^{(t-1)}), \end{aligned} \tag{10}$$

where r_1 and r_2 are uniformly distributed in $[0,1]$. c_1 and c_2 represent acceleration parameters. The inertia weight ω is updated as $\omega = \omega_0 - \frac{(\omega_0 - \omega_1) \times t}{t_{max}}$. $p_{best\,i}$ denotes the better position of the ith particle compared to its history up to the tth iteration, while g_{best} represents the best position within the swarm up to the tth iteration.

3.2.3. Problem

FCM's nonlinear optimization based on fuzzy set theory iteratively improves the initial cluster centers to approximate final cluster centers close to the actual ones. However, it might trap local minima due to local search methods. Deviation of the final cluster centers from the actual ones can compromise FCM's clustering results. In contrast, population-based PSO is a global optimization algorithm that employs random search techniques but might have limited clustering performance.

3.2.4. PSO-FCM

To overcome FCM's local minima trapping and achieve better clustering results, we harness the strengths of both FCM and PSO. In particular, the PSO-FCM algorithm uses FCM's objective function (6) as the fitness function and PSO's global search method to find cluster centers.

The PSO-FCM algorithm utilizes particles in PSO to represent potential solutions for FCM's cluster centers. The positions of particles in a swarm of Q particles encode the cluster centers $\mathbf{z}$. Each particle q is defined as $x_q = (d_{q1}, d_{q2}, \cdots, d_{qC})$, representing candidates in the swarm (Q) for clustering the data. The updated dimension values representing cluster centers generate $\mathbf{z}$ by decoding g_{best} when PSO recognizes an accepted cluster center or reaches a predefined number of iterations. The convergence of both algorithms toward the same objective function for optimal clustering drives the minimization of fitness functions in PSO-FCM. This fusion of FCM and PSO, through PSO-FCM, capitalizes on the advantageous features of both. Below, Algorithm 2 summarizes the PSO-FCM algorithm.

Algorithm 2 PSO-FCM algorithm

Input: $t_{max}, m, c_1, c_2, \omega_0, \omega_1$.
  Initialization
  $x_q^{(0)} = (d_{q1}, d_{q2}, \cdots, d_{qC}), v_q^{(0)} = (v_{q1}, v_{q2}, \cdots, v_{qC})$
  $pbest_q = x_q{}^{(0)}$
For each particle
  Calculate the $fitness$ of particle.
$temp = \min\{fitness(pbest_1), fitness(pbest_2), \cdots, fitness(pbest_Q)\};$
$gbest = temp;$
Repeat until t_{max} iterations are reached
    Update v_q and x_q.
    Calculate the membership u_{qj}.
    Update the $fitness$ of the particle;
    If $fitness(x_q^{(t)}) < fitness(pbest_q)$
      $pbest_q = x_q^{(t)};$
      Update p_{best};
    if $fitness(pbest_q) < fitness(gbest)$,
      $g_{best} = p_{best_q}$.
  Decode g_{best} to obtain cluster centers $\mathbf{z}$.

In computing the fitness of each particle q, we first derive the cluster center z_q from the particle's position representation. Subsequently, we calculate the membership degree u_{qj} for each data point x_q using Equation (8). By utilizing these cluster centers and membership degrees, we evaluate the $fitness$ of each particle q using Equation (6). Notably, the minimization of the fitness function in PSO-FCM aligns with minimizing the objection function J in FCM. Both algorithms define the same objective function, thereby aiming for optimal clustering. PSO-FCM leverages the strengths of both FCM and PSO, utilizing their favorable features to minimize the fitness function in pursuit of achieving optimal clustering. Equations (9) and (10) update the velocity v_q and position x_q of each particle q.

3.3. Modulation Order Identification Using Circle Radius Ratio

Each point in an MQAM constellation diagram is surrounded by circles of varying diameters, which are determined by their distance from the constellation center. Different orders of QAM signals exhibit characteristic ranges of circle diameter values. This property allows us to utilize circle radii within the constellation map for the purpose of MQAM signal classification and identification. In the absence of noise interference, a noise-free 16QAM's constellation map displays a point with the highest amplitude corresponding to a circle with radius r_{max}, while the point with the lowest amplitude corresponds to a circle with radius r_{min}, as shown in Figure 2. In a standard constellation plot, the ratio of the maximum to minimum circle radius is defined as $R_b = \frac{r_{max}}{r_{min}}$.

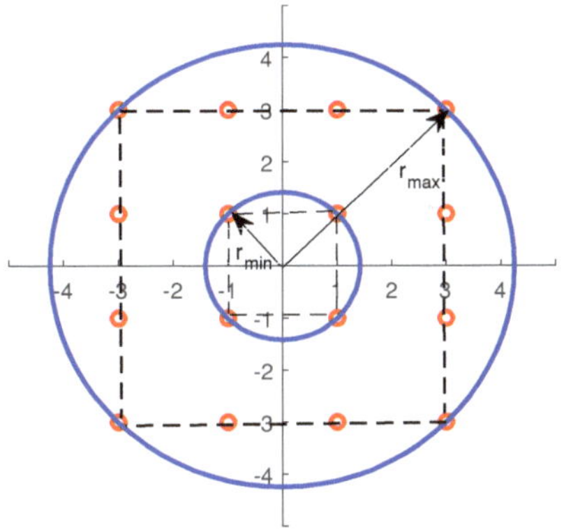

Figure 2. 16QAM modulation constellation with inner radius (r_{min}) and outer radius (r_{max}).

After applying the clustering algorithm to obtain the reconstructed signal's constellation diagram, we calculate and sort the distances between the cluster center and the starting point in descending order. The top W distances are averaged to determine the maximum circle radius, while the bottom W distances are averaged to determine the minimum circle radius. The R_b values of different MQAM modulation signals are categorized into distinct ranges based on predefined standard values. The categorization is as follows:

$$\text{MQAM} = \begin{cases} 4QAM & : \ 0.0 < R_b \leq 1.6 \\ 8QAM & : \ 1.6 < R_b \leq 2.6 \\ 16QAM & : \ 2.6 < R_b \leq 3.5 \\ 32QAM & : \ 3.5 < R_b \leq 5.6 \\ 64QAM & : \ 5.6 < R_b \leq 8.1\,. \end{cases} \tag{11}$$

Noise can lead to inaccuracies in the initial determination of cluster centers through adaptive subtractive clustering based on the signal-to-noise ratio. The update of semi-supervised fuzzy mean clustering affects the positions of cluster centers but not the number of cluster centers. Consequently, the number of cluster centers in the reconstructed constellation map may not correspond to the actual number of modulation points. By employing the radius method on different circles of the constellation map, we can calculate radius values, mitigating the impact of an incorrect number of cluster centers. This approach does not affect the final recognition result and enhances the classification accuracy.

4. Simulations Results

In this section, we present the numerical results obtained through MATLAB simulations of SN-SC, FCM, and PSO-FCM. Table 1 provides an overview of the simulation parameters employed in our study.

Table 1. Parameter values used in the simulations.

Algorithms	Parameters	Values
SN-SC	K_a	1
	K_b	1.5
	λ	0.4
	N	3000
PSO	c_1,c_2	1.5
	Q	30
	ω_0, ω_1	1.1, 0.5
	ε	10^{-5}
	t_{max}	300
FCM	m	2
	W	2

In the low-SNR scenario (SNR = 4 dB), the FCM algorithm is susceptible to becoming trapped in local minima, as depicted in Figure 3. When the FCM algorithm, which relies on a fuzzy clustering objective function, is used, this tendency can cause some cluster centers to shift within the constellation. This sensitivity to initialization and the resulting misplacement can lead to substantial errors during the decision-making and demodulation processes. While the PSO-FCM algorithm demonstrates superior clustering performance compared to FCM, it still encounters challenges in fully mitigating the issue of local optimization, as shown by the presence of local optima in Figure 4.

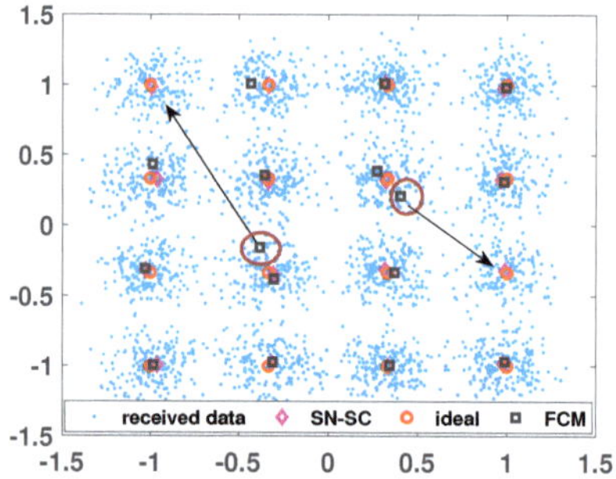

Figure 3. 16QAM received signal modulation at SNR = 4 dB with clustering centers for SN-SC and FCM.

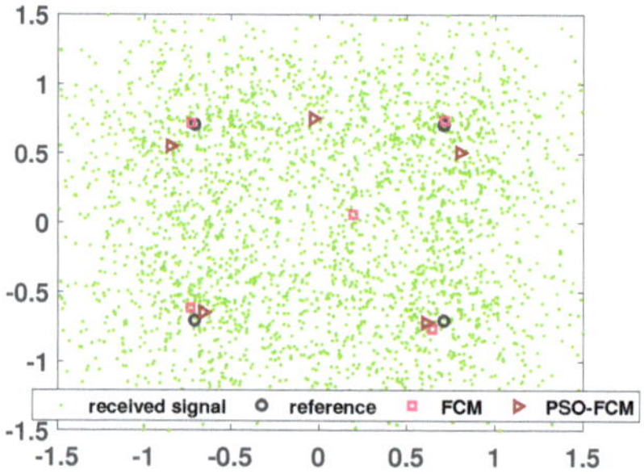

(**a**) 4QAM, SNR = 0 dB

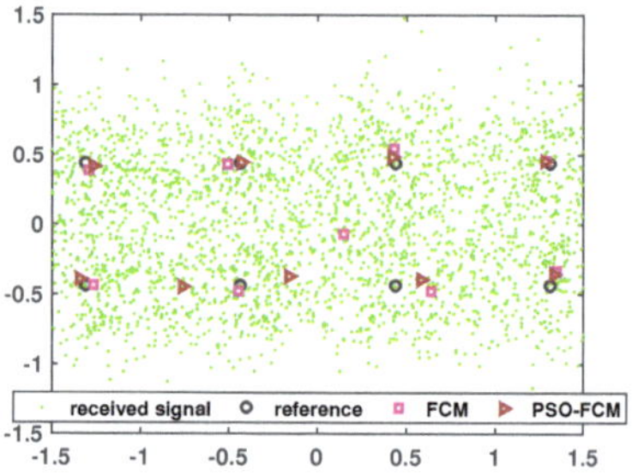

(**b**) 8QAM, SNR = 0 dB

Figure 4. *Cont.*

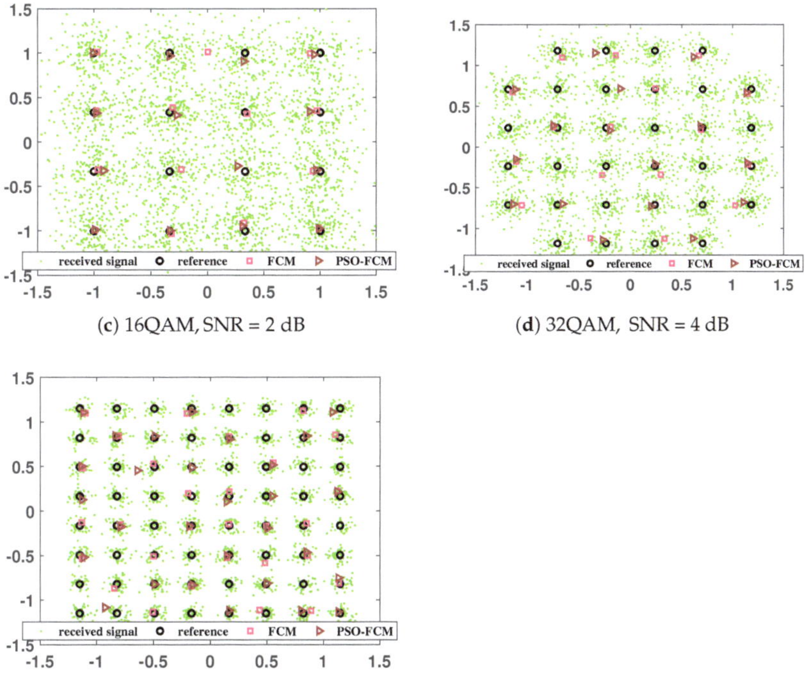

(**c**) 16QAM, SNR = 2 dB

(**d**) 32QAM, SNR = 4 dB

(**e**) 64QAM, SNR = 6 dB

Figure 4. The clustering performance of FCM and PSO-FCM; 4QAM with SNR = 0 dB, 8QAM with SNR = 0 dB, 16QAM with SNR = 2 dB, 32QAM with SNR = 4 dB, 64QAM with SNR = 6 dB.

In Table 2, we present the average number of cluster centers obtained by SN-SC (#1), SC with $r_a = 0.22$ (#2), and SC with $r_a = 0.33$ (#3) for 4QAM, 16QAM, 32QAM, and 64QAM digitally modulated signals under varying SNR scenarios. Algorithms #2 and #3 based on the SC method perform well in clustering 16QAM and 4QAM signals; however, their reliable classification performance cannot be guaranteed for other modulation schemes. In contrast, algorithm #1 demonstrates its suitability for diverse modulation signals and outperforms algorithms #2 and #3 in overall classification performance.

Table 2. Comparison of clustering results for different-order QAM signals under various SNR situations using the SC algorithm and the SN-SC algorithm.

Type	0 dB			2 dB			4 dB			6 dB			8 dB			10 dB		
	#1	#2	#3	#1	#2	#3	#1	#2	#3	#1	#2	#3	#1	#2	#3	#1	#2	#3
4QAM	**2.9**	13.1	4.9	**3.8**	12.6	4	**4**	11.9	4	**4**	5.9	4	**4**	4	4	**4**	4	4
8QAM	**6.8**	14.5	6.2	**7.6**	15.4	6.2	**7.9**	14.2	6.5	**8**	10.2	6.8	**8**	8	7.2	**8**	8	8
16QAM	**13.6**	18.9	7.6	**15.2**	16	9.1	**15.8**	16	10.2	**16**	16	11.8	**16**	16	12.8	**16**	16	14.5
32QAM	**19.4**	19.8	8.3	**23.8**	22.1	8.8	**27.4**	24.8	10.2	**30.5**	27.8	11.6	**31.6**	29.9	12.2	**32**	31.7	12.5
64QAM	**23.5**	23.5	10.2	**26.6**	26.4	12.1	**29.9**	27.7	12.8	**33.1**	29.2	12.8	**45.8**	32.1	13.1	**63.6**	33.9	13.3

Table 3 presents the clustering performance of the FCM and PSO-FCM algorithms. The results demonstrate that the PSO-FCM exhibits a reduced number of occurrences of local optima compared to the FCM algorithm across all modulation schemes. This suggests that the PSO-FCM algorithm is more effective in identifying the global optimum compared to the FCM algorithm.

Table 3. Clustering results of two clustering algorithms with various constellation datasets.

Modulation Type	No. Classification	Method	No. Local Optima
8QAM	8	FCM	10 (6.7%)
		PSO-FCM	5 (3.3%)
16QAM	16	FCM	21 (14.0%)
		PSO-FCM	9 (6.0%)
32QAM	32	FCM	82 (54.7%)
		PSO-FCM	73 (48.7%)
64QAM	64	FCM	127 (84.7%)
		PSO-FCM	121 (80.7%)

The studies used the PSO-FCM and FCM algorithms to find modulation in 4QAM, 8QAM, 16QAM, 32QAM, and 64QAM signals. Figure 5 illustrates the modulation recognition rates for MQAM signals, showing that PSO-FCM generally achieves a higher modulation identification rate compared to FCM. Moreover, upon analyzing the results depicted in Figure 6, it becomes apparent that the FCM algorithm converges more rapidly. PSO-FCM converges more slowly than FCM due to the simultaneous optimization of particle positions and membership values in the PSO-FCM hybrid.

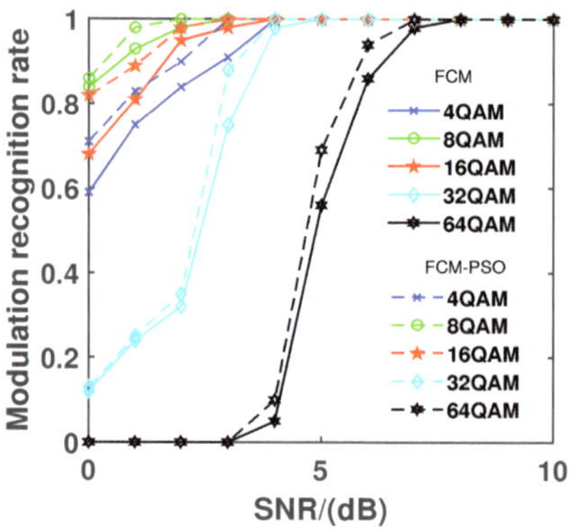

Figure 5. Modulation recognition rate of FCM and PSO-FCM across varied SNRs for multiple QAM signals.

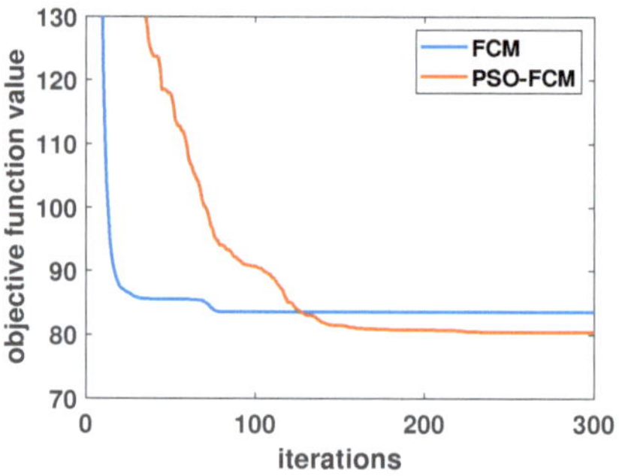

Figure 6. Iterations vs. objective function value; 16QAM, SNR = 2 dB.

PSO introduces additional complexity in the PSO-FCM compared to the traditional FCM algorithm due to the augmented computational load per iteration. In PSO-FCM, there is an inclusion of supplementary complexity multiplication and addition operations. Specifically, each iteration in PSO necessitates $4QC$ complex multiplications and $6QC$ complex additions, where Q denotes the number of data points and C represents the number of dimensions. These extra computational operations in PSO-FCM potentially contribute to slower convergence compared to FCM. The objective function value of the PSO-FCM algorithm gradually diminishes and eventually falls below that of the FCM algorithm, indicating superior optimization performance to some extent. Consequently, the choice between algorithms requires consideration of the trade-off between additional complexity and optimization effectiveness.

5. Conclusions

This paper presents a novel PSO-FCM algorithm designed specifically for accurately identifying modulation orders within MQAM schemes. This hybrid approach integrates the SN-SC algorithm for initial cluster center obtainment and combines FCM and PSO techniques to enhance precision in determining modulation orders. By evaluating fitness using FCM's objective function and analyzing the ratio between maximum and minimum cluster center radii, the algorithm effectively discerns various MQAM modulation schemes. The simulation results validate the algorithm's superior performance, especially in accurately identifying modulation orders even in low-SNR scenarios. This robustness underscores its potential practical application in real-world communication systems where precise QAM modulation order identification is crucial.

Author Contributions: Conceptualization, Z.Q., H.Z., J.L. and H.S.; methodology, Z.Q. and H.S.; writing—original draft preparation, Z.Q.; writing—review and editing, H.Z., J.L. and H.S. All authors have read and agreed to the published version of the manuscript.

Funding: This research was funded by the National Natural Science Foundation of China under the grant number U1604160.

Institutional Review Board Statement: Not applicable.

Data Availability Statement: The original contributions presented in the study are included in the article, further inquiries can be directed to the corresponding authors.

Conflicts of Interest: The authors declare no conflict of interest.

References

1. Ali, A.K.; Erçelebi, E. An M-QAM signal modulation recognition algorithm in AWGN channel. *Sci. Program.* **2019**, 6752694. [CrossRef]
2. Azzouz, E.E.; Nandi, A.K. Automatic identification of digital modulation types. *Signal Process.* **1995**, *47*, 55–69. [CrossRef]
3. Abdelbar, M.; Tranter, W.H.; Bose, T. Cooperative cumulants-based modulation classification in distributed networks. *IEEE Trans. Cogn. Commun. Netw.* **2018**, *4*, 446–461. [CrossRef]
4. Xu, J.L.; Su, W.; Zhou, M. Likelihood-ratio approaches to automatic modulation classification. *IEEE Trans. Syst. Man Cybern. Part C (Appl. Rev.)* **2010**, *41*, 455–469. [CrossRef]
5. Hashim, I.A.; Sadah, J.W.A.; Saeed, T.R.; Ali, J.K. Recognition of QAM signals with low SNR using a combined threshold algorithm. *IETE J. Res.* **2015**, *61*, 65–71. [CrossRef]
6. Mobasseri, B.G. Constellation shape as a robust signature for digital modulation recognition. In Proceedings of the IEEE Conference on Military Communications MILCOM 1999, Atlantic City, NJ, USA, 31 October–3 November 1999; pp. 442–446.
7. Mobasseri, B.G. Digital modulation classification using constellation shape. *Signal Process.* **2000**, *80*, 251–277. [CrossRef]
8. Yin, C.; Li, B.; Li, Y.; Lan, B. Modulation classification of MQAM signals based on density spectrum of the constellations. In Proceedings of the 2010 2nd International Conference on Future Computer and Communication ICFCC 2010, Wuhan, China, 21–24 May 2010; Volume 3, pp. 57–61.
9. Fuchs, C.; Spolaor, S.; Nobile, M.S.; Kaymak, U. A Swarm Intelligence Approach to Avoid Local Optima in Fuzzy C-Means Clustering. In Proceedings of the 2019 IEEE International Conference on Fuzzy Systems (FUZZ-IEEE), New Orleans, LA, USA, 23–26 June 2019; pp. 1–6. [CrossRef]
10. Zha, Y.; Wang, H.; Shen, Z.; Shi, Y.; Shu, F. Intelligent identification technology for high-order digital modulation signals under low signal-to-noise ratio conditions. *IET Signal Process.* **2023**, *17*, e12189 . [CrossRef]
11. Jajoo, G.; Kumar, Y.; Yadav, S.K. Blind signal PSK/QAM recognition using clustering analysis of constellation signature in flat fading channel. *IEEE Commun. Lett.* **2019**, *23*, 1853–1856. [CrossRef]
12. Lu, F.; Shi, Z.; Su, R. Communication signal modulation mechanism based on artificial feature engineering deep neural network modulation identifier. *Wirel. Commun. Mob. Comput.* **2021**, 9988651. [CrossRef]

13. Cheng, Y.; Shao, S. Communication modulation recognition method based on clustering algorithm. *J. Phys. Conf. Ser.* **2021**, *1827*, 012153. [CrossRef]
14. Askari, S. Fuzzy C-Means clustering algorithm for data with unequal cluster sizes and contaminated with noise and outliers: Review and development. *Expert Syst. Appl.* **2021**, *165*, 113856. [CrossRef]
15. Li, G.; Qin, X.; Liu, H.; Jiang, K.; Wang, A. Modulation Recognition of Digital Signal Using Graph Feature and Improved K-Means. *Electronics* **2022**, *11*, 3298. [CrossRef]
16. Nayak, J.; Swapnarekha, H.; Naik, B.; Dhiman, G.; Vimal, S. 25 Years of Particle Swarm Optimization: Flourishing Voyage of Two Decades. *Arch. Comput. Methods Eng.* **2022**, *30*, 1663–1725 . [CrossRef]
17. Ying, L.; Ning, L. Improved change detection method for flood monitoring. *J. Radars* **2017**, *6*, 204–212.
18. Kao, Y.; Chen, M.H.; Hsieh, K.M. Combining PSO and FCM for dynamic fuzzy clustering problems. In Proceedings of the Swarm Intelligence Based Optimization: First International Conference, ICSIBO 2014, Mulhouse, France, 13–14 May 2014; Revised Selected Papers; Springer International Publishing: Berlin/Heidelberg, Germany, 2014; Volume 1, pp. 1–8.
19. Ezugwu, A.E.S.; Agbaje, M.B.; Aljojo, N.; Els, R.; Chiroma, H.; Elaziz, M.A. A comparative performance study of hybrid firefly algorithms for automatic data clustering. *IEEE Access* **2020**, *8*, 121089–121118. [CrossRef]
20. Gad, A.G. Particle swarm optimization algorithm and its applications: A systematic review. *Arch. Comput. Methods Eng.* **2022**, *29*, 2531–2561. [CrossRef]

MDPI AG
Grosspeteranlage 5
4052 Basel
Switzerland
Tel.: +41 61 683 77 34

MDPI Books Editorial Office
E-mail: books@mdpi.com
www.mdpi.com/books

www.ingramcontent.com/pod-product-compliance
Lightning Source LLC
LaVergne TN
LVHW072318090526
838202LV00019B/2304
* 9 7 8 3 7 2 5 8 3 8 1 9 6 *